AUGUST WILSON

A LIFE

PATTI HARTIGAN

Simon & Schuster
New York   London   Toronto   Sydney   New Delhi

Simon & Schuster
1230 Avenue of the Americas
New York, NY 10020

First Simon & Schuster hardcover edition August 2023

SIMON & SCHUSTER and colophon are registered
trademarks of Simon & Schuster, Inc.

For information about special discounts for bulk purchases,
please contact Simon & Schuster Special Sales at
1-866-506-1949 or business@simonandschuster.com.

The Simon & Schuster Speakers Bureau can bring authors to
your live event. For more information or to book an event, contact
the Simon & Schuster Speakers Bureau at 1-866-248-3049
or visit our website at www.simonspeakers.com.

Interior design by Lewelin Polanco

Manufactured in the United States of America

1   3   5   7   9   10   8   6   4   2

Library of Congress Cataloging-in-Publication Data has been applied for.

ISBN 978-1-5011-8066-8
ISBN 978-1-5011-8068-2 (ebook)

For my mother, Nancy Irene Hartigan,
and for all mothers whose love is
both tender and fierce

There is a way under, around or through any door.

—AUGUST WILSON

CONTENTS

AUGUST WILSON

Prologue

To arrive at this moment in my life, I have traveled many roads, some circuitous, some brambled and rough, some sharp and straight, and all of them have led as if by some grand design to the one burnished with art and small irrevocable tragedies.

—AUGUST WILSON

On March 22, 2003, under a somber gray sky, August Wilson walked slowly up the steps of St. Benedict the Moor church, the grand, imposing Roman Catholic cathedral on Crawford Street at the base of Pittsburgh's Hill District. The temperature was in the low fifties, typical for early spring in Pittsburgh, but an unforgiving drizzle added a nip to the air. Wilson had cut short a trip to Syracuse to be back in Pittsburgh that day. He sported a black turtleneck and a brown tweed jacket, topped by a trench coat to keep away the chill. His signature Borsalino fedora shadowed the deep circles under his puffy eyes; his neatly trimmed beard was more salt than pepper.

He hadn't originally planned on spending the day back home in Pittsburgh. His latest play, *Gem of the Ocean*, was about to make its world premiere in less than a month at the Goodman Theatre in Chicago. He had finished a very rough draft and he would rewrite during rehearsals, the same way he had revised the other plays in his ambitious ten-play cycle about African Americans in the twentieth century.

Gem was the ninth play in the cycle. He had one more to go, and he already felt the pressure of completing the goal he had set for himself so long ago. He had also foolishly agreed to write and perform a one-man autobiographical show for a benefit fundraiser at the Seattle Repertory Theatre. He hadn't written a word, and he had just two months left before he had to get up on the stage and play himself as a young man. He was a perennial procrastinator, but standing on the steps of that church, looking up toward the Hill District, he was burdened by grief and memories, many of them painful. He had mourned his mother, Daisy Wilson, at this very church twenty years ago, almost to the day. He knew he was going to pay tribute to her in his one-man show, and he had already thought about what to say. "There will come a day when you will suffer the most profound grief imaginable," is what he eventually wrote. "And you look up and you find out that all them years you been living on your mother's prayers and now you've got to live on your own."

This church, so noble and grand, evoked images from the past. As a boy, Wilson had attended the parochial school at Holy Trinity in the Lower Hill District, but the school was demolished during an ill-informed period of urban renewal in the late 1950s. Several parishes merged to form St. Benedict the Moor, named for an Italian Franciscan friar who was born of African slaves and celebrated for his charity. The church commissioned a giant statue of its patron saint in 1968, the same year as the assassination of Martin Luther King Jr. The eighteen-foot-tall landmark faces with its arms stretched in welcome to the people of downtown Pittsburgh, its back turned on the Hill District. The orientation of the statue of a saint with African blood turning its back on his people had infuriated Wilson the day it was unveiled. It still did.

But he was here to bury one of his friends, not resurrect old grievances. Wilson never missed a funeral. His life and his work reinforced the notion that attention must be paid to history, to ancestral roots, to family, and to friends, both celebrated and obscure. He stopped briefly outside the church to greet Nate Smith, the legendary labor leader who had famously laid down in front of a moving bulldozer in 1969 to protest the absence of Black union workers at the Three Rivers Stadium construction site. Smith's bald head glistened, his mournful eyes rimmed red. Wilson had been an impressionable young man in his early twenties when Smith led thousands in protest marches in downtown Pittsburgh, ultimately forcing the mayor and the union leaders to develop a plan to admit Blacks and women into the city's entrenched trade unions. Smith was one of his heroes back then, but today the two men met as peers, fellow mourners.

While Smith was organizing protests, Wilson was living in a shady basement apartment on Crawford Street, just a block over from St. Benedict's. He was an aspiring young poet, a high school dropout who loved words as much as he loved the sweet smell of a woman's perfume in the late-night hours. He wrote poetry on a manual Royal Standard typewriter. That typewriter had been replaced long ago, and the apartment building had been demolished. But he had forged deep friendships with his fellow poets back then. He had found his vocation right here on these streets by becoming one of a quartet known as the Centre Avenue Poets: Chawley Williams, Nicholas Flournoy, Rob Penny, and Wilson. Swept up in the Black Nationalist Movement, they aimed to change the world with poetry and plays, by giving the people a voice.

And that is what brought Wilson, now an acclaimed playwright, winner of two Pulitzer Prizes, a Tony Award, and numerous honorary degrees, to the steps of this church, not far from where he had grown up the son of a single mother in a two-room flat with no indoor plumbing. He was back home to bury Rob Penny. A small, wiry man with an infectious grin, Penny had preceded Wilson at Central Catholic High School, the elite exam school in Oakland, a neighborhood that is a stone's throw from Carnegie Mellon University and miles away in mindset from the Hill District. Despite rampant racism at the school, Penny had been able to succeed because he was the fastest runner on the track team—and whip-smart, too. Wilson was accepted two years after Penny's graduation; he withdrew after barely a year, tired of the racist notes that were left on his desk and the jokes played at his expense. Penny graduated and was a celebrated star athlete. Years later, Wilson saw him take a dare from a group of teenagers hanging out in a park. The upstarts thought they could beat the old man with the graying dreadlocks in a hundred-yard dash. Penny won. He always won.

The two former Central Catholic students had been brothers back when they were aspiring young artists. They had bonds. They had a past together. Back in the 1960s, Penny called himself Brother Oba, which means "king" in the Yoruba and Bini languages of West Africa. Wilson took the name Mbulu, the name of a town in Tanzania. Together in 1968, the two men launched Black Horizons Theatre, creating art from the ashes of the fiery demonstrations that rocked Pittsburgh after the assassination of Martin Luther King Jr. They were poets and dreamers who subscribed to the principles of Amiri Baraka's Black Arts Movement, which espoused that theater and art could empower the Black community.

Penny was able to turn his poetry acumen and community activism into a teaching slot at the University of Pittsburgh's newly formed Department of Africana Studies in 1969. There was no place for Wilson in the department, but he didn't begrudge his friend his good fortune. Penny, at least, had graduated from high school. Wilson continued to struggle as a penniless poet and playwright for many years, while Penny enjoyed the perks and acclaim of academe. Penny went on to become chairman of Africana Studies in 1978, serving until 1984 and remaining an esteemed professor until his death of a heart attack on March 16, 2003. Wilson, on the other hand, worked every odd job from dishwasher to short-order cook. His first nibble at theatrical success came in 1982, when his play *Ma Rainey's Black Bottom* was accepted to be developed at the prestigious Eugene O'Neill Theater Center in Waterford, Connecticut. He included his Pittsburgh friends in that small moment of triumph: Penny and another Pitt professor, Curtiss Porter, traveled to Waterford to see the play. Wilson continued to invite his Pittsburgh brothers to his Broadway openings, and he also celebrated their achievements over the years.

Back in the day, Penny had taken to wearing dashikis, while Wilson wore musty tweed sports coats he bought at the St. Vincent de Paul thrift shop; a coat went for thirty-five cents and a tie cost a nickel. Now his tweed had a better pedigree, but Wilson still related to the young man who shopped the bargain stores.

Before Wilson set foot in the church, Penny's family sent a message to him. All the mourners were invited to say a few words about the departed. Except August Wilson. Wilson believed in speaking well of the dead. He spoke at funerals of folks he barely knew, impoverished street characters he gave a few bucks to when they were down on their luck. Not speak at Rob's funeral? He told his younger brother Richard Kittel that he was crushed.

Many of his contemporaries saw him during the services and noticed that his legs buckled, ever so slightly. His lips sank downward, making his mustache seem like a deep frown. Sala Udin, an actor from the old days who had gone on to a career in local politics and activism, saw the normally self-restrained Wilson weep openly over the coffin. Mark Clayton Southers, an aspiring playwright, noted that Wilson was inconsolable. He didn't know that his idol August Wilson had been silenced—because of his own success. Wilson was aware that the people who had been his dearest friends in the old days resented his acclaim. Some of them had suggested to one another, privately, that he had somehow "sold out" because of his commercial success on Broadway. When he gave his controversial speech "The Ground on Which I Stand," in 1996, he was shattered that many of his friends from the theater failed to support him publicly. The fiery speech called for the creation of more Black theaters and denounced "color-blind casting" as demeaning to Blacks. Many of the "Wilson Warriors," the actors who made their livings performing in his plays, were silent. That stung more.

Wilson had noticed over the years that the more successful he became, the more distant his former brothers grew. Poet Nick Flournoy, however, had remained true to their friendship, even as he continued to work primarily as a community activist. But Wilson knew others questioned his loyalties. He knew they envied his success. But he also knew that he was still the guy who wrote in basements and restaurants, even if he could afford the penthouse suite. His reception at the funeral accentuated the conflicting emotions about the city he celebrated in his plays. "I have this sort of love-hate relationship with Pittsburgh," he once said. "This is my home and at times I miss it and find it tremendously exciting, and other times I want to catch the first thing out that has wheels."

When he exited the church with his fellow mourners, he had trouble containing the deep lump in his throat and the steady flow from his watery eyes. A crowd had gathered at Freedom Corner, directly across the street from the church. Wilson was just a boy in the 1950s when developers encroached on the lower part of the Hill District, threatening to destroy the bustling multiethnic enclave where he grew up. The developers razed the Lower Hill to put up the Civic Arena, displacing thousands of people and creating a wasteland of urban blight. In the 1960s, protesters put up signs saying "NO Redevelopment Beyond This Point," drawing a line at the corner of Centre Avenue and Crawford Street. The spot became known as Freedom Corner, a place where protesters gathered to begin marches for social justice and racial equality. Nate Smith had launched many of his protests there. His name was inscribed along with those of other civil rights leaders in the monument that was finally built on the spot in 2001.

Wilson's younger cousin Renee Wilson, his uncle Frank's daughter whom he barely knew but who had grown up to be a crackerjack community activist, had called him some time earlier. She had organized a group called People Against Police Violence to protest the deaths of five Black men killed by Pittsburgh police. She had scheduled a demonstration for March 22. The victims' stories sounded like anecdotes from a Wilson play. One of the dead was a twelve-year-old boy who was shot in the back while fleeing from police after a car robbery. Renee Wilson was dedicated to the cause of "No justice, no peace," and she asked her famous cousin to attend the protest. He declined her request. He had planned to be in Chicago on that day, working on his play.

Renee had also called Rob Penny. She had taken a writing class with him at Pitt and he had encouraged her to keep writing poetry. She asked that he speak at the rally. He agreed to attend, but he would not speak.

As it turned out, Penny was there, but in a coffin. Renee had planned on starting the march downtown earlier in the day, but out of respect for Penny, she postponed the beginning of the demonstration until after the funeral. Wilson must have been aware of the symbolism of the moment. Like his cousin, he had harbored dreams of changing the world, but he had had to leave Pittsburgh to do it. He had walked those same streets when he was a young man, but even though he had almost accomplished what he set out to do when he started writing his cycle of ten plays, some of his former friends had branded him as the one who had turned his back on the community, just like that statue of St. Benedict the Moor.

The hearse went one way, and the protesters another. Wilson had written plays that dramatized the reasons for the protest his cousin was leading. He had done his part. He had found his song and shared it with audiences all over the world, but he hadn't expected to pay such a high, personal price. He looked across the street at the protesters and looked at the hearse. He followed the funeral procession. It was time for another generation to take over the struggle.

CHAPTER ONE

The Blood's Memory

When your back is pressed to the wall, you go to the deepest part of yourself, and there's a response—it's your great ancestors talking. It's blood memory.

—AUGUST WILSON

In the dark hours of June 9, 1923, shots rang out on Spear Tops Mountain, a craggy peak in Spear, North Carolina, an isolated hamlet in the Toe River Valley section of Southern Appalachia. Sarah "Eller" Cutler undoubtedly heard the cussing and hollering outside her weatherworn homestead, a wooden cabin perched halfway up the mountain. She had raised many children in that cabin with no indoor plumbing or electricity, but her husband, Jacob Cutler, had died more than a decade earlier and her sons had moved on, likely finding work in the local mica mines or the bustling lumber industry. On this particular night, Eller was living with her daughter, Zonia, and her three young children. Faye was six years old, Daisy was three, and Detroit (who later went by Ray) was just a year old. The sound of gunfire on the mountain was an aberration: it wasn't often that villagers from the tiny town of Spear made the trek up the ragged path to Eller's property, which was only accessible by climbing more than a mile up a rocky trail that began at the Vance Bros. general store. In late spring, the path would have been overgrown with tangles of laurel and encumbered by unruly branches that jutted out from the dogwoods, oaks, and chestnut trees. This was not a well-groomed pathway for a casual walk in the woods, and the clatter must have been alarming. At fifty-five, Eller was a strong independent woman, the daughter of a former slave who was well aware that hers was the only Black family on the mountain, which heightened the danger. Undoubtedly, she scrambled to check on her grandbabies to make sure they were safe.

She also likely heard the animated voice of Willard Justice, a fifty-year-old single white farmer who lived nearby with his sister and her two sons. Eller and Justice weren't strangers. They had a connection that would cause any woman to worry in 1923. And on that night, there were at least a half dozen armed men up on the mountain.

By the end of the night, Justice was mortally wounded. He had been shot twice, with bullets hitting him in the chest and abdomen. He made his way down the mountain to the offices of Dr. W. B. Burleson, the county physician. Bleeding profusely, he managed to dictate his last will and testament, demanding that the gunmen be prosecuted for "shooting me without a cause." He died at 4:30 a.m. on June 11, 1923, and he was buried the next day in Yellow Mountain Cemetery just outside Spear. The stream that flows through the mountain hollow is now known as Justice Creek.

That much is documented, but the story has taken on a life of its own in the oral history passed down by the natives of this mountainous region. According to published reports, five lawmen had a warrant to arrest Justice and claimed that he was a fugitive and shot first. But that's where the various stories diverge. Justice, on his deathbed, insisted that he was shot "without cause." In one tale, Justice was tied to a cart and dragged down the mountain. Another claims that Justice was scalped, which is clearly apocryphal according to the medical details on his death certificate. Other stories imply that Justice was headed for the Cutler home at the time of the murder. According to mountain lore, Justice was a regular visitor at the Cutler's austere abode. One tale claims that he was infatuated with one of the Cutler women. Another legend claims that he was paying for female companionship and that Eller Cutler ran the kind of house that would make good Christians blush. The law of the land was not kind to women in 1923: they could be imprisoned for anything from adultery to

keeping a disorderly house. And miscegenation, which had been prohib-
ited in North Carolina since 1873, was declared a felony in 1921, making
the stories even more loaded.

Eller was made of strong stuff and refused to leave the mountain after
her husband died. She inherited her grit from her father, Calvin Twitty,
who was born into bondage on a plantation in Rutherford County, North
Carolina. In 1864, a man named Calvin was left as "property" in the will
of plantation owner Robert Gwynne Twitty. In that same will, the plantation owner's daughter received a tract of land worth $8,000, "three Ne-
groes," and a piano. The instrument was a gift from her father and she
likely practiced her études in the parlor of the Big House while her father's
enslaved workers labored in the fields. Many years later, Calvin Twitty's
great-great-grandson August Wilson would turn a piano from the ante-
bellum era into a searing image of slavery and its tortuous hold on future
generations. That play is called *The Piano Lesson*.

By 1880, Calvin Twitty had settled in Bakersville, the Mitchell County
seat in the heart of the mountains about fifty miles north of Rutherford.
He had married a woman named Martha and had eight children, includ-
ing Eller, who was born around 1868, five years after the Emancipation
Proclamation. He identified himself as an illiterate farmer, but he was a
savvy man who fought for his rights. He claimed that he fought in the
Civil War, serving for about two years with Company F in the 40th U.S.
Colored Infantry. When he applied for his superannuation, officials in
Washington at the Record and Pension Office denied his claim, contending there was no record of his service. This was not unusual, since names
were often misspelled and escaped slaves who enlisted often did not provide their real names.

But by the time his claim was denied, he no longer needed the money.
He had demanded restitution after his son William was killed in a gruesome accident on a runaway log train in November 1891. William had
an accident insurance policy of $5,000, and after the accident, the Rich-
mond and Danville Railroad awarded his father another $5,000 "as a

compromise," according to newspaper accounts. He walked away with $10,000, a sum that would be worth a shade more than $306,000 today. The story of Twitty's financial bonanza was reported in newspapers all over North Carolina, although little was made of his son's tragic death. One oft-republished—and racist—account noted, "The old darkey has gone to his humble mountain cabin worth $10,000, and feeling much richer than our neighbor, Mr. Vanderbilt." Years later, his great-great-grandson would celebrate the stories of ordinary men like Calvin Twitty who did extraordinary things against all odds.

Eller shared her father's steely resolve. She made a good match when she married Jacob Cutler in 1884. He was born around 1835, and he had been married before, to a woman named Jane. He and Jane lived on a sizeable tract of land he had purchased in Watauga County, North Carolina, and when he began his second marriage with Eller, he also owned the land on Spear Tops Mountain. After he died, Eller stayed put, even after the gruesome murder took place steps from her home. She was accustomed to the rugged territory. Spear is nestled between the Blue Ridge and Iron Mountains. The Toe River snakes through the region; it takes its name from Estatoe, the daughter of a Cherokee chief who drowned herself in the river when her lover was killed as they attempted to run off together. In 1923, there were only 611 people living in the Toe River Township and most of them lived in the hollow below the mountain. In those days, widows often moved in with other relatives, but Eller was fiercely independent. There was plenty of clean water from the streams fueled by Cutler Falls, the one-hundred-foot cascading waterfall about a mile up the 4,900-foot peak. No one remembered when the falls was christened, but Eller and her offspring had always known it to bear the name of their family, the odd Black landowners living among a handful of poor white families.

Eller worked in some capacity for Dr. Burleson. As a midwife or "granny woman," she was inured to mountain life and undaunted by the blood and pain of childbirth. Granny women in Southern Appalachia were healers who used herbs and spiritual practices to treat all sorts of wounds, as well as bring babies into the world. Zonia, her youngest daughter, lived off and on in the family homestead. Born in 1896, she later told her children that she had gone back and forth to nearby Tennessee, where she worked as a domestic servant for a branch of the Vance family, the well-heeled clan that owned the country store and the Tar Hill Mica Mine, which provided jobs for many of the local men. Zonia also told her children that she had been raped several times by a white man and that Daisy and Detroit were the result of sexual violence. The family believed that Faye had a different father, a Black man with whom Zonia had a consensual relationship. Eller is listed as the midwife on all three of her grandchildren's birth certificates, which are labeled with the stark word "illegitimate."

Life was anything but easy for Zonia, and it took a worse turn after the murder on the mountain. Justice had had a brush with the law—and it did involve the Cutlers. In April 1923, Eller and Justice were charged with an unspecified crime, but Justice was dead by the time the case got to court. A year later, in April 1924, Eller appeared in court with her daughter "Zone" (a misspelling of Zonia) listed as a codefendant. The two women were accused of "keeping a bawdy house," and a dozen witnesses testified against them, including the deputy sheriff who led the group that shot Justice. The two women were convicted and ordered to pay court costs of $171.25, a princely sum in the mountains in those days. They were also sentenced to six months in jail. It is not clear if they served time, but if they did, they would have been incarcerated in the women's section of the Avery County Jail, located eleven miles away in Newland. But the conviction alone added to the stigma already surrounding Eller and her daughter.

At the same time Eller and Zonia faced charges, racial tension was rampant in the area. In 1923, violence erupted in nearby Spruce Pine after a Black laborer named John Goss was accused of rape and a mob of white residents stormed the labor camp, aiming to "run the Blacks out of the county." Goss, who was working on a chain gang at the time of his arrest, was sentenced to death by an all-white jury that deliberated for five minutes. This was the prevailing attitude that Eller was up against when she and Zonia appeared in court on the charges of "keeping a bawdy house." The truth remains a mystery, starting with the initial charges and continuing through the death of Willard Justice and the trial. Was Justice a fugitive or was he murdered for being friendly with Black women? Was Eller running a "bawdy house" or was she framed by her neighbors?

Mountain folk still talk about the Cutlers. Spear remains a town that time forgot. The general store is still there, a gathering spot where you can buy a mousetrap or a carton of milk, a hammer or a hero sandwich. There is an abandoned gas station and an abandoned mica factory. The trail to Spear Tops Mountain is even more overgrown than it was in Eller's time. The land is now the property of the Southern Appalachian Highlands Conservancy, which hopes to preserve its natural splendor. The trail is posted and blocked off by a fence that is easily circumvented.

Halfway up the mountain today, the stones of Eller's chimney remain on the site of her homestead. The Cutler family laid its roots in those hills, and the land below Spear Tops Mountain is still known as Cutler Hollow. Eller valued the land that bore her name. She died on that mountain at age sixty-seven in 1935, and her body, weathered by age and a hard life, was carried down the narrow path before she was most likely buried in an unmarked grave at the AME Methodist Cemetery in nearby Plumtree, where Black people were laid to rest. The graveyard is not far down the road from Yellow Mountain Cemetery, the white people's cemetery where Willard Justice's body was put away in a "decent manner."

Eller's great-grandson, August Wilson, almost certainly did not know what happened on Spear Tops Mountain that night in June 1923 or in the months that followed. His grandmother, Zonia Wilson, died when he was five, and he told interviewers he barely knew her. The little he knew about Eller was passed on by his mother, Daisy Wilson, who was one of the children sleeping in the cabin the night of the murder. She described Eller as sturdy, but stern, a tough taskmaster who insisted her grandchildren work to keep food on the table.

Wilson told interviewers that his mother was the daughter of sharecroppers who demanded she quit school after sixth grade to help in the fields, but Zonia was not a sharecropper. There were no sharecroppers in the Toe River Valley. Eller and Jacob owned the land.

Wilson repeatedly said that he didn't do any historical research for his plays. He wrote from what he called "the blood's memory," which was his way of saying that he felt the pulse of his ancestors. He just *knew* what they must have endured. He listened to his characters talk, and he wrote down what they said. One of his most memorable characters is Aunt Ester (or ancestor), who figures in four of his plays. In each play, she is as old as slavery, her birth dating back to 1619, the year the first slave ships sailed into North America. Wilson has called her his most important character, the matriarchal force that holds his series of ten plays together. She is "the embodiment of African wisdom and tradition," he said, a spiritual healer who can make people whole. In *Gem of the Ocean*, she leads a man struggling with his conscience to the mythical City of Bones, where he meets his ancestors, discovers his self-worth, and heals his soul.

Wilson said that Aunt Ester "resembles any Black woman in her 70s—someone you wouldn't look twice at if she stepped outside." She could have been Eller Cutler. Aunt Ester is a healer who leads people to redemption. Eller was a granny woman who soothed wounds and delivered babies. When Wilson wrote the character of Aunt Ester, he was likely thinking of all the "aunts" he had while growing up in Pittsburgh, friends of his mother who watched out for all the children in the neighborhood, as his great-grandmother did in Spear.

Aunt Ester is the blood's memory.

Wilson also likely didn't know that his great-grandmother's brush with the law happened around the same time that a racist mob stormed the labor camps in Spruce Pine. He may never have heard of the name John Goss, the Black laborer accused of rape, but his great-grandmother certainly had. As she faced her own trial, she was well aware that a member of a chain gang had been sentenced to death on the scantest of evidence. Herald Loomis, the central character in Wilson's masterpiece, *Joe Turner's Come and Gone*, was a haunted figure who had survived seven years of enforced labor.

The blood's memory, again.

Wilson never visited Spear. He almost certainly never saw the will in which Calvin Twitty was listed as property, along with a piano. His mother and grandmother never returned to Spear after they moved north. But Wilson wrote a play about a piano and created a character who could have been his great-grandmother. He knew his family was descended from slaves even before he heard Aunt Ester talking. And he knew that his grandmother Zonia tried to leave her troubled past behind her when she married and left Spear Tops Mountain for good.

In 1928, Zonia began a serious courtship with Bynam Wilson. He came from Cleveland County, seventy miles to the south. He was a bit of a mystery and had secrets of his own. Born in 1896, he had disappeared from his home in Cleveland County, where he was married to a woman named Mary Young. They had at least two children: Everett Mills in 1918 and Lucille in 1924.

His family later recalled that he vanished, leaving his children behind. On the 1930 U.S. Census, Mary Young reported that she was widowed. Maybe she believed that, maybe she didn't. But in 1928, Bynam was in Toe River Valley, romancing Zonia. He was a wanderer, at least that's how his grandson, August Wilson, memorialized him in a poem many years later, placing him among a generation of men, born of former slaves, full of rage and a desire to roam free. In the poem, Wilson depicted his grandfather as a bird, giant and fierce. Wilson also named one of the most mystical characters in *Joe Turner* after his grandfather. The character Bynum is a seeker, a man who binds lost souls together.

The blood's memory, again.

The mythical grandfather of the poem was a man who sired many children, passing on a noble legacy to his offspring. Whatever his past, Bynam captivated Zonia Cutler. Zonia later told her children that Eller didn't like the match, but she didn't say why. Eller didn't want her daughter to leave Spear Tops Mountain. But the first wave of the Great Migration of Blacks moving north had just begun. Faced with racism, Jim Crow laws, and little economic opportunity, more than 1.6 million African Americans left the South for the North between 1910 and 1930. African Americans living in the rural South headed north to such cities as New

York, Chicago, Pittsburgh, and Detroit. Zonia left her past behind, but she could never forget her conviction in court with her mother and its consequences.

So early on Monday morning of July 9, 1928, Bynam and Zonia walked into the train station in Newland, also the site of the Avery County Jail. They bought two one-way tickets to Elizabethton, Tennessee, the seat of Carter County, just across the state line. They sat in the "colored" waiting room and later rode in the "colored" car. People from Spear frequently made the thirty-mile journey through the mountains and across the state line. Young couples whose parents disapproved would often elope to Elizabethton, where they could get a marriage license and tie the knot far enough away from the probing eyes of neighbors and court administrators who knew everyone born in those parts. Upon arriving in Elizabethton, the couple found their way to the courthouse. There were two other couples in line, so they waited patiently while the others exchanged their vows before a justice of the peace. Zonia and Bynam got their license. He signed the document with an X. The couple took their vows before P. P. Williams, a minister of God.

They had no intention of returning to Spear. The North beckoned. Zonia had had to make a choice before she got on that train: leave her three children with Eller or take them along to an unknown future. She left them with their grandmother. Faye was ten, Daisy was eight, and Ray was six. Eller, who was now sixty, needed help around the house. She was always short on money. She and her grandchildren lived a subsistence life, and she could be a stern disciplinarian, even though she did the best she could to keep them clothed and fed.

They lived off the land and the meager wages Eller earned as a midwife and as an assistant to Dr. Burleson. They canned and preserved apples from the trees outside their cabin. They salted hog meat and saved it for the winter. They gathered water from the clear stream—Justice Creek—that flowed through the mountain. And there wasn't much choice when it came to schooling. Eller never learned to read or write, and she signed an X in place of her name when she was presented with legal documents. She sent her grandchildren to a segregated one-room schoolhouse in Elk Park. Located twelve miles from Spear, the school was the only place where Black children could learn their ABCs.

Years later, Daisy had bad memories of the school. She told stories about being chased and taunted by white children as she made her way to and from the building. But she didn't have a choice. She attended school in Elk Park or she didn't go at all. Teased and bullied, she may have felt a sense of relief when Eller pulled her from school after she had completed sixth grade. Eller needed her grandchildren to help around the homestead. But Daisy later regretted her lack of education. She knew the power of literacy, and she vowed that her own children would receive the education she never had.

She also must have wondered about her mother. Why had she left her and her siblings with their grandmother? The family legend says that after Bynam and Zonia eloped, they walked all the way from Tennessee to Pittsburgh. But the 1930 U.S. Census has the couple living in the tiny town of Rock, in Mercer County, West Virginia. Bynam was working as a loader at a coal mine, and Zonia was a homemaker. They did not go back to North Carolina, but Zonia's sister Lillian and her husband, Arthur, who had moved north, returned to Spear to live with Eller and the children, bringing with them stories of a place called Pittsburgh, where you could hear music any night of the week and buy clothes and groceries in proper stores. People rode around in streetcars, and most of the homes had electricity and radios.

Daisy must have imagined Pittsburgh as a magical place, so different from the cabin she had called home her entire life. And then on May 9, 1935, Eller died of chronic myocarditis. Her death certificate notes that she passed away in her home. She was carried down the mountain, the procession following the same path on which the dying Willard Justice had been carted a dozen years earlier. Her granddaughters Daisy and Faye would have made the shroud; her grandson Ray likely built the coffin. Uncle Arthur escorted Eller's three grandchildren, teenagers now, to Pittsburgh. None of them would ever return to Spear.

CHAPTER TWO

The Crossroads of the World

*I happen to think that the content of my mother's life—her
myths, her superstitions, her prayers, the contents of her
pantry, the smell of her kitchen, the song that escaped from
her sometimes parched lips, her thoughtful repose and
pregnant laughter—are all worthy of art.*

—AUGUST WILSON

When Daisy Cutler arrived in Pittsburgh in 1937, she discovered a
bustling, smoke-filled city that was a stark contrast to the home-
spun world she knew. In Spear, she had to trek a mile down the mountain
to buy staples like sugar or flour. Here, there were shops on every corner. The city's three majestic, albeit polluted, rivers—the Allegheny, the
Monongahela, and the Ohio—made Toe River look like a stream. And
the people: there were so many of them. In 1930, there were only about
1,400 people residing in Toe River Valley, and only a handful of them
were Black. In contrast, Pittsburgh's population was bursting at around
670,000, with 8.2 percent of them Black. Since 1910, the city's Black population had more than doubled from 25,623 to 54,983 in 1930. Most of
these newcomers had made the Great Migration north from Southern
states like North Carolina.

This was the kind of place where she could blend in.

Years later, her son imagined her arrival in the Steel City. He wrote
that she was "wide-hipped and full of grace . . . already marked by the

turbulence of Black life in the South, and coming North she was hopeful and willing to engage America on its own terms and its moral obligation to live up to the words of its creed so as not to make a mockery of its ideals."

When she was finally reunited with her mother and a stepfather she barely knew, she had a choice. How would she identify herself in this new place? Zonia and Bynam had settled into married life, and they had added two more children to the family: John D., born in 1932, and Frank, born in 1934. Zonia would soon give birth to a boy named George. The younger children all shared Bynam's surname, and Zonia was also a Wilson. Daisy may or may not have known that the puritanical word "illegitimate" was written in bold ink on her birth certificate, but she had been called "bastard" in Spear more times than she cared to remember. This was a chance for a rebirth, a christening. She didn't hesitate to adopt Bynam's surname. Neither did her North Carolina siblings. None of them knew the identity of their biological father.

Daisy and her sister, Faye, cemented their independence by moving into a boardinghouse on Clark Street in the city's Hill District, which at the time was a bustling world unto its own within a larger metropolis. The neighborhood, while primarily Black, was a melting pot of nationalities that included Greeks, Jews, Syrians, Italians, and Irish. August Wilson would later describe it as "an amalgam of the unwanted" with "each ethnic group seeking to cast off the vestiges of the old country, changing names, changing manners . . . bludgeoning the malleable parts of themselves. Melting into the pot. Becoming and defining what it means to be an American." This was a place where the thousands of Blacks who had made the Great Migration, including Daisy and her siblings, could take new names, forge new identities, and shake off painful memories.

The Hill, which came to be known locally as "the crossroads of the world," had an all-Black radio station. Its weekly newspaper, the *Pittsburgh Courier*, was one of the most prestigious Black newspapers in the country, with a nationally acclaimed team of sportswriters and photography by Teenie Harris, a renowned artist whose work is now exhibited at museums, including the Carnegie Museum of Art.

It was also a cultural epicenter. The neighborhood boasted several movie theaters, with uniformed ushers seating moviegoers at the New Granada and Roosevelt Theatres. A jazz renaissance began in the Hill's many clubs in the 1920s, and by the time Daisy arrived, the music thrived in the area's clubs and dance halls. Racketeer Gus Greenlee—who was raised in Marion, North Carolina, not far from Spear—was the owner and proprietor of Crawford Grill No. 1, a smoke-filled, lively space in the Lower Hill that was almost a city block long with three floors and a central revolving stage in the main room. Greenlee opened a companion club, Crawford Grill No. 2, in 1943. Jazz legends and big bands blew tunes late into the night, with performances into the early morning at such after-hours venues as the Musicians Club and the Bambola Social Club. Such stars as Louis Armstrong, Ella Fitzgerald, and Dizzy Gillespie headlined at the big downtown theaters and then socialized at the Crawford Grill, which was a popular gathering spot during its heyday. Pittsburgh's native-born jazz stars like pianist and band leader Earl "Fatha" Hines, singer Lena Horne, and pianist Mary Lou Williams drew crowds when they came home to perform. The Hill was the place to be, the center of the city's Black cultural life. When famed entertainer Bill "Bojangles" Robinson visited Pittsburgh in 1940, he did the requisite VIP tour, but ended up shooting billiards at Pat's Place, the popular pool hall in the Hill District. Hill residents closely followed the careers of such homegrown artists as Billy Eckstine; one of Eckstine's schoolmates at Pittsburgh's Peabody High School was a future artist named Romare Bearden, who went on to create stirring collages that captured the pathos and passion of the era.

The Hill was the kind of place where anything seemed possible, and newcomers like Daisy and her siblings could build lives of their own. Daisy's younger brother Ray likely would have been destined for a life in those mica mines if he had remained in Spear, but in this multiethnic community, he saw new opportunities and was encouraged by his stepfather. The two grew close. One day, Bynam sat the young man down and told him that his skin was light enough for him to "pass," showing his stepson how to style his hair so that it was shiny and slick. He had been named Detroit Ray at birth, but he dropped Detroit and became simply

Ray. In 1942, he registered for the U.S. draft as Ray D. Wilson, born in Mexico. He was more specific when he applied for veteran compensation in 1950; he pinpointed his birthplace to Aduro, Mexico. Apparently, the paper pushers in Pennsylvania failed to notice that Aduro, Mexico, does not exist.

Ray found work as an auto mechanic, a trade in which Mexican immigrants were favored by customers in Pittsburgh. He didn't speak a word of Spanish, but apparently, no one questioned his made-up country of origin. The city was teeming with newcomers, after all. One day, his younger brother Frank visited him at work and walked in through the front door of the auto shop. Ray pulled him aside and told him to enter through the back door like the rest of the "colored people." Frank never visited his brother at work again. When Ray died in 1971, his siblings showed up at his wake. Ray's wife and her relatives had never known that he was Black. This story became part of the family lore, passed on from cousin to cousin.

By 1940, Faye had married and had two children, but Daisy remained single at age twenty. She eventually settled into a two-room rear apartment at 1727 Bedford Avenue in a two-story brick row house built in 1841 that had a dirt backyard. Louis and Bella Siger, a Jewish couple, operated the mom-and-pop store Bella's Market in the front of the house. The flat had no hot water and, when Daisy moved in, it had an outhouse in the backyard. Dr. Albert Goldblum, a family practitioner (who later became a dermatologist) known as Doc to the neighborhood children, lived across the street, and the brothers Frank and Johnny Butera, who were of Italian descent, repaired watches and shoes in the house next door. This stretch of Bedford Avenue was a village within a village, where everyone knew one another's business and where families stayed for generations.

Daisy may not have married, but she was setting down roots in this community. On April 17, 1941, she gave birth to her first baby, a girl she named Freda. She had desperately wanted a boy, and she likely chose to name her infant after Frederick August Kittel, a white Bohemian-born baker she had met in the neighborhood. Kittel was not Freda's father, who many in the family say was likely a Black man from the Hill. But Daisy had already begun a tempestuous relationship with Kittel, a European pastry chef twenty-four years her senior who had been married for two decades to Maryanna "Jenny" Jodzis, a Polish immigrant.

Despite the unlikely match, Daisy quickly gave birth to two of his children, Linda Jean in 1942 and Donna in 1944. Kittel showed up every now and then but had little to do with the raising of the children, beginning a pattern that would last throughout the children's youth. Daisy may have hoped that Kittel would leave his wife, but he had been married by a Roman Catholic priest, and divorce was forbidden in the church. Perhaps Kittel promised her they would marry when his wife died. That would be a long time coming.

Even if Kittel wouldn't marry her, Daisy longed for a son, and she finally got her wish on April 27, 1945, when she gave birth to a boy she named Frederick August Kittel Jr. She nicknamed him Freddy. He later, like his mother, changed his name, choosing to become August Wilson. Kittel Sr. believed the boy was his son, but there was no way to be entirely certain at the time; DNA testing was not introduced until the late 1970s. Freda, after all, had a different father from her siblings. As Freddy grew up, he felt the void of a missing father, and some in the family suspected that he secretly wondered if a man who neglected his children could really be his biological father. But Daisy always said that Freddy was Kittel's son.

Life couldn't have been easy for a large family in two spare rooms with no hot water and an outhouse in the backyard. Daisy bathed the children in the kitchen, where she heated water on the stove and poured it into a large galvanized tub. The landlord eventually installed a toilet in the mid-1940s, but Daisy would have to wait until 1953 for a bathtub and a hot-water heater. But she embraced motherhood, dedicating herself to her children's "prosperity and growth," as her first son later observed. "She knew and taught that we all have our hands in the soup, that we all make the music play just so, that we can make of our lives what we will."

In 1947, Daisy gave birth to a girl named Barbara. Kittel was not the father—and he knew it. At twenty-seven, Daisy was already raising four children under the age of six, doing all the cooking and cleaning and scolding and comforting on her own. The growing family subsisted on welfare checks, plus whatever meager amount Kittel contributed. After giving birth to Barbara, she left the baby at the hospital and returned home empty-handed. Young Freda, who was barely six at the time, was inconsolable. She conspired with her cousin Richard Walker, the son of Daisy's older sister, Faye. The two children implored Aunt Faye to take the baby, and she agreed, raising the child as one of her own. August Wilson later dedicated his play *The Piano Lesson* to his brothers and sisters. Barbara's name is not among them, although he did have contact with her as an adult.

Life at home was far from luxurious, but Daisy made sure her children were always busy. She loved cards and board games, and the family played tag and other running games in the backyard. The kids made go-carts out of milk crates and fashioned brooms into bats for stickball. They listened to shows on the radio. The older sisters did chores, and as Freddy grew, he had to pitch in, too. Some days, Daisy would send him around to the front of the house to Bella's Market, where he could pick up a loaf of bread on credit. He later told a friend that Bella put her hand on her scale while weighing the meat. But Bella Siger was a vital part of the community. Her husband, Louis, died in 1945, and she purchased the building at 1727 Bedford Avenue, becoming the landlord. She let the family take home groceries when they couldn't pay, so the family shopped there when needed, even if the store was more expensive than larger markets.

Daisy doted on Freddy and reveled in the fact that he learned to read by the time he was four. She had only a sixth-grade education, but she valued literacy as necessary for growth and success. Her mother and stepfather were illiterate. Their opportunities, even after they left Toe River Valley to seek a better life, were limited. She regretted that she had had to leave school early, so she pushed Freddy. When he was five, she marched him down to the modest Hill District branch of the Carnegie Library on Wylie Avenue, where he got his first library card. From that minute on, he read everything he could get his hands on: "editorials, essays, advertisements, instruction manuals, magazines, comic books, newspapers," he said in a speech. There weren't a lot of books at home, but Freddy took all of the Hardy Boys books out of the library and borrowed his sisters'

Nancy Drew mysteries. He preferred the Nancy Drew mysteries; even at such a young age, he was a discerning reader. He used his paper library card so often that it frayed until it was velvety soft. One day he lost it, and he sobbed. "I thought I was cut out of the world of books forever, because I lost my card. No more books for you. But they said, 'You can get another one,' so I did," he said shortly before he died.

Not long after he was born, his grandfather Bynam disappeared. Zonia lived across the street at 1712 Bedford Avenue with Charley and Julia Burley. Julia was Daisy's best friend, and the two women talked every day, playing cards while the neighborhood children romped freely in the backyard at 1727. Kittel was an absent presence in the family, and Charley Burley became a sort of surrogate father to Daisy's children. Burley was a former champion welterweight and middleweight boxer who compiled a career record of eighty-four wins and a glowing reputation as one of the greatest all-around fighters in the sport. But he never got a shot at a world title and ended up supporting his family as a sanitation worker for the city of Pittsburgh.

He made an impression on young Freddy, who grew up enamored of professional boxers. Burley picked up garbage by day, but at night when he went out to listen to jazz in the thriving local clubs, he dressed to the nines, his Florsheim shoes shined, his hat tilted, and his jacket and tie crisp. "I grew up without a father, and the male image that was in my life was Charley Burley," Wilson said years later as an adult. "And that's what being a man meant to me, to be like him. I wanted to grow up and dress like him. He wore those Stetson hats and things of that sort, and I couldn't wait until I got to be a man to be like Charley Burley. Everybody always called him Champ. And for a long while I was growing up, I thought he was the champion." He later modeled his most famous character, Troy Maxson in *Fences*, after the Champ.

And Julia Burley was like a second mother to the Kittel children—but in the Hill District, she was just one of many women who watched out for the local youngsters. "Any one of the adults could tell you to do anything, and you did it quicker than if your mother told you to do it," Wilson said when reminiscing about his childhood. "If Miss Pearl or Bella or Julia or Sadie said to do something and you didn't do it, and they told your mother, it was twice as difficult."

One of those neighborhood ladies made a significant difference for Daisy and her children. Miss Sarah Degree was a devout Catholic who took it upon herself to convert all of the local kids and make sure they were indoctrinated into the Church. One day, she was walking down Bedford Avenue, and she saw Daisy's four young children playing in front of their brick house. She said, "Where is your mother?" Miss Sarah told Daisy, in no uncertain terms, that her children needed to find God. From that day on, Freddy and his siblings went to church every Sunday with Miss Sarah. "Sunday morning, you would see Miss Sarah coming down the street with forty kids. And she had 'em all in a line, and she would take 'em all to church," Wilson recalled. She also held Sunday school at her house—every day of the week during the summer months. Daisy's children made the pilgrimage to Miss Sarah's house, which was blessed with what seemed to Freddy to be a thousand statues of saints. "At six o'clock, there's Miss Sarah teaching us about the Bible. We had to sit there in this hot room in the middle of the summer with Miss Sarah and this huge chart that she got from somewhere, teaching us stories from the Bible and making us say the Rosary every night at seven o'clock."

As an adult, he remembered Miss Sarah with fondness and respect. "I've been threatening to write the bishop of the Archdiocese of Pittsburgh a letter, because we need to honor her in some way: Miss Sarah Degree Gymnasium or Miss Sarah Degree House for Wayward Women," he told an interviewer in 1987, a year after she died. "There's no question: If she was white, they'd have a Miss Sarah Degree Child Care Center or something. I swear I believe that."

With that kind of influence in the neighborhood, it made complete sense that Daisy would send her children to Catholic school. The parochial schools provided a solid education, she thought, and her children started out at Holy Trinity School, one of four Catholic parishes on the Hill. It was located on the Lower Hill, at the corner of Fullerton Street and Centre Avenue, less than a half mile from the family's home. In kindergarten, Freddy stood out because he was already devouring books like a miniature scholar. "We came to school to learn to read, but he came to school already reading," said Sala Udin, a childhood friend a few years older. But the star student did not show off. He never waved his hand in the air when one of the nuns asked a question. But if called upon, he always knew the answer.

The nuns ran a tight and punitive ship, keeping the students in place by rapping them on the knuckles for a tiny infraction, worse discipline for a larger one. And they also dished out a form of subtle, yet emotionally scarring, punishment on some of their students—the ones who looked like young Freddy. The parish had been traditionally white, but it was recruiting members of the Black community at the time, so the classes were mixed, but the racial makeup of the student body was new to the nuns.

Daisy was a loyal parishioner who volunteered at the church, and priests knew that she struggled to feed and clothe her large family. Daisy had a good relationship with the monsignor at Holy Trinity, and the parish helped the family financially, including support for tuition.

Freddy had his own problems. He kept to himself on the playground. He was arguably the smartest kid in the class, but he had trouble communicating. "He was a great stutterer, and that automatically made him a little dorky," said Reginald Howze, Sala Udin's younger brother who was in the same grade as Freddy. It took patience for other children to converse with him because sometimes it took him a few minutes to spit out a sentence. "When he would get frustrated trying to say something, he would make jerky movements trying to get his words out," Howze recalled.

Things were rocky at home, too. In 1950, when Freddy was five and so proud of that library card, his grandmother Zonia died. Her husband, Bynam, eventually turned up in Waterloo, Iowa, where he died alone in 1980. His obituary notice said that there were no known survivors, but his family was alive and well in Pittsburgh. It's not clear whether Zonia took ill before or after he left Pittsburgh, but her last years were difficult. The family buried her in Greenwood Cemetery, a pleasant, tree-lined resting place about nine miles north of the Hill District. Her grave is marked with a simple flat stone, inscribed "Zonia Wilson, 1896 to 1950." She is commemorated with a simple word: "Grandma."

Freddy barely knew the ghost of a woman who lived across the street with "Uncle" Charley and "Aunt" Julia. His older sister, Freda, had a closer relationship with their grandmother, and she later told relatives that Zonia had a haunted look and seemed to suffer from mental illness. She died far from Spear Tops Mountain, the place she had fled several decades earlier. She told her children that she had been raped. She had been tried and convicted in court with her mother. She knew that Willard Justice had been murdered. The man who had rescued her, Bynam Wilson, had gotten up and left Pittsburgh, the same way he had left another family in North Carolina. Many years later, August Wilson named one of the characters in *Joe Turner's Come and Gone* after his grandmother. The character of Zonia is an eleven-year-old girl who shows up in a boardinghouse with her father, Herald Loomis, a man who is "at times possessed." She clings to her father's hand, as if afraid she might lose him.

Daisy did her best to provide a stable home for her family, but money was always tight with all those mouths to feed. She sent the children out to the charity food truck when it made its visits to the neighborhood. The year after Zonia died, she gave birth to another child, a boy named Edwin. He was also Kittel's son. Kittel was still rarely around and when he did show up, the family never knew what to expect. He was an accomplished baker who claimed to have once worked at the Waldorf Astoria, but he also had a fondness for cheap wine in massive quantities. He might come bearing boxes of pastries from the bakeries where he worked or he might show up angry and drunk, slurring his words and hurling racist insults at the children, who ran cowering to hide in the closet. Those times, Daisy would yell for everyone to take cover, while sending one child off to fetch Charley Burley from across the street. It is not clear what he promised Daisy, but he was neglecting the children financially, and Daisy had a temper of her own. In May 1952, she took Kittel to court for "Failure to Support Children Born out of Lawful Wedlock." He was ultimately ordered to pay child support. She gave birth to another child, Richard, in August 1954, and promptly sued Kittel again for "adultery and bastardry." He was ordered to pay an extra $7.50 a week in child support.

It is unclear whether young Freddy or any of the children were aware of their mother's financial and legal battles with Kittel. Daisy strongly believed that her children should not be burdened by her hardships, past and present. But Freddy was keenly aware of how hard she had to work as a single mother and of the fact that the man who was said to be his father was barely present. He rarely, if ever, talked about Kittel later in his life, but those closest to him could see that he was haunted by abandonment issues. "That was something that deeply wounded him, about not having a relationship with his father," said playwright and television writer James Yoshimura, a close friend and confidant. "It was more than bitter. We are all bitter if rejected, but there was something very psychically wounded there. It was the fuel that propelled him into how deep he wanted to develop the patriarchal characters in his plays."

But if he bore scars from growing up without a father, August Wilson also idolized his mother as the most principled woman he knew, and grew angry if anyone dared criticize her. He was enamored when, as a young reader, he discovered Langston Hughes's poem "Mother to Son," which made him realize, in a way, that his mother had a life outside of her relationship with him, that she had struggled but that she had dreams, too, and that she would never give up. It begins "Well, son, I'll tell you: / Life for me ain't been no crystal stair."

His childhood memories of growing up in her home fueled his plays, as well as the stories he told to anyone who would listen, over and over again. One day, the whole family was at home listening to the Top 40 on the radio. The deejay announced a contest that offered a brand-new Speed Queen washing machine for the prize. The question was easy: "What product has the slogan 'When it rains, it pours'?" Daisy quickly wrote the station phone number down on a slip of paper and sent her daughter around front to Bella's Market. She told her to call the radio station and say, "Morton Salt." She practically pushed her out the door: "God damn it," she said, "just go do what I told you." A few minutes later, she heard the deejay announce, "We've got a winner." She had won. The family eagerly anticipated the arrival of that brand-new machine.

It didn't come. When the radio station owners found out that Daisy was Black, they offered her a certificate to get a used washing machine from the Salvation Army. She said no. Her best friend, Julia Burley, urged her to swallow her pride and take the prize. "Daisy, go get the used washing machine. Then you won't have to be wringing out them clothes on your hands." But Daisy was adamant. "Something is not always better than nothing," she told her kids. And then she began saving for a washing machine she could buy with her own money. She put a mayonnaise jar on the counter in the kitchen. Freddy understood that his mother was taking a stand, but he also knew that he wouldn't be getting any spare change for a while. "She reached into her apron and took out a dime," he told an interviewer. "She said, 'That is the first ten cents toward the eighty-nine dollars for a Speed Queen washing machine.' I went, 'Oh man, no more nickels for me.'"

Freddy was always observing events around him, and he absorbed every detail, even if he kept his thoughts to himself. He noticed that white customers at Woolworth's carried out their purchases in paper bags, but the cashiers refused to give bags to the Black customers. When he grew up, he was known to ask for a paper bag when he bought something as small as a pack of gum.

He was a bit of a loner as an elementary school student. But he and the other children were savvy enough to know when something big was happening in the neighborhood. They heard the adults whispering words like "demolition" and "relocation." A major "urban renewal" project was slated for the Lower Hill. In 1955, the Pittsburgh City Council voted to redevelop the area where Holy Trinity was located and where many of Freddy's schoolmates lived to make way for the new Civic Arena. There were some eight thousand people living in the area at the time, representing one-fifth of the Hill's total population, coexisting with around four hundred thriving businesses. Representatives from the city's Urban Redevelopment Authority began knocking on doors, informing residents that the city planned to take the properties by eminent domain to make way for the $21 million project. Residents would have to relocate. Of the 1,885 total families living in the Lower Hill at the time, 67.1 percent were Black, and 32.9 percent were white.

Rumors flew through the neighborhood. "To kids, this was frightening," said Sala Udin. "Will I have a new school? Will I have to find new friends? Why are they tearing our neighborhood down? Why not just fix it up?" Many of the neighborhood's cherished landmarks were slated for the wrecking ball: Crawford Grill No. 1, the YMCA, and the Bethel AME Church. Freddy and his friends may not have loved school, but it was a jolt to hear that Holy Trinity was to be demolished and the students would relocate to St. Richard's School on Bedford Avenue, outside the line of the demolition area. Most of the Black families moved to the Middle and Upper Hill, with 29 percent relocated to public housing, including Udin's large family. Most of the white families moved out of the neighborhood entirely, settling in Pittsburgh's white enclaves like Mt. Washington and Mt. Lebanon. Daisy Wilson's home at 1727 Bedford was not in the demolition zone. And the two-room apartment had become more deluxe. The neighbors upstairs had moved out, so the Wilson family cut a hole in the ceiling and built stairs to combine the upstairs and downstairs, giving Daisy and her children two more rooms.

Despite the upheaval, school did not change much with the move to St. Richard's. It was still not challenging enough for a bookish boy. In fourth grade, the teacher handed out a book on the first day. Freddy took it home and devoured it, page by page. He asked the teacher for another book. She said, "No, we're going to go through that book for the whole year." He clung closely to his cherished library card, which would get him all the books he wanted for free. The nuns noticed his precocity—and his aloof attitude, which could have just been a mask for shyness or social anxiety. He stuttered, after all. "The nuns said I was either going straight to the top or straight to the bottom," he remembered.

Freddy kept to himself for the most part, and the school bullies knew to stay away from him. "He had a reputation of being unpredictable and having a bad temper," said classmate Reginald Howze. "You didn't mess with him." He didn't get into fights often, partly due to the fact that his classmates were aware of his sudden temper and kept a distance. "He used to put his tongue between his teeth and growl when he got angry," Howze said.

But things weren't entirely intolerable for the star student. He had begun writing stories about whatever fancy turned his active mind. In sixth grade, he had Sister Mary Christopher, who inspired him and supported him. "She would stop the class and say, 'Frederick wrote a story, and he's going to read it for the class,'" he said. "I wanted to make it good. She was very, very encouraging."

A trip to buy a new pair of shoes was a grand occasion, and it was his one memory of a special outing with Kittel. The baker took the boy downtown to buy a pair of Gene Autry boots. Before they went into the store, Kittel handed Freddy a handful of coins and told him to jingle them in his pocket, to make it look as if he had money to spare. This memory would stick with him, but not out of fondness for Kittel. He understood the implicit message: a Black boy needed to appear well-off or he could be suspected of criminal activity. He never forgot it.

Kittel named him as his son in his will when he died in 1965, but he left out Freda, who everyone in the extended family knew had a different father from Daisy's other children. Yet when he became a prominent playwright, August Wilson rarely mentioned his father—except in an intimate, curious letter he later wrote to his friend Jean Passannante in which he wondered whether his father, whoever and wherever he was, had commissioned a photographic portrait he had of his mother, taken the year he was born. Certainly, as a boy, he didn't dare raise the issue. His mother was the center of his universe. He lived in a matriarchal society, and all his "aunts," whether blood relatives or pillars in the neighborhood, were to be respected and never questioned.

The same was true at school. He butted heads again with the seventh-grade teacher at St. Richard's, Sister Mary Eldephonse. Freddy was not a fan, and the dislike was mutual. He had been the star student who got to read his stories aloud in Sister Mary Christopher's class. But he had a feeling this new teacher was out to get him. He later said that he sleuthed around, listening to adult conversations and trying to figure out

why she was so different from his other teachers. He said that he discovered that his teacher's real name was Agatha, and he determined that she
didn't have a vocation and had joined the sisterhood to run away from
her parents. He had already begun making up narratives for people he
encountered. He didn't dare confront her with his tale, but his attitude
showed that he had no respect for her. She frequently sent him out of the
class to sit in the principal's office, but the principal, a nun named Sister
Ann Catherine, was also the eighth-grade teacher. He sat in her class and
listened, and when she gave tests, he asked to take them along with the
older students. "I was the only one who got all the answers right," he said.

But he still had to endure some time with Sister Mary Eldephonse,
who made a lifelong impression on him. He craved the role of Joseph in
her Christmas pageant, which was his first introduction to theater. But Sister Mary Eldephonse cast a white girl named Nancy Ireland as Mary and
a boy who, like Freddy, stuttered as Joseph. Nancy was his seventh-grade
crush. He wrote her love letters and left them on her desk, unsigned. He
had taken to writing poetry, and he penned lyrical verse expressing his
youthful desire. He later quoted one such poem, the work of a lovelorn
adolescent infatuated with a fetching classmate and enamored by flowery
words. The short poem reads like a long, drawn-out sigh.

Despite his flair for flowery verse, the young Cyrano de Bergerac
didn't even get a speaking role in the Christmas pageant. When he retold
the story years later in his one-man show, *How I Learned What I Learned*,
he complained that the boy playing Joseph had a speech impediment, but
he didn't mention that he, too, stuttered at the time. His friend Howze said
Wilson didn't get over his speech difficulty until years later when he was
a young poet reciting his work at coffeehouses and galleries. As an adult,
Wilson did not broadcast the fact that he stuttered as a boy; he didn't mention it to his collaborator Todd Kreidler while they were working on *How
I Learned* together. But in the show, he tells a story about a friend who
was turned down for a job as a disc jockey. The friend is convinced he is a
victim of racism, but when he speaks, he trips on his words and is hardly a
good fit for a job as a radio broadcaster. The anecdote always gets a laugh,
but Wilson was curiously silent about his own difficulty.

It is possible that the nun deliberately slighted Freddy because she disliked him, but it is equally possible that she didn't think he was capable of a lead role. Instead, he was assigned to play the cymbals. The school didn't own any cymbals, so they had to borrow them from another school. During rehearsals, Freddy simply clapped his hands. He did get to spend time with Catherine Moran, a waiflike white girl from a poor family who was assigned the role of the narrator. He forgot all about his love for the heartthrob Nancy Ireland and devoted his attention to the narrator.

On the night of the pageant, they consummated their love with a kiss just before the play began. It was a coming-of-age moment for young Freddy, who would later develop a reputation as a Casanova. But this preteen moment was pure innocence. "Brief. Electric. The kiss was witness and sanction and it deepened our conspiracy," he wrote. "And I knew that years later I would have to travel through the province of unsettled schoolboys searching for the fleshy comforts of conquest. The wild, exclamatory music of sorority girls in full surrender and secret knowing of riotous muscle. But here, now, that kiss held us in the conspiracy of boundless joy."

That kiss, so forbidden by the rules of the St. Richard's nuns, was an act of rebellion and a defining moment for the socially inept but brilliant boy. Maybe this theater thing had potential. Maybe being an outcast didn't mean you had to be a nobody. Maybe he could find his own way in the world, Sister Mary Eldephonse aside.

He held on to that realization of his self-worth. Life at home had changed dramatically as well, mostly for the better. Kittel had been showing up less around 1727 Bedford Avenue. He took a place in the background after Daisy met David Legion Bedford—a large, gray-haired man with a troubled past. In 1931, when Daisy was eleven and still living on the mountain with Eller, Bedford had been involved in the robbery of a drugstore on the Hill. A talented football player, he was trying to get money to attend Pitt. The robbery went awry, and he shot and killed Harry Siegel, an employee working his first night as manager. Bedford was sentenced to life imprisonment and sent to the Western State Penitentiary, an imposing brick structure about four miles north of downtown Pittsburgh.

Bedford became a model prisoner who created programs to educate his fellow inmates. He made neckties in the prison work program, and the guards trusted him enough to allow him to keep scissors in his cell. He had a spotless record while imprisoned. He was accused of participating in a prison riot in January 1953, but another inmate defended him and testified that Bedford not only did not participate, he protected several inmates who took cover in his cell. After serving twenty-three years, Bedford's sentence was commuted in 1954 by Pennsylvania governor John S. Fine.

Bedford must have been charmed by Daisy Wilson. She had a bunch of kids, but he stepped in to join the family and support them. He had a car, and the family began doing the grocery shopping at stores outside the Hill, where their choices were not limited to one overpriced market. He had a job working sanitation for the city. He got home at four in the afternoon, and Daisy had dinner on the table for the whole clan at five. There weren't a lot of presents on Christmas morning, but Daisy and Bedford always fetched the biggest tree they could fit in the house, and Daisy cooked in earnest, making family favorites like fried chicken and greens and sweet potato pie. The children no longer feared sudden appearances by Kittel. David Bedford was a calming, stabilizing influence and there is a bit of him in Troy Maxson from *Fences*, who tells a tale about going to prison for murder and coming out determined to make an honest living and support a family as a sanitation worker. The children no longer had to run to line up at the food truck, bringing home powdered milk and government cheese. Bedford had a steady income, and they were more comfortable than ever before.

In 1958, when Freddy was in seventh grade, the Hill District was still in disarray over the urban development. White families were fleeing. Businesses were closing. The family moved to Hazelwood, settling at 303 Flowers Avenue, a two-family house in a white neighborhood a few miles south of the Hill District. It was bigger than the apartment, with more room for the kids to spread out. Daisy enrolled Freddy at St. Stephen's, the local parochial school. He was the only Black boy in his class. They were in the neighborhood for a few days when Freddy got a lesson in life. In the Hill District, most families struggled to make ends meet, but they all looked out for each other, Black, white, Arab, Jew. The adults scolded and harangued the kids, but they also cared for them. Before the Lower Hill was razed, he had lived side by side with people of all races and ethnicities.

So he didn't expect what happened one night shortly after the move. Someone threw a brick through the window of their new house. There was a note attached. It said "Stay out nigger."

CHAPTER THREE

Something Is Not Always Better Than Nothing

From my early childhood, books have always been an important part of my life. That has carried over in my adulthood and I have often fallen asleep with a book in my arms where there should have been a woman. I have stained the pages of books with coffee, ketchup, water, mustard, bourbon and more than a few times with tears.

—AUGUST WILSON

On a muggy morning in September 1959, Freddy put on a jacket and tie and picked up his book bag. He walked out the door of the family's new home at 4738 Sylvan Avenue, a few blocks away from their former home on Flowers Avenue. The family had stayed on Flowers Avenue for only a few months; that nasty, racist note was not a one-time occurrence. One night, hoodlums smashed the windshield of David Bedford's car, and the family had had enough. They were now settled into a new rental home, which had three bedrooms and was far more comfortable than the flat on the Hill. The backyard looked out on the smoky towers of J&L Steel, which was perched a few blocks away on the banks of the Monongahela River. The plant provided jobs for many in the neighborhood, and its blast furnaces emitted clouds of dark, sulfurous air. (In the 1940s, the

Pittsburgh air was so polluted that the city was shrouded in dark clouds all hours of the day. That started to improve when Mayor David L. Lawrence began efforts to clean up the air in 1946, reducing smoke pollution significantly in the next twenty years, but the air in Hazelwood was murky when the family lived there.) The plant wasn't particularly welcoming to Black workers, who struggled to get union cards. The new neighborhood, however, was welcoming to the Wilson family, and Freddy had made a few friends on the street. "Looking back on it, those very important years from twelve to eighteen years were spent in a place with Little League teams and middle-class experiences," he said. "You could sleep with your windows open, and a friend could come stick his head in your window to wake you up."

But an impressionable teenager does not forget a brick being thrown through the window, and the experience certainly made the already circumspect Freddy more guarded, especially in unfamiliar places.

It was his first day in a new school, and as he walked out the door that morning, he most likely didn't know that the story of a Black family encountering racism in a middle-class white neighborhood was playing to great acclaim in New York. Lorraine Hansberry's *A Raisin in the Sun* had opened on Broadway in March 1959 at the Ethel Barrymore Theatre. It was directed by a man named Lloyd Richards, the first Black man to direct on the Great White Way. The play introduced white audiences to the lives of a Black family for the first time, and a significant number of Black people went to the theater to see it, also a first. "Never before in the entire history of the American theater had so much of the truth of Black people's lives been seen on the stage," James Baldwin wrote of the play. Freddy's only experience with theater, however, had been that Christmas pageant in seventh grade.

Broadway was certainly not on Freddy's mind that morning. At five foot seven and 175 pounds, he had grown into a sturdy boy with broad shoulders, strong arms, and powerful fists. He still had a reputation for being hot-tempered, but he was also a stellar student capable of work years above his grade level. This was an opportunity he couldn't pass up. The monsignor at St. Stephen's had agreed to sponsor him at Central

Catholic High School, the prestigious all-boy college-preparatory school in the tony Oakland neighborhood of the city. That meant the parish paid his tuition. Students had to have excellent grades to get in, and Freddy landed a highly desirable spot. This was a great honor, and Daisy held on to great hopes for her eldest boy. He would go to college. He would study law at Notre Dame—at least that's what Daisy hoped. She repeatedly reminded him that he had an IQ of 143; she expected him to use it. Central Catholic, known for its high standards and superior instruction from the Christian Brothers, was the first step toward that dream. Established in 1927, the school had a student body of 1,800 boys from more than fifty parishes in 1959. Its motto was to "inspire boys to become men of faith, men of scholarship, and men of service."

Freddy must have been well aware his mother was banking on his success as he walked over to Second Avenue to catch the streetcar. Oakland is just a few miles from Hazelwood, but the neighborhoods are strikingly different. Known as Pittsburgh's center of higher learning, Oakland boasts the leafy campuses of the University of Pittsburgh and Carnegie Mellon University.

Freddy's bus came to a stop at 4720 Fifth Avenue. The day was already scorching hot, and the pea-soup air that gave the city its nickname Smoketown added to the oppressive heat. When he looked up at the building, he saw an imposing Flemish Gothic structure, with soaring towers and buttresses. Almost all the students arrived in streetcars or hitched a ride to the school, and they climbed the steps and entered through the massive Fifth Avenue front doors. Few of them looked like him. There were only a handful of African American students in his grade. But the school boasted its own library, and Freddy had already devoured hundreds of books at the Hazelwood and Hill District branches of the Carnegie Library.

The students at Central Catholic were tracked—placed in classes based on their academic ability—starting on the first day. Freddy had taken the school's placement exam, and he was placed in 3F, the third-highest rank. He walked up the four flights of stairs to the freshmen classrooms, passing through the cavernous stairwell in which every noise echoed. He was one of about forty boys in his class—and the only Black student in the room.

His homeroom teacher was Brother Vincent, a bespectacled man with a shock of white hair. Like all the other Brothers, he wore a floor-length black robe and a white collar. Every day, he called the class to order for morning prayers and the Pledge of Allegiance.

The school was stifling, especially on the fourth floor. At Central Catholic, the teachers, all Christian Brothers, moved from class to class, and the students stayed in their homerooms. It was a long time to sit still. For study hall, the freshmen were marched downstairs to the auditorium, a stuffy, dark expanse with stained-glass windows blocking out any natural light. The day dragged on, but Freddy was encouraged when Brother Dominic, the English teacher, showed up to lead the class. English was his favorite subject.

Lunchtime, on the other hand, was torture. He didn't know any of the other students, and they weren't particularly friendly. He sat alone at his own table because none of the other students would sit with him. "It was like I was contaminated or something," he told an interviewer. But one day he was quietly eating his lunch alone, and a student named Tom Kennedy sat down at his table. He was a star on the freshman football team. Kennedy didn't say anything. He just sat there. "He ate his lunch. I ate my lunch. I came in the next day, and there's like four guys sitting at the table. I'm like, 'That's my table.' Now, I didn't have anywhere to sit. I had to eat my lunch standing up. I liked it better when I had my own table, at least I had a table. I thought, 'This ain't working.'"

At recess, the boys were not allowed to run around and play ball or just hang out. They were required to walk in a counterclockwise circle, single file, in the courtyard behind the school. The goal was to encourage quiet contemplation—but for Freddy, it was anything but peaceful. Years later, he described this ritual as torture. The students had to walk with their eyes looking straight ahead, and the taunts began almost immediately. A potato chip bag "accidentally" hit him in the back. Someone stepped on the back of his shoe.

As an adult, he remembered experiencing shock at this treatment. The Hill had been an "amalgam of the unwanted," a melting pot of people who helped each other out and watched each other's children. Here, he was singled out as the "unwanted" student. "The neighborhood I grew up in was very mixed, there were white, black, all sorts of people. So going from there to Central Catholic at fourteen was really the first time I had confronted anything like . . . racism, actually."

Daisy was enthusiastic about all the doors Central Catholic would open for her prolific child. When he complained about the school, she likely told him about another Black boy from the Hill District, Rob Penny, who had gone to Central Catholic. He was a star athlete, the standout sprinter on the track team who won a chestful of medals and awards. Penny graduated in 1957, two years before Freddy enrolled. Samuel Howze, whom Freddy had known from his days at Holy Trinity and St. Richard's, also attended Central Catholic, but he was a few years older. Later Freddy learned that Howze (who changed his name to Sala Udin in the 1960s) felt the school was a breeding ground for racism, encouraged by the Christian Brothers. One day in the cafeteria, Howze and his handful of Black friends sat down at their table to find a note: "This is Negro history week. Invite a nigger to lunch." By this point, Howze and his friends were seething. They pinpointed the troublemakers, who were snickering at another table. They rushed them all at once, upending the table and starting an all-out brawl. Shortly thereafter, Howze was "invited to find another school."

While Freddy did not witness that fight, he was aware of it and the culture in which it was allowed to happen. His introduction to the elite world of preparatory school was bracing, and every day was another lesson that this cold-blooded environment was the distinct opposite of the warm melting pot of the Hill District. He arrived almost every morning to find a note on his desk saying "Nigger, go home." He tore the notes up and pretended nothing had happened. That is how he started every single day—until the day he, like Howze, couldn't take it anymore. Freddy was known for doing a slow boil and eventually exploding. One morning, Brother Vincent called the class to order and, on cue, all of the boys stood to say the Pledge of Allegiance. The boys recited in unison, but when they got to the part "One nation under God," Freddy heard it. The student behind him substituted the N-word for the word "nation." He turned around, grabbed the boy by the shoulders, threw him to the floor, and started punching him, hard. Pandemonium broke out, and at the end of the day, there were about forty boys waiting to attack him when he left the building. The principal sent Freddy home in a cab, for his own protection.

And it kept happening. Freddy would hold his anger in, until one day he would explode and he'd end up in a cab again. But he didn't take a cab to school in the morning. Sometimes, his tormenters would be waiting on the steps of the school, ready to jeer at him as he made his way through the door.

Unlike Rob Penny, the Hill District athlete who had thrived at the school, Freddy couldn't even catch a break with sports. He tried out for the football team, but didn't make the cut. They told him he was too small. At five seven and 175 pounds, he was hardly small. His stepfather, David Bedford, a high school football player himself before he got into trouble with the law, tried to intervene, but the coaches wouldn't budge.

The only outlet Freddy had at the school was Brother Dominic's English class. Freddy found great pleasure in reading and writing, and Brother Dominic became a mentor. The teacher encouraged Freddy's writing and told him he could be a successful author. Freddy was already thinking of writing as a career. One day, at age fourteen, he walked into the Hazelwood branch of the Carnegie Library on his way home from playing basketball. He discovered the "Negro" section, a collection of thirty or so books. He picked up a sociological tract and read the phrase "the Negro's power of hard work." He always remembered how that phrase struck him. "That word 'power' was magical. I had never seen or heard of it associated with the word Negro before. Even though the context of its usage was in explaining the Negro's suitability for slavery, it didn't matter. I wrenched it from its place in the text and set it separate in my mind in a high place." He thought of that word "power" when he worked after school cutting the lawn for a neighbor named Herbert Douglas, who had gone blind after suffering a heart attack at forty-one. His disability did not hinder him and he built a successful parking garage business in Pittsburgh. His son, Herbert Douglas Jr., had won the Bronze medal for the long jump at the 1948 Olympics. Freddy respected his neighbor's perseverance and wanted to do a good job. "I was proud of the fact that a blind man trusted me to cut his lawn, and I am afraid after reading that line about the Negro's power of hard work, I didn't so much cut Mr. Douglas' lawn as plow it," he said.

At fourteen, he alternated between wanting to be the next heavyweight champion of the world or the next Hank Aaron. One day, when the Milwaukee Braves were in town, he waited at the ballpark to shake the hand of Hammerin' Hank. But he was also a regular habitué of the library. He spent hours reading in the "Negro" section, discovering other possibilities while reading Langston Hughes for the first time. "One thing I took beyond all others that that shelf of books gave me was the proof that it was possible to be a writer," he said of his time in the library. He sought out any Black writer he could find. He took out *The Complete Poems of Paul Laurence Dunbar* and returned it—three decades later. He rethought everything that had ever happened to him and his family and reevaluated every encounter he had had with people in positions of authority: "the teachers, the principal, the policeman, the mailman, the landlord, the grocer, the pharmacist, the people in the welfare department, the clerks in the department stores, the fireman, the streetcar conductor, the insurance man, the furniture salesman." They were all white. That led him to think about his mother and her forebears. "I began to understand how it was my grandmother and grandfather came to be in Spear, N.C. I began to understand the profound implications of slavery."

He also read Ralph Ellison's *Invisible Man*, which changed the course of his trajectory. "It opened a world that I entered and have never left," he said of the novel. He discovered, there on that shelf of thirty-odd books, that he could become a writer.

He was armed with that new sense of self-discovery when he handed in an English class assignment for Brother Dominic, who was teaching poetry writing. He wrote a poem about a Black man, and he deliberately used the word "Black" and not "Negro." That did not fly with Brother Dominic, who called his star student in for a discussion. Freddy was proud of his work and fashioned himself as a budding Langston Hughes. But his mentor had other thoughts. "You shouldn't just write about Blacks," he told his fourteen-year-old student. "You should write about universal sub-jects." Later, Freddy would realize how wrong that was because it implied that the Black experience was outside of the universal experience. In fact, he would dedicate his career as a writer to dispelling that wrong-headed notion. But he wanted to please his favorite teacher, so he started writing nature poems. That period did not last long, but the misguided advice nagged at him. He was a young writer in search of his voice, and he iden-tified more with the books he was reading than with the style of poetry writing that he was being taught.

While he was struggling internally, the daily insults persisted. After almost making it through the year, Freddy exploded. Shortly before his fifteenth birthday, he saw a nasty note on his desk for the last time. He stormed into the principal's office. "I'm gonna quit," he said. "I'm gonna quit." The principal ran and got Brother Dominic, who tried to convince him to stay. But Freddy was done. He was done with the snickers, the jabs, the "accidental" kicks during the ritual walk at recess, the loneliness. All of it. He announced he was leaving, and he walked out.

His mother was not pleased. There was quite a scene when he got home. She lectured him about her dream for him to become a lawyer. She drummed in how he was the smartest of all of her children, how she had worked so hard to get him into that school, that she had done everything she could to make sure he would succeed. As adults, his siblings said that Daisy was hardest on her eldest son because she expected the most from him. He probably looked at his feet while she screamed at him because he had taken to staring downward and scrunching his shoulders at Central Catholic. In the school's 1959–60 yearbook, he stands in the back row of his homeroom photo, gazing at the ground. Daisy gave him an ultimatum. "Well, okay if you're not gonna be a lawyer, go down there and learn how to fix cars or something," she told him. Her brother Ray, the "Mexican," fixed cars. He made good money.

That is how he ended up at Clifford B. Connelley Trade School, a pub-lic vocational high school in the Hill District that had been teaching car-pentry, plumbing, and automotive trades skills to both Black and white students since it opened in 1930. Unlike vocational technical schools today, which now boast programs to prepare students for such white-collar professions as computer science and engineering, Connelley was a stopping point for students who were ill-equipped for college. When Freddy showed up at the school, he learned that auto mechanics was full. So was the auto body shop. He was assigned to the sheet metal shop, where he sat, day after day, making tin cups.

The point of the school was to provide students with the skills to earn a living in a trade; academics were secondary. But the school did require the students to take academic classes in the afternoon, and when Freddy first entered the classroom, he was appalled. "They're doing fifth-grade work! Half the kids can barely read," he told his mother. He clashed with the sheet metal teacher, and one day, the teacher knocked him off his stool. He told his mother, "I don't want to be an auto mechanic. I don't want to make tin cups."

He transferred to Gladstone High School, which was conveniently located just across the street from his house on Sylvan Avenue in Hazelwood. The commute was easy enough. But he was confused and disappointed in himself. He was also bored. The classes weren't challenging for a boy who had already read more books than most of the teachers. He wasn't impressed with the school, but at least no one was leaving nasty notes on his desk.

And there was one particular teacher who fascinated and infuriated him at the same time. The history teacher was a Black man Wilson later referred to as Mr. Biggs. Every day after class, he would take off his sport jacket and put on a smock. The students could see that it was a stockboy uniform. He was a tenth-grade history teacher who moonlighted as a stock boy and also worked as a soda jerk over the summer. He must have been saving his money for a bigger dream; he wanted to be someone in life. He didn't want to teach history to surly tenth-grade students.

Freddy sensed Mr. Biggs was the kind of Black man who wasn't comfortable in his skin. He didn't like the Black students and turned a blind eye when white students lied about having completed their homework assignments. But Mr. Biggs ran an after-school club to prepare students to apply for college, and Freddy joined, sensing an opportunity. One major assignment was to write a research paper on a historical figure. He decided to write about Napoleon. He admired the fact that he was a self-made emperor. Plus, he had taken Napoleon as a nickname with his friends in Hazelwood. They went to pick apples at an abandoned orchard in the area, and each took a name. One boy called himself Tarzan because he was a good climber. A kid named Earl was Daniel Boone because he was a scout. And Freddy was Napoleon because he was the leader. The other boys looked up to him. Whenever they were unsure of the plan for the day, they asked him, "What do we do next?"

So Freddy left school that day and started to research his paper. He worked tirelessly on it. He called it "Napoleon's Will to Power," a phrase he took from a line by Victor Hugo. He read book after book, even though he knew most of the kids in the class were copying their papers straight from the encyclopedia. He was so proud of his work that he hired his sister to type it for him on a rented typewriter. It was twenty pages long; he knew, because he paid her by the page. It had a long section with footnotes. It was a classy piece of writing.

He handed it in, expecting to get nothing but praise—and a top grade. The next day, Mr. Biggs asked him to stay after class. Freddy was excited. Finally, maybe someone besides Brother Dominic would recognize his intelligence and talent. He walked into the room, and Mr. Biggs showed him the paper. He had written an A and an E (the grade for failure at the time) at the top of the title page. Freddy was confused. "I'm going to give you one of these two grades," Mr. Biggs said. "That doesn't make much sense to me," Freddy replied. Mr. Biggs flipped through the pages, all twenty of them, and said, "Where did you do your research?"

Freddy pointed out that all of his sources were listed in the bibliography. Mr. Biggs replied, "Well, you have some older sisters. Is it possible that they could have written this paper?" By this point, Freddy was writing papers for his sisters—and they were paying him to do it. He told Mr. Biggs that, yes, he had written the paper and his word should be enough to prove it. Mr. Biggs leaned back in his chair, circled the E on the title page, and handed the paper back to Freddy, who was incensed.

Freddy tore the paper to shreds, threw it in the wastebasket, and stormed out of the room. He didn't go back to school the next day. He was on strike. The morning after he tore up his paper, he stood beneath the basketball hoop in the playground at Gladstone High School, an imposing brick building set on a slight hill at the corner of Sylvan and Hazelwood Avenues. Even though his house was right across the street, the kitchen was in the back, so his mother could not see him. He dribbled the ball with ferocity. He shot. Again and again. He was hoping that the principal would see him and ask why he wasn't in class. He was hoping Mr. Biggs might see him, too. It didn't happen. After a few days, he gave up. For the rest of his life, he would go on the defensive if he perceived that anyone was undervaluing his work. The incident with Mr. Biggs was more than just a failure of an adult to encourage singular achievement. It was a defining moment that would color his interactions as an artist later in life.

"I dropped out of school, but I did not drop out of life," he said of that pivotal period. Every morning, he got back on the same streetcar that took him to Central Catholic in Oakland, but he got off at the main branch of the Carnegie Library, a stately, white-pillared building with vaulted ceilings. He was naive enough to think that the library, built by the steel magnate Andrew Carnegie, held every book in the world. He remembered being handed one book to slog through for the entire year in fourth grade. "I felt suddenly liberated from the constraints of a pre-arranged curriculum that labored through one book in eight months," he said. Every day, from 9:00 a.m. to 3:00 p.m., he read voraciously, books on "cultural anthropology, theology, the Civil War, slavery, furniture making, photography, airplanes, automobiles, trains and boats, agriculture, culinary art, pottery and table manners." He read biography. He read W. E. B. Du Bois's *The Souls of Black Folk* and Booker T. Washington's *Up from Slavery*. He read the Emancipation Proclamation and the U.S. Constitution. He may have been a high school dropout, but he was more convinced than ever that he was going to be a writer.

But he could keep his secret from his mother for only so long. Even though he came home every day promptly at 3:00 p.m., as if he had been at school just across the street from their home, Daisy eventually figured it out—and all hell broke loose. She was so furious she made him sleep in the basement. Her genius eldest son was fifteen—and a high school dropout. "My mother was through with it," he said. "My entire academic career, I never got anything less than an A. Out of all her kids, I was the one with the most potential. This is what the nuns would tell her. They'd say, 'Mrs. Kittel, he's either going straight to the top or straight to the bottom. There is no middle ground for him.'" Daisy never forgot that. She screamed, "Just like they said, straight to the bottom!"

She wasn't easy on her eldest son, who had been her hope for upward mobility. "She told him he was no good, that he would amount to nothing," his sister Linda Jean told the *New Yorker*. "It was relentless. It was an agony for him. He suffered many indignities. He was often denied food. She would take the food out of the refrigerator, put it in her bedroom, lock the door, and then go out. He was made to live in the basement for a while. She said he was dirty. She didn't want him in the house upstairs."

He took his mother's criticism hard, but he was at sea. He picked up odd jobs, but continued to read and dream of becoming a writer. In 1962, when he was seventeen, he enlisted in the U.S. Army at his mother's insistence. He later told his friend the novelist Charles Johnson that he got frustrated and quit. "Being a proud and hot-blooded young man, he left when he was told he was still too young to apply for officers' training school," Johnson wrote. According to other accounts, he was allowed to take the exam and his score was "off the charts," but he was not accepted into the training program. Later in life, he didn't talk much about his experience in the services or clear up the various versions of the story. There are no military records on file at the U.S. National Archives for a Frederick August Kittel, but all accounts say that he left the army after a year.

Later, he was dismissive of the army as one of the only viable choices for young Black men. "Anyone who goes into the army and makes a career out of it is a loser," he said. "They sit there and are nurtured by the army and they don't have to confront life." In *Fences*, the young, talented athlete Cory joins the marines after his father throws him out of the house. He wanted to be a football star, but the military was the best option available to him once he was on his own. At the end of the play, however, Cory decides the military is not the career for him. "I got six [years] already," he says. "I think that's enough."

One year was certainly enough for Freddy. After he got out of the army in 1963, he went off to Los Angeles with a man named Horace, one of his sister's ex-boyfriends. Horace was a pharmacist, and he set Freddy up with a job in a drugstore. The City of Angels was alluring to the young man at first. He later wrote a poem called "LA 1963." In the beginning of the poem, he is enchanted with the city; it is full of beautiful women and ripe with possibility. But he eventually became disillusioned and remembered that waitresses in Los Angeles would call him "boy," which angered him. Years later, he became enraged when anyone said, "What'll you have, boys?" when taking a restaurant order. He left Los Angeles at the end of the year, and he didn't talk much about his experience. His poem, brimming with optimism at first, ends tersely, and Wilson got out of Los Angeles and returned to Pittsburgh, which felt like home.

CHAPTER FOUR

A Period of Reinvention

His art was anchored in lacerations and a latticework of scar tissue.

—CHARLES JOHNSON

One late afternoon in January or February 1964, Peggy Martin was sitting at the return desk of the University of Pittsburgh library, which was located in the school's huge, landmark Cathedral of Learning at the time. She had recently flunked out of the university, and her mother had told her she wasn't allowed back in the house unless she had a job. At nineteen, she was a bookish young woman despite her academic failure, and she was well-suited for a job in the library. That day, she looked up at the window opposite the desk. The sun was about to set, and the window was covered with moisture. She saw a young man standing there, bathed in a watery glow. "I was mesmerized," she said. "I was like, 'Who is that god over there?'"

She beckoned him over, and he said he was looking for some books. He introduced himself as August and readily admitted that he wasn't a student, but he hadn't been able to find certain books at the main branch of the Carnegie Library, just a few blocks away. For some reason, she immediately trusted him and got the books. The two made a deal. He could ask her for books, she would sign them out, and they would meet at the entrance to the library for the exchange. He always brought them back, and a friendship was born. They were both voracious readers. She was reading Freud, so he did, too. They both read the Welsh poet Dylan Thomas. He requested books by the historian John Hope Franklin, including *From Slavery to Freedom* and *The Free Negro in North Carolina, 1790–1860*, which held particular interest to him given his mother's roots. Martin decided to learn three new words a day, and when August found that out, he did the same thing. Their sentences were full of outrageously long and obscure words.

They were not romantically involved, but they had a bibliophile affair. Martin was a young white woman who had befriended Black students at Pitt, and she later surmised that the man—who called himself August, not Freddy—likely saw her with her Black friends and intuited that he could trust her. (He hadn't officially rechristened himself as August Wilson yet, but he was no longer going by his given name with new friends.) He was a frequent visitor to the Carnegie Library, which is adjacent to the Pitt campus, and he had taken to hanging around the campus and had noticed a pretty young white girl eating lunch with the Black students in the cafeteria. When they finally met, he never told her he was a high school dropout. He just had a certain magnetism that made her feel special. He focused his eyes on her as if she were the only person in the world, even if they were simply sharing new words one of them had discovered in a book. August Wilson had that effect on women from an early age, and he would use it for the rest of his life.

He had continued to read voraciously when he returned to Pittsburgh from Los Angeles. The City of Angels had been an eye-opener for him. Outside of his home cocoon, he saw how the rest of the world lived, and he wasn't sure he liked it. And at nineteen, he was searching for a purpose. Life had changed with his family. His mother had moved twice: first to Homewood and then back to the Hill District, where she settled in a house at 1621 Bedford Avenue, a few doors down from where he grew up. She would live there for the rest of her life. She was still partnered with David Bedford, but she was about to use her wiles to get something out of Frederick Kittel, the absentee father of her children. His wife, Maryanna Jodzis Kittel, passed away on January 6, 1964. Daisy Wilson went into action. She and Kittel went to the courthouse in nearby Butler County and got married on May 1, 1964. They chose the courthouse carefully; it was far enough outside of Pittsburgh so Kittel's brothers would not be aware of the union. Interracial marriage had been legal in Pennsylvania since 1780, but it wouldn't become legal nationwide until the 1967 *Loving v. Virginia* Supreme Court decision struck down laws banning miscegenation.

Daisy's son Richard concluded that the marriage was Daisy's ploy to get dependent benefits for her children. "My mother was very practical and pragmatic, and she wanted to do the best she could for us," he said. "We were her life." At any rate, Kittel did not move in with Daisy after the marriage; she was still living with David Bedford. A few months after the civil ceremony, Kittel filed for divorce, stating that he had suffered indignities that rendered his "condition intolerable and life burdensome." The divorce never went through; after Kittel's initial petition for divorce, he dropped the case and did not file any further paperwork with the courts.

It is unclear what Daisy's eldest son knew of the negotiations with Kittel. The young man who now called himself August was declaring his own independence at the time, and he had always had a small, nagging suspicion that Kittel might not be his biological father. He didn't talk about it, but some family members speculated about it privately years later. On March 5, 1965, he moved out of his mother's home and settled in a furnished basement apartment at 85 Crawford Street, a stone's throw from St. Benedict the Moor church and not far from the Connelley Trade School, where he had halfheartedly made tin cups. He worked odd jobs, and he adopted a sartorial style that was more akin to the 1940s than the turbulent 1960s. He bought woolen coats from the St. Vincent de Paul thrift shop, and he always had his shoes shined, a lesson he had learned from Charley Burley. He smoked a pipe, completing the tweedy image. "He was always in businessman appropriate. Everyone else was wearing boots and army fatigues," his younger brother Richard said. He would walk down the street reciting poetry to himself, and more often than not, he had an armful of books he had gotten from Peggy Martin, along with yellow legal writing pads. He was cultivating an image of a romantic poet. "A lot of people thought there was something wrong with my brother," Richard Kittel said. They either thought he was a lawyer—or the neighborhood nut.

Daisy Wilson was not happy with her son's chosen vocation. When he told her he wanted to be a writer, she looked at him fiercely and said, "How you gonna eat?" She hounded him about other men his age from the neighborhood who had made something of themselves, in her view, at least. "She thought I was a failure," he told an interviewer. "She was always pointing to Sidney—Sidney McClanahan, who worked down at the Ford plant. She'd say, 'Look at Sidney. He's making eleven dollars an hour.' Sidney had a house, a car. He was a success. I had nothing."

She didn't care much for his poetry, either. When a brothel in the neighborhood burned down and three prostitutes died in the flames, Wilson wrote a tribute called "The House of the Seven Whores." He went home one day and recited the poem to his mother. Daisy was not amused. She was furious. If her son frequented such establishments, she didn't want to know. At the time, he was looking for love and inspiration wherever he could find it. He later told Charles Johnson, who became a close confidant after they met at the Seattle Repertory Theatre in 1991, that he once took sage advice from a prostitute, who told him, "If you want to be a writer, you better learn how to write about me." It took him a while to realize that she was telling him to write about residents of the Hill, in their voices and in words they would use.

At the age of twenty, Wilson was one of about fifty-five thousand African Americans living in the Hill District, a neighborhood that he later likened to "a third-world country," given the poverty, life expectancy, and high infant-mortality rate. But to a twenty-year-old aspiring writer, it was a place teeming with life, a stage on which the human comedy played itself out—junkies and artists, hookers and hoodwinks, fruit vendors and con men, every single one of them looking for opportunity. And some found it. Lena Horne had spent five formative years there, and guitarist and singer George Benson grew up there, busking and playing in unlicensed nightclubs at an early age. Wilson later marveled at the vitality of the area: he remembered walking the streets that boasted "nine drugstores . . .

three wallpaper and paint stores, two lumberyards, a live fish market, four funeral homes, eighteen barber shops, thirteen beauty shops, and one hundred and forty-seven bars." It also had eighty-two churches and the Mainway Supermarket, which charged exorbitant fees because it could. Wilson steered clear of the supermarket and rarely worshipped, preferring instead to write in restaurants and cafés, beginning a tradition he would continue for the rest of his life. He jotted down thoughts on napkins, receipts, and random scraps of paper. So often was his pen on paper that the older men who observed him later told him they thought he was drawing. They never imagined a young Black man would be writing florid verse, especially a high school dropout.

And in April 1965, the boy who had been called Freddy renounced all childish things and officially rechristened himself. The elder Frederick Kittel, a hard-and-heavy alcoholic, was dying of cirrhosis of the liver, and for reasons of her own, Daisy took him in, sending David Bedford to sleep in the basement. On paper, she was his wife, and her vows had stated "until death do us part." Kittel got the couch in the living room. Wilson told the *New Yorker* that he had one last visit with his absentee father, who reminisced about his days in the U.S. Army during World War I. But the old man was as volatile on his deathbed as he was during his lifetime: "He suddenly looked up and said, 'Who are you?'" Wilson recalled. "He basically chased us out of there, but for a couple of hours we had a great time." Wilson later wrote a lukewarm tribute called "Poem for the Old Man," which begins with him painting a picture of a man who knew his way around women.

Kittel Sr. died on April 1. He left each of his five "beloved" children $659.01. The eldest sister, Freda, had a different father, as did Barbara, the daughter Daisy had sent away to live with her aunt; neither one was included in Kittel's will. He tried to keep Daisy from inheriting his small estate, but she contested the will and later received a settlement of $8,000. The family did hold a wake for Kittel at a funeral home in Homewood, and his obituary notice identified him as Daisy's husband and the father of six of her children. It also included his brothers Rudolph and Emil as next of kin. The family arranged for a requiem mass, but they buried him at St. Stanislaus Cemetery, in a pauper's grave with no headstone. There is one unmarked grave between Kittel and his first wife, Maryanna Jodzis Kittel, who was also buried in the "singles," or pauper's, section. The two remain separated in death, just as in life.

Years later, when he was already a famous playwright, Wilson told and retold the story of what happened on April 1, 1965, never mentioning Kittel's death that day. He had twenty dollars in his pocket because his sister Freda had paid him to write a paper for her. His three sisters had all graduated from high school, which gave Daisy pride. Her three sons never did. Freda was the only one of her children to go to college. She was a student at Fordham University in New York, and the paper was called "Two Violent Poets: Carl Sandburg and Robert Frost." He took that twenty-dollar bill, engraved with the jowly face of Andrew Jackson, and traded it for a used Royal Standard manual typewriter, which was probably twenty years old. He bought it at McFarren's Typewriter Store on Liberty Avenue downtown and carried it a long way home to the Hill, making the trip on foot because he didn't have any money left for bus fare. In his oft-told version of the story, he sat down in front of the machine, loaded a piece of onionskin in the slot, and rolled it up. He looked at the blank sheet of paper and typed out various versions of his name. August Kittel. Frederick Kittel. Frederick August. He thought of his mother and typed again. Frederick Wilson. August Wilson. He stopped when he got to August Wilson. He was already using the first name August with new friends like Peggy Martin. It worked. He liked the sound of it. He went by that name for the rest of his life, although he didn't change it legally until 1981. He told this story over and over, and the timing of the tale is perfect, even if it meant he left his mother to handle the funeral details while he went shopping for a typewriter. The symbolism was beautiful, and by repeating it so often, he made the story an indelible part of his legend. And he ended his poem to his father with a look toward the future, noting that he was exploring new opportunities but would someday distinguish himself as a writer.

This was a period of reinvention. The boy who called himself Napoleon while playing with his friends in Hazelwood began speaking with an affected Welsh accent, an homage to Dylan Thomas. He mastered the art of code-switching, speaking like a British poet at times and conversing in street language when appropriate. He became fast friends with three other poets on the Hill: the activist Nick Flournoy, the recovering heroin addict Chawley Williams, and Rob Penny, who had preceded him at Central Catholic. This was a turbulent time, and revolution was in the air. Two years earlier, Martin Luther King Jr. had led his March on Washington and gave his "I Have a Dream" speech. Malcolm X was assassinated in February 1965. The next month, peaceful protesters were beaten and tear-gassed during the Selma-to-Montgomery freedom march, an atrocity that was broadcast on live television and became known as "Bloody Sunday." Many of the Pittsburgh poets were writing angry, militant verse. Not Wilson. He was writing flowery, ornate poems about a young man's love conquests and failed attempts at romance. He was focused on becoming a poet, not a revolutionary. Years later, he wrote about being a self-conscious artist holed up in his basement apartment worrying about aesthetics and words. In his introduction to a 1991 collection called *Three Plays*, he wrote, "As I bedded down each night with my immortal self, the guns of social history and responsibility that went boom in the night and called the warriors to their stations went largely ignored."

The newly minted August Wilson was young and impressionable and wanted to make new friends in this exciting life of freedom. He sympathized with the street people and junkies in the neighborhood and allowed them to shoot up in his Crawford Street basement flat. Chawley Williams, a streetwise man who ran numbers when he wasn't dealing drugs, protected him. "When I met August, I was in the drug world," Williams told the *New Yorker*. "Here come August. He's sensitive, he's articulate, he has talent, he's trying to write. And the hustlers of the streets is at him. They could get him to do things, 'cause he wanted to belong. He would allow them to come to wherever he stayed at to eat, to get high and shoot their dope, to lie up with different women. They were trying to get him to get high. I put a halt to that." Later Wilson paid tribute to Williams in his one-man autobiographical show, thanking the elder poet for pushing away the pushers. He described one incident in which the baritone-voiced Williams slammed a junkie against the wall when he offered to share dope with Wilson. "That's August, man, that's August. Don't you never offer him none of that shit." He also partially modeled the title character in his play *King Hedley II* after Williams.

Williams introduced Wilson to a friend named Cy Morocco, who couldn't read but was a generous soul who would become one of the models for the gentle idiot savants who create the soul of Wilson's plays, such as the trumpet player Gabriel in *Fences* or Hambone in *Two Trains Running*. The day they met, Wilson shook Morocco's hand and said, "Nice coat." Morocco gave it to Wilson. "No, man, I just said I liked it." Morocco flashed a snaggletoothed grin, ran back to his apartment, returned wearing another coat, and asked Wilson what he made of the latest article in *Time* magazine. Wilson later learned that Morocco was illiterate and asked for summaries so that he could pretend he read the article himself. He also told everyone he could play the saxophone, but when he performed at open mike nights, he could barely spit out a note. "He was a joke among the musicians," said Pittsburgh composer and jazz musician Nelson Harrison. "When he came around with the saxophone, everyone would run." Morocco later became unhinged and wandered the streets. Wilson dubbed him "the original homeless man," and did all he could to take care of him. The police would occasionally pick him up and bring him to jail to force him to take a shower; they gave him used clothes as well. Wilson thought of him often in later years. "He was an African lost in America," he wrote in *How I Learned*. "Cause when you're African in America there's adjustments and things that you have to make. . . . But Cy had trouble making that adjustment." Morocco remained a generous soul; he didn't have much, but he collected rocks and gave them away to his friends even when he was homeless.

A young woman named Barbara Peterson lived next door to Wilson at 85 Crawford Street. She was an aspiring artist, but she had been rejected by Carnegie Mellon University. In his one-man show, Wilson was direct about why he thought she was denied admission: she was Black. Peterson got a job modeling for an introductory painting class at the university, and while she sat still in her pose, she listened, good and hard. She went home and painstakingly followed the professor's instructions, and she later showed him her portfolio. The professor was so impressed that he got her a full scholarship. She went on to become the director of art for the Pittsburgh Public Schools. "That was my first real lesson in life," Wilson wrote in *How I Learned*. "I said, 'August, there's a way under, around, or through any door.'"

Her boyfriend was in jail at the time, and Wilson and Peterson began a romantic relationship—until the boyfriend was released from jail. She had purchased two chickens. She cooked one and put the other in Wilson's freezer. She came to get the chicken out of the freezer the night she left him. It made an impression, and he always thought of her as someone who knew her way around obstacles.

He had many female companions during those formative years. And he was writing, always writing. He wrote where he ate. One favorite haunt was Eddie's Restaurant, where he would nurse one cup of coffee for hours until the owner, Eddie T. Owens, kicked him out. Owens took pity on the young writer and gave him a job. He lasted all of a day. "He took a break to write and sat in the booth to work on whatever he was writing," Owens's daughter Valerie Johnson said at the time of her father's death in 2000. "My older sister caught him and reported him to Eddie, who said, 'You're not here to write.'" Despite his dismal job performance, Wilson later used Eddie's Restaurant as the model for the setting in his 1992 play, *Two Trains Running*, which unfolds during the heated year of 1969.

Wilson found other places to write when he was kicked out of the restaurant. He wrote at Pat's Place, the local pool hall where the elders gathered. The seniors called him Youngblood: He used that name for a character in his early play *Jitney!*. He had picked up Claude McKay's novel *Home to Harlem*, which mentioned that railroad porters would stop at a pool hall named Pat's Place while in Pittsburgh. He sought out the elders and absorbed their chatter. "They talked philosophy, history; they discussed whatever the topic of the day was—newspapers, the politics of the city, the baseball games, and invariably they would talk about themselves and their lives when they were young men," Wilson said. He had an excellent memory, and he remembered every word. But he was still writing like a romantic English poet, and it wasn't until later that he put the language and expressions of these elders to use in his plays.

He had a string of odd jobs: dishwasher, stock boy, short-order cook. He sold eggs door-to-door with his younger brother Richard. He quit many of these jobs when he encountered the slightest hint of racism. In *How I Learned*, he recounts quitting a job at a toy store before he even started. The manager had told him he would shoot him if he stole anything, so he walked away. "I quit. Motherfucker." He stormed off a landscaping job because his boss accommodated a white woman who refused to let Wilson mow her lawn. He resigned on the spot, only then realizing that he was fourteen miles out of town and had to walk home. He quit a job at Klein's Restaurant, a tony place known for its fresh lobster and garlic puffs, after the manager berated him for being twenty seconds late. The daily indignities made a huge impression on Wilson as a young adult and contributed to his determination to prove the bigots wrong. He knew he was smarter than these men in charge who did not trust him, and the insults stung. He later created characters who had suffered similar slights. Troy Maxson, the lead character in *Fences*, played on a Negro League baseball team, but he could not move up to the Major Leagues because of the color of his skin. He ended up as a trash collector, a job he felt was beneath him. Wilson felt the same way about his jobs.

And he was earning just enough to pay the rent—or not. When he first met Chawley Williams, the older man gave him the name of a lawyer to call when he went to jail. Williams didn't say "if," he said "when." That was not lost on the young Wilson. "As a twenty-year-old Black man in the Hill District in Pittsburgh in 1965 you going to jail," he wrote. "The opportunities on Centre Avenue in 1965 was the opportunity to die an early death. Opportunity to buy some dope. Opportunity to steal something. And if you're lucky, an opportunity to maybe find a girlfriend."

And that is how he ended up in jail. He took a young lady home one night, supposedly to listen to his record collection. But the landlord had padlocked the door because he was behind on the $25 rent. He called the lawyer, who told him it was fine to break open the padlock. But the lawyer was wrong: the apartment was furnished, and it was illegal to enter a furnished apartment after being evicted. Wilson was arrested, and he spent three formative days in jail. He was okay with the other inmates until night set in and the cells were locked. He heard a lone voice singing. When the song was over, another inmate down the corridor called out a suggestion, asking for the man to sing a tune. It's not clear what the suggestion was. Wilson described this incident in *How I Learned*. In the original, unpublished version, he remembered hearing "Just Friends," a tune popularized by the white jazz trumpeter Chet Baker. He wept when he heard the mournful lyrics. But in the posthumously published version of the play, the scene is changed. In this version, Wilson hears "After You've Gone," a Bessie Smith classic. Many of the stories in that "autobiographical" play are greatly exaggerated, and clearly, the script was edited for publication after his death, perhaps to emphasize his love for the blues. Either way, whatever song he heard touched him deeply. Warm tears fell onto the cold floor of Wilson's cell. He had fashioned himself as a great writer and here he was in jail, like a petty criminal. But that lone voice, that artistry, got him through the night. When he was finally released, he vowed to remember the power of art, the power of a Black man singing through the darkest of nights. He was even more committed to his dream. He was, after all, a genius bound for greatness, and he ended up in jail for $25 in back rent. The incident made his desire to prove his worth to the world even greater.

Wilson soon discovered two different kinds of music that changed his life forever. He was a frequent patron of the St. Vincent de Paul thrift shop, where he bought 78 rpm records for five cents each to play on his antique Victrola. One day in 1965, he walked into the store and bought an old 78 record with a yellowed label on it. It was Bessie Smith's "Nobody in Town Can Bake a Sweet Jelly Roll Like Mine." He took it home and played it, and his world changed. Her strong contralto filled the room, and Wilson discovered the blues.

Nobody in town can bake a sweet jelly roll like mine, like mine
No other one in town can bake a sweet jelly roll so fine, so fine
It's worth lots of dough, the boys tell me so
It's fresh every day, you'll hear 'em all say
Don't be no dunce, just try it once. You'll be right in line.

"The universe stuttered and everything fell to a new place," he later wrote. He said that he played the record twenty-two times, marveling in music that spoke to him and his culture. He was not trained musically, but he heard something in Smith's bravado, so full of persistence and sexual confidence as she unabashedly cooed about her "sweet jelly roll," a euphemism for sex. The blues genre, which was not popular in Pittsburgh's vibrant music scene, moved him in a way that nothing else ever had. It connected him to the past, evoked what he later called the "blood's memory." In the introduction to *Three Plays*, he recounted his epiphany when he played the old album over and over again:

> Suffice it to say it was a birth, a baptism, a resurrection, and a redemption all rolled up in one. It was the beginning of my consciousness that I was a representative of a culture and the carrier of some very valuable antecedents. With the discovery of Bessie Smith and the blues I had been given a world that contained my image, a world at once rich and beautiful, and at crucial odds with the larger world that contained it and preyed and pressed it from every conceivable angle.

In that moment, he discovered his muse. "The blues gave me a firm and secure ground," he wrote. "It became, and remains, the wellspring of my art."

During these years, he never stayed in one place very long; Crawford Street was not his only home after he moved out of Daisy's house. He moved in and out of boardinghouses in the neighborhood, but he didn't really understand the residents of those humble homes until he heard

Bessie Smith's voice. "I began to look at the people in the rooming houses differently," he recalled later. "I had seen them as beaten. I was twenty, and these were old people. You could never have told me there was a richness and a fullness to their lives. I began to see it." He began to appreciate Black life on its own terms.

He came to believe that the blues expressed Black life in its fullest, and the music had an indelible influence on his later plays. The blues, he later said, "is the best literature that the Blacks have. It's certainly at the bedrock of everything I do, because it's the world and the people. The music comes out of Black life as created by Black people."

Interestingly, "Jelly Roll" was the B side of the Columbia blue label 78 rpm single, which was released in September 1923. Wilson never mentioned the A-side track, a sultry tune called "If You Don't I Know Who Will" in which Smith lets her lover know that if she doesn't get "furs and things" and "diamond rings," she has another paramour waiting to deliver. Wilson became fixated on the B side, and it became part of the lore he constructed about his formative years. The song that had touched a nerve when he was briefly in jail, "After You've Gone," was a Bessie Smith signature tune. She sang with joyful ribaldry about her empty bed and string of bad lovers, and her worldly, wise, ain't-nobody's-business attitude hit the young Wilson in a familiar place.

When he discovered that record, he was living with a waitress he had become infatuated with at Pope's Restaurant. Everyone called her Snookie, but her real name was Willa Mae Montague. She introduced him to marijuana, and he liked it. She was separated from her husband, Billy, when they met, and before long, Wilson moved into her place. He took her on dates at the Oyster House in downtown Pittsburgh; a fish sandwich cost just thirty-five cents. Life was good. He had a job in the mail room at Kroger, where he had access to free paper and pens. Wilson was in love with Snookie, and he later memorialized the short-lived relationship in *How I Learned*. As he tells it, Snookie showed up for a Valentine's Day date with her estranged husband. In the play, Wilson says Billy pulled a gun on him, activating Wilson's flight-or-fight instinct. It is a great story, but it isn't true. "I never saw Billy with a gun," Montague said. In fact, the two men became great friends and visited her together. She got tired of both of them and ended up with another man, Reginald Howze, Wilson's boyhood friend. But the embellished story meshed perfectly with the myths Wilson cultivated later in his life.

Wilson was learning more about the Hill District. One night in 1966, he was on his way home and came across a crowd outside the Crawford Grill at the intersection of Kirkpatrick Street and Wylie Avenue. People on the Hill knew that there was a window on the side street where they could stand and hear the music, even if they couldn't afford a ticket. There were two hundred people on the street that night, listening to John Coltrane work his magic on the saxophone. Wilson was mesmerized standing on the street with his neighbors. It was another life lesson for the young poet. "It remains one of the most remarkable moments of my life," he wrote in *How I Learned*. He and the other listeners were "stunned into silence by the power of art and the soaring music of John Coltrane and his exploration of man's connection to the divinity. And the power of possibility of human life." At that moment, he became converted to jazz. Previously, he would shrug when he saw his contemporaries walking around with Coltrane or Archie Shepp albums, saying, "Aw, man, it ain't got no words! If it didn't have any words, I wasn't that interested." He observed the power the music had over that crowd and viewed it as a force that "enabled them to survive these outrageous insults that American society has forced on them." He was young. He wanted to be a writer. "This is what I want my art to do," he told himself. And he went out and bought some Coltrane albums to add to his growing music collection.

Sadly, Coltrane would die a year later of liver cancer, but his music inspired Wilson. He was searching—for a voice, for a woman, for a philosophy, for the elusive thing that would define his life. That same year, he went to see a free screening of *The Battle of Algiers*, Gillo Pontecorvo's stunningly brilliant and brutal depiction of the Algerian people's fight for independence against the French. Wilson was on his way to the screening at the New Granada Theater on Centre Avenue when he ran into his younger brother Richard, then in seventh grade. He took him along, and after the screening, they had a long conversation about the film, which was told in documentary style. Richard remembers his older brother telling him that people needed to take responsibility to achieve liberty. "You can't be a drug addict. You have to clean yourself up," Wilson said.

Wilson had a special fondness for Richard, the baby of the family. Richard had fair skin, even lighter than Wilson's. Since Daisy had moved back to the Hill, he attended the Epiphany School, near the Civic Arena where the neighborhood had been demolished. At the end of each school day, the white students would turn one way and head for Fifth Avenue to go to their homes downtown. Richard turned the other way toward Centre Avenue and the Hill District. "I went with all the Black kids, and I was questioned about that by the white kids," he said. Wilson faced the same kind of questions, and he understood the confusing situation for his younger brother. Wilson identified as Black, and he encouraged his younger sibling to feel just as comfortable with his racial identity and to ignore the questions.

When he was in middle school, Richard frequently stopped by his older brother's apartment to play with the typewriter. Wilson always rented furnished apartments, and his prized possessions were the typewriter and his massive record collection. Some in the neighborhood thought that Wilson was Richard's father, given that he dressed in a suit jacket and tie and carried himself like a distinguished gentleman. He read his poetry aloud to his younger brother, who noticed the affectation in his brother's voice when he recited his verse. "He had two voices," Richard said. Over the years, Wilson offered Richard fatherly advice, sometimes solicited, sometimes not. His younger brother got caught in a cycle of petty crimes; he was arrested more than twenty-two times and spent years in and out of the penitentiary. Wilson never lectured, but he believed in self-determination and he frequently told his brother to reinvent himself. "He told me to be my own man," Richard said.

Wilson was working on that concept himself, starting with changing his name. He wanted to be seen and heard for who he was and to be appreciated for his poetry. He and his fellow poets began taking road trips, reading their work at local coffeehouses and bars. In 1966, the Hill artists got a home of their own when the Halfway Art Gallery opened a storefront on Centre Avenue. It was the brainchild of Chawley Williams and a visual artist named Ewari "Ed" Ellis, who took the idea to Reverend Richard Martin, a missionary from St. Stephen's Episcopal Church of Sewickley, a suburb about thirteen miles northwest of Pittsburgh along the Ohio River. The priest had set up a storefront office on the Hill, but he was having difficulty attracting people to his self-described "parsonage." The gallery changed that. It was funded by the church, but it was run by the artists. It became a gathering spot for the community, with poetry readings, jazz sessions, art exhibitions, and activist meetings on any given night. When it opened, Wilson recited Dylan Thomas's poem "Should Lanterns Shine" from memory.

It was there that Wilson and his fellow poets came up with the name Centre Avenue Poets' Theater Workshop; together they established what they called "the Centre Avenue tradition." They put out a magazine called *Signals*. In 1968, Signals Press published a journal called *May We Speak*, edited by poet Gerald Rhodes and featuring the work of eight African American Pittsburgh poets, including Wilson and his cohorts Rob Penny, Charles P. (Chawley) Williams, and Nick Flournoy. Wilson's verse was lofty and full of references from the classical Western canon. But the titles of his contributions to the journal show an increasing political consciousness from his earlier work when he ignored the "guns of social responsibility." The volume includes four Wilson poems: "Christmas and Cassandra," "The Dark Christmas," "To Whom It May Concern," and "For Malcolm X and Others."

"To Whom It May Concern" is a sensual love poem that ends:

Or rather only imagine we fall off,
The imagination being the only
Link to the shadow, and the clothes being
Quite similar to the storm, the arrangement
Of the town, with the church
At the centre, and the bell, ringing.

The Malcolm X poem is opaque, with the young Wilson imagining "a flock of saints / Run ground as thieves." He is troubled "in the gloom / and glutton of this time."

> I live and turn my wheel,
> And move from place to place,
> Always forward, never behind,
> No foot except my own
> Carries my dangerous hand
> That never knew blood
> Or love enough to stroke a cat.

Many years later, in his speech "The Ground on Which I Stand," Wilson introduced himself as a man who was rooted in the Western tradition "pioneered by the Greek dramatists" but, more important, he stressed, he was anchored in the Black Power Movement and the Black cultural nationalism of the 1960s. Both influences are present in these early poems.

In February 1968, the Afro-American Institute of Pittsburgh, a community activist group, staged a three-day celebration of Malcolm X, who had been assassinated three years earlier. It included art exhibits, a fashion show, and jazz workshops, culminating at the Savoy Ballroom on the Hill, with a keynote speech by playwright-activist Amiri Baraka (who began writing as LeRoi Jones but changed his name to Amiri Baraka sometime after Malcolm X was assassinated in 1965). Wilson was also one of the speakers at the event, and, at twenty-three, he wowed the crowd with his powerful rhetoric. "When you see a revolution going on—and it's your revolution—you don't get out the way. You join in," he told the crowd. Later in his play *Two Trains Running*, a recently released prisoner named Sterling tries to convince the patrons of a diner to attend a rally celebrating Malcolm X's birthday at the Savoy Ballroom.

Baraka's presence at the event was transformative for Wilson and the Centre Avenue Poets' Theater Workshop. The activist/artist gave a thundering oration, urging the crowd to join him in the Black Nationalist

Movement. He also brought along the Spirit House Movers, a spoken-word collective that added a backing track to his militant speech. Wilson had never seen a play before, apart from the Christmas pageant in seventh grade. But Wilson became a devotee of Baraka's fiery poetry. He had a copy of *Black Magic: Poetry, 1961–1967*, a collection published in 1967. "I wore that book out," Wilson said. "The cover got taped up with Scotch tape, the pages falling out. That was my bible. I carried it wherever I went."

While Wilson was initially struck by the poetry, he soon became aware of Baraka's groundbreaking plays. *Dutchman* had won an Obie Award in 1964, and he had followed it up with such plays as *A Black Mass*, an origin story based on the myth of Yakub (Baraka used the spelling Jacoub) as espoused by the Nation of Islam. Baraka had founded the Black Arts Repertory Theatre/School in Harlem in 1965, which in its short-lived existence was a larger, more established version of the Halfway Art Gallery. He then founded Spirit House, a combination theater/artists' community in Newark, New Jersey.

A seed was planted at the celebration for Malcolm X. "We talked about doing theater, because theater was part of our name," Wilson said about conversations with his poet friends. And then came April 4, 1968. Martin Luther King Jr. was assassinated in Memphis. Riots broke out the next night in the Hill District and other areas of Pittsburgh, as they did in cities across the nation. Newspapers reported "gangs of Negroes" looting, destroying property, and throwing firebombs. On the second day of the disturbance, looters swarmed the Mainway Supermarket on Centre Avenue; a few hours later, it was torched to the ground. "It was the first place to burn because the owners overcharged us and they were disrespectful and the people hated shopping there," Wilson wrote in *How I Learned*. (A friend, the photographer Frank Floyd Hightower, staged a photo of Wilson, then twenty-three, standing among the smoldering wreckage.) Governor Raymond P. Shafer and Mayor Joseph M. Barr called a state of emergency and enforced a curfew. Thousands of rifle-bearing National Guardsmen and Pennsylvania State Police were called in to patrol the streets of the Hill District. More than six hundred people were arrested.

Around this time, Wilson and Rob Penny began hanging around with members of the Black Action Society (BAS), a student activist group at Pitt. They came up with the idea of starting a theater modeled after the arts organization Baraka had founded in Harlem. They called it Black Horizons Theatre. None of them knew much about theater. Wilson said he didn't see his first professional production until 1976, when the Pittsburgh Public Theater mounted Athol Fugard's *Sizwe Banzi Is Dead* (with electric performances by Joe Morton and an older actor named Joe Seneca, who went on to appear in Wilson's first Broadway play, *Ma Rainey's Black Bottom*). But Wilson and the others had heard Baraka stir the crowd earlier that year, and so they set out to put on plays. The fledgling troupe held meetings at a place called the Pan Fried Fish restaurant on Wylie Avenue. It had the best fish sandwich in town, but the owners were two cantankerous brothers who couldn't be bothered to name the place or put up a sign, so it became known as Pan Fried Fish. Wilson would arrive early for meetings so he could go hang out at the jitney station next door.

The new theater company included many artists from the neighborhood: Hightower, the photographer; Sala Udin; and Curtiss Porter from Pitt's BAS. Porter contends that BAS had received university funding and that, as chairman of the BAS program committee, he initially funneled money to the new theater. The company secured a place to perform at the A. Leo Weil Elementary School on Centre Avenue. The troupe needed a director, but since no one volunteered, Wilson was chosen by default. He didn't know any better, and he was committed to the idea that art could empower Black people.

Wilson later told his friend Nelson Harrison, a jazz musician who was pursuing a doctorate in psychology at Pitt at the time, that he had no idea what to do when he first sat down with the actors. They looked to him for direction, so he said, "Read the play." They finished and looked at him again. His response was "Read it again."

He later marveled at the troupe's naiveté and idealism. They thought they were inventing Black theater, while they were continuing a long tradition. "It never occurred to us that there had been [Black] people doing theater before us," he said years later. "Every day we walked into Walter Worthington's record store, never knowing that twenty years before he'd had a theater, the Pittsburgh Negro Theater. Had we known, we could have tapped into that. No institution had developed out of that for us to fit into. It was our failure to access our history, and a failure on their part not to hand it on, to preserve cultural values. We missed each other."

And so Wilson went into directing with no knowledge of the craft or its history. He took out a book on directing from the library and learned how to direct on the job. The first play the company mounted was Baraka's *A Black Mass*, which is the furthest from an August Wilson play as could be. In this Frankenstein-like tale, the Black magician Jacoub brings the "White Beast" to life, and the creature turns out to be an evil monster brutally seeking world domination. The play ends with a frenetic scene, orchestrated by throbbing music by the eclectic jazz artist Sun Ra, with the new race storming the audience while a narrator delivers a stark warning: "There are beasts in our world. Let us find them and slay them."

The play, which is rarely revived, was a prophetic choice. It inverts the notion that black is bad and white is good. Wilson was obsessed with language, and he often talked about the different words associated with black and white. In fact, he devoted an irreverent scene on this topic in *How I Learned*, pointing out that "black" means "outrageously wicked, dishonorable, connected with the devil, menacing, sullen, hostile," while "white" means "outstandingly righteous, free from blemish, moral stain or impurity."

Black Horizons Theatre was a community theater in the very spirit of the word "community." Wilson solicited donations from churches and local businesses—$10 here, $25 if he got lucky—and the price of admission was affordable at fifty cents a ticket. Children came and sat on their parents' laps or ran around the auditorium. The company learned as it went along. They were committed to the kind of theater that would empower the people. In the summer of 1968, the *Drama Review*, an academic quarterly put out by New York University at the time, published an issue called "Black Theatre." The Pittsburgh neophytes were desperate for plays to mount, and someone got a copy of the journal, which included essays and plays by such writers as Baraka (still going by Jones), Ed Bullins, Sonia Sanchez, and Ben Caldwell, among others. Wilson later said they did every play in the volume. After a while, the periodical was also held together with tape.

The journal also included several scholarly essays, notably an opening piece by the poet Larry Neal called "The Black Arts Movement." He defined the movement as the "aesthetic and spiritual sister of the Black Power concept," a drive toward "self-determination and nationhood." He called for "a radical reordering of the western cultural aesthetic" and, most important for Wilson, "a separate symbolism, mythology, critique, and iconology." Wilson scoured the dog-eared pages of this volume repeatedly and absorbed those ideas, particularly the idea of creating a separate mythology. He later applied it not only to his work, but to the narrative he created about his own life.

He was already building the "myth of August Wilson," with the tweed jackets, the affected accent, the obscure verse. The singular persona may have been intriguing before the turmoil of 1968, but this image was out of sync with the turbulent time following King's assassination. Curtiss Porter remembers one reading at the Halfway Art Gallery, where Wilson recited poems with titles like "For Once a Virgin." His fellow poets were reading verse in the militant spirit of Baraka. Porter recalls Wilson being laughed off the stage for verse that was pretty but lacked revolutionary fervor, only to be consoled by his friend Rob Penny. He was deeply scarred by the rejection. "He felt left out of the Black Arts Movement," said dramaturge Todd Kreidler, a close confidant later on. The people wanted rage; Wilson was offering broken hearts and classical references. He couldn't please anyone. At another poetry reading, after he recited an ode in an accent that made him sound like an Oxford don, a man stood up and confronted him. "You didn't write that," he said. Wilson was taken aback. "I go, 'Excuse me, yes, I did. I did write that.' But the guy kept insisting that I didn't write it."

He was a young autodidact searching for his voice, and the world was changing around him. He had read the poets in the Western canon and was particularly fond of Dylan Thomas and John Berryman, a tortured soul acclaimed for his confessional style. Much of Wilson's early poetry concerns deeply personal moments of revelation, guilt, sexual desire, and sorrow.

He straddled two worlds in more ways than one. As a biracial man, he was not easily characterized. Wilson chose his mother's culture and never considered any identity other than Black. Later in his life, he would bristle when grilled about being biracial. Colleagues in the professional theater community, both Black and white, whispered behind his back about his heritage, but he never wavered from his self-definition as a Black man. Unlike his uncle Ray, he never considered passing. He was raised by Daisy in the Black community, and he was Black, period. But the people who snickered at his poetry reading saw something different. They saw a light-skinned tweedy chap with a grandiose accent and a slight stutter reading verse that didn't speak to them. No matter how Wilson viewed himself, his contemporaries acknowledged that he appeared different from the regulars at the Halfway Art Gallery, many of whom had adopted African names and proudly wore dashikis and kufi caps. "August wasn't really Black. He was half-and-half," Chawley Williams said. "He was too dark to be white, and he was too white to be dark. He was in no-man's-land. I knew he was lost. I was lost. Kindred brothers know one another. We were trying to become men. We didn't even know what it meant."

He did, however, manage to get two poems, "Muhammad Ali" and "For Malcolm X and Others," published in *Negro Digest* in 1969. He had been sending out poems to various publications for three years, and they always came back with rejection slips. The Malcolm X poem, of course, had been published by Signals Press, but this was a national publication (which later changed its name to *Black World*). The Muhammad Ali poem, he later said, takes its inspiration from an African praise song:

Muhammad Ali is a lion.
He is a lion that breaks the back of the wind.
Who climbs to the end of the rainbow with three steps
and devours the gold,
Muhammad Ali with a stomach of gold,
Whose head is a lion.

The year of his first professional publication began dramatically when Wilson's friends from BAS took over Pitt's computer center in January 1969 to protest racial inequality and demand that the school recruit more Black students, hire more Black faculty, and create an Africana studies department. After only six hours, the students not only received amnesty, but the university chancellor agreed to seven of their demands. The prospect of a new department at the university delighted the poets and activists at Black Horizons Theatre. They had been doing the work. Maybe there would be faculty opportunities for them. Wilson, after all, had haunted the campus for years, reading every book he could get his hands on, thanks to his friend Peggy Martin. But when the university established its Department of Africana Studies later that year, Rob Penny got a job teaching. Curtiss Porter, who had been one of the leaders of the protests, became chairman. The new department brought in Bob Johnson, a professional dancer who made his Broadway debut in the rock musical *Hair*. August Wilson got nothing. Porter claimed he tried to find him a position but could not push another hire through the administration. Wilson felt misunderstood and left out, just the way he was wounded when people laughed at his poetry.

But at the same time, Black Horizons had taken off. Wilson, along with members of Black Horizons and Pitt's Black Action Society, took a road trip to Oberlin College in Ohio. Their goal was to help Black students at the small liberal arts college to organize and to introduce them to the Black Arts Movement. In footage from the visit, a bearded Wilson is smoking a cigarette and wearing a wool coat and maroon turtleneck, walking on the leafy campus with his friends Rob Penny and Curtiss Porter, among others.

After just one season, the company had made a small amount of money. Wilson wanted to use the funds to buy a van so the troupe didn't have to scrounge around for transportation, but some of the other company members wanted to split the money among themselves. "August was pissed and hurt, so he cashed out," his friend Kreidler said. The work was also exhausting. "Doing community theater was very difficult—rehearsing two hours a night after people got off work, not knowing if the actors were going to show up," Wilson told an interviewer. "Because of having to rely so much on others, I said, 'I don't need this.'"

He took his share of the money and went to New York to visit a girl-friend, Brenda Burton, who grew up in the Hill District and now was a student at New York University. He was deeply in love. During that trip, the couple conceived a child. They married soon after on July 5, 1969. Wilson listed his occupation as a laborer, and she said that she was a sur-vey aide. He was twenty-four; Burton, a tall regal woman who carried her-self with confidence, was just eighteen and three months pregnant at the time. A reception was held at the home of Elder Joseph Burton, the bride's father. Wilson's father-in-law was a respected entrepreneur on the Hill; he owned Burton's Place Father and Son, a popular chicken restaurant, and Burton's Recreation Parlor, a pool hall. Burton, who was widowed in 1961, was well-known on the Hill for his standards: he ran the only pool hall in Pittsburgh where profanity was forbidden. (In his play *Seven Guitars*, Wilson gives a nod to his father-in-law; one of the characters is searching for a friend, and he looks for him at Joe Burton's Pool Hall. In his last play, *Radio Golf*, Elder Joseph Barlow is an elderly citizen who fights to main-tain the traditional values of the Hill district.)

Wilson, meanwhile, was still writing in restaurants and picking up odd jobs. He compartmentalized his life. His friends from the arts scene rarely saw his wife. She didn't attend poetry readings or rehearsals and Wilson didn't discuss his marriage. Years later, in interview after inter-view, he brushed over this period, even though it was a time of major life events. David Bedford died on August 27, 1969. Bedford had done time for his mistakes, and he came out of prison a new man, becoming a community leader and a role model for Daisy's children. Wilson consid-ered him more of a father than Kittel. He stuck by Daisy, even when she married Kittel and took him in while he was dying. Bedford was loyal, and Daisy's children looked up to him. Wilson never said a bad word about Bedford, and neither did his siblings.

Wilson was about to become a father himself. Sakina Ansari was born January 22, 1970. Wilson was delighted with everything about his baby girl, whose name means "spirit of tranquility" in Arabic. He doted on his daughter, his brother Richard said. His wife was a member of the Nation of Islam, and Wilson tried to live up to her strict moral standards—but never could. He wore the requisite black suit and bow tie, and he sold the Muslim newspaper *Muhammad Speaks* on the streets of the Hill. His sister Freda told the *New Yorker* that he never managed to sell more than a few copies but concluded that his efforts had "put him in touch with the way Blacks think, the way the Black and white worlds treated each other."

He also wanted to create the two-parent household he never had. He later said that he believed in the Black Muslim movement and embraced its philosophy, but he struggled with its rigid lifestyle. He liked to watch football and have a beer, but that conflicted with his wife's stringent religious beliefs.

And so, again, he found himself straddling two worlds. He still liked hanging around with his fellow poets, and he went to poetry readings and other events on his own. One afternoon when Sakina was still in diapers, Wilson was walking on the Pitt campus when he saw a bearded, bespectacled Black man sitting outside playing the flute (but not very well). There was something jaunty and cosmopolitan about his confident demeanor. So Wilson introduced himself. He could sense the man was an artist. His name was Claude Purdy, and indeed, he had traveled around the world doing professional theater, far from the modest community productions of Black Horizons Theatre. Both men were gifted raconteurs, and they talked for hours. Purdy had just returned stateside after fifteen years abroad, with six of those spent at the American Theater of Paris, where he acted and directed with such avant-garde theater luminaries as Philip Glass, Lee Breuer, and JoAnne Akalaitis. He had also spent five years in residence at the University of Ibadan in Nigeria, working with John Pepper Clark and the heroic playwright Wole Soyinka.

The two men became instant friends, and Wilson told Purdy about Crawford Grill, where they later met for a jazz session. Before long, Purdy and his new girlfriend, Elva Branson, had taken over Black Horizons. Wilson started showing up again to watch rehearsals. He sensed something different about this man, and Purdy also saw a budding playwright in his new poet friend.

One night in 1971, Purdy, Rob Penny, and Wilson went to the Soldiers and Sailors Memorial Hall across from the Pitt campus to see Alice Coltrane in concert. The opening act was an original dance theater production of *Isis and Osiris*, choreographed by Bob Johnson, the dancer recruited to teach at Pitt's Department of Africana Studies, with music by composer Nelson Harrison. The troupe had had only two rehearsals, and the dancer playing Isis was about eight months pregnant. Still, the performance received a long standing ovation. It was a sign that Pittsburgh was ripe for new and innovative work by Black artists. Johnson had started the Pittsburgh Black Theater Dance Ensemble in 1970. He would soon become a close collaborator with Wilson and Purdy.

But all the time Wilson was spending at the theater and writing in restaurants was taking a toll on his marriage. As a Muslim, Brenda didn't hang around at the theater or attend openings at the Halfway Art Gallery. And she was frustrated with a husband who earned money washing dishes and selling eggs on the street. But in Wilson's mind, he wasn't a menial worker. He was a writer. Richard Kittel worked side by side with him washing dishes for a time, but after work, Wilson would change into his tweed coat and tell anyone who asked that he was a writer. "He had the tools of the trade," Kittel said. "He never deviated from it."

But Brenda Burton—and Daisy Kittel—did not approve, nor did they believe in his declared vocation. "It was a source of pain for him," Todd Kreidler said. "His mother saw him as a street hoodlum. She couldn't see what he was trying to do. He was trying to politicize the community."

Despite her disapproval, his mother was the bedrock for his belief system. And his wife was the mother of his child, the love of his life. But things fell apart in 1972. In September of that year, she filed for divorce. According to documents filed in the Common Pleas Court of Allegheny County, Wilson failed to show up for several hearings, and the divorce was granted in April 1973. Earlier that year, the Pittsburgh Housing Authority moved to evict the couple from their apartment in the Arlington Heights public housing development. The Housing Authority had reduced the monthly fee from $88 to $53, but the couple still owed three months in back rent. They had qualified for the housing based on a combined annual income of $3,000.

Wilson was devastated by the divorce. "She moved out with the baby," his sister Linda Jean Kittel said. "The shock and pain were unbearable to him. In a nutshell, she thought his writing was a waste of time, he wouldn't amount to anything." Later, Wilson did not like to talk about the marriage, other than to quote Abraham Lincoln and say, "A house divided against itself cannot stand." He also said he bore her no ill will and that she was a good person. Richard Kittel said that Burton kept to herself and did not make an effort to become part of the family, yet it is still odd that Wilson's friends on the Hill never got to know his wife. He talked about his daughter, but he didn't share any details about his marriage with his contemporaries.

Burton took the baby and moved in with her father, who paid for her to continue her education at the Shadyside School of Nursing. She ultimately became a nurse, but Wilson was crushed. This was the lowest point of his life to date. This was personal. He wasn't clean enough or pure enough—or at least that was the message he absorbed. "It was pure trauma. Pure hell," said Kreidler, who was one of the few people the mature Wilson trusted enough to talk to about this period of his life.

In fact, in three of Wilson's plays, religion plays a part in the dissolution of a marriage, although it is Christianity not Islam. In *Ma Rainey*, Toledo's wife leaves him after she starts going to church. "Soon she figure she got a heathen on her hands," the character says, adding that he didn't blame her. Wilson never forgot that Daisy told him he was "dirty" when he dropped out of school. In *Fences*, Rose discovers a new life in the church after her husband cheats on her. But the most potent example is in *Joe Turner's Come and Gone*. At the end of the play, the central character, Herald Loomis, is finally reunited with his wife after he served seven years on a chain gang. Now aptly named Martha Pentecost, she appears at the end of the play, stern and sanctimonious and *"dressed as befitting a member of an Evangelist church,"* according to the stage directions. She tells her estranged husband, "You done gone over to the devil." She recites Psalm 23. Herald ultimately finds salvation in himself and he willingly surrenders their daughter, Zonia, to his former wife. But in doing so, he finds what the character Bynum describes as "his song." The last line is optimistic as Bynum tells Loomis, "You shining. You shining like new money." Someday, Wilson would be, too.

CHAPTER FIVE

A Road Marked with Signposts

*I called to my courage and entered the world of Romare
Bearden and found a world made in my image. A world
of flesh and muscle and blood and bone and fire. . . . A
spirit conjured into being, unbroken, unbowed, and past
any reason for song—singing an aria of faultless beauty
and unbridled hope.*

—AUGUST WILSON

At the beginning of 1973, Wilson was not shining—and he did not
have any money. He had been evicted. His wife had left with their
baby. His friend Claude Purdy left Pittsburgh for Los Angeles with his
girlfriend, Elva Branson. They wanted to try to make a break in the film
industry, and they left Black Horizons Theatre in the hands of Wilson. It
floundered and slowly sank. By the mid-1970s, it folded entirely.

Wilson was devastated by the failure of his marriage. His brothers and
sisters saw that he was heartbroken. He missed Sakina and wrote poems
about her with titles like "Season of Sadness." He longed for the daily life
he had with her, seeing her when she woke up in the morning, curious
and energetic. Years later, he still felt the wound of being abandoned by
a woman he truly loved. He talked about the loss many years later with

Charles Johnson, who had written a novel called *Oxherding Tale*. In the picaresque novel, a light-skinned escaped enslaved person passes as white and is living as a free man; he purchases a slave named Minty, his lover from his days on the plantation. He aims to free her, but she is deathly ill, and he is devastated when she passes away. Wilson was shattered by the death scene because it reminded him of his own grief, and he wrote a blurb for the 2005 paperback reprint of the novel. "I laughed. I cried. I thought. I marveled," he wrote.

But Wilson's heartache also sparked a burst of creativity. He was beginning to absorb the advice that friends like Purdy and Rob Penny had been giving him: drop the pretense and unleash your authentic voice. Don't try to be Dylan Thomas: be August Wilson. He started thinking, hard, about the banter he heard in Pat's Place and at the jitney station, about men sitting around signifying and telling lies. He later had a realization about the florid verse he wrote as a young poet. "I didn't value and respect the speech pattern," he said. "I thought that in order to make art out of it you had to change it. I was always trying to mold it into some European sensibility of what the language should be."

That changed for him one day in 1973 when he sat down and wrote what he called his "Morning Statement."

It is the middle of winter
November 21 to be exact
I got up, buckled my shoes,
I caught a bus and went riding into town.
I just thought I'd tell you.

It's simple, to the point, nothing extraneous. He put aside the grandiose language, the Biblical references, the genuflections to Greek mythology. He found *his* voice. "The poem didn't pretend to be anything else," Wilson told interviewers. "It wasn't struggling to say eternal things. It was just claiming the ground as its own thing. For me, it was so liberating." Before he wrote that poem, he waged a battle with every word. "I was wrassling with poems," he once said. "I'd see them as if it was war, and I was a general. You only get the initial moment of creation once. I would have the initial impulse but I didn't know how to craft it."

He decided to take a stab at playwriting. He had been directing for years, and his friend Rob Penny was a prolific playwright. Wilson had read the poets in the Western canon, but it hadn't led to great success as a poet. He consciously decided not to read classic dramatic literature: no Chekhov, Shakespeare, Tennessee Williams, Eugene O'Neill, Arthur Miller. His friend Nick Flournoy had urged him to come along one day in 1965 to see a thirty-minute excerpt from Eugène Ionesco's absurdist play *Rhinoceros* at the Fifth Avenue High School. He was underwhelmed. "What the hell is this?" he asked. "There was nothing to relate to in it."

He was searching for his own voice, and he was still straddling two worlds. He was also beginning to feel the limitations of poetry. "I would describe my poetry as intensely personal," he reflected. "I needed something as big as a play because my ideas no longer fit in the poems, or they fit in a different way, for myself only. I needed a larger canvas that would include everyone."

And he needed an outlet for the void left by the loss of his marriage—and his loss of daily contact with Sakina. Fueled by pain, he wrote his first play, *Recycle.* That summer, he and Penny were invited to start a neighborhood theater for youth in Hazelwood, where Wilson had lived as a teenager. The two poets had a grandiose plan to start seven theaters in seven different communities, and they hoped this effort would lead to the realization of that dream. They met with youngsters at the Glen Hazel Recreation Center. They were planning to stage one of the plays they had done with Black Horizons—something by Baraka, Ed Bullins, or Benjamin Caldwell—but the teenagers asked to produce a stage version of *Super Fly*, the 1972 blaxploitation crime drama that glorified drug dealing and violence. This was certainly not what they had intended, by a long shot. Penny later said that Wilson wrote the adaptation, turning the story of cocaine dealer Youngblood Priest into an anti-drug crusade. Other sources contend that Penny wrote the script but got frustrated and left the direction to Wilson. Either way, the community embraced the production, with teenagers and their parents pitching in to make costumes and sets.

Despite what some leaders of the Black community thought of *Super Fly*, the play was a thundering success in the community. Wilson and Penny named their new venture Ujima Theatre. The name was derived from Ujima, which is the third principle of Kwanzaa and stands for collective work and responsibility. They suggested other plays for the young people to perform, and Wilson took the opportunity to stage *Recycle*. The play (which remains unpublished) was inspired by a murder Wilson had witnessed outside a local bar. The bartender had gotten into an argument with a customer and shot him on the street. A nurse ran to the victim and performed CPR, to no avail. The man died, bleeding on the sidewalk. Wilson followed the nurse (who was Black) and heard her say, "The niggers are killing one another these days." When a bartender asked her about the fate of the man, she said, "Yeah, he's dead. I beat on his chest." He resurrected that memory in his play, which opens in a bar, where a man and a woman are having a conversation.

Wilson recruited his friend and off-and-on girlfriend Maisha Baton to perform the play with him, with Penny directing. In an interview many years later, she said that the play incorporated two distinct styles: the male character, a poet, speaks in flowery language, and the woman character, a nurse, speaks what she called "the poetry of Black Pittsburgh." The play opens with the woman repeating the line Wilson had overheard on the street: "I beat on his chest." A man enters, and the two actors converse, with the woman dismissing the man with plain language while he woos her with florid praise. Years later, Baton reconstructed the dialogue from memory. The female character says, "What kind of woman would mess with a nigger like you? I bet you ain't even got a woman." The man replies, "I want a woman to smile at me and be softly interested in my visions, herself to hum and purr from moaning. Her eyes soft and wet with laughing."

The woman rejects the man at first, perhaps for his affectation and highfalutin language. One of the reasons Brenda Burton had left Wilson was because she couldn't feed her baby with pretty words and dreams of literary success; after the divorce, she, like Wilson's character, pursued a career in nursing. That experience is echoed in the play. Wilson was also expressing his artistic conflict at the time. He had spent countless hours poring through yellowed copies of poems from the Western canon, and he had absorbed their formal language and even adopted what he saw as the proper way for a gentleman poet to dress. But he had another voice inside him, the particular cadence and speech pattern he had heard growing up on the Hill, as well as in Daisy's kitchen.

That inner turmoil exploded onstage during the only performance of the play that summer in 1973. After Baton spoke the first line, the man appeared in the bar and she laughed at him. The character was not happy about it, which was in the script. The man was supposed to reply with his line. But in the performance, Wilson, acting the part of the man, got riled up. He reached out and slapped Baton, hard. She was astonished and said, "What the fuck is wrong with you?" She said that the audience stared at them as if to ask, "What is wrong with the two of *you*?" The actors collected themselves and got through the performance, but the audience was not impressed. Some years after that dismal production, Wilson and some friends set out to film *Recycle*, but the film was not finished due to lack of funding and the play was never performed again.

Even though Wilson later said that he turned to plays because his poetry was too private and personal, *Recycle* was an attempt to exorcize his pain over the breakup of the marriage with Burton. His peers could see that he was crushed, and the tepid response to the single production ripped at his confidence.

He was in mourning for his marriage, but he refused to be a "daughterless" man. He visited Sakina as often as he could after the breakup. He took her out for ice cream; she remembers he would let her order whatever she wanted while he sat and jotted down notes on the paper place mats. He adored her, but he was self-absorbed and focused on his ambitions as a writer during their outings. He found an opening in the fence surrounding the Pittsburgh Zoo, and they would slip through since he didn't have the cash to pay the admission fee. He bought a book about origami and taught her the art of paper folding. He took her to rehearsals when he was working on plays, but one day, the script called for swearing. Burton dressed Sakina in modest Muslim garb. One of the actors pulled Wilson aside and told him it was inappropriate for his daughter to hear such language, so she had to stop accompanying him when he was working in community theater. He brought her to visit his mother. Once, when she was around the age he was when he learned to read, he bet her a dollar she couldn't spell her own name. She did, and he proudly gave her the money.

But these visits weren't the same as living with his daughter. And since Black Horizons was languishing, he didn't have an artistic home. He turned back to poetry and began working on a series of poems about a nineteenth-century outlaw nicknamed Black Bart. Meanwhile, another theater with the same goals as Black Horizons was founded at Pitt in 1974. In 1969, a teacher named Vernell Lillie arrived in Pittsburgh from Houston to pursue graduate studies in English at Carnegie Mellon University. While working on her doctorate, she joined the Africana Studies department at Pitt. In Houston, she and her husband had run a theater that was firmly rooted in the Black Arts Movement. Lillie had no intention of staying in Pittsburgh, but she discovered a vibrant city with a thriving Black arts scene. There was visual art at the Halfway Art Gallery. A visionary named William Strickland had founded the Manchester Craftsmen's Guild in 1968 to teach ceramics to underprivileged youth. Bob Johnson had launched the Pittsburgh Black Theater Dance Ensemble in 1970. Lillie was so engaged in the arts scene that she later marveled that she managed to complete her studies. And so she was persuaded to stay in Pittsburgh to start Kuntu Repertory Theatre, which filled the gap left by the dissolution of Black Horizons. Kuntu takes its name from the Bantu languages of Africa, and it means "way" or "mode." The theater's mission was to reflect "the cultural tradition of Africa in which the artistic creations in dance/movement, drama, music, visual arts, and words are entwined as a single unit."

Lillie admired plays written by Penny because they fit neatly into the theater's aesthetic and its goal to use theater to promote social change. Kuntu's first season in 1974 opened with Penny's *Little Willie Armstrong Jones*, a play about a businessman in the Hill District who struggles to maintain financial security and family stability in a troubled community. Lillie always thought Penny would be the breakout playwright from the Pittsburgh crew, not Wilson. But Wilson was itching to be involved. He hung out at Penny's office at Pitt any chance he got, and along with Penny and Baton in 1976, he formed the Kuntu Writers Workshop, an informal seminar for all writers—young, old, experienced, or amateur. The group met on the weekends in the offices of the Africana Studies Department at Pitt. Wilson was in charge of the poets and Penny mentored the playwrights. Wilson had spent years trying to discover his own voice, and he was gentle with the aspiring poets who sought his advice at the workshop. "He could, just with a twinkle of his eye, listen to someone read a poem and ask the right questions," Lillie said. "He would ask, 'What did you mean to say?' 'Where do you want to go with this?' He never said, 'You ought to change this.'" Later in his life, Wilson provided similar encouragement to young emerging artists.

But he was still asking questions of himself: What do you want to say? What is the best medium? He took a stab at writing short stories, and in 1975, he penned "The Greatest Blues Singer in the World." He had conceived a long story about the "social context of the artist," but he just wrote one sentence. "The streets that Balboa walked were his own private ocean, and Balboa was drowning." That was it. Wilson later quoted this tale during interviews, noting that he had said everything he had to say on the subject. He also became known for first drafts of plays that went on for more than four hours, with long, poetic monologues that stopped the action. The irony was not lost on him.

He became more and more fascinated with playwriting, even though the sole production of *Recycle* had been an abject failure. He still had hopes for *Recycle*, which was part of a trilogy he called "The Wood of the Cross." The other two plays were *Placebo*, written in 1978, and *The Coldest Day of the Year*, written in 1977. Each of the plays featured the man and the woman, whom he fashioned as Everyman and Everywoman at different stages of their relationship. Wilson was attempting to explore the phenomenon of passing time. The couple is young in *Recycle*, and they have reached middle age in *Placebo*. The three plays remain unpublished, and copies of *Placebo* have vanished, but St. Paul actor Terry Bellamy read all three. In *Placebo*, the woman is pregnant and the man encourages her to keep the baby, even though she is reluctant to bring a child into the world. This is a theme that shows up in his later play *King Hedley II*.

The Coldest Day of the Year, the third play of the cycle, depicts the couple as senior citizens. The one-act play is reminiscent of *Waiting for Godot*—although Wilson said he never read other playwrights. He also said he did not go to the theater, so it is highly unlikely he had seen Samuel Beckett's masterpiece of existential theater.

In the thirty-seven-page play, a man and a woman meet on a park bench, sharing a poor man's communion and reminiscing about old lovers. The language, like much of Wilson's early poetry, is stilted and formal. Like the tramps in *Godot*, the characters end one scene promising to come back tomorrow, and, of course, they do. In the last scene, the man has a long monologue about a romance gone sour, a forebear of the long speeches that would become Wilson's trademark in his mature plays. Wilson was still smarting over the breakup with Burton, and he also had other failed relationships with women, yet in this early attempt at playwriting, the male character finds companionship with a battered old woman who appreciates his language, and they walk off together into an uncertain future.

That third play in the trilogy was not produced until many years later, but Wilson was working on other scripts at the same time. Lillie was looking for plays to produce for the Kuntu Repertory Theatre, and he offered her a play called *The Homecoming*. Lillie directed it on a bill of three one-act plays performed at Schenley High School in October 1976. The other two plays were *Wine in the Wilderness* by Alice Childress and *A Question Mark on Your Face* by Rob Penny.

Dedicated to Blind Lemon Jefferson and other unnamed blues singers, *The Homecoming* takes place in an abandoned train station in rural Alabama. Obadiah and Leroy, two Black men in ragged clothes, await the arrival of their friend, bluesman Blind Willie Jefferson. The unseen character of Blind Willie Jefferson is clearly modeled after Lemon Henry "Blind Lemon" Jefferson. The blind son of sharecroppers in Coutchman, Texas, he recorded such hits as "Match Box Blues" and "See That My Grave Is Kept Clean" for Paramount Records, the leading producer of blues records at the time. He died an untimely death in Chicago in 1929 at the age of thirty-six; the usual story surrounding his early passing is that he froze to death in the middle of a Chicago blizzard. It is possible that the other half of the name of Wilson's character was inspired by two other famous musicians, Blind Willie McTell and Blind Willie Johnson.

In the seventeen-page play, two white recording agents from the North appear at the station. They are looking for bluesmen to make albums and money for their production company. The two men, Irving and George, are hardly subtle. They wear their racism on their sleeves and flaunt their white privilege. When Obadiah and Leroy turn the tables and pull out a gun, George threatens to call the police and get them arrested. The two Black men recall how their friend, Blind Willie Jefferson, was lured up north by white producers who tempted him with tales of fancy women with painted faces, picture shows, and the promise of so much money he could light cigars with dollar bills. The dialogue of all four characters is contrived, perhaps deliberately, but probably not. A train does pull into the station, and Blind Willie's corpse is delivered in a coffin. Obadiah and Leroy avenge their friend's tragic death by forcing the visiting producers into the train station and nailing it shut, leaving them to starve to death. Blind Lemon Jefferson's music plays as the lights go down. The plot is stark and gruesome, and the characters are stereotypes who speak stilted dialogue.

This was not the first time that Wilson had written about the exploitation of Black musicians by white producers. He repeated it in several early poems, including a paean called "Mr. Jelly Roll Morton." Ever since he had discovered Bessie Smith as a young man in 1965, he had collected stories about the profiteering commercial music industry that failed to compensate Black artists adequately and appropriated their music at the same time. (Morton did make some recordings with a white band called the New Orleans Rhythm Kings. Among music historians, this is actually considered one of the few early examples of a genuine interracial collaboration.)

Lillie's production of The Homecoming didn't lead to new opportunities for Wilson, but in November 1976, he saw Athol Fugard's Sizwe Banzi Is Dead at the Pittsburgh Public Theater. The theater had opened on the Northside in Pittsburgh in 1975, bringing regional theater to a city that had a declining professional theater scene since Broadway tryouts had stopped coming to town. Wilson and his friends had done their small part in keeping community theater alive, and the new Pittsburgh Public was an addition to the cultural landscape of a city that had become known nationally as unfriendly to professional theater. Its first season did not offer much that interested Wilson, with productions of Tennessee Williams's *The Glass Menagerie*, *One Flew Over the Cuckoo's Nest*, and *Twelfth Night* with Leonard Nimoy as Malvolio.

But Wilson had heard of Fugard, the white South African playwright who had risked his life writing plays that revealed the atrocities of apartheid. Written in 1972 in collaboration with the actors John Kani and Winston Ntshona, *Sizwe Banzi* is a one-act about the dehumanizing passbook laws in South Africa that restricted travel and employment for non-white citizens. After acclaimed productions in Capetown and London, the play opened on Broadway in 1974, and Kani and Ntshona shared a joint Tony Award for Best Actor in a Play. Pittsburgh Public's production was directed by Woodie King Jr., who founded the New Federal Theatre in Manhattan, a showcase for such playwrights as Ed Bullins and Ntozake Shange. Wilson later said it was the first professional production that impressed him. He cited this production as a turning point in his life as an artist. He was particularly inspired by the monologues. "I thought, 'This is great,'" he said about his reaction to the play. "I wonder if I could write something like this?"

The Homecoming was a precursor to *Ma Rainey's Black Bottom*, which Wilson started writing that year. He initially intended to write about Bessie Smith in a Chicago recording studio, but decided that enough had already been written about the blues legend that had inspired him. He had recently acquired a fresh remastering of Ma Rainey's albums and decided to change the character to the Mother of the Blues. He first began writing it in 1976, and at that point, it was about her confrontation with white producers in a recording studio in Chicago. He let it sit and came back to it a few years later, when he added another act about her sidemen hanging out in the band room waiting for the singer to show up. But *Ma Rainey's Black Bottom* wouldn't come to fruition until 1982.

He also discovered another pivotal influence during this period. He came upon the works of Romare Bearden, the great American artist known for his mixed-media collages celebrating the everyday lives of African Americans. Bearden was born in Charlotte, North Carolina, but his family later moved to Pittsburgh. Wilson never met the artist, but he vividly remembered the night he was introduced to his work. His friend Claude Purdy purchased a copy of *The Art of Romare Bearden: The Prevalence of Ritual*, a lavish coffee-table art book first published in 1973. Purdy invited Wilson over for dinner one night in the fall of 1977, and after their meal, he laid out the book, holding it reverently in his hands. Wilson remembered the moment the same way he recalled hearing Bessie Smith sing for the first time. Bearden's work spoke to him and inspired him to attempt to achieve something similar through words. "What for me had been so difficult, Bearden made seem so simple, so easy," he wrote in the introduction to Myron Schwartzman's 1990 biography of the artist. "What I saw was Black life presented on its own terms, on a grand and epic scale, with all its richness and fullness, in a language that was vibrant and which, made attendant to everyday life, ennobled it, affirmed its value, exalted its presence. It was the art of a large and generous spirit that defined not only the character of Black American life, but also its conscience. . . . My response was visceral. I was looking at myself in ways I hadn't thought before and have never ceased to think of since." He recognized the beauty in the faces and postures of the people who were ennobled in Bearden's collages. They looked like the faces of his aunts and uncles, of all the elders who fed him and loved him and scolded him as a youngster in the Hill District. "He showed me a doorway," Wilson wrote. "A road marked with signposts, with sharp and pure direction, charting a path through what D. H. Lawrence called 'the dark forest of the soul.'"

Since *Recycle* had flopped, he turned back to directing, and Lillie finally gave him the opportunity when she hired him to direct a production of Ed Bullins's *In New England Winter* for Kuntu Rep in 1977. Bullins, along with Baraka, was one of the few role models for the aspiring playwright. Bullins had served as the Minister of Culture for the Black Panthers in Oakland, producing protest theater. He had also won a Guggenheim Fellowship for playwriting and an Obie Award for his 1975 play, *The Taking of Miss Janie.* By 1977, Bullins was working on a series of plays he called "The Twentieth Century Cycle," aiming to produce twenty plays about a group of young African Americans who came of age in the 1950s. *In New England Winter* was the second play in that series, and it focused on the troubled, immutable bonds between two half brothers. In a 1971 review of *In New England Winter, New York Times* critic Mel Gussow noted that he was looking forward to the next eighteen plays. Wilson surely took note of this grandiose goal, although contemporaries said that Wilson wasn't impressed with Bullins's playwriting skills and felt that he could do better and write a cycle of his own.

His production did not go well, and Wilson clashed with Lillie during rehearsals. He knew he wasn't likely to direct for her again soon, but he had yet another project of his own in the works. At Purdy's suggestion, he went back to his poems about Black Bart and aimed to refashion them into a Western musical called *Black Bart and the Sacred Hills.* He had become fascinated with the nineteenth-century outlaw Charles Earl Boles, a white Englishman who called himself Black Bart. Black Bart was a flamboyant character who robbed stagecoaches and left poems at the scene of his crime. The unlikely combination of poetry and thievery amused and intrigued Wilson, and he had spent several years writing verse about the bandit, inventing a zany, psychedelic tale about a charismatic fugitive who takes to the hills and supposedly turns water into gold. In his version, Black Bart is African American, and he is surrounded by electric angels who protect his operation from the citizens in a nearby town, which is populated with a multicultural group of prostitutes, lawmen, barkeeps, and cowboys. When he decided to take a stab at turning the play into a musical, he recruited friends like Bob Johnson and his sometimes girlfriend Maisha Baton to collaborate. The group held late-night brainstorm sessions that Baton described as "sheer artistic madness." Baton was assigned to write lyrics, and the group called in local musician Nelson Harrison to write the score. "It was fun, but it was mad," Baton said. "It was an artistic collaboration that had no long-range goal."

While they were working on the project, Claude Purdy and Elva Branson returned to Pittsburgh from Los Angeles; they had given up on trying to break into Hollywood and soon joined a new theater called Pittsburgh City Players. Branson recalled that Purdy had been searching for a project that he could call his own, a play that would cement his reputation in the theater. He became obsessed with the *Black Bart* project and pressed Wilson to complete the musical version. The group was clearly influenced by Ishmael Reed's 1972 novel, *Mumbo Jumbo*, a revolutionary masterpiece of magical realism that Purdy and Wilson had read and dissected and discussed. Purdy, in particular, was captivated by Reed's work; he had met the writer in New York and his enthusiasm prompted him to urge Wilson to write the musical.

Purdy wasn't alone. Johnson had originally wanted to put together a production about Stagger Lee, a Black pimp who reigned in St. Louis in the late nineteenth century and was immortalized in folklore and song. Johnson recruited musician Harrison to write the score and wooed Wilson to write the script. Nothing ever came of that project, though, but Johnson became more and more determined to produce *Black Bart*.

In the spring of 1977, both Johnson and Purdy were pushing for a production. Johnson sent the script to Peter M. Carnahan, the director of performing arts for the Pennsylvania Council on the Arts. He got a "Thanks, let me know if it is ever produced" reply. The team had been hoping to get grant money. They drew up a production budget, with an estimated $186,729 in preproduction costs and $23,866 in weekly expenses. Johnson repeatedly urged Harrison to write songs for the show, which called for a gigantic multicultural cast.

They were all dreaming. The idea that the group could raise tens of thousands of dollars for an off-the-wall musical by an unknown playwright was outrageously optimistic. But they scheduled auditions anyway, putting out a "Wanted" poster calling for a multiracial cast to try out for "A New Musical Satire by August Wilson." The auditions were held in early May at the Pitt student union. The production was slated for a July opening. The team couldn't raise the money, and the dream was put on hold.

At the time all this was unfolding, Wilson was directing *In New England Winter* for Lillie. But his friend Purdy was restless. He had spent time in Minneapolis, where he had directed *The Great White Hope*. While there, he became involved in the founding of the Penumbra Theatre Company, a fledgling troupe located at the Hallie Q. Brown Community Center in St. Paul. The center had received a $150,000 cultural grant through the federally funded Comprehensive Employment and Training Act (CETA), and Purdy joined forces with Lou Bellamy, Penumbra's founder.

By fall 1977, it was clear that there wasn't going to be a grand production of *Black Bart* in Pittsburgh anytime soon. Purdy was asked to direct Penumbra's first production, so he packed up and moved to St. Paul. Wilson lost his mentor yet again. Penny was firmly in place at Pitt, where he had an office and professor's salary and the prestige that came with the title. Wilson was on chilly terms with Lillie of Kuntu Repertory Theatre. Near the end of the year, Purdy invited Wilson to come out and see his first production at Penumbra, Steve Carter's *Eden*. The play, which had been produced by the Negro Ensemble Company in New York the year before, showcases a Caribbean immigrant who is horrified to discover his daughter has become romantically involved with an African American. The story was based loosely on Carter's parents.

Purdy saw great potential in Penumbra. A group of actors in the Twin Cities was mobilized, and the nascent troupe saw an opportunity to define their own aesthetic: raw, gritty, realistic, unapologetic. He wanted Wilson to join him there. He knew his friend was stagnating in Pittsburgh. And Purdy was still eager to produce *Black Bart*, one way or another. He secretly hoped Penumbra would take on the project. He also had his eyes on the Guthrie Theater in Minneapolis. The theater had been established in 1963 by Sir Tyrone Guthrie, and it set the standard for resident theaters that were sprouting up all over the country, thanks to an influx of cash from the Ford Foundation. The idea was to create professional theater within a community, far from the commercial demands of Broadway. Purdy lured Wilson with promises of potential theater opportunities—and a plane ticket. Wilson didn't travel much, but he sensed Purdy's enthusiasm, and he accepted the invitation. He knew nothing about Minnesota, and he didn't expect to stay long. But he was eager to see this new theater, which sounded more professional than Black Horizons. He wasn't succeeding in Pittsburgh. He had nothing to lose.

CHAPTER SIX

Learning to Listen

I was sitting in a room with sixteen other playwrights. It was the first time I had been in a room with that many playwrights, and since I was sitting there, I said to myself, "I must be a playwright, too."

—AUGUST WILSON

n January 1978, Wilson boarded that plane for Minneapolis. It wasn't exactly the ideal time to visit the Twin Cities, where winter temperatures rarely hit above twenty degrees during the day and usually hovered in single digits at night. But Wilson was ready for something different. He had been writing poetry for more than a dozen years, and even though he had directed plays and tried his hand at playwriting, he wasn't getting anywhere. And Claude Purdy was his greatest champion, urging him to continue working on his dramatic voice. Purdy did not lack for confidence, and he was searching for a play that would help him make the leap from small, scrappy theaters to bigger stages. He saw this enclave in the Midwest as fertile ground for his creative spirit.

Purdy asked his new girlfriend, Jacqui Shoholm, to drive him to the airport to pick up his friend that day. They had barely made introductions when Wilson asked if they could go to the Washington Avenue Bridge, which spans the Mississippi River and connects the east and west campuses of the University of Minnesota. He wasn't interested in it as a typical tourist attraction; he had no desire to plunge his toes in the Mighty

Mississippi. The poet John Berryman had jumped to his death from that bridge in 1972, and Wilson wanted to pay his respects. Attention must be paid. Shoholm gave them the car, and the two men went off to reflect at the site of the tragedy.

Wilson stayed with Purdy at the Commodore Hotel for a few days. The grand hotel, located in the heart of St. Paul's tony Cathedral Hill district, was founded in 1920 and hosted such luminaries as F. Scott Fitzgerald at its basement speakeasy during the Prohibition Era. The hotel's storied bar was open for business during Wilson's stay there. He went to see *Eden* at Penumbra Theatre several times. The play had won awards in New York and Los Angeles, and Wilson was captivated. The production was gritty and raw and more professional than the plays he had directed in Pittsburgh. The Hallie Q. Brown Community Center was housed in the Martin Luther King Jr. multiservice facility on Kent Street, about half a mile from where Wilson was staying in St. Paul. It was built in 1972, and its executive director was a theater aficionado who had the foresight to include a professional stage in the complex, which also offered day care, medical services, senior programs, violence prevention groups, as well as arts and recreation programs. Wilson was intrigued; this was far better than the auditorium of the A. Leo Weil Elementary School in Pittsburgh, where Black Horizons had performed.

He also got to know Shoholm, Purdy's new girlfriend. She was a city planner responsible for allocating the federal CETA grants and had been instrumental in awarding the grant that launched Penumbra. She was a white single mother and a theater buff. She had seen Purdy's 1976 production of *The Great White Hope*, which was performed at the Downtown Dinner Theater in Minneapolis and starred Ernie Hudson, who went on to become an acclaimed character actor in film and television. She and Purdy had fallen for each other. One morning, she joined Purdy and Wilson for breakfast at a local café. The two men immediately launched into their usual patter. They could talk for hours about the day's headlines or the books they were reading. They became absorbed in each other's company, oblivious to the fact that they were leaving Shoholm out of the conversation. She asked Purdy if he had something for her to read. He always carried a briefcase full of scripts and articles. He gave her Wilson's one-act play *The Coldest Day of the Year.* She read it while the two men conspired, and by the time she was finished, tears were streaming down her face. "This guy is the real thing," she thought at the time.

She introduced Wilson to her best friend, a white social worker named Judy Oliver. Oliver cooked him dinner one night, and he asked her to read *The Coldest Day of the Year.* She was captivated by his "true heart." He later reconstructed their conversation. "I said, 'Here is who I am.' I carried it around with me and quoted from it all the time." Oliver was as taken with the short play as Shoholm had been a few weeks earlier.

Soon after, he moved out of the Commodore to stay with Oliver at her apartment at 587 Grand Avenue, a stately brick building on a main thoroughfare in St. Paul's Ramsey Hill section, which boasts the mansions of residents who settled in the city during the Gilded Age. The apartment was within walking distance of pubs and restaurants that welcomed a writer nursing a single cup of coffee for hours. The two clicked. With long brown hair and aviator glasses popularized by feminist icon Gloria Steinem, Oliver was a steady force who made a living nurturing others.

Wilson spent hours with Purdy discussing *Black Bart* and returned to Pittsburgh invigorated by the visit and eager to work on the script. Bob Johnson, the choreographer, was also keen to move forward. He had sent the script to Joseph Papp, the theater impresario and founder of New York's legendary Public Theater and the original producer of the counter-culture musical *Hair*, before it transferred to Broadway. Johnson had performed in the Broadway production. But Papp wasn't interested in *Black Bart*, and Johnson received a polite "Thanks but no thanks" note from Lynn Holst, the Public's play development coordinator.

Wilson didn't stick around in Pittsburgh for long. He had smelled opportunity in the Twin Cities—and he had become smitten with Judy Oliver. On March 5, 1978, he flew back to St. Paul and officially moved in with Oliver. On that same day thirteen years earlier he had moved out of his mother's house to the basement flat on Crawford Street. His mother wasn't happy about his life choices then and she was still not convinced about his burning desire to become a writer, but she blessed the move. It would get him off the streets and away from the characters he called his friends.

Wilson was accustomed to living in the Black community in a city where things moved fast and there was a hustle on every corner. St. Paul was starkly different. There were more than fifty-five thousand Blacks living in Pittsburgh's Hill District when he left, about the same number as the entire Black population of the state of Minnesota at the time. Life was slower, the people were more polite, yet more reserved. Wilson had always been an outside observer, and he settled into the same role in his new home. He started showing up at Penumbra, but he sat in the back of the theater, chain-smoking Marlboro Lights and watching rehearsals from the last row. "He was the dude in the shadows," actor Abdul Salaam El Razzac said. Wilson kept largely to himself while at the theater. He was "a friend of Claude's" who smoked incessantly and always had a legal pad and pen, taking notes. He didn't dress like a thespian: his shirts were pressed, and his shoes were shined. Few knew what he was doing there, a quiet presence in the background.

At the time, the artists at Penumbra were making it up as they went along. There was electricity in the air. They knew they were creating something unique and necessary, but they didn't know then that the fledgling organization would have a significant influence on the state of Black theater nationwide. They were just a bunch of young visionaries—all with day jobs—who wanted to put on plays that reflected their life experience. The operation was led by founding artistic director Lou Bellamy, with Purdy as the principal director. Purdy shaped the aesthetic that the theater continues today. Penumbra's productions are gritty, bold, real, visceral. As director, Purdy went for the jugular.

In addition to *Eden*, the theater's inaugural 1977–78 season included Bullins's *The Taking of Miss Janie* and works by African American playwrights Horace Bond, William Wells Brown, and Gus Edwards. As Wilson watched quietly from the back row, he was introduced to serious dramas that addressed racial equality head-on. But the season also included an unlikely production of the Neil Simon comedy *The Odd Couple*.

It was directed by Bond, who added a twist: the mismatched roommates Felix and Oscar were played by a white actor and a Black actor, suggesting that race played a role in their constant quibbling. The advertising for the production read "Until you've seen 'our' odd couple, you'll never know how outrageously funny *The Odd Couple* can be." The nascent theater was looking for an audience, and comedies do better at the box office than political dramas. "We were attempting, I think, to get broader audiences," said Lou Bellamy. "You couldn't always get audiences giving that pessimistic view of where we think we are in this world. So we were attempting to still get the message out there but to sell some tickets and let some people have some fun too."

It was a heady time, and even though Wilson remained in the shadows during his first year in St. Paul, he watched the theater grow. The federal CETA grant enabled Penumbra to pay the actors $150 a week, and Bellamy insisted that they all participate in every show, even if they were not cast. Everyone had to audition, and those who did not get roles were required to assist with sets or costumes, tech, or box office. They rehearsed whenever they could, and they were one big dysfunctional family, fueled by artistry and idealism and often under the influence of marijuana or booze. As with any small group, there were fights and romantic triangles. It was hard to keep up with who was sleeping with whom. Lou Bellamy's brother, Terry Bellamy, was one of the core actors, and he said that some days actors would arrive and shouting matches would erupt over money, lovers, or bruised egos.

And in the early days, the theater was hardly sensitive to feminist issues, even though the second wave of feminism was in full swing. Most of the key members were male, and actress Faye M. Price, who was with the company at the beginning, described her experience as "being a female in an all dick theater." They were not doing plays by writers like Adrienne Kennedy or Ntozake Shange, whose landmark choreopoem, *for colored girls who have considered suicide / when the rainbow is enuf*, debuted in 1976. Penumbra did not produce it until 1999. "The Black Arts Movement was clearly a very male movement," Price said. "There were a lot of men and me. Or me and one other woman." She said she was relegated to roles playing "a mother or a prostitute or a ho-ish mother who was a prostitute." She said she never felt threatened, but she was "aware how much my, not my sexuality, but my sex . . . was used in a show."

Even though Wilson was still an outsider at Penumbra, he did join the company members when they met after rehearsals at local watering holes to discuss plays or poetry or, as they described it, to "tell lies." He was settling in and finding a new group of artists. Penumbra provided a place where these young artists could be themselves. Playwright Carlyle Brown remembered it this way: "It was a place where the artists were Black people telling stories, and there was a kind of level of explanation that you didn't have to go through. You didn't have to explain yourself or justify yourself to convince people you were human. You could just work on your play."

The Twin Cities were known to be a place where interracial relationships were accepted. Wilson settled into life with Judy Oliver easily. The pair became inseparable from Purdy and Shoholm, another interracial couple. Shoholm had a son about the same age as Sakina, who was now eight, and as things grew more serious with Oliver, Wilson knew he had to introduce Sakina to his new girlfriend. He arranged a trip to Disney World. Sakina was excited but surprised when Oliver accompanied them on the trip. "It was like, 'Wow, you're in Disney World, and here is my new girlfriend,'" she said.

Wilson could afford the trip because, at thirty-four, he had a regular, salaried job for the first time in his life. Through her work as a city planner, Shoholm connected him with a new theater program at the Science Museum of Minnesota in downtown St. Paul. Wilson was hired to write plays that illuminated the exhibits. The plays, which have not been produced outside of the museum, included titles like *Eskimo Insult Duel* and *How Coyote Got His Special Power and Used It to Help the People*. It was not a particularly taxing job, nor was it artistically rewarding. He did, however, have some fun with the dry subject matter. In *Profiles in Science: William Harvey*, a one-act play about the seventeenth-century British physician who discovered blood circulation, Wilson has the actor playing the title role break down the fourth wall and address the audience. The actor says he doesn't like playing the genteel British gentleman and would rather play the wildly controversial and temperamental Swiss physician Paracelsus (even though the two scientists were not contemporaries). It is quite possible that Wilson had read "La rosa de Paracelso," Borges's short story about the mad scientist who was also said to be the inspiration for Mary Shelley's *Frankenstein*. Either way, the writing is spritely, and clearly Wilson had found a way to inject humor into the educational material.

One day, a senior curator called Wilson into his office and showed him a discovery he had made decades earlier. He had done nothing of great import since. It was his way of telling Wilson not to stay in a day job just because it was comfortable.

After he had been on the job for about a year, an actress in the Science Museum company got a real gig, performing in a local production of a play called *Snow in the Virgin Islands*. Wilson went to see it to support his friend Linda Varvell, but he wasn't impressed. "I could write a better play than that," he told her. "She looked at me like, 'Oh, yeah.' She didn't believe me." He spent ten feverish days finishing *Jitney!*, his play about the cabdrivers he had observed back on the Hill. He was enamored of the actress and dedicated *Eskimo Insult Duel* to her. Many years later, he was giving a speech in St. Paul, and he heard someone in the audience shout out. It was Linda Varvell. "She said, 'Do you remember me?' I was like, I could never forget you."

Back in Pittsburgh, choreographer Bob Johnson was still intent on getting *Black Bart* produced. So was Claude Purdy, who had a contact at the Inner City Cultural Center in Los Angeles. The center was founded by C. Bernard Jackson in 1965 in the wake of the Watts Rebellion and aimed to provide arts opportunities and training for minorities who were all but locked out of the white film industry that dominated the City of Angels. Purdy arranged for a reading of *Black Bart* there in May 1978. The eager team from Pittsburgh flew out for the production, which was a complete disaster. "It was a mess," Shoholm said. But it was a learning experience. Purdy and Wilson met regularly to discuss changes to the rambling, psychedelic script. Shoholm would come home from her job at city hall and find the two of them huddled together in a cloud of smoke, ashtrays overflowing and ideas pouring out in the haze, which was redolent with the skunky scent of marijuana. The two were attached at the hip: when they weren't talking about *Black Bart*, they were discussing subjects ranging from Buckminster Fuller to Romare Bearden to Joseph Campbell. Wilson had already expressed an interest in building a mythology for Black people in his work, an idea he had picked up from Larry Neal's essay on the Black Arts Movement and from the writings of Maulana "Ron" Karenga, an activist and cultural philosopher known for creating Kwanzaa in 1966. Wilson and his Pittsburgh poet friends had studied and debated Karenga's philosophy and found one requirement lacking. "The one thing which we did not have as black Americans—we didn't have a mythology," he said. "We had no origin myths." His discussion with Purdy about Campbell solidified his urge to use his writing to establish a Black mythology. Years earlier, he had told his younger brother Richard that all disenfranchised people should create their own mythology and celebrate it.

Purdy was a huge influence on the local theater community in general and on Wilson in particular. They and their partners were together constantly, and the two couples formed a friendship that was the closest thing Wilson had to family away from Pittsburgh. They celebrated holidays and birthdays together. Both couples had stormy relationships, though. The men were serial womanizers; their affection for women and sex was not a secret in the small, close-knit theater community. At some point, Sholholm became aware of her husband's philandering and believed Oliver had figured it out about Wilson at some point as well. The interns at Penumbra knew well enough to concoct stories about who was with whom when spouses or partners called. They began each day by figuring out what lies they had to tell when they answered the phone.

But by all accounts, Oliver was Wilson's muse. "She was lively and funny and smart and really dug August," Wilson's friend James Yoshimura said. "He had told me about his first wife and how that had devastated him. Judy helped him put his soul back together." As a social worker, she knew her way around the world of nonprofit organizations, and she encouraged Wilson to send his scripts out for various awards. Purdy's apartment on Selby Avenue became Grant Central. Sholholm, an experienced city planner, would write the grants, and Oliver mailed them, kissing the envelope for good luck. That luck didn't come readily. Script after script was returned, and Wilson didn't take it well. Once, he picked up a rejected script and threw the envelope across the room in disgust. He wrote until all hours of the evening. "Sometimes I can hear him clicking on the keys," Oliver said of his late-night sessions at the typewriter. "It sounds like a lullaby."

His friend Rob Penny had sent him a brochure from the prestigious Eugene O'Neill Theater Center in Waterford, Connecticut, scribbling the words "Do this!" on the pamphlet. In 1979, Wilson applied with two scripts. He sent a television treatment of the still-unproduced *The Coldest Day of the Year* to the center's Television Conference and submitted *Black Bart* to the National Playwrights Conference. Both were rejected. He submitted *Jitney!* in 1980 and it was also rejected. He figured the reader must have been wrong, so he submitted it again the next year: same response.

But he persevered, with Purdy as his champion. Purdy spent several years nagging Lou Bellamy at Penumbra to produce *Black Bart*, but Bellamy was not impressed with the script or its author. Wilson chain-smoked. He did not easily fit into the Midwest relaxed pace of life. "He had all this East Coast energy," said actor James Craven. "He would go from zero to sixty in a heartbeat."

Craven, in fact, was from the Twin Cities, but he was one of the only local Black actors who had left to get formal acting training. He was a self-described "fuck-up" in high school, and in order to graduate, he interned at the Guthrie Theater in Minneapolis to get his last six credits. The "fuck-up" ended up appearing onstage in *Julius Caesar*. The powers that be at the prestigious Guthrie took a liking to him and helped him get a full scholarship to study drama at Carnegie Mellon University in Pittsburgh. While he was there from 1971 to 1977, he met Purdy, who was living in the area at the time. The first time Craven saw him, Purdy was playing a sitar and smoking weed. They became fast friends, and Purdy introduced him to Wilson.

Craven came back to his hometown in 1978, the same year Wilson had made his pilgrimage. He was cast in a production of David Rabe's

Streamers, and one night, he was surprised to see Wilson and Purdy back-stage after the performance. They were talking about a theater named Penumbra, but Craven didn't want to stay to be a part of it. He went to New York, only to return later and join Penumbra's acting company. Purdy got him in. "Lou Bellamy said, 'I don't trust this guy. He is crazy,'" said Craven, who went on to appear in many of Wilson's later plays, although the two were like fire and water. Craven never bought into the "myth of August," and he was never cast in a Wilson production on Broadway.

But Purdy did buy into that myth—and he hoped Wilson could be his springboard to bigger and better gigs for himself. In 1981, Purdy finally convinced Penumbra to produce *Black Bart*. It had fourteen musical numbers and a multicultural cast of twenty-six actors. It required a motorcycle onstage. Before it even opened, the press release drew snickers from the local critics. It read:

> A musical satire set in the mythical town of Little Egypt. Black Bart, Alchemist and Master Sorcerer, has carved out a retreat called the Sacred Hills and is reported to be making gold out of water. Pharaoh Goldstein, the Regional Representative of the Culturally Independent Adults (CIA), enlists the help of Chauncey Riffraff III and Master Divine in devising a scheme to penetrate the Sacred Hills, which are guarded by invisible Electric Angels. After several misguided attempts, they secure the services of Bart's archenemy Kid Sampson. At their encounter, Bart and Sampson engage in a magical duel.

And it's more complicated than that brief summary.

Wilson had seen a production of Amiri Baraka's *Great Goodness of Life: A Coon Show*, a larger-than-life satire about the trial of a middle-aged Black man that ends in a horrifying ritualistic murder. Wilson was struck by the satirical form. "It's wild and zany and it is extremely effective," he told Joan Herrington, a theater professor at Western Michigan University and author of *"I Ain't Sorry for Nothin' I Done": August Wilson's Process of*

Playwriting. "Baraka takes his anger and makes art out of it. It's funny and it gets its point across. Baraka wanted to make everything big."

And *Black Bart* is certainly big: in fact, it's gigantic. The musical opens with a monologue by a character named Horsefeathers, a Native American whose first word is "How." He rages about the relics that were stolen from his people and put in museums. Horsefeathers was played by a young Black actor named Marion Isaac McClinton. Purdy and Wilson spent hours and hours refining the outrageous plot, and Shoholm remembers their writing sessions as smoke-filled, hilarious brainstorms. Wilson later said the musical was a modern take on Aristophanes's *Lysistrata*, but he failed to realize that it was being performed at a time when women were deeply engaged in second-wave feminism. One critic pointed out that "there is a large cast of whores, all dressed Bob Fosse–style in corsets, garters and stockings."

On opening night, there were women from several nonprofit foundations in the audience. They walked out early and didn't leave quietly, offended when a character named Norma Jean sang a tune about snaring a man who could get her out of poverty. A Chinese character named Ping Pong spoke in broken English. Stereotypes abounded. The whole thing was a phantasmal mess. One critic described it as a "cartoon-like parody," noting it was "a little bit of everything, a few crumbs of something and quite a lot of nothing." Wilson was striving for the magical realism of Ishmael Reed's *Mumbo Jumbo*, but it wasn't clicking onstage. One night, the motorcycle caught on fire, and those who hadn't already left ran screaming from the theater. It was not an auspicious debut for Wilson in his new town. Lou Bellamy was furious. "I will never do a play by that August Wilson ever again," he said at the time, fuming. But Penumbra would go on to produce all of Wilson's plays, over and over again.

Years later, Wilson was amused by the memory of *Black Bart*. "It's zany. I think it would make the greatest musical. It is crazy. That might be a future project," he said in early 2005.

Wilson weathered that disaster. He was honing his craft. The play has the long monologues Wilson became known for later, and it is full of biblical references and nods to the classics and Greek mythology. Despite this less than successful debut, he was loving his life in his newly adopted home. He eventually quit the Science Museum to focus on his own writing. Oliver knew the executive director of a social service agency called Little Brothers of the Poor, located in a modest brick building across the river on East Lake Street in Minneapolis. They were looking for a chef, and Oliver recommended Wilson, who had cooked barbecue and worked at many restaurants over the years. He made breakfast and lunch for the staff of sixteen employees, working from 9:00 a.m. to 3:00 p.m. and spending the rest of the day writing.

Wilson fit right in and relished cooking for the staff. On holidays, he would make special theme meals. He and several staff members played in a local softball league. His two brothers, Edwin and Richard Kittel, were now living in St. Paul, and they joined the team. Over the years, they had each gotten into scrapes with the law, and when they were released from prison, Daisy sent them to stay with their older brother, who had yet to make a big name for himself, but at least had a stable lifestyle. Wilson played shortstop, and he hit like a powerhouse, despite the fact that he had trouble running the bases because he chain-smoked. One spring, the staff took a weekend retreat, and Wilson posed for photos dancing the cancan, cigarette hanging out of his mouth. He bonded with an employee named Mike Morgan, who had recently retired from a career in professional boxing. He was no Charley Burley, but his record was respectable—20-12, with five knockouts. On Monday mornings, he and Wilson would meet outside the kitchen in the dining room and reenact the fights from the weekend. They recited the play-by-play, fists flying in the air as they recounted the match.

Wilson was earning about $5 or $6 an hour, according to Mike Henley, the executive director who hired him. Oliver supported the couple with her earnings as a social worker, but it wasn't always easy; they rolled pennies for extra cash and filed for bankruptcy in 1981. Wilson appeared at the Minnesota Second Judicial Court on March 31, 1981, and officially changed his name from Frederick August Kittel to August Wilson. He and Oliver married on April 25, in a ceremony at a waterfront condo that belonged to friends of Sholom. Purdy and Sholom stood as witnesses.

The newlyweds chose to have their reception in the dining room at Little Brothers. Wilson's family members were there, including Sakina. Daisy came from Pittsburgh and beamed in the photos.

According to Henley, the couple had a flair for drama. "They would have verbal arguments and then make up," he said. "They loved each other, but it was challenging sometimes because he was attracted to other people and he always had an eye for women. That must have been challenging for her." Even early in the marriage, his colleagues at Little Brothers were aware that he wasn't the most faithful of husbands. Later, Henley looked back fondly on those simple days. "He enjoyed the time to cook, write, be with friends," he said. "Once he became famous, it was nice that he got a lot of attention, but he missed the ease he had at Little Brothers. When he became a public figure it changed a lot of things for him. He used to describe the years at Little Brothers as the best time of his life."

But even during that simple time, he was still aspiring to write the Great American Play. He applied for a fellowship at the Playwrights' Center in Minneapolis, submitting *Jitney!*, the play he had turned to in earnest in 1979 after Linda Varvell challenged him to write a better play. He won the fellowship, which was funded by the Jerome Foundation and included a $2,400 annual stipend. The playwrights also had access to actors and directors to perform staged readings of their plays. Many of the playwrights took their time before they had readings, but Tom Dunn, then the executive director, said that Wilson had readings every two or three weeks. "He was older than the other playwrights, and he did a great job challenging them," Dunn said. Lee Blessing, who went on to write *A Walk in the Woods*, was a fellow that year, too.

Jitney! was given a staged reading at the Playwrights' Center, and it was markedly different from Wilson's earlier work. It didn't have the "Americanized Homeric dialogue" that the critics complained about in *Black Bart*. For the first time, he captured the rhythm and cadence of the people he observed in Pittsburgh. He wasn't putting words in their mouths. He was listening to them. He was becoming part of a long literary tradition: like Beckett and Baldwin, he had to leave his home in order to capture its essence.

He spent many hours at the center, which is housed in an old church at 2301 Franklin Avenue in Minneapolis. That year, the organization acquired two IBM Selectric typewriters, the state of the art at the time. Wilson took advantage of those machines, and he often frequented the space when he wasn't working at Little Brothers. Wilson always showed up dressed like a professional: coat, tie, shoes shined. He was clearly from out of town, but at the same time, he had found an artistic home. And when he attended his first meeting at the center, he felt validated as an artist. He had arrived. He was a playwright now.

One of the members of the center's board of directors was an executive at Target, which originated near St. Paul, its first store opening in 1962 in Roseville, Minnesota, long before it became a national chain of superstores. Tom Dunn was not shy about asking his board members for help of any kind. This executive agreed to offer assistance to the playwright fellows and allowed them to send their scripts to the Target business offices, where office workers made copies on their professional Xerox machines. Shortly after Wilson became a fellow, he sent over a draft of his expanded version of *Ma Rainey's Black Bottom*, which was about the length of four one-act scripts. Soon after, Dunn heard from Target. He said, "I got a call from this guy's secretary, and she said, 'We are confused, we have scripts but we can't tell if it is two or three or four plays or what. It is by August Wilson.' We said, 'Yep, that is one script.' When I told August, he said, 'Are you suggesting I cut it down for the photocopiers?'"

This was a fertile period, despite the huge disappointment with the disastrous *Black Bart*. He wrote a play called *Fullerton Street*, which is set in 1941 and tells the story of Moses Lee, who made the Great Migration with his wife and parents, relocating from the South to the industrial North. (Wilson submitted this unpublished play to the O'Neill in 1981, but it was rejected.) A Playwrights' Center newsletter described it this way: "Oppressed by the socioeconomic conditions and memories from his past, he enlists in the Army in an effort to obtain first class citizenship by helping America win the war. After a bittersweet homecoming and his dream of social and economic equality is shattered, he is forced to choose between his blind allegiance to his principles or the negotiation of compromise." The blurb is clearly written for marketing purposes, and the play remains unpublished, even though it was given a staged reading at the Playwrights' Center.

The play was significant because Moses's mother dies. "That was the first person I killed off in any of my plays," he told an interviewer years later. "I remember her name was Mozelle, and I remember when I wrote the scene of Mozelle dying, I was crying, and the tears were falling on the page, and I was trying to write, and the ink was getting all screwed up." He would kill off many characters over the course of his career, but the first one left him bereft. "It was like, 'Mozelle is dead.' I had lived with her for so long." Two other characters die in the play, and a bereft Moses screams at Death. The play is unpolished and lacks the long monologues Wilson later mastered, but it foreshadows his obsession with mortality, particularly a scene in which his most famous character, Troy Maxson in *Fences*, wrestles with Death.

Wilson was also working on a trilogy called *Dangerous Music*, which was summed up as an examination "of three major wars on American society and explores the conflicts generated by changing cultural values." He had planned to write a trilogy about the blues, which included *The Homecoming* and his first, twelve-page draft of *Ma Rainey*. He never wrote the third play. "I was going to write three plays about the blues, but I abandoned that," he said. At any rate, as Wilson matured as a playwright, he was committed to exploring cultural values and how they affected the lives of Blacks in Pittsburgh.

His imagination was fueled in this new place. The cold Midwestern winters sparked his creativity. He held the first staged reading of *Ma Rainey* at Little Brothers, a place where he felt at home. He had started writing the play in 1976, but it was originally a one-act with the blues singer in the studio. "I wasn't a playwright," he said of his original effort. "I was just scribbling on paper bags." But Wilson had the epiphany at the Playwrights' Center during his first meeting. "I must be a playwright, too," he had thought. He started to listen to characters in scenes that played out in his mind. "I dug up the paper bags on that play I was writing, and I said, 'Maybe I'll go down in the band room and see what's going on down there.' There were three guys like sitting down in the band room. This other guy walks in, and he's wearing glasses, and he's carrying a newspaper, I'm like, 'Excuse me man, I'm writing a play here. Who are you?' That was Toledo. He was in the bathroom. Now I got four guys instead of three. That's when I learned you could do that. You could send them offstage." Toledo was a piano player and the only one of the four musicians who could read. Wilson imagined Toledo and the other characters talking and let them take control of his fertile imagination, and he would end up working that way for the rest of his life. This new approach enabled him to open up the world of the play, which had originally been a slight sketch about the intrepid blues singer. "It became a different play," he said. "The people who play the blues and jazz have made a tremendous contribution to music, but we know very little about who they are; too often we view them in a glancing manner. I tried to show that Blacks in America have different cultural responses than white America, that there is a system of values that will sustain a man once he has left his father's house." He was paraphrasing a James Baldwin quote, which he often referred to over the years, but interestingly, sometimes he changed the quote to "values that will sustain a man once he has left his *mother's* house," not his *father's* house.

It was a time of epiphanies for Wilson. Every day, after he cleaned up at Little Brothers, he would either go to the Playwrights' Center or to a local watering hole to write. "One day, I was at a place called Nora's," he said. "I got there at three o'clock." He wrote one of *Ma Rainey*'s most explosive scenes sitting there. Near the end of the play, the central character, Levee, pulls out a knife and stabs at the "white man's God." He has already told a horrific story about his mother being raped and his father being lynched, and he rages at another character, a trombonist who is a man of faith. "I was writing about Levee stabbing God, and I looked up and the shift had changed," he said. "It's like ten o'clock. I was sitting there for seven hours."

That scene led to an even more cataclysmic ending, and the notes scribbled on paper bags became a play that originally ran four hours and had the long, poetic monologues that became Wilson's signature. It was given a staged reading at the Playwrights' Center, with actor Terry Bellamy playing the role of Levee, the hotheaded trumpet player in the scene written at Aunt Nora's. People were beginning to notice that the guy who hung out in the shadows was paying attention.

Some of the actors got together to film Wilson's first play, *Recycle*. Terry Bellamy was in it, but his brother, Penumbra artistic director Lou Bellamy, didn't want to have anything to do with Wilson, who almost chased off his theater's funding sources with the calamitous *Black Bart*. The film project, which was directed by Purdy, ran out of money, and the crew never completed filming, but Wilson was not giving up. He kept trying to get a play accepted at the O'Neill. On December 1, 1981, Wilson and Oliver finished yet another application for the O'Neill. This time, Wilson sent a short screenplay called *Why I Learned to Read*. It never got anywhere. He was so eager he also sent the pages of *Ma Rainey*, which was a rambling script that had been rewritten many times in bars like Sweeney's or Aunt Nora's. Oliver brought it to the post office, kissed the envelope, and sent it off.

CHAPTER SEVEN

The Launchpad of American Theater

Your belief in yourself must be greater than everyone else's disbelief in you.

—AUGUST WILSON

ate one afternoon in May 1982, Wilson emerged from a van and stepped onto the pristine grounds of the Eugene O'Neill Theater Center in Waterford, Connecticut, a bucolic seaside town known for its pristine beaches, oceanfront mansions, and crispy fried clams. He had boarded the van in front of the Yale Club in Midtown Manhattan, sharing the ride with a group of playwrights, directors, and designers. It seemed like a reunion for some of the travelers, who paired up in seats and immediately fell into easy conversations about mutual colleagues or productions that had closed off-Broadway. Most of them were dressed in casual weekend attire—weathered jeans, flowing skirts, sandals or sneakers. Wilson, however, sported a khaki safari jacket and a page boy cap, a signature look he had cultivated when he had moved from Pittsburgh to St. Paul. He sat in the back with the other smokers, lighting cigarette after cigarette and inhaling deeply until the burning tip touched his tar-stained fingertips. He spent three hours writing notes on a yellow legal pad.

The bus came to a stop on the circular drive in front of the mansion, a grand twenty-four-room estate with a lush, rolling lawn that cascades down to the waves of Long Island Sound. The building reminded Wilson of the magnificent palaces on Summit Avenue in St. Paul, except here the view boasted a vista of the Atlantic Ocean instead of the Mississippi River. This was all new to him, and he took it in quietly, standing to the side and observing every detail like a photographer contemplating the right angle for the perfect shot. He had been dreaming of arriving here—the prestigious O'Neill, the so-called launchpad of the American theater—ever since Rob Penny had sent him that brochure a few years back inscribed: "Do this!"

Wilson had read everything he could about the O'Neill, but there was nothing like being there. The O'Neill was founded in 1965 by George White, a young Yale School of Drama graduate who had grown up in Waterford. In 1963, White learned that a vast waterfront property, formerly the estate of the railroad magnate Edward Hammond, had been donated to the town of Waterford. He formed a nonprofit foundation and leased the land and buildings from the town for $1 a year, and two years later, he invited a group of playwrights to attend the first annual National Playwrights Conference. It was named for Eugene O'Neill, the four-time Pulitzer Prize winner and the only American playwright to win the Nobel Prize in Literature. O'Neill had grown up in the area and spent much of his boyhood in the nearby Monte Cristo Cottage, where he set both *Ah, Wilderness!* and *Long Day's Journey into Night.*

The heady early years were full of fistfights and fury, as young, often inebriated off-off-Broadway writers clashed with established mainstream playwrights and critics. Eventually, though, the center became established as a safe haven where new work could be developed outside the commercial chaos of New York. By the time Wilson arrived, there were three theaters on the campus: the Rose Barn Theater, the outdoor Amphitheater, and the Instant, an outdoor space with bleacher seating (it has since been renamed the Edith Oliver Theater). Such eminent writers as John Guare, Derek Walcott, Wendy Wasserstein, and David Henry Hwang launched or developed their careers there. It was known as a retreat where writers could showcase and shape their plays. Artistic director Lloyd Richards came on board in 1969, bringing with him the gravitas of a long career in the theater and a solid commitment to shielding writers from the pressure of the marketplace. Among playwrights, both fledgling and established, the O'Neill was the gold standard, the entrée into professional theater circles.

Wilson, who was still working as a cook for the Little Brothers of the Poor, was fueled by ambition. In his heart, he was a playwright, even if he was still unknown outside of Pittsburgh and St. Paul. For him, writing was a force necessary for survival. He was not above working blue-collar jobs, but that was to put food on the table. He fed his spirit with words. And he wanted to succeed as a playwright. He had, of course, applied to the National Playwrights Conference five times—and was rejected five times. That didn't stop him from applying again. Like many writers, he had unbridled faith in his ability, but deep inside, he also battled self-doubt.

His wife kept him going, bolstering his confidence after every rejection, encouraging him that his day would come. She once wrote a letter to the editor of the Minneapolis *Star Tribune*, chastising the paper for failing to review the premiere of Wilson's musical, *Black Bart*, deeming the oversight a "blatant attempt to disregard Black theater and its playwrights." She celebrated with him when the sixth application to the O'Neill turned out to be the charm.

And now Wilson was determined to prove her right as he stepped off that bus onto the gravel driveway at the O'Neill. He, like some other playwrights, carried the acceptance telegram that had been sent weeks earlier by Lloyd Richards:

CONGRATULATIONS YOUR PLAY HAS BEEN SELECTED FOR THE 1982 NATIONAL PLAYWRIGHTS CONFERENCE. LETTER FOLLOWS.

LLOYD RICHARDS, ARTISTIC DIRECTOR

That electronic missive had been followed by a packet of information from Jean Passanante, Richards's assistant, telling him to buy a plane ticket to New York and file for reimbursement later. The O'Neill contract provided room and board, transportation to and from the conference, and a $1,000 stipend. Wilson called Passanante and told her he couldn't afford the fare; he didn't tell her that he and Oliver had filed for bankruptcy the year before. He was broke, but he would have walked to the O'Neill if that was what it took. His bank account was empty but his passion was deep, and he knew that this was his big chance.

Wilson kept his financial situation—and his feelings—to himself on that bus ride and during the next four days of the preconference, the annual gathering at which the selected playwrights read their scripts to the assembled theater professionals. He felt out of place. "People showed up, and they all started hugging each other," he said of his introduction to the center. "I didn't understand that. It took me a while to get up to speed on that." In the back of his mind, he was wondering, "Did they really mean me? I felt they had the wrong guy. Did they make a mistake? Seriously. Later I found out that I wasn't alone. All the playwrights felt that way."

Richards, the O'Neill's artistic director and dean of the Yale School of Drama since 1979, presided over the event like a mandarin mentoring a group of eager, yet inchoate, students. Short and bespectacled with a salt-and-pepper beard and a Buddha belly, Richards was an inscrutable figure with a theatrical history that inspired Wilson. He was best known for directing the acclaimed 1959 Broadway production of Lorraine Hansberry's *A Raisin in the Sun*, the first Black man to sit in the director's chair on the Great White Way. He was a legend, a mentor, a powerhouse who could provide an entrée into prestigious theaters. Richards was guarded about his age and never revealed it, prompting the playwrights and O'Neill staffers to play a sort of parlor game trying to guess how old he really was. That summer, he was sixty-three; Wilson was thirty-seven.

Richards and Wilson didn't immediately become fast friends at the preconference, even though there were only three African Americans in the room. (The other was director Dennis Scott.) But Richards had his eye out for Wilson that weekend. He had championed *Ma Rainey's Black Bottom* during the conference selection process, even though it was bloated at four hours long, heavy with lengthy, poetic monologues, but not so precise on structure or plot. It was two one-act plays sewn together with the seam showing. Director Constance Grappo, the screener who initially read the script, had described it as "a story well-told and worth telling," but she also outlined her reservations in her reader's report. "I feel it could use some editing, especially at the end," she wrote. "The main characters are interesting but the telling of their respective 'stories' is not well set up and could be subtler." The play made the cut from several hundred scripts, which were read by two screeners and then brought to the selection committee members, who read about thirty or forty plays. It wasn't a shoo-in, but Richards pushed for it. "My sense was that it was possible that it hadn't been read completely by some of the people because it looked like a telephone book—it was huge, and the typeface was very small," Passanante said.

Richards, who worked steadily in the theater and had just helped usher Athol Fugard's *A Lesson from Aloes* to Broadway, was looking for a fresh Black voice, or as some who knew him well called it, "The Great Black Hope." He sensed potential in Wilson's script, and he wondered who could have written a play infused with characters who embodied such an uncanny blend of fury and grace. Richards said that Wilson's dialogue reminded him of the animated conversations he had overheard while working as a young man at a barbershop in Detroit. "The characters were alive," he said. "They were people I had met in the barbershop on Saturday mornings, talking about baseball, philosophy, politics. You'd hear humor, imagery, poetry—the poetry of oppressed people who have to create a sense of freedom in their words, people living more in their vision than their actuality."

Richards didn't immediately recognize Wilson when he walked into the first preconference reading on Saturday morning. He studied the faces of each playwright as they filed into the room. Wilson, with his light skin and safari attire, parked himself in the corner, head down, legal pad in hand. But when Richards heard him mumble a few words, he knew this was the man who had written *Ma Rainey*.

On the first day of the preconference, Richards gave each of the playwrights a treasured jacket. The jackets were inscribed with the O'Neill Center's logo—a line drawing of playwright Eugene O'Neill sporting a toothbrush mustache (that many of the O'Neill's inner circle complained was reminiscent of Adolf Hitler)—and the word "playwright." Many playwrights held on to theirs for years, even when they left the theater and moved on to lucrative careers in film or television. Wilson cherished his: it meant he had made it.

Richards didn't direct plays himself at the conference because he ran the entire event; it's hard to be a general and a sergeant at the same time. He also kept his thoughts to himself, maintaining a calm presence that could be unnerving to playwrights who craved attention and feedback. When asked for advice, he was known to simply say, "Be where you are." Some directors, actors, and playwrights nicknamed him Buddha. Others called him Yoda. They held contests to see who could make him laugh— or even crack a smile.

Richards kept Wilson at a distance during the preconference, a reflection of his persona as the inscrutable, all-knowing sage. But the other playwrights and artists didn't warm up to Wilson, either. "The O'Neill is like a club," said director Steve Robman, a Yale School of Drama graduate and an O'Neill regular. "It's a terrific place if you are a member of the club. If you are not, it is not so fun."

And Wilson was decidedly not a card-carrying member of any club. During the communal meals in the mansion's cafeteria, he took a table in the corner. If someone asked to join him, he was friendly and polite, but he didn't seek anyone out. Right after breakfast each morning during the preconference, the playwrights and creatives gathered in a small screening room in the production cottage, where pillows were strewn on the floor and ashtrays were filled to the brim. The preconference readings were a kind of playwright boot camp: an opportunity for those with abundant egos to show off and a version of hell for those with even a shred of self-consciousness. Each playwright read his script aloud, including the stage directions. "You could lay on the floor and bring a pillow and close your eyes, but you could not snore," said Minnesota playwright Lee Blessing, who developed *A Walk in the Woods* at the O'Neill. "You would hear blah, blah, blah, blah and blah, blah, blah. It was the dullest possible way to hear a play." The readings went from early morning to midnight, and it was not uncommon for someone to step outside briefly and return with glassy eyes, the musky smell of marijuana fresh on their clothing. Playwrights arrived with bottles of whiskey, and the unwritten rule was that they had to share.

Wilson sat by himself during the first day of readings, but he noticed that others were nodding off and softening the boredom with booze. Some playwrights droned on in a monotone; others overacted. Negative criticism from the crowd was verboten. Richards insisted on good manners. Sometimes Wilson felt as if he needed toothpicks to keep his eyes propped open. But like everyone else, he listened, courteously, through a day and a half of readings. As a seasoned poet, he had recited his work before large crowds at poetry readings in Pittsburgh bars and county jails and had performed for surly teenagers in parks and elementary schools. But this was different. These people were leading the life he wanted to lead. They were *real* playwrights, directors, and professional journalists. Michael Feingold, the dramaturge assigned to his play, was the senior critic at the *Village Voice*. Edith Oliver was the celebrated theater critic for the *New Yorker* and she was a beloved yet tenacious dramaturge at the conference. The dramaturges played an important role: they served as editors who looked at structure, context, themes, and language and supported the efforts on rewrites. Richards, of course, was the all-knowing pioneer who was directing a play on Broadway the year Wilson began his ill-fated short tenure at Central Catholic.

His turn to read came on the afternoon of the second day. Richards handed him a note on a square piece of paper: "Could you read *Ma* next?" it said. Wilson kept that small slip of paper in his files for the rest of his life. No one knew what to expect when he walked to the podium with a script as thick as an encyclopedia. Wilson was an enigma. One of the playwrights had seen him emerge from the shower the night before, cigarette in hand. That was his claim to fame that day. *He smoked in the shower!* The most anyone had been able to learn about him was that he said he was a short-order cook who did not go to the theater and (supposedly) had never had a play produced. He spoke slowly, with a mesmerizing cadence. He held on to words in a way that could be mistaken for affectation, but that was, more likely, a cover-up for an ever-so-slight stutter. He had been in front of an audience before, sometimes to an appreciative crowd, but other times to a room full of hecklers. "How did I feel?" he said of that moment years later. "I felt ready."

Wilson stood at the podium, tapping his foot nervously. He looked down at the worn pages. He had typed the play on the Olivetti 93 DL he had bought for a princely $330 when he moved to St. Paul in 1978. He hated that typewriter; it skipped spaces and didn't type heavily enough. But he could practically recite his own words without the script, especially the long monologues. He began with the introduction to the play, which opens with a description of Chicago in 1927 and ends with a paean to the blues and its ineradicable connection to African Americans. He extolled "its warmth and redress, its braggadocio and roughly poignant comments, its vision and prayer, which would instruct and allow them to reconnect, to reassemble and gird up for the next battle in which they would be both victim and ten thousand slain."

Wilson got the attention of everyone in the room. "*Ma Rainey* is very long, and we were settling in for what we thought was going to be a very long afternoon," said Passanante. The play opens slowly, setting the scene for a recording session with blues legend Ma Rainey and her sidemen. A few pages into the play, the character named Levee enters. He is a young, flamboyant trumpet player with a passion that is fiery and dangerous. Wilson's characters live in his head; he hears them speak. And he had been listening to Levee for a long time. Wilson's friends in St. Paul contend that he had, in part, modeled the role after his friend Terry Bellamy, a fiercely talented yet temperamental actor (who quit a later production of *Ma Rainey* shortly after it opened). His demeanor changed when he got to Levee's entrance. People reclining on the floor at the O'Neill sat up to listen.

"He inhabited every character," Passanante said. "He was rocking on his feet. It was a once-in-a-lifetime experience, seeing a room full of slightly resentful, dubious playwrights and directors watching someone transform with so much passion and conviction." One playwright used the word "transcendent," as if Wilson were hearing the characters singing in his head, right there in the room. Richards took note, but the neutral expression on his face didn't change.

But *Ma Rainey* was a wake-up call for director Amy Saltz. "When you listen to four plays a day for four days, you can get a little stoned, a little stupefied," she said. "We were all exhausted. People would take little naps—and not on purpose. But all of a sudden this incredible force burst open the doors of that tiny little room."

Saltz, like Wilson, was a newcomer to the O'Neill. Despite an established career in New York and at regional theaters nationwide, she had not been able to wrangle a job at the O'Neill until she finally got invited in 1982. She was the only female on the directing staff that summer. At five foot two, she was dwarfed by the male directors, many of whom towered over six feet tall (with the exception of Richards, who was small in stature but powerful in his presence). And, like Wilson, she was an outsider. After Wilson's reading, she initiated the beginning of what would become an enduring friendship. She smoked at the time, and so did he. They both liked bourbon. "The O'Neill was an intimidating place for newcomers, and we were both outsiders," Saltz said. The O'Neill is isolated geographically, a sprawling oceanfront estate several miles from the nearest state package store, which is Connecticut's name for a liquor store. Saltz, unlike most of the artists at the conference, had a car. She and Wilson found a package store. As her friendship with Wilson developed, she took to keeping a bottle of bourbon in the car's trunk, for moments when they both needed something strong.

Saltz would later direct *Joe Turner's Come and Gone*, Wilson's masterpiece, at the O'Neill. During that first weekend in 1982, she noticed something about the soft-spoken man who took the rituals and customs of ordinary Black people and raised them to mythic proportions. Saltz realized that he lived his own life the same way. "August was a mythmaker," she said. "He created myths about himself. Sometimes it was hard to know what was real and what was part of the myth." Wilson told her he was two years older than he really was. He claimed he had never had a play produced and that he had no experience in theater, when, in fact, *Black Bart* had received a full, albeit disastrous, production at Penumbra. He had directed numerous plays with the Black Horizons Theatre in Pittsburgh and had directed and acted in his 1976 play, *Recycle*. He cultivated the image of a neophyte who sprang, fully formed, into a playwright. Later, when he became a theatrical legend and won strings of awards, he did not dispel these self-perpetuated myths that were cemented as his celebrity grew.

But even that first summer, some were suspicious—or jealous—of the aura that seemed to be growing around Wilson. Despite its reputation as a sheltered harbor for artists, the O'Neill can be a nerve-racking place for playwrights, who are under a constant spotlight. In the early days, they all craved attention from the inscrutable Richards. Everyone worked hard to gain his praise, and after the preconference, the playwrights went home to revise their scripts for six weeks. They returned, rewrites in hand, for the actual Playwrights Conference in July. James Nicholson, who was there in 1982 with his play *Proud Flesh*, had the perception that Wilson stood out from the crowd. "He was the anointed playwright," Nicholson said. "He acted like a nobody, but it was obvious he was Lloyd's pet. He told everyone he was just a short-order cook who wrote this play. That was a myth." Richards made a point not to single out any playwright in public, but many years later, Wilson told his friend Charles Johnson that Richards had pulled him aside and said, "You are the one I was looking for."

Wilson may have sensed that others were looking at him askance, but he was used to it. Senior citizens in his neighborhood in the Hill District used to think he was an odd duck, walking down the street in a tweed coat, a book in one hand, a pipe in the other. He didn't go out of his way to cozy up to the other playwrights that summer, but he developed warm friendships with Saltz and Bill Partlan, the director assigned to *Ma Rainey*. He settled in to the conference and adapted to the unique ethos of the place.

During the four weeks of the conference, the O'Neill campus becomes a sort of commune, where actors, directors, and designers all live, eat, and sleep together. In 1982, they were housed at nearby Mitchell College in a bare-bones dormitory appropriately nicknamed "The Slammer." The dorm rooms were spare, with circa-1960s cinder-block walls and cold concrete floors. Thin mattresses topped metal frames, and torn plastic coverings crinkled at the slightest touch. It was nearly impossible to sleep at night, given the lack of air-conditioning, the broken window screens, and the constant clattering of typewriters as playwrights rewrote into the night. The coed bathrooms were crowded, with shower stalls separated by tiled dividers. That's where Wilson became famous for perching a cigarette on top of the divider, soaping up, and stopping to take a long, slow drag.

He also became known for his unquenchable affection for women. For Wilson, the O'Neill was like the freshman year in college that he never had. He emerged from the shower one afternoon, towel wrapped around his waist, Marlboro between his lips, and noticed a young woman brushing her teeth. He casually informed her that the two things he loved most in life were baseball and sex. She politely turned down his not-so-subtle offer, but the two later became friends. He passed notes to the actress Julie Boyd during meals, professing his admiration and calling her his "white China doll." At twenty-one, she had just finished her first year as a graduate student at the Yale School of Drama, and she was young and new to an environment like the O'Neill. She was flustered by his advances. "He was persistent," she said. "He was really persistent. At first, I didn't even know who he was. I don't even know this old guy. But it was never about power. It was never physical, just notes written on little napkins." The two eventually became platonic friends, and Wilson stopped writing the notes.

Late one night, he did consummate a flirtation with a woman who worked in the office, only to be interrupted by an unsuspecting observer who accidentally walked in on their dalliance. Rumors spread fast at the insular O'Neill, and there was plenty of whispering at breakfast the next morning.

But Wilson was single-minded when it came to the work, and that didn't go unnoticed, either. "He was intense," said director Barnet Kellman. "He seemed to be burning like an ember, an energy glowing. He was older than the other playwrights, and the affect was one of experience. He had lived some shit."

And *Ma Rainey* did, in fact, spring from both anger and love. Set in a Chicago recording studio in 1927, the play centers on the sidemen who are waiting for the legendary blues singer to show up for a recording session. Levee, the flashy trumpeter, wants to bust out of the music he considers to be "old jug band shit." He has written some songs and wants to sell them to the white producers in charge of the session. The musicians bicker and feud and tell stories in the band room. In the studio, they are treated like second-class citizens despite their skill and experience. The manager refers to them as "boys," a disparaging term that infuriated Wilson during the year he spent in Los Angeles in 1963. The studio is freezing cold. When Ma Rainey and her entourage finally arrive, they are trailed by a policeman threatening arrest. Levee later erupts when he feels he is being cheated by the producer, who had agreed to buy his music. The underlying theme is the exploitation of Black musicians by the white recording industry.

Kellman was spot-on in his observation that Wilson was burning inside. He felt an ancestral connection to the blues since that day in 1965 when he repeatedly played the old 78 recording of Bessie Smith's "Nobody in Town Can Bake a Sweet Jelly Roll Like Mine." His play celebrated the music that embodied his very being, and it castigated the money-grubbing producers who used the music to fill their pockets and not their souls. This was not new territory for him, of course. His 1976 play, *The Homecoming*, explored the exploitation of Black musicians and was a crude precursor that set the scene for *Ma Rainey*. And his early poem "Mr. Jelly Roll Morton" describes a young man's passion for the music and his sympathy for the musicians, who were underpaid, underappreciated, and largely forgotten.

Ma Rainey is a much more mature spin-off of those earlier works about the blues. And Wilson found an unlikely friend at the O'Neill who understood his passion for the blues tradition, a pot-smoking, fun-loving photographer named Vinnie Scarano, who was paid $100 plus room and board to photograph the Playwrights Conference for six weeks every summer. Wilson and Scarano would go down to the beach occasionally to smoke a joint and talk about music. Wilson took his guard down when discussing his play—and his future—with Scarano. "That is not going to happen to me," he said, comparing himself to the exploited musicians in his play. "As an artist, I am going to retain all the rights to my work, and I am not going to get ripped off."

Wilson was making lasting connections that would bolster his career.

One day, Richards introduced him to Benjamin Mordecai, the recently hired managing director of Yale Rep. At thirty-seven, Mordecai was the same age as Wilson but had much more professional experience. He had cofounded the Indiana Repertory Theatre in Indianapolis and served as its producing director for eleven years before joining Yale Rep. A bespectacled man with a chinstrap beard, Mordecai was a practical numbers cruncher—methodical, exacting, and exceedingly patient with artists. Although seemingly different, he and Wilson struck up an immediate friendship that would last for the rest of their careers.

Even though Wilson was a newcomer at the O'Neill, he was fiercely protective of his work, passionately attached to every word. Every monologue was like an appendage of self. At the preconference, his director, Bill Partlan, and his dramaturge, Michael Feingold, sent him home with pages and pages of suggested cuts. When Wilson returned six weeks later, he had made few, if any, of the suggested changes. The problems with the play were clear to the seasoned professionals. At more than four hours, it was too long, despite its incantatory poetry and striking imagery. It still read like two separate one-act plays. The first act featured the sidemen waiting for the arrival of the star, and the second act was about the explosions that occur after she arrives. In fact, Wilson had written the first act in 1976 and tabled it. Later, when he was itching to get a coveted spot at the O'Neill, he added the second act. Partlan and Feingold wanted to massage the script so that both acts fit together into an organic whole. They weren't just cynical or jaded by the fact that no producer would mount a play that ran longer than the time it takes to fly from Minneapolis to New York. The play itself stopped cold every time the action was interrupted with an eloquent, but meandering, monologue.

Wilson, however, was resistant. "He said that he had to hear it in front of an audience first," Partlan said. The schedule at the O'Neill is a stressful race against time. The actors have four days to rehearse, and one of those days is eaten up with such technical issues as lighting and sound. After the fourth day, the actors perform a staged reading, script in hand. Playwrights can make changes at any time, and the new pages are printed on different-colored paper and inserted into the script. Wilson did not make any changes during the rehearsals, but he filed away suggestions made by the actors and the creative team.

And the actors were not a silent bunch. Charles S. "Roc" Dutton was playing Levee, and he was an outspoken, intimidating presence. Dutton had been convicted of manslaughter as a teenager in Baltimore and spent seven years in jail. When sentenced to six days in solitary confinement, he said he read an anthology of work by Black playwrights, which included *Day of Absence*, Douglas Turner Ward's 1965 "satirical fantasy" about what happens in a Southern town when all the African Americans disappear overnight. He was inspired and found his calling. A few years after his release, he enrolled in the Yale School of Drama and became one of Richards's protégés. Even before he went on to work in film and television, he was a legend in his own mind, proudly embracing the epithet "jail to Yale." And Ma Rainey's paramour, Dussie Mae, was played by a young Yale School of Drama student named Angela Bassett.

Like Richards, Dutton was struck by the characters in the play, but he didn't immediately recognize Wilson as the author until he heard him speak. "We heard these stories," he said. "We knew this dialect. It was so full of Black folklore. I remember wondering if white folks were going to get it."

Partlan and Feingold sat Wilson down over lunch after the first long read-through. "The writing was beautiful, but it was story after story after story," Partlan said. "He defined it like jazz: there were solos and riffs by each character. We told August that we would get to a point where we couldn't hear another story and needed to move forward with the action."

Wilson had heard this before, but still, he resisted. Partlan had to ease up. The whole premise of the O'Neill is to support the playwright. In the real world, if a play doesn't work, a director can sometimes use smoke and mirrors to cover up the flaws. At the O'Neill, the goal was to bring the problems to the surface so that the writer could discover the solution himself. Partlan agreed to stage all four hours, but he asked Wilson to consider cuts after watching the first performance. And he had one request. "You are not allowed to pace in the back of the theater," he said. He had seen Wilson leaving the theater to sneak a cigarette at other O'Neill performances, which he thought was counterproductive in this case. "You are to sit in the middle of the audience and notice when the audience is leaning forward and when it is leaning back."

Wilson complied, and after the first performance, he stayed up all night and approached Partlan the next day and handed him "huge cuts" that clipped an hour and a half off the play. At the O'Neill, plays get two performances. Wilson's second performance was slated for that night, the coveted Saturday-night slot when theater types from New York train in to see new work. Partlan had one last rehearsal that day, which was supposed to be two hours long. He broke Actors' Equity rules and had the cast stay longer so that they could learn the new staging and work on transitions.

The performance was at 8:00 p.m. in the Rose Barn Theater, a sprawling wooden space where actors have to project to the rafters. The barn has a quasi-Elizabethan quality—narrow seats packed tightly together, claustrophobic. Saturday audiences were large, and often filled with out-of-towners. Wilson's mother had come in from Pittsburgh. His wife was there, along with friends from Pittsburgh including Rob Penny and Curtiss Porter. Wilson was nervous. From the time he learned to read at age four, his mother had told him he was destined for greatness, and he had disappointed her time and time again, prompting her to banish him to the basement when he dropped out of high school. At sixty-two, she remained the most important influence in his life and he desperately sought her approval, even as a grown man.

Another person in the audience that night was a critic named Frank Rich from the *New York Times*. At thirty-three, the Harvard-educated Rich had been the *Times* theater critic for just two years, but he had already gained a reputation as a sharp-tongued scribe who could make or break careers. He had come to the O'Neill ostensibly to see what it was all about. The press office was aware of his presence, as were Richards and O'Neill founder George White. During his visit, Richards introduced Wilson to Rich. Wilson later informed Feingold of the introduction. As the longtime theater critic for the *Village Voice*, Feingold knew everyone involved in the New York theater world. He was amused to learn about the introduction. "God bless you," he said to Wilson. "Your innocence will save you."

Before his visit, Rich had been schooled in the rules of the O'Neill: Critics were welcome, but the Playwrights Conference was a shelter for writers. Soft features were okay, but no reviews. Period.

It was a hot evening, and the actors were pumped and caffeinated after the afternoon's lengthy rehearsal. Dutton was on fire, his large frame decked out in a crisp black jacket and bow tie. The atmosphere was charged, and unlike the performance the day before, the play zipped along. The audience members leaned forward in their seats, and at the play's explosive conclusion, they leapt to their feet.

After the performance, Wilson met with his guests and made sure his mother got back to her hotel safely. Scarano slipped him a joint as a celebratory gift. For the duration of the conference, Wilson finally began to relax among his peers. He went to Chuck's, a local waterfront bistro, and drank until the wee hours of the morning. He joined the parties on the beach, where playwrights and actors were known to skinny dip even when the fog rolled in off the ocean. He played softball on the O'Neill lawn, smoking cigarettes at shortstop and awing everyone with his prowess at bat.

One day near the end of the conference, Wilson had a long, closed-door discussion with Richards, which made a few of the other playwrights bristle. Some referred to Wilson as Richards's favorite child, but actress Julie Boyd, for one, didn't care. "If you were doing something wrong, you knew it was okay if you were with August," said Boyd, who stayed close friends with Wilson for years. "Yes, he was the favorite child. But guess what? He had the goods."

Like the other playwrights and actors, Wilson stayed until the end of the conference. He spoke very little at the public critiques that followed every play. These sessions were guided by the Richards Rules: constructive criticism only, delivered with gentility. The playwrights were coddled like sensitive children, long before the days when "Everyone Gets a Trophy" became the methodology of helicopter parenting.

Wilson was thoroughly enjoying his last weekend at the O'Neill at breakfast on Sunday, August 1. Some of the playwrights came up to congratulate him; others were chilly. The *Times* had arrived. There, on the front page of the Sunday Arts and Leisure section, was an article with the headline "Where Writers Mold the Future of the Theater." It started out simple enough, beginning like a feature about Richards and the O'Neill process. But then it turned a corner and discussed three plays Rich had seen during his visit to the O'Neill. Rich, it turned out, had broken the rules. This was no puff piece; it was a full-blown review. First, he praised *A Knife in the Heart*, Susan Yankowitz's surreal play about a grisly murder. He also had kind words for Nancy Fales Garrett's *Playing in Local Bands*.

Rich saved Wilson for last. And it was a rave like only Frank Rich could rave. He extolled the long monologues that had vexed some artists at the O'Neill, noting that Wilson had "the talent to go all the way and write them like music." He marveled at Wilson's rich language, noting, "It is quite unusual in 1982 to find a playwright who is willing to stake his claim to the stage not with stories or moral platitudes, but with the beauty and meaning of torrents of words." He echoed the opinion of many who had been in the theater that night. "I was electrified by the sound of this author's voice," Rich wrote. He compared Wilson to none other than Eugene O'Neill. "Mr. Wilson," he concluded, "is the kind of writer who fulfills the Conference's goal to replenish our theater's future—yet, eerily enough, he works in the same poetic tradition as the man who inspired the O'Neill Center's mission and who gave American theater its past."

Wilson, of course, was delighted. He sent a copy of the piece to his mother, wondering if, finally, this was enough to make her accept her son's chosen profession. But the gossip mill at the O'Neill went into full gear. Directors and playwrights were appalled. Rich, of all people, they said, had betrayed the very foundation of the O'Neill, where all playwrights were supposed to be equal. Some suspected Richards had deliberately invited Rich on that weekend, knowing he would see *Ma Rainey*. Rich said that isn't true. "Lloyd never gave me instructions," he said. "I picked it blind." He was so blown away that he felt compelled to write, he said. He did clear the piece with O'Neill founder George White, but he insists there was no conspiracy with Richards.

But Wilson suspected Richards had a hand in garnering the good press. Many years later, he laughed at the suggestion that Richards was shocked—shocked!—when the rave review appeared in the *Times*. "Lloyd knew what he was doing," Wilson said.

Despite the efforts of everyone involved—and Rich's effusive praise—the team never really worked out all the kinks in the play, which is not Wilson's best effort. It is still bloated at about an hour too long, and it still, in Partlan's words, has speech after speech after speech. Subsequent productions of the play have dragged, and Wilson was dissatisfied with a 2005 production at the Seattle Repertory Theatre. A 2003 Broadway revival starring Dutton and Whoopi Goldberg was a critical and box office disaster and closed prematurely after nine weeks.

But shortly after the piece ran, Wilson got a call from an agent, Helen Merrill, a powerful force in the theater who launched and nurtured the careers of numerous playwrights, designers, and directors. It turned out someone else had been in the Rose Barn Theater that Saturday night at the O'Neill: a producer who was looking to get his hands on a Broadway musical production. Of course, it was against the Richards Rules for producers to approach playwrights during the conference, which was a running joke among the playwrights. They were wary of taking calls or messages from theater impresarios while on the grounds, but were eager to talk to them the minute they left the conference. Playwright Jeffrey Hatcher remembers one colleague joking, "Can we have a phone in the bus back to New York?"

But after the piece ran, Wilson was peppered with messages from the commercial theater world. "The whole time I was there, my wife would call once, but one day I had twelve messages on the board," Wilson said. This was before the days of cell phones, and telephone messages were tacked to a bulletin board in the main office. "I went to Michael [Feingold] and showed him. He said, 'Come on, man. This is so and so and this is so and so. If you go and see this guy, bring your lawyer.'"

The producer interested in a musical adaptation quickly sent Wilson a contract, and Wilson carefully studied what many would have thought to be a bountiful offer. The document had a clause saying the producers could fire the writer and take on another author at any time, for any reason. It was more similar to a Writers Guild of America contract issued to Hollywood screenwriters than the type used by the Dramatists Guild, which represents playwrights. The deal came with $25,000, a significant amount of money, and Wilson and Oliver were still struggling with their finances after the bankruptcy. But fire the writer? Wilson was furious and parted ways with Merrill, the undisputed most influential representative for emerging playwrights who had once famously claimed, "I *am* the theater." The contract was exactly what *Ma Rainey* was about: powerful executives exploiting the artist and his or her work for their own profit. Wilson ripped up the document and called Richards for advice. The director had expressed an interest in producing the play at Yale Repertory Theatre, with certain changes. Theatrical seasons at regional theaters are planned and announced well in advance, so the earliest this could happen would be 1984, giving Wilson time to make revisions.

He had left the O'Neill bursting with energy. He was already at work on another play, a story set in the 1950s about a disillusioned former baseball player named Troy Maxson. He called it *Fences*. He briefly held on to his job at Little Brothers of the Poor, where he enjoyed cooking meals for the staff at the social service agency. On days when he had trouble focusing, he walked around the skyways in St. Paul, listening to the characters who played a constant song in his head. He liked the skyway system, which connects building to building and protects pedestrians against punishing winter conditions. When the weather got nippy, he wore his O'Neill jacket and remembered what passed through his mind the day he received it: "I must be a playwright, too."

CHAPTER EIGHT

Living on Mother's Prayer

It is only when you encounter a world that does not contain your mother that you begin to fully comprehend the idea of loss and the huge irrevocable absence that death occasions.

—AUGUST WILSON

Wilson arrived back in St. Paul buoyed by the O'Neill experience—and that glowing review. He committed Rich's piece to memory, and he could still recite it, word for word, more than two decades later. "Although I haven't yet found out where drama critics go to die, I do know where they go to be reborn," he would say, quoting the first sentence of the "feature" that launched his career. Rich was praising the O'Neill as an incubator for playwrights and a balm for jaded critics hungry to discover fresh voices.

But reviews (or reviews masked as features) could not pay the bills. Despite all the attention at the O'Neill, Wilson's financial situation hadn't changed. But he did have a production in the works, this one back home in Pittsburgh. The choreographer Bob Johnson had not given up on trying to produce Wilson's work, even though he had been unsuccessful with *Black Bart.* Johnson teamed up with a fledgling organization called the Allegheny Repertory Theatre to direct and produce *Jitney!.* The theater had only been around for two years, and Johnson convinced them to produce his friend's work. The effort had a "Gee, we have a barn, let's put on a show" quality to it. The perky press release noted that Johnson "was eager to see one of his chum's works get a full-scale production."

Wilson had learned the importance of a dramaturge when he was at the O'Neill, and Johnson was more than willing to take on that role and encouraged changes to the short, one-act script, including advocating for a sharper ending. Wilson was agreeable to some of the changes, but he also had one request before he flew to Pittsburgh. In a September 27, 1982, letter to Johnson, he asked his friend to make sure he had money to pay him because he was short on cash. He also noted that he wrote the letter while high on marijuana.

Johnson capitalized on Wilson's recent residency at the O'Neill in his advertisement for auditions, describing Wilson as "the 1982 recipient of the Eugene O'Neill International Playwright Award." It sounded good, even if it was stretching the truth. He ended up casting a few of the actors from the Black Horizons Theatre days, including Sala Udin and Curtiss Porter. Udin was initially reluctant to play the role of Becker, the former steel mill worker who runs a jitney station in the Hill District. He was planning on leaving town to move to California, but changed his mind after he read the script. "I thought, 'What the hell am I doing crying at a play?'" he said. He stuck around and played the part.

The production took place at the Fine Line Cultural Center at 3300 Fifth Avenue in Oakland, a little more than a mile away from Central Catholic, where both Wilson and Udin had refused to put up with racism and dropped out. The play opened on October 29, and the first weekend was slow, with an audience composed mainly of friends and relatives of the cast. But then the local papers published two favorable reviews. The critic for the *Pittsburgh Post-Gazette* raved about the "breathtakingly realistic cast." After that, you couldn't get a ticket. Black Horizons had never gotten coverage in the mainstream press, and the publicity brought out crowds. Residents of the Hill District flocked to the theater, many of them seeing a professional play for the first time. Wilson took Daisy to the show, escorting her in a jitney. These marginally legal independent cabs were essential to the city's Black community, since taxi drivers for licensed companies often refused to take customers to the Hill District,

citing perceived danger. The jitney driver told Wilson that he waited outside the theater every night to take audience members home, and most of
them left the theater in tears.

The play sold out and was extended two weeks. This was Wilson's first
big success, on his home turf, no less, and he reveled in it. Written in 1979,
Jitney! was still a rough sketch, as it hadn't undergone the scrutiny that *Ma
Rainey* received at the O'Neill. It lacked the long monologues of Wilson's
signature style, but Wilson captured the rhythm and essence of the jitney
drivers he had listened to for years. Audience members heard their voices
onstage; they recognized the characters and understood their frustrations
and aspirations. Originally set in 1971 during the Vietnam War, the play
unfolds in a jitney station owned and operated by Becker, played by Udin.
The drivers sit around waiting for fares to call the station number, COurt
1-9802, which was, in fact, the real number for the jitney station across
from Pan Fried Fish. By the time the play was produced, that jitney station
had closed, but the number was etched in Wilson's mind.

In the play, the jitney station is on a block in the Hill District that is
scheduled for demolition, and Becker plans to close the business, leaving
his drivers jobless. The demolition of the Lower Hill had made an indelible impression on Wilson. The play centers on a group of men who sit
around "telling lies," seemingly at war with one another, but also deeply
connected, not unlike the bickering sidemen in *Ma Rainey.* Fielding is a
former tailor with a drinking problem, and Becker threatens to fire him
every time he catches him with an open bottle. Turnbo is a gossip with his
nose in everybody's business. Shealy is a local numbers runner who takes
bets off the phone at the station. Wilson's mentor, Chawley Williams, ran
numbers as well, but he called himself a "digitarian." Youngblood is a Vietnam veteran who wants to buy a house and settle down with his girlfriend,
Rena. Youngblood is the name the senior citizens gave to Wilson when he
was an aspiring poet listening to their stories.

Becker's son, Booster, shows up halfway through the play. In his early
forties, Booster has just been released from jail after serving twenty years
for murdering his white girlfriend, who had lied and accused him of rape.
To Booster, it was a crime of honor. But to Becker, it was a disgrace. He

had hoped his son, a star student, would go on to a white-collar job and not end up in a prison uniform. In the original one-act play, Becker refuses to speak to his son, who comes to make amends when he is paroled.

Wilson later revised *Jitney!* (taking off the exclamation point) and fleshed out the characters. But the original play struck a chord with the city's Black population, who saw their lives depicted onstage. The SRO audience was mostly Black, Udin said, with parents bringing along their children, no matter how young. His own family attended many times. Becker dies offstage in the end, and during the final scene, Udin's two young children were inconsolable. "They were saying, 'Daddy is dead. Daddy died,'" he said. Their mother had to convince them that it was just a play.

The *Pittsburgh Press* declared *Jitney!* the "best premiere of a previously unproduced play" in its year-end wrap-up. The production's spectacular success boosted Wilson's ego and pushed him to keep working on rewrites of *Ma Rainey*. He was also racing to complete the draft of his new play, *Fences*, in time for the December application deadline at the O'Neill.

And life at home in St. Paul had gotten more complicated. By this point, he and Oliver had moved to a first-floor duplex at 756 Hague Avenue, a quiet side street with modest houses and well-tended lawns. Sakina was in seventh grade, and she moved from Cleveland to live with Wilson and Oliver. In Cleveland, she lived with her mother and attended a mostly Black school. It was a culture shock to arrive in St. Paul, where the Black population was so small. She was being raised as a Muslim, and when she arrived in St. Paul, she was wearing the headscarf and modest clothing of the faith. She had to adapt to a new culture and to a stepmother who had no biological children. She took to wearing sweaters and jeans and became friends with Jacqui Shoholm's son, Damon, who was the same age. They both attended Highland Park Middle School.

It was a stressful living situation, however, as Sakina shared her father's temperament, and there were many battles between her and Oliver and between father and daughter as well. She learned early that she had to share her father with others—and that, first and foremost, he was dedicated to his work. He wanted to be the kind of father he never had. He took her to movies. He taught her origami. But work came first. She knew it, and he knew it. He later dedicated *Joe Turner* to her, and the inscription is telling. "To my daughter, Sakina Ansari," he wrote, "with love and gratitude for her understanding."

Wilson was writing furiously during this period, and he finally quit the job at Little Brothers of the Poor to focus on playwriting. In early March 1983, he was awarded the prestigious Bush Foundation Fellowship for Artists, one of ten visual and literary artists to receive an award of $20,000 with up to an additional $3,000 in travel and production costs. (The comparable award in 2022 is about $56,000.) The Minneapolis *Star Tribune* announced the awards on March 13. But this was not a time to celebrate. Back in Pittsburgh, Daisy Wilson was fighting a losing battle with lung cancer. Wilson and Oliver flew to Pittsburgh to be at her bedside. They left Sakina in St. Paul, and she didn't understand why she couldn't visit her grandmother one last time. She was devastated. Wilson's younger brother Richard had left St. Paul earlier to care for his mother. Wilson wasn't always at his mother's side at her home at 1621 Bedford Avenue while he was visiting. He spent part of each day meeting friends and conducting business. He arrived back from one of these trips around 4:00 p.m. on March 15. Daisy died an hour later, three days after her sixty-third birthday. Richard remembers his sister Freda saying to her, "I'm sorry you didn't have a good life." Even on her deathbed, Daisy Wilson remained no-nonsense and, in her pragmatic way, optimistic. "Of course, I had a good life," she said. "I didn't have to bury any of you."

Among the extended family, there is a story that, as Wilson stood at his mother's deathbed, he asked her if Kittel was really his biological father. As the story goes, she replied that, yes, absolutely, he was. Wilson never discussed that moment, and it could be true or simply the imagined stuff of family lore. Either way, Wilson bristled when the subject of his father arose. But he offered a clue to his feelings in a poem that appears on the opening page of the published version of *Fences*:

When the sins of our fathers visit us
We do not have to play host.
We can banish them with forgiveness
As God, in his largeness and laws.

Wilson's focus was on his mother, though, and this was not the time to dwell on Kittel Sr., who had been dead for almost two decades. Ever practical, she had left instructions for her funeral, and Wilson threw himself into making the arrangements. He was well aware that he had forged his own path, not always pleasing her with his choices. But he was committed to following her wishes after she died. Years later, he remembered running around Pittsburgh, talking to the undertaker and the florist and making sure the music was just right. Funerals mattered to him, but this burst of activity also gave him a way to postpone his grief, at least temporarily. If he had things to do, he didn't have to sit down and face the enormous hole that her death left in his life. At thirty-seven, with a second wife and a teenage daughter and a career that was about to blossom, he still worshipped his mother. She had been a sharp critic, and perhaps that is why he always aimed to please her and make her proud. As a child, Mother's Day in his neighborhood was a grand occasion. It was an obligatory church day, and Hill residents wore paper carnations pinned to their Sunday best. A red flower signified that your mother was still alive, and a white flower meant that your mother had passed. Most of the children sported red flowers, but a white flower indicated that a youngster suffered from what Wilson called "a mysterious and unfathomable condition," the incomprehensible experience of a motherless child.

Wilson later remembered the few days after her death as a blur, as if he were on autopilot, a natural defense mechanism to stave off the grief. There was a two-day wake, and Daisy was buried at Greenwood Cemetery. Her mother, Zonia's, grave rests in an adjacent section of the cemetery; it's a short walk in a straight line between the two burial sites.

When Wilson returned to St. Paul, he vowed to hold a birthday party for his mother every year in the Hill District. He was finally finding his way, but he was unmoored, as if the ground underneath his feet had shifted. He kept his feelings to himself, though, and didn't talk much about his mother's death at the time. He changed the subject if it came up with peers at the Playwrights' Center in Minneapolis in the weeks after the funeral. Daisy had been his guiding star, even though she made it clear that she disapproved of his vocation. Even as an adult, he never felt he was good enough to please her. She dismissed his aspirations to be a writer and criticized him even when he shared news of his first published poem, a major accomplishment for a young man in the Hill District. "She's like, 'That's nice. How you gonna eat?'" he said a few months before his own death. "I said, 'Ma, you don't understand.' She goes, 'Okay, you're a writer.' I say, 'Phew.' She says, 'If that's what you want to be, then write something and put it on TV. Then I'll say you're a writer.'"

But he had finally been able to please her in her later years. She had smiled for photographs at his second wedding. She had seen *Ma Rainey* at the O'Neill and rode in a jitney to see her son's premiere in Oakland. And she had not complained in her dying moments; she was content. Her children were survivors.

But ever since Wilson had read Langston Hughes's "Mother to Son," he had been aware that Daisy had a life outside of her children. He considered her early life in Spear, North Carolina; he knew it had been difficult, but just how much he knew isn't clear. He later said that the adults of her generation—the parents who had made the Great Migration—deliberately hid the difficult parts of their past from their children. "They sheltered us from a lot of the indignities they suffered," he said. "I think it's wrong, but there are some things you don't want to tell your kids." Nevertheless, a world without his mother was "an alien place," even if she was "a fiercely independent and stubborn woman, full of contradictions"—and hard on her eldest son. Thirteen years after her death, he described his grief this way: "It is a world in which all the known references are dismantled and the cartographers labor day and night redrawing the maps. It is a world in which you are lost, like Hansel, in what D. H. Lawrence called the 'dark forest of the soul,' where you battle for light and clarity while looking for sharp and good directions."

Daisy left her estate, which included her home at 1621 Bedford Avenue, a few doors down from where Wilson grew up, to her six children, excluding Barbara. The siblings decided that Freda, the eldest, would handle the estate. Wilson wasn't interested in property. But he did hold on to a cherished keepsake: a photograph of his mother taken in a studio the year he was born. He later described the image to his friend Jean Passanante from the O'Neill, when she was about to give birth to her first child. He marveled at Daisy's beauty and the fact that she was carrying him the day the photo was taken.

The photo reminded him of a part of her life he never really understood. It made him think of his father. Who was he? Did he love Daisy? Did he pay for the portrait? He imagined the man who fathered him loved her spirit and the fact that she was carrying a child, a beacon of new life. He went on to say that he hoped, wherever his father was, that he was aware that she cared for her children and gave them a life full of promise.

Kittel died in 1965, and Wilson wrote the letter in 1986. He was conflicted about his relationship to Kittel, but there is no doubt: he wanted whoever fathered him to adore his mother, the same way he did.

Years after Daisy's death, Wilson said that he suffered the "most profound grief imaginable," but he also had an epiphany. "You look up and you find out that all them years you been living on your mother's prayers and now you've got to live on your own," he wrote. And so he continued to forge ahead with his career. He applied for—and won—a coveted slot at New Dramatists, the playwrights organization located in Manhattan. Founded in 1949 by playwright Michaela O'Harra (with support from such theater legends as Howard Lindsay, Richard Rodgers, Russel Crouse, Oscar Hammerstein II, John Golden, Moss Hart, Maxwell Anderson, John Wharton, Robert E. Sherwood, and Elmer Rice), New Dramatists provides support for playwrights and is a leading developmental lab for new theater works. Playwrights are selected for a seven-year residency, and the center foots the bill for staged readings of their work. Tom Dunn, from the Playwrights' Center in Minneapolis, took over as director of New Dramatists in 1981.

Since its founding, New Dramatists had exclusively supported New York–based writers, but Dunn established a national residency, which opened the door for Wilson to apply. Wilson was accepted unanimously by the committee that reviewed applications, and his seven-year residency began in the spring of 1983.

New Dramatists is housed in an old church on West Forty-Fourth Street, in the heart of Hell's Kitchen. There are three bedrooms on the third floor, where out-of-town playwrights can live when they are in New York. The third floor is known as "Seventh Heaven," named for the 1922 play produced by New Dramatists' patron and cofounder John Golden. Wilson made his first visit for the annual spring luncheon in May 1983. At the time, the three rooms were named the Pierre, the Plaza, and the William Inge. Wilson chose the William Inge as his home away from home. It was the best of the lot, with two small rooms. There was a double bed in the bedroom and a desk and a daybed in the adjoining room. At any given time, there might be three playwrights staying overnight, and the traffic up and down the stairs to Seventh Heaven was often heavy, with playwrights bringing lovers up to the rooms on the third floor. Like the O'Neill, New Dramatists was a free-for-all, where writers could crash, romance, write, or party into the late-night hours.

Wilson arrived at New Dramatists and immediately fell into the ethos of the place. He joined a group that went to a retreat at the home of Zilla Lippmann, the president of the New Dramatists board and the niece of producer John Golden. She was the driving force behind the creation of Seventh Heaven. She hosted a group at her mansion on Long Island, once the home of New York mayor Fiorello La Guardia. It was a wild weekend. Someone brought marijuana. Someone shared cocaine. Booze flowed. Casey Childs, the artistic program director, said that Wilson was quiet. He chain-smoked and spoke in monosyllables for most of the weekend. On Saturday night, the group was gathered around the table, partying late into the night. Playwright Peter Dee, who was a member of New Dramatists, said he was going to bed and left. About ten minutes later, he reappeared, dressed in Lippmann's nightgown, shower cap, and slippers.

He had night cream on his face. In the morning, he denied the whole thing. And no one told Lippmann about the impersonation.

That incident was typical for New Dramatists. The playwrights, used to writing in a vacuum, bonded as a group. It was like summer camp, all year round. Playwright Sherry Kramer, who now teaches playwriting at Bennington College, made New Dramatists her home in the early 1980s. She enjoyed going down to the kitchen on the second floor in her pajamas and bidding good morning to the staff.

Dunn was notorious for his questionable management style. He always had a deal going on. Once, he managed to get a collection of "free" IBM Selectric III typewriters. No one really knew where he acquired them or how, and in the early 1980s, these machines were the top of the line. Everyone at New Dramatists loved those machines. Stan Chervin, the artists services director, sent one to Wilson in St. Paul, prompting an engaging letter in reply about all the typewriters Wilson ever owned, beginning with the Royal Standard he bought for $20 with money from his sister Freda. He got his second machine after a thief stole a typewriter but had no use for it. The thief asked around to see if anyone might be interested in buying it; Wilson paid $15 for it. His sister Freda gave him another typewriter for his thirtieth birthday, but he absentmindedly left it on a bus.

Wilson could turn a story about a typewriter into a myth, which wasn't lost on his colleagues at New Dramatists. They noticed early on that he was a fabulist: he changed his stories to suit his audience. He told one of his fellow playwrights that he was bedding three women in St. Paul and they had threatened to go to the police to report him. He went to workshops of plays and told people that he had seen only four plays in his entire life. The next night, he said it was nine. But in those years at New Dramatists, he was happy and carefree. He had been welcomed into the world of professional theater, but he had yet to debut on Broadway and to achieve the status—and burden—that comes with fame.

That part of Hell's Kitchen was run by the Irish gang known as "The Westies." New Dramatists had two people on the payroll that nobody had ever seen. It turned out that both of them were dead, and the money went to the Westies for protection. Wilson loved the intrigue, and he loved the characters that hung around the gritty neighborhood. He bonded with the superintendent of the building, who lived next door. The two men would sit on the stoop, deep in conversation. Once, when New Dramatists held a fundraiser, the playwrights were asked to write four-minute plays for the benefit. Wilson's contribution was called *The Janitor.* In the short piece, a janitor is sweeping the floor and then stops and picks up a microphone and starts talking. Wilson gave him a voice—and opinions and thoughts and intelligence. "I came up with the idea of the janitor who is someone whom this society ignores and someone who may have very valuable information, someone who has a vital contribution to make, and yet you have relegated him to a position where they sweep the floor," Wilson said.

Since most of the playwright fellows lived in New York, Wilson was often the only person living upstairs in Seventh Heaven. One weekend, he was staying at New Dramatists and had the whole place to himself. The resident cat, whose name was Ziggy, followed him from place to place. He and Oliver had a cat named Maxwell, and Wilson thought that Ziggy really liked him, but then he realized that the cat had not been fed in days. He went out and bought some 9Lives.

Wilson was settling in to the life of an itinerant playwright. He had been invited back to the O'Neill for the 1983 National Playwrights Conference for a workshop of *Fences*, and this time, he knew what to expect at the preconference weekend. He had one goal before he got on the van to Waterford. He needed to stock up on scotch. When he arrived at the pickup location, he spotted someone he had never seen before. He seemed unfamiliar with the routine, with the same apprehension that Wilson had experienced the year before. He was James Yoshimura, a writer from Chicago who had attended the Yale School of Drama. He had an athlete's build. After a brief introduction, Wilson told Yoshimura that they needed to get some liquid sustenance in order to make it through the long weekend. Yoshimura was up for the chase. They found a store, pooled their money, and bought a large bottle of scotch. They didn't wait until they arrived at the O'Neill to open it. By the time the van deposited them at the mansion, they were smashed. And they became fast friends.

Like Wilson, Yoshimura was raised Catholic and came from a large family. His parents converted when they were forced to live in an internment camp for Japanese Americans during World War II. "That does not work for birth control," Yoshimura said. "I am the middle of eleven children." His family was one of only three Asian families in a predominantly German-American Catholic parish on the North Side of Chicago. "You are the *other*," he said of his childhood. "August could empathize with that. He knew what the 'other' was. We shared this friendship. It wasn't like we would discuss Catholicism. This was just how we grew up. We never felt part of the mainstream of the faith that we were baptized into." They bonded quickly over their common outlier status. They shared an irreverent spirit—and a taste for Marlboro Lights and fine scotch.

During his first year at the O'Neill, Wilson was stunned to see all the theater people hugging one another, but now he was one of them. He took it upon himself to initiate his new friend to the summer camp experience. "The bottle of scotch made the preconference much better," Yoshimura said. And they were willing to share. "We made a lot of friends." Yoshimura needed liquid encouragement to get through the process of reading his play aloud before strangers. He was there with *Ohio Tip-Off*, a drama about seven athletes on a minor-league basketball team who are vying to make it to the NBA. The team has four Black players and three white players. Wilson did not question his new friend's subject matter, but he did question the way he read his play for the group. "I read my play very badly, and he laughed aloud about how bad I was—while we were still sharing our scotch." Wilson did not tell Yoshimura that he had been at the O'Neill the summer before (nor that he had become the controversial star after the Frank Rich piece ran in the *Times*, nor that he was in discussions about bringing *Ma Rainey* to Broadway). When Yoshimura found out, he asked Wilson about it. "He was humble. He didn't want to talk about it."

Wilson, who later went on to make strong public statements about the need for a Black director to direct a film version of *Fences*, nurtured

Yoshimura. He never suggested that Yoshimura should not be writing Black characters. His friend played basketball, and he was writing what he knew. "All of our discussions were about aesthetics," Yoshimura said. "It was never a matter of color. He was like, 'If you write it, you write it. If it doesn't work, you gotta fix it.' " Wilson told other playwrights the same thing over the years. Laura Maria Censabella, a playwright who was also a jazz singer, came to the O'Neill with her play *Jazz Wives Jazz Lives.* The characters included Black jazz musicians that she based on her friends and colleagues in the jazz world. Some critics at the O'Neill questioned whether she, as a white woman, should write Black characters. Wilson defended her; she was writing from her own experience. Because of his support, the griping stopped.

Wilson had different issues with *Fences.* It clocked in at more than four hours when Wilson read it at the preconference. "My impression was, this guy can write, but he hasn't heard of the two-hour limit," Yoshimura said. "It took two hours to get through the first act."

Yoshimura was the perfect partner for Wilson at the O'Neill, where, in addition to learning about playwriting, he enjoyed the college experience he had never had. The two bonded over sports. Wilson was still obsessed with the 1965 boxing showdown between Muhammad Ali and Sonny Liston. Ali unexpectedly knocked out Liston early in the first round, leading to suspicions that the fight was rigged. Wilson could dissect that match for hours, and Yoshimura was a willing audience. "He was an encyclopedia of boxing. He knew all these fighters, their styles, their records. It was remarkable to listen to the guy."

When Yoshimura's wife showed up to visit, Wilson made sure to teach their young son how to hit a baseball with a tree branch, a skill he had learned on the streets of the Hill District. They were improvising, onstage and off. Yoshimura had written a play about basketball, but the O'Neill rules on staging were that everything was modular; designers could only use wooden cubes to build sets. The actors held scripts in hand, and the blocking was primitive. But Yoshimura felt that a basketball was a crucial prop for his play. Lloyd Richards relented, and the two friends went out and bought a brand-new basketball. Yoshimura, along with Wilson and the cast (which included a young up-and-comer named Samuel L. Jackson), took the new ball out into the gravel parking lot and played with it so it would look used and scuffed-up.

This endearing friendship was formative for both men. Yoshimura had been told that he would succeed only if he wrote plays about Asian Americans, but Wilson assured him that was nonsense. Yoshimura tried to engage him on the subject of father-son relationships, since that is the foundation of *Fences*. Wilson, who was willing to talk about any subject for hours and to enact a recap of the Liston-Ali fight, shut down when asked about his father. Yoshimura intuited that his friend was "deeply wounded" and didn't push the issue.

Bill Partlan was again assigned to direct Wilson's play, and Edith Oliver, the theater critic for the *New Yorker*, was the dramaturge. At the pre-conference, they both told Wilson that the play needed cuts. They made suggestions, but again he said he wanted to see it first before excising any scenes or monologues. Wilson had never studied dramatic structure. He had directed for Black Horizons, but as a writer, he did not consider how his plays would translate to the stage. He was learning fundamental rules such as the fact that an actor can't be soaking wet in the rain at the end of one scene and then appear at the top of the next scene in fresh new clothing and dry hair.

After the first performance, he stayed up all night and cut forty-five minutes from the script. (Helen Hayes had been in the audience that night, and she left after the first act, saying, "I think I've had enough theater for one night.") Wilson took out a long monologue about bones walking on water, a poetic piece of writing. Partlan told him to hold on to it. The monologue would be the foundation of a moving speech in *Joe Turner*.

The play revolves around the tragic hero, Troy Maxson, a former slugger in the Negro Leagues who never got a chance to play in the Major Leagues because of the color of his skin. At its heart, the play is about the confrontation between Maxson and his son Cory, a theme that Wilson had explored in *Jitney!* as well. At the end of the play, Troy dies, and his brother, Gabriel, who was wounded in World War II and is mentally disabled with a metal plate in his head, wants to send his brother off to St. Peter in heaven. He blows his trumpet, but no sound comes out. The stage directions say it all. *"He begins to howl in what is an attempt at song, or perhaps a song turning back into itself in an attempt at speech. He finishes his dance and the Gates of Heaven stand open as wide as God's closet."* With that, Gabriel lightens up and says, "That's the way that go."

On the second night of the performance at the O'Neill, the fog from the Atlantic Ocean rolled in at the end of the play. This was a common occurrence. Eugene O'Neill wrote about the fog in his masterpiece, *Long Day's Journey into Night*. "How thick the fog is," he wrote. "I can't see the road. All the people in the world could pass by and I would never know."

At the O'Neill, the natural setting was magical. The weather changed just as Gabriel, played by Howard E. Rollins Jr., went to play his trumpet. "The fog came in, and the lights pierced through the fog," Partlan said. "I sent Howard up the ramp that leads to the door in the barn to usher Troy into heaven. It was magic. I can still see and feel it today."

The wallop of that final scene became a sort of touchstone at the O'Neill. Other playwrights aspired to achieve that emotional depth. At the end of the preconference when Wilson first read his play, he and playwright John Patrick Shanley got drunk together one night. Shanley said, "You son-of-a-bitch. You wrote that stage direction at the end of that play," referring to Gabriel blowing the trumpet. "You son-of-a-bitch. Nobody can touch that."

Wilson had written the play to prove a point. After *Ma Rainey*, he had heard criticism that he was incapable of writing a well-made play built around a tragic hero, in, say, the style of Arthur Miller or Tennessee Williams. After the second performance of *Fences*, he felt he had achieved that goal. And so, when it was over, Wilson was able to relax, free of the stress that was common for writers before their play was produced. He and Yoshimura were not afraid to break the unwritten O'Neill rules. In fact, they egged each other on. One rule was that everyone in residence attend all performances, out of respect for the writer. But they skipped a production by a playwright they considered to be a "pompous asshole," convincing a production assistant to drive them to the nearest package store. Wilson was thirty-eight and Yoshimura was thirty-three at the time. "This is the age when guys drink," Yoshimura said. "You're writing and you don't have any money, you can't afford a good time. A little alcohol helps. We bought a box of wine, one of those things where they put really cheap wine in these plastic bladders with a little spigot. We hid out in the production office and sat around getting drunk with our box of wine. We didn't feel bad about it one bit."

The summer ended on a high note for both men. Since Wilson had not been able to cement a satisfactory Broadway deal for *Ma Rainey*, Richards added it to the 1983–84 Yale Repertory Theatre season. The season also included the twenty-fifth-anniversary production of Lorraine Hansberry's *A Raisin in the Sun* and a new play by South African playwright Athol Fugard, whose work Wilson had admired a decade earlier in Pittsburgh. And Yoshimura's play *Ohio Tip-Off* was set to be produced at Baltimore's Center Stage.

Back home in St. Paul, Wilson and Oliver moved to a second-floor apartment at 469 Selby Avenue, a grand thoroughfare lined with shops and restaurants. Sakina moved back to Cleveland to live with her mother, who had remarried. Claude Purdy and Jacqui Shoholm lived a half block away in St. Paul. The couples were constant companions when Wilson was in town. They all knew that this was Wilson's chance to make his big breakthrough, and Wilson made a promise to Purdy. He told him that he would buy him a new Mercedes when he made his first million; in turn, Purdy promised to buy Wilson an island someday.

But Wilson wasn't home all that often. He had taken to staying in New York, rooming upstairs at New Dramatists. When he was there, he and playwright Sherry Kramer would go out for inexpensive dinners in Times Square and then walk around the Theater District, people-watching as the crowds gathered outside theaters during intermission. One night, Kramer turned to Wilson and said, "Someday, our plays are going to be in these theaters." His reply struck her as sad. "Your plays may be done here, but mine won't," he said, implying that because he was a Black man, his plays

wouldn't be on Broadway. "The irony is all of his plays have been done and
he has a theater named after him," Kramer said after Wilson died.

True to his word, Wilson hosted a birthday party for his mother in
Pittsburgh on March 12, 1984, the first of an annual tradition. His siblings and extended family attended, and these events were important
to Wilson, who wanted to keep the memory of his mother alive. As the
years passed, though, his relatives were there less to honor Daisy than
to bask in his fame. He was the glue that kept the family together. His
sister Freda Ellis graduated from Fordham University, the only one of
the siblings to graduate from college. She earned her master's in education from Pitt and had a long career teaching. She remained on the Hill,
raising two children at 1615 Bedford Avenue, close to where her mother
had lived when she died. Freda was always around when Wilson visited
his hometown. Wilson remained close with his youngest brother, Richard, who eventually moved to Erie, Pennsylvania. Wilson often asked
Richard to read his work and described the baby of the family as his first
critic. But families, especially big ones, often have their share of sibling
issues, and some of Wilson's other siblings went years without talking
to one another.

Wilson was always the star attraction at the birthday parties, and his
repository of stories was growing. In March 1984, he was poised to leap
from being an obscure poet to becoming a nationally acclaimed playwright. True to his word, Richards was directing *Ma Rainey* at Yale Repertory Theatre. This was a breakthrough for Wilson, as it would be for any
playwright, but Wilson viewed the production as more than just a milestone in his career. In an elegiac letter he wrote to Richards on March 1, he
linked the music of Ma Rainey to his grandmother and all Black men and
women throughout history in the U.S. and in Africa. Ma Rainey's sensual
voice, he wrote, enabled him to understand the richness and fullness of
his grandmother's life and evoked the many Black people who worked
and suffered under Jim Crow laws in the South. The letter continues like
a free-form poem, carrying their song through Trinidad and Jamaica,

Louisiana and Tennessee, Texas and North Carolina, and, finally, to the villages of Africa.

In this one-page, single-spaced letter, Wilson pays tribute to his grandmother Zonia Wilson. She died when he was five, but he embraced the fact that her life and her resilience made his own possible. The letter serves as both a thank-you to Richards and as a sort of mission statement. He is writing for the grandmother he barely knew and for all the ancestors. The play, then, represented the "blood's memory," and he dedicated the published version to Daisy.

Yale Rep was a new experience for Wilson, a well-oiled professional theater that lacked the summer camp atmosphere of the O'Neill and the anything-goes spirit of community theater. Perched on Chapel Street in the heart of New Haven, Yale Rep occupies the former Calvary Baptist Church, a stately building in the Gothic revival style that was built in 1846. A short flight of stairs leads to two sets of fire-engine-red doors. The opening-night crowds at the Rep were a mix of friends and family; the theater typically "papered" the house with distinguished professors and theater mavens, donors and board members. The local critics sat in the aisle, making it easier for them to run out at the curtain call to write furiously to meet an overnight deadline.

Wilson surrounded himself with family and friends for the opening on April 6, a tradition he would continue for the rest of his life. Judy Oliver and Sakina were there, along with friends he had met at the O'Neill and New Dramatists. Wilson didn't know it at the time, but there was an aspiring producer in the theater that night. Robert Cole was a twenty-something theater enthusiast who, in 1979, had started a small acting school in New York called the Michael Chekhov Studio, but by 1984, he was trying to become a producer. As a young, green aspirant with no experience, he had been unable to secure the rights to any plays and he was searching for an unknown playwright to produce so he wouldn't have to vie against deep-pocketed, established names in the industry. Like Richards, he was looking for a playwright to "discover," so he had been going to places where new works were developed. He had seen *Ma Rainey* at the O'Neill two years earlier, so he went to Yale to see it again. If this didn't work out, he was going to quit the business and find a new profession. But he was blown away by the play, which he said "exploded on every level." He searched for Wilson after the performance and offered to produce the play on Broadway. Wilson politely referred him to his agent, who at the time was Shirley Bernstein, the sister of maestro Leonard Bernstein.

An answer was not immediately forthcoming. Wilson had no idea who Cole was, and he was increasingly wary of commercial offers. As it turned out, in order to transfer the Yale Rep production to New York, a producer had to arrange the rights through the theater, not through Wilson's agent. Wilson wasn't in a hurry. At the O'Neill, dramaturge Michael Feingold had warned Wilson to be wary of producers, and he had already turned down one offer.

The local reviews were glowing. Writing in the *Hartford Courant*, Malcolm L. Johnson began by declaring that "August Wilson's funny, poetic, stabbing re-creation of the world of Black blues back in the '20s should go on to take its place as a major American play of the '80s." At this point in his career, the national press was invited to review the first productions of his work at regional theaters; that would change later. And Wilson now knew that, despite local raves, there was one review that could propel his play to Broadway. And he got it on April 11, when Frank Rich struck again. "Mr. Wilson has lighted a dramatic fuse that snakes and hisses through several anguished eras of American life," he wrote in the *New York Times*. "When the fuse reaches its explosive final destination, the audience is impaled by the impact. Mr. Wilson is a major find for the American theater."

After the review ran, some twenty-one established Broadway producers contacted Richards to offer to bring the play to New York. None of them had seen the production. That made Wilson suspicious. How could a producer express interest, sight unseen? The neophyte Cole was still determined to win the rights, even though he was an unknown. He got in touch with Benjamin Mordecai at Yale Rep. Mordecai offered to have him team up with another set of producers, Elizabeth McCann and Nelle Nugent. After a meeting, they dropped out of the project, so Mordecai set Cole up with Bernie Jacobs and Gerald Schoenfeld of the powerful

Shubert Organization. If they approved of Cole, Yale Rep would grant him the rights to produce the play.

They gave him the green light, and Cole immediately began working on the production. It cost $700,000 to move it to New York, with mostly the same cast. It was set to open at the Cort Theatre in October. For Wilson, this period was a whirlwind. He was beginning a stretch of time when he would regularly be working simultaneously on two or three plays in different stages of development. Shortly after he left New Haven, he was back at the O'Neill Center for the National Playwrights Conference, where he was debuting *Joe Turner*, which he had begun writing in late 1983. He was also rewriting *Fences*, which was penciled in for a production at Yale Rep in 1985. The O'Neill, which had been intimidating when he first arrived in 1982, was now a respite, where he could focus on a single project, among the company of former strangers who had now become friends.

After the summer at the O'Neill, he was about to get his introduction to the fast-paced world of commercial theater, where he would be at the mercy of press agents and tight production schedules. He still had his oasis at New Dramatists, where he could stay for free during the Broadway rehearsal period. The two-room suite on the third floor, with its shared bathroom and modest kitchen on the lower floor, was like a home away from home. But the producers provided him with a new place to stay, the Hotel Edison, a fading art deco hotel on Forty-Seventh Street in the heart of the Theater District. It had its own theater, which was the longtime home to the revue *Oh! Calcutta!*, the risqué all-naked show. There was no room service and patrons could not find ice machines at the end of every hall. It was popular with high school student groups in town for the New York experience. All of this amused Wilson. He took an instant liking to the modest place, and from then on, he stayed at the Hotel Edison whenever he was in New York.

The production of *Ma Rainey* wasn't beginning anew, as most of the cast remained the same. Richards replaced an actor playing the white music producer, because he had been "difficult." He also recast the actor playing the tiny role of a policeman for similar reasons. Joe Seneca repeated his stint as Cutler, a role named after Wilson's great-grandmother Eller Cutler, who died on the mountain ten years before he was born. Robert Judd was Toledo, the piano player and the only one in the band who could read. Leonard Jackson played Slow Drag, the bass player who appeared to be as dim as his name, but hid a harsh intelligence. Dutton, of course, repeated the role of Levee; his Yale Rep performance had been singled out by Rich, who wrote "this young actor brings the audience to a deathly silence in a bitter, corrosive speech that ignites the play's climax." In the play, Levee bellows, "Where the hell was God when all this was going on?" Cutler, the trombonist, has just told the story of a Black minister who was humiliated by white men when he got off a train at the wrong station.

Wilson had respect for the role the Black church played in the community, but he was suspicious of institutions. He knew that particular scene would strike a nerve, and when he was working on the play at Yale Rep, he had sought advice from the production's musical director, Dwight Andrews, who was both a musicologist and a chaplain. "That speech shuts down the empty religiosity that August fiercely hated," Andrews said. "He hated the phoniness of it. He wanted to lift the curtain off the empty churchiness that does not address race and freedom and equality." In that scene, Wilson was exploring the question of whether it is possible for the divine to exist in the midst of evil. It was a daring move for him to curse God, and that scene invariably infuriated the church ladies at Sunday matinees, who stormed out because they objected to Levee's blasphemy. It stunned white audience members as well; as Levee storms against an unjust God, he is blunt. "He a white man's God," he says. "Jesus hate your Black ass!" Wilson deliberately named this character Levee, a reference to the Great Mississippi Flood of 1927, when Black work crews were forced at gunpoint to throw sandbags on the levees as the river's waters rose. When the levees were breached, scores of workers were swept away in the deadly deluge.

Dutton did a slow boil in the role, but he didn't carry the show by himself. The resplendent Theresa Merritt repeated her majestic performance from Yale Rep in the title role, decked out in a fabulous froufrou gown. Richards called on actress Ebony Jo-Ann to be her understudy; she was a regular performer at the O'Neill who was known for providing context for African American history when white directors did not understand a script written by a Black playwright.

Richards also wanted to replace the actor playing the small role of Ma Rainey's nephew, Sylvester. The singer insists that her nephew introduce her recording, even though he suffers from a debilitating stutter, just as the young Wilson had. Richards asked for a meeting with Cole. "He said, 'Here is what I would like you to do. I want to cast my son in the role of Sylvester,'" Cole said. His son was Scott Davenport Richards, who had graduated from Yale University and had grown up going to the theater. Cole agreed, but insisted that the younger Richards audition. "I talked to Lloyd privately after the audition when Scott was not in the room," Cole said. "There was an awkwardness as far as his presence. He was acting too much. Lloyd agreed and said, 'I will get him there.'" It was not uncommon for Richards to do favors for his family. His wife, Barbara Davenport, had her play *Piano for Sale* accepted at the O'Neill in 1986, and more than a few of the O'Neill regulars questioned whether the play deserved the coveted slot.

Scott Richards had played the role of Sylvester at the O'Neill in 1982. His older brother, Thomas, was originally cast, but he decided to play saxophone on a cruise ship for the summer, so Scott replaced him. Originally Scott was not that impressed with the play. "My brother and I were raised in the Black revolutionary theater. We didn't feel the play was telling us anything new," he said. "I felt like, 'Yeah, yeah, yeah. I know this.' But I realized after college that the world I grew up in was new to many people. The more I got to know, I felt the play was addressing things in ways that were new."

After the first few rehearsals, the director kept his promise to Cole. He coached his son. "He took me home and said, 'We got to work on some things,'" Scott Richards said. "I eventually found what would be a good and successful performance. I had some catch-up work to do with the rest of the cast." As a director, Richards asked questions. He didn't do line readings. He peppered his son with questions that day, and his son felt he understood the character better. But that didn't stop theater colleagues and O'Neill regulars from questioning why he got the role.

The play was set for a pre-Broadway tryout at the Annenberg Center in Philadelphia, September 10 through September 30. Everyone from the production was booked to stay at the Sheraton in downtown Philadelphia. One night, Theresa Merritt was locked out of her hotel room. She had a history of being treated poorly in hotels, and she was furious. Wilson later remarked that it could have been a scene from the play: the star gets mistreated by an industry that exploits Black artists. She left the hotel, and the general manager of the production got her a room at the Hilton. Wilson was incensed by what had happened. But Scott Richards insisted that he was in the bar with other cast members when the incident occurred. He said that the hotel had a new computer system that automatically locked guests out of their rooms if their bill had not been paid. He said it was a glitch in the system. "I don't think it was a personal thing," he said. "It was a computer error. But she was reacting to a history of racism." So was Wilson. The incident was just one of many he had witnessed or experienced himself over four decades.

The play received a rave in the *Philadelphia Daily News*, although critic Nels Nelson had some reservations. Describing it as "far from a perfect play," he wrote, "It is messy, noisy, excessively verbal, a bit quirky and sometimes unintelligible." But then he went on to say, "The American theater has a new master of the vernacular who converts plain language and mundane situations into coruscating statements and profound emotions with seeming ease."

Fueled by the praise, the cast and crew went to New York, where the play was set to open on October 11. Other plays on Broadway at the time included David Mamet's *Glengarry Glen Ross*, David Rabe's *Hurlyburly*, and Tom Stoppard's *The Real Thing*. Musicals included *Dreamgirls*, *La Cage aux Folles*, and *Sunday in the Park with George*. A young comedian named Whoopi Goldberg was set to open a one-woman show at the nearby Lyceum Theatre two weeks later. The comedian would later headline an unfortunately ill-conceived revival of *Ma Rainey* in 2003, even though she is not a singer.

The unflappable Richards was an old pro on the Great White Way. He had most recently transferred two Yale Rep productions of plays by Athol

Fugard to Broadway, *A Lesson from Aloes* and *"Master Harold"* . . . *and the boys*. But the process was new to Wilson. He nervously attended all nine previews. On the first night, he went outside at intermission to smoke. "I was always the first one out of the theater," he said. "But this time some guy beat me out the door, looked up and down, said, 'What a piece of shit' and walked away. I wanted to yell, 'Don't you be throwing my stuff on the ground!'" When the rest of the audience filed out, however, Wilson overheard not only positive reactions, but outright raves.

His family flew in for opening night. Sakina told her teacher that she had to miss school because her father had a play opening on Broadway, but her teacher didn't believe her. Sakina had seen the play when it opened at Yale Rep, but the New York experience was eye-opening for a fourteen-year-old girl. Wilson, along with his daughter and wife, rode to the opening-night party in a limousine. The star-studded affair was held at Limelight, the trendy nightclub downtown on Twentieth Street that had opened to great fanfare in 1983. Limelight was housed in a former Episcopal church built in the Gothic revival style with a pointed nave roof and a red door reminiscent of the Yale Rep building. "Everyone felt relief," Scott Richards said. "It was pretty astonishing."

As per tradition, producers read reviews aloud at opening-night parties—if they are positive. When the first edition of the *Times* arrived, the crowd listened intently. Once again, Frank Rich raved. "The play is a searing inside account of what white racism does to its victims—and it floats on the same authentic artistry as the blues music it celebrates," he wrote. Not all the reviews were as glowing, but Rich's was the one that mattered. Douglas Watt of the New York *Daily News* called it "stirring and entertaining," but found it more of a "padded-out, though vivid, slice of life than a full-fledged play." In the *New York Post*, Clive Barnes kvetched that "nothing much happens." While he praised the actors, he added, "They are playing in a play that is never really there." But Wilson was drawing from the oral tradition, and the seemingly random conversations of Black men at jitney stations or in band rooms bore deep significance to their character, culture, and past.

The play had certainly come a long way from the original one-act that Wilson had scribbled on paper bags, but it could easily be cut by thirty minutes (or even an hour), as director George C. Wolfe did in the flawed 2020 film adaptation. The two one-act plays were still not quite woven together, and half of the first act is spent waiting for the arrival of Ma Rainey. And despite the title, the play is not primarily about the singer; it is about Levee, the tempestuous trumpet player. Any production of the play relies on the performance of the actor in that role: without a strong Levee, the play implodes. With this first Broadway endeavor, though, Wilson established his signature style. The plot is less important than the monologues that interrupt the action, and that is where Wilson's writing sings. Ma Rainey is a force in the scenes she has, insisting on her dignity and worth as an artist, but Dussie Mae is thinly drawn eye candy. The male characters dominate. The first act ends with Levee's monologue about witnessing his mother being gang-raped by a group of white men when he was just eight years old. He tried to fight them off and ended up getting slashed with a knife; he bares his chest to show the scar. His father later takes steps to avenge the crime, but he is caught and hanged and set on fire. It's a powerful scene that brings an otherwise slow first act to a thundering close, and it foreshadows what is to come in the second act.

Levee simmers in the second act. After he shocks his fellow musicians with his blasphemy—"God can kiss my ass!"—the play hurtles inevitably toward the final scene. Toledo accidentally steps on Levee's brand-new Florsheim shoes, and Levee, in a rage, stabs him. He isn't acting out of anger over a pair of scuffed shoes: he is unleashing the rage about his mother's rape, his father's murder, the white producers who double-cross him, a world in which he can't get a break. He and his fellow Black men are, as Toledo says, "leftover from history." Levee's rage is enough to jar an audience out of complacency, but the overlong play stops and starts before reaching that final primal scream. But in 1984, Wilson's voice was new and refreshing and sorely needed in professional theater, and the poetic monologues overshadowed the play's weaknesses in structure and plot. Wilson was still learning his craft, and while *Ma Rainey* is hardly his best work, it was remarkable nonetheless because he was speaking truth in a way that was rare on a Broadway stage.

The editors at the *Times* acknowledged that fact by lavishing the play with attention. The paper published three long features after the play opened, including one about the four sidemen. The piece extolled their close relationship, explaining that none of them were musicians, but that Dutton learned to play rudimentary trumpet. Seneca played the trombone in parts of the production, but the other two actors only learned the rhythm. Most of the play had recorded music arranged by Dwight Andrews, who had been with the production since Yale Rep. The piece gushed about their tight-knit bonds. "The four men, who come from diverse backgrounds and have very little to do with each other after the curtain falls, still aren't quite certain why they work so well together," it read.

The truth was, they weren't all that tight. Jackson, the bass player, and Dutton did not get along. The atmosphere backstage was tense and heated. Dutton was known to be a bit egotistical among the cast members, which made for a difficult time in the greenroom. It was no secret that Dutton had a hot temper and could be as intense and fiery in real life as he was onstage. But the actors clicked when they were performing, and the ensemble spirit made the play work.

After the reviews were out and the play was deemed an artistic success by the white commercial theater establishment (if not a financial one), Wilson started thinking more about his future in the theater. He was tired of agents. Mordecai and Richards decided to help him out. They met with Wilson at the law offices of John Breglio, a powerful entertainment attorney known for getting the best deals for his clients. Breglio's office was on the thirty-first floor at 1285 Avenue of the Americas, the home of the prestigious law firm Paul, Weiss. He was one of the most high-powered entertainment attorneys in the business, representing a who's who of musical theater artists including Stephen Sondheim, Tommy Tune, and Michael Bennett. The meeting was initially awkward. Breglio gleaned that Wilson had been nettled by some of the criticism of the play, notably its unwieldy structure and lack of a cohesive plot. During that initial meeting,

Wilson told him that he had already written *Fences*, his attempt to write a traditional play about a Black family with a strong tragic hero, a cohesive plot, and an ending that packs a punch. Breglio was also aware of what he described as "Shubert Alley loose talk about anti-Semitism" in Wilson's portrayal of the recording industry executives who exploit Ma Rainey and her band. Certain high-level producers objected to the way those characters were written. But Breglio had seen and loved *Ma Rainey*. He agreed to take on Wilson as a client on a contingency basis, waiving his usual steep hourly fee. He believed in this playwright. They began a relationship that lasted until Wilson's death in 2005.

Wilson was reserved during that first meeting, but this was his first major step toward controlling his own creative process and ensuring ownership of his work. When he returned to St. Paul in December, he was a bit of a local celebrity, no longer just the short-order cook who wrote in bars and restaurants. And despite what Lou Bellamy of Penumbra Theatre said about Wilson after the *Black Bart* debacle, he had decided to stage *Jitney!*. Claude Purdy was assigned to direct. Judy Oliver did not have to write letters to newspaper editors to get coverage this time. Those days were over.

Before the play opened, actor Terry Bellamy described Wilson as "the Black Shakespeare" in a pre-publicity interview with the Minneapolis *Star Tribune*. Peter Vaughan, the same critic who had spewed vitriol on Penumbra's production of *Black Bart*, wrote a rave review of *Jitney!*, noting that the play "simmers and boils through its uninterrupted 90 minutes."

Wilson's star was rising. He was the darling of the O'Neill and had been deemed a genius by the *New York Times*. He was in and out of New York and was becoming a regular patron of the Hotel Edison, which was just a block away from the Cort Theatre, where *Ma Rainey* ultimately played for 276 performances. The production lost all of its investment, which was not uncommon for a straight play on Broadway. "The street's postmortem was that it was too great a stretch for a predominantly white Broadway audience," John Breglio wrote in his memoir, *I Wanna Be a Producer: How to Make a Killing on Broadway . . . or Get Killed*. In fact, Breglio estimated that "more than 90 percent of all plays on Broadway lost either all or most of their investments."

It was, however, a critical success and received three Tony Award nominations: Best Play, Best Featured Actor for Dutton, and Best Featured Actress for Merritt. Richards was not nominated. The ceremony was held on June 2 at the Shubert Theatre, and hopes were high. But *Ma Rainey* did not win any statues that evening; the Best Play award went to Neil Simon's *Biloxi Blues.* Wilson was gratified, however, to win the New York Drama Critics' Circle Award for Best Play. That award was first given in 1936 and is the second-oldest drama award in the U.S. after the Pulitzer Prize. Bestowed by a committee of critics from the New York metropolitan area, the award is not presented with televised fanfare, but it is highly respected in the theater community. It validated Wilson's debut. Awards, he later noted, "are useful. They empower you. They add fuel to the fire." They can also be humbling. He won a little-known prize called the Theater of Renewal Award for *Ma Rainey*, but since he had hoped to win the more prestigious accolades, he shrugged it off and did not even attend the ceremony. "That's nice," he said and tossed the medal in a box and forgot about it. But after he failed to win the big, glittery statues, he retrieved the modest trophy and displayed it on his desk. It was a lesson in humility.

The producers had been hoping that a win at the Tony Awards would lead to a surge at the box office, but when the statues didn't materialize, the play closed abruptly on June 9, which was a disappointment to everyone involved, including its star. "There were nights when I felt I could have jumped a little higher, been more keyed up," Dutton said.

But the Broadway run opened up Wilson to a new world. While the play was still running, he stopped in to see the show whenever he was in New York and visited the actors backstage after the explosive ending. One night, a member of the audience appeared at the stage door, asking for the playwright. It was Hank Aaron. The former Milwaukee and Atlanta Braves right fielder said that he wanted to meet the man who had written a play that spoke to him so clearly. The two men shook hands, and Wilson said, "You know, Mr. Aaron, this isn't the first time we've actually met." Wilson had always been a sports fan, and Hammerin' Hank had been one of his heroes while he was growing up in Pittsburgh. Aaron was surprised, since he didn't remember meeting the playwright. Wilson smiled and said, "When I was 14, and a big fan of yours, I waited outside the Pittsburgh dugout for the pleasure of shaking your hand. And now you've come to shake mine. It seems we've come full circle." It had been a formative moment for the boy who was searching for heroes who looked like him. In *Fences*, the father and son argue about the superstar status of a certain slugger: Hank Aaron.

CHAPTER NINE

A Fastball on the Outside Corner

Some people build fences to keep people out . . . and other people build fences to keep people in.

—AUGUST WILSON

t was an unseasonably chilly evening in New Haven on May 3, 1985. The moon was full but hidden behind clouds. The opening-night audience at Yale Repertory Theatre, however, was lit up with anticipation.

This night was a big one for Wilson. *Fences* was opening, with none other than James Earl Jones in the lead role. This was a career-defining moment, a chance for Wilson to prove he was more than a one-hit wonder. *Ma Rainey* had been a critical success, but not a financial one. Since he had first brought that play to the O'Neill, he had heard grumblings that it was too long and too unstructured with its succession of monologues that peaked to a tragic crescendo. He intuited that some critics would prefer to see him write a traditional well-made play, with a tragic hero and classical plot and structure. He heard it from colleagues at the O'Neill, too. "All of these people who are used to theater kept trying to tell me my work should be something different," he said. "I asked myself, 'Do I really know how to write that play?' So I wrote *Fences* in answer to the challenge that I'd given myself." He was going to prove those naysayers wrong.

Wilson was often uncomfortable sitting in the theater, even with Judy Oliver and Sakina there for support. He couldn't smoke. At intermission, he headed straight for Chapel Street, where he chain-smoked several cigarettes, down to the filter. A few days earlier, he had written a poem called "Home," dedicated to the Yale Repertory Theatre. In one stanza, he uses a baseball metaphor to describe his journey. The poem is a tribute to Yale Rep and the many paths he had to travel to find an artistic home. He salutes the theater in the last stanza and makes a humble offering of what he describes as a "bloodless execution of the alphabet."

Wilson read his poem for the cast and crew before curtain on opening night and then took his aisle seat in the theater. Malcolm L. Johnson, the critic for the *Hartford Courant*, was again in the audience that night. So was Frank Rich, but his review would not run until May 7. Johnson started his review with a sentence that Wilson would remember for the rest of his life. "This is no sophomore slump for August Wilson." He knew he still had some work to do on *Fences*, but he was not going to write one play and then fade into obscurity. *No sophomore slump.*

That night, he wrote a thank-you note to Lloyd Richards. He said that he had taken the first step toward writing *Fences* forty years earlier, the day he was born. He noted that while the play was not autobiographical, it came close to his life and to the neighborhood of his youth. He told Richards that he wished his mother, Daisy, could have been at the opening and then went on to say that the play represented his uncle Frank and Richards's uncle Charlie and all the other men who he had known who lived noble lives despite economic and social hardships. He wrote it, he noted, as a paean to their lives. He ended with an endearing thank you—and he dedicated the published version of the play to Richards, "who adds to whatever he touches."

The play, set in Pittsburgh in 1957, honors the elders Wilson had observed in the Hill District, but particularly his stepfather, David Bedford, and his mentor, Charley Burley. He originally conceived the play with a single image that came to him. He imagined a man standing in a yard, not unlike his own yard at 1727 Bedford. He was holding an infant. "The first lines I wrote was 'I'm standing out here in the yard with my daughter in my arms. She's just a wee bitty little ole thing. She don't understand about grownups' business, and she ain't got no mama.'" He started to wonder who this man was and why he was holding a motherless child. This was the way he worked: he started with an image, a lyric from a classic blues tune, a painting, or a single line of dialogue and then developed a story around it.

He would work this way for the rest of his life. In the case of *Fences*, he came up with his tragic hero, Troy Maxson, a former slugger in the Negro Leagues who was good enough to hit homers off Satchel Paige but who peaked before Jackie Robinson broke the color line in Major League Baseball in 1947. He is a sanitation worker in Pittsburgh who, like David Bedford, did time in the penitentiary for murder, but settled down and started a family with his wife, Rose. He makes $76.42 a month and fights to be promoted from picking up garbage to driving the truck, but when he wins that battle and gets the job, he sits in the driver's seat, isolated and alone. He feuds with his son Cory and stops him from getting recruited to play college football. The two have one of the most explosive father-son confrontations in American dramatic literature. Cory asks him, "How come you ain't never liked me?" and Troy explodes.

> Like you? I go out of here every morning . . . bust my
> butt . . . putting up with them crackers every day . . . 'cause
> I like you? You about the biggest fool I ever saw. (*Pause.*)
> It's my job. It's my responsibility! You understand that?

Cory cringes at the rebuke, but Troy isn't simply being cruel. He is teaching his son how to survive, a lesson he learned through hard experiences. He is telling him that as a young Black man, he needs to watch over his shoulder. "Don't you try to go through life worrying about if somebody like you or not," Troy says. "You best be making sure they doing right by you. You understand what I'm saying, boy?" Wilson bore scars from his own fatherless childhood, but in Troy, he created a strong father figure who may not have been emotionally nurturing, but who stuck around and taught his son the ways of the world. Troy has also reconnected with

Lyons, his adult son from a previous relationship. He cares deeply for his brother, Gabriel, a World War II veteran who had "half his head blown away" and has a metal plate in his skull. Troy used Gabriel's $3,000 disability settlement to buy his house, and he lives with the guilt of knowing, at fifty-three, that he wouldn't have "a pot to piss in or a window to throw it out of" if it weren't for his brother's injury.

The play is well-made in every way. Troy's downfall is his affair with a woman named Alberta, who dies while giving birth to their daughter. He brings the baby home, and his confrontation with Rose brings down the house. "A motherless child has got a hard time," she tells him. "From right now . . . this child got a mother. But you a womanless man." That line stops the show, every time. He doesn't only lose his wife. He also loses the close relationship he had with his best friend, Bono, a fellow sanitation worker who is disgusted with Troy's infidelity.

As time passes, Rose finds solace in the church, leaving Troy to fend for himself. She is another example of a typical Wilson woman, modeled after his mother. Wilson gives her a powerful monologue that resonates with women in the audience, but he doesn't give her the agency to get up and leave. He would say that he was depicting a typical housewife from the 1950s who stays with Troy, regardless of what he does, just the way Daisy kept running back to Kittel, even when he failed to pay child support and showed up drunk. She stands by her man, even if she gives him the holy silent treatment for the rest of his life, but Wilson does not grant her the independence to throw him out.

There is, however, redemption at the end of the play after Troy dies. Cory, who has spent six years in the military, comes home for the funeral and meets his little sister, Raynell. Gabriel tries to blow his trumpet and is beside himself when he can't make a sound. But then, in the ending that left the audience speechless at the O'Neill, the clouds lift and the skies open up in a flash of heavenly light. For all his flaws, Troy has made it through the Pearly Gates.

After the Yale Rep opening, everyone was waiting for the reaction in the *Times*, and the review ran the following Tuesday. While Rich described the play as "absorbing" and praised individual monologues, he noted that, at times, the secondary characters "sound like stock replicas of the characters of paradigmatic white family plays (starting with Arthur Miller's)." Rich's review was uncanny. He saw exactly what Wilson was doing. "The reason for the shortfall in *Fences* may be that Mr. Wilson has now learned more—maybe too much—about playwriting," he wrote. He added, "As Mr. Wilson's extraordinary voice can be too tidily fenced in by his generic dramatic carpentry, so Lloyd Richards's production also seems constricted."

The day after that review ran, Wilson, Jones, and several of the actors did a talkback with the audience. Someone asked Wilson if he had modeled his play after Arthur Miller's *Death of a Salesman*, and he said he hadn't read it. The talkback audience was full of Yale Rep regulars, including some who liked to quibble. There is a moment in the play right after Troy tells his wife about his affair; Gabriel enters and hands Rose . . . a rose. She holds it throughout the scene. Someone in the audience objected to that bit of symbolic business, and Wilson replied that it was his favorite part of the play. One woman in the discussion said, "I haven't known that many Black people in my life, so I came expecting to feel separate from the play. Instead, I found my whole life shown up there on the stage—my parents immigrated from Portugal." Wilson would repeat that anecdote over and over for the rest of his life, sometimes changing "Portugal" to "Poland," sometimes to "China." There is a certain irony in the fact that he felt compelled to repeat that story about his characters' "universality." No one would ever feel the need to say that about, say, Shakespeare, but critics and audience members were so stunned to discover that Black characters could be "universal." Of course they were.

Wilson had not been home for seventy-three days, and when he got back to St. Paul he wrote Richards another letter on June 25, 1985. He was proud of the play and had begun to feel that he was making an important change in American theater.

But all was not well behind the scenes. Like Rich, producer Bob Cole thought *Fences* was too tidy, and he suggested changes in the script. The play, he determined, was too commercial, too traditional, too kitchen sink. He audaciously suggested that he work with Wilson as a script adviser. On June 27, 1985, Wilson fired off another letter to Richards. He rejected Cole's suggestion and said that he trusted Richards. He knew the play needed some work, but he had already toiled at the rewrites under Richards's direction. Cole passed on the opportunity to produce *Fences* on Broadway, a mistake his wife later called the most expensive one he ever made. She told him: "I have the f-word for you. It's *Fences*." According to James Earl Jones, many other prospective producers came to see the play, but they left saying, "Well, it's a play about a Black family. We don't know if that will work in the commercial theater."

Jones had his own problems with the play. The actor was in South Africa during the summer of 1985, and he sent Richards a nine-page, handwritten critique of the play. He disliked the actor playing Troy Maxson's mentally impaired brother, Gabriel, and demanded a replacement. He said the entire play depressed him and left him depleted, while also adding that the "negative edge" of the character of Troy, while frustrating and depressing, also challenged him to "realize a frightening human aspect of heroism—the only aspect really worth sharing with an audience." That said, he also felt that the play did not come to a resolution, in part because his character dies offstage before he reconciles with his son. He compared it to *Othello*, in which the title character has a climactic death scene. He said he could do the play for six months if Wilson changed the script to address his perceived problems. "Could they be solved," he wrote, "I think my depression could be a healthier one and less futile."

The legendary actor is a self-defined recluse, but he was certainly not shy with his opinions. Wilson had said he wrote the role of Troy Maxson with Jones in mind. He recalled hearing that deep, resonant voice while crafting the play. Jones outright rejects that notion. "I immediately dismissed that," Jones said. "That is not possible. He doesn't know me well enough to write with me in mind. What does that mean? I appreciated that he wrote a role that I could do. In fact, I hadn't had anything to challenge me since *The Great White Hope* [in 1967]."

Wilson did not workshop a play at the O'Neill that summer, but he popped in for a visit and offered support and writerly advice to his friend James Yoshimura, who was working on a new play called *Union Boys* and had called his friend when he was struggling with rewrites. "I said, 'Where are you, August?' and, boom, he was there," Yoshimura recalled. "He helped me with a certain moment in the second act; it needed to be funny. That is the kind of guy he was. He was very generous."

Wilson was working on his own rewrites, and Richards was frustrated that he had not been able to secure a Broadway producer for *Fences*. He believed in the play and his cast and wanted to see it move beyond the Yale Rep production. It was at this moment that he dreamt up the idea that would shape his work with Wilson for the next decade. If a Broadway producer was not willing to take a chance on *Fences*, he could take another crack at the play and direct it at another regional theater. He told Benjamin Mordecai that he wanted to see how the play would progress in "the protected environment of the nonprofit theater."

At the same time, the Goodman Theatre in Chicago asked Yale Rep to release the rights to the play for a Goodman production in the winter of 1986. The Goodman was in between artistic directors at the time. Gregory Mosher had recently departed to become director of theater at New York's Lincoln Center. Before he left, he had announced the Goodman's 1985–86 season, which included a revival of John Guare's *The House of Blue Leaves*, directed by Jerry Zaks, set for a February 1986 opening. But Mosher had since decided to mount that production in New York instead of Chicago, leaving the Goodman with a hole in its season. Robert Falls had been appointed the new artistic director, but he had yet to officially begin what would turn out to be a long and illustrious career with the storied regional theater. On October 3, the Goodman announced that it would present a new production of *Fences*, with a week of previews beginning on January 31, 1986, and opening a four-week run on February 10. Under the headline "*Fences* Gets New Look for Goodman," the *Chicago Tribune* reported that Richards would direct "a separate, Goodman production, with new rewrites by the author and a new cast fully rehearsed in Chicago." The paper added that, so far, "there are no plans to present this *Fences* version elsewhere, either before or after its Chicago run."

But that changed three weeks later. Richards and Mordecai had negotiated a new deal that included Yale Rep. The Goodman announced that the cast now featured the original stars, James Earl Jones and Mary Alice, and that the play was a joint production by the Goodman and Yale Rep, not a separate Goodman production. That announcement led to speculation that Richards was hoping Broadway producers might take another look, since he was keeping Yale Rep in the mix rather than handing the rights over to the Goodman. At any rate, this coproduction model was a stroke of genius, particularly for a writer like Wilson, who was still learning about dramatic structure and who benefited enormously from seeing his work performed onstage. The Goodman production enabled him to rewrite and refine, a perk that is rarely available to other playwrights. It was a win-win for both theaters: the Goodman, which was in transition, filled its gap with a star-studded production with a renowned director, and Richards invented a model that would enable Wilson to further develop his plays in the nonprofit regional theater. He would expand on that model in the years to come, opening it up to other theaters, but not without controversy.

At the same time that *Fences* was set to run at the Goodman, another production of the play was rehearsing at the GeVa Theatre Center in Rochester, New York. It was directed by Wilson's friend Claude Purdy with a completely different cast and design team. This was an anomaly. Richards never allowed other directors to stage Wilson's work until he had brought what he considered the "definitive" version to Broadway. Richards later told colleagues that he recommended Purdy to direct subsequent productions of Wilson's plays, but only after Purdy had seen his version on Broadway, suggesting that Purdy would simply repeat his directorial choices.

The GeVa production opened on February 22 and went unnoticed outside of the area, although it received a rave in the local paper, the *Democrat and Chronicle*, which hailed the play as "expertly constructed, splendidly produced and created for enduring significance." Judy Oliver and Jacqui Shoholm went to see the Rochester production as well as the one at the Goodman. But the GeVa production came and went, and neither Richards nor Wilson ever mentioned it when discussing the history of the play, despite its success in upstate New York.

Their focus at the time was on Chicago. There was a lot at stake in the Goodman production. Richards and Wilson were still hoping to attract a Broadway producer. In fact, the day before the opening, Wilson told Richard Christiansen, the so-called "dean of Chicago theater critics," that the production provided not only an opportunity for a "second viewing," but also "a chance to give producers another crack at the play." Wilson also told the critic that, despite his success with *Ma Rainey*, he was still not able to earn a living as a writer. By this time, however, he had received generous fellowships from both the Jerome and Bush Foundations, so he was no starving artist.

The cast and creative team remained the same, with one exception. Richards had capitulated to one of James Earl Jones's demands. He replaced actor Russell Costen with Frankie Faison in the role of Gabriel, despite the fact that Rich from the *Times* had described Costen as "particularly formidable."

The play opened on Monday, February 10, a seasonably frigid day in Chicago with temperatures in the low teens and winds whipping at ten to eighteen miles an hour. But the reception was warm at the theater that night, as Jones's star power brought high expectations. Christiansen raced to meet the *Tribune*'s crippling overnight deadline, and he did not disappoint. He, like the critics in New Haven, compared the play to *Death of a Salesman*, likening Troy Maxson to Willy Loman. He had nothing but praise for Jones—and his character. Troy Maxson, he wrote, "is a man of almost mythic power and nobility who, despite personal failings and life's limitations, is still fit for heaven's gates." The production, he said, will "live long in memory." He, like Jones, had reservations about the crucial final scene, noting that "it could use some refinement in its writing and direction." Still, he ended his review by genuflecting to the playwright: "August Wilson, it is clear, can write like an angel."

The play had staying power, and so did Wilson. In fact, at the time, Wilson was harboring hopes that *Ma Rainey* would be adapted for the large screen (that didn't happen until 2020, when Netflix released a screen adaptation starring Viola Davis and Chadwick Boseman, with direction by George C. Wolfe). He also said that he was working on a musical called *Mr.*

Jelly Roll, about the great ragtime and jazz pianist Jelly Roll Morton, who had been the subject of his earlier poem. He was anticipating a workshop in the fall of 1986, but that never happened. He didn't elaborate, but the Broadway producer Margo Lion had commissioned him to write the book for a musical about the great pianist. Wilson eventually changed the name of the musical to *St. Louis Blues* and wrote a slim book about Jelly Roll Morton showing up in St. Louis for the 1904 Louisiana Purchase Exposition (more commonly known as the St. Louis World's Fair). His attempt to write another musical was halfhearted and not fully realized. Lion told Wilson it was a "beautiful poetic play" about "a stranger who came to town and every five pages or so there would be a cluster of Jelly's music," but it wasn't what she had in mind and she rejected the script. Wilson put it in a drawer and vowed to get back to it someday, but it was never produced.

Wilson was simultaneously working on rewrites of *Joe Turner's Come and Gone* and polishing *The Piano Lesson* for the coming summer's National Playwrights Conference at the O'Neill. He was now in that period during which he had three projects going at once. He had written the first draft of *Piano Lesson*, which he conceived as a play about a piano passed down in an African American family and what it symbolized. He had written it the previous winter and fall, in time to submit it to the O'Neill by the December deadline. But two months later in February, he had his eyes on the prize. He hoped that the Goodman production of *Fences* would attract a Broadway producer.

It just so happened that Carole Shorenstein Hays, the well-heeled daughter of San Francisco real estate magnate Walter Shorenstein, aspired to become a producer and was in the market for a new play. She was a dilettante with a substantial family fortune—and a mercurial temper of equal size. She saw *Fences* at the Goodman, but as often is the case with Wilson, there are two stories detailing how she got to Chicago to see the play. According to the play's star, Jones, theatrical icon Carol Channing saw the production and urged her friend Hays to see it. According to John Breglio, the powerful entertainment attorney who represented both Wilson and Hays, it was he who encouraged the young producer to see the play. He knew that other producers had passed on a Broadway production, and he claims that he was the true matchmaker.

At any rate, Hays immediately identified with the family saga. "I realized that no matter what your station, whether you are wealthy, educated, poor, illiterate—all families wrestling with anxieties and hostilities tend to work them out the same way," she said. "All families have the power structure of parent and child. All families have rivalry. Background is irrelevant when it comes to families in crisis."

She particularly related to the father-son relationship. "Troy Maxson was my father," she said of the play's main character. "'My gosh,' I thought. 'How did they get that?' Here was a character I knew and understood, that I empathized with very deeply." The similarities, however, are not readily apparent. Wilson was aiming to depict a Black man as a loyal, dependable provider, the kind of strong paternal presence he had never known as a child. "I don't know first-hand what a father-son relationship is all about," he told Christiansen, "but, unlike the kind of Black feminist perspective you see in *The Color Purple*, I'm trying to show in *Fences* one Black male who stayed with and was responsible for his family." He was not just reacting to the deep hole in his own childhood experience, but he was also providing a counterpoint to the abusive father depicted in Alice Walker's 1982 Pulitzer Prize–winning novel, a man who beats, rapes, and impregnates his daughter. He wanted to explode the stereotype of the deadbeat Black father figure. Troy Maxson, he said, "is trying as best he knows to be a responsible person."

Hays's father, on the surface, could not be more different. He had built a $400 million real estate empire in San Francisco and had bought the Golden Gate and Orpheum Theaters and acquired the lease on the Curran Theater, along with his business partner, the producer James Nederlander. Hays had been raised with everything a girl could want, including an education at the prestigious Crystal Springs Uplands School in Hillsborough, California. "I thought it would look good on my engagement announcement," she once said of her schooling. She attended New York University but did not graduate and breezily admitted she was a terrible student. But her father was willing to finance her dream to become a producer, no strings attached. "We've never looked at what Carole does as a profit center," he told a reporter. "We've looked at it as part of our contribution to the arts and the community. We've set aside certain sums for her to use." He gave her the money to put up 100 percent of the financing for *Fences*, an unusual arrangement that included no other investors. He also gave strict instructions to Mordecai, who handled the business side of Yale Rep. "Don't you ever make my little girl unhappy," he said.

Jones saw an ally in this diminutive thirty-eight-year-old producer. He and his agent, Lucy Kroll, set up a private meeting with Hays following the wrap of the Goodman production. The legendary actor laid out his problems with the play, particularly his belief that the father-son relationship is unresolved. He brought the inexperienced and eager producer into his confidence, confessing that he left the theater depressed after each performance when he went home to his young son, Flynn Earl Jones. "I would look at him and say, 'Does this have to happen—this desperate, wordless, physical confrontation between a father and son, so choked with words they can't speak that they risk killing each other?'" He told Hays about his relationship with his own father, Robert Earl Jones, who abandoned his family shortly after his son was born. Jones later reconciled with his father, but the scars ran deep. He solidified a bond with Hays, which would later lead to turmoil. Theater troupes often refer to the team for each production as "family." The *Fences* family was dysfunctional and would soon experience a bitter struggle for control.

But Wilson was buoyant. His second Broadway production was in the works, and Hays had free rein with her father's money. She began planning for a pre-Broadway run at the Curran Theater in San Francisco for the following February, with a Broadway opening a month later. But Richards had been uncertain that the Goodman production would yield such success, and he had scheduled yet another production for a run at the Seattle Repertory Theatre. While Jones and the company were finishing up the final performances in Chicago, he was in Seattle working on *Fences* with a completely different cast. Samuel L. Jackson played the role of Troy's older son, Lyons; the cast also included Gilbert Lewis as Troy, Keith Amos as Cory, Frances Foster as Rose, and William Jay as Gabriel. All of those actors went on to successful careers in television and film, but did not become part of the tight circle of actors who became known as the "Wilson Warriors." Jackson's film career skyrocketed, but he later appeared in a 2022 Broadway revival of *Piano Lesson*. The Seattle production received rave reviews with minor reservations. Tim Appelo of the *Seattle Times* noted that the play's "main flaw"—the poetry—was also its "chief glory," concluding that "this is realism at its most lyrical" and noting that Jackson had perfect pitch in the secondary role. Joe Adcock in the *Seattle Post-Intelligencer* began with an exclamation—"Such richness!"—and then continued with a breathless review that compared Wilson to Aeschylus, Sophocles, and Euripides.

The Seattle production went unnoticed by East Coast theater professionals, who did not yet recognize the high quality of the nation's growing network of regional theaters. The Seattle run is often left out of the history of Wilson's most commercially successful play. But the fact that Richards had initiated the production indicates that he was getting more serious about the plan that would take fruition with Wilson's subsequent plays. He would direct different productions in theaters across the country, honing Wilson's overwritten, cumbersome scripts into tight packages that ideally ran under three hours. (Broadway theatrical unions charge overtime for any play that runs longer than two hours, fifty-nine minutes.)

Both Richards and Wilson were in overdrive for the next few months. Immediately after the Seattle production, they convened in New Haven, where *Joe Turner* received its world premiere at Yale Rep on April 29. A few weeks later, Wilson was back at the O'Neill for the preconference session for *Piano Lesson*, which he developed that summer at the National Playwrights Conference. Wilson was immersed in the busiest and most fertile period of his career. He was rarely in St. Paul, and his colleagues, both male and female, knew that he frequently enjoyed the company of female companions—some quickie affairs and other more long-term relationships that dragged on and off for years. It is not clear whether Judy Oliver knew what was happening on the road, but Wilson's constant absence from home surely put a strain on the marriage. He didn't hide his affairs at the O'Neill or at New Dramatists, where inhibitions were relaxed. Even though he repeated the same stories over and over again to anyone who would listen, he knew how to draw an individual into his personal orbit, making the listener feel as if she were the most important person in his world. Few of his contemporaries will discuss his infidelities on the record, but they were not a secret among those who worked with him.

At the same time, he was becoming a sought-after playwright among leaders at the nation's regional theaters. Peter Altman, then the producing director of Boston's Huntington Theatre Company, had seen *Ma Rainey* on Broadway and he attended a preview performance of *Fences* at Yale. He recognized a huge talent and wanted to be part of the development team. The Huntington, founded at Boston University in 1982, had done little to attract Black audiences, and Altman saw an opportunity to nurture an astonishing new voice in American theater—and to reach out to Black theatergoers as well. He approached Richards and Benjamin Mordecai to discuss *Fences*, but the team was already sewing up plans for the Goodman production and hoped to make it to New York. Not deterred, Altman asked about upcoming projects, and Richards told him about *Joe Turner.* Altman offered Richards the opening slot in his 1986–87 season. That further solidified the development system that Wilson would use to his advantage for all of his plays. They would open at a string of regional theaters that grew to include Huntington, the Goodman, the Mark Taper Forum in Los Angeles, and Arena Stage in Washington, D.C. The arrangement provided both a financial and artistic advantage for everyone involved. In the 1980s, the days of pre-Broadway tryouts for straight plays in commercial theaters were coming to an end. It was too expensive and too risky to preview a play out of town. The resident theater network offered a safe and more affordable place to see the work onstage. And for Wilson, who had learned to make the most of the development process at the O'Neill, it was a writer's dream.

On the surface, everything seemed ideal. Wilson was hopscotching from one production to another, and he was receiving terrific reviews and conducting high-profile interviews in every city where his plays were produced. Newspaper articles always accentuated the Wilson-Richards partnership, comparing it to the relationship between playwright Tennessee Williams and his frequent collaborator, the director Elia Kazan. Richards was portrayed as the experienced sage who was mentoring the younger playwright and shaping his raw talent. Wilson never publicly objected to this portrayal, but behind the scenes, tension was brewing. The playwright had not received princely compensation for productions of his early plays. With Black Horizons, the creative team shared whatever profits, if any, came in at the box office. More likely than not, they came up short and put their own meager funds into the productions. When *Ma Rainey* was produced on Broadway, Wilson had agreed to an unusual arrangement with Richards. The director received 16.6 percent (or one-sixth) of the author's royalties from subsidiary rights, in perpetuity. Sometimes the playwright retains 100 percent of the subsidiary rights, but in some cases, it is not uncommon for the first director of a new play to receive a share of the royalties. But that share is usually between 5 and 10 percent. (Directors of musicals, such as Tommy Tune, Michael Bennett, and Bob Fosse, often received a higher percentage, because their work undeniably defines the final artistic product.) In the case of *Ma Rainey*, though, Richards's cut was exceedingly generous. The director, however, had spent two years helping Wilson craft a drama out of what was essentially two one-act plays that were short on exposition and structure and heavy on monologues. Richards felt that he had helped shape the play and deserved a significant share of future earnings, which included movie and television rights, as well as productions in regional theaters.

But now Wilson had entertainment attorney Breglio to manage his contracts. Breglio was extremely protective of his clients, especially Wilson. And now that *Fences* had secured a Broadway producer, Wilson and Breglio requested a new agreement. In a letter dated April 22, 1986, they offered Richards 5 percent of the author's royalties for a limited period of time, contingent on Richards directing a "first-class production." Wilson had privately told friends that Richards was taking too much of his money, and the letter was an attempt to make the financial arrangement more equitable to what other playwrights received.

Richards did not take that request well.

He waited to reply until after *Joe Turner* had opened at Yale Rep on

April 29, to mostly enthusiastic reviews (although Rich of the *Times* suggested that the play needed more work to make it the masterpiece it would
eventually become). On May 5, Richards fired off a three-page response
to his lawyer, Gary DaSilva of the New York firm DaSilva and DaSilva. He
did not pull any punches. "For openers," he wrote, "I found the letter to be
inaccurate, non-perceptive, demeaning and insulting." Noting that he had
a "short fuse and little tolerance for the power plays of the industry," Richards excoriated Breglio and what he called his "negotiating techniques."
He described Wilson as "a unique and talented Black poet and a story-
teller with few peers" and offered his summary of their work together on
Ma Rainey, Fences, and *Joe Turner.* In each case, he wrote, "August has a
meaningful impulse and a basic situation populated by fascinating characters who reveal themselves through interaction and storytelling. There
is a story but not always a through line or a fully realized theme. My work
with August begins there. We search for the theme then rearrange, re-
adjust, cut, add or I ask him to rewrite so that we can dynamically and
dramatically reveal, illuminate and explode the material bringing it to full
theatrical realization." After this work is done, he continued, "practically
any director can do it."

His work, he said, went far beyond the usual role of a director and he
was uniquely qualified to do it. "There is not anyone that I am aware of
who could have or would have realized his potential and that of his work
in the way that our collaboration has done," Richards wrote, adding that
he did not take a fee during the National Playwrights Conference or at
Yale Rep, but that he expected compensation if the work went beyond
Yale. He also implied that he had made it possible for Wilson to work full-
time as a playwright. He did not elaborate, but Wilson had received many
grants. (In fact, in November 1986, he would be one of ten artists to receive the prestigious Whiting Award, which came with a grant of $25,000.
The nominators for the awards were anonymous.)

In the long missive, he did not sway from his commitment to Wilson.
"I respect the writer and love the man," he wrote. "That will not change
and is not subject to negotiation. As Bynum in *Joe Turner's Come and*

Gone would understand, binding people together with their work is my song. It costs me a piece of myself but it's a joyous price to pay."

Richards also defined the unique development process that would guide his work with Wilson for the next decade—and pinpointed the reasons for its necessity. "We are all conscious of the Commercial Theatre's attitude toward serious plays and of their feeling about serious plays concerning minorities. They are not considered a good risk." He had learned that firsthand with *Fences*. Despite the rave reviews, Richards had initially been unable to attract a producer. "I stood with a close associate who owns theatres and produces. He and his wife had just seen *Fences* and his wife was still in tears. He explained that he could not consider producing the play." That experience spurred him into action. "These circumstances have led me to explore and develop the rich possibilities of the Regional Theatre Circuit as was done with *Fences*. It may be the real future for August's work and that of many other playwrights." Richards was right about that and he and Wilson would use it to great advantage over the next ten years. But Richards did not concede an inch on the issue of compensation.

Breglio fired back a week later, and Wilson stayed out of the fray, leaving the lawyers to work it out. Wilson attended the National Playwrights Conference that summer with *Piano Lesson*, and he and Richards joined forces in September 1986 on the production of *Joe Turner* at Boston's Huntington Theatre. No one at the Boston theater noticed anything unusual or strained between the two men, but there was an unspoken rift that they managed to keep to themselves. A year later, Wilson would reach out to his mentor with a typewritten letter written on July 6, 1987, noting that there had been tension between the two in Boston and they should talk about it to clear the air.

It's not certain if they ever addressed the money issue face-to-face rather than through their representatives, but in December 1986, Wilson and Breglio prevailed. Richards signed an agreement granting him 5 percent of the royalties, not 16.6 percent. Richards, who was known as a calm, unflappable Buddha to students and playwrights, had seethed during the negotiations, and like Wilson, he never forgot a perceived indignity or insult. This was the first crack in his relationship with Wilson, although the press was still playing up the "father-son" dynamic. The argument over the royalties had changed Wilson. He was beginning to demand greater control over his work, which would only intensify as he gained acclaim in the theater world.

But the rift over the money was put on hold during the rehearsal period for *Fences* in San Francisco at the beginning of 1987. The two men became allies in a troubled backstage battle over control of the script. Hays had hired a seasoned general manager, Robert Kamlot, to oversee the production. James Earl Jones had already wielded his influence with Hays, creating an odd power dynamic in the rehearsal room. Jones still wasn't satisfied with the ending and complained that several serious scenes were eliciting laughter from the audience. Hays met with Jones, Richards, and Wilson to relay these concerns, but according to Jones, the director and playwright refused to budge. Jones felt he was "being stonewalled and became more and more frustrated." He deepened his allegiance with Hays. "She was white, Jewish, rich, and young, and I saw something personal in the subtly negative way she was dealt with," he wrote in his autobiography, hinting that there might be a measure of male chauvinism and anti-Semitism involved in the disagreement.

The play began previews on Thursday, February 6, and opened to mostly positive reviews a week later. Breglio (who also represented Hays) flew out for the opening. Despite the reviews, Hays and Kamlot were concerned. Some of Hays's subscribers (to a Broadway subscription series at the San Francisco theaters her father owned) had complained about the play. They said it was too long, and they were put off by Wilson's frequent use of the N-word, which, in context, was appropriate for the characters to use. Troy uses it in the second line of the play as he banters with his best friend, Bono. Jones agreed with Wilson and Richards on that point. That was how men of that generation talked to each other; they took back a word that had been intended as a slur and made it their own, using it specifically with other Black men. But Jones was still secretly lobbying for other changes. After the opening, Hays and Kamlot met with Breglio and gave him a heavily marked-up script, highlighted in pink and yellow. Anything highlighted in pink was a "recommended change," and everything in yellow was a "required change." Breglio's client list included many theatrical legends and impresarios, and he later insisted that he had never seen a producer mark up a script and demand such hefty changes (although it is not uncommon). Wilson and Richards said they had their own rewrites in mind. As a powerful entertainment attorney, Breglio often put his clients together to work on a project, and in this situation, he encouraged Hays and Wilson to work it out. While the show was in previews in San Francisco, he thought the conflict was resolved and flew back to New York, assuming that the show was on course to open on Broadway.

But the trouble was only beginning. A week after the opening, Richards anticipated a stalemate and announced he was going back to New Haven. Hays asked him to reconsider, so he stayed, which Hays said she appreciated. On February 13, she wrote again, emphasizing that she was confident they could collaborate to create a beautiful play.

The détente did not last long. Jones sided unconditionally with the producer. He had deep respect for Richards, but he and Hays still didn't like the ending of the play and felt that the father-son conflict was unresolved. In Act 2, Scene 4, the family dynamic has changed. Rose is raising Troy's out-of-wedlock baby and has found a new purpose in the church (her stoic, silent holier-than-thou stance was reminiscent of Brenda Burton's rejection of Wilson years earlier). At the end of the scene, Troy has a violent confrontation with his son Cory. They fight over a baseball bat, but when Troy gets control, he cannot bring himself to strike his son. Cory leaves the house, clearly for good. The scene ends with Troy taking on Death, the specter that has hung over the play. "It's between you and me now! Come on! Anytime you want! Come on! I be ready for you . . . but I ain't gonna be easy." The lights go down and come up on the scene that begins the morning of Troy's funeral, culminating in the now famous moment when Gabriel tries unsuccessfully to blow his horn.

Jones remained frustrated that the father and son never got to reconcile their differences face-to-face. This was personal for him. He knew

Wilson was averse to editing his work, and he saw that Richards was struggling with the backstage battle. The director was in charge at the O'Neill, the Yale School of Drama, and Yale Rep, yet he was being challenged by a rookie producer. One day during a discussion about script changes, Jones remembers Richards saying, "How does it feel not having power at all? Not good. You have all the power, and then suddenly you have none."

The next week, Hays and Kamlot raised the stakes. She had never produced a new play before, and she wanted to establish a reputation as a forceful decision-maker. She was at once a wealthy tenderfoot and a mercurial, controlling meddler. She may have been spending her father's money, but she made it clear that she could flex her muscles. She knew precious little about nurturing artists: that was Richards's specialty. But she knew what she wanted, and she also had Jones—the man who voiced Darth Vader and brought down houses with his commanding Othello—whispering in her ear.

Hays suggested an alternate ending in which Cory sings a song that his father had taught him. Wilson and Richards were emphatic about keeping the ending as it was. However, they agreed to stage the different endings on alternate nights, but that didn't change Wilson's mind. Courtney B. Vance was a twenty-six-year-old actor and a student at the Yale School of Drama whom Richards had tapped to stay with the production in San Francisco and make his Broadway debut as Cory. He was "a young green kid at the time" and was demoralized by the acrimony of the backstage drama. He was intimidated by Richards but impressed by his refusal to budge. The director sided unconditionally with Wilson. "He said, 'I will not go against my playwright,'" Vance said.

On Wednesday, February 25, Hays sent Richards a two-page memo, outlining four important changes. The first was telling: she wanted to restage Jones's curtain call to bring more attention to him. Curtain calls for straight plays are fairly standard. The star always comes out last, so it is odd that, of all things to nitpick, Hays wanted to find a way to showcase Jones even more. He was not only her star; he was also her comrade in arms. She also wanted to cut ten minutes and asked for clarifications of certain details. This list included an item calling for Wilson to change Rose's line about taking care of Troy's baby. It was incomprehensible that she wanted to change the play's most famous line—"You a womanless man"—which evoked shouts of "You go girl!" from the balcony. It remained in the script.

Hays also asked how Troy died, noting that it was a critical shortcoming. Throughout the entire play, Troy wrestles with death and in his last scene he speaks directly to the Grim Reaper, foreshadowing his passing and the funeral at the end of the play. The stage directions say, *"Troy assumes a batting posture and begins to taunt Death, the fastball on the outside corner."* That was enough for both Richards and Wilson.

She continued to insist on changing the ending. During the intermission of the performance on Thursday, February 26, Hays relayed, through her general manager, that she was considering canceling the Broadway transfer if she did not get her way. Richards asked Kamlot to book him a flight back to New Haven, where he would work until a decision was made. The next morning, Hays called Richards and "threatened [him] because he was leaving." She called back forty-five minutes later and apologized and urged him not to go.

By Saturday, Richards had not received a definitive answer, and he had had enough. He flew back to New Haven, but not before writing an impassioned six-page missive to Wilson. The fiery handwritten note took an avuncular tone, but the message was fierce. He said that he had heard two things expressed ad nauseam during the long discussions. The first was about the critics: it was imperative that *Fences* be a "hit." The second concerned the amount of money invested. "These are the forces," he wrote, "that have been and are even more desperately driving the machine that is *Fences*." He also put some of the blame on the critics, noting that, in order to be deemed a hit, the play must have "excited, entertained and if at all possible dazzled and you must certainly have provoked to thought beyond their ability to completely understand and approve in the fifteen minutes between the end of the play and their first headlines." In those days, critics for daily newspapers raced out of the theater before the curtain call and got back to the newsroom to write in time for the first edition, often leaving them an hour or an hour and a half to write. Some were brilliant at it, others not so much, and the system didn't do anyone any favors. But even though many producers bemoaned the process, they also encouraged it, sending press representatives to newspaper offices to get copies of reviews to read at the opening-night party. They also combed through the reviews to extract glowing quotes, often lifted out of context, to appear in their advertisements. Producers, too, had a deadline to meet.

Richards, however, was understandably not fond of the system, particularly with a Wilson play. "The fact that a play lingers, haunts, and contents like a down-home meal is too late and therefore in the circumstances irrelevant," he wrote. His disillusion exposed the worst of "commercial" theater, which he described as an attractive prepackaged product with strict constraints. It must have a star. It must be entertaining, but topical enough so that well-heeled audience members could discuss it at meetings or parties. It must clock in at two and a half hours.

Richards had a card to play with Hays, but his disgust with the workings of commercial theater may have kept him from using it. As much as they complained about it, the Broadway machine placed undue power in one review—that is, in the *New York Times*. Frank Rich had catapulted the Richards-Wilson partnership to Broadway with his lavish praise of *Ma Rainey*. He had liked *Fences* in New Haven, but he thought it was too tidy, too dramaturgically well-made. Richards could have waived that review—and the *Ma Rainey* raves—and explained that the most important critic in New York had already signaled that he was going to write a positive notice, but had also expressed reservations. It wouldn't help to make the play even more neat and conservative, Richards could have argued. It could have been the perfect power play, especially with an inexperienced producer, but Richards didn't use that argument. He had made clear his disgust with the Broadway system and the need to appease the critics in his letter to Wilson. He was not about to support the system he despised. The stalemate dragged on.

Hays ultimately decided to move ahead with the New York run, but the tempest had only just begun. The play was set to open on March 27 at the 46th Street Theatre. Rehearsals were testy, though, as Hays was still demanding control over the script, bolstered by her exacting general manager and encouraged by her iconic star. The rest of the cast had been left out of the contretemps, but it was impossible to ignore at this point. Vance was reticent to make waves, which made his onstage confrontation with the commanding Jones all the more powerful. He brought a breathtaking innocence to the role of a son who just wants his unbending father to like him. Vance kept to the sidelines. "I was a little boy and nobody talked to me," he said. But between San Francisco and Broadway, he learned that the little girl playing Raynell in the last scene was going to be replaced with her understudy. She had been playing the role since the Yale Rep production, and Vance was loyal to her and furious that she wouldn't make her Broadway debut. It was Jones who had suggested the casting change; the understudy was light-skinned, which would telegraph that Troy's lover was most likely a white woman, making his infidelity a double betrayal. Jones wanted the understudy to take over, but Vance wanted the original girl to get a chance to perform on Broadway, even if she had grown too old for the role. "It was a bitter, bitter fight," Vance said. He shared his anger with Richards, who told him, "Courtney, in forty years I've never seen anything like this." It was yet another battle, pitting the producer and the marquee star against the playwright and the director. The little girl was recast.

Vance was crushed by the power struggle. "He couldn't understand why we were so fractured," Jones said of the conflict. "For him, it was devastating that we weren't getting along and that there were lawyers involved. Yale had made sure that mess stayed away. That was what the ivory tower was about. It was a mess, and he questioned his faith in everybody, including me. I broke his heart when he found out I was part of the revolt, if not the instigator of it."

The atmosphere in the rehearsal room in New York was quiet yet combustible, as if one wrong word could ignite a fiery showdown. And the situation grew more and more volatile as opening night approached. After the show began previews, the producer held a notes session, and she and Kamlot insisted vehemently that all of their changes be incorporated in the script. At the time, many in the commercial theater world knew Wilson as a shy, soft-spoken man of few words who usually deferred to his director. But the producer and her manager had crossed a line. Wilson had the temperament of a steam engine that can hold only so much water before it explodes. And his steam engine was cranked too high. Wilson lunged at Kamlot, but his colleagues kept him from pummeling the general manager. "Some words were exchanged between August and the general manager," Jones said. Jones had a theory about what was going on beneath the surface of the fight. "August didn't like white men, including our producers. He didn't like his father, and his father was white. I don't think he ever came to terms with that. He certainly didn't in his writing."

In fact, Jones had lobbied both Wilson and the producer to take out a line that Troy says to Cory, who wants to be recruited to play football in college. "The white man ain't gonna let you get nowhere with that football noway," Troy tells his son. He also complains about his own failed attempts to become a star in Major League Baseball. He says, "If they got a white fellow sitting on the bench . . . you can bet your last dollar he can't play! The colored guy got to be twice as good before he get on the team." Jones objected to that attitude. "I said, 'I don't need to say that,' but I didn't win. It was a problem for me on the page. If he would write about his father that would be one thing, but to have that seeping through Troy's consciousness his whole life is a pain in the ass."

Jones did not confront Wilson about his relationship with Frederick Kittel, but it was on his mind during the rehearsal process. "I was always on guard about it with August," he said. "I didn't know to what extent he was really in control of it. By control of it, I mean does he wake up every morning hating his father?" It was a question many asked about Wilson, but he refused to address the question, even before he became famous. He didn't talk about his father with Claude Purdy and Jacqui Shoholm, his best friends in St. Paul, and he certainly wasn't going to discuss it with Jones, who was trying to take control of his play. Wilson's parentage was none of Jones's business, and it certainly was not a factor in rehearsals. But Jones, like others in the gossipy theater world, speculated privately about Wilson's family background. Jones readily admits that there was no love lost between the two of them, even though he believed that Wilson had written the best stage role for him in decades. "I didn't like him," he said directly. "The doors were shut. You couldn't get in. I only knew the Black August

Wilson. I would like to have known the white August Wilson. He fought desperately to keep it at bay. He is genetically a white man as well as a Black man, and he did the best job of any artist I know of keeping them separate."

Jones's attitude, expressed years later, would surely have infuriated Wilson, who guarded his heritage closely. He chose to be Black, and he was Black. He defined himself. That was the end of it. He changed the subject whenever it came up. And Jones knew the subject was taboo, but that didn't stop him from speculating. Wilson was perceptive, and he later resented Jones's attitude and what he considered the veteran actor's tendency to defer to the white theater establishment rather than use his clout to change the system.

Jones also pointed out that both he and Wilson were married to white women at the time (as was Richards). Jones married actress Cecilia Hart, who played Desdemona to his Othello on Broadway, in 1982. And as the voice of the iconic Darth Vader in the first three *Star Wars* movies, he delivered the famously misquoted line, "No, *I* am your father," to a son who recoiled at the revelation.

Meanwhile Hays, who appeared to be a dabbler, exercised her producer's clout. She couldn't fire the playwright, so she fired Richards even though the production was inching closer to opening night. Jones stepped in as de facto director, and Wilson fumed. "She had to fire them to get control of the production again," Jones says. "I am not a director, but I had to function as a director at least until the lawyers worked it out."

Because Breglio represented both Wilson and Hays, he patched together a solution to avoid conflict of interest. He put together two teams of lawyers at his firm, Paul, Weiss, to represent each of them individually, and he acted as the middleman. Eventually, after a few days, a truce was reached. Wilson continued to work on the script and Hays backed off her demand to rewrite the ending. Breglio was working from Key West, where he was on vacation with his family, and he later intuited that both Hays and Wilson blamed him for suggesting they work together. "I realized later that I was an easy scapegoat since I was far from the fray and it's always easier to blame the lawyers (if not kill all of them)," he wrote in *I Wanna Be a Producer*.

Fences opened on March 26 to rave reviews. The play enjoyed a run of 525 performances. But all was not forgiven on opening night. The key players were still simmering, and the idea of all of them in one room pretending to make nice at a traditional opening-night party was absurd. Wilson and members of the cast booked a room at Sardi's, and they celebrated together as the reviews came in, first watching the television critics and waiting for the indispensable *Times* review. Rich admired the changes the team had made since he had first seen the play, even if he was still itching for a less traditional structure that did not invoke "the clunkier dramaturgy of Odets, Miller and Hansberry on this occasion." But he gave glowing reviews to the performers and to the poetry, once again anointing Wilson as "a major writer, combining a poet's ear for vernacular with a robust sense of humor (political and sexual), a sure instinct for crackling dramatic incident and a passionate commitment to a great subject."

After all the rewriting—and the meddling—*Fences* remains Wilson's most financially successful and popular play. It is also, however, his most conventional, rooted in a familiar structure. Maxson is an archetype: the Everyman with a tragic flaw. *Fences* lacks the deep mysticism of Wilson's later plays, in which the characters are haunted by four hundred years of bloody history. It does not reach across the ocean to Africa nor evoke the ghosts of the Middle Passage, and its characters are planted firmly in the soil of Pittsburgh in 1957. That said, it was remarkable for so memorably bringing a Black family to life on Broadway in a way that hadn't been achieved since Hansberry's *A Raisin in the Sun*. It's seamlessly constructed, and the monologues—Troy's epic battle with Death and Rose's declaration of self—are precursors of the soaring soliloquies to come. It's perfectly packaged in its universality, and the play, more than *Ma Rainey*, established Wilson as *the* voice of African American theater of his generation. Wilson knew he had strayed from his spiritual and poetic muse in writing a play to please audiences—and to prove himself to his critics and colleagues. He later said, without a second of hesitation, that it was his least favorite of all of his plays.

Audiences lapped it up, despite Wilson's self-criticism. In fact, according to Breglio, *Fences* was one of the most financially successful dramas of all time. Like *Ma Rainey*, it won the New York Drama Critics' Circle Award for Best Play. And on April 16, 1987, it was awarded the Pulitzer Prize for Best Drama. It beat out Neil Simon's *Broadway Bound* and Lee Blessing's *A Walk in the Woods*, which was also developed at the O'Neill by a fellow playwright from Minnesota. Wilson was the first resident of Minnesota to win the Pulitzer for Drama.

Wilson attended the Pulitzer Prize luncheon that spring, which was in its fourth year of being held annually at the Low Library at Columbia University. At the event primarily known for honoring journalists (most of whom were white), Wilson sought out Rita Dove, the second African American to receive the Pulitzer for Poetry for her collection *Thomas and Beulah*. (Gwendolyn Brooks was the first, in 1950.) Dove's prizewinning collection was a series of semi-fictional poems about her grandparents, a topic that reminded Wilson of his own heritage. On the day that he was winning the most prestigious prize for U.S. playwrights, his mind turned to one person: his mother, Daisy. He noticed Dove, who was wearing a light blue dress she had purchased for $20 at a Goodwill store, sitting at another table. He wrote her a letter a few years later and told her Daisy would have been proud of her and of what her success represented for all Black women who were once little girls. He said Daisy would have put her in the same category as Ralph Bunche or Nat King Cole or Lena Horne and she would have taken pride in her own life and been proud of her own accomplishments. The letter touched Dove so much that she kept it—and the envelope it came in.

Wilson had a conversation with Dove after the luncheon, and he modestly confided in her that he had started out as a poet and that she had achieved what had once been his dream. The event itself was more of a journalism affair than a literary gathering. It was "quasi low-key and elevated" at the same time, Dove said, noting that "everyone was so busy being cool." She and Wilson shared a moment of connection. "We recognized that we had come a long way to get to this place, and I loved the warmth that he exuded," she said. "It felt like, here we are, the two unlikeliest suspects who have worked against assumptions of who we were in terms of our race. It felt like an energy bubble to be in this spot together."

Wilson, too, treasured the moment, and he later wrote a poem called "Meeting Rita Dove at the Pulitzer Luncheon." He sent it to her after she was appointed U.S. Poet Laureate in 1993. The first word of the poem is "blood": She reminded him of all the ancestral women in his lineage. She evoked the blood's memory. He was delighted that she had achieved what he had set out to do on the streets of Pittsburgh and ended the poem with a genuflection that came straight from the heart.

Wilson was at a high point and was busier than he had ever been. Claude Purdy had directed a production of *Ma Rainey* at the American Conservatory Theater in San Francisco that spring, and Wilson was traversing the country overseeing regional theater productions of *Joe Turner* while preparing for the upcoming world premiere of *Piano Lesson* at Yale Rep. He was home in St. Paul when he got the word about the Pulitzer, and he shared the news with Purdy and Shoholm. They, along with his wife, had supported him while he was still an unknown writer given to hanging out in bars and chain-smoking. *Ma Rainey* was playing at Penumbra in St. Paul, in a production directed by Purdy and starring his friend Terry Bellamy in the explosive role of Levee. Everyone in St. Paul said the role was tailor-made for Bellamy, a strapping, mustachioed man with a fierce independent streak and a hot temper.

And the awards kept coming. The man who had sent his plays off to theaters and to the O'Neill only to be rejected over and over was now quite literally the talk of the town. Minnesota governor Rudy Perpich proclaimed May 27 to be August Wilson Day at an event held at the Martin Luther King Center, the home of Penumbra Theatre not far from Wilson's apartment. St. Paul mayor George Latimer also proclaimed it to be August Wilson Day in Wilson's adopted home city. A crowd filled the small, stifling King Center gymnasium that evening. Wilson wiped sweat off his brow before the ceremony and asked if he could smoke. Richards was there and his words did not reveal any ongoing friction after their battle with their Broadway producer or with each other over the director's compensation. "This is a talent the theater must support," Richards said, adding, "There is no law, no money that can call talent into being."

Wilson, who was still digesting the lessons he had learned from the fight to control his work with *Fences*, was demure and modest that evening. Fidgeting at the podium, he said that St. Paul "is not my home, but it has been the place where I could discover the voice inside me." Judy Oliver also spoke briefly, noting that Wilson's success had changed both of their lives for the better. "Now we can pay our bills," she noted, deadpan. She wasn't kidding.

This was the first time the state had declared a day honoring a playwright, and it was just another in this year of firsts. *Fences* was nominated for six Tony Awards: Best Play, Best Direction of a Play, Best Lead Actor (Jones), Best Featured Actress (Mary Alice), and two for Best Featured Actor (Courtney Vance and Frankie Faison, who played Gabriel). The 41st Annual Tony Awards were presented in a live broadcast from New York's Mark Hellinger Theatre on June 7.

It was a cloudy, drizzly evening, with temperatures in the high fifties. Wilson escorted his wife and Sakina to the ceremony. They stayed at the Hotel Edison, where Wilson was now a familiar face. He was still on chilly terms with producer Hays and reserved an unspoken disdain for Jones. But the event turned out to be a joyous occasion. Jones and Mary Alice won in the acting categories, and Richards won for directing. Wilson took the award for Best Play. When Glenn Close and William Hurt presented that award, Hays was the first to make it to the stage. Far along in her first pregnancy, the dainty producer wore a billowy pink silk maternity gown that was designed by Pauline Trigère and adorned with a poufy, girlish bow on the bodice. Wilson took the microphone first, and he thanked his daughter, his family, and "all the Troy Maxsons." He thanked Richards, "one of the giants of American theater." He saved his final tribute for his wife, acknowledging, "most importantly, my wife, Judy Oliver, who has been there at three o'clock in the morning, when the rest of the world has been asleep."

When he was finished, he ceded the microphone to Hays, who had a dazed look on her face. Many years later, she claimed she "saved" *Fences*, but on the night of the Tony Awards she could muster only one sentence. Looking overwhelmed, she looked out at the audience and whispered in a thin, nasally voice, "I think I'm going to give birth right now."

That's the way that go.

CHAPTER TEN

Shining Like New Money

*You should always respect what you are and your culture
because if your art is going to mean anything, that is where
it comes from.*

—ROMARE BEARDEN

In July 1987, Wilson received a letter at home in St. Paul that began with the salutation, "Revolutionary Greetings, Mbulu." It could only be from one person: his old friend, the poet and playwright Rob Penny, an Africana Studies professor at Pitt. Now that he had achieved fame with *Fences*, Wilson never mentioned the name from the old days, but Penny always remembered. He was writing to invite Wilson home. The playwright had granted Pittsburgh's Kuntu Repertory Theatre permission to produce *Ma Rainey's Black Bottom* in September, with Vernell Lillie directing. The team had petitioned Pittsburgh mayor Richard Caliguiri to declare September 26 August Wilson Day to coincide with the opening of the production. He had already been feted by officials in St. Paul, and now Pittsburgh was honoring its native son.

Fences was still on Broadway; *Joe Turner* was making the rounds of the regional theaters before a Broadway run, with a production at Arena Stage in Washington, D.C., in October; and his latest play, *The Piano Lesson*, was set to debut at Yale Rep in November. His first triumph, *Ma Rainey*, was enjoying an extended run at the Los Angeles Theatre Center, in a production directed by Claude Purdy and starring St. Paul actor Abdul

Salaam El Razzac. Wilson jetted from city to city, stopping in to visit the O'Neill even though he didn't have a play there that summer.

He was back in St. Paul on August 5. The St. Paul City Council had invited him to speak at its meeting and to accept a proclamation officially honoring him. Wilson gave a speech so elegant that council member Janice Rettman likened his words to "The New Colossus," Emma Lazarus's famous poem. "It could be to St. Paul what the inscription on the Statue of Liberty is to America," Rettman said of the speech. Mayor George Latimer vowed to hire a calligrapher to inscribe Wilson's words on a banner to display in his office. Wilson began by saying he had lain awake all night searching for the right words to say, but in fact, he ended his remarks by recycling, almost word for word, the poem "Home," which he had written as a tribute to Yale Rep two years earlier. He just replaced a few words at the end with "I walk up to the city of St. Paul," not Yale Rep. "I have carried in my pockets to bargain my passage memories, acorns and a wild heart that plies its trade with considerate and alarming passion," he began. He ended with a baseball reference that had been so apropos when he was speaking about *Fences*. "As I remember now, as remembering then, the time I batted .400 and sent 11 home runs crashing into windows of the houses behind the park. I remember to touch each base nonchalantly—the same bases as in life, the same object: to find a way home, even at the start. So I walk up to the city of St. Paul. I enter. I take off my hat and I hang it up. I'm here. I'm home." The once-shy playwright was getting used to these kinds of events and used stock phrases over and over again. The poem he wrote for Yale Rep may be hanging on a wall somewhere in the Twin Cities.

But even though he sang the praises of his adopted city, Wilson was rarely there, given the demand for his work and simultaneous productions. In fact, that summer, he and John Breglio had hopped into a stretch limousine and were chauffeured from Breglio's Midtown Manhattan office to a sprawling estate in Englewood, New Jersey, a tony community that was a hotbed for celebrities with cash to spare. A twenty-minute drive took them from the theater district to "Bubble Hill," a sprawling estate on five acres. Comedian-actor Eddie Murphy had bought the ten-thousand-square-foot home for a reported $3.5 million in 1985 and more than doubled the size of the mansion, equipping it with a bowling alley, a home theater, seven bedrooms, thirteen bathrooms, an indoor and outdoor pool, plus a professional recording studio. In 1987, Murphy, who was raised in Brooklyn and spent a year in foster care, was a Hollywood wunderkind. He had smashed box office records with *48 Hrs.*, *Trading Places*, and *Beverly Hills Cop.* He was sitting pretty: at twenty-six, he was a superstar at Paramount Pictures, and the studio would roll over backward for its most lucrative actor. It turned out that Murphy, who cut his teeth in New York stand-up before earning acclaim as a cast member on *Saturday Night Live*, had seen *Fences* on Broadway, and he wanted to star in a film version. His manager had called Breglio to request a meeting to inquire about buying the screen rights. Murphy was too young to play Troy Maxson, the James Earl Jones role, but he had his eyes on the role of Cory.

Wilson and Breglio enjoyed themselves on the ride to Bubble Hill, settling into the plush seats of the limousine and then laughing about the vastness of Murphy's massive, yet somewhat empty, estate. A giant garage housed more cars than one person could possibly ever need. They were ushered into the library, which boasted a full-length portrait of Murphy over a fireplace. (Coincidentally, *Fences* star James Earl Jones has a full-length portrait of himself over his fireplace at his rambling estate in rural upstate New York; he, however, is in character and costume for the title role in *Othello*.) Murphy was a bachelor at the time, and Bubble Hill was a slang term for "party."

Murphy kept his guests waiting and when he eventually appeared, he was "quite nervous and extremely deferential to August," Breglio said, noting that Wilson was amused by the actor's demeanor. Wilson laid out his ideas for the film. Breglio recalled that an enthusiastic Murphy readily agreed to the terms, but Wilson later described a somewhat testy exchange. He informed Murphy that he wanted a Black director, to which Murphy replied, "I don't want to hire nobody just 'cause they're Black." Wilson replied immediately, "Neither do I." That was the end of it, and Paramount sealed the deal, paying Wilson $1 million to option the rights to the play and an additional six-figure sum for a screenplay. The deal was announced in early September, and the comedian was in no hurry to start production. "Eddie Murphy thinks that *Fences* is so good, it's ir-relevant when we make it," his manager Bob Wachs said shortly after the announcement. But nobody expected that thirty years would pass before the film was eventually made—and without Murphy. The impasse was over Wilson's demand for a Black director. Wilson later wrote, "I wanted to hire somebody talented, who understood the play and saw the possibil-ities of the film, who would approach my work with the same amount of passion and measure of respect with which I approach it, and who shared the cultural responsibilities of the characters."

The seven-figure sale of the rights hit the newspapers a little more than a week before the celebration in Pittsburgh, and Wilson's connection with the biggest African American box office star only increased the play-wright's cachet. He was in Washington, D.C., rehearsing the Arena Stage production of *Joe Turner*. Wilson wanted to be a constant presence at the rehearsals, so he sent his older sister, Freda, to speak in his place when the Pittsburgh City Council honored him with a proclamation at its meeting on Monday, September 21. She addressed the council, listing her brother's accomplishments and celebrating his hometown roots. "August Wilson," she said, "speaks for the ghetto, the Hill. The greatest compliment we can pay him is to recognize him as our bard, the voice of our dreams and dra-mas set in different eras of time."

Wilson did take time away from rehearsal to attend the opening-night performance of *Ma Rainey* and to be feted at a post-performance recep-tion in Pittsburgh on September 26. Kuntu Repertory set up a whirlwind two-day schedule for the playwright, with back-to-back interviews and an appearance at a local high school. By this point, Wilson was used to meeting the press and to giving advice to aspiring young writers—he had, after all, learned how to give the same eloquent but recycled speech to a new audience. But he was still living and traveling modestly. He sub-mitted a three-day expense account for his Pittsburgh visit and was re-imbursed for the small amount of $97.92. He took one of his meals at Kentucky Fried Chicken, and his brother Edwin Kittel drove him to his appointments. Wilson never learned to drive, and friends and family readily chauffeured him.

The play was performed at the Stephen Foster Memorial, the land-marked performing arts center in the heart of the Pitt campus. The Gothic revival building sits in front of the university's towering Cathedral of Learning, where Wilson once borrowed books on the sly with the help of a friendly and supportive library aide. A flight of granite steps leads to the grand entrance, with its two sets of imposing red doors; the memorial building boasts two theaters as well as a shrine to its eponymous composer, Stephen Collins Foster. Dubbed "the father of American music," Foster was a songwriter known for his popular parlor music, but many of the songs in his oeuvre were performed in minstrel shows. In that sense, his work (which included such tunes as "Camptown Races," "Oh! Susanna," and "My Old Kentucky Home") was a stark contrast to the African American blues music Wilson celebrated in his plays—specifically, *Ma Rainey*.

Nevertheless, that history was in the background on the night of the celebration. Wilson's friends drove him to the event in a 1920s Jaguar, after taking a spin around the Hill District so he could see his old haunts. He arrived wearing a sharp black suit and listened politely during a reading of the mayor's proclamation before the play began. The laudatory document read "August Wilson, as poet and playwright, as a genius and gentleman par excellence, has raised the Pittsburgh experience to a national and international spotlight of dazzling creativity." During intermission, the members of Kuntu Rep presented Wilson with a poster-sized plaque honoring his work. The balding and bearded playwright who had learned how to speak to crowds was, on this occasion, at a loss for words. "It is very hard to express the eloquence of the heart," he said, before the full house broke out in spontaneous applause. At the Pulitzer ceremony, he had told Rita Dove that she had achieved his dream, but this hometown celebration had been his lifelong dream. He had wanted to prove himself to the nuns, the teacher who accused him of plagiarism, the elders on the Hill . . . his mother. This was Pittsburgh, and this celebration was the one that choked him up.

After the performance, friends and colleagues from his early days feted him at a jam-packed reception. It was held at Pitt's Forbes Quadrangle, a hall that sits on the former site of Forbes Field, once home to the Pittsburgh Pirates. It was there that a teenage Wilson first shook the hand of Hank Aaron. But on the night of the gala, he was the star player.

Poet Maisha Baton, who had performed with Wilson in his semi-autobiographical play *Recycle*, began with a passionate speech. "You have always been consistently who you are. I think there's a lesson there," she told her friend. "Even [to] people who did not like the fact that he was August, he was *himself*." She also noted that he was secure in his Black identity and his commitment to celebrating the Black experience. The reporter for the *Pittsburgh Courier*, the city's prestigious Black-owned newspaper, took that as an opportunity to mention that "Wilson is of mixed parentage, a white father and Black mother." Wilson hated those kinds of references, because he identified 100 percent with his Black heritage. His colleagues in the professional theater world knew not to raise the subject with him because it was a sensitive topic. The reporter for the *Courier* did not have that inhibition. Baton also implied that Wilson had not always been fully accepted in Pittsburgh's Black cultural circle. "As Pittsburghers, no matter how jive we may be at times, you are someone that Pittsburgh— Black Pittsburgh, I know—is proud of."

Again, Wilson struggled for the right words to say. His speech was full of "abrupt starts and intense and cautious" pauses. "Perhaps this is the most extraordinary day of my life," he told the crowd of hundreds of admirers. "I have so many, many mixed emotions. So many things—people I haven't seen in 20 years, I see here. There's so much going on inside me, I can't properly express. . . . I want to say thank you." Wilson had been calm and composed when he accepted his Tony Award on national television and he could recite years-old poetry with strangers, but back on his home turf, the place that mattered most, he was almost lost for words.

Rob Penny, who had known him since his beginnings as a poet and had cochaired the August Wilson Day committee, had no doubts about his friend's accomplishments, which he extolled in his poetic, prepared remarks. "Yo, Bro," he began, before comparing Wilson's contributions to Black culture to those of Ma Rainey, Josh Gibson, Sojourner Truth, Sterling Brown, and Amiri Baraka. He placed him in the blues pantheon, along with Blind Lemon Jefferson, Billie Holiday, and Julio Finn. "Quiet as it's kept, his song has always been right there in his throat," Penny said. "In the Book of the Blues, it is written that in the beginning was the sound: August Wilson, a great artist, has utilized the sounds of his song to put us in the mood of life."

Wilson was surrounded by reporters and photographers during the event, but the next day, he joined his family privately for a noon Sunday mass at St. Benedict the Moor church on the Hill. He sat in a pew with his family, quietly observing, but after the Gospel reading and the sermon, the pastor announced that Wilson was present and asked him to say a few words from the pulpit. The churchgoers leapt to their feet and applauded, which he had come to appreciate in the theater but did not expect at a church service. He composed himself and said, "Coming back implies going away." He then talked about his mother, Daisy, who "founded a community of people" and he thanked her for "her justice and dignity." He also paid tribute to his friends at the church, saying they always helped him, despite their own struggles. He carried the communion wafers to the altar with his niece and nephew and then snuck out early, unnerved by the spontaneous attention. He stood on the sidewalk and smoked until his family and friends joined him after the service.

The day after the mass, he left Pittsburgh to return to Washington, D.C., for *Joe Turner* rehearsals at the Arena Stage to prepare for an early-October opening. The play, set in 1911, in some ways echoes the story of his ancestors. The elders in his family didn't talk much about the past and he only had sketchy details about life on Spear Tops Mountain and of his great-grandmother Eller Cutler, but the characters and plot of *Joe Turner* hold a mirror up to his heritage.

Wilson said he got the inspiration for the play while thumbing through the pages of *National Geographic* in 1983. He was up late at the apartment on Selby Avenue in St. Paul sitting at the desk he had fashioned from a wooden door atop two filing cabinets. That makeshift desk was just as important to him as the Royal Standard typewriter had been two decades earlier. "The moment that I got my desk was the most liberating moment of being a writer," he said. "I had a space to write in. It wasn't temporary. It was truly liberating, the biggest thing that happened to me." He cherished the midnight hours at that desk, and that night he was working on a poem about a former enslaved man who was searching for his lost family. But then he came across an image of *Mill Hand's Lunch Bucket*, the Romare Bearden collage. He had been inspired when he first discovered Bearden, whose art evokes the richness and beauty of the African American experience. "In Bearden I found my artistic mentor and sought, and still aspire, to make my plays the equal of his canvases," he once wrote.

This particular image intrigued him. "It showed a man coming down the stairs of a boardinghouse reaching for his lunch bucket, a woman with her purse apparently going out, and a child sitting at a table drinking a glass of milk," he said. "And in the center of the painting was this man with a hat and coat who was sitting in this posture of abject defeat." He started writing about the painting, depicting Pittsburgh at the beginning of the twentieth century as "the sons and daughters of newly freed African slaves wander into the city." He later told Todd Kreidler that he wrote feverishly into the night, ending with a sentence that would inspire his next play. "Foreigners in a strange land, they carry as part and parcel of their baggage a long line of separation and dispersement which informs their sensibilities and marks their conduct as they search for ways to reconnect, to reassemble, to give clear and luminous meaning to the song which is both a wail and a whelp of joy." It is the last sentence of his eloquent preface to the play.

He continued to ponder the man in the overcoat and hat in Bearden's collage. Who was he? Why was he bowed over in abject defeat? "I wanted to find out who this man was, so I began to write a short story called 'The Matter of Mill Hand's Lunch Bucket,'" he said, explaining that the act of writing became a process of discovery. "After about twelve pages, I abandoned it and began to write a play. I did not quite understand what the play was about until I was listening to a song by W. C. Handy called 'Joe Turner's Come and Gone,' in which Handy said that the story of the blues could not be told without the story of Joe Turner." Joe Turney, not Turner, in fact, was the brother of Tennessee governor Peter Turney, who served from 1893 to 1897; he was notorious for enslaving men for seven years on his chain gang. When women discovered their husbands or lovers had disappeared, they lamented in song:

> *Dey tell me Joe Turner's come an' gone—O, Lawdy!*
> *Tell me Joe Turner's come an' gone—O, Lawdy!*
> *Got my man—an'—gone.*

> *Come wid his fo'ty links of chain—O, Lawdy!*
> *Come wid his fo'ty links of chain—O, Lawdy!*
> *Got my man, an' gone.*

He originally named the play after the Bearden painting, but at Richards's request, he changed the name in a later draft. The play is set in a Pittsburgh boardinghouse. Migrants from the South flock to the city; they are not that far removed from slavery. The boardinghouse is a lively place, with tenants coming in and out of a homey kitchen permeated with the aroma of warm biscuits and fried chicken. The itinerant residents seek a new identity, a chance to seize opportunities their parents never had. Seth Holly, the freeborn proprietor, is an entrepreneur who dreams of opening a tinsmith shop, a path to prosperity. A high-spirited guitar player named Jeremy Furlow hopes to make his fortune playing in clubs rather than building roads. Mattie Campbell pines over a lover who abandoned her and yearns for a lasting romance. Mollie Cunningham wants to make it on her own—she has had enough of men who wander off. Seth, who was raised in the North by free parents, sees his tenants "coming up from the country carrying Bibles and guitars looking for freedom." He has no patience for Jeremy, in particular. "That boy done carried a guitar all the way from North Carolina. What he gonna find out? What he gonna do with that guitar? This is the city." Wilson's grandmother and mother arrived in Pittsburgh from North Carolina with similar hopes for a fresh start. Zonia Wilson arrived in 1929, Daisy Wilson in 1937. They may not have carried Bibles or guitars, but they lived in boardinghouses and eventually learned the ways of the city.

The boardinghouse hums along under the skilled hands of Bertha Holly, Seth's wife. She welcomes the wanderers who step into her kitchen, including the white traveling peddler Rutherford Selig. (The name choice is uncanny: Wilson's great-great-grandfather Calvin Twitty was enslaved on a plantation in Rutherford, North Carolina.) Selig shows up in the first scene and Bertha immediately offers him a biscuit and a cup of coffee. Apart from the two music industry professionals and the policeman in *Ma Rainey*, Selig is the only white character to appear onstage in Wilson's cycle. He explicitly wanted to shine the spotlight on Black men and women, but white characters are an unseen, ominous presence in all of his plays. They control the recording industry in *Ma Rainey*, and in *Fences* they put up roadblocks in Major League Baseball, making it impossible for Troy to break the color barrier. In *Joe Turner*, an unseen labor boss demands a portion of Black workers' wages in order for them to keep their jobs. Wilson told the playwright Douglas Post that he was conscious of these unseen characters as he wrote, and that he had a backstory for each of them.

But Selig is a complicated character. Known in the Black community as the "People Finder," he takes names of missing people and charges a dollar to find them. Some value this service, but Bertha is skeptical, even if she welcomes him at her table. "This old People Finding business is for the birds," she says. "He ain't never found nobody he ain't took away." And Selig comes from a long line of "People Finders." His great-grandfather worked on a slave ship, ferrying Africans across the ocean. His father was in the business of capturing people who escaped slavery. Selig sells pots and pans door-to-door, so he knows where people live, enabling him to reunite Black people who were separated from one another during the Jim Crow era. His history is tainted, and it is debatable whether his work is truly benevolent or simply expedient. But Wilson defended the character: "He's not evil at all," he told an interviewer. "In fact, he's performing a very valuable service for the community. The fact that his father was a 'People Finder' has no bearing on Selig's character." Wilson was aware that some interpreted Selig as a profiteer, so he brought him back later in *Gem of the Ocean*. He likened him to the "guy who opens up a hardware store in the Black community. He's got a long history of involvement."

But while Selig is accepted in the boardinghouse, the order is upset when a newcomer appears, an "old wild-eyed, mean-looking" man named Herald Loomis. He looks as if he "killed somebody gambling over a quarter," and Seth takes an immediate dislike to him. It is later revealed that Loomis spent seven years working on a chain gang; he was pressed into illegal bondage by Joe Turner.

Loomis shows up with his eleven-year-old daughter, Zonia. Wearing a dark hat and cloaked in a long woolen coat, *"he is unable to harmonize the forces that swirl around him,"* his dejection mirroring the mood of the man sitting at the table in Bearden's painting. Loomis is searching for his wife, who left his daughter with her mother and took off for Pittsburgh while he was laboring in chains. Zonia, of course, was Wilson's grandmother's name. She left her three children with her mother and traveled to Pittsburgh with Bynam Wilson. Her children came north almost a decade later, after Eller Cutler passed away on the mountain.

He paid tribute to his grandfather by naming a pivotal character Bynum, a clairvoyant conjure man who on the surface is given to "old mumbo jumbo nonsense" and "heebie-jeebie stuff," but who is actually a binding force who helps Loomis discover his roots and find his "song." Wilson didn't know the real Bynam, who disappeared from Pittsburgh and ended up dying alone in Black Hawk County, Iowa, in 1980, unbeknownst to his family. His obituary said, "There are no immediate survivors." Bynam had also left another family behind in North Carolina before he married Zonia in 1928. Wilson had written an ode to his grandfather, and he was a beloved part of the family lore. His mother had taken the name Wilson, and Bynam was a part of the family, whether he was present or not. Wilson understood that his grandfather had what he called the "walking blues," which is also the name of a blues standard written by Son House and recorded by such artists as Robert Johnson and Muddy Waters. In *Fences*, Troy's friend Bono asks, "Ain't you ever heard of nobody having the walking blues?" He explained it this way: "They walk out their front door and just take on down one road or another and keep on walking."

The fictional Bynum, however, is a searcher and a healer who connects Herald Loomis to his past and, thus, helps him bring about his own salvation. Loomis is broken—by the loss of his wife and by the chains he wore for seven years. He is seeking closure with his wife, but he is also looking for a way to "reconnect and reassemble." The landlord Seth sees him as a dark and evil force, but Bynum understands his search, as he, too, is searching for his "shiny man," an elusive supernatural being who is the answer to his own "search for life." The play is set in a well-made, naturalistic boardinghouse replete with the smell of fresh bread, but it is also a conduit to centuries of history that stretch back to the first slave ships crossing the Atlantic Ocean to Jamestown in 1619. While the boarders go about everyday routines like visiting the outhouse and eating Sunday supper, they are also linked to mystical rituals and a shared past. At the end of the first act, the boardinghouse residents break out into an African juba, singing and dancing in an ecstatic demonstration of rhythmic hand clapping and knee slapping. The scene is joyous and entirely unexpected, and all the residents participate, except Loomis, who at first objects, but then suffers a spasmodic fit. He speaks of "bones walking on top of the water." Bynum is the only character who reaches out to Loomis, and he guides him through his terrifying visions. The act ends with Loomis unable to move, lying prostrate on the floor. "My legs won't stand up," he says. "My legs won't stand up."

The bones represent the Middle Passage, but the image is also biblical. Wilson had had enough catechism drummed into him in his early years, yet he was suspicious of organized religion—even though he acknowledged its significance as a pivotal binding force in the Black community. During rehearsals for *Joe Turner*, he consulted musical director Dwight Andrews, whom he had first met when Andrews was a theology and music theory student at Yale, as well as pastor of the Black Church at Yale. Andrews was the resident expert on both music and theology. "He looked at me with a cynical eye because I was a minister, but he respected it and ran his biblical questions by me," Andrews said. He, like everyone else in the room, was stunned the first time the actors read the scene with the bones walking on water. He recalled the "Valley of the Bones" story from Ezekiel 37, in which the Lord raises the bones of the people of Israel. According to the scripture, "There was a noise, a rattling sound, and the bones came together, bone to bone." The story is different in Wilson's play, but it is equally miraculous. "He took the material he needed for his own circumstances," Andrews says. "He wasn't trying to be a theologian, but there was a nexus between the biblical story and the Middle Passage." Wilson said repeatedly that his mission was to create his own mythology, in his life and in his work, and he drew inspiration from many sources.

Wilson had submitted the play, still titled *Mill Hand's Lunch Bucket*, to be developed at the O'Neill in the summer of 1984. There were twenty-two playwrights in residence that summer, and Wilson, back for the third time, was part of the inner circle. His friend Amy Saltz was assigned to direct the play, and she immediately knew that she was in over her head. "I was intimidated by *Joe Turner*," she said. "It is arguably his best play, but I didn't think I was the right person to direct it." Wilson was a good camper at the O'Neill. He accepted every director assigned to his work. It was only when his plays moved outside of the O'Neill cocoon that he insisted on Black directors. But Saltz readily admitted that she didn't understand the play's deep mysticism. At a design meeting, Wilson talked about the Bearden painting, which he had yet to mention to Saltz. It helped her comprehend the play much better, but even years later, she still thinks she did not do the play justice.

Saltz was particularly flummoxed by the juba scene at the end of the first act. But Ebony Jo-Ann was in residence that summer. The dynamic young actress had understudied Theresa Merritt in *Ma Rainey*, and she was anything but shy. She had a small role in *Joe Turner* and took it upon herself to school the director. "August would walk in circles and smoke cigarettes in the background and throw his hands up in the air and say, 'I just write. I just write,'" she said. "I am like, 'What in the name of heaven?' I didn't get upset with Amy. There was no possibility she knew what she was dealing with. Amy would say things like 'What do y'all do?' What do you mean, 'What do *we* do?'" Jo-Ann stepped in and worked with the actors on the juba choreography.

Claude Purdy was also there that summer, and he played the role of Bynum. Angela Bassett played Martha Pentecost, Loomis's estranged wife who shows up at the end and rejects him because he isn't clean enough—or Christian enough—for her. But he slashes his chest in a ritual baptism, and the play ends with Bynum saying one of those killer final Wilson lines: "Herald Loomis, you shining! You shining like new money!"

At the O'Neill, it was clear that the play was too long, which was not a surprise to anyone. That summer, Wilson took long walks on the beach, often headed for Fred's Shanty, a fried-fish place about two miles away from the O'Neill. One day, he caught up with Carl Capotorto, a twenty-five-year-old aspiring writer with an MFA in playwriting from Columbia University. (Capotorto went on to create the role of Little Paulie Germani on the television classic *The Sopranos*.) Capotorto was a bit in awe. He had heard Wilson read *Joe Turner* at the preconference. "It was the first time we were alone together," Capotorto recalled. "He said, 'I have come up with a career plan for myself. I am going to write one play about the Black American experience for every decade, from the beginning of the twentieth century to the end.' I was younger. I had no pattern in my head like that. I had no such big idea about a career pursuit. This was the summer of 1984. It sounded like a new idea."

Wilson mentioned the idea a few months later to a feature writer for the *Pittsburgh Press* in November, saying simply, "As it turns out, I am writing a play for each decade of the 20th century and trying to isolate the most important ideas that confronted Blacks." Later, however, he made the story of the conception of his ten-play cycle a bit more dramatic. He told interviewers that the idea dawned on him at a friend's seder. "The first words of the ceremony were 'We were slaves in Egypt,'" he told the *New York Times* about a seder he attended in 1986. "I thought this is something we should do. Blacks in America want to forget about slavery—the stigma, the shame. That's the wrong move." The connection was spot-on, but he had already come up with his ambitious plan.

The play underwent many revisions at the O'Neill, and it debuted at Yale Rep two years later, opening on April 29, 1986, at the same time that Wilson and Richards were drawing up plans with Hays to produce *Fences* on Broadway. By this point, Wilson was a familiar face at the Rep. Richards had provided a safe haven for him, as well as for Athol Fugard, who also debuted his work in New Haven before Broadway. Charles S. Dutton came back to his alma mater to play the towering role of Herald Loomis, paired with Ed Hall as Bynum, the conjure man. "There's nothing like sitting down to write a play and knowing it's going to be produced," Wilson said at the time. "If every regional theater would only commit themselves, not to a play, but to a playwright. That's what makes me. You can fail and your life won't disappear." Still, on the eve of the opening, he told a reporter that he was "worried about disappointing that audience" and pretended to be a theater patron begrudgingly putting on his coat and heading off to see yet another play by August Wilson.

He didn't need to worry about failing and disappearing—at least in terms of the critical reception. Rich again made the sojourn to New Haven and he found what he felt was missing in *Fences*. The play, he wrote, "is at once a teeming canvas of Black America at a specific moment in time and a spiritual allegory with a Melville whammy." He added that the relationship between Loomis and Bynum adds "a metaphorical force new to Mr. Wilson's work," which was precisely the intent. He did have reservations about the ending (which was becoming a common theme with the first productions of Wilson's plays), which mirrors the final scene in Act 1. But the review, yet again, cemented Wilson's growing reputation.

Wilson was buoyed by the reception to *Joe Turner* when he arrived at the O'Neill that summer of 1986 to work on his fourth play in the cycle, *The Piano Lesson*. He was keeping an exhilarating but grueling schedule. He left the O'Neill and went straight into rehearsals for the next production of *Joe Turner* at Boston's Huntington Theatre. This was the next of several stops in the development process: the play was also scheduled to run at Arena Stage in Washington, D.C., and the Old Globe Theatre in San

Diego. Richards was expanding on the idea he had dreamt up for *Fences*, which marked a change in the League of Resident Theatres, the umbrella organization of the nation's professional theaters. (Resident, or regional, theaters are professional nonprofit organizations outside of New York that produce a series of plays, usually offering a subscription series. Audiences are local and loyal. Because of their nonprofit status, these theaters raise funds from patrons and local businesses and often receive grants from foundations and government sources. This business model enables these institutions to take chances on new plays outside of the commercial pressure of Broadway.) The concept of touring the same production to nonprofit houses before a Broadway run was solidifying, and administrators at some of the nation's top theaters were increasingly seeing the Richards-Wilson system as the wave of the future.

"The Broadway system is a relic. It's just about moribund," Huntington managing director Michael Maso said before the Boston opening. He added that the regional theaters are the place "where serious theater and serious playwriting are being nurtured." He and some, but not all, of his colleagues applauded this model because it allowed new dramas to succeed based on merit, not on commercial success. "Success or failure in conventional commercial terms is irrelevant in all the terms that really matter to serious theater," Maso said. "Broadway is for expense-account ticket purchases. Great plays that don't fit the mold can fold on Broadway in two weeks—even if they're good or even great plays. But they're labeled 'failures,' and what a helluva way to nurture theater."

While the Huntington wasn't focused on commercial success, the administrators didn't have to worry. The play opened on September 27 to a packed house. Charles S. Dutton had other commitments, so he was replaced with Delroy Lindo in the role of Herald Loomis. Angela Bassett repeated the role of Loomis's wife, Martha Pentecost. Boston, with all its universities, boasts a sophisticated audience, and many in the house that night were stunned and mesmerized by the bones scene that ends Act 1, when the juba ends and Loomis falls into a paroxysm of tremors. Lindo nailed the character, looming like a haunted shadow in his tattered hat and long black cloak. *Boston Globe* critic Jay Carr described him as "an ax blade, ready to fall." The second act packed just as powerful a punch and an even more dramatic conclusion. By the time Bassett appeared, looking stern and haunted, the audience was pumped. And when the play reached its galvanic climax when Herald Loomis slashes his chest as a way of freeing himself of his chains, the audience leapt to its feet seconds after Bynum said, "Herald Loomis, you shining! You shining like new money!" Maso was right: you couldn't pay for the kind of response the play received from the audience and the press. Carr began by calling the play "one of the most powerful and important plays on Black (or white) American life in years." Wilson was reaching back to a communal African past and the character of Bynum was more than just full of "mumbo jumbo nonsense." He was a link to the tribal past where medicine men healed wounds both physical and spiritual.

Many of the names in the play have significant meaning. Wilson named his character Herald, not Harold; he is a messenger of personal and spiritual freedom that is yet to arrive. His estranged wife, Martha, now goes by the last name Pentecost, a reference to the Christian holiday that takes place fifty days after Easter to commemorate the biblical story about the Holy Spirit descending upon Jesus Christ's followers and apostles.

Wilson said repeatedly that if he had never written anything but *Joe Turner*, he would be satisfied, and the reception in Boston confirmed his belief in the play. The play is deeply personal. While Herald Loomis exorcised his demons, Wilson purged some of his own. Martha Pentecost, dressed *"as befitting a member of an Evangelist church,"* is unforgiving and buttoned-up, imploring her estranged husband to walk the walk of a committed Christian. She sternly rebukes Loomis for not being Christian or devout enough, which echoes back to Wilson's experience in his first marriage to Brenda Burton.

He also includes two scenes with Loomis's daughter, Zonia, and a neighborhood boy named Reuben. The scenes are seemingly extraneous to the rest of the plot, but in one, Zonia shares her first kiss with the boy. It is a moment of pure innocence in an otherwise troubled world, the promise of a future the other, more seasoned characters cannot imagine. Wilson had a thing for such coming-of-age moments; he later described his own first kiss as a "conspiracy of boundless joy."

Wilson had dedicated the play to Sakina, and the character of Zonia is a valentine to the women in his family. But the other female characters in the play are thinly drawn archetypes or objects. Bertha is a no-nonsense homemaker who keeps the household together with her cooking and compassion. Mattie Campbell has one goal in life: to find and keep a man. Jeremy outright tells her, "A woman like you need a man," and, "A woman can't be by her lonesome." Mollie Cunningham swings in the opposite direction: she doesn't trust men, but if one materializes, she is willing to go along for the ride. Jeremy objectifies both young women, and Bynum tries to school him by describing the ideal woman: a mother. "Your mother was a woman," he tells Jeremy. "That's enough right there to show you what a woman is. Enough to show you what she can do. She made something out of you. Taught you converse, and all about how to take care of yourself, how to see where you at and where you going tomorrow." Wilson was still idealizing Daisy, but had yet to create a fully realized independent woman.

It's mind-boggling to consider Wilson's schedule and peripatetic life during this period. He was constantly crisscrossing the country as he worked simultaneously on several plays. He was relatively "free" during December for the holidays, but after the new year, he was on the road with back-to-back productions: *Piano Lesson* opened January 9 at the Huntington, followed by the pre-Broadway production of *Joe Turner* at San Diego's Old Globe Theatre, which opened on February 9. Meanwhile, *Fences* was still selling to SRO audiences on Broadway, and Billy Dee Williams replaced Jones in the role of Troy in February. Wilson did not have a personal assistant at the time, and his nonstop schedule was daunting.

Amid this whirlwind, Wilson's first priority was *Joe Turner*. With its images of bones walking on water and the glorious juba scene that caps the first act, this was not typical Broadway fare in 1988. *Les Misérables*, which had won eight Tony Awards the year before, while *Fences* won four, was still waving its red flag before sold-out crowds. At the time, tourists were flocking to see the chandelier fall in Andrew Lloyd Webber's most recent spectacle, *The Phantom of the Opera*, which opened amid much hoopla in January 1988. That show relied on pyrotechnics and stage wizardry, while Wilson's jaw-dropping juba scene was powered by a cappella voices and rhythmic movement. Wilson is specific in his stage directions: "*The Juba*," he writes, "*is reminiscent of the ring shouts of the African slaves. It is a call and response dance. . . . It should be as African as possible, with the performers working themselves up into a near frenzy. The words can be improvised, but should include some mention of the Holy Ghost.*" Like director Amy Saltz, Dan Sullivan, the *Los Angeles Times* critic, did not get it, either, when he saw it at the Old Globe in February, the last stop before Broadway. He started his review by noting the importance of the "networking that is going on among regional theaters," rather than opening with the play itself. Sullivan admitted that he just didn't understand it. "It left this viewer fretful, as when a friend recounts an incident that obviously had enormous emotional repercussions for him, and you, the listener, only half understand its significance," he wrote. "Something hasn't been communicated." *Joe Turner*, he concluded, "is a major play, but part of it escaped this viewer."

But it was a work of sheer brilliance, and the failure of a white critic to grasp its significance underscored the importance of telling this particular story. Wilson wrote *Fences* to assuage his critics, but he wrote *Joe Turner* to honor the ancestors. Wilson was taking bold steps with both form and content.

Out of all the plays in the Wilson oeuvre, *Joe Turner* crystalizes everything he aimed to do when he set forth on his decade-by-decade exploration of the African American experience—and it gels with many of the lessons he learned in his own life. In a way, the characters of Bynum and Herald Loomis reveal two sides of the playwright. Bynum is a creative force; he says he binds people together with their "song," and in doing so, he connects them with their pure soul, unsullied by centuries of brutality and inhumanity. He is driven by the urge to guide people to shed their literal and metaphorical chains and discover their true value. His "shiny man" enables him to do this work, as he explains in Act 1, Scene 1:

There was lots of shiny men and if I ever saw one again before I died I would know that my song had been accepted and worked its full power in the world and I could lay down and die a happy man. A man who done left his mark on life. On the way people cling to each other out of the truth they find in themselves.

He could be Wilson explaining his own work. For both Bynum and Wilson, this task was sacramental, but it came with a price. "I don't do it lightly," Bynum says. "It cost me a piece of myself every time I do." Wilson would say the exact same thing years later to his friend Charles Johnson, noting that every play took a little piece of himself.

Unlike Bynum, Loomis has lost his song—and his identity. He is haunted by seven years on a chain gang that robbed him of his family and his humanity. He is unmoored when he enters in Act 1, Scene 1. The stage directions describe him as *"a man driven not by the hellhounds that seemingly bay at his heels, but by his search for a world that speaks to something about himself. He is unable to harmonize the forces that swirl around him, and seeks to recreate the world into one that contains his own image."* Wilson was writing plays at a time when Blacks rarely saw their own image onstage, on television, in advertisements, in the books read aloud in elementary schools. In drama, they were often relegated to the maid or the janitor, the hooker or the drug dealer. Wilson sought to change that, just as Loomis was searching for a "world I can fit in."

The brooding character repeatedly expresses this desire. His transformation begins during that majestic scene where he sees the bones walking on water. In his vision, they begin to take on flesh, and it is this resurrection of his ancestors that connects him to his history and to his place in the world. "They Black," he says. "Just like you and me. Ain't no difference." He is stunned by the recognition that he is part of a sacred history, that he is not alone, that he is connected.

But at the end of the scene, he collapses and is unable to stand up. His search isn't over. He tells Bynum that he needs to see his wife again before he can become whole. It is only when he finally sees her that he can rebuild his own life. Martha Pentecost's fierce words set him free. "I woke up one morning and decided you was dead," she tells Loomis. "Even if you weren't, you was dead to me. I wasn't gonna carry you with me no more. So I killed you in my heart. I buried you. I mourned you." That rejection— so brutally honest and so resonant with Wilson's own experience in his first marriage—enables Loomis to resurrect himself. The bloodletting ritual at the end symbolizes his rebirth. Wilson's stage directions define the image: *"Having found his song, the song of self-sufficiency, fully resurrected, cleansed and given breath, free from any encumbrance other than the workings of his own heart and the bonds of the flesh, having accepted the responsibility for his own presence in the world, he is free to soar."* The image is breathtaking.

Anticipation for the Broadway opening was high. Wilson had, after all, won the Tony and the Pulitzer the year before. *Joe Turner* was set to open on March 27, 1988, at the Ethel Barrymore Theatre on West Forty-Seventh Street, the same stage where Lorraine Hansberry's *A Raisin in the Sun* debuted nearly thirty years earlier. *Fences* was still playing to SRO crowds around the corner—and it was a rare feat for any playwright to have two shows on Broadway at the same time. *Fences* had just celebrated its one-year anniversary, with a gross of $11 million, setting an all-time record for a non-musical in the Theater District. Billy Dee Williams, who had not been onstage in nine years, received less than flattering reviews for his performance as Troy, but fans of his movies flocked to the theater. Jones had warned his replacement about the tendency for audience members to shout out during performances. During one matinee, Jones had agreed to carry Carole Shorenstein Hays's infant daughter onstage, instead of the doll he usually used as a prop. Hays wanted her daughter to get an Actors' Equity card, and the one-time appearance would qualify her. The scene is pivotal, as Jones's character is asking his wife, Rose, to raise his love child, conceived with a woman the audience never sees. The baby began to fuss, and its snowy little arm poked out of the blanket. A woman sitting near the stage interpreted this as a clue to the racial identity of Troy's lover. She shouted, "I knew that bitch was white!"

Wilson, though, had turned all of his attention to *Joe Turner.* Two weeks before the *Joe Turner* opening, Romare Bearden died on March 12 after suffering a stroke at New York Hospital. He died on Daisy Wilson's birthday, and Wilson's play was mentioned in the *Los Angeles Times* obituary that ran in numerous papers nationwide. Wilson had always wanted to meet the painter, but never had. He once walked by Bearden's home at 357 Canal Street in lower Manhattan, but he was too nervous to climb the five flights to Bearden's walk-up loft. "I have often thought of what I would have said that day if I had knocked on his door and he had answered," he wrote in an homage to the artist. "I probably would have just looked at him. I would have looked, and if I were wearing a hat, I would have taken it off in tribute." But Bearden's passing was an omen: Wilson had recognized his people—his uncles, Charley Burley, the men at Pat's Place—in Bearden's collages, and now it was his job to make sure their stories were told on the stage.

When the play opened two weeks later, the reviews were almost universally ecstatic. Frank Rich in the *Times* put his hands together in a critical expression of gratitude. "There are occasions of true mystery and high drama, and they take Mr. Wilson's characters and writing to a dizzying place they haven't been before," Rich wrote. He was entranced, not befuddled, by the juba scene and by Herald Loomis's physical collapse at the end of the first act. "The clash between the American and the African shakes white and Black theatergoers as violently as it has shaken the history we've all shared."

The opening-night party was a joyous affair. Wilson was now attracting marquee names to his opening nights; photos of a beaming Richards and Wilson celebrating with actress Jean Stapleton and choreographer Debbie Allen went out over the wires. Veteran producer Elliot Martin (who coproduced with Vy Higginsen, Ken Wydro, and Yale Repertory Theatre), spent $106,000 on advertising after the opening, sure that he had a box office hit as strong as *Fences*. But the audience did not materialize. After less than a month of performances, the production was siphoning money; it cost $96,000 a week to run, but it was taking in less than $60,000 a week. The producers announced that the show was going to close on April 24 if business didn't pick up. *Ma Rainey* had closed abruptly after 276 performances, but *Fences* was still going strong. Wilson was now inured to the unpredictable financial vagaries of commercial theater. No matter how good a show is, if it isn't making money for the producers, it gets shuttered quickly. No doubt, this was a tense time, and it wouldn't be the only time in his long career that he faced a show closing. But after word hit the press, the box office rebounded, and the play remained open.

The persistence paid off. Wilson received the New York Drama Critics' Circle Award for Best Play, and the production was nominated for six Tony Awards: Delroy Lindo for Best Featured Actor in a Play; L. Scott Caldwell, Kimberleigh Aarn, and Kimberly Scott for Best Featured Actress in a Play; Lloyd Richards for Best Direction of a Play; and Best Play. The ceremony, hosted by Angela Lansbury, was held on June 5 at the Minskoff Theatre; Caldwell was the only one who took home the statue that night. Wilson lost to BD Wong for *M. Butterfly*. His old friend from the O'Neill, Lee Blessing, also lost for *A Walk in the Woods*. The producers shut *Joe Turner* down on June 26, after only 105 performances. But Wilson would later say that he wished he had won the Pulitzer and the Tony for *Joe Turner*, not *Fences*.

Wilson's hectic schedule meant that he was rarely home in St. Paul with his wife. When he was home, he returned to a new level of comfort. When he won his Pulitzer, he and Oliver were living in a modest second-floor apartment at 469 Selby Avenue, a street lined with popular restaurants and shops. One day, Wilson and Oliver buzzed the doorbell of their friends Claude Purdy and Jacqui Shoholm, who lived a half a block away. They urged them to come down to see the new BMW they had purchased.

Wilson never sat behind the wheel; he took public transportation or relied on friends for rides. But he liked the car, even if Oliver did all of the
driving.

About a month later, they arranged a dinner date with their friends
at Tommy K's, one of their favorite restaurants on Selby Avenue. They
strolled to the restaurant together, but before entering, Wilson stopped
in the parking lot. He pointed out a brand-new, shiny taupe Mercedes
190E. "Claude, check out that car," he said. Purdy replied that it was beautiful. His friends were confused. Wilson had just bought a BMW, and he
certainly didn't need two cars. Years later, Jacqui Shoholm still marveled
when she remembered what happened next. Wilson handed Purdy the
keys, and said, "Yeah, man, it's yours." Shoholm wept. Purdy was working
regularly in the regional theater, sometimes directing Wilson's plays after
the Broadway productions, but the couple still struggled financially. They
were raising Jacqui's son, Damon, and on top of standard living expenses,
they had to save for Damon's college expenses.

This act of kindness didn't come out of nowhere. Wilson did not forget the promise he had made to Purdy a few years earlier: he had vowed
to buy his friend a Mercedes when he made his first million. He kept his
word after he sold the option for *Fences* to Paramount. He also insured
the car for six months. "He knew we were broke, and he was extremely
generous," Shoholm said.

Oliver continued to work as a social worker, and she wanted a permanent home in the neighborhood they both loved. She took charge, and the
two decided on a five-thousand-square-foot Victorian home at 472 Holly
Avenue, a quiet side street in the elegant Ramsey Hill neighborhood. It
was just blocks away from the shops, restaurants, and bars on both Summit and Grand Avenues. McSweeney's, a popular Irish pub where Wilson
liked to write, was just a few blocks around the corner. Called the William
George House, the stately stone mansion they bought was built in 1895
and was once the home of Louisa McQuillan, the wealthy grandmother
of St. Paul native son F. Scott Fitzgerald. The Wilson and the Fitzgerald
clans couldn't be more different: While Wilson's grandmother Zonia was
eking out a subsistence living on Spear Tops Mountain, Louisa McQuillan

was living off the fortune of her husband, an Irish immigrant, who made his money in the wholesale grocery business. Both men wrote American classics, but from distinctly different points of view.

The house, with a wraparound porch and crenellations above a bay window, stands back from the quiet street and is surrounded by well-pruned shrubbery. In the 1940s, it had been converted to a boardinghouse, and it needed a major renovation when Wilson and Oliver purchased it in 1988. Oliver took the lead. The house is located in a National Historic District, which makes renovations no small feat. Oliver had to abide by the byzantine rules of the historic district, and she painstakingly restored the house to its Victorian splendor. She was adamant that Wilson have a grand space for his writing room, and she converted the third-floor attic to a front-to-back office, with gleaming wood floors and abundant natural light. He moved his makeshift desk, the file cabinets topped by a wooden door, to the third floor.

Oliver also devised a special homage for her husband during the renovation. He frequently told stories about his early years growing up on Bedford Avenue in a two-room, cold-water flat. He shared common bathrooms with other playwrights at the O'Neill and at New Dramatists, and he had never had a bathroom of his own. She hired a tile mason to design a tribute in a new third-floor bathroom. The floor is a brilliant white, with a diagonal strip of tiles spelling out the name "August" in red uppercase letters. The background is gray, with a bold black border that contrasts brilliantly with the white tiles of the rest of the floors. Subsequent owners have left the bathroom floor intact.

The couple began living a little larger, but at the same time, Wilson was rarely home to enjoy his new abode. He took some time to look at colleges with Sakina, who toured the historically Black Howard University in Washington, D.C., and Morgan State University in Baltimore. She chose Morgan, and she remembers her father took her out for a prime rib dinner after the tour. He didn't pay her college tuition, however. Her maternal grandfather, Elder Joseph Burton, was a successful entrepreneur who owned a pool hall and chicken eatery in Pittsburgh. He had a fourth-grade education, and he put aside money for his granddaughter's college tuition. When she moved out of the dormitory, he paid her rent as well. Burton lived long enough to attend some of his former son-in-law's plays on Broadway, and his pool hall is mentioned in *Seven Guitars*. Wilson admired him, despite the breakup of his marriage. And even though he wasn't paying tuition, he kept a close eye on his daughter's college education, questioning her about the texts she was reading and the classes she was taking. Once, she called and proudly told him that she was a member of a Black action society at Morgan and that the group was studying Timbuktu. She thought he would be pleased, but he told her to start her lessons with her grandmother and work back to Africa. "It didn't make any sense to me for her to know all about Timbuktu and know nothing about her grandmother," he said. "I felt she'd have a better sense of who she was and her current situation." When she graduated in 1994, Morgan awarded him an honorary Doctor of Humane Letters.

Wilson and Oliver never had children, although a friend from the O'Neill said that Wilson once asked her if it was a deal breaker in a marriage if one partner wanted children and the other didn't. He told her that he did not want another child at that time, and his friend was struck by the poignancy of his query. By all accounts, Oliver was beloved among his theater colleagues, and many who knew him before he was famous credit her for encouraging him and being his sounding board. But at this stage of his career, family did not come first. His star was rising, and he was single-mindedly focused on his next play, *The Piano Lesson*.

That level of absorption has to put a strain on any marriage, along with the constant travel. At the time, he admitted that he couldn't remember where he actually lived. "I like St. Paul and I plan to stay there," he told one interviewer. "But my wife may have to quit her job and travel with me."

CHAPTER ELEVEN

What Do You Do with Your Legacy?

> *Everybody got stones in their passway. You got to step over them or walk around them. . . . All you got to do is set them down by the side of the road. You ain't got to carry them with you.*

—**AUGUST WILSON**

ate one night in 1984 or 1985, Dwight Andrews got a call from Wilson, who breathlessly explained that he had the story for a new play. "Hey, man, there's this piano," Wilson said. And then there was a long pause. "There are some ghosts in the house, and this guy is trying to get the piano out of the house so he can sell it and get some land." Andrews was confused. "I thought August was high. I said, 'What are you talking about?' It didn't make sense." By the end of the conversation, Andrews was still a bit befuddled, but he was also thrilled. "I sensed an opportunity to tell the story of every Black person today. What is your value: Your material goods or the sacrifice of your ancestors? It hit me in my gut as being so truthful to the dilemma of the Black community."

When he called Andrews, Wilson just had the germ of an idea. He had come across Romare Bearden's *The Piano Lesson (Homage to Mary Lou)* in a gallery, and he turned to a friend and said, "This will be my next play."

The artist's evocative 1984 print depicts a woman in a blue gingham skirt, bending over a girl playing the piano, perhaps practicing scales in the low register. A metronome sits on a doily on top of the instrument; a framed image of an older woman—a grandmother, perhaps—hangs on the wall. Wilson was struck by the image. What was the provenance of the piano? Who were these people? The piano, Wilson knew, was a symbol of gentility on Southern plantations. (There was, after all, a piano bequeathed in Robert Twitty's will in 1864.) Wilson took one look at the Bearden print and knew there was a story there.

He always started a play with an idea—or a question. In this case, the Bearden painting aroused questions about ancestry. Wilson began to wonder: What happens when you deny the past? He knew from the painting that there would be a woman and a young girl in the play—and a piano. "I thought that the woman would be a character trying to acquire a sense of self-worth by denying her past," he told a reporter. "And I felt she couldn't do that. She had to confront the past, in the person of her brother, who was going to sweep through the house like a tornado coming from the South, bringing the past with him." The piano came to represent their shared history, providing a link to their ancestors and to Africa. "Then the question became: What do you do with your legacy? How do you best put it to use?" As he had done with the play that became *Joe Turner*, he named the new play after the Bearden painting. This time the title stuck.

He developed *Piano Lesson* at the O'Neill in the summer of 1986. As usual, it was very much a work in progress. Set in Pittsburgh in 1936, the play focuses on a brother and sister's fight over the piano they have inherited. Berniece keeps the piano in her Pittsburgh home; she polishes it every day. Her brother, Boy Willie, blows in from Mississippi late one night. He doesn't lose any time announcing that he plans to sell a truckload of watermelons to raise money to buy a parcel of land down south. Boy Willie's entrance is energetic and audacious. He takes the tired stereotype about African Americans and watermelon and turns it on its head, using it to his advantage: he is going to make a fortune selling the fruit in Pittsburgh's upscale white neighborhoods.

And the piano is more than just eighty-eight keys; it is an elegantly carved instrument that represents the siblings' ancestral legacy. *"On the legs of the piano, carved in the manner of African sculpture, are mask-like figures resembling totems,"* the stage directions note. *"The carvings are rendered with a grace and power of invention that lifts them out of the realm of craftsmanship and into the realm of art."* Two generations back, the portraits were carved by the siblings' great-grandfather, an enslaved person named Willie Boy. The slave owner Robert Sutter had traded Willie Boy's wife and young son for the piano. The faces of their ancestors are depicted on the rich wooden panels, crafted by a man who missed his family.

Years later, his grandsons, who were born after emancipation, broke into the Sutter estate and reclaimed the piano. Boy Charles, who was Berniece and Boy Willie's father, was murdered in the aftermath. Now, in 1936, the siblings are engaged in a tug-of-war over the instrument. Boy Willie wants to sell the piano to buy land in Mississippi, but Berniece refuses to part with it. She also never plays it: "She say it got blood on it," her uncle Doaker explains. The siblings' struggle represents two different approaches to life: Do you refuse to face the past and let the piano gather dust or do you seize it for an opportunity for a better future? The two siblings grapple with those questions, and Wilson himself didn't know the answer at first.

Wilson wrestled with the resolution to that dilemma long after his midnight call to Andrews. As he worked, though, he heard one voice for the role of Boy Willie: Charles S. Dutton, who had played Levee in *Ma Rainey* on Broadway and played Herald Loomis at Yale Rep (but not in subsequent productions). Dutton played the role at the O'Neill, where Steve Robman directed and Michael Feingold served as dramaturge. Robman concerned himself with blocking the long, unwieldly play—that is, getting the actors from place to place. He knew the play was too long, but by now, everyone at the O'Neill understood that Wilson was averse to cuts until he saw his work onstage. "It was obvious he would do them when he was ready," Robman said. Years later, he still thinks the final version of the play would have benefited from further pruning. "Some of the plays are too long, but the guy's prose is so enticing. Most directors think they can't take the scalpel to his work. The stuff is too good," he said. Wilson frequently said that he didn't sit down and "write" at the beginning of his process; first, he listened to the characters. Given the length of his scripts, one O'Neill director was fond of saying, "I wish sometimes he would tell them when to shut up."

Feingold became Wilson's sounding board, and as theater critic for the *Village Voice*, he had a certain gravitas and asked keen, probing questions. In particular, he helped Wilson clarify the backstory, which was convoluted with so many generations of two families, several deaths, and one ghost. He drew a family tree and showed it to Wilson, who said, "You know, you skipped a whole generation!" Wilson realized he needed to clear up the story; that was what the O'Neill was about.

Wilson made many changes to the play, but the final version of the plot still remains knotty. Willie Boy's grandsons—Boy Charles and his brothers, Doaker and Wining Boy—reclaimed the piano on July 4, 1911, while the Sutter family was out celebrating Independence Day. They were asserting their independence in a different way. Boy Charles, in particular, felt that the piano represented his family's history; he couldn't be free until he took possession of it and passed it on to his children. Doaker and Wining Boy successfully carted the piano to a safe place, but for some reason that is never fully explained, Boy Charles stayed behind at the Sutter home, which was then owned by Robert Sutter's grandson. When Sutter discovered the piano missing, he and a posse of men burned down Boy Charles's house. Boy Charles fled and jumped on a train called the Yellow Dog; he hid in a boxcar with four hobos. Sutter and his cohorts stopped the train and set the boxcar on fire, killing the men inside, including Boy Charles. Two months later, one of Sutter's cronies fell in his well and drowned. The locals attributed his death to the "Ghosts of the Yellow Dog," saying that the five men who burned to death on the train were exacting their revenge.

Fast-forward to 1936. Sutter's grandson falls into a well and dies. His death is steeped in superstition: the Ghosts of the Yellow Dog have struck again. Boy Willie is given an opportunity to buy Sutter's land, which represents a chance for poetic justice as well as economic independence. He needs to sell the piano to raise enough cash for the purchase. Berniece refuses to sell. She is still mourning her husband, Crawley, who was shot dead three years earlier in Mississippi. A group of men, including Boy Willie and Crawley, snuck out one night to retrieve a load of wood they had stolen from a work site. They were caught in the act, and Crawley was killed in the fracas. Berniece blamed her brother. At the end of Act 1, she breaks down and pounds on Boy Willie's chest. Her meltdown is interrupted when her eleven-year-old daughter, Maretha, screams: Sutter's ghost is haunting the house.

The presence of the specter created two conundrums. How do they exorcize Sutter's ghost and the bloody legacy it represents? And who gets the piano? At the O'Neill, Wilson didn't provide the answers. The play ended with Boy Willie trying to fight off the ghost. "In the original ending, I never said what happened to the piano," he told theater scholar Joan Herrington. "To me, it wasn't important. The important thing was Boy Willie's willingness to engage the ghost in battle. Once you have that moment, then for me, the play was over."

But at the O'Neill, it wasn't over for the audience. What, after all, is the point if the ownership of the piano is left unresolved? Wilson talked to another playwright in residence that summer, who encouraged him to think about what happens after the lights go down on the final scene. He eventually determined that Boy Willie conquers the ghost and walks out the door, leaving the piano—and its legacy—with his sister. But it took many rewrites to get to that point.

After the O'Neill workshop, Wilson was deeply engrossed in the *Fences* imbroglio as well as the first productions of *Joe Turner*. He returned to *Piano Lesson* in November 1987, when it made its world premiere at Yale Rep, directed by Richards. Wilson had written the role of Boy Willie for Dutton, but the actor could not perform in the Yale production because he was filming *Crocodile Dundee II* at the time. Samuel L. Jackson stepped in and created the character, but he was replaced by Dutton in subsequent productions. Jackson became attached to Boy Willie, though, and understudied Dutton when the play moved to Broadway. Years later, he made it no secret that he struggled with alcohol and cocaine addictions at the time, and his disappointment over losing the role triggered his substance abuse disorder. "I was pretty much devastated that I wasn't going to make my Broadway debut, drowning myself in a drug-fueled kind of craziness and ended up in rehab, which, you know, started a whole other journey for me," he said in retrospect. (He made a successful recovery and went on to star in Quentin Tarantino's 1994 neo-noir crime film *Pulp Fiction*, which catapulted him to international stardom. He got another chance at *Piano Lesson* in a 2022 revival, giving a scene-stealing performance in the smaller role of Doaker.)

The Yale Rep production opened on November 27, 1987, to mixed reviews. Wilson had always been adamant about one aspect of the ending. "I wanted Boy Willie to demonstrate a willingness to battle with Sutter's ghost, the ghost of the white man—that lingering idea of him as the master of slaves—which is still in Black Americans' lives and needs to be exorcized," he wrote in a feature for the *New York Times*. But at Yale, the ending was murky and inconclusive; Richards used hokey effects to emulate the ghost, and the ending played like an old-time horror movie. It did not find a way to meld the naturalism of Berniece's parlor with the supernatural notion of a haunted house. Rich of the *Times* called the play "unruly and unfinished," adding that the "clumsily managed cathartic climaxes of both acts are as yet unsupported dramatically by what comes before." But the top critics were becoming accustomed to the development system that Richards had worked out, and reviews took into account that the production was essentially a work in progress. Rich also noted, "These flaws co-exist with some of Mr. Wilson's most virtuosic and easeful writing to date." Since the success of *Ma Rainey*, most critics took notice of Wilson's enormous gift and were encouraging, rather than dismissive. His work was filling a void that was painfully obvious in the homogeneous nonprofit and commercial theater world, and his unique way of working enabled critics to act as dramaturges rather than executioners. He got a pass few other playwrights received.

Since Richards was the dean of the Yale School of Drama in addition to being artistic director of Yale Rep, his MFA students were often assigned plum acting and design jobs in Yale Rep productions. A design student named Constanza Romero was tapped to create the costumes for *Piano*

Lesson; the team also included students Christopher Akerlind on lighting and J. Scott Servheen on sound. Wilson, now forty-three, was drawn to the twenty-nine-year-old Romero. When Sakina traveled to New Haven for the opening, Wilson took her out to lunch to meet Romero. "My dad made a point that he wanted me to meet her," she said. "I didn't know why he wanted me to meet her, but he asked me what I thought. I'm like, 'She's okay.'" She thought it was odd.

Others noticed that the two had grown close. Akerlind, the lighting designer, was good friends with Romero, and he detected the sparks. The mutual attraction was undeniable. "We were working on a great play with great people, and there was a sizzling frisson in the rehearsal room," he said.

Wilson was never in one place for long in those days; he was preoccupied with simultaneous productions all over the country. And *Piano Lesson* was far from finished. Richards and Benjamin Mordecai had worked out an even more intense series of productions in theaters across the country. With Dutton back in the role of Boy Willie, the play opened at Boston's Huntington Theatre in January 1988, two months before *Joe Turner* opened on Broadway. During the Boston run, Huntington managing director Michael Maso noted a significant change in the playwright. At a production meeting in New York, "he made it clear that he was in charge of his work," Maso said. "It was a change in terms of his public behavior." Wilson was no longer letting Richards talk for him; he was speaking up for himself.

But the play was still having trouble, especially in the second act. Kevin Kelly, the longtime drama critic for the *Boston Globe* who was not known for pulling punches, wrote a supportive review that applauded the play's potential, lauding its "promise and power," while noting that it "has yet to find directness and clarity."

But Wilson was opening up a world that the overwhelmingly white theater community had never experienced. With every new production of the play, it was clear that Wilson had captured not just a particular moment in time, but four centuries of African American history. The seemingly idle banter of the secondary characters was rich and revealing: Doaker, the uncle who owns the house in Pittsburgh, has worked on the railroad for twenty-seven years (first lining track and then as a cook) and his tales echo the stories Wilson had heard at Pat's Place. Another uncle, named Wining Boy, is an itinerant musician who brings the blues to life when he sits down at the piano. Berniece's suitor, Avery, is a pastor who works days as an elevator man. Her daughter, Maretha, represents the next generation; like the little girl in Bearden's painting, she is learning to play the piano, even though her mother won't touch the keys. Boy Willie's friend Lymon is a country boy who had run-ins with the sheriff back in Mississippi; like Jeremy Furlow in *Joe Turner*, he seeks opportunity—and romance—in the North.

Wilson also must have heeded the criticism of his female characters. Berniece is buttoned-up and paralyzed by grief, but she also works hard to provide a better life for her daughter. While Mattie in *Joe Turner* cannot live without a man, Berniece rejects that notion. "You trying to tell me a woman can't be nothing without a man," she tells Avery when he pressures her to marry him. "But you alright, huh? You can just walk out of here without me—without a woman—and still be a man. That's alright. Ain't nobody gonna ask you, 'Avery, who you got to love you?' " She isn't having it.

The cast was as good as it gets, but still, Richards was not able to finesse the final scene's ambiguity. The play just switched gears at the end. "The theater suddenly erupts into *The Exorcist*: thundering noise, fluttering curtains, eerie light, showing us a kind of spectral gallery of grieving Black ancestors against the Pittsburgh sky," a befuddled Kelly wrote. "Hokey, I mean strictly as stage business, and certainly a disservice to the mythic power Wilson is suggesting." Kelly was dead-on: the final scene played like a parody of a cult B-horror movie.

The play went on hiatus for a year while Richards and Wilson worked on other projects. Rarely home, Wilson was an absent presence in the house on Holly Avenue, and he was seldom at the desk in the third-floor office Oliver had lovingly restored for him.

Overseeing productions of his plays all over the country, he finally hired an assistant, a young woman named Emily Kretschmer, whom he had met a few years earlier while she was working at a half-price ticket

booth in St. Paul. She took over his travel arrangements and business correspondence so that he could have more time to write.

The team returned to the play in 1989, when it opened on Martin
Luther King Day at the Goodman, which had become a pivotal stop for
Wilson since the triumphant production of *Fences*. Richards, who was almost seventy at the time, had taken a fall, and he asked his son, Scott, to
join the production as assistant director. The creative team had the same
frustrating problem; Wilson was digging in his feet. "It was hard to pin
August down as to what the ending was," Scott Richards said. Still, the
reviews were mostly glowing—the Minneapolis *Star Tribune* compared
Wilson to Eugene O'Neill and the *Chicago Tribune* noted that Wilson's
language "soars with lyric beauty"—but the ending was still unresolved. It
still wasn't clear who kept the piano.

The play was billed as a "work in progress," so audience members
knew they were not seeing a finished product. Reviewers were entranced
by the depth of the characters and the musicality of their dialogue, but
continued to be perplexed by the play's mix of naturalism and the supernatural. The preacher, Avery, cannot pray the ghost away. Berniece must
embrace her past—and her ancestors—by playing the piano. She must
own her heritage in order for the ghost to depart.

The creative team was still wrestling with that scene. What should
she play? How would she make the ghost disappear? Wilson wasn't sure,
and Richards wasn't about to tell him what to do, so the team turned to
Andrews. He tried spirituals. He tried hymns. Nothing worked. Finally,
he made a suggestion. "She doesn't play anything," Andrews determined.
"She kinetically just bangs on the piano with everything in her being. She
bangs like a train, clickety-clack, and that invokes the ancestors." Wilson
put it in his stage directions this way: *"It is an old urge to song that is both
a commandment and a plea. With each repetition it gains in strength. It is
intended as an exorcism and a dressing for battle. A rustle of wind blowing
across two continents."*

Berniece calls out to the ancestors as she bangs on the keys, and the
unseen ghost rages in a burst of wind that nearly blows the curtains off the
windows. The cacophonic sound worked, but after all that supernatural

wrestling with the ghost, the play just ended. At the beginning of the play, Berniece was too frightened of her past to confront the legacy of the piano. Boy Willie embraced the history, but instead of clinging to it, he wanted to use that legacy to build a prosperous future. But Boy Willie, more than Berniece, understood the deep significance of the wood carvings. In a way, he was a stand-in for Wilson's belief that African Americans need to keep their history alive.

Wilson had felt that way at the seder he had attended a few years earlier and realized that the Passover meal was a way of remembering the legacy of slavery in Egypt and the hope for redemption with the final line, "Next year in Jerusalem." He put that idea into the character of Boy Willie, who tells his sister to teach her young daughter about her legacy and instruct her to honor it. "If you want to tell her something, tell her about that piano," Boy Willie says. "You ain't even told her about that piano. Like that's something to be ashamed of. Like she supposed to go off and hide somewhere about that piano. You ought to mark down on the calendar the day that Papa Boy Charles brought that piano into the house. You ought to mark that day down and draw a big circle around it . . . and every year when it come up throw a party. Have a celebration." (The speech eloquently sums up the play, but it also shows the murkiness of the backstory. Earlier, the characters note that Boy Charles stayed behind and never went back home with the piano.)

By the time Boy Willie gets to that speech, his character has evolved and he understands the symbolic significance of the family heirloom. But Wilson still hadn't come up with an ending when the production moved to the Old Globe Theatre in San Diego in May 1989. It was tighter and more focused than it had been at Yale, but just as frustrating. Writing in the *Los Angeles Times*, critic Sylvie Drake summed up the problem: "Everything up to that point has been so cleverly calibrated that Wilson's decision to leave these questions unanswered feels like an unconsummated act."

Wilson was still struggling with the ending during the summer of 1989, but he took time off to attend the first National Black Theatre Festival in

Winston-Salem, North Carolina. The six-day event was the brainchild of Larry Leon Hamlin, artistic director of the North Carolina Black Repertory Company. Hamlin enlisted poet Maya Angelou as chairwoman, and the two ultimately raised $600,000 for a festival that attracted ten thousand people with thirty performances by seventeen Black theater companies. Wilson and television mogul Oprah Winfrey were the guests of honor at the opening-night gala, which attracted a who's who list of Black theater artists, including Ruby Dee and Ossie Davis, Louis Gossett Jr., Roscoe Lee Browne, Cicely Tyson, and Woodie King Jr.

Wilson was in his element. During an interview at the host hotel, he said, "This is the kind of thing I've sat around for the last 10 years saying should happen." He hoped that the festival would generate an "artistic agenda of where Black theater should be going." And Black theater was hurting. Hamlin came up with the idea while researching an article on Black theater in the South, and he discovered what he described as "this terrible scream of pain, of torture, coming out of those theaters." The problem was primarily financial; even though Hamlin identified two hundred Black theaters, many of them struggled to make ends meet. Foundation money had dried up since the 1960s and '70s, when it was fashionable for large foundations to fund Black theaters. Many of the theaters also suffered from mismanagement, and they operated in isolation. In contrast, the League of Resident Theatres provided a support network for the nation's large institutions, which were almost universally run by whites and often bolstered by university affiliations.

The festival confirmed what Wilson had been thinking as he traveled from regional theater to regional theater, and the conversations he had there would later have profound significance when he became a controversial public intellectual. But the six-day festival was also a joyful gathering and a scene for reunions and parties. His old friends from the Penumbra Theatre were there, represented with *Malcolm X*, a solo show that Wilson had written years earlier for the theater and that had been performed in schools in Minnesota. Actor Terry Bellamy played the civil rights activist.

The local hotel became a meeting spot for attendees, the place "where you stand around and see people you haven't been able to find for two years," according to Lou Bellamy of Penumbra. One day, Wilson was expecting a letter and went to the reception desk to retrieve it. The attendant said he didn't have it. Words were exchanged, and Wilson, who was not a small man, leapt over the desk to confront the employee. "This was a mild-mannered dude, and he ran that dude into the office and he locked the door," said Bellamy, who heard the commotion and intervened. "I said, 'August, let's get out of here. You can't be doing that.'"

Theater artists are notorious for gossip, and word of the altercation spread rapidly. Wilson, of course, was an honored guest who boasted awards and financial success many attendees would never achieve. He already had a reputation for a volatile temper, and the scene in the lobby confirmed it. The fracas with the hotel employee was characteristic. Wilson could keep his temper in check with members of the media and arts dignitaries, but he was known to erupt in rage over everyday frustrations: a waitress delivering the wrong order, an admirer taking a photo, an assistant forgetting to deliver a message. Some were unforgiving, including many who witnessed the outburst at the hotel. But his longtime friends Jacqui Shoholm and Claude Purdy were more empathetic. "Claude understood it," Shoholm said. "The raw anger. That comes from living in poverty and striking out against racism every single day, pillar to post, and feeling like nothing is ever going to go in your favor." In this way, Wilson was like Levee in *Ma Rainey*: He didn't explode because Toledo stepped on his shoes. His rage had been building for decades.

But while Wilson could lash out at underlings for mistakes or perceived slights, he had cultivated an uncanny ability to remain calm and composed in public situations where his demeanor mattered. The year before, in October 1988, he was the featured guest on Bill Moyers's PBS series *A World of Ideas*. The thirty-minute segment was filmed at the Playwrights' Centre in Minneapolis, not at Penumbra Theatre in St. Paul, which caused some sniping in the Twin Cities theater community. Even then, everyone wanted a claim to Wilson's success. During his discussion with Moyers, he credited his mother for bringing the poet inside him to life. The interview was a big deal for the playwright. The series was notable for introducing thoughtful writers to the screen and had featured interviews with such literary luminaries as Chinua Achebe, Derek Walcott, Toni Morrison, and Maxine Hong Kingston. The interview with Wilson could have gotten confrontational at times, given the line of questioning, but Wilson remained calm and thoughtful. Moyers got stuck on the notion that Blacks in America need to embrace the mores of the dominant culture in order to succeed. Wilson's lifework was to assert that Black culture is unique and worthy of art. Moyers pressed the issue, finally asking, "Don't you have to adopt American values, American—" Wilson gently and politely interrupted him. "We got the American part together the first hundred years we were here," he said. "We would not be here had we not learned to adapt to American culture. Blacks know more about whites in white culture and white life than whites know about Blacks. We have to know because our survival depends on it. White people's survival does not depend on knowing Blacks. But we still have our own way of doing things, even though we are Americans."

Moyers also pushed Wilson to discuss his mixed-race heritage and asked three questions about his white father. Again, Wilson deflected him, noting that he had always been Black. "The cultural environment of my life, the forces that have shaped me, the nurturing, the learning, have all been Black ideas about the world that I learned from my mother." His soft-spoken yet firm tone made it clear that he wouldn't entertain further probing. He remained cool when Moyers poked him several times by suggesting that Blacks in America should aspire to the kind of bland, upper-middle-class life depicted on *The Cosby Show*. The queries negated Wilson's mission to honor the Black people he knew on the Hill, not doctors and lawyers who had assimilated. But Wilson knew he was being filmed for a national audience, so he simply said that the show "does not reflect Black America to my mind." In other situations, he might have become more heated, but Wilson was savvy and wasn't about to lose his calm demeanor. When he was talking to the tweedy journalist with the White House pedigree and slight Texas twang, he spoke like a professor himself. In conversations with his theater friends, he would code-switch between the voices of his characters and the jargon of academe. And he stayed seated when Moyers asked a final tone-deaf question that in other circumstances would have made him explode. "Don't you grow weary of thinking Black, writing Black, being asked questions about Blacks?" Moyers asked. Wilson barely flinched as he got in the last word. "How could one grow weary of that?" he replied. "Whites don't get tired of thinking white or being who they are. I'm just who I am. You never transcend who you are. Black is not limiting. There's no idea in the world that is not contained by Black life. I could write forever about the Black experience in America."

By January 1990, *Piano Lesson* was nearing the end of its long development process in the regional theater. It opened a ten-week run at the Doolittle Theatre in Los Angeles on January 18, and while the cast remained largely the same, there was one notable difference. It now had a definitive ending. Berniece keeps the piano, and Boy Willie goes back to Mississippi, promising to return if she ever stops playing it. The headline for the *Los Angeles Times* review was telling: "'Piano Lesson': Harmony at Last."

The artistic team had a generous ten weeks to polish the play before it opened on Broadway in April. Wilson took time off to keynote an event called "A Conversation with August Wilson" at the Kinsey Auditorium in Los Angeles's Exposition Park. Sponsored by the California African American Museum, the discussion was supposed to center on the state of Black theater. But Wilson knew he was in the City of Angels and that Hollywood producers were likely to be in the audience. He quickly changed the topic to the dearth of Black film directors. He pointed out that several recent movies about Blacks, including *The Color Purple*, *A Soldier's Story*, and *Bird*, were all helmed by white directors. "White people have set themselves up as custodians of our experience," he said. He knew exactly what he was doing and who was in the audience. Los Angeles is a one-shop town, where it's impossible to pivot without running into someone in the "industry." Wilson brought up the subject of *Fences*. He had completed a first draft of the screenplay, but the movie wasn't moving ahead because of his insistence that Paramount hire a Black director. "Until the industry is ready to hire a Black to direct [Robert] DeNiro or [Robert] Redford, Blacks should at least be able to direct their own experience," he said. Wilson did not have the contractual power to insist on a Black director, but by making his demand public in the city where it most mattered, he was putting pressure on an industry that understood his growing acclaim as the nation's preeminent Black playwright. It turns out that Paramount film production vice president Kevin Jones, who is Black, was in the audience. He later played the company line when he told the *Los Angeles Times*, "The reality is that the studio wants August's cooperation and wants him to work with the director, but we also want the best director for the job." Wilson would remember that response. This was not the end of his standoff.

After the *Fences* debacle, Wilson and Lloyd Richards had become increasingly suspicious of producers. And Richards was about to have more time on his hands to focus on directing. At the end of January, he announced that he would be leaving his posts as dean of the Yale School of Drama and artistic director of Yale Repertory Theatre in June 1991. He had held both positions since 1979; Yale usually had a ten-year tenure for deans, but Richards had agreed to stay an extra two years at the request of Yale president Benno C. Schmidt. Richards planned to remain on board at the O'Neill Center. When asked about his future plans, he answered in typical Buddha fashion: "I will go on to what I must do next," he said. "Which is more of the same."

In this case, that meant shepherding *Piano Lesson* to Broadway. The powerful Shubert Organization had lost money on *Joe Turner*, which made the search for a new producer challenging in many ways. But Jujamcyn Theaters, a producing and theater-ownership company, was looking for an important play to reopen one of its theaters. The organization was completing a $2 million restoration of the Ritz Theatre on West Forty-Eighth Street, which was renamed the Walter Kerr Theatre, in honor of the longtime *New York Herald Tribune* and *New York Times* drama critic. The collaboration between Jujamcyn and Wilson's team began with Jack Viertel, who had been Frank Rich's roommate at Harvard. A former theater critic and arts editor for (the now defunct) *Los Angeles Herald Examiner*, Viertel had worked as a dramaturge for the Mark Taper Forum in Los Angeles before joining Jujamcyn as creative director in 1987. He had read *Piano Lesson* at the Mark Taper and was captivated. He is a blues enthusiast, so he was drawn to the script. His boss, Rocco Landesman, agreed to invest in the Broadway production. Viertel had never met Wilson, so when he saw the playwright on the opening night of *Piano Lesson* at Yale Rep, he introduced himself. He gushed about the play, coming across as a star-struck fan. "I said to him that a certain passage in the play had so knocked me out that I didn't care what else was in the play. We had to produce it," Viertel told *Pittsburgh Post-Gazette* critic Christopher Rawson. Viertel said it took him days to get over that scene. Wilson was nonchalant and said, offhandedly, "Oh, I took that out." He hadn't actually taken it out, but he was having a bit of fun with a novice producer.

The play closed at the Doolittle in Los Angeles on April 1 and was set to open at the newly renovated Walter Kerr Theatre on April 16. But before the play even opened, the show received the kind of free publicity that would make press agents turn cartwheels of glee. On Thursday, April 12, four days before opening night, Wilson was sitting at the Café Edison in his home away from home when he was in New York. The café was known as the Polish Tea Room because of its Eastern European menu. Wilson was treated like family by the café's proprietors, Harry and Frances Edelstein, and he held court at a back table in a dingy corner of the coffee shop's smoking section, where two faux Corinthian columns held up the hammered-tin ceiling. Wilson called the place "The Spot," a no-nonsense, inexpensive eatery where he could sip a cup of coffee all day and fill the ashtray. He was in the middle of an interview with Peter Vaughan, the theater critic for the Minneapolis *Star Tribune*.

Wilson's assistant, Emily Kretschmer, burst into the café and inter-rupted the interview. "By the look on her face, I thought something was wrong," he said. Quite the contrary. She had just received word that he was awarded his second Pulitzer Prize in Drama, this time for *Piano Lesson*. "It's a surprise. It's great!" the usually soft-spoken playwright said while Vaughan's tape recorder was rolling. "Now there's two, and I get to go to the luncheon again. Wow!"

Later that day at the Walter Kerr, a reporter from the *Washington Post* pointed out that he was among an elite group of playwrights with two Pulitzers, including Tennessee Williams and Edward Albee. (At the time, only four others had achieved that honor: Eugene O'Neill, Arthur Miller, Thornton Wilder, and George S. Kaufman.) "That's good company to be in," Wilson told the reporter. "I think my mother would be proud to know that the content of her life is worthy of the highest accolades."

She would also have been thrilled to learn that her dropout son had been awarded an honorary high school diploma signed by Robert Cronenberger, director of the Carnegie Library of Pittsburgh. It had been awarded to him at an event at the Hill District library on October 10, 1989. His sister Freda picked it up for him. The official document, embossed with the library seal, says: "This certifies that August Wilson has satisfactorily completed the Course of Study and is therefore entitled to this Diploma." He prized this honor, perhaps more than the numerous honorary doctorates he received, and later referred to himself as "a graduate of the Carnegie Library."

After Wilson learned about his second Pulitzer, he and Richards posed for photographs at the Walter Kerr, by the piano onstage. The photographer shouted, "Tinkle the keys," to which Wilson replied, "I don't play." The photos of Wilson and Richards at the piano capture their relationship at the time. The bespectacled Richards sits at the keys, a serious expression on his face as he gazes directly into the camera. Wilson, wearing his signature page boy cap, stands behind him, with a hint of an amused smile on his face.

The play opened to positive reviews a few days later. The cachet of the Pulitzer added excitement to opening night. At the time, it was rare for a play to win the prize *before* opening in New York, which was a testament to the increasing stature of regional theaters. Now a play didn't have to open on Broadway to earn accolades. It was also on the minds of the New York critics, who mentioned the award early in their reviews. The play had come a long way since the early days at Yale when the creative team was searching for music to play in the final scene with the ghost and Richards was struggling with how to stage the supernatural elements without resorting to contrived hocus-pocus. The reviews were almost universally positive, with the usual caveats about Wilson's tendency to overwrite the tangents—an "O'Neill-like excess" is how the *Times* described it. The play ultimately received five Tony Award nominations: Wilson for Best Play, Richards for Best Direction, Dutton for Best Performance by a Leading Actor in a Play, Rocky Carroll for Best Performance by a Featured Performer in a Play, and S. Epatha Merkerson for Best Performance by a Featured Actress in a Play. It didn't win any of the awards; Frank Galati won Best Play for his epic adaptation of *The Grapes of Wrath*.

Piano Lesson exemplifies Wilson's strengths—and weaknesses. The symbolism is deep, and the characters are richly drawn, with poetic monologues that soar. At the same time, the backstory is overly complex, which makes it hard to follow. Feingold had the right approach to dramaturgy: a family tree and a timeline would be helpful to keep the characters straight.

Wilson was not one of those artists who claimed he didn't read reviews. He read them. Sometimes he learned from them. But he was certainly not prepared for a scathing review that came out in the *New Republic* on May 21. Headlined "The Lesson of 'The Piano Lesson,'" the review was written by Robert Brustein, staff critic and also artistic director of the American Repertory Theater (ART) based at Harvard University. Richards had replaced Brustein as dean of the Yale School of Drama after his contract was not renewed by then Yale president A. Bartlett Giamatti. Brustein, who had founded Yale Rep, did not go quietly. He complained in the press that Giamatti planned to "deprofessionalize" the department. He also said that changes to the program "could constitute a serious loss to the American theater."

Brustein did not review the first three Wilson productions that premiered at Yale. "Protocol required that I hold my tongue about the progress of a theatre I founded and the conduct of my successor," he wrote. But he did comment in a 1988 *New York Times* article about a trend he called "McTheatre"—that is, the process of using the regional theater as a sort of tryout circuit to develop new plays for Broadway. He counted Richards and Wilson as the biggest offenders, even though ART had produced the musical *Big River*, which went on to the La Jolla Playhouse in San Diego before opening on Broadway. Jules Feiffer's *Grown Ups* and Marsha Norman's *Night, Mother* and *Traveler in the Dark* had also gone to Broadway after premiering at ART. The issue of whether nonprofit theaters should produce plays that are bound for the commercial world of Broadway was debated widely in the press. It is commonplace now, and ART, under the leadership of Diane Paulus, premieres Broadway-bound works regularly.

Copies of the review were circulated in the insular theater community, as Brustein wrote with acid ink about an award-winning play by the country's preeminent Black playwright. In several thousand words, Brustein hit every possible nerve. Dismissing the play as "an overwritten exercise in a conventional style," "a kitchen-sink production," and "much ado about a piano," he attacked the very thing Wilson was trying to do, which was to pay homage to ordinary Black Americans. Brustein carped that Wilson's characters "sit on the edge of the middle class, wearing good suits, inhabiting clean homes" and "never come on like menacing street people screaming obscenities or bombarding the audience with such phrases as 'Black power's gonna get your mama.'" He compared the humor to the sitcom *The Jeffersons*. He proclaimed that "Wilson is reaching a dead end in his examination of American racism," but predicted that his next play, *Two Trains Running*, "will probably be greeted with the same hallelujah chorus as all his other work."

Brustein ended the review with a parting salvo at Richards. "I will simply ask how much attention such an artistic director can pay to his own institution when he has spent the last three years staging a single play in five different theatres, before producing it and directing it on Broadway?" The review scandalized Wilson's ever-growing theater circle, as well as the large group of actors, designers, and playwrights who had been Richards's students at Yale and his protégés at the O'Neill. Richards was known for his inscrutability. Although he had a temper in private, he rarely flinched publicly at criticism, and in this case, he remained silent.

Wilson, however, gave a measured response to the *New York Times*, which devoted an entire piece to Brustein's review. He hearkened back to his interview with Bill Moyers, noting that he had once been asked if he grows tired of writing about the Black experience. "Has anyone ever told a white playwright to write about Blacks?" Wilson asked. "There's no idea that cannot be contained in Black life. It's full and it's flourishing, like anyone else's life. How can that be limiting? Was it limiting to Chekhov to write about his people?"

Wilson's response may have been civil, but the wound cut deep, and it would not be the last of it. But Wilson would get his chance to battle it out with Brustein. He would reference the language of the review in the introduction to another play several years later. And he would keep working. His next play, *Two Trains Running*, had received its premiere at Yale Rep that spring, and it was on the same development trajectory at regional theaters nationwide. That would not change.

But one constant in his life was about to change unalterably. Since *Ma Rainey* had been accepted at the O'Neill in 1982, Wilson had been married to his work and rarely home. The fall before *Piano Lesson* opened on Broadway, Oliver produced a weeklong run of his early plays, *The Homecoming* and *The Coldest Day of the Year*, as a benefit for St. Paul's Model Cities Health Center. He made a rare trip home for the opening. He was touched by her efforts and told a reporter that *Coldest Day of the Year* was his favorite of all of his plays.

But Wilson's serial infidelity was well known among theater professionals who gossiped about him in private. Surely this wasn't lost on Judy Oliver, who spent most months of the year living on her own in St. Paul. No one in the theater or in his family had a bad word to say about Oliver. She was smart. She was loyal. She was not flashy or overly extroverted, but she provided stability and a strong foundation for Wilson when he was a struggling writer. But a marriage with an absentee partner cannot last forever.

Wilson's life had grown increasingly complicated since he had introduced Sakina to the costume designer Constanza Romero over lunch in New Haven. As the creative team worked on *Piano Lesson*, Wilson's relationship with Romero deepened. On July 19, 1990, a terse statement in the *New York Times* announced the dissolution of Wilson's second marriage. Wilson blamed the divorce on his work and was gracious in his brief comments, which were most likely designed to stop any chatter in the gossip columns. He said that he had only been home about three months a year for the past five years. "It's real hard to maintain a marriage and do the work at the same time," he said. "I was never there for her." He said he planned to move to Seattle, an arrangement he worked out with Oliver, according to friends. The two remained friends and talked intermittently after the breakup. Oliver cut off ties to their mutual friends and colleagues, however, and Lou Bellamy said she showed up at Penumbra one night with a man who was the spitting image of Wilson. She moved on with her life and, to this day, does not want to talk about her marriage. As for Wilson, he was deep into revisions of *Two Trains Running*, which had premiered at Yale Rep in March. The dedication in the published version of that play is sweet and to the point: "This one's for Judy."

CHAPTER TWELVE

Pick Up the Ball

How beautiful it is and how easily it can be broken.
—TENNESSEE WILLIAMS

When the announcement of his divorce appeared in the *Times*, Wilson was already in the process of moving to Seattle. At thirty-two, Romero was thirteen years younger than Wilson. She grew up in California, but Wilson did not want to move to the Golden State. He had spent that year in Los Angeles as a young man and left dejected. Since his triumphant Broadway debut with *Ma Rainey*, he had received plenty of offers to write screenplays, but turned them all down. He didn't want to become another washed-up playwright who worked on scripts that never got made or were written by committee. He had seen what happened to Charles Fuller, whose *A Soldier's Play* won the 1982 Pulitzer Prize for Drama; Fuller wrote the screenplay for the film adaptation of his play (called *A Soldier's Story*, it was directed by the white director Norman Jewison and starred Howard E. Rollins Jr.). Fuller was nominated for an Academy Award for Best Screenplay Based on Material from Another Medium, but after that, his screenplays never went anywhere. Wilson didn't want to write one play and then essentially disappear in the machinery of Tinseltown. "Where's Lonne Elder?" he asked a reporter from the *Guardian*, referring to the writer who started as a playwright, was lured to Hollywood to write the screenplay for *Sounder*, and then got disillusioned. "Where's Joseph Walker? They go, 'They're in Hollywood.' And I go, 'Oh,

I see.' I wanted to have a career in the theater." And, of course, he was still smarting over the *Fences* film deal, which had not come to fruition with a Black director. He had written his first-draft screenplay and expected to hear from Paramount about a production in June, but the deadlines kept changing. He wasn't budging; he had learned from his mother that something is not always better than nothing.

Wilson was putting St. Paul in his past. It would be two years before the divorce from Oliver was finalized, but both of them were moving on with their lives. Wilson had not been a good husband the second time around; he knew that. But the two handled the split without acrimony. Oliver had been a pillar of support for Wilson's work, but she hadn't signed up for fame and fortune. She compartmentalized her life, which was particularly painful for Shoholm, who had shared a decade of her life with her best friend. But for Oliver, that period was over, and she did not want to talk about it. Shoholm wasn't the only person who was hurt. Lloyd Richards's wife, Barbara Davenport, found the situation extremely awkward. "My mother was friends with Judy until there was no Judy," Scott Richards said. "She was not terribly pleased."

Wilson moved on rather quickly himself. He was not a nester; he was happy living in hotels and writing in bars and browsing around bookshops. The couple decided on Seattle without much debate. "We were not shopping around," Romero said. "August doesn't travel well, even though he had traveled constantly for twenty years. We made our decision and stayed. We didn't know anyone. We just knew each other. We found a house to rent. He is a walker and he could walk to the bank and the grocery store. He could go out and get his coffee. He's independent in this area, which is very important to him."

Wilson found a warm welcome at Chameleon Bookstore, a quirky, overstocked place owned by former Peace Corps volunteer Al Frank. One day, Wilson and Romero walked into the shop, and Frank immediately took to them. He was their first friend in the city. Since they didn't have children and were on the road so often, they didn't make a lot of friends at first, and Frank was a listener and a raconteur who was mesmerized by Wilson's long, rambling stories. Frank was a free spirit who described Wilson as "half big brother and half mentor."

Wilson eventually rented a house in the Capitol Hill neighborhood of Seattle. Located on a steep hill, it was originally known as Broadway Hill, after the main thoroughfare that runs through the bohemian neighborhood. The area is home to many of the wealthiest streets in Seattle, and Broadway is dotted with taverns, coffee shops, and restaurants, which suited Wilson's penchant for sipping an all-day coffee and chain-smoking as he wrote or chatted with one of the baristas in the town that popularized the term. The weather was another thing entirely. The dreary rain was depressing. But Wilson was on the road with *Two Trains Running*, so he wasn't around much to experience seasonal depressive disorder.

Two Trains had debuted at Yale the previous March, and it was touring regional theaters. But Wilson was still privately toying around with *St. Louis Blues: A Blues and Jazz Musical Featuring Mr. Jelly Roll Morton*, the musical he had written for Broadway producer Margo Lion in 1986. Lion had optioned the rights to a series of Library of Congress interviews that the ethnomusicologist Alan Lomax conducted with jazz pianist Jelly Roll Morton. Wilson's play focused on an incident that was recorded in the interviews. Morton had told Lomax that he did not attend the St. Louis World's Fair in 1904 to compete in a piano competition because he expected the New Orleans pianist Tony Jackson would be there and would inevitably win. Wilson took that historical footnote and expanded it into a musical with a cast of twelve and twenty-five songs, all standard tunes popularized by Morton. In the musical, Morton shows up in St. Louis for the competition, but he never makes it to the World's Fair. He and pianist Jackson face off in a saloon, and the contest is ruled to be a tie. The local gambling boss kills a character who is a salt-of-the-earth pillar of the community, and Morton leaves town after the funeral. The cast includes a group of church ladies, as well as a single mother who is Morton's short-lived love interest.

As musicals go, it was rather slight, and Lion passed on producing

Wilson's book. She switched gears and hired George C. Wolfe to write the book instead.

But Wilson didn't give up on the project after Lion pursued other options. He and Claude Purdy got together with musical director Dwight Andrews, Wilson's colleague from Yale who had joined the faculty of the Department of Music at Emory University in 1987. They had several meetings with the university's Theater Emory and had plans to apply for grants from numerous sources, including the National Endowment for the Arts and the Meet the Composer foundation. Andrews said the team knew that they couldn't just do a jukebox musical featuring Morton's music, but they never figured out who would write original music and lyrics. "One of the first things we confronted was August's rich imagination," Andrews said. "How do we confront his wonderful language and transform it into a lyric and song and compress it into a much smaller amount of words? That was the conceptual challenge." They discussed whether they needed to bring on a lyricist, but Wilson was proprietary about his work. He was inclined to write the lyrics himself.

This was a departure for Wilson. While music infused his dramas, he was adamant that they were not musicals and rejected suggestions that he turn *Ma Rainey* into a musical. But he was interested in reaching the musical theater audience and further exploring the music he loved in another format. The three collaborators met with administrators at Theater Emory in Atlanta to discuss the project, and they eventually submitted a proposal to hold a workshop in the spring of 1991, with a cast of seven professional actors, along with a company of ten to fifteen students from Emory and Atlanta's predominantly Black colleges. They were also banking on Wilson's growing fame. Wilson mentioned the workshop in interviews and was excited about the prospect; Purdy was just as gung ho. He and Wilson had worked together on the comically calamitous production of *Black Bart* in 1980, and Purdy thought his friend had another big, boisterous musical in him, one that showcased the music he loved and featured an all-Black cast. But it never materialized. Wolfe's musical, *Jelly's Last Jam*, premiered at the Mark Taper Forum in March 1991. It was a smash hit on Broadway in 1992 with a cast led by Gregory Hines, Savion Glover, and Keith David (who later appeared in Wilson's *Seven Guitars*).

Wilson filed his script away. He had not mastered the musical theater format, and he also knew that nobody was going to produce another musical about the same subject. Plus, his heart wasn't in it anymore; the project distracted him from his cycle of plays. He didn't think about it—or mention it—again. He did, however, think he should return the $10,000 commission he had received from Lion, but never did.

He was seething about the prolonged stalemate with the film adaptation of *Fences*. It had been three years since he had sold the option for the film rights, and the movie remained unproduced. He wrote a scathing essay headlined "I Want a Black Director" for the October 1990 issue of *Spin* magazine. The special issue was guest-edited by filmmaker Spike Lee, who had made a name for himself with *She's Gotta Have It* and *Do the Right Thing*. He was at work on his next film, *Jungle Fever*. The director was as vocal as Wilson was reserved, but they wholeheartedly agreed on the issue of Black directors directing films about Black culture and history. It made sense that Lee and the magazine gave Wilson a platform to take a public stand. In his essay, Wilson laid out his case that Black Americans share their own unique culture and sensibilities. "We are an African people who have been here since the early 17th century," he wrote. "We have a different way of responding to the world. We have different ideas about religion, different manners of social intercourse. We have different ideas about style, about language. We have different aesthetics. Someone who does not share the specifics of a culture remains an outsider, no matter how astute a student or how well-meaning their intentions."

The provocative piece called out Hollywood producers as well as Eddie Murphy, who had been dismissive of the idea when they sealed the deal. (Ironically, the issue also included a long interview of Murphy, conducted by Lee.) Wilson noted that Black Americans are frequently questioned about their ability and qualification in all fields, regardless of their experience and expertise. "The skills of Black lawyers, doctors, dentists, accountants and mechanics are often greeted with skepticism, even from other Blacks. 'Man, you sure you know what you doing?'" Wilson wrote.

The magazine drew a lot of media coverage, mainly because it featured the thirty-three-year-old wunderkind as editor of a music magazine founded and published by Bob Guccione Jr., the son of the founder of *Penthouse*, the porn periodical. Guccione granted the director full control. "We shook hands and I told him it would be the Blackest issue they've ever had . . . which wasn't very hard to do," Lee wrote in his editor's note.

The whole issue was explosive, but it was Wilson's piece that was excerpted on the op-ed page of the *New York Times*, where it received even more attention and laid the groundwork for positions Wilson would take later in his career. It created quite a buzz in Hollywood and theater circles. The man who had oft been described as low-key and laid-back had taken a controversial stand. Paramount had agreed in March to hire a Black director, but Wilson wasn't holding his breath. He didn't care if it meant his movie didn't get made, and he did not back down. At the same time, Lee staged a public protest against the plan by Warner Bros. to have Canadian director Norman Jewison helm a film about Black Nationalist icon Malcolm X. Like Wilson, he insisted only a Black director could do the film right. "No white in the world can appreciate being a Black. So no white director can do a good job on Malcolm X," he said. Lee went on to direct the 1992 film *Malcolm X*, which starred Denzel Washington.

Fences star James Earl Jones disagreed vehemently with both Lee and Wilson on this issue, and Wilson's persistence meant Jones would be too old to play the role he had originated on Broadway by the time the film was made. "There's too much attention paid to the wrong issues," Jones told the *New York Times* in 1991. "Let's just damn the torpedoes and get it done."

The theater gossip channels were still abuzz when Wilson arrived in Boston a few weeks after the publication of the piece. He was there to work on *Two Trains*, which he had been rewriting since its premiere at Yale in March 1990. This was his 1960s play, set in the era when he was hanging out on the streets of Pittsburgh learning to become a poet and a man. The Yale program had included a brief author's note: "It is 1968 in

Pittsburgh. . . . Here there is hope refreshing itself, quickening into life. Here there is a drumbeat fueled by the blood of Africa. . . . There are always and only two trains running. There is life and there is death. Each of us rides them both."

At Yale, the play was set a month after the assassination of Martin Luther King Jr. The production was billed as a "work in progress," which was code for "Critics be kind and constructive." Wilson himself was well aware that, for the first time, he had not subjected this play to the development process at the O'Neill and that the play was in rough shape. Kevin Kelly of the *Boston Globe* wrote that the play's eight scenes "fail to accumulate into a compelling climax, principally because there's an odd lack of definition." But as usual with Wilson, the critics did not write as if they were seeing a finished product, but rather a first draft with enormous potential. The play, Kelly wrote, not able to resist riffing on the title, "is waiting at the station. Humming. Ready to roll. And perhaps roar."

After seeing the play onstage at Yale Rep, Wilson felt that the timing was a distraction, so he rewrote it and set it in 1969. "Setting it in 1968 put too much pressure on the play," he said. "Most people remember that year because of the [Martin Luther] King assassination and the [Robert] Kennedy assassination. I don't deal with any of those things in the play, so the smart idea was to change it to 1969." He had lived through that era, though, and he was more interested in capturing the spirit of the time rather than the historical facts, which were well documented elsewhere. "By 1969, there was a new Black man on the scene, with some new power to work his ideas," was the way he explained it. "I am just going to go with that. I wrote the play simply to say that."

Wilson took the title from an old blues song: "There's two trains running / But there's not one going my way." The image represented a choice for Black Americans in 1969: assimilation versus cultural separatism. In many ways, it is a "typical" Wilson play, with long monologues and characters who sit around signifying. Like all of his plays except *Ma Rainey*, it is set in Pittsburgh, in a diner across the street from West's Funeral Home and Lutz's Meat Market, two businesses that actually existed. The diner—where you can get meatloaf with two sides for $2.35 and play

Aretha Franklin on the jukebox for a quarter—is a neighborhood gathering place, much like the gypsy cab station was in *Jitney!*. The restaurant's owner, Memphis Lee, came north from Mississippi in 1936 after he was cheated out of a land deal by a group of scoundrels who also killed his mule. The neighborhood is scheduled for redevelopment, and he aims to sell his restaurant to the city for $25,000 so he, like Boy Willie in *Piano Lesson*, can go back to Mississippi and reclaim his land. The regulars include Wolf, a numbers runner who uses the diner as an office; Holloway, a retired housepainter turned armchair philosopher; West, the funeral director whose wife has walked out on him; and Hambone, a wounded soul with a singular refrain: "He gonna give me my ham. I want my ham." Years ago, Hambone had painted a fence for Lutz, the meat market owner, and was promised a ham as payment, but he was only offered a chicken. He wants justice, paid in meat. Every day, he asks for his ham, and every day, he doesn't get it. Even though he appears to be a lunatic, he is the soul of the play. He wants dignity. He wants to be valued for what he is worth. The ham represents his forty acres and a mule.

On the other hand, Risa is the inscrutable waitress—and the sole female character—who slashed her legs with a razor to ward off unwanted advances by men. The play never reveals her backstory, and she has little to say or do, except fry up the chicken and pour bottomless cups of coffee. The character is inscrutable—and underdeveloped. While Wilson gave Berniece in *Piano Lesson* a sense of self-determination, he barely gives Risa a voice, much less a personality. She is the weakest of all of his female characters. She disfigured her body as a message that she didn't want to be objectified, which in its essence is fascinating, but Wilson never reveals why. Was she abused in the past? It is hard to believe she is making a bold feminist statement, since she allows herself to be ordered around by Memphis and the customers in the diner, who always seem to be asking her to fetch some sugar. Is she reserved and subservient because she suffers from post-traumatic stress? Or has she built a wall for self-preservation? Wilson never answers any of those questions.

As in other Wilson plays, the equilibrium is shaken with the appearance of a stranger, in this case a young, idealistic parolee named Sterling, who is fresh out of prison and looking for a job and some action. Death is an omnipresent force. The neighborhood is mourning Prophet Samuel, a charlatan preacher with gold rings on his fingers who is laid out to rest at the funeral home across the street. Meanwhile, Sterling tries to convince Risa to attend a birthday celebration in memory of Malcolm X at the Savoy Ballroom, a real event that Wilson actually attended in 1969. Sterling is just as interested in Risa as he is in Black Nationalism; he has taken to the taciturn waitress and wants to lure her out on a date. Risa loses her steely demeanor in Act 2, Scene 4, when she gives in to Sterling's unsubtle advances and slow dances with him as the lights go down. She is literally scarred, but she finds her happiness in the arms of a man, just like Mattie Campbell, the boarder in *Joe Turner* who connects with Herald Loomis at the end of the play.

The real prophet of the story is an offstage character named Aunt Ester, a woman who lives at 1839 Wylie Avenue and who is said to be 322 years old with the healing power to "make you right with yourself." (There is no 1839 Wylie in Pittsburgh. Wilson chose the number because it was the year of the Amistad slave rebellion. Today, there is a memorial to Wilson on the site where 1839 would be.) Holloway urges Sterling to knock on her red door and ask for guidance. This is the first mention of Aunt Ester—or ancestor—in the Wilson canon, and Wilson brings her back in three later plays. It turns out that she is really 349 years old, as old as slavery in the United States. (Wilson meant for her to be born in 1619, the same year that slave slips landed at Jamestown, but he originally set the play in 1968. For the math to work, she should be 350 years old, but Wilson neglected to change the number when he changed the setting to 1969.) Aunt Ester represents the past, the tradition, the history, and she is a symbolic guidepost during a turbulent time when the future is uncertain. When Sterling and other characters seek her advice she has one message: "If you drop the ball, you got to go back and pick it up. Ain't no need in keeping running, 'cause if you get to the end zone, it ain't gonna be a touchdown. . . . You got to go back and pick up the ball." Wilson later said that Aunt Ester was the most important character, holding all of his plays together.

In the six months between the world premiere at Yale and the

September 1990 opening at the Huntington, however, Wilson had not done much rewriting, except to change the year of the action. There was one major casting change, however. Samuel L. Jackson was out in the role of Wolf, a numbers runner akin to Wilson's Pittsburgh mentor, the poet Chawley Williams, the self-described "digitarian." He was replaced by Anthony Chisholm, who would later become a member of a tight group that called themselves the "Wilson Warriors" and appeared over and over again in his plays. Many of them credit Wilson with giving them a path to financial stability, and more than one of them paid their mortgages and children's college tuitions because of the steady work they got acting in the Wilson canon.

But the play was still more like a series of character sketches than a cohesive story. Kelly wrung his hands in print, noting that "it's an evening of long, rambling, sometimes informative, sometimes idly charming anecdotes," not "a dramatic whole." And of course, the headline writers couldn't resist: " 'Trains': All Steamed Up, No Place to Go" was the headline of Kelly's review. Critics and copy editors could not resist obvious puns: "Two Trains Still Stalled at the Station," read another headline. The play, no doubt, "needed to get on track." Even though the story unfolds at a time when Wilson and his friends were steeping themselves in the Black Arts Movement, the play read as if Wilson were keeping the fever of the time at a distance; perhaps it was still too close and too deeply personal for him to examine fully. Sterling represents that "new Black man in 1969" who is not going to stand outside the market to get what he is owed but who is instead going to take it. In 1969, Wilson was trying to be that man himself. He was searching for his voice, and he had yet to find it. As a young man, he had, in a way, been looking for his own Aunt Ester. He was writing florid verse and was frustrated when audiences laughed at his work. He tried to satisfy Brenda Burton with a halfhearted attempt to embrace the Nation of Islam. He was raised in Daisy's home and subjected to racism at Central Catholic, but his peers questioned his ethnicity. He couldn't win. But he always cherished the strong Black women in the neighborhood who provided a moral compass, women like Miss Sarah Degree who insisted that he and his siblings study catechism. (Wilson

mentions Miss Sarah Degree as an aside, when West says she was the oldest person he ever buried.) Aunt Ester is a tribute to all those women. She
is the true source of knowledge. As he emphasized in *Piano Lesson*, without knowing the past, there is no future.

Wilson was self-aware enough as a writer to know that the play still
needed work. His other plays had seemed to flow magically from those
voices in his head directly to the page. This one was different. "You start
at the beginning each time you sit down," he said. "Nothing you've written
before has any bearing on what you're going to write now."

He compared the process to his favorite sport, boxing. "It's like a
heavyweight fighter," he said. "You've gotta go out and knock the guy out.
It doesn't matter if you're undefeated. There's another guy standing there,
and you have to go out again, and you have to duck his punches, and do
all the rest of whatever it is you do."

Wilson was still rewriting the play and fighting that fight when *Two
Trains* opened in January 1991 at the Seattle Repertory Theatre, a major
institution in his new hometown. He had rethought the character of Hambone, who originally died in the first act. He liked him too much to kill
him off so early in the play, however, so he added another scene for him
in the second act. Some critics had complained that there was too much
talking and not enough plot. Wilson rarely answered his critics directly,
but he later said, "My plays *are* talky; I say shut up and listen. They are
about Black men talking, and in American society you don't too often
have that because the feeling is: 'What do Black men have to say?'" And
even if the play meanders, the male characters are wise, and their stories
matter. In one scene, Memphis and Holloway discuss the fate of a boy who
was shot by the police and whose family never received justice.

The opening night of the Seattle production turned out to be aus-
picious in an unexpected way. Wilson was standing in the lobby when a
local writer approached him, stuck out his hand, and said, "Welcome to
Seattle." It was novelist Charles Johnson, who had won the National Book
Award for *Middle Passage* in 1990. Wilson was touched; aside from Al
Frank at the bookstore, no one else had extended such a warm welcome.
The encounter turned out to be the beginning of a beautiful friendship.

The two writers soon began meeting regularly for dinners that stretched way beyond midnight. They convened at the Broadway Grill on Capitol Hill, an idiosyncratic bistro that was a haven for the city's gay community as well as a neighborhood mainstay. Frequented by a diverse clientele of young and old, grunge and Goth, straight and gay, tie-dye and tweed, the quirky room boasted pinkish walls, an ornate glass chandelier, and a menu that included grilled chicken and whipped yams. Wilson and Johnson always asked for a table in the smoking section in the back, where they "would order organic Sumatra French roast coffee and a platter of chicken nachos with black beans, olives, and guacamole." And then they would talk into the night.

Johnson was three years younger than Wilson, and so they shared more than just their careers as writers. They both knew what it was like to be young, Black, and brilliant while growing up in the 1950s. They both believed in ritual. They frequently exchanged gifts before digging into their meal. In addition to being an author, Johnson is also a cartoonist, so Wilson presented him with books like *The Complete Far Side* by Gary Larson and *The Complete Cartoons of the New Yorker*. In turn, Johnson gave his friend a collection of stories by Jorge Luis Borges, since he knew Wilson admired the Argentine author. Wilson frequently cited Borges as an inspiration, and he was clearly influenced by the short story writer's uncanny blend of fact and fantasy and his mastery of magical realism.

Wilson opened up to Johnson in ways he didn't with journalists like Bill Moyers. In his essay "Night Hawks," Johnson recalled the significance of their connection. "This experience, we both knew, was extremely rare in the lonely, solitary lives of writers, especially those considered to be successful by the way the world judged things, so we sometimes looked at each other as if to say, 'How did *you* happen?'" Sitting at a late-night bohemian eatery with another Black writer, Wilson could pull down his mask and allow vulnerability to slip through. He told Johnson that he spent two weeks in deep depression after every Broadway opening. Sakina confirmed that. "My dad hated openings," she said. He always invited his family, and he ended up scurrying around to make sure everyone had their tickets and their hotel rooms. "It was stressful. Instead of taking the opportunity to enjoy his work, he worried about everyone else. He didn't care for the parties or the attention, either," she said.

Each play, it seems, took a little piece of his soul, and he was able to explain that to Johnson in a way he couldn't with most people. "Every page—indeed every paragraph—had been a risk," Johnson wrote. "Every sentence had been a prayer." Wilson told him that he wept one day when he could not remember when or why he had received one of his many honorary degrees. The man eating grilled cedar plank salmon over dinner did not have to project the image of the strong Black male who had overcome a rough-and-tumble childhood. He could unmask the sensitive artist who was afraid of dogs and who wondered, deep down, if art really matters. "Nothing we've done changes or improves the situation of Black people," he told Johnson one night. "We're still powerless and disrespected every day—by everyone and ourselves. People still think Black men are violent and lazy and stupid. They see you and me as the exceptions, not the rule."

Johnson, a practicing Buddhist who had grown up in a middle-class family in Evanston, Illinois, provided a sounding board for the playwright, who had always found comfort and inspiration in his friendships with male artists—Chawley Williams and Rob Penny in Pittsburgh and Claude Purdy in St. Paul. Wilson was a spiritual man who did not subscribe to any organized religion; he recognized the power of the church in the Black community, but he questioned blind faith and dogma. In that way, he was like Levee, cursing God. He was still haunted by the breakup of his first marriage, when he felt he wasn't good enough for his strict Muslim wife. But he was a searcher, and Johnson offered kernels of wisdom from Eastern philosophy, including a quote Wilson cherished from the Bhagavad Gita, which is part of the ancient Hindu epic, the *Mahabharata*: "Your right is to action alone; never to its fruits at any time."

Those lingering dinners provided an anchor for Wilson when he was in Seattle—which wasn't often. *Two Trains* was making its way around the country's regional theaters, with productions at the Old Globe Theatre in San Diego in March 1991 and at the Kennedy Center in Washington, D.C., in November that year. Wilson had grown more and more protective of his work, and he frequently checked in on regional productions

Zonia Wilson, August's
maternal grandmother. She
married Bynam Wilson, and
they left Spear, North Carolina,
to start a new life in Pittsburgh.

Wilson, then using his birth name of Frederick August Kittel, at Pittsburgh's Central
Catholic High School, back row center, with his head down. He quit after less than a year
because of racist taunting.

3

Wilson and Pittsburgh's Centre Avenue Poets, as they called themselves: (*left to right*) Chawley Williams, Rob Penny, Wilson, Maisha Baton, and Nick Flournoy.

4

An aspiring writer, Wilson worked with the Little Brothers of the Poor until 3:00 p.m., when he left to write in restaurants. Executive director Michael Henley is next to Wilson.

5

Wilson and his mother, Daisy, at his wedding to his second wife, Judy Oliver. Wilson's daughter Sakina is behind Daisy.

6

Wilson and Oliver at the Eugene O'Neill Theater Center, where Wilson made his break-through. Oliver helped support him as he sought to become a playwright.

James Earl Jones played Troy Maxson in *Fences*. Jones loved the role but clashed with Wilson as the play made its way to Broadway.

After winning a Pulitzer for *Fences*, Wilson won another for *The Piano Lesson*. By then, he and director Lloyd Richards (*right*) had created one of the most significant partnerships in American theater history.

7

Delroy Lindo (with Angela Bassett) gave an indelible performance as Herald Loomis in Wilson's masterpiece, *Joe Turner's Come and Gone*. Wilson said that the play was the best thing he ever wrote.

Charles S. "Roc" Dutton, who went from jail to Yale, in *Joe Turner*. He also played Levee in *Ma Rainey's Black Bottom* and Boy Willie in *The Piano Lesson* on Broadway and appeared in other roles at the O'Neill Center.

At the Dartmouth summit, playwright Ntozake Shange (*left*) was a spiritual force. Wilson's third wife, Constanza, stands alongside him as he holds their daughter, Azula.

Wilson with Lou Bellamy, left, and Claude Purdy at the Penumbra Theatre, where Bellamy staged Wilson's disastrous musical *Black Bart and the Sacred Hills*. Purdy directed many of Wilson's plays in regional theater.

After he broke with Richards, Wilson chose Marion McClinton (*left*)
rather than Purdy as his director of choice.

Wilson bonded with Todd Kreidler, his assistant on *King Hedley II*. He asked Kreidler to
cowrite and direct his one-man show, *How I Learned What I Learned*.

Pallbearers at Wilson's 2005 funeral, left to right: Kreidler, Anthony Chisholm, unidentified, Kenny Leon, and Wilson's brother Richard Kittel.

15

Wilson's older daughter, Sakina, at Wilson's childhood home in Pittsburgh, now restored as a community arts center.

16

17

A few weeks after Wilson's death, Broadway's Virginia Theatre was renamed in his honor.

Viola Davis (*seated, far left*) and Denzel Washington (*seated, center*) on the set of the Broadway revival of *Fences*. Washington has committed to filming all of Wilson's plays.

of plays that had already debuted on Broadway. Sometimes he couldn't keep track of his own schedule. Once, he was on the East Coast working on a production at the Huntington while Lloyd Richards was on the West Coast directing a different play. Wilson flew to San Diego to meet with Richards, but the director had just left town. Wilson gave in to his exhaustion: he got a hotel room and slept for four days.

The production at the Old Globe was bittersweet. Actor Ed Hall, who had given a transcendent performance as Bynum in *Joe Turner*, was struggling in the role of Holloway. Earlier in Boston, he had trouble remembering his lines and had to make belabored efforts to stand up or sit down. Wilson had been dazzled by Hall's performance as Bynum, but now he and Richards were alarmed by his frailty and decided to recast the role. Richards was fiercely loyal to his actors, and as a young man, Hall had had a walk-on role in the 1959 Broadway debut of *A Raisin in the Sun*. The actor and director went way back, and the decision was not an easy one for Richards. A few years later, a similar casting decision would lead to trouble, but in this case, both Richards and Wilson agreed that they had to replace Hall, who died that July of a long, protracted illness. Death was a theme in the play, and Wilson never missed an opportunity to honor the dead; he spoke glowingly of Hall in a *Boston Globe* tribute, describing him as "the consummate actor" who should have won a Tony Award for his spellbinding performance in *Joe Turner*.

The subject of death was always on Wilson's mind and it would end up central in his next play, which he was already creating in his head while he was crisscrossing the country. At this point, he was envisioning a play called *Moon Going Down*, set in the 1940s in a turpentine processing camp in Georgia. "It would have an all-male cast, and their life within the camp would reflect the societal pressures outside," he told Richard Christiansen of the *Chicago Tribune* in February. "Each man would be capable of killing the others."

This was typical Wilson. He had heard the characters of his previous plays talking to him, and now he was listening in on these men. And he couldn't always control what they said—and to whom. By December, he had changed direction for a single reason: a woman walked in. He remembered that moment by re-creating the conversation he had with the characters. "The guys looked up and said, 'Hey man, you said this was an all-male play. What the hell she doin' here?' Hey, I don't know. 'Well get out of here! You don't belong here.' She says, 'I want my own scene.'" Wilson decided to add a woman to the cast of characters. But that wasn't the end of it. "Then a man knocks on the door, and he had a chicken under one arm and a radio under the other. And she opened the door and called him by name and said, 'Come on in.'"

Wilson dropped the turpentine camp and set his 1940s play in Pittsburgh, with the original characters, along with the woman and the man with the chicken. He changed the title to *Seven Guitars*, and he never finished the play about the turpentine camp.

All of this was going on in his head as he readied *Two Trains* for its Broadway opening, which was set for April 1992. He was also finalizing the divorce with Oliver. The paperwork was filed on March 24. Oliver filed, citing "an irretrievable breakdown of the marriage relationship." At the time, she was employed by the St. Paul Urban League. The two worked out a deal, with Oliver receiving a total settlement of $1 million. That included a percentage of Wilson's creative rights on his first four plays through 1995. Wilson was a man who was true to his word, and he must have insisted that the lawyers work out the numbers so that the bottom line came down to a clean million. When they were first married, the pair scraped to get by, went through bankruptcy, and ultimately ended up buying and restoring a gorgeous historic property in an upscale section of St. Paul. As Wilson said when he won his first Tony Award, Oliver had been there with him at 3:00 a.m. when everyone else was asleep. She licked the envelopes of his play submissions and kissed them for good luck. They remained friends. And then she disappeared from the August Wilson orbit.

On April 13, 1992, three weeks after the divorce was finalized, *Two Trains*, the play he had dedicated to his ex-wife, opened at the Walter Kerr

Theatre on Broadway. *Piano Lesson* had debuted there as well. The critics unwittingly provided plenty of blurb material for the production's marketing team: "vivid and uplifting" in *Time*; "unassailable authenticity" in *Variety*; and "easily Mr. Wilson's most adventurous and honest attempt to reveal the intimate heart of history" in the *Times*. Two performances stood out: Larry Fishburne as the young parolee and Roscoe Lee Browne as Holloway, the retired housepainter and self-appointed philosopher. (He had replaced the late Ed Hall.) At the time, Fishburne (who later changed his professional first name to Laurence) was known for starring roles in the films *School Daze* and *Boyz n the Hood*. He was not yet the icon he would become after his commanding performance in the 1999 blockbuster *The Matrix*, but his captivating role in *Two Trains* was a huge draw and he later walked away with the Tony Award for Best Featured Actor in a Play. Browne, a veteran of both Shakespeare and television who boasted a rich voice and natural stage presence, had an uncanny command of the stage.

But despite these two performances, the flaws in the play were evident. Even though it had been rewritten over two years of productions in the regional theater, it was still a series of vignettes with little action. Frank Rich of the *Times* put it this way: the play, he wrote, "sometimes seems the battered survivor of a conventionally grueling road tour." Inaction was not the only problem. Wilson had not been able to humanize his one female character, Risa, who remained not just enigmatic, but devoid of spirit. She was a nonentity until someone needed a cup of coffee or a bowl of beans. Perhaps Wilson knew this and perhaps that is why he listened when "a woman walked in" while he was imagining his next play. He was certainly aware that some critics and academics, many of them women, thought his female characters were stereotypical and limited to the role of mother or lover. That wasn't true of the dynamo Ma Rainey, but she was not the central character in *Ma Rainey*, despite the title. Risa was an enigma. Wilson had certainly known strong, independent women in 1969; the poet Maisha Baton had stood up to him when he smacked her in the face during the ill-fated performance of *Recycle*. He failed to re-create that spirit in *Two Trains*.

He may have been aware of this failing. He was having misgivings about his career and his meteoric rise to success. Shortly after the opening, he had a heart-to-heart conversation with Jujamcyn creative director Jack Viertel at the Café Edison. Wilson confessed that he wasn't satisfied with *Two Trains*; he felt that if you moved the scenes around, it wouldn't make any difference. To some extent, he was right. The characters tend to declaim, and as poetic and commanding as they are, the long speeches do not move the plot forward. But while Wilson struggled with the ending of *Piano Lesson*, he nailed the ending of *Two Trains*. After Hambone dies in his sleep, Sterling takes what Hambone had spent nearly ten years seeking: he breaks into Lutz's Meat Market and steals a ham and tells West to put it in the casket as the lights fade to black. It is the perfect conclusion.

Wilson was feeling weighted down by the enormity of the task he had created for himself. He told Viertel that he was thinking a lot about the career of Tennessee Williams. The playwright, of course, was a theatrical phenomenon in the 1940s and '50s, with a prodigious output of such Broadway hits as *The Glass Menagerie*, *A Streetcar Named Desire*, and *Cat on a Hot Tin Roof*. Like Wilson, he partnered primarily with a single director, Elia Kazan. But Williams went into a downward spiral in his later years, suffering from depression and alcohol and drug abuse. He died tragically in 1983 at age seventy-one, alone in his suite at the Hotel Elysée in Manhattan. This made Wilson wonder about his own career path. "I've told the world that I'm going to write these ten plays," he said to Viertel. "At a certain point, Tennessee Williams's career fell down the elevator shaft because his personal obsession became so much that he was writing about things that only he could really appreciate or care about. So I'm looking at how he did it to make sure I don't do it." In that moment, Wilson was concerned. Williams, after all, exorcised his personal demons and his family trauma in his work. In his earlier plays, Wilson wrote from the "blood's memory," but *Two Trains* was set in the formative years after he left his mother's house and learned to become a man. Williams's career was a cautionary tale. Wilson had lived through a lot, but he became more and more determined not to let it destroy him.

As he confessed to Charles Johnson, he was wondering whether art really mattered—at least when it came to social change. *Two Trains* takes place a year after the assassination of Martin Luther King Jr. sparked riots in Pittsburgh. Wilson had lived through that turmoil. He had seen the National Guard swoop down on the Hill District. When he was working on *Two Trains* in San Diego in March 1991, an eighty-one-second amateur video of a Black man named Rodney King being beaten by four Los Angeles police officers was aired by news media all over the world, creating outrage over police brutality. On April 29, 1992, two weeks after *Two Trains* opened on Broadway, a jury in Los Angeles acquitted all four police officers of assault in the King beating and acquitted three of using excessive force (they could not reach agreement on the fourth officer). The verdict uncorked the fury that was already simmering in the Los Angeles African American community; six days of rioting destroyed neighborhoods and left more than sixty people dead and several thousand injured. The National Guard was called in to restore order. The uprising—and the pent-up rage—were familiar territory to Wilson. He remembered Pittsburgh in 1968, and his play was set in the aftermath of that turmoil.

Two Trains closed on August 30, 1992, after 160 performances. It was nominated for the Tony Award for Best Play and was a finalist for the Pulitzer Prize but did not win either. It did receive the New York Drama Critics' Circle Award for Best American Play, an award that Wilson treasured and had won for each of his Broadway productions. Fishburne was the only member of the cast to win a Tony, for Best Featured Actor in a Play. (Coincidentally, *Jelly's Last Jam* was up for Best Musical that year but lost to *Falsettos.*) And if Wilson was worried about his work having meaning, Fishburne eloquently gave him a reminder in his acceptance speech at the Tony Awards ceremony. He summarized exactly what Wilson was doing when he gave thanks to all who had passed before him. "I'd like to thank . . . my ancestors, the mothers of my mothers, the fathers of my fathers, who speak so eloquently and seem to come to life and breathe through the works of the poet warrior, my elder brother August Wilson," Fishburne said.

For once, Wilson didn't have a new play already in the development process, and he had more time to focus on *Seven Guitars* but was still traveling
to see productions of his work at regional theaters. In May 1993, he found
himself in St. Paul to attend a performance of *Piano Lesson* at Penumbra
Theatre, his old stomping ground. Marion McClinton, an actor and playwright who had played the narrator in the ill-fated production of *Black Bart*
a decade earlier, was the director. Born in 1954, McClinton was nine years
younger than Wilson, but they shared a similar, hardscrabble background.
McClinton grew up in the Selby-Dale section of St. Paul, which at the time
was considered a gritty neighborhood like the Hill District in Pittsburgh.
They each had strong, tenacious mothers, and both attended parochial
school. Both were whip-smart, and both quit school to protest overt racism. McClinton left the University of St. Thomas in St. Paul after his freshman year because the school hosted a "faux-slave day," where students were
auctioned off and held captive for the day. He never graduated from college,
and he spent his early adulthood trying to find his way as an artist.

McClinton was out of town the night Wilson showed up to see his
interpretation of *Piano Lesson*. McClinton was anxious, since Wilson was
notorious for his temper, especially when he felt that his work wasn't being
served. Another actor told him that Wilson "flipped out" when he saw
the production, and McClinton was initially devastated, until he learned
that Wilson "flipped out" in a good way. A few years later, Wilson said
that McClinton's production was his favorite staging of the play. Another
friendship was born.

And life was more relaxed in Seattle. He was still focused on theater
and his cycle of ten plays, but he didn't have a deadline looming for his
next opening. Film offers poured in through his attorney, John Breglio,
but Wilson turned all of them down. Most of the offers were for biopics
examining the lives of such African American legends as Jackie Wilson,
Sam Cooke, and Muhammad Ali, and Wilson wanted to focus on original
work, on his own ideas.

He didn't need a fancy place to develop those ideas, either. But in September 1993, he bought the second house he would ever own, a three-
story home at 1412 East Aloha Street, a leafy spot in the upscale section

of Seattle's Capitol Hill. Built in 1903, the residence had a spacious front porch, the perfect setting for long, rambling conversations. A majestic staircase led to his office on the second floor, an aerie similar to the one he had had at the house on Holly Avenue in St. Paul (without his name tiled on a bathroom floor). Wilson stored books and awards in that space, but he didn't write there. When he was creating, he retreated to the half-finished basement, where he set up a simple desk and installed a punching bag to work out his energy, when needed.

He liked the confines of the basement, the purr of the furnace, the musky air. The furnishings in the rest of the house, at first, were minimal. Romero was eager to decorate the new home, but she didn't push it. Now that they had been living together for several years, she knew when to nudge Wilson and when to leave things alone. The piano from the set of *Piano Lesson* took up a corner of the living room; later, the jukebox from *Two Trains* was displayed nearby. Wilson didn't care about sofas or formal dining tables. He would disappear into the basement and work into the late night, and during the day, he would sit outside one of the cafés on nearby Broadway. He crossed the street if he saw one of the many dog-loving residents out for a stroll with a beloved pet; he never got over his fear of dogs. He still didn't drive, and he was fond of Seattle's public transportation system. He could always pick up a bus if he had to get somewhere in another part of the city. And he quit smoking. Romero didn't smoke, and Sakina had always wanted him to quit, as she grew up fearing a late-night phone call from the hospital. He didn't use the patch or nicotine gum. He just stopped cold turkey.

By December 1, 1993, he had finished the first draft of *Seven Guitars*. He sent it off to the O'Neill Center for consideration in the next National Playwrights Conference. He didn't ask for special treatment; he played by the rules and applied just like all the other playwrights. (He surely didn't have to; August Wilson was now synonymous with the O'Neill, one of its biggest stars, and he had an unspoken, open invitation to work there, even with an unfinished draft.) He had learned his lesson from *Two Trains*; the vigorous developmental process at the O'Neill helped him to see more clearly and led to more cohesive work. Of course, his play was accepted.

In the meantime, Wilson and Richards had reached an agreement to film a teleplay of *Piano Lesson* for *Hallmark Hall of Fame*. Shooting was set to take place in Pittsburgh during the summer of 1994, beginning just after the playwrights conference. Wilson had had a few months to slow down, but that summer his life became peripatetic again, with several simultaneous projects.

But the O'Neill was still home for him, even though he discovered one change when he arrived for the conference in July 1994. The playwrights had formerly been housed in "The Slammer," the antiseptic, Spartan dorms at nearby Mitchell College. They now had new digs at the Seaside Sanatorium. Set on the shore of Long Island Sound a few miles from the O'Neill campus, Seaside is an imposing three-story brick fortress designed in 1934 by architect Cass Gilbert. By the time the playwrights arrived, the sprawling Tudor Revival compound had fallen into disuse; its brick facade was covered with green moss, and the once manicured lawns were patchy and bare in spots. Its most endearing feature was the seawall at the edge of the property; on clear summer nights, playwrights would convene there to share a bottle, a cigarette, or a pungent joint.

The setting was a mix of former splendor and current squalor, and since the playwrights all had active imaginations, they imagined grotesque scenes from the storied building's past. They convinced themselves that the complex was a former psychiatric hospital—and told macabre tales to go along with that theory. "It was a building that clearly had been built I think in the nineteenth century," playwright Lee Blessing said in *The O'Neill: The Transformation of Modern American Theater*. "Metal gates blocked some of the stairwells. It felt like Shutter Island. Creepy. We were all on the first floor. If you went down to the basement, I'm told you could see equipment that had been used to, uh, help people with mental and emotional problems over the years."

In fact, the facility was originally built to treat children with tuberculosis. When sun and fresh-air treatments for the disease were replaced with new medications, the facility was used as a home for the elderly, then a hospital, and finally a school and home for intellectually disabled individuals. Seaside was included in a 1965 book about state institutions called *Christmas in Purgatory: A Photographic Essay on Mental Retardation* by Burton Blatt and Fred Kaplan. The book exposed abusive conditions at some state schools, but it singled out Seaside as a paragon of compassionate, dignified care. The authors held Seaside up as the ideal model compared with the other abhorrent institutions chronicled in the book.

But it made a better story for the playwrights to say—and come to believe—that they were living in what they called an "insane asylum," complete with instruments of torture in the basement. It's what they do: they create drama and make their own mythology. By the summer of 1994, Wilson was a bit of a mythical figure himself at the O'Neill. He had been anointed the "Chosen One" his first summer in 1982, but he had gone on to prove his worth.

The O'Neill can be unnerving for first-time playwrights, as Wilson learned when he was a neophyte. During the summer of 1994, a young playwright named Herman Daniel Farrell III was in residence with *Bedfellows*, a drama about the slippery world of New York politics. (His father, Herman Daniel Farrell Jr., was a New York State assemblyman, representing West Harlem, Inwood, and Washington Heights from 1975 to 2017. He unsuccessfully ran in the New York Democratic primary for mayor of New York in 1985, losing to Ed Koch.) On the first night at Seaside, Farrell joined a group of playwrights who had gathered to share some Jack Daniel's, and he began to feel more comfortable as the evening wore on. Around 11:00 p.m., Wilson shuffled in. "He was wearing slippers, black socks, and Bermuda shorts," Farrell said. "He comes in and says, 'Mind if I join you? I am August.'" Of course, no introduction was needed, but Wilson wanted to make the younger playwrights feel at ease. "He said, 'I am so glad I got in. I was so excited when I got the telegram from Lloyd.' We were all looking at him as if there was any doubt he would get in. He was trying to remind us that he is a regular guy."

Wilson turned out to be an impeccable housemate. The playwrights lived on the first floor, with rooms near where the old nurses' station used to be. Even though they ate meals at the O'Neill Center, they shared a communal refrigerator that mysteriously always seemed to be stocked with beer. Wilson bought it, according to Douglas Post, who was back at the conference for the third time with his play *Drowning Sorrows*. Even though Post was a veteran, he was still a bit unnerved by the process in which playwrights are put under the spotlight and their works are subjected to critiques by veteran Broadway actors and directors. Wilson's camaraderie put him at ease. "I never got a sense that he wanted to be treated differently," Post said. "I never got a sense that Lloyd was showering more love on him than anyone else. Because Lloyd did not necessarily shower a lot of love. Every summer I went there, Lloyd would look at me, and I always felt like I was the mistake." Wilson, on the other hand, accepted all the playwrights as peers.

At the preconference that year, the playwrights did not receive the traditional jackets with the O'Neill logo that many had come to treasure over the years. Apparently, there was no money in the budget. But one day during the conference, the jackets suddenly appeared; an "anonymous donor" had paid for them. Post and the other residents of the sanatorium knew who it was: the guy in the slippers and Bermuda shorts who also went out on beer runs for the group.

Wilson was there to work, though, and he kept to himself quite a bit, strolling around the grounds in his signature khaki coat and page boy cap. Amy Saltz was once again assigned as his director. She had been both bedazzled and befuddled when she had directed *Joe Turner* several years earlier, but she was immediately drawn to *Seven Guitars*. Set in 1948, *Seven Guitars* is a composition for seven characters who play off one another like a well-tuned septet. "It was a world that I could understand," Saltz said.

At the O'Neill, playwrights are given four days of rehearsal, followed by two staged readings. They sweat and work until the performances are over, and then they are free to let loose and turn the rest of the experience into a sort of postcollegiate frat party. Several of the playwrights had already had their performances when Wilson was rewriting. One foggy night, a group of them gathered on the seawall with a bottle of something strong. They noticed the light was on in Wilson's room, and they could see him sitting at his desk, working. He was listening to music, the blues, and they could hear the bittersweet sound of the chords and the clacking of the keys on his typewriter. The mix of the fog and the music—blurred by the booze—created a sort of painterly image, and the playwrights got up from the wall and approached the building. Post got the idea to serenade Wilson, and all at once, the group broke into a round of "You Are My Sunshine." Wilson stopped what he was doing. "He put his elbows on the window and looked out at us and smiled," Farrell said. "It was beautiful." He went back to working and the other playwrights went back to drinking. Wilson later described the moment to Richards and said he was honored and inspired by his fellow playwrights.

That kind of camaraderie was the norm at the O'Neill in those days, and a sense of calm mixed with melancholy set in after the final critique by the entire O'Neill community. Most playwrights found the discussions brutal, and Wilson was no exception. But after his critique, he took time to relax under the old beech tree on the grounds. One afternoon, a somewhat timid young woman named Lucy Thurber approached him. She was twenty-three and working as an electrician for the playwrights conference. She had recently graduated from Sarah Lawrence College, but she had grown up poor in Western Massachusetts. *Seven Guitars* had touched her. "I come from a rural white background, and he was writing about the African American experience, but it was the first time I saw the people I loved onstage," she said. She told him she wanted to write about her background, so Wilson asked about her upbringing. "I come from poor white trash," she told him. He immediately stopped her, mid-sentence. "He said, 'Are they really trash? Is your mother trash? Are the people you love trash?'" He then went on to tell her something that changed her life. "You should never use the narrative that is being given to you," he said. "That is a false narrative about who you are and the people you grew up with. Don't let their language define who these people are," he told her. He then asked her for more details. She told him that her people could drink three cases of beer and still stand up. They could run from the cops and not get caught. "Start there," he said. "You give them their own language and allow them their own mythology. Do not let them be owned or defined by the greater narrative that is being forced on them." Thurber had been scared to approach Wilson for weeks, but she took his advice to heart and wrote a cycle called *The Hill Town Plays*, which celebrate her hard-scrabble background and culture. She won an Obie Award for her cycle in 2014. (The Obie Awards are similar to the Tony Awards and celebrate achievement in off-Broadway productions.) Wilson also gave her a copy of Toni Morrison's Nobel lecture, which the writer had delivered in December 1993. He signed it, "To Lucy, continue courage."

Wilson could have been talking about himself when he gave that advice to a young, aspiring playwright. He was frequently approached at the O'Neill, especially after his play had already been performed and he seemed open to conversation. One day, the playwright Post found him sitting alone under the beech tree. Wilson did not have the beatific smile from the night of the serenade. He was deep in thought. Post assured him he didn't want to talk about his play, but wanted him to perform in a parody he had written for the Playwrights' Cabaret, to be held at Blue Gene's pub on the O'Neill campus the following week. Every summer, the actors put on a cabaret, but this summer, the playwrights had banded together to stage their own performance. And Post had written a role for Wilson.

At first, Wilson said no. Period. He wrote. He did not perform. But he eventually agreed, and the next week, he starred in a skit called *Dunking Sadness*, a short parody of Post's play. Wilson played himself as an inebriated playwright who keeps mumbling about winning the Pulitzer Prize—twice—but most important, he boasts that he once made Lloyd Richards laugh. This was an in-joke among O'Neill habitués; Richards rarely played his cards, and it was considered a coup if you could get him to smile. The skit centered on Wilson's attempt to remember just what he said to elicit a chuckle and he got the final line—and the last laugh. The reluctant actor was the star of the show. It is not clear whether Richards thought it was funny, but Wilson later recited lines from the parody when visiting friends in New York.

Richards had more serious matters to consider than the playwrights' spoof. In addition to running the conference, he was preparing to direct the teleplay of *Piano Lesson*. Wilson had written the script, and he was also a producer on the project. Several cast members for the teleplay were in the O'Neill company that summer, which was convenient given the tight scheduling. The conference wrapped on July 30, and preproduction began in Pittsburgh on August 4. Wilson had had a break after the lukewarm reception to *Two Trains*, but he was back to his demanding schedule, as was Richards.

The two men had been collaborating this way now for more than a decade, but this schedule was hair-raisingly tight. Post and other playwrights did not notice any tension between Wilson and Richards during the conference. Richards, after all, was Buddha, a man who never lost his temper or buckled under stress, at least in public. Wilson was focused on *Seven Guitars*, but *Piano Lesson* was the first of his plays to be filmed for a national audience. His hopes of getting *Fences* filmed with a Black director were still unrealized, and he was well aware that more people would see a teleplay on national television than would see a film in a movie theater. "There's no question the largest audience is on TV," he told his hometown paper, the *Pittsburgh Post-Gazette*. "More people will see the production . . . than have seen all of my plays, all over, everywhere." The expected television audience was thirty million viewers. The pressure was on.

The production team was warmly welcomed in Pittsburgh, as Wilson was now a local hero, the hometown boy who made it to Broadway. He had specific Pittsburgh references in all of his plays, except *Ma Rainey*, which he set in Chicago. The local papers followed the production closely, and 168 locals played extras in the teleplay. Wilson was particularly enthusiastic about being able to cast two hometown legends as extras: union organizer and activist Nate Smith played a minister, and photographer Teenie Harris had a cameo as a neighbor. But not everyone in Pittsburgh, especially in the Hill District, was a fan of the way Wilson depicted his old haunts. Prior to the filming, the Pittsburgh Public Theater had mounted a production of *Two Trains*. In the play, the undertaker West is depicted as a moneygrubbing businessman who would steal the jewelry off corpses before laying them in the ground. But there was a real West Funeral Home on the Hill, run by a well-entrenched Black family that nurtured the community and often buried poor people for free. After the opening in Pittsburgh, the granddaughter of Thomas L. West Sr. wrote a scathing letter to the *Post-Gazette*, complaining that Wilson didn't really know "the characters of the Hill" and that he had insulted "the memory of the Hill forefathers and their current descendants." In her letter, Thomasina L. West wrote that her grandfather and his sons "never let the dollar sign interfere with their commitment of serving the people of the community, regardless of their financial status." When asked to respond, Wilson said that it was obvious that he was not writing about the real Thomas West. So why did he use the name? "Why not?" he asked, somewhat cavalierly. "There are West funeral homes all over the world. There are a dozen of them in Atlanta alone."

Wilson had the same attitude about using the Lutz Meat Market name. In *Two Trains*, Lutz refuses to give Hambone his ham as payment for a job well done. But in real life, Karl Lutz, who was white, was a beloved fixture in the Hill community, and most of his employees were Black, which was rare for white-owned businesses in the area at the time. His prices were fair; his meat was high-quality. But again, Wilson just picked the name; he was not writing about that particular business owner. The nitpicking frustrated him. "I never consciously modeled a character after anyone," he said. When *Two Trains* was playing in Boston, an Italian-Swiss television crew was doing a story about Wilson. The crew went to Pittsburgh and asked everyone on the Hill if they knew a man named Hambone who went around asking for a ham. They were repeatedly told no, but they continued their search. "They somehow thought, 'He couldn't have written that, there had to be a guy.' They went around trying to find him and then they wouldn't believe it when people told them no. I was so mad when I found that out," Wilson said years later.

But he was still loyal to Pittsburgh, and he had insisted that the *Piano Lesson* teleplay be filmed on his home turf. He also said that he was thrilled to have Richards behind the camera. Richards, he also noted, had always been his first choice to direct the film version of *Fences*. But tension between the two men arose during preproduction of the teleplay, which had an estimated $4 to $5 million budget. Richards is credited as the director (he also has a cameo in a gambling scene). Wilson is credited as the author of the play and teleplay, as well as a producer. That title gave him more clout than Richards, and he was using it. His daughter was hired as a costume assistant, and his brother Edwin worked on the crew as well. And Wilson became more of a micromanager than he had been in the theater.

At a production meeting, a designer named Patricia Van Ryker described her vision for the piano, mentioning that it would be carved with images of plantation life. But the piano is the central symbol. In the introduction to the play, Wilson was quite specific. *"On the legs of the piano, carved in the manner of African sculpture, are mask-like figures resembling totems,"* he wrote. As the play unfolds, it becomes clear that the carvings are a tribute to the ancestors.

Van Ryker's suggestion infuriated Wilson. "He was screaming," she told the *New Yorker.* "'How dare you do this! You're insulting my relatives! My race!' It was like I'd thrown kerosene on him." Richards was appalled. "I don't function dictatorially," he said. "I don't give directives. I saw August in a position of power. I knew I couldn't work *for* him."

During the shoot, Wilson was also overprotective of Sakina, who at twenty-four was getting a taste of the entertainment business and relishing the opportunity. Richards suggested that Wilson write some lines for her so that she could make some additional money as an extra. She is seen in the opening of a gambling scene along with Richards; she is on camera for just a few seconds. "I remember even then, he was being so protective," she said, before echoing her father's voice. "'What are you gonna be doing? You better not be sitting on some man's lap.' I thought, 'I am twenty-four years old and you're telling me I better not be sitting on some man's lap?'"

The timing of the film was unfortunate, not just because it overlapped with the O'Neill. Wilson and Romero had set a date to make their relationship official. She had planned an intimate wedding in the backyard of their home on East Aloha Street for August 20, but Wilson was at the O'Neill and in Pittsburgh in the weeks leading up to this major life event. He did manage to get back to Seattle on August 15 to apply for the marriage license, but by that point, the details were set. The decor had been arranged, and Chef Jim Watkins from a restaurant called Organica had been hired to cater a dinner for sixty guests. Romero had chosen a vintage orange-red outfit, but a few days before the wedding, Wilson had not even decided what he was going to wear to the ceremony. (He ended up wearing a blue suit.) Most couples take a little time off before and after the festivities—and plan that thing called a honeymoon. But Wilson, Sakina, Richards, and family members blew in from Pittsburgh, as if the wedding were a quick break from film production, not a life ritual.

He invited his friend James Yoshimura to Seattle for the ceremony. The day of the wedding, Yoshimura put on his best suit and showed up at Wilson's house. Wilson gave him the grand tour, leading him up a majestic staircase to the spacious second-floor office, with big windows, a massive fireplace, and an imposing desk. Wilson had bought the house more than a year earlier, but books were still sitting in piles on the floor. "This is supposed to be my writing room," Wilson said. He then led his friend back down the elegant staircase, past the kitchen, and into the basement. "Next to the hot-water heater and the furnace, there was a little portable table with a typewriter on it," Yoshimura said. Wilson gestured at the table. "This is where I write. I can't write upstairs. It's too nice."

It was only then that Wilson turned to his friend and said, "By the way, can you stand up for me?" He was asking Yoshimura to be his best man—on the day of the wedding. "I am telling you, the guy sometimes makes you just want to pick something up and knock him in the head," Yoshimura said. He was probably not alone in that thought. The small religious ceremony was held in the backyard before close friends and family. Richards gave a speech; Romero was his former student at Yale. Yoshimura, who makes his living with words, would have spent hours composing an appropriate toast if he had had the time, but he came up with something on the spot. The dining tables were set up in the (still-unfurnished) living room and arranged informally in a zigzag pattern, without the traditional table for the wedding party. Yoshimura made some impromptu remarks about how brilliant it was for the couple to include everyone at the head table. Despite being put on the spot, he was thrilled for his friend, who had come so far since the days when they pooled their pennies to buy a box of wine. Now Wilson was living in an elegant home, wearing a tailored blue suit, and standing next to his bride.

But the choice of a best man was an afterthought, as if Wilson had not spent any time thinking about the wedding or helping with the planning. A few days after the event, Richards and Wilson and the others involved with the filming of *Piano Lesson* flew back to Pittsburgh to complete the shoot. No honeymoon, no time to kick back with his bride. Work came first, which was a harsh reality for those closest to Wilson—and a cruel message to send when making a commitment.

Richards had spoken eloquently at the wedding, but he was beginning to wonder about the changes he saw in his protégé, who at forty-nine was no longer a young man. Richards wasn't, either. At seventy-five, he had already had a hip replacement and his health was up and down.

They wrapped the film on October 1, after twenty-five stressful days of shooting. The *Hallmark Hall of Fame* production aired on CBS on February 2, 1995. Wilson had predicted it would be seen by thirty million viewers. He thought of his mother. He could still feel her searing disappointment when he was a struggling poet. He could still hear her voice taunting him, "You be a writer when you get something on television!" The day it aired, he looked up at the sky and said, "Look, Ma, I did it."

"You a Big Man"

*An artist must be free to choose what he does, certainly, but
he must also never be afraid to do what he might choose.*

—LANGSTON HUGHES

In December 1994, Lloyd Richards underwent surgery to remove a
blockage from his carotid artery, which supplies oxygenated blood to
the frontal lobe of the brain. It is a dangerous condition that can lead to a
stroke or even death. On the day of the surgery, Richards's wife, the former dancer Barbara Davenport, and her two sons gathered in the waiting
room at Manhattan's Mount Sinai Hospital. Scott Richards, who had appeared as Sylvester in *Ma Rainey* and assisted his father on *Piano Lesson*,
was pursuing a Master of Fine Arts at New York University's Tisch School
of the Arts. Thomas Richards, who along with his brother had spent sum-
mers at the O'Neill, had settled in Italy and was an "essential collaborator"
with the experimental theater director Jerzy Grotowski. Lloyd Richards
was seventy-five, and the family had nursed him through other health
issues, including a hip replacement years earlier. They were used to waiting rooms and remained fairly calm in the antiseptic space where family
members of patients watched the clock and leafed through old issues of
Time magazine.

The trio was settled in when suddenly an agitated man burst into the
waiting room. It was Wilson, who had not been invited to sit vigil during
the operation. "He was incredibly nervous," Scott Richards said. "He was

breathing heavily and shuffling and seemed almost panicked. He seemed more upset than we did. I think he was incredibly scared." The family members were surprised to see him, but they weren't bothered by his presence. Over the years, he had become part of the family and had often been a dinner guest at the Richardses' brownstone on the Upper West Side of Manhattan. He had been there one night when Scott had a heated argument with his mother, and it wasn't a big deal because the family felt comfortable with him.

But there in the waiting room, Wilson was out of sorts. Because of the surgery, Richards had to withdraw from the upcoming production of *Seven Guitars*, which was set to open January 21, 1995, at the Goodman Theatre in Chicago. Richards had seemed in good health the previous summer at the O'Neill and during the filming of *Piano Lesson* in Pittsburgh, disagreements with Wilson aside. But this was life-or-death surgery, and Wilson was clearly terrified. "My guess is that he felt vulnerable, and I think that scared him on some level," Scott Richards said. "He might have felt some level of abandonment as well."

The surgery was successful, but Scott Richards thinks the medical emergency may have made Wilson realize that his relationship with the director who had shepherded five of his plays to Broadway might not last. Their arrangement had already shifted when Richards retired in 1991 as artistic director of Yale Repertory Theatre and dean of the Yale School of Drama. When Richards stepped down, Wilson wrote an eloquent tribute honoring the director at one of the many events celebrating his long career. "In the old days, in ancient Greece, in Africa and China, and all over the world, when you wanted to learn something, you left your village, your town, your hamlet, and went to sit at the feet of the master of what you wanted to learn," he wrote. "In 1982, I left my home in St. Paul and came to sit at the feet of Lloyd Richards. It was crowded. But I made a little space for myself and sat down. I came to learn about theater and in the process learned so much more."

Richards was a free agent now, and he didn't have control of the Yale Rep stage, which is why the pair had opted to premiere *Seven Guitars* in Chicago. The two men, along with Benjamin Mordecai, had discussed setting up a production company to mount Wilson's plays. In fact, around the time of Wilson's wedding in August, the three had hired an attorney to set up a general partnership agreement to produce *Seven Guitars*. They had proposed a unique profit-sharing formula: Wilson would receive 50 percent; Richards would get 35 percent; and Mordecai would receive 15 percent. In November, Wilson's attorney, John Breglio, had suggested an even higher share of 52 percent for the playwright, lowering Richards's take to 33 percent. Richards's attorney, Gary DaSilva, described this proposal as "incredulous and unacceptable." They had argued over profit sharing when *Joe Turner* was being produced, and they were back at it. Wilson and Mordecai quickly agreed to go back to the original formula.

The negotiations continued while Richards recuperated from his surgery and Wilson worked on *Seven Guitars* in Chicago. The team had brought on Walter Dallas, then artistic director of the New Freedom Theatre in Philadelphia, to replace Richards for the Goodman production. Dallas, a bald, bespectacled man who was two years younger than Wilson, was a laid-back director known for infusing joy into the rehearsal room. He was a stark contrast to the inscrutable Richards, and Wilson developed a brotherly kinship with Dallas, as opposed to the father-son relationship he shared with Richards. Wilson had once told *Vanity Fair* that he considered Richards to be a father figure. "Now Lloyd is old enough to be my father," he said. "Having grown up without a father, that has a lot to do with my relationship with him. I always view him in a fatherly way. You know, you want to please Pop. You want Pop to be proud of you."

But the father-son relationship, however genuine at first, was beginning to fray. At some point, children demand their independence. Sometimes, the break is smooth and without friction, but other times, the bond can break like a bone, sharp and painful. In this case, the proposed production partnership was creating hostility. While the profit split was uneven, the original plan was that each man would have one vote and that the partners would equally share decision-making and control. But while Richards was recovering in New York, he began to suspect that he was going to be cut out of a long-term partnership entirely. Wilson's attorney had requested that the playwright maintain the right to break any deadlock on creative decisions among the partners, rather than requiring unanimity, as originally planned.

On January 16, 1995, less than a week before opening night at the Goodman, Richards fired off a missive to Wilson and Mordecai. He outlined the long history of his work with the playwright and his "large role in creating and pursuing the paths for the work." He said that he was the one who had suggested the partnership, and that all three had agreed to an equal division of power. Yet Richards clearly sensed that his power was diminishing. "I fully realize that as August has gained knowledge and affirmation he might want to feel a greater control of his own and his work's destiny," he wrote. "Yet he might fail to recognize that he has always had that." He referenced "the father thing or authority figure thing, real or alleged; fact or images of power." He went on to say that new realities "create a center of power in one person and erode the original concept of Partnership." He described the new arrangement as the "August Wilson Company, funded by others and utilizing their services," not a genuine partnership.

In the meantime, Wilson and Mordecai had privately formed their own agreement to launch a partnership called Sageworks, and two days after he wrote his letter, Richards declined to participate because he "found nothing there to entice him." The son had struck out on his own, leaving the father behind to recover from major surgery.

Years later, Constanza Romero said that she believes Wilson called Richards to tell him that he was forming the company with Mordecai alone. But Richards felt burned. He had created the structure to develop new plays at various regional theaters before bringing them to Broadway. After the split, Richards confided in Courtney B. Vance, the former Yale student who originated the role of Cory in *Fences*. "Lloyd told me, 'Courtney, I set up this whole regional theater network so that all I needed was a playwright. I'd been waiting for a playwright so we could go around to all the regional theaters, work the play, and come on into New York.'" That wasn't entirely true; Richards initiated the regional theater circuit idea out of necessity, when he couldn't attract a producer for *Fences*. But Richards had shepherded his protégé since the day he showed up at the O'Neill, and now, when he was free of any strings that attached him financially and professionally to Yale, he had been cut loose.

Richards said he never discussed the split with Wilson but contended that the production company was initially his idea. His son Scott does not mince words. "It was a betrayal, and he was rightfully resentful," he said, adding that he had nothing to say about Mordecai, whom Richards had hired at Yale Rep and pulled in to manage Wilson's productions in the regional theaters. He felt it was a double-pronged betrayal with Wilson: Richards had welcomed him into his family. "My father didn't hang out with people other than his family," his son said. "He did not have buddies. He did not go out to the bars. He would do his work and go home. August became part of the family because we were at the same events all of the time."

The summer before the dispute over the new production company, Wilson and Richards had seemed to be on cordial terms when Wilson workshopped *Seven Guitars* at the O'Neill. Amy Saltz was tapped to direct again, and while she was captivated by the world Wilson had created, she knew the play was in rough shape and needed major surgery. "When he gave it to me, it wasn't a play," she said. "It was a lot of speeches. There were wonderful stories, but there was no play. There was no driving action." That had been the problem with *Two Trains*, which was one reason Wilson went back to the place where it all began for him.

Set in 1948, *Seven Guitars* opens as a group of friends gather after the funeral for blues singer Floyd "Schoolboy" Barton, who was murdered after returning from Chicago to Pittsburgh to reunite with his former lover Vera. (She is the woman who walked into Wilson's head when he was formulating the all-male play about the turpentine camp.) Floyd's hit record, a tune called "That's All Right," plays on the radio. The play originally began with Floyd and Vera dancing in the backyard of a house modeled after Wilson's boyhood home at 1727 Bedford. This early version led up to Floyd's murder and ended with his death, followed by a scene after his funeral. At some point, Wilson moved the last scene to the beginning, so that the audience immediately knows there has been a murder but doesn't know how it happened. The rest of the play is a flashback. The structure is Wilson's homage to his hero Jorge Luis Borges. He had discovered the Argentine writer in the *New Yorker* magazine, and he was struck by his stories that revealed the end at the beginning, leaving the reader to put together the pieces as they turned the pages. Even though the outcome was clear, the mystery was in the telling of the tale. "You're intrigued, because you know what is going to happen," he said of this Borges technique. "The intrigue is how this happened. I thought that it would be a great way to write a play." He added Borges to the list of creative influences he described as "The Four B's": Bearden, the blues, Baraka, and Borges.

Wilson had initially tried Borges's method of storytelling in an early version of *Fences*, which began with Troy's funeral and then went back in time to tell the rest of the story. But he dropped that idea and chose to write a linear tale. He was intent on starting at the end with *Seven Guitars* when he workshopped the play at the O'Neill. And even though he had become a theatrical powerhouse since he and Saltz first shared bourbon back in 1982, he was clear that he wanted the diminutive director to do her job and take the reins. "He still wanted to learn," she said. "He was open to hearing anything and everything about his play. He said, 'You are the director, so direct. It is your job.' He wanted the input. He wanted the feedback."

So Saltz did her job. Wilson had written his usual poetic monologues and had created seven characters who formed a makeshift urban family. (Wilson deliberately set the play at his childhood home, where he was one of seven children, even though his sister Barbara did not live with the clan.) Floyd had walked out on Vera when he moved to Chicago to make it big in the music industry, and now that he has a hit record, he has several goals. He wants Vera back, and he wants to convince her to go to Chicago with him for another recording session. He will prove himself and become a star. He also wants to convince his two sidemen, drummer Red Carter and harmonica player Canewell, to join him in another recording session in Chicago. He also wants to prove his worth.

Louise is Vera's no-nonsense neighbor, and her young niece, Ruby, has just arrived from down south, where she got into trouble with dueling lovers and "her little fast behind." Her lover Elmore shot and killed her other paramour, Leroy. Elmore is in jail, and Leroy is in his grave. She is pregnant, but she doesn't know which man fathered her child.

Hedley is the man carrying a chicken that Wilson had envisioned when he first dreamt up the plot; he's angry and put-upon and is a prophet in his own mind. He imagines that the jazz cornetist Charles "Buddy" Bolden, who died in 1931, is going to resurrect and give him enough money so he can buy a plantation in his native Jamaica. He peddles chicken sandwiches and cigarettes on the street, but he yearns to father a messiah who will "lead the black man out of bondage," a visionary akin to the Jamaican Pan-Africanist Marcus Garvey. He repeatedly says he aspires to be a "big man."

Each character plays his or her own note, and together they create their own kind of music. That was Wilson's vision, anyway. But at the O'Neill, the playwright had merely cobbled together a series of vignettes; he still had not fashioned it into a cohesive drama. Saltz was primarily concerned with the character of Vera, who was sorely underdeveloped. The character needed more material to become a vital life force rather than another two-dimensional figure like Risa in *Two Trains*. Wilson was easily convinced. Given the criticism of his female characters, he knew this was his chance to write a strong woman who was more than just a waitress or a wife. Saltz pressed him, and he went off to the old sanatorium building to write.

One day, he showed up at rehearsal with a rewrite. "He was shaking," Saltz said. He handed her a page. It was a new speech for Vera in Act 1, Scene 2, in which she explains to Floyd how she felt when he abandoned her. "Floyd touched me here," Vera says. "And he touched me here and he touched me here and he kissed me here and he gave me here. . . ." It rises to a soul-shattering crescendo, and it is now one of the most memorable monologues in American theater. Actors regularly use it for auditions. Wilson was nervous about it, though. "He didn't know whether it was good or not," Saltz said. "He had just written it and it was still so raw."

He kept writing until the day of the first performance, which was set for Friday, July 15. The play had been rehearsed in the center's outdoor amphitheater, the perfect setting for an operatic drama that unfolds in a Pittsburgh backyard. The alfresco stage provides a feeling of spaciousness. But the forecast was for rain, so the cast and crew had to scurry to remount the production in the Rose Barn Theater, an enclosed space that can feel claustrophobic on a hot summer evening. Saltz had five hours to reconfigure everything, and Wilson showed up with more pages. He had restructured the entire second act. It was chaos, but they finished in time for the actors to break for dinner. After the rehearsal, Saltz asked Wilson why he had cut a pivotal scene in which the young Ruby willingly gives herself to Hedley so he can father a child before he dies. She doesn't tell him she is already pregnant; she is giving him a gift. Wilson was confused. He had intended to leave that scene in the play, but in the frantic rush to restage the show, those pages had gotten lost. At the O'Neill, rewrites are printed on different-colored pieces of paper and inserted into the script. Saltz and Wilson searched through boxes and boxes of discarded pages until they eventually found the scene.

That night, the cast gathered in the greenroom of the barn for a prayer circle, led by actor Tommy Hollis and joined by cast member Charles S. Dutton of *Ma Rainey* and *Piano Lesson* fame. A few minutes later, they gathered in the wings while Richards gave his traditional opening speech to the audience. "The energy was coming off of them," said Saltz, who joined them in the wings. "They were led by Roc [Dutton], who was like a bull who could lift the Empire State Building off its foundation. He was pacing in this little area behind the stage, and everyone else started doing the same thing. It was their version of preparing. It was extraordinary. They knew they were birthing an August Wilson play, and they couldn't wait."

But even after that titillating moment at the O'Neill, the play still needed work six months later when it went into rehearsal at the Goodman in January. Wilson had not rewritten *Seven Guitars* after the playwrights conference the summer before, as he had done with his other plays. "I think I meant to rewrite it but I never could," he said. "I never got around to it. So I just said, 'Ah, I'll do it in rehearsal.' And I discovered a new way of working and that is in the heat of the moment, in rehearsal, doing the rewrites."

He had a luxury that most playwrights don't have, since the top administrators at his preferred regional theaters understood that his plays were works in varying degrees of progress. In this case, he was working from a very rough draft. Amy Saltz had pushed him to flesh out the play at the O'Neill, but he hadn't completed the job. Sakina was worried about the pressure and the stress of this in-the-moment way of working, but Wilson walked into the rehearsal room with an aura of confidence and control. Colleagues immediately noticed a difference. Dwight Andrews, the musical director on three of Wilson's earlier plays, sensed that the playwright stood on equal footing with director, Walter Dallas, and at times, it wasn't clear which man was in charge. "August began to assert more of a directorial role and input," Andrews said. "And in a sense that complicated the rehearsal process. It seemed like we had two directors. August was asserting himself more and more in the process. It was a challenge for everyone." For instance, Wilson accompanied Andrews to the recording studio to oversee his music selections for the play. That had never happened before; in the past, Andrews did his work in the studio and then played it for Richards and Wilson for their approval. "He wanted to hear what I was doing," Andrews said. "I felt like I had his attention in a way I wasn't sure I knew what to do with. Lloyd trusted me. He didn't look over my shoulder."

Dallas, however, didn't mind this collaborative process. He preferred to create an environment in which everyone had a voice: actors, director, and playwright. "It's usually an open forum," he said. "We all sit in there. I've never been one of those directors who has said to the playwright, 'Now don't talk to my actors. These are my actors and you have to talk through me.' My feeling is that the playwright is the source." Wilson became an active, leading participant in the rehearsal process and made direct suggestions to the actors that, in the past, he had channeled through Richards.

Opening night was on Saturday, January 21, a bitterly cold evening with temperatures in the mid-twenties and wind gusts peaking at twenty-five miles per hour. It was typical Chicago winter weather that kept people home. Sakina remembers that turnout was lower than expected, especially for an opening night of a world premiere. She continued to worry about her father and the pressure that came with mounting an unfinished play. The stress got to him, which he often unleashed with anger. At one post-performance gathering, Andrews was having drinks with Wilson and several others from the production. "Some critic or someone went up to August and said, 'I thought there would be more music.' It was like lighting a fuse and watching a nuclear explosion. He blew up," Andrews said. Wilson screamed at the intruder. "I don't write musicals. I write plays!" He was infuriated and insistent that his work not be confused with "Black musicals," even though he had written the unpublished and unproduced musical, *St. Louis Blues*. "If you could have seen the rage—he turned purple. It terrified everyone. I got a deeper appreciation for how intense the anger could be and where his fault lines were," Andrews said.

Wilson's back was up against the wall with this play. It wasn't just an issue of the endless rewrites. Apart from *Jitney!* and *Black Bart*, this was the first time he hadn't opened a new play in the familiar environment of Yale Rep, and the first debut that was not helmed by Lloyd Richards. The strain was evident, and the play also still needed work. He asked Saltz to come out to the Goodman. He needed the comfort of a director he had known for more than a decade, because he was well aware that *Seven Guitars* was not ready for Broadway. And this play was particularly important to him, since it is set at 1727 Bedford and he pays tribute to his mother in his playwright's note, penning a line he would return to again and again: "I happen to think that the content of my mother's life—her myths, her superstitions, her prayers, the contents of her pantry, the smell of her kitchen, the song that escaped from her sometimes parched lips, her thoughtful repose and pregnant laughter—are all worthy of art."

The play, which was still much too long at three and a half hours, concludes with another of Wilson's wrenching wallops. In the end, the character Hedley kills blues singer Floyd Barton. It is an accident. Floyd has buried money he got from robbing a loan office, and Hedley stumbles on him when he is digging it up. Hedley, a tubercular curmudgeon who admits that "it is not all right in my head sometimes," thinks Floyd is Buddy Bolden, who has resurrected to give him money to buy a plantation. When Floyd refuses to hand over the cash, Hedley slits his throat with a machete. Floyd was in the wrong place at the wrong time, and Hedley was delusional. That scene was painful for Wilson to write.

He had procrastinated, and he was still wrestling with the script at the Goodman. "You have to assemble all your strength and all your courage and get all that together, and it's going to be a battle. It's going to be painful," he said of the writing process. The act of writing the scene with Hedley reminded him of a line said by Bynum, the mystical man in *Joe Turner* who binds people together. Bynum's calling is spiritually and mentally draining. "Bynum says, 'I don't do it lightly. . . . It costs me a piece of myself every time I do it.' And sometimes I feel like that: It costs you a piece of yourself. You just have to be willing to pay that price: to get this guy [in this case, the character of Hedley] to talk with me and to try to understand someone who would kill another human being, try to understand someone who so casually would slice him—what, where, how, who, why?"

Richards was the one who gently asked Wilson those questions in the past, but Dallas was more like a brother than a Buddha. It showed in the work. The critics were lukewarm, but forgiving, as they had learned that Wilson's plays evolved as they moved from theater to theater. Writing in the *Pittsburgh Post-Gazette*, critic Christopher Rawson noted that the play is "far from finished," adding that "details remain confused and major revelations are muffled." While the play needed work, two performances stood out: Ruben Santiago-Hudson as the harmonica player Canewell and Viola Davis as Ruby, the young woman who got into "man trouble" back home in Alabama. Davis was a young, emerging artist at the time. She went on two decades later to win both a Tony Award and an Academy Award for her performance as Rose in a stage revival and then film version of *Fences*.

The designers sensed tension in Chicago. Lighting designer Christopher Akerlind, who had been a student at the Yale School of Drama under

Richards, detected a different alchemy between Wilson and Dallas, and he felt it was reflected in the design. The set, he thought, did not have a necessary "patina of age" and was unexceptional. "It felt non-epic," Akerlind said. "The whole idea of the cycle has something mythic and epic about it, and you have to find a way to push some edge out of it in a non-operatic way. In Chicago, it did not feel electric enough." He missed Richards.

Wilson was reminded of his longtime collaborator when the teleplay of *Piano Lesson* aired on February 2, 1995, to great acclaim. *Seven Guitars* closed at the Goodman on February 25, the day after he was feted at city hall by Chicago mayor Richard M. Daley. At the celebration, he told reporters he would like to see another of his plays filmed for television, and when asked which one, he replied, "Put them all in a hat and pick one." It would be more than two decades before another film of a Wilson play was produced for the small or the big screen.

Wilson had six months before *Seven Guitars* was set to open at Boston's Huntington Theatre in September, and he and Mordecai were eager to get Richards back as director. On April 25, Mordecai wrote to Richards on Sageworks letterhead offering him the same contract he had for directing *Two Trains*. But when Richards was at Yale, he was paid less than his usual professional fees for all productions that began at Yale Rep, because his salary made up the difference. He was insulted by the offer and replied two days later, demanding his professional fee, which was much higher than union scale. Mordecai had also asked him to serve as a consulting producer to Sageworks for this production only. But Richards was still simmering about being left out of the partnership and replied that the suggestion "hardly seemed tactful." He also noted that the offer "made no mention of an assistant." Richards was a stickler for detail, and his ego was already bruised.

Eventually, they worked out a deal, and Richards signed on to direct. All three men showed up in Boston for rehearsal in late August. The Huntington made special housing arrangements for Richards, who was still frail after his operation. There had been two casting changes over the summer. Keith David was now playing the role of Floyd, and veteran South African actor Zakes Mokae was playing Hedley. Dutton had been planning on doing the play, but he dropped out because he had a movie deal. Delroy Lindo, who had played Herald Loomis in *Joe Turner*, was approached, but he was noncommittal. Mokae seemed the perfect choice. He had a long history with Richards. While at Yale Rep, the director had nurtured the work of Mokae's longtime collaborator Athol Fugard. Mokae appeared at Yale Rep in the 1980 revival of Fugard's *Boesman and Lena*; the 1982 world premiere of *"Master Harold"* . . . *and the boys*; and the 1985 revival of *Blood Knot*, in which he and Fugard were reunited onstage for the twenty-fifth-anniversary production. Mokae won a Tony Award for his performance in *"Master Harold."* He and Richards were tight. Wilson was also familiar with Mokae, and he said he wrote the role of Hedley with the actor in mind.

But in Boston, Mokae struggled during rehearsal. As a South African, he had difficulty mastering Hedley's Jamaican lilt. Hedley is what Wilson called a "spectacle character," akin to Gabriel in *Fences* and Hambone in *Two Trains Running*. These characters appear to be off-kilter, but underneath their eccentricities, they harbor a deep wisdom. Mokae couldn't grasp the essence of Hedley, a man who is angry at all the slights he has been dealt as a Black man in America. He has a painful backstory and vents his rage upon anyone who will listen and vows that the Black man will rise up and avenge his white oppressors.

Mokae had difficulty learning his lines. Even though Wilson claimed he had heard Mokae's voice when he wrote the role, the essence of the character was lost because the actor couldn't master the dialogue. As rehearsals went on, the situation became more and more tenuous, and Wilson grew more frustrated.

On opening night, Mokae went onstage with the script in hand. The Huntington diplomatically announced that he needed the script because Wilson continued to rewrite and because Mokae joined the cast late, but that wasn't the real story. He was struggling. Wilson was out of his comfort zone, too. His frustration grew, night after night. The stage manager's production notes are full of complaints about Mokae. The creative team talked to him repeatedly and worked lines with him privately. The overall sense was that he was reading, not acting. He was "tired" and "muddled and full of repetitions," stage manager Jane E. Neufeld wrote. One night, he was discovered nodding off during the performance.

Richards was loyal to his crew of actors, and his ties with Mokae went deep. He wanted to give him time to grow into the role. But Wilson's anxiety was rising. On October 4, a few days before the Huntington production closed, he sent a two-page fax to Richards with criticisms and suggested that Mokae was not up to play the role.

He was not alone in his concern. "I loved Zakes," said Keith David, the actor playing Floyd. "He was a great guy. But the truth of the matter is, the play was suffering. With August, you've got to know those lines." Wilson was used to a development process in which it was all about the play, not about struggling actors. Wilson said the same thing in his missive to Richards, noting that Mokae was impeding the actors and making the audience struggle to comprehend the play.

But Wilson went beyond just defending his play. He made suggestions that would usually belong to the director, outlining changes to the blocking and the use of props and how the actors interact with one another in specific scenes. This was a marked difference in the way the two men had worked together in the past. Richards asked the questions. Wilson answered them. Huntington managing director Michael Maso, who had known Wilson since the theater first produced *Joe Turner*, noticed a dramatic difference. "August made a decision that 'I am going to make sure it is clear that I am in charge of my own work. There are other people, but I'm in charge, and ultimately the final word is mine,'" Maso said. The playwright even put that idea into *Seven Guitars*. When the blues musician Floyd is strung along by his white manager, his friend Canewell tells him he needs to take charge of his career and his music. "You a big man, Floyd," Canewell tells his friend. "People supposed to treat you like a big man." Maso once quoted that line to the playwright, changing it to say, "August Wilson is a big man." Wilson gave him a look, as if to say, "You're bad. We've been talking too much." He then said "something about how much he needed to be led in the beginning, needed to be told, knew that he was a student. And then at some point, he wasn't," Maso said.

The cast and creative team had a few weeks between the last

performance in Boston and an upcoming run at the American Conservatory Theater (ACT) in San Francisco. The questions about Mokae were still very much on the table. Richards, who was loyal to a fault, did not want to let Mokae go. Richards's agent, the venerable Lucy Kroll (who, eighty-five at the time, also represented James Earl Jones), sensed that trouble was brewing between Richards and Wilson. On October 17, a week after the Huntington production closed, she sent a supportive letter to Richards. "There is something in August's life that he does not wish to confront and he is angry and has not found the answers," she wrote. "This translates into his work and when he resolves his personal struggles he will find the artistic answers." She added that any great work of art needs harmony, implying that Wilson was just as wounded as Mokae. "It is this harmony, this blending, that August does not have in his life. And one does not know what his life has been and what it took to come where he is." She encouraged Richards to keep working with Wilson to achieve a peaceful accord. "Your help will be so much more meaningful as he can't hear you now with all that is whirling in his inner life."

The creative team had a significant amount of work to do before the debut in New York. They all arrived in San Francisco to rehearse for the ACT production, which was set to begin previews at the Marines' Memorial Theatre on November 9. The official opening was Wednesday, November 15, and Mokae was still not at the top of his game. The reviews were mixed. While most critics admired Wilson's characters and poetic monologues, they also pointed out that the play dragged on far too long, still clocking in at three and a half hours. The play, wrote Robert Hurwitt in the *San Francisco Examiner*, "contains an overabundance of Wilson's signature weaknesses, not the least of which is a propensity to repeat himself at considerable length." By this point, critics were aware that they were seeing a Wilson work in progress and kept their commentary to constructive criticism. Hurwitt described the production as "one stop on the pre-Broadway shakedown cruise." However, the critics could not help but expose the difficulty Mokae was having with the role. The actor, Hurwitt wrote, "draws his portrait of this complex and contradictory character with great care, but with such intensity that his timing seems to drag out some of his scenes unnecessarily." Peter Haugen of the *Sacramento Bee* emphasized the actor's "fuzzy enunciation," noting that "his dreams seem like inconsequential madness when they ought to foreshadow danger."

That was precisely the kind of reaction Wilson did not want to hear— and he read reviews religiously. Wilson's anxiety was rising. One day at the theater, he picked up an oversized postcard advertising the play and wrote down two words in neat block letters: "HELP ME." In an interview with the *Examiner* a few days before the opening, he had explained that the character of Hedley "has a lot of truth in what he says, but nobody listens because they think he's crazy." Wilson had made up his mind. Mokae had to go.

The night of the opening, Wilson and Richards met in the theater. The subject was no secret: Wilson wanted to fire Mokae. Richards was against it, especially right in the middle of the San Francisco run. Scott Richards explained, "You can't really fire people on the spot. I think there was a difference in an understanding of process. Writers have process and so do actors. August was less patient and less understanding of that."

To Richards, this wasn't about one actor who couldn't learn his lines. It was about a friendship and an unbreakable bond he had forged with Mokae over years of kinship, both on and off the stage. He had spent years supporting Mokae in his fight against apartheid in South Africa. So when Wilson demanded that Mokae be fired, Richards did what he rarely did. He exploded. The two men had a shouting match that could be heard outside the theater. In this case, Wilson had the power. This time, he was the producer, along with Mordecai and their company, Sageworks. He and Richards were alone in the room, but word of the heated confrontation spread in the insular San Francisco theater community. Actress Julie Boyd, Wilson's "white China doll" from the O'Neill, was in town doing another play, and she had seen *Seven Guitars* on opening night. She heard about the battle the day after it happened, and she, like many O'Neill and Yale veterans, was crushed. It was a rare display of anger for Richards. "It was probably one of three times he showed that kind of anger in fifty years," said Boyd, who studied under Richards at the Yale School of Drama.

From that point on, his relationship with Wilson was changed indelibly. They still had a play to fine-tune for Broadway, but by most accounts, they barely spoke to each other for the rest of the pre-Broadway run. Mokae was informed of the decision after the blowup. He was offered the chance to complete the San Francisco run, but he left abruptly, giving his understudy only four hours to prepare before curtain. The San Francisco production closed on December 23 and moved on to Ahmanson Theatre in Los Angeles, where it was set to open January 19, 1996.

The rift was not healing; if anything, the chasm between the two men was widening. Wilson ended the year with a stern, almost patriarchal letter to Richards, written on Sageworks letterhead. He criticized the actors and, in doing so, took a swipe at the direction, claiming that it was second-rate and diminished his play. He didn't have anything good to say about the actors, either, noting that they were not a unified ensemble and seemed to be competing for attention. He said the mediocre production lost sight of the values at the core of *Seven Guitars*—truth, responsibility, and justice.

Wilson came up with his own solution. He suggested that he give the actors notes during rehearsal in Los Angeles, a job that was normally the purview of the director, not the playwright. He requested a meeting with Richards as soon as possible in Los Angeles.

This could not have sat well with Richards. He was the director. He was in charge. He was the trainer, and Wilson was the neophyte boxer. Richards later described how he felt to actor Courtney Vance. "Every playwright that I've worked with eventually wants to direct, they want to act, they want to write, they want to do the lights, they want to do the sound, they want to do everything," he said. "Basically, August Wilson wanted to be me. And he cannot be me."

But both men masked their differences when discussing the play with the press. The *Los Angeles Times* ran a preview of *Seven Guitars* on Sunday, January 14, 1996, a few days before the official opening. The article repeated the old story about Richards being the father figure to the unformed genius he "discovered." Both men were interviewed, and Richards talked as if nothing had changed. He summed up Wilson's oeuvre in one word: "truth." And he indicated that their partnership would continue, in part because it was so vital to bringing African Americans into the theater. "Richards concedes that as far as he and Wilson have traveled together, and as far as they may still have to go, there are people they have yet to reach," arts reporter Jan Breslauer wrote. She then quoted Richards: "It has been a conscious effort on my part to acquaint the nation in total with his work. Hopefully the theaters that we went to [will] do a follow-up, not only one event that would attract a Black audience. No, one is never satisfied."

They successfully hid the impasse from the press, but word of the feud was spreading in the theater community. People began to take sides. Dutton owed his "jail to Yale" career to Richards, and he vehemently stood behind his director. "How can you dump the guy who brought you to the dance?" he later asked. "I completely believe that if it wasn't for Lloyd there would have been no August." "If it wasn't for Lloyd, there definitely would have been no Charles Dutton." Vance and musical director Andrews agreed. And Dutton was right: Wilson was working as a cook and writing in restaurants before Richards nurtured him at the O'Neill and beyond. He was naive about the elemental dynamics of playwriting and staging. And Richards honed the scripts in his quiet way, asking probing questions. At the same time, Wilson was one of a kind. Richards, for all his talent, had not been able to shepherd other writers to such acclaim, and no other writer in the history of the American theater had undertaken such a massive project. They were both right. And they were both wrong.

And that is why Boyd and some others felt like the children of divorce. Ruben Santiago-Hudson felt the repercussions of the feud in rehearsals. "It was hard for me to figure out who to follow now," he said. "Some of [Richards's] power had been removed so he didn't sit as high as normal in a way. His throne didn't have the luster it had prior to him being moved from being a producer. It was odd. It was like my parents were breaking up." The children of the theatrical "divorce" didn't want to take sides, but they desperately wanted the two partners to get back together. The partnership had been played up by the theater community and the media—and by Wilson and Richards themselves—as a father-son relationship. But Wilson was thirty-seven years old when he first went to the O'Neill. He was hardly a child, even at the start, and now he was an icon in his own right. Richards was furious during their argument, but he remained polite publicly after the rift. "He learned a lot of things under me, and I let him into everything," Richards would say a year before his death in 2006.

In the end, the split was inevitable, preordained in Wilson's own work. He wrote poetry about legendary bluesmen who lost ownership of their music. His Ma Rainey character was a demanding diva, but she insisted on control of her art. Floyd Barton was hoodwinked by the music industry, and he died without getting a chance to stake his claim on his songs. This was personal to Wilson. After he had been pressured to change his ending and his vision during the *Fences* debacle, he had sworn he would never lose power again. He didn't need a trainer anymore. He needed to be his own man—"a big man," like his characters Floyd Barton and Hedley wanted to be.

Despite the rift, work on the play continued. Since he had first workshopped it at the O'Neill, Wilson had cut it down from four and a half hours to a shade over three hours. During the run of the regional theaters, entire monologues had been cut, only to be put back in days later. A speech about insomnia was originally delivered by Louise, the upstairs neighbor, but it ended up in the mouth of Vera, Floyd's wary onetime lover. Wilson beefed up the character of Hedley, even after he dismissed Mokae, his model for the role. He pared down the character of Canewell, the sideman, who, as played by Santiago-Hudson, dominated the stage. Wilson cut one of Canewell's monologues in Boston, and the actor was crushed. He didn't speak to Wilson for three days. "I don't know if I'll do another play for a while. It's too hard, too painful," Santiago-Hudson said shortly after the Los Angeles run closed on March 10.

The emotional toll of the long ride was hard on everyone, actors included. The actor who replaced Mokae, Roger Robinson, could be temperamental, prone to what the cast called "Rogerisms." During the Los Angeles run, he hung up on Richards, who had called him to discuss complaints from the cast. But Wilson and Richards were still putting on a good face when they did pre-publicity for the Broadway opening on March 25. Both men were interviewed for a story that ran March 24 in the *New York Times*. Reporter Bruce Weber referred to "their mutual affection," but noted that it had "a bristly element."

That was one way to describe it. On opening night, March 28, 1996, Richards and Wilson were not speaking to each other. The atmosphere inside the Walter Kerr Theatre on Forty-Eighth Street was frigid. Wilson's family, as usual, was there, as were such A-listers as Gregory Hines and Laurence Fishburne. Wilson was with Romero that evening; she had designed the costumes. The playwright had dedicated *Fences* to Richards, but this one was for his third wife—"without whom my life would lack the occasion of poetry that her presence demands."

After the performance, Wilson met with Amy Saltz at the Hotel Edison. They were walking through the lobby on the way to the cast party when they ran into Richards. She was stunned by the encounter. "It was a very cool reception between the two of them," Saltz said. She had known both men since 1982 and had never seen either of them so icy. "Oh my god, it was awful. They grunted at each other."

The cast party was nothing special. This was, after all, the pair's sixth outing on Broadway, and the overall consensus was that this play was solid, but not a masterpiece. "The feeling was like, 'We've done this before,'" said Scott Richards. "There wasn't a sense that this was a great triumph." He didn't notice anything overt about the rift between his father and Wilson. "When things are a huge success, everyone is buddy-buddy," he said.

The reviews that trickled in were mostly positive, with some complaints. Vincent Canby of the *New York Times* hailed "a play whose epic proportions and abundant spirit remind us of what the American theater once was." Clive Barnes of the *New York Post*, however, pulled out the music clichés and wrote, "It's like a session number with great riffs but a less than interesting melody." The play, while a bit overlong, had rich characters and a resonant story. Certainly, the female characters were strong, independent women who stood up for themselves; Vera's monologue stands on its own. Hedley was another one of Wilson's wounded warriors, even if the casting of the role had led to the breakup of a great theatrical partnership. The play was solid, if not brilliant, and it holds a strong place in Wilson's cycle. And despite all the backstage trauma, *Seven Guitars* would go on to win the New York Drama Critics' Circle Award for Best Play and was nominated for eight Tony Awards (only Santiago-Hudson won). It closed less than six months later on September 8, but was presented by several regional theaters the following year.

Photographs from the opening-night party show Wilson smiling directly at the camera, his arm around the shoulders of a beaming Rosalyn Coleman, who played Ruby. A photo taken a few minutes later depicts the actress with the bespectacled Richards, his face stern. Andrews, the musical director who had known Richards since their days together at Yale Rep, noticed the tension between the two men. Near the end of the party, Richards approached him and asked to bum a cigarette. The director had quit smoking years earlier. The two went outside to the alleyway. Richards took long, deep drags. Andrews knew what was going through his mind. "August was like Lloyd's other son," he said. "Their relationship went so far beyond the productions and plays. Lloyd felt kicked to the curb." They stood outside, and Richards quickly finished his smoke, inhaling all the way to the tip. Later he would tell Andrews that he could work *with* Wilson, but not *for* Wilson. But there in the alleyway, he turned to Andrews and summed up his experience working on *Seven Guitars*. "I don't think I'll ever do *that* again." He threw the cigarette butt on the ground and stomped it out, decisively.

CHAPTER FOURTEEN

The Ground on Which I Stand

> The Negro is sort of a seventh son, born with a veil, and
> gifted with second-sight in this American world. . . . One
> ever feels his twoness—an American, a Negro; two souls,
> two thoughts, two unreconciled strivings; two warring
> ideas in one dark body, whose dogged strength alone keeps
> it from being torn asunder.
>
> —W. E. B. DU BOIS

After all the backstage drama, Wilson was ready for a break. "I'm going home," he told the *Pittsburgh Post-Gazette* in early June, shortly after the 1996 Tony Award ceremony. Things had gotten even more heated after the New York opening. Richards and his attorney had threatened to sue Wilson and Sageworks in a dispute over the director's share of the proceeds for *Seven Guitars*. Their two lawyers, Albert DaSilva and John Breglio, agreed that they wanted to avoid a public dispute and were able to work it out behind closed doors. The conflict had gotten ugly and exhausting, and Wilson said he wasn't "going to do anything" over the summer, except perhaps tinker with the screenplay for *Fences*. That task didn't excite him. "I'm not sure I want to invest my life and spirit in the making of a movie," he said. "Arthur Miller says the best way to deal with

Hollywood is to drive to the border, throw the script over, grab the money and leave." He wanted to get away from it all. The whole mess with *Seven Guitars* had been tortuous, and he needed a break from the theater, where all eyes were on him and everyone had an opinion.

It didn't work out that way.

He had agreed to give the keynote address at the eleventh biannual Theatre Communications Group (TCG) conference, slated for late June in Princeton, New Jersey. The TCG conference attracts a veritable who's who in American nonprofit theater, with top directors, designers, administrators, actors, and producers mingling with aspiring artists from small venues. While it features a jam-packed schedule of panel discussions and roundtables, it is also a gigantic social event where theater professionals network, reconnect, trade notes, and gossip. The forums range from such non-sexy topics as fundraising and audience development to headier issues like censorship and cultural diversity.

Wilson had first attended the conference in 1984, a few months before *Ma Rainey* opened on Broadway. That year, actor Judd Hirsch gave the keynote address on the topic of "Other," and Wilson was intrigued. By 1996, the theater was still grappling with that issue. Despite some progress, the members of the League of Resident Theatres still had a long way to go when it came to representing diversity in their boardrooms and offices, as well as on their stages. The time was ripe to rip off the Band-Aid and take a deep look at the state of the nonprofit theater. TCG, the umbrella organization for the nation's regional theaters, was in the midst of a transition. Founded in 1961 with a grant from the Ford Foundation, the organization was launched to support the growing network of professional theaters around the country—which provided the counterpoint to the notion that American theater was rooted in the commercial confines of Times Square. For twenty-three years, it had been run by executive director Peter Zeisler, a cofounder of the Guthrie Theater in Minneapolis and a well-known pioneer in the regional theater movement. He put the organization on the map, establishing *American Theatre* magazine, the national conference, and TCG Books, an independent publisher of dramatic literature.

Zeisler not only built the organization, he also micromanaged it and established himself as *the* voice of regional theater. When he retired in 1995, his successor, John Sullivan, wanted to shake things up. At the time, philanthropic organizations like the Ford Foundation and the Lila Wallace-Reader's Digest Fund were encouraging theaters to diversify with large grants to support plays by people of color and to encourage "nontraditional" casting. Ten years earlier, in 1986, the Actors' Equity Association had established the Non-Traditional Casting Project in an attempt to push theaters to hire actors of color and actors with disabilities. The actors' union defined the concept as "the casting of ethnic minority and female actors in roles where race, ethnicity, or sex is not germane." It was the topic du jour, and Sullivan saw a need to address it head-on. He recruited the husband-and-wife team of Ken Brecher and Rebecca Rickman to help shape the conference. Brecher, an anthropologist by training, was well-known in the arts world for his commitment to diversity. He had been an associate artistic director of the Mark Taper Forum as well as the executive director of the Boston Children's Museum, where he revamped the institution from top to bottom to make it a welcoming place for all families. He challenged other arts institutions in that city to look at their boards, staffs, and programming—and he was not always thanked for his outspoken appeals. Rickman was a well-respected curator of contemporary art. The first thing Brecher and Rickman did was to invite Wilson to deliver the keynote. "We said, 'Are we correct in thinking you have something to say to this group of people?'" Rickman said. Wilson initially turned the offer down, but after some thought, he regretted his decision. The invitation, however, was still open, and he agreed to speak. "I have been waiting a long time for this," he told the couple. They didn't ask him to elaborate and had a feeling whatever he said would provoke discussion—or better yet, controversy.

Sullivan loved the idea. He knew there was tension brewing in the theater world over who had access to funds and programming. He wanted to invite conference attendees to address issues surrounding multiculturalism. "We just *had* to talk about it. People who had not been a part of the TCG world were pushing and wanting access, so this seemed like a great opportunity to get the issues on the table," Sullivan said twenty years later.

The organizers did not give Wilson suggestions or talking points, but they knew that the playwright, at the very least, would captivate the audience and generate a heated discussion. "I think he wanted it to be a surprise," Rickman said of his speech. "I knew that he felt it was going to be a very important occasion." This was a rare chance for Wilson to speak to this particular group of colleagues, which included many of the most powerful and well-heeled producers of American theater. He didn't take it lightly. After *Seven Guitars* opened, he went to Pittsburgh, where he was revamping his 1979 play, *Jitney*, for the Pittsburgh Public Theater. While there, he peppered the actors with questions about their experience working in regional theater. He was particularly interested in how they felt about nontraditional casting. Actor Anthony Chisholm was one of the "Wilson Warriors," Black actors who appeared regularly in Wilson's plays. He was an artist, but he was also a realist. He wanted to act, period. "I have no problem with nontraditional casting," Chisholm told Wilson. "I play a creature, and as an actor, I play a character from the soul out." Wilson felt differently. He argued that African Americans have their own unique culture and that nontraditional casting erased their humanity. He had immersed himself in that culture in Daisy's kitchen. It was why he still kept insisting on a Black director for the film of *Fences*. He and Chisholm agreed to disagree.

He discussed these issues with Romero, too. "As part of the process of developing his plays, he would go from one repertory theater to another," she said. "As he traveled through these different theaters, he was welcomed by everybody, but he never thought that this was somewhere where he could, as he put it, 'hang his hat.' He never felt like he was at *home*. He always felt like a guest. An important guest, but a guest nonetheless." He labored over his speech, writing and rewriting, the same way he did with his plays.

On June 26, he arrived at the McCarter Theatre Center on the campus of Princeton University, wearing a tailored gray suit and a maroon tie. Quitting smoking agreed with him; he looked trimmer and healthier than he had in the recent past. As usual, he was better dressed than most of the attendees, many of whom wore bohemian chic for the networking event.

The keynote was held in McCarter's Matthews Theatre, a 1,100-seat grand space that was built in 1930 as a home for the Princeton Triangle Club. Thornton Wilder's *Our Town* had its world premiere there in 1938, and Paul Robeson played Othello on the stage in 1942. The keynote took place at the beginning of the event, so theater professionals who hadn't seen one another in years were meeting and greeting. Excitement was in the air as more than 550 conference attendees filed into the auditorium. Wilson drew a crowd, and almost everyone in the room was aware of the stand he had taken over *Fences* and of his stature as the nation's preeminent Black playwright.

The room quieted down quickly when Wilson took the podium. This wasn't the jocular raconteur who hung out in smoky jazz bars that some people were expecting. This was a somber and serious intellectual commanding attention. He started out with a definitive declaration. "I wish to make it clear from the outset that I do not have a mandate to speak for anyone," he said. "There are many intelligent Blacks working in the American theater who speak in a loud and articulate voice. It would be the greatest of presumptions to say that I speak for them. I speak only for myself and for those who may think as I do." From the very beginning, Wilson exuded a sense of urgency. He had been holding in his frustration for years, and his recent split with Richards was a move to gain ultimate control of his own work. Now he wanted that same kind of clout in the nonprofit theater world at large.

Many who were in the theater that day remember a few highly controversial sound bites from the speech, but it was a carefully thought-out, nuanced, and occasionally meandering argument. Wilson began by establishing his place in the theater as something akin to what W. E. B. Du Bois called "twoness." He said he was a product of the Western theater tradition, beginning with the Greek dramatists and moving forward through Shakespeare, Shaw, Chekhov, and O'Neill. But he was also a product of Black history, influenced by Nat Turner, Marcus Garvey, and Elijah Muhammad, among others. The Black Power Movement of the 1960s, he said, was "the kiln in which I was fired." He was laying the groundwork. As a Black man, he could not separate the art from the artist. "I have strived to

live it all seamless—art and life together, inseparable and indistinguishable," he said.

Noting that he was a "race man," he said that he learned culture in
his mother's kitchen at 1727 Bedford Avenue and that Black culture is
distinct from white culture and equally deserving of art. He defined
two kinds of Black theater: first, the kind that originated in the "big
house" and was meant as an entertainment for white slave masters;
and second, the kind that provided spiritual substance for Blacks in the
slave quarters. "I stand myself and my art squarely on the self-defining
ground of the slave quarters and find the ground to be hallowed and
made fertile by the blood and bones of the men and women who can
be described as warriors on the cultural battlefield that affirmed their
self-worth."

By this point in his life, Wilson was an accomplished orator. His
speaking voice may have been soft, but he had a commanding presence.
The speech wandered from theme to theme at times, but Wilson's language soared to the same lyrical heights as the monologues in his plays.
It soon became clear that he was taking on the very power structure of
the nonprofit theater, which was designed for whites, run by whites, and
attended by whites. Wilson was demanding equal opportunity—and
funding—for Blacks to run their own professional theaters. About a third
of the way through the keynote, he castigated one—and only one—theater
director: Robert Brustein, the founder and artistic director of the American Repertory Theater in Cambridge, Massachusetts, and drama critic for
the *New Republic*. Brustein, who also founded the Yale Repertory Theatre
and was replaced by Lloyd Richards after he was fired from the position,
was a self-appointed defender of what he deemed to be unassailable artistic standards. A tall, imposing figure with a keen intellect who wrote
with acid ink, Brustein had long insisted that theater is a meritocracy,
not a democracy, and he was an outspoken critic of attempts to achieve
cultural diversity through the funding of arts education and audience
development initiatives. Wilson cited a 1993 *New Republic* article called
"Unity from Diversity," in which Brustein wrote, "Funding agencies have
started substituting sociological criteria for aesthetic criteria in their

grant procedures, indicating that 'elitist' notions like quality and excellence are no longer functional."

That suggestion rattled Wilson and many others in the arts world. Wilson also read reviews, and he had a long memory. And he would never forget Brustein's scathing review of *Piano Lesson* in 1990. Like other Black artists, Wilson knew that he risked being labeled an "angry Black man" if he lashed out, but now, under the auspices of a national theater conference, he had the perfect platform for a response.

And he was direct and to the point. "Quite possibly this outpouring of works by minority artists," he said, "may lead to a raising of standards and a raising of the levels of excellence, but Mr. Brustein cannot allow that possibility." He had to pause here for a long round of applause. "I say raise the standards and remove the sociological conditions of race as privilege, and we will meet you at the crossroads, in equal numbers, prepared to do the work of extending and developing the common ground of the American theater." He was interrupted by applause yet again.

After working in the nonprofit theater for more than a decade, Wilson was standing his ground and demanding equality in the theater at all levels: boards, administrative staffs, ushers, actors, designers, and playwrights. But he eventually got to the part of the speech that is most often remembered. He took a stand against color-blind—or nontraditional—casting, which he declared was "an aberrant idea that has never had any validity other than as a tool of the Cultural Imperialists who view their American culture, rooted in the icons of European culture, as beyond reproach in its perfection." Many audience members had been with him until this point, but he was speaking to a group of theater professionals who sincerely felt they were providing opportunities for Black actors by casting them in parts traditionally played by whites—roles like Romeo or Juliet or Willy Loman or Big Daddy. Wilson was essentially telling them that not only had they been doing everything wrong, they were insulting Black culture. At the same time, actors of color in the audience were finally getting the chance to take on some of the meatiest roles in Western theater—and work steadily. Many actors supported nontraditional casting, as long as it was done with cultural awareness. Anthony Chisholm had told Wilson that, and since the concept was introduced in 1986, it was slowly being adopted by both regional and Broadway theaters. In 1988, Phylicia Rashad (who later appeared in a Wilson play) replaced Bernadette Peters as the Witch in Stephen Sondheim's *Into the Woods*. A year earlier, Filipina singer Lea Salonga took on the role of Éponine in the Broadway production of *Les Misérables*. The actors' union viewed such examples as progress. When Wilson dismissed and denigrated the concept, the room suddenly became divided and the enthusiastic applause gave way to stunned silence.

Wilson also called for more funding for Black theaters, urging foundations and philanthropists to stop devoting precious resources to encourage white-led institutions to diversify and to direct those grants to Black theaters instead. He pointed out that of the sixty-six members of the League of Resident Theatres (all represented at the conference), only Crossroads Theatre in New Brunswick, New Jersey, could be described as a Black institution. This assertion quieted the room, yet again. Wilson was espousing an idea that W. E. B. Du Bois had promoted in 1926 in his magazine, *The Crisis*. Du Bois called for a "real Negro theater" that operated on "four fundamental principles": "1. About us. 2. By us. 3. For us. 4. Near us."

Wilson said many things in this long speech, but given the audience, the main takeaway was his criticism of color-blind or nontraditional casting. He also connected the state of the theater to the state of the world. "Where is the common ground in the horrifics of lynching?" he asked. "Where is the common ground in the maim of the policeman's bullet? Where is the common ground in the hull of a slave ship or the deck of the slave ship with its refreshments of air and expanse?" He was using imagery from his plays, invoking scenes that were all too familiar to him as a Black man who grew up on the streets of the Hill District. But this was long before the age of cell phone cameras, when videos of police brutality against Blacks became readily available. Two and a half decades later, the very same theaters that were represented in the audience that day issued "diversity statements" and developed initiatives and plans after the Black Lives Matter movement emerged as a cultural and political force. But in

1996, Wilson was not yet preaching to the converted, and many in the audience were startled by his candor.

Wilson's strong stance against nontraditional casting diverted attention from the rest of the speech, and in the aftermath, it was one of the only things that people in the audience remembered and discussed. In hindsight several years later, he regretted making that point. "I think I would leave the colorblind casting alone," he told an interviewer in 2003. He hadn't changed his mind, but he realized it became a "lightning rod" that distracted from everything else he was saying. "I would still have said it, but I would have talked about it the next week," he said.

He had divided the audience, and at the end, he tried unsuccessfully to bring them back together. He abruptly switched gears and ended his speech with a call for unity, encouraging all theater professionals to work together to create equity. "The ground together: We have to do it together," he said. "We who are capable of those noble pursuits should challenge the melancholy and barbaric, to bring the light of angelic grace, peace, prosperity and the unencumbered pursuit of happiness to the ground on which we all stand."

The response was immediate—and electric. Wilson received a standing ovation, although many in the audience disagreed with his rejection of color-blind casting. The theater lobby was abuzz with heated debate after the speech. Conference planner Rickman ran into Stephen Albert, the managing director of Houston's Alley Theatre at the time and a former administrator at the Mark Taper Forum in Los Angeles. "He was shocked," Rickman said. "People felt they were being told that all the work they were doing was not only not successful, but it was actually preventing the things that should happen from happening. It wasn't anti–August Wilson. It was the shock of 'We have been trying so hard to do the right thing and now someone comes along saying it is all wrong. So what are we going to do?'"

The speech upended the entire conference. The requisite panels on such management topics as funding and advocacy were upstaged by Wilson's manifesto. Director Benny Sato Ambush organized two impromptu discussion sessions held under a big tent and attended by about a hundred participants. The meetings went on for hours. "It blew the conference up," Ambush said. "Everything about the normal schedule took a back seat to the overwhelming importance of reacting and responding to that speech. You could feel everybody being set off while he was talking." As for Wilson, he later told the *Los Angeles Times* that the speech was "the proudest moment of my life."

Wilson was not after all going to enjoy a quiet summer of rest and relaxation. For months after, the speech was the most talked-about topic in both the nonprofit and commercial theater worlds. Brustein, for one, was not going to take the criticism quietly, and he quickly published a fiery response in a column in the *New Republic*, which was reprinted in the October 1996 edition of *American Theatre*, along with a rebuttal by Wilson. Both essays were predictable. Dismissing the speech as a "rambling jeremiad," Brustein took on Wilson point for point—and also defended his honor. He first objected to Wilson's stated allegiance to Black Nationalism and questioned why Wilson did not include Martin Luther King Jr. in his list of people who shaped his aesthetic. He also took on Wilson for asserting that the nonprofit regional theaters routinely excluded Black playwrights, noting, "I fear Wilson is displaying a failure of memory—I hesitate to say a failure of gratitude because all of Wilson's plays were produced at mainstream theaters." He also implied that Wilson had singled him out, at least in part, because he had written negative reviews of his plays. He criticized Wilson's outright rejection of color-blind casting, but on that point, Brustein was not alone. Wilson had a few supporters who also objected to the practice, but many, if not most, actors and directors supported the idea that a person of any race could take on roles traditionally played by whites, as long as the role was not a culturally specific character and was approached with sensitivity to race. But even though many of his colleagues agreed with him on that point, Brustein deliberately chose incendiary language. "By choosing to chronicle the oppression of Black people through each of the decades, Wilson has fallen into a monotonous tone of victimization," he wrote. He was not simply critiquing the speech; he was rejecting and misinterpreting Wilson's life goal, which was to celebrate Black people and their culture, not to portray them as victims.

In his parting salvo, Brustein deemed Wilson to be a divisive separatist given to "rabid identity politics and poisonous racial consciousness." He again invoked the memory of King. "I don't think Martin Luther King ever imagined an America where playwrights such as August Wilson would be demanding, under the pretense of calling for healing and unity, an entirely separate stage for Black theater artists. What next? Separate schools? Separate washrooms? Separate drinking fountains?"

Wilson refuted Brustein's deliberately incendiary response and repeated many of the arguments in his speech. He continued to call for foundations to fund Black theaters. And he hit right back on the references to King. "It is Brustein's failure to imagine a theater broad enough and secure enough in its traditions to absorb and make use of all manners and cultures of American life that contributes to the failure of the American spirit that permits King's challenge to go unmet. We issue the challenge again. We cannot afford to fail."

The dispute continued in the December issue of *American Theatre*, with other theater professionals weighing in. It was the talk of the insular theater world, where everyone loved a good fight between two giants of the industry. Wilson was taking on a hallowed institution, but outside the world of theater, it might have remained an academic argument between two skilled men of letters. But Wilson had revealed the unspoken truth in the rarified world of the arts: despite some progress in other realms of society, the arts in general, and theater in particular, remained an exclusive arena. The nation's theaters were run primarily by white men, and the boards and staffs of these publicly funded institutions were overwhelmingly white.

Wilson received a standing ovation after his speech, yet he sensed that many of his actor friends didn't have his back in this fight, mainly because of his stance on color-blind casting. His friend Mordecai, however, was steadfastly loyal and defended him publicly, describing the speech as "eloquent, honest, and brave." But there was one sentence in the speech that went largely unacknowledged during the public brouhaha that followed. Wilson put out a call for Black theater artists to "confer in a city in our ancestral homeland in the southern part of the United States in 1998, so that we may enter the millennium united and prepared for a long future of prosperity." Paul Carter Harrison, a playwright and theater professor at Columbia College Chicago who had written the afterword to the published collection of Wilson's first three plays, took note. He connected with Don Evans, professor of theater and African American studies at the College of New Jersey, and Victor Leo Walker II, a theater professor at Dartmouth College. They joined forces to convince Wilson to host such a gathering. They met with Wilson for dinner in September, after *Seven Guitars* closed on Broadway, but did not come up with a concrete plan. Wilson said that he had received more than a dozen requests from university professors and administrators, foundation program officers, and theater administrators who had expressed interest in convening a national Black theater conference. He wasn't interested. He turned them all down. At the very least, he agreed to continue talking with this group, but he was noncommittal about his participation.

Meanwhile, his speech continued to generate interest and coverage in the media. On October 4, a *Boston Globe* theater columnist (the author) made a "modest proposal," suggesting that solo performance artist Anna Deavere Smith interview both men in a public forum. The column was reprinted in *American Theatre* magazine. Smith was celebrated for her one-person shows *Fires in the Mirror* and *Twilight: Los Angeles, 1992*, in which she single-handedly portrayed multiple characters based on interviews with people involved in racial disturbances in New York and Los Angeles. At the time, Smith was traveling on the presidential campaign trail, working on a piece about the 1996 presidential election between President Bill Clinton and Senator Bob Dole. She got a phone call from the *Los Angeles Times* theater critic Don Shirley, asking her what she thought of the debate. Since she was researching the history of presidential elections, she initially thought he was referring to the famous Lincoln-Douglas debate of the nineteenth century. She had heard nothing about the feud between Wilson and Brustein.

After reading both men's commentaries, she started thinking about the impasse between the two theater luminaries. She was inspired by "A Rap on Race," the 1971 discussion between anthropologist Margaret

Mead and author James Baldwin. She thought, perhaps, that she could elicit a similar conversation between the two men. "Wilson had the fire of Baldwin, and Brustein had the candor of Mead," she said. Smith was about to start a residency at New York University's Tisch School of the Arts, and she envisioned getting the two men in "a nice conference room," where they could discuss their differences—and similarities, there were a few, after all—face-to-face. Both men tentatively agreed to meet if she would moderate, but her unostentatious plan for an intimate gathering was quickly derailed. Her assistant, who was charged with arranging the details, accidentally got Brustein's name wrong during a phone conversation. She called him "Mr. Bernstein," and he refused to participate in a conversation at NYU.

Smith still thought it was a good idea, so she contacted Sullivan at TCG. He was more than enthusiastic and suggested booking Town Hall, a historic 1,500-seat theater on Forty-Third Street in New York. From there, Smith's idea of a reserved conversation took on a larger scale. TCG scheduled the "debate" for January 27, 1997, making sure it was a Monday, when theaters were dark and actors and other theater professionals would be free to attend. TCG also hired a public relations firm that hyped the event like a boxing match, promising something akin to the "Fight of the Century." Tickets sold out fast, and scalpers sold tickets at a premium— all for a gentlemen's quarrel. The glitterati snapped up tickets; the audience included Whoopi Goldberg, Vanessa Redgrave, and William Styron, among others.

The atmosphere outside the theater was electric on the evening of the debate, despite the fact that temperatures hovered in the low twenties and a wintry mix chilled the air and made for treacherous travel. The overflow crowd clamored to get into the theater, overwhelming the ushers and causing a half-hour delay in the start time. Outside the theater, a giddy Henry Louis Gates Jr. described the event as the "Thrilla in Manila," comparing it to the 1975 boxing match between Muhammad Ali and Joe Frazier. In fact, the event itself had a more pedestrian title: "On Cultural Power: The August Wilson/Robert Brustein Discussion." Smith had never imagined an event of such scale and hype. She was taken aback when she was asked to work with the public relations agency handling the event. The press rep created the boxing match sales pitch and was even taking bets. "Wilson will take the fight," he told an astonished Smith.

TCG executive director Sullivan set the tone in his opening statement. "It has been some time since I made my way through a phalanx of paparazzi and representatives of the Revolutionary Worker's Party," he said. In the first half of the event, which was frequently interrupted by hoots from the audience, both men gave opening statements. Brustein, wearing the requisite professorial tweed coat and a black turtleneck that he later said made him sweat under the bright stage lights, repeated the same arguments he had made in his essays. He called to mind the ancient Greek philosophers: Plato, he said, viewed theater as a form of political action, while Aristotle defined it as a way to explore "the workings of the human soul, which has no color." He agreed with Wilson about the need for more Black theaters and more foundation support for such institutions, but he also took a jab at the playwright, whose work was developed and produced in mainstream theaters run by white men. "If Mr. Wilson knows of a worthy Black theater that isn't being properly funded," he said, "he could give it instant recognition by rewarding it one of his world premieres." He summed up their differences as "inclusion versus exclusion" and "integration versus separatism."

Wilson, wearing a tailored suit and tie, repeated many of the arguments he had made in his original speech, citing the statistic about sixty-six members of the League of Resident Theatres that included only one Black theater. "We are not advocates of separatism, as Mr. Brustein claims, but rather we are seeking to be included," he said. He deliberately did not mention the hot-button issue of color-blind casting. He had already realized that it had been a mistake to include that issue because it overshadowed all of his other points.

There were few fireworks during the first half of the event, and during the intermission, Smith was deflated. She had hoped to moderate a real discussion between the two men and open up what she viewed as a vital conversation about race relations in the theater. Instead, she was bombarded. "TCG staffers descended upon me as if I myself were a boxer about to be eaten alive, with many notes scrawled on pieces of paper, meant to help me pick up the pace, ask provocative questions, and make the event more exciting," she said. "There were also 3 x 5 cards with questions from the audience—headless, voiceless, presenceless questions."

Perhaps because of that pressure, the second half of the event was even more unruly—and had better sound bites. Brustein responded to Wilson's remarks by saying, "I think you have probably the best mind of the seventeenth century." Wilson came right back: "Are you aware that in the seventeenth century we were slaves; African Americans were slaves. You are aware of that?" Smith had to intervene and instruct the audience to stop shouting.

Smith read questions submitted by the audience, and one participant couldn't help but pose the question that many talked about but dared not ask Wilson to his face. "It was a question about your own background, and to what extent you recognize the part of you which is white." This question infuriated Wilson. He had deep feelings about his parentage, but he chose to keep those feelings to himself and to define himself on his own terms. He gave his usual answer. "I make this self-definition of myself as a Black man. And that's all anyone needs to know."

One question brought up nontraditional casting, which Wilson had hoped to keep out of the discussion. It was just one piece of his position, yet in the insular theater community, it had become the focal point that distracted from his larger argument. Many of the audience agreed with Brustein on this point, and Wilson privately wanted to dial back his original strident attack on the practice.

But by taking questions from the audience, the organizers allowed the "debate" to deteriorate into the realm of silly. Smith read one flippant question that mocked the seriousness of the issues. "I am an actor of mixed cultural heritage," it began. "My mother is Jewish of Austrian-Polish descent. My father is Black, mixed with a bit of Scots, Irish, and Native American Indian. Both of them were highly involved in CORE in the 1960s, and my father is currently president of a chapter of the NAACP. I was raised in a predominantly Chicano neighborhood in Los Angeles. Where does someone of my background fit into the American theater?"

Wilson refused to take the bait. "However that person wants to define themselves, fine," he answered.

Many in the audience had come expecting fisticuffs, and they were disappointed. Some felt like the event was a sham: it was ostensibly about race, but the participants were all beneficiaries of the mainstream theater world. "This is an academic exercise for the white folks and those handful of Black folk who have made it in the white theater," Elmo Terry-Morgan reflected later. At the time he was an associate professor of Theatre Arts and Afro-American Studies at Brown University. Terry-Morgan, who is Black, also thought the whole affair was a fleeting fad. "This will all blow over, and it will be back to business as usual."

During one moment near the end, both men reached common ground and agreed that initiatives that directed grants to white-run theaters to diversify, including a program run by the Lila Wallace-Reader's Digest Fund, were counterproductive. They also agreed that those grants would be put to better use by funding Black theaters to produce Black plays. That one instance of agreement generated enthusiastic applause.

The event had been billed as an entertaining sporting match, and everyone onstage knew that nothing much had been accomplished. Smith gave the two men a chance to sum up what they had learned, and Brustein blurted out, "I learned that behind Mr. Wilson's anger, he is a teddy bear." The minute he said it, he wished he could take it back. Wilson replied, "I consider myself a personable person, but I assure you, I'm a lion." And that was the end of it.

Smith was dejected. "I thought it was a failure," she said. She had started out wanting to initiate a genuine meeting of the minds, but she had been pressured to pick up the pace and amp up the volume. The next day, the *New York Times* ran a sort of play-by-play on the front page, and the article did not even mention her participation. "This is how we get written out of history," she said after years of reflection. "I put this whole thing together and I am not even in this article. That is the first time I ever used that expression: this is how women get written out of history." This had long been a criticism of Wilson's plays, which was not lost on Smith.

For his part, Wilson walked out of the theater and immediately went to a dinner at the West Bank Cafe on West Forty-Second Street. Constanza Romero had been in the audience, but she was in the first trimester with her first (and only) child and had the flu. She had a burning fever and had lost her voice. "I was so worried about the baby," she said. "He didn't have me for that. I was all caught up in that. You have a fever and you're pregnant. I'd never been pregnant before, and I was melodramatic. We were both in totally different worlds." This wasn't her fight, and she needed to rest. She and Wilson had used the occasion to tell Sakina about the pregnancy, and she was digesting that news. Sakina had had her father to herself for twenty-seven years, and the news of a new half-sibling disarmed her. So Wilson went alone to the restaurant, where some fifteen to twenty Black academics and theater professionals had gathered for a post-debate meal and discussion. The purpose was not to dissect the debate, which had been underwhelming, but to attempt to solidify plans for a national Black theater conference. Smith had been invited, but after the debate, the organizers knew she would not show up.

The "debate" dominated discussion in the theater for a few days, but since it had been a disappointment, the chatter died down. None of the issues—which were real and substantial—were resolved, and nothing much changed in the institutional theater over the next decade. Brustein later said that neither one of them had wanted to participate, but neither felt they could back out. "Both August and I thought this was a bad idea, but we didn't have the courage to say no," Brustein said. "I actually felt very fond of him, and I felt it was a shame that we had to be in front of the audience expecting a blistering confrontation." Wilson agreed that the event didn't even come close to a debate: the issues got lost in the preposterous promotion.

He did, however, react strongly when the New Yorker ran a piece on February 3. Written by self-described "race man" Henry Louis Gates Jr. and titled "The Chitlin Circuit," the ten-page article began by reconstructing the history of the Wilson-Brustein feud, but it was really about a different kind of theater entirely. It explored what is more accurately called the "urban theater" circuit, which mounts enormously popular productions of populist melodramas with titles like My Grandmother Prayed for

Me and *Beauty Shop*. These formulaic plays are presented in theaters in Black neighborhoods and marketed exclusively on Black radio. They are as far away in mindset from places like the Town Hall or the McCarter Theatre Center as they could be. Unafraid to flaunt stereotypes, they frequently feature a family in crisis and stock characters: a staunchly religious grandma, her wanton daughter, and a couple of grandkids who are faced with the evils of sex, drugs, and firearms. They play exclusively to Black urban audiences—and rake in hundreds of thousands of dollars at the box office. Shelly Garrett, the producer and author of *Beauty Shop*, told Gates that his play netted $600,000 a week in Atlanta. (Garrett, known as "the Godfather of Urban Theater," also claimed that *Beauty Shop* was seen by more than twenty-one million people during a ten-year span, grossing $33 million from 1987 to 1997. Its spin-offs—*Beauty Shop Part II*, *Barber Shop*, and *Laundromat*, were equally popular at large urban venues.) These producers did not care about the relative value of grants from the Lila Wallace-Reader's Digest Fund or the Ford Foundation. They sold out huge venues and made boatloads of money. And audiences loved what they were selling. Professionals in the mainstream "legit" theater, however, looked down on these broad melodramas; they distinguished their work as the "real" art, while viewing urban theater as lowbrow entertainment for the masses.

Wilson was furious about the article. He had granted a long interview to Gates, who barely quoted him in the piece. And Gates elicited biting quotes from many of Wilson's colleagues. "If O.J. can play a Black man, I don't see any problem with Olivier playing Othello," said playwright Amiri Baraka, who had been one of Wilson's early role models. And an unnamed source blamed Wilson for the lack of opportunity experienced by other Black playwrights. "Once the white mainstream theater found a Black artistic spokesman, the one playwright who could do no wrong, the money that used to go to autonomous Black theater started to dry up," this source said. A few years later, the Negro Ensemble Company founder and artistic director Douglas Turner Ward said essentially the same thing in an interview with the *Miami Herald*.

And Gates also brought up the thorny topic of Wilson's racial identity.

He questioned his Blackness. "He neither looks nor sounds typically Black—had he the desire he could easily pass—and that makes him Black first and foremost by self-identification," Gates wrote. Wilson had been hearing this all of his life, and now here he was, reading it in the esteemed literary pages of the *New Yorker*, the magazine where he had discovered his beloved Borges. He felt that he had stuck his neck out to defend Black theater, and his very identity was being challenged yet again. He later told Dartmouth professor Walker that he had more respect for Brustein than he did for Gates.

The piece and the aftermath of the debate further convinced Wilson's colleagues of the need to convene a Black theater conference. But Wilson was not an easy sell. Romero, after all, was pregnant with their child, and she was not a retiring sort who subsumed her needs for her spouse. Wilson told Walker and Paul Carter Harrison that he could only commit to attend a conference if Romero agreed to accompany him. Walker had already garnered the support of Dartmouth College. William Cook, chair of the university's theater department, was on board. They offered Wilson a ten-week residency at Dartmouth as a Montgomery Fellow. He would be required to teach and Dartmouth would provide institutional support for the conference. After months of discussions and dinners, in May 1997, Wilson finally agreed to participate and lead the conference, which was then scheduled for March 1998 at Dartmouth. He had been hoping to convene the summit in the "ancestral homeland" in the South, but no Southern institution offered to host the event. "Why Dartmouth?" he said. "Because Dartmouth was willing."

Wilson left most of the planning to the academics because, for once, he was focused on his family. Romero gave birth to a daughter on August 27, 1997. At fifty-two, Wilson was getting a second chance at fatherhood, and he was enchanted. He cut the umbilical cord after the birth, and he marveled at the miracle of it all. "He was mesmerized," Romero said. "Our birth announcement was August's hand around her little chest. It was like the birth of Venus." They called their daughter Azula Carmen Wilson. Romero had originally wanted to call her Sula, after Toni Morrison's 1973 novel, but it sounded too much like a nickname for Ursula.

Azul means "blue" in Spanish, and Wilson's most famous character, Troy
Maxson from *Fences*, sings a song about a dog named Blue. And so they
came up with Azula, which the bilingual Romero laughed about a few
years later. "In Spanish, that's like blue-a," she said. Wilson did not have
a new play scheduled in the coming year, so he was able to revel in par-
enthood. He handed out cigars to his friends and treated himself to one
to celebrate. Unfortunately, the occasional cigar led to more frequent
smokes, and before long, he went back to his old habit.

Wilson had committed to the Black theater summit, but he let the
academics handle the details while he took time off to spend with his new
daughter. The organizers had hoped to attract major philanthropic spon-
sors, but during the planning stages, they learned that the Ford Foundation was about to pledge $1.5 million to a somewhat related project called
the Institute on the Arts and Civic Dialogue, a combination think tank and
artist colony that aimed to promote discussion about social and political
issues through the arts. It was a joint project between the American Repertory Theater and Harvard's W. E. B. Du Bois Institute. The project was
to be headed by Anna Deavere Smith. Brustein, of course, ran the American Repertory Theater, and Gates was the head of the Du Bois Institute.
Wilson and his partners felt burned—and also realized that they didn't
have a prayer of getting that kind of grant from the Ford Foundation.

But they forged ahead anyway and eventually raised $250,000, which
included $60,000 from the Rockefeller Foundation and a grant of $15,000
from the National Endowment for the Arts. The conference was eventually sponsored by the Ford Foundation as well. The organizers put
together a list of participants, which included directors, producers, playwrights, and professionals from other fields with knowledge of fundraising and organizing. It wasn't easy compiling the list, and the organizers
tried to be as democratic as possible. The goal was to gather a mix that
represented various age groups, genders, and professions. They capped
the list at forty-five people and required that all participants stay for the
entire event, which was slated for March 2–7, 1998, at Dartmouth. Some
prominent members of the Black theater community could not commit
to the entire time, including Baraka, playwright Pearl Cleage, and director

George C. Wolfe. As the group discussed names, Wilson pulled his weight only once. The organizers suggested inviting Lloyd Richards, and Wilson said, "I don't think this is a good meeting for Lloyd." His name was crossed off the invitation list, even though Richards was the first Black man to direct on Broadway and had run the Yale Repertory Theatre, the Yale School of Drama, and the Eugene O'Neill Theater Center. Clearly, the wound was still raw.

The goal was to keep the working group small enough so that it could actually accomplish something, but the organizers opened themselves up to criticism from the start. Before the meeting even took place, theater professionals who weren't invited—Black and white—lobbed accusations of sexism, homophobia, and separatism. "They're styling it as if they're defining theater for the next century," Andrea Hairston, chairwoman of the theater department at Smith College in Northampton, Massachusetts, said at the time. "It's a little pompous to think that we need a bunch of boys gathering in the woods in New England to define how things should go and then the rest of us will follow." Hairston, who is Black, also pointed out that the performing arts faced obstacles that went beyond the issue of race: increased competition from electronic media, diminishing resources from public and private sources, and shrinking arts education in the public schools. "Theater is the art of change, and I'm not interested in distinguishing between Black theater and white theater and multicultural theater and women's theater and queer theater," she said. "That's just pointless, diversionary bull." She was not alone in her criticism.

Undeterred, the group decided to call the gathering a "summit" rather than a conference, taking a cue from the 1905 Niagara Movement Summit, a pivotal meeting led by W. E. B. Du Bois and William Monroe Trotter that laid the foundation for the National Association for the Advancement of Colored People. They adopted the name "On Golden Pond": The National Black Theatre Summit. Dartmouth owned the Minary Conference Center in Ashland, New Hampshire, a retreat center on the banks of Squam Lake that was not far from the setting for the 1981 film *On Golden Pond*. The area has a rich history; it was a stop on the Underground Railroad on the way to Canada as well as a shelter for African Americans who had escaped slavery. George Washington's former enslaved person Ona Judge lived in the area after escaping from bondage.

Despite all the backstage quibbling, the participants convened at Dartmouth on March 2, during one of the coldest winters in recent history, even by New Hampshire standards. At the opening-night ceremony, Wilson sat at the head table, bouncing Azula, who was six months old at the time, on his knee. When she got fussy, he handed the baby to Romero, who disappeared from the room, infant in her arms. She had agreed to spend ten weeks in wintry New Hampshire with a new baby in tow, but Azula had a cold, and Romero's chief concern was the health of her child. She spent much of the time in the background.

The participants stayed at first-class accommodations near Dartmouth in Hanover and rode a bus to the Minary Center in Ashland. The trip took about an hour and fifteen minutes. No one really knew what to expect, but this was not a rarified group; the irreverent jokes began immediately. Elmo Terry-Morgan from Brown was sitting next to playwright Ntozake Shange on the bus, and he turned to her and said, "Is we free yet?" But the first day was less than auspicious. Very little was accomplished because of the huge personalities in the room. "The first day we spent nine hours doing nothing but arguing back and forth," Walker said. Woodie King Jr., founding director of New York's New Federal Theatre, was particularly argumentative, and he was especially critical of Lou Bellamy, the founder of Penumbra in St. Paul, where Wilson got his start. Bellamy could be pushed only so far before he exploded, and the conference organizers were concerned that their attempt to come up with a serious agenda would be derailed by clashing egos.

Tension was rife when the attendees arrived for the second day. But before the session even began, playwright Shange retreated into the kitchen and grabbed a broom. With her singular dramatic flair, she started sweeping the room, speaking in a mix of Spanish and Portuguese for a good ten minutes. The performance artist Idris Ackamoor began playing impromptu percussion as she swept, and then she opened the door and brushed all the dust outside. It had been snowing, and the storm suddenly halted. Out of nowhere, King started to choke. He eventually got his breath back, but he stopped haranguing the other participants. After that spur-of-the-moment ritual, the attendees got down to business and held panel discussions on everything from fundraising and marketing to playwriting and dramaturgy.

The event was held in private, but the public was invited to a final National Black Theatre Conference at the Hopkins Center on the Dartmouth campus on March 7. The organizers didn't know what kind of crowd would show up, but the room was filled with three hundred artists, academics, students, and interested members of the public. The group had not solved the issues about the funding and visibility crisis in Black theater, but it had come up with two tangible projects. It announced a partnership with Dartmouth's Tuck School of Business; the school would provide scholarships for Black theater artists to attend its summer Minority Business Executive Program. Many small Black theaters in communities nationwide struggled with the financial end of operations, and the program aimed to provide management tools for administrators. The group also announced the formation of the African Grove Institute for the Arts (AGIA), a service organization to support and sustain Black theaters. The institute took its name from the African Grove Theatre, a Black theater established in New York in 1821. The theater was memorialized in Carlyle Brown's *The African Company Presents Richard III*, a play that was developed and produced by Penumbra in 1988. In the play, the members of the Black troupe compete with a white theater while they are both producing *Richard III*. The police shut down the Black theater, and its founder, William Henry Brown, vows to write his own plays for Black people and about Black people. Wilson was a fan of the play and espoused its message. The name of the new institute was a tribute to those early efforts.

After the public event, the attendees gathered for a closing dinner. It began with the usual speeches, but then Shange took the stage and performed an original, twenty-minute poem called "Beneath the Necessity of Talk." Shange, of course, is known for the free verse she made famous in *for colored girls who have considered suicide / when the rainbow is enuf*, and she knew how to command a room. She got a prolonged standing ovation. Wilson was the last speaker of the evening, and for once, he knew he had been upstaged. "I am not following that," he told Walker. He did take the stage and said, "Sister, you just brought it down. You put an exclamation point on it."

After the rough beginning, the summit led to the formation of AGIA, but Wilson still thought it should have been convened in the "ancestral homeland," rather than at a conservative Ivy League school in the heart of New England. The group approached Dwight Andrews, who had recently taken over as the artistic director of the National Black Arts Festival (NBAF) in Atlanta, which was scheduled for July. Andrews agreed that the NBAF could cover 75 percent of the cost of another summit, which would coincide with the festival. Wilson's rewrite of *Jitney* was already slated to be a key attraction at the festival.

The second summit, held July 12–15, amassed a wider range of participants and included a closed-door session for more than thirty artistic directors of Black theaters. This time, there was a panel discussion focused on the urban theater circuit; the organizers realized that urban plays were extremely profitable, and they put aside their elitist assumptions in order to learn about the circuit's business strategies. At the summit, the group also announced a partnership between AGIA and the Getty Research Institute in Los Angeles; Black theater artists would be given residencies at the Getty, partnering with the goal of preserving, stabilizing, and sustaining Black cultural organizations.

Wilson signed on as chairman of the AGIA board, but he did not fund the organization out of his own pocket. Walker left Dartmouth and became AGIA president, and Keryl McCord, a seasoned theater administrator, was appointed vice president. The organization staged town meetings in cities all over the country, and for a few years, it was able to sustain itself through foundation support and individual contributions. But the leaders discovered that the needs were different in every community, and those needs ran deep. Unlike Theatre Communications Group, which supports itself with a publishing arm, a magazine, and membership dues from large regional theaters, AGIA relied solely on donations. The partnership with the Tuck School of Business was dissolved in 2001, and the relationship with the Getty did not last long. Wilson felt that the Getty was using his name and the clout of other well-known Black writers to tout its "diversity" efforts rather than genuinely trying to help.

And Wilson, while committed to the goals of both summits, had three more plays to write to complete his cycle. The excitement and energy generated at the summits was difficult to sustain, and grant money for Black theaters and AGIA started to dry up. Black theaters were facing deeper financial difficulties than they were when Wilson first gave his speech in 1996. Crossroads Theatre canceled its 2000–2001 season, citing a $2 million deficit. Such theaters as Jomandi Productions in Atlanta and the Inner City Cultural Center in Los Angeles were struggling. Wilson was disheartened. In 2002, he noted that there were now sixty-seven members of the League of Resident Theatres, but since Crossroads had gone bankrupt, there were no Black theaters in the league. After all that convening and communing, Wilson felt the situation hadn't improved: it had gotten worse. He summed it up in a 2003 interview: "The concrete results of Black gains—I don't see any, none."

CHAPTER FIFTEEN

A Master Jitney Driver

We need these stories. They matter. They mean so much
to so many different people. They're honest and they say,
"This here is our place," a place that is inherited, just like
our blood and bones.

—MARION ISAAC MCCLINTON

While Wilson was embroiled in what did not turn out to be the "Debate of the Century," he was simultaneously working on a rewrite of *Jitney!*, the play that started it all. Wilson's career took off after the wildly successful semi-amateur production in a scrappy basement theater in Pittsburgh in 1982. He had put *Jitney!* in a drawer and forgotten about it.

But Pittsburgh audiences remembered. Of all of Wilson's plays, it is his most infectious and endearing and, despite its tragic underpinnings and an out-of-nowhere death at the end, it is hilariously funny. The jitney drivers are salt-of-the earth souls who work hard for a living and just want to get by. The father-son feud at the heart of the story is as universal as the paternal struggle in *Fences*, making it nearly impossible not to feel an instinctive kinship with the characters. Director Marion Isaac McClinton put it this way in his introduction to the published script: "It did not matter if they were Black, white or Martian, that they [the audience members] were not watching a play—they were watching their own lives acted out before their very eyes."

Eddie Gilbert took over as artistic director of the Pittsburgh Public

Theater in 1993, and when he talked to audience members, they all had one request. They wanted to see *Jitney!* again. Never mind that it had played at a much smaller theater more than a decade earlier. People remembered it. And so he invited—or perhaps implored—Wilson to remount it. The playwright had come a long way since he wrote the play at an Arthur Treacher's Fish & Chips shop in St. Paul, so he agreed to expand the play for a production at Pittsburgh Public in June 1996. It had, after all, been rejected by the O'Neill not once but twice, and despite its popularity, Wilson wanted to beef it up. (It lost the exclamation point in the process and became known as *Jitney.*)

He decided to rewrite during rehearsal, the same way he had done with *Seven Guitars*, even though that experience had been fraught with tension. He was also privately working on his TCG speech late at night, but he had become a master multitasker and juggled both projects at once. As originally written, the play was only ninety minutes long, and it lacked Wilson's signature monologues. This time, rather than cut a script from four and a half hours to a more palatable (and producible) three hours, he wanted to expand the story and flesh out the relationships that were mere outlines in the one-act version.

When things went sour with *Seven Guitars*, it was clear that Wilson's relationship with Richards was over. There was no question that he would choose another director for future productions, and for *Jitney*, he tapped McClinton, the actor and playwright from St. Paul who had performed in Penumbra's *Jitney!* as well as in *Black Bart*. But interestingly, Pittsburgh Public announced McClinton as the director in August 1995, *before* Wilson and Richards began their feud over whether or not to fire Zakes Mokae from the *Seven Guitars* cast. Richards had been ill, and Wilson was worried about the future even before the contretemps between them reached the point of no return. He had done six plays with one director, and feud or no feud, he was already contemplating a change.

The choice of McClinton seemed natural enough. But this decision left many in Wilson's orbit scratching their heads. If the playwright were to make a break with Richards, why didn't he choose his longtime director and confidant, Claude Purdy? The director, after all, had lured him to

St. Paul and championed his work, convincing Penumbra's leadership to let him direct the ill-fated *Black Bart*. Richards typically recommended Purdy to direct subsequent productions of Wilson's plays, *after* his "definitive" version debuted on Broadway (which was a sort of backhanded compliment). Purdy became the director of choice for later productions of Wilson's plays at regional theaters, and he had directed acclaimed productions in San Francisco, Los Angeles, Houston, Pittsburgh, as well as London. He had accompanied Wilson to the O'Neill in 1984, the summer *Joe Turner* was workshopped, and played Bynum Walker, the play's mystical life force, in the O'Neill staged reading.

Purdy was not a dilettante; he was the real deal when it came to directing. A rangy, bearded man with a penchant for jaunty hats and an impeccable sartorial style, he had ideas about plays, and he didn't just blindly follow the text. He challenged actors. Richards, on the other hand, was an enigmatic director who asked actors questions and stuck strictly to the script; ever faithful to the playwright, he did not impose his own interpretation on the plays he directed.

That difference is most likely the reason why Wilson chose McClinton. Purdy was five years older than Wilson, while McClinton was nine years younger and, perhaps more important, readily agreeable to bow to the playwright's wishes. While Wilson had told interviewers that Purdy was his first choice to direct his plays after they debuted on Broadway, their relationship frayed over the years. According to actors from St. Paul, the two men feuded, but they took the precise source of their dispute to their graves. Purdy's widow, Jacqui Shoholm, never knew the exact cause of the friction between the men. Wilson's choice of McClinton bruised Purdy, who had been loyal to a fault and once carried a copy of *Black Bart* in his briefcase—just in case a theater producer would agree to read it. And he understood Wilson's characters in a way that few other directors did. Early on, when Wilson was still a green playwright, Purdy explained the heart of the plays to Lou Bellamy, artistic director of Penumbra. "These people are never to be laughed *at*. They are not funny," Purdy instructed Bellamy. "They tend to, inside of themselves, be hilarious in terms of dealing with each other, but the cumulative effect of their interaction can never allow anyone to laugh *at* them. They must laugh *with* them." Bellamy said that single explanation guided his approach to Wilson's plays ever since.

But over the years, Wilson grew increasingly angry at Purdy for taking liberties with his plays. Wilson was exacting about productions of his work. After he became successful, he traveled the country to check in on productions at regional theaters. He didn't react well when he felt his work was misinterpreted. Purdy directed the St. Paul premiere of *Ma Rainey* at Penumbra in 1987 and a later production in 1996. Actor Terry Bellamy played the trumpeter Levee in both productions (although he quit the second production shortly after it opened). In the scene in Act 2 where Levee romances Dussie Mae, Purdy directed Bellamy to go hot and heavy, veering toward an R-rated interpretation. Dussie Mae enters the band room and flirts with Levee, who puts his hands on her buttocks. But Wilson's stage notes are explicit: *"He moves to kiss her as the lights go down in the band room and up in the studio."* The attention turns to Ma Rainey in the recording studio as she talks to Cutler, the trombonist and bandleader. It is an important scene and contains one of the most oft-quoted bits of dialogue in the play (although the actual Ma Rainey never said such a thing). Ma tells Cutler:

> White folks don't understand about the blues. They hear
> it come out, but they don't know how it got there. They
> don't understand that's life's way of talking. You don't sing
> to feel better. You sing 'cause that's a way of understand-
> ing life.

In Purdy's staging, the lights were left on in the band room, so while Ma Rainey was speaking, the audience could see Levee and Dussie Mae making out. Wilson blew a fuse when he saw the rehearsal. "They were supposed to do a dance, and Claude had me grinding on her for twenty minutes," Bellamy said. "August was like, 'What are you doing to my play, man?' and Claude was like, 'I got artistic ideas too, motherfucker.'" Wilson was adamant that the sexy business had to go. Bellamy is convinced that the rift between the two men began in that moment, but he is not sure whether Purdy was not chosen because he took liberties. "Lloyd read the words, and Claude was like, 'Throw some of this away. You gotta breathe it and digest it.' Playwrights don't want to hear that," Bellamy said. He said that Wilson told Purdy, "If you want to direct my play, you can't do that." (Oddly, in the posthumous 2020 film version of *Ma Rainey*, the same scene goes even further; the two characters make love on a piano, a steamy bit of action that is decidedly not in Wilson's original script. The playwright surely would have objected, and that scene would not have made the final cut.)

Wilson could not control Purdy. After *Joe Turner* debuted on Broadway, Purdy directed a coproduction of *Joe Turner* with the American Conservatory Theater and the Los Angeles Theatre Center in 1989. It starred stage and television icon Roscoe Lee Browne as Bynum and James Craven, a Penumbra veteran, as Herald Loomis. (Anna Deavere Smith was also in the cast as one of the women in the boardinghouse.) The production of *Joe Turner* was well-received.

Browne and Craven both admired Purdy as a director. The three men thought that the play, which is set in 1911, would make a great shoot-'em-up Western opera, somewhat akin to the Wild West setting for *Black Bart*. They suggested the idea to Wilson, who not only objected to the idea, he exploded. "*Black Bart* didn't work out for him, and he didn't understand that it was a worthy idea to pursue it in other things," Craven said. "Claude understood about *Joe Turner*, in terms of it being a Western." Of course, the adaptation never happened.

Wilson had another blowup when Purdy directed *Joe Turner* at the Alley Theatre in Houston in 1991, with Craven and Browne reprising their roles from San Francisco. In one scene, the brooding Herald Loomis has a brief romantic interaction with Mattie Campbell, a fellow boarder. In the script, it is a short encounter at the end of Act 2, Scene 3, and according to the stage directions, Loomis *"finds he cannot"* just before the lights fade to black. Purdy had other ideas. In Houston, he had the two actors undress completely. When Wilson saw the production, he went ballistic. "August said that Claude was trying to turn his play into a porn show, and Claude said it was art," Craven said. "But two Black people naked? August hit the roof."

Bellamy and others in St. Paul said there may have been another, more personal reason that caused a deeper chill in the relationship between playwright and director, but the men guarded their secrets closely. When it came time to pick a replacement for Richards, though, McClinton was the easier choice. They could disagree, but Wilson maintained the final say. They had an easy rapport. And both men worshipped—and feared—their mothers. In his elegiac 1996 *New York Times* essay, "Living on Mother's Prayer," Wilson wrote, "Of all human relations, that of a mother and child is the most primary, the most fundamental. It is also sometimes the most complicated and is often, given the nature of human life, an embattled relationship." At fifty-one, he was still his mother's son. And at forty-two, so was McClinton. While McClinton grew up in a two-parent household, both men had mothers who pinched pennies so their sons could attend parochial school. He echoed Wilson's sentiments about the death of his mother. "I don't have the human guide that was guiding me through life and helped me get back to the direction of the light," he said of her passing. She also ruled the household, the same way Daisy Wilson did. "You didn't take on Lenora McClinton," McClinton told the *Los Angeles Times* in 2000. "She was tenacious, indefatigable—the only person who ever scared me." The two men clicked. They spoke the same language. And McClinton was more prone to defer to Wilson than Purdy. It worked.

During the *Jitney* rehearsal period, residents of the Hill District who had been involved with the original 1982 production threw a welcoming dinner for the cast and crew. Anthony Chisholm, who played the alcoholic driver Fielding, remembered that it was hosted by a group of senior women from the Hill District—"older than our mothers," he said—and that scores of guests packed into a house for a family-style party. About a half dozen women circulated through the crowd with posters displaying photographs and reviews from the 1982 production. The gathering culminated with a group prayer conducted by a priestess of the Yoruba religion. All the guests, including adults and children, held hands while she performed a libation, pouring wine on the floor. She offered a prayer for *Jitney*. "It was like we were wishing it a long life and blessings from the spirit," Chisholm said. "The experience was really uncanny."

While Wilson rewrote during rehearsal, he aimed to heighten the dramatic tension in the father-son conflict. His plays are always a mix of comedy and tragedy, and Wilson wanted to emphasize the gut-wrenching, universal struggle between fathers and sons. He had brushed over that theme when he wrote the play in 1979. In the original, Becker and Booster confront each other only once, and the father rejects the son. When Becker dies at the end, Booster is suddenly proud of his old man, but there is no indication why he has a change of heart. Wilson acknowledged that problem at Pittsburgh Public, and he added another scene between the father and son. "When I wrote the play 17 years ago, I did not know what the father and son would say in a second scene," he admitted. He simply killed the father off in the end so he didn't have to write another scene with them together. "Coming here, I feel confident to write them another scene." The new scene illuminated the relationship, but the characters still needed to be further fleshed out.

The actors playing the jitney drivers also didn't have much to work with. Their characters had a way with jabs, but they were one-dimensional. They complained to Wilson that they needed monologues, otherwise it wouldn't be a signature "August Wilson play." Wilson fielded ideas from them. He had gotten close to Chisholm when he played Wolf, the numbers runner, in *Two Trains*. At the time, Wilson was going through five packs of cigarettes a day. Chisholm was also a heavy smoker at the time, and they would meet outside during breaks to have a cigarette. The two men shared stories about their families. Chisholm also had a strong mother who valued education; his mother, Edith Chisholm, made him memorize and recite poetry when he was growing up in Cleveland. During *Jitney* rehearsal breaks, Chisholm told Wilson about his father, who worked as a luggage carrier for the railroad, but moonlighted as a tailor. "We got into a conversation about families, and I told him about my father, who was a red cap on the railroad but had great tailoring skills and started making clothes for traveling band members. August said, 'I like that; can I use it?'" Chisholm said. "One day he handed me a wonderful, brand-new scene, and I was so happy; it rounded out my character. Fielding wasn't just an alcoholic; he'd had a whole other life." The expanded character was once a tailor who dressed Pittsburgh-born jazz vocalist Billy Eckstine and pianist and bandleader Count Basie. By the time Wilson was finished with revisions, he added seven monologues. He also cut extraneous and repetitive lines.

The discussions with the actors continued throughout the rehearsal process, which included field trips. Wilson took some of the actors on a long tour of the Hill District. It was a sweltering day, with temperatures well into the nineties, but they saw his childhood home on Bedford Avenue and stopped in at Eddie's Restaurant, where Wilson had worked briefly before he got fired for spending all of his time writing in the corner and mumbling to himself. They visited the barbershop where the young Wilson got his hair cut, and Chisholm recalled talking to an elderly barber who remembered the playwright as a boy. "The guy was about one hundred years old, and August seemed to shrink down into a little seven-year-old," Chisholm said.

One night, they went to the Crawford Grill and ran into Wilson's poet friends Rob Penny and Chawley Williams. Wilson was usually one to talk into the late hours of the evening, but he cut the evening short and told Chisholm it was time to leave. "We have to go," he told the actor. "I'm ready to go back to my writing. My batteries are charged now." Chisholm automatically thought he was talking about the *Jitney* script, but he was working on "The Ground on Which I Stand," the speech that launched the firestorm in the theater world. As he often did, Wilson was multitasking that spring, working on the speech and the play at the same time. Chisholm asked him to recite the speech then and there, but Wilson, who often went into character spontaneously and recited entire monologues from his plays, demurred. He promised to send a copy of the speech to Chisholm when he was finished polishing it. Chisholm and the rest of the theater world heard about it soon enough.

The Pittsburgh Public production opened on Friday, June 14, 1996, to ecstatic reviews, and the *Pittsburgh Post-Gazette* later named it the best play of the year. Originally scheduled for a six-week run, it was held over and ran well into September, playing to standing-room-only crowds just like the original production had a decade and a half earlier. The rewriting had paid off. But Wilson's relationship with McClinton had soured. According to Chisholm, Wilson did not ask him to continue with the production, which was slated to move to another theater. McClinton went home to St. Paul, and he was despondent.

Wilson wasn't finished with *Jitney*, and he had a plan that he had been keeping to himself. During the debate at Town Hall, Brustein had challenged Wilson to mount one of his world premieres at an African American theater. Wilson did not respond directly to that quip, but in fact, he had already promised to mount the revised *Jitney* at Crossroads Theatre in New Brunswick. At the time, Crossroads was the only African American theater in the League of Resident Theatres, the theater that Wilson had referred to in his speech. Founded in a New Brunswick loft in 1978, Crossroads was kick-started by a Comprehensive Employment and Training Act grant. In 1986, it presented the world premiere of *The Colored Museum*, a seminal satirical work by the director George C. Wolfe (who would direct the 2020 film adaptation of *Ma Rainey*). Wilson did not flaunt his arrangement with Crossroads during the debate, and the theater held off announcing the production until January 29, two days after the Town Hall event. "I'm kind of glad it didn't come up at the debate, because it would have been tit for tat," Crossroads artistic director Ricardo Khan said after the announcement was made. "But that's exactly what he's doing. He's launching his play here."

With McClinton sent unhappily back to St. Paul, Wilson turned to Walter Dallas, the director who had stepped in to direct *Seven Guitars* when Richards was ill. Dallas directed the production of *Jitney* that opened at Crossroads on April 13, 1997.

At Crossroads, Wilson added a scene to magnify the impact of Becker's sudden death at the end. In the original version, he was defeated and was just going to accept the fact that the neighborhood was being demolished and close the station. But in this new scene, Becker holds a meeting to discuss how to fight back and save the business. That scene made clear that Becker is a community leader who took the kind of action that his son could respect.

He also changed the time of the play from 1971 to 1977. One of the jitney drivers is a Vietnam War veteran trying to buy his first home and start a life with his fiancée. Wilson wanted the action to take place after the Fall of Saigon in April 1975, so the focus was not on antiwar efforts, but rather on the veteran's attempt to get a fresh start. He made a similar change with *Two Trains*, when he moved the setting from 1968 to 1969 in order to distance the story from the tragic assassination of Martin Luther King Jr.

Wilson was trying to dig deeper than he had before on an issue that was somewhat too close for comfort. He certainly wasn't aiming for slapstick comedy. At Crossroads, Dallas mined the material for every laugh, including cheap ones that weren't called for in the script. Some of the actors who were in the Pittsburgh production bristled at the new direction. "It was like he was playing for the Chitlin Circuit," said Chisholm, referring to the enormously popular, over-the-top comedies. Stephen McKinley Henderson played the gossip Turnbo. In one scene, his character has a conversation with Rena, who is engaged to the Vietnam veteran Youngblood. Dallas instructed Henderson to circle the couch and wiggle his bottom. "He was practically twerking," Chisholm said. Henderson did not want to play it that way. "I said, 'Can the character have some dignity?' And Walter said, 'What are you talking about? Turnbo has no dignity.'"

Wilson's purpose was to turn everyday people into kings and queens, but the direction did the exact opposite. Producers and theater administrators who came to see the production were turned off by the broad comedy. The actors hated having to perform in that style. Critic Christopher Rawson of the *Pittsburgh Post-Gazette* was diplomatic. "In general, director Dallas sets a sunnier tone," he wrote, comparing what he saw at Crossroads to the production at Pittsburgh Public. "I miss the tension. Laughs sometimes upstage drama."

Nevertheless, the infectious play, which is Wilson's most likeable and accessible work, proved to be director-proof. The Crossroads production played to SRO audiences. The same production, with most of the same actors, was remounted at Dallas's New Freedom Theatre in Philadelphia in June 1998, and it was a linchpin of the National Black Arts Festival in

Atlanta in July of that year. With each production, Dallas directed the actors to go a little bit further with the broad comedy. "Walter would say, 'I love what you are doing, but let's see if we can make it a little bit funnier,'" Chisholm said. "He had groomed his audience at the Freedom Theatre for that over-the-top slapstick humor. It was a laugh-fest." Every night, the theater was packed with people roaring uncontrollably. The actors knew it didn't serve the play, which is a tragicomedy. "It got so ridiculous that, to tell you the truth, we were laughing at our own words like on a television variety show," Chisholm said.

Wilson was scrupulous about attending openings of his plays and eventually he would put a stop to the yuk-a-minute direction. But he snuck in a trip to the National Arts Festival in Grahamstown, South Africa, in late June. He had been commissioned to teach a playwriting class, and he brought Sakina along with him. He had only been there a few days when he was approached by a Pittsburgh actor and aspiring playwright named Mark Clayton Southers, who was appearing at the festival. Southers delivered a difficult message. Nick Flournoy, one of the original Centre Avenue Poets, had passed away at the age of fifty-eight. Wilson was inconsolable. Of all of his friends from Pittsburgh, Flournoy was the most loyal and true; he never resented Wilson's success. He worked as a community activist and never had much money, and Wilson would quietly slip him cash when he visited Pittsburgh. Wilson told Sakina that he was crushed that he couldn't attend the services at the Hill District's West Funeral Home, which he had immortalized in his play *Two Trains*.

When Wilson returned, he went straight to Atlanta to check in on the *Jitney* production and attend the second National Black Theatre Summit. He had heard the actors griping about Dallas, and he agreed with their criticism. He told Dallas that he would not be directing future productions and asked McClinton to come back as director. The cast was thrilled. "We got Marion back. It was a victory," Henderson said. "Nobody thought he would be asked back, but he was ready." McClinton had been disconsolate when he had been let go, but he was vindicated and eager to return. "August knew when it had gone too far," Henderson said of the bawdy production that milked every possible below-the-belt gag.

Many of the same cast members convened for a new production at Boston's Huntington Theatre that October, and Wilson was ready for a complete shakedown. "We're going to scrap everything," he told the *Pittsburgh Post-Gazette*. "We're going to start over and I'm going to do some rewrites, particularly the Becker-Booster scenes [the father and son]. I want to rethink the whole character of Booster. I wrote that 18, 19 years ago, and I think maybe if I reimagine it, now that I'm more mature, they'll say different things."

He had worked at the Huntington on four plays with Richards, and he was comfortable rewriting there. The changes to the script were significant. The father and son encounters were more confrontational, and Wilson provided a backstory that deepened the understanding of the rift between the two men. In earlier productions, Booster is a stereotypical, smarmy ex-con who shows up with a girl glued to his arm shortly after he is released from prison. She is clearly a rent-by-the-hour attraction who serves no purpose in the plot, and her presence cheapened Booster's dignity and added to the criticism that Wilson's female characters were one-dimensional and stereotypical. But in Boston, the courtesan was gone. Wilson expanded the monologues and created a backstory for Booster, making his prison sentence all the more tragic. As a youngster, he was a whiz kid at science, winning first prize in the local science fair three years in a row. He earned a scholarship to Pitt, which in the 1950s was not a particularly welcoming place for African American students. Becker invested his hopes in his brilliant son, and he was shattered when his son ruined his future by murdering a white woman who falsely accused him of rape. To Booster, the crime was about principles. To Becker, it was a mark of shame. The father disowned his son and refused to attend the trial, while his wife sat in the front row every day, weeping and praying. She died shortly after the guilty verdict. Now, twenty years later, both men blame the other for her death. Booster says his mother died from neglect while Becker says she died of grief. Wilson heightened the stakes. "You are my son," Becker says, echoing Troy in *Fences*. "I helped to bring you into this world. But from this moment on . . . I'm calling the deal off. You ain't nothing to me, boy."

He also expanded the story of Youngblood, the Vietnam vet, and his fiancée, Rena. In the original play written in 1979, Rena is a cardboard character. She becomes jealous when Youngblood starts hanging around with her sister, but she is meek and unconvincing in her confrontation. But in this new version, Wilson made her fiercely independent. When she learns that Youngblood was touring houses with her sister so he could use his veteran's benefits to buy a home, she doesn't shower him with tearful gratitude or congratulate him the way she did in the original. Instead, she says what any partner would say about being left out of such a monumental purchase. "A *house*?" she asks, incredulous. "You bought a house without me!" She adds, "Don't surprise me with a house that I didn't even have a chance to pick out!" They iron it out, but the relationship is on equal footing. In 1993, coincidentally or not, Wilson bought the antique Victorian on East Aloha Street in Seattle, a year before he married Romero.

Because of these changes, the Boston production was much sharper than it had been in any of the previous cities, and Wilson and McClinton were working together harmoniously. They bounced ideas off each other in rehearsal, bringing a sort of electricity to the process that had been missing when Wilson worked with Richards. By this point, many of the *Jitney* actors had been together on and off since 1996, and the ensemble was seamless. McClinton had proven himself, and he and Wilson began doing interviews together. McClinton had officially replaced Richards as the director of choice. Purdy was sidelined to secondary productions in regional theaters. He never directed a Wilson premiere other than *Black Bart*.

Jitney was a smash hit in Boston and made the *Boston Globe*'s list of top ten plays of the year. But Wilson was still not finished tinkering, and now that he had a director he trusted, he continued to work on the script when it debuted at Baltimore's Center Stage the following March. Sakina lived in the Baltimore area and she participated in the rehearsal process. Wilson had considered cutting the confrontational scene between father and son, but Sakina objected and told him that the father couldn't just dismiss his own son without hearing him out. The scene made its way back into the play.

By this point, the production was becoming a well-oiled machine, and it continued to play to standing ovations and sold-out houses. It broke the record for attendance and single-ticket sales at Center Stage, making it the most popular show in the theater's history at the time. McClinton took to calling it "the little engine that could." Writing in the *Washington Post*, critic Lloyd Rose heralded it as nothing short of the salvation of American theater. "Wilson mourns for a whole culture, and the fullness of his feeling makes you realize how pinched and childish the emotional range of most American plays is. Our dramatic tradition consists largely of self-pity, resentment, frustration, finger-pointing and self-righteousness, little puddles splashed away to nothingness by a flood like this."

What was once a little play that Wilson dashed off had become a tour de force. *Fences* made a fortune on Broadway, but the other plays did not. *Jitney*, however, was not only raking in ticket sales at the box office, it was stirring audiences. Wilson had hit his stride. Under Richards's tutelage, he had learned dramatic structure, and it is not by accident that his poetry soared when he wrote about father-son relationships. He had been scarred as an impressionable child, and now he was a father of an adult daughter he had been separated from when she was a baby. He had also become a father again during the play's long road since the Crossroads production in 1997. He rarely saw his toddler, though—which was a high price of his success, but also his personal choice. Work first; honeymoon, wife, baby second.

The play continued to travel from city to city, receiving the same popular appeal at Chicago's Goodman Theatre in June 1999 and at the Mark Taper Forum in Los Angeles in January 2000. With past productions, the Mark Taper was often the last stop before a new Wilson play opened on Broadway, but much to his disappointment, Wilson was not able to entice a producer to bring it to the Great White Way. "No one stepped forward and said, 'Hey, I want to do this on Broadway,' which I find puzzling in the sense that it's done good box office every place it played," he said. McClinton was more direct in saying that the lack of interest had everything to do with race. "Whenever you're working on a show written by an African-American, you run up against a lot of resistance," he told the *New*

York Times. "Old ideas die hard, and I think in the commercial world they die harder."

Wilson had not had a play on Broadway since *Seven Guitars* in 1996, but he resigned himself to open *Jitney* at New York's Second Stage, a 299-seat off-Broadway theater. The production was set to open in April 2000. He was working on a new play called *King Hedley II* at the same time, which was surely bound for Broadway, so in some ways, the smaller theater was a blessing because it lowered the stakes and the demands on Wilson's time. "The only reason *Jitney* didn't go to Broadway was because it wasn't supposed to go to Broadway," Henderson said in retrospect. "If *Jitney* had gone, *Hedley* would have taken another year. If the clock had a year added to it, the canon would not have been completed. August had the time he had, and the clock was ticking." (*Jitney* was eventually revived on Broadway in 2017, in a pitch-perfect production that received rave reviews and won the Tony Award for Best Revival of a Play.)

And Wilson had other things on his mind at the time. He had been invited to give a speech at the Heinz Lecture Series in Pittsburgh on March 20, 2000. He was always home in mid-March to host a family party in honor of his mother's birthday, an annual tradition since she died in 1983. But even though he was Pittsburgh's favorite playwright, he wasn't smiling when he took the lectern at the Carnegie Music Hall. Dressed in a somber dark suit, he began by thumping the podium with his open hand forty-one times. Some audience members started clapping in unison, not sure if Wilson was about to lead a rhythmic chant. But then he stopped and said, "The old world's in a hell of a fix when an unarmed man is shot 41 times for looking up and down the street." He was referring to the murder of Amadou Diallo in New York the year before. The story haunted him. He went on to deliver a fiery ninety-minute speech about racism and the dismal economic and social conditions that African Americans faced. The *Pittsburgh Post-Gazette* described it as "a 90-minute angry assault," but it was not an empty rant. He chronicled police violence against Blacks and said to a stunned audience, "We've replaced the [lynching] rope with bullets" fired by "rogue cops who act with impunity. We are tired of bleeding." He did not mince words, noting that federal civil rights laws had not been enforced and contending that Blacks were still being treated as "marginal human beings."

This was not the jovial Wilson locals had seen extolling the benefits of reading when he celebrated the Hill District library a few years earlier. Wilson ended his speech with an appeal to future generations. He asked all Americans "to find the courage to solve this problem as not to burden our children and grandchildren." The speech brought to mind the young poet addressing the crowd at the party for Malcolm X back in 1969. The Heinz Lecture Series was not usually controversial or even political. Funded by Drue Heinz, the philanthropist and widow of ketchup magnate H. J. Heinz II, and cosponsored by the Carnegie Library, it was primarily a forum for such authors and artists as Michael Chabon, Isaac Stern, Louise Erdrich, and David Sedaris, not for activists. But since his "The Ground on Which I Stand" speech, Wilson had transformed himself into a public intellectual. He still savored smoky jazz sessions where he would recite poetry with friends and acolytes, but he was also more willing to use his eloquence and platform to speak directly about the inequality he had experienced and of the social ills that continued to plague the country.

But when he returned to New York for the opening of *Jitney*, his focus was on putting on the best production possible. Broadway or off-Broadway, the lights shone brighter in New York. Friends and family were there for the opening at the small theater on the corner of Forty-Third Street and Eighth Avenue, on the fringe of the city's Theater District. A few days before the opening, the theater staged a benefit performance for the African Grove Institute for the Arts. Honorary chairmen included Phylicia Rashad, Angela Bassett, Laurence Fishburne, Danny Glover, and Delroy Lindo. After the play opened officially, the reviews were positively glowing, with headlines like "*Jitney*: Why Must This Ride Ever End?" Writing for the Associated Press, Michael Kuchwara declared that this was Wilson at his "explosive best." Most of the critics singled out the tight ensemble and Wilson's flair for dialogue that makes the characters seem so familiar that the audience feels as if they have known them forever.

Ben Brantley of the *New York Times* pointed out the skillful dialogue, so smooth and eloquent that it sounded like an "urban symphony." But

Brantley also zeroed in on the play's main flaw. Despite all the rewrites, the ending still felt forced. In the original play, Wilson killed off the father to avoid a direct confrontation with his son, and in the new version, the father still dies at the end in a freak accident. In his grief, Booster seems to resolve all the old wounds, and the ending, Brantley pointed out, "feels hammered on, with the nails showing." He was correct. Wilson had a thing for funerals; a wake goes on for days in *Two Trains*, *Seven Guitars* begins with a funeral, and *Fences* ends with one. But in the case of *Jitney*, Becker's death is abrupt and seems fashioned for a neat and hopeful ending. Nevertheless, the ending still unfailingly packs a punch, and both Chisholm and Henderson said they received a standing ovation after every single performance—and the ensemble played multiple cities in several years leading up to the New York production.

Jitney took home the New York Drama Critics' Circle Award for Best Play, making it the seventh time Wilson had won the coveted award. And despite the fact that he couldn't find Broadway investors, *Jitney* ran for five sold-out months at Second Stage and then transferred to the larger Union Square Theatre, where it played another six months. It then went on to the National Theatre in London, where it was equally successful.

Wilson had not been this busy since the first few years after he made his debut at the O'Neill, and at fifty-five, he was maintaining the schedule of a much younger, much hungrier playwright. But even though he repeatedly told interviewers that he would like to spend more time at home, he was already immersed in productions of *King Hedley II*. At age three, Azula had taken to calling him "the slippery guy." Romero had come up with the term because he was there one minute and then slipped away the next. It stuck. When he published the print version of *Jitney*, he dedicated it to his young daughter, with a coda that speaks for itself: "For Azula Carmen Wilson who burst upon the world clothed in the light of angelic grace. You are more blessing than I deserve."

CHAPTER SIXTEEN

The Struggle Continues

You can only close if you opened.
—AUGUST WILSON

The peripatetic production of *Jitney* that ultimately opened in New York had begun its long journey at the Pittsburgh Public Theater—and the theater wanted Wilson back. Artistic director Eddie Gilbert invited Wilson to open the institution's new O'Reilly Theater, a $20 million performing arts venue that was billed as the "crown jewel" of the city's downtown Cultural District. This was a big deal, and Wilson agreed to debut *King Hedley II* at the theater's grand opening in December 1999. It would be the Pittsburgh Public's last play of the twentieth century and its first play in the grand new building.

Wilson said repeatedly that he was humbled and honored by the gesture. How could he turn down such an honor from the institution where he had seen his first professional play in 1976? Of course he said yes. There was only one problem: he hadn't written the play.

And so he found himself back in Pittsburgh on October 27, 1999, about to start rehearsals of a play that wasn't finished. Wilson had promised Gilbert that the play would be ready for the historic opening, but the draft was just as rough as the raw plays he workshopped at the O'Neill. He didn't have the luxury of a workshop this time. The theater construction was nearly complete, and he couldn't back out. He was a man of his word. But he didn't perform well under external pressure. He procrastinated. He had long discussions about some issue that infuriated or delighted him. He went to the coffee shop and smoked cigarettes. He talked about the play, but he didn't write it.

He had enlisted McClinton to direct, now that the two men had settled whatever differences they had during the first production of *Jitney*. They had just finalized the cast three days earlier, and rehearsals were set to begin in two days. Wilson knew he would be rewriting round the clock until the first preview in December, and he had asked the theater to set up a printer in his hotel room.

Wilson was fiddling with the remote control for the television set when someone knocked on the door. A gangly young white man with rectangular glasses and a gee-shucks manner sidled in and introduced himself as Todd Kreidler from the Pittsburgh Public. At twenty-five, Kreidler was an aspiring director and playwright himself, and he was currently Gilbert's assistant. He had directed a few productions for the Public's Young Company. Part of his job description was to serve as assistant director for three mainstage productions a year. McClinton brought his own assistant director, so Kreidler was assigned to work as Wilson's personal assistant instead. He assumed the role would involve fetching coffee and chauffeuring the playwright. He didn't hide his initial disappointment, but his colleagues at the theater chided him. "Do you realize that people would cut their eyes out to have this opportunity?" they told him. Kreidler had no choice but to accept this role, even if he thought it was a demotion. But he also had a genuine interest in people. While Wilson was reserved and somewhat inscrutable, Kreidler was the kind of young man who would strike up long, inconsequential conversations with strangers at the grocery store. With Kreidler, a simple "Hi, how are you?" could elicit a lengthy response.

And so Kreidler was game for a philosophical conversation about electronics when he walked into the hotel room that day in October. "Do you know anything about remote controls?" Wilson asked him out of the blue. He then launched into a complaint about the device's design. Even though the majority of people are right-handed, he thought that the buttons were placed in a way that made the controller easier for left-handed people to navigate. It was a quirky observation, but Wilson could obsess for hours about small, seemingly insignificant details. And he was kvetching to the perfect person. Kreidler had a similar temperament, and the two fell into a long lament about remote-control devices, televisions, and electronics. Wilson was more than twice Kreidler's age, but the two immediately forged a comfortable rapport. It didn't hurt that Kreidler smoked and was unfazed by the smoky haze in Wilson's room.

About an hour into their conversation, the phone rang. It was McClinton. Wilson was late for the preproduction meeting at the theater; Kreidler had been sent to drive him. As they were leaving the hotel room, Kreidler noticed something that Wilson had typed that appeared on the computer screen. It read, "The man in the green hat walked into the ballroom." At that moment, he realized that maybe the job wasn't so bad after all. "I was like, oh my god, that is August Wilson's writing. That is like hot type." Kreidler etched that short sentence—and the date, October 27, 1999—into his memory.

At first glance, they made an unlikely duo—a quiet, distinguished Black man of a certain age who always dressed professionally and a twenty-something white man who looked like an overgrown teenager and had a loud, earsplitting laugh. But they soon discovered they had more in common beneath the surface. Growing up outside of Pittsburgh in what he considered to be the underclass, Kreidler had had a chilly relationship with his father, a used-car salesman who did not seem to know the phone number to his emotions. His father lived apart from the family, and Kreidler and his younger brother were raised primarily by his mother and her parents. His grandfather took on the paternal role, but there was never enough money and his mother returned to teaching to support her two children. Kreidler worshipped his mother the way Wilson idolized Daisy. He understood what loneliness and poverty can do to a child, and he still had a piece missing that should have been filled by a father's love. Wilson had the same void. And Kreidler was a rebellious youth, a self-described "angry young man," frequently in trouble. "If I had been a young Black man, I would have suffered more," he said. Unlike Wilson, he did manage to graduate from Duquesne University's McAnulty College of Liberal

Arts in 1996, but he spent just as much time reading books for pleasure as he did for studying for class. He was becoming his own man when he met Wilson, and both fashioned themselves as outsiders. Wilson had been mentored by Chawley Williams at Kreidler's age and later by Lloyd Richards, and because he was often on the road away from his immediate family, he saw an opportunity to turn the tables and become a mentor himself. The relationship worked.

Wilson liked to hold forth, telling and retelling the same stories to rapt audiences. Women, in particular, were often taken in by his spell. Kreidler was a ready listener, and he also was more than willing to focus on any conundrum, however obscure, as if the future of humanity depended on its resolution. He had rough edges and a big heart, and he came along at a time when Wilson was beginning to feel alienated by his own success. It is not coincidental that Wilson began the preface to the published edition of *Hedley* by citing "The Greatest Blues Singer in the World," the one-sentence story he had written years earlier. "The streets that Balboa walked were his own private ocean, and Balboa was drowning." During this period, Wilson needed a human anchor, someone to trust unconditionally, now that Richards was out of the picture. It soon became clear that Kreidler could fill that void.

And the pressure was on. Wilson was well aware of the symbolic significance of the upcoming world premiere of *Hedley* at the new theater, which was already being billed as the event of the year in Pittsburgh. Designed by celebrated architect Michael Graves, the new 650-seat theater had been in the works for years and was the biggest addition to the Pittsburgh cultural landscape in decades. The spotlight was glaring, and it represented the blessed curse of his success. Like it or not, he had been anointed the "hometown hero." In March 1999, when he was home for the annual birthday party he hosted to honor Daisy, he gave a speech at the celebration of the centennial of the Hill District branch of the Carnegie Library. Along with extolling libraries and books and knowledge, he addressed both the youth and the elders still struggling in a world of inequality. He was formulating the story of *Hedley*, which is set in 1985 during an era he didn't quite understand, and he urged young people to take charge of their lives and of their communities. "You have to make your spirit larger and stronger," he said. "It doesn't get larger by killing your brother. It doesn't get stronger by disrespecting your elders. The book does not say to steal your grandmother's TV to buy dope."

The awards kept coming, distracting him from his work. In June that year, Wilson had been ranked number one on the *Pittsburgh Post-Gazette*'s annual list of the city's most powerful culture brokers—even though he hadn't lived there in two decades. On September 29, he was awarded the National Humanities Medal by President Bill Clinton; other recipients included Aretha Franklin, civil rights historian Taylor Branch, Steven Spielberg, Norman Lear, and Graves, the architect of the new theater. "I was at Hillary's table at the dinner," Wilson told the *Pittsburgh Post-Gazette*. "I met Aretha Franklin!" But his daughter Azula, then two-and-a-half, was most impressed with the ribbon and the medallion. "Daddy, medal on," she told him on the rare occasions when he was at home in Seattle. He spoke to his daughter frequently on the phone when he was on the road, and she would begin the conversation by saying, "Pittsburgh, far away."

He had missed so many important moments with Sakina. He wanted to be more present in his second daughter's life, but he was under enormous pressure to finish the cycle, a burden that was compounded with being chosen to inaugurate the new theater.

So Kreidler walked into that room—and into his life—at precisely the right time. It also helped to have someone young around to consult on *Hedley*. Wilson's previous plays had focused on past decades, and he glorified earlier eras and old-fashioned values like loyalty, dignity, and the importance of family and community. He could understand those mores, but he never understood the 1980s. He spent that decade working on his plays, creating a name for himself in the American theater. He was disconnected from the culture. He didn't go to the theater or the cinema often. He didn't see a Shakespeare production until he saw Ralph Fiennes's Tony Award–winning performance in *Hamlet* in 1995, and he was underwhelmed at best. But despite his disengagement with popular culture, he was a voracious reader who followed the news fervently and tried to understand the tenor of the times. He was disoriented by what he read about the 1980s, particularly the rise of rap and gangsta culture and the dismemberment of the traditional family in the African American community. He and Charles Johnson shared this disillusion. The era of "hip-hop, misogynistic gangsta rap and profanity-laced ghetto lit sometimes made our souls feel like they needed to take a shower," Johnson wrote in his essay about their friendship.

Since Wilson felt disconnected from that decade, he struggled with how to write about it. Before he wrote *Hedley*, he had said he planned to listen to the music of the era for inspiration and vowed to familiarize himself with rap. But he didn't. He listened to the blues instead. Why? He believed rap music was rooted in the blues. "All the ideas and attitudes that hip hop generation people in the '80s had, that's where they got it from. They got it from they daddies. It was rooted here," he said during an interview with the esoteric magazine the *Believer*. He peppered his younger brother Richard with questions about the period as he struggled to make sense of it. He was most concerned with the loss of a connection to the past, which is front and center in *Hedley*. "It's not so much a breakdown of the family in the play, but a break with the tradition of the extended family," he said. "It's the connection with the grandparents that is broken that causes many of the problems in the play."

Kreidler, it turned out, was a good sounding board, particularly about rap culture. (He later wrote the musical *Holler If Ya Hear Me* about slain rapper Tupac Shakur.) Wilson aimed to write a Greek tragedy, focusing on a vengeful central character whose downfall is determined by fate. He first envisioned the title character as a man with a long, 112-stitch scar etched in his face. He asked the usual questions he posed when creating a new character. How did he get the scar? Who was he? Wilson began by setting the play in 1985, in a Pittsburgh backyard similar to the setting in *Seven Guitars*. He said that he envisioned his mother's home at 1621 Bedford Avenue, the place where she died.

He was determined to use this play to better understand the ethos of the "gangsta" decade that he and Johnson deplored. "When I look at the situation of Black America in 1985, I want to see where these kids got these guns," he said in an interview in 1997, when the play was still germinating in his mind. "I personally think I can trace it all back to

Bernhard Goetz in his paranoia shooting those four Black kids on the subway, two of them in the back. He was seen as heroic." (In 1984, Goetz, a resident of Greenwich Village who owned an electronics business, shot four Black teenagers on a New York subway, claiming they were trying to rob him. The young men said they were merely panhandling, and one was left paraplegic and brain-damaged after the shooting. Goetz, dubbed the "Subway Vigilante," was initially celebrated by some people for taking a stand against the spike in urban crime during the crack epidemic of the 1980s.) Shortly after that, Wilson pointed out, copycat crimes against Black youth occurred in New York and New Jersey, with youngsters being beaten with baseball bats or shot. "I think the Black kids said, 'Wait a minute, we're under attack here,'" Wilson hypothesized. "And they went out and got guns. They armed themselves because they were under assault. Now, unfortunately, they are using the guns on each other."

Against that backdrop, he also decided that, for the first time, he wanted to tie the characters in *Hedley* with characters from *Seven Guitars*. The title character in *King Hedley* is a thirty-six-year-old man with that monstrous scar on his face. He lives with his mother, Ruby, and his wife, Tonya. In *Seven Guitars*, Ruby was a twenty-five-year-old newcomer to Pittsburgh described as an "uncommon woman" who "exudes a sensuality that is electric." When she left Alabama for Pittsburgh, she was secretly pregnant, carrying the child of her boyfriend, Leroy. She had been entangled in a love triangle with Leroy and a gambler named Elmore, who murdered Leroy in a jealous rage. Ruby migrated north to escape the scandal and live with her aunt Louise. She had no trouble acclimating to Pittsburgh and grew fond of a delusional old man named Hedley, who fantasized about fathering a messiah. She did him a favor and had sex with him, allowing him to believe that the child she was carrying was his.

In the thirty-seven years between the two plays, Ruby gave birth to King and built a career as a blues singer. She was frequently on the road, so Aunt Louise raised her son, who grew up resenting his mother's neglect. He also believed that the Hedley from *Seven Guitars* was his biological father. He never knew the first Hedley, but he idolized him, although Wilson inexplicably never explains why.

Life wasn't easy for King in the time period between the plays. His scars go deeper than the one on his face. He felt abandoned as a child, and he struggled to prove his worth, both to himself and to the world. He "strives to live by his own moral code." King began a feud with a neighborhood strongman named Pernell, who dared to call him "champ," not King. "I ain't gonna be nobody's champ today," he thought. Pernell sensed King's animosity, which prompted him to slash King's face with a razor; it took a doctor four hours and 112 stitches to sew up the wound. This was another insult, so King murdered Pernell. Revenge was part of his code. His girlfriend at the time turned state's evidence against him. She died when he was in jail for murder.

All of that happened before *Hedley* begins, and while the backstory may have been clear in Wilson's mind, the labyrinthine tale is a chore to untangle, even for those familiar with *Seven Guitars*. At the beginning of *Hedley*, King is out of prison and wants to get his life back on track and build a family with Tonya, his wife of several years. At least, he says that: he still mourns his dead girlfriend and continues to visit her grave. He is a deeply conflicted character who wrestles with all of it: the murder, the scar, the seven years in prison, the betrayal and death of his lover, his yearning for a father he never knew. At the same time, he aims to convince himself that all of his past actions are justified. "I ain't sorry for nothing I done," he says.

The plot gets even more knotty when Elmore (an offstage character from *Seven Guitars*) shows up. He has remained in Ruby's life as her "longtime, but sporadic flame." He tells King that he murdered Leroy many years ago, and he also reveals that Leroy was King's biological father, not the man whose name he cherishes. Violence is inevitable when King learns the truth and comes face-to-face with the man who murdered his father.

Here again in this byzantine tale, Wilson is digging deep into the archetypal father-son conflict he addressed in *Fences* and *Jitney*. This time he is writing a character who grew up not knowing his father's identity. Perhaps because he and Kreidler both had father issues, Wilson began to rely on Kreidler as a sounding board for rewrites. One day during rehearsal, he asked Kreidler to consult with him outside during a smoking break. He was having trouble with a particular scene involving a character named Stool Pigeon. This character is a sixty-five-year-old former harmonica player who has become a pack rat. In *Seven Guitars*, he was the sideman Canewell. Wilson fashioned Stool Pigeon as a Greek chorus who sometimes directly addresses the audience.

Wilson was vexed by a pivotal moment between Stool Pigeon and King. He knew the dialogue needed to pack a punch. He showed his notes to Kreidler, and the two men stood outside under an awning, drawing arrows on the script as they considered where to move lines and what words to keep in Stool Pigeon's monologue. The pages were covered with notes and marks, and after a brief period of intense consideration, Wilson was satisfied. He was nearsighted, so he held the pages up to his face and flashed his rare, but demonstrative grin. "We did it, man," he told his protégé. "That took only fifteen minutes." He paused. "Three years and fifteen minutes."

Wilson thrived on this sense of discovery in rehearsal, but he did not always approach the process with the same urgency as the rest of the creative team. As he and Kreidler grew closer, they would often disappear during rehearsal breaks. Wilson realized he had a rapt audience with this young man who was eager to break into theater and become a playwright himself. As they stood outside smoking, Wilson regaled Kreidler with his repertoire of stories. One day, he launched into tales about his time working at Little Brothers of the Poor. He remembered one of the cooks, a man supposedly in his nineties who was taking a geometry class and carrying on with two girlfriends at the same time. That led to stories about the Science Museum of Minnesota. He told Kreidler about the curator who cautioned Wilson not to stay in a dead-end job writing plays about dinosaurs or he would risk becoming a dinosaur himself. That particular story may have been Wilson's way of telling Kreidler to find his own voice, to carve his own path. At any rate, this conversation was interrupted by McClinton, who came storming out of the theater. "What are you two doing? Are you ever coming back to rehearsal?" he bellowed. They had been outside for three hours. From that day on, Kreidler referred to these kinds of moments as "August Wilson time." He said, "You fall under the spell of his storytelling, and hours become days."

Living on "August Wilson time" may have been engaging and entertaining, but it wasn't helping the play. *Hedley* was unwieldy and confusing, and everyone involved knew it. The play, as usual, was too long at more than three and a half hours, and given its overlap with *Seven Guitars*, the plot was confusing. The title character lacked motivation, and Wilson's attempt to turn it into a Greek tragedy was contrived. The play was cast at the last minute, and Wilson wasn't entirely satisfied with some of the actors. Only one actor, Charles Brown as Elmore, would continue with the production after it left Pittsburgh. Wilson was stressed, and when he was in the rehearsal room, he could be demanding, revealing his frustration in a way he had never done when he was working with Richards. "He had that ability to chill a room," Kreidler said. "He welcomed collaboration, and if you were going to collaborate with him, you had to be willing to step into the fire."

And the stakes were high. By this time, Wilson was keenly attuned to the continued criticism that he did not write strong female characters. He wanted to say something important through King's wife, Tonya. She had been a teenage mother, and now at thirty-five, she sees her teenage daughter repeating all of her mistakes. Tonya is pregnant with King's child, but she looks around and sees a community in which young Black men are carrying guns, going to jail, or—even worse—killing each other or being killed by the police. She doesn't want to bring a child into that world. Wilson wrote a monologue for Tonya that remains a classic in American theater; it's another that actors often use for auditions. Tonya confronts King when he objects to her getting an abortion. She explodes, taking him down in a showstopping speech.

> I'm thirty-five years old. Don't seem like there's nothing left. I'm through with babies. I ain't raising no more. I ain't raising no grandkids. I'm looking out for Tonya. I ain't raising no kid to have somebody shoot him. To have his friends shoot him. To have the police shoot him. Why

I want to bring another life into this world that don't respect life? I don't want to raise no more babies when you
got to fight to keep them alive.

Wilson knew when he had hit the right notes, and that speech is exactly what he was trying to say in the entire play, the same sentiment he
shared with Charles Johnson. In the eighth play of the cycle, he gives a
woman a powerful voice: she refuses to take any more pain, any more
violence, any more heartache.

He was depicting a community in crisis, and to emphasize the depths
of that communal despair, he killed off Aunt Ester, the matriarchal, mythical character he introduced in *Two Trains* (and would incorporate in two
later plays, *Gem of the Ocean* and *Radio Golf*). She is the revered elder
who tells a character in *Two Trains* to "go back and pick up the ball" and
reminds the characters in *Gem* that they have a "duty to life." But in *Hedley*, the troubling situation is too much for her. "The path to her house is
all grown over with weeds," Stool Pigeon says in the prologue. "You can't
hardly find the door no more." The community is in chaos. Stool Pigeon
hoards old newspapers, and their headlines depict senseless violence:
"Man Bludgeons Schoolteacher"; "Man Stabs Assailant"; "Teen Killed in
Drive-By." In this world, it seems that young people are not heeding the
wisdom of the ancestors, and Aunt Ester dies of a broken heart. Stool Pigeon announces her death at the end of the first scene of the play. "Lock
your doors! Close your windows! Turn your lamp down low! We're in
trouble now. Aunt Ester died!" The wind howls, and the lights go out all
over Pittsburgh.

As in all of his plays, he had the characters in *Hedley* relive some of his
own experiences. In one scene, King tells his friend Mister about a teacher
who once told him he was destined to be a janitor. Wilson never forgave
the teacher who accused him of plagiarism. King also recounts a series of
indignities while doing menial jobs. He gets a job at a toy store, and his
boss immediately warns him not to steal anything. "Got one job the man
told me he was gonna shoot me if he caught me stealing anything," King
says. "I ain't worked for him ten minutes. I quit right there. He calling me

a thief before I start." The same thing happened to Wilson as a young man. He never got over those early wounds and demanded respect.

But he relished telling those stories from his youth, perhaps as a sort of therapy or perhaps simply to procrastinate. During rehearsal breaks, he repeated the story about the toy store to Kreidler, who lapped it all up. Kreidler started writing down the vignettes on scraps of paper and napkins and the wrappers of empty cigarette packets. He also shared Wilson's rage on certain issues, such as the tragedy of Amadou Diallo, the unarmed twenty-three-year-old Guinean immigrant who was fatally shot with forty-one bullets by four New York City Police Department plainclothes officers in February 1999. "Forty-one bullets!" Wilson would bark at Kreidler. Wilson, of course, had used that tale as an example of police brutality a few months later during his speech at the Heinz Lecture Series, but when he discussed it with Kreidler, the two came up with a novel idea. Wilson could write and perform a one-man, autobiographical show, which would start with Wilson throwing ping-pong balls at the audience, hurling them out one by one and counting until he got to forty-one. Kreidler wrote that idea down, too. Like Wilson, he had a capacious memory, and he had a feeling the stories would come in handy later. This easy camaraderie cemented the growing bond between the two men, and Kreidler was often the first person Wilson would consult when he showed up at rehearsal with new pages.

As opening night neared, the excitement around the production grew in Pittsburgh. That December, the rest of the world was zeroed in on the approaching millennium—and the fears it engendered of computers crashing and potential doom. Survivalists were stocking up on guns, food, and medical supplies, while teams of computer programmers were working triple time to fix any potential bugs that might cause computers to run amok when the calendar rolled over to the year 2000. But for Wilson, the real deadline was opening night. On December 5, 1999, the *Pittsburgh Post-Gazette* published a sixteen-page special section dedicated to the opening of the theater. Of course, it included a long profile on Wilson, who indicated that, despite all the hoopla, he couldn't wait to get home to Seattle. "I've spent three months home this year," he said. "I've seen my share of the cities of this country. The idea is to stay home more." He echoed that idea repeatedly, but somehow never managed to stay home for long. At the same time, he couldn't hold back about how thrilled he was to inaugurate a theater in the place where he once read poetry in storefront galleries and produced plays in an elementary school auditorium. He said it was the highlight of his career.

The play opened to great fanfare on Wednesday, December 15. Wilson and Romero attended a preperformance dinner at the Duquesne Club, the elegant establishment a few blocks from the theater that bills itself as "the premiere private club in Pittsburgh." The guest list of about one hundred included major benefactors along with theater professionals. When the diners left the club and arrived at the theater for the sold-out performance, Wilson and Romero paced outside in the chilly drizzle while the crowd inside buzzed about the sparkling new building. According to the *Pittsburgh Post-Gazette*, some attendees whispered about the length of the play, which with Wilson is always an issue. "Sure enough, at intermission a chunk of the crowd headed for the hills (at more than three and one-half hours, *King Hedley* pleaded for surgery)," the *Post-Gazette* reported. "But the consensus was that Wilson and ensemble were in top form and the seats were surprisingly comfortable." The play received a standing ovation, and many of Wilson's friends attended, including actor Stephen McKinley Henderson, playwright John Henry Redwood, Claude Purdy, and Pitt professors Rob Penny and Vernell Lillie.

Despite its overcomplicated plot, the play received a positive—and exceedingly forgiving—review by Christopher Rawson in the *Post-Gazette*. "Bear down, buckle up and kick back—there's a long, thrilling haul ahead," it began. He described the play as a "craggy, thickly forested mountain of a tragedy," yet allowed that it was not yet finished. While noting that the play was dark, gritty, and unrelentingly long, Rawson put it in the same category as such masterpieces as *Long Day's Journey into Night* and *King Lear*, because all three are "centered on the search for identity, responsibility and guilt in the most painful place—the family." *King Lear? Long Day's Journey?* The play was a mess and desperately called out for the dramaturgical surgery done at the O'Neill.

The play received mixed notices from national critics who attended to review both the new building and Wilson's latest installment in his decade-by-decade cycle. Even after subsequent rewrites, *Hedley* remains the weakest and most turgid play in Wilson's cycle. He said he did not understand the 1980s, and it shows on the stage and on the page.

By this point, reviewers were used to Wilson's method of honing his plays as they traveled to regional theaters across the country, and they were more magnanimous toward his raw, unfinished works than they would be with any other playwright. And Wilson was treated like theater royalty in his hometown. Rawson reviewed the play not once, but twice, and while glowing, he did note that there is a downside to seeing a world premiere of an August Wilson play. "No Wilson play is as good in its first production as it will be later, after he's further refined it," he wrote. That kind of understanding would have been unheard of during the golden era of pre-Broadway tryouts, and it didn't account for the fact that audiences were essentially paying to see a work in progress. Sophisticated theatergoers went to the O'Neill for that experience, where the ticket prices were low and audience members knew what they were getting.

After the opening, Wilson had planned on going straight home to Seattle for the holidays, but he had received an invitation he had to accept. President Clinton had invited him to the gala reception at the White House to ring in the millennium, and he and Romero were headed to Washington, D.C., to join a guest list that included boxer Muhammad Ali (the subject of one of Wilson's early poems), actor Robert De Niro, astronaut and senator John Glenn, music producer Quincy Jones, Olympian Carl Lewis, and poet Rita Dove (whom he met and admired when he won his first Pulitzer Prize for *Fences*). Wilson was feeling good about himself and brimming with confidence. When asked shortly before the *Hedley* opening how he felt about the coming of the millennium, he said, "This is perfect. This is when I'm living. I'm fast approaching the age of those guys I used to see on Centre Avenue, the elders. I wouldn't trade this. I've *earned* it, every year of it."

But before he left for the gala, he had one bit of business to finish. He knew that his protégé, Kreidler, aspired to be a playwright himself. He arranged to have lunch with Kreidler at the Seventh Street Grille. After they ordered their meal, Wilson handed Kreidler a gift. The wrapping paper was clumsy and crinkled; clearly, Wilson had wrapped it himself. Kreidler was emotional. Back on October 27, he had thought he was being handed a second-rate job, but instead, he had found a kindred spirit and a role model. He opened the box and saw an elegant Pelikan fountain pen, inscribed with the message: "To Todd, for the blank pages of the hymnal awaiting the testimony of the witness." Kreidler wasn't often lost for words, but he had to swallow hard before he said, "Wow, I've never had a fountain pen. How do you get the ink in?" Wilson waited a moment—a dramatic beat—and answered, "Todd, man, that's the easy part."

When Boston's Huntington Theatre announced its 1999–2000 season, it simply listed "The August Wilson Project" for the last slot. The playwright and the Boston producers were not sure if *Hedley* would be ready for the May 24, 2000, opening and planned on mounting a production of *Fences* if the play wasn't finished. But Huntington producing director Peter Altman determined that the play was "ready enough." He said, "We knew it wasn't going to be perfect, but we wanted to help get it out there." Wilson was still wrestling with the structure, length, story line, and clarity. The invitation to inaugurate the O'Reilly Theater had short-circuited his usual meandering process, but the artistic staff at the Huntington were forgiving. "Art takes as long as it takes," Altman said.

This time, Wilson had his new protégé at his side. After *Hedley* closed in Pittsburgh, he implored Kreidler to accompany him on the road, as the play was slated for several cities before eventually opening on Broadway. Kreidler took a half cut in his "already meager pay" and had what he describes as "the greatest adventure of my life." He had been on a plane only once before, and he happily joined the Wilson entourage. They bounced ideas off each other, and Kreidler continued to write everything down.

It was clear in rehearsals that the play was raw, with a few soaring monologues, but a head-scratching plot. Wilson and McClinton collaborated closely and stayed up late at night in their rooms near the theater, debating how to solve the play's cumbersome problems. "There was a lot of volatility in the process," Altman said, noting that Wilson had a much more interactive relationship with McClinton than he had had with Richards. "It wasn't that [Wilson and McClinton] had an argumentative relationship. Everyone knew something had to happen, but nobody agreed on what was the best thing to do." He likened their intense relationship to two jazzmen playing, riffing off each other's ideas.

But it was clear that Wilson simply didn't understand—or like—the 1980s, and his attempt to create a tragic hero was weak. King lives by his own code of honor, but he can't find his way in the world. He dreams of opening a video store with his friend Mister, but since he is short on cash, he resorts first to selling stolen refrigerators and then to robbing a jewelry store. He wants desperately to prove his self-worth in a world that discounts him. "I want everybody to know, just like my daddy, that you can't fuck with me," he declares at the end of Act 1. But later, it is Tonya who tells him how to be a man, and her definition hearkens back to *Fences*, which unfolds in an era that Wilson embraced and understood. She tells him that he is headed on a path that will lead him straight back to the penitentiary. If she is going to give birth to his child, she wants him around and reliable, end of story. "It ain't for you to go out of here and steal money to get me things," she says. "Your job is to be around so this baby can know its daddy. Do that. For once, somebody do that. Be that. That's how you be a man, anything else I don't want."

This was a woman who refuses to blindly stand by her man, which is progress for Wilson, but the play was still wobbly. Wilson spent hours talking about the play with McClinton and Kreidler, settling in to a table in the smoking section at Ann's Cafeteria, a bacon-and-eggs eatery on the same block as the Huntington. It was a low-key place with laminate counters and scratched-up floors that was owned by a local Greek couple who welcomed Wilson as a regular when he was in town. Wilson knew he had to focus on *Hedley*, but he was always preoccupied. He was beginning to feel the pressure of completing his cycle, and even though he was deep into a play already in production, his mind had moved on to the next play, which would be set in 1904 and eventually called *Gem of the Ocean*. One day he met Kreidler at Au Bon Pain—or "The Spot," which is what they called their favorite diner in each city they visited. Wilson suddenly started talking about Aunt Ester, the character he had just killed off in *Hedley*, at the age of 366. "There's a lot of things I don't talk about. I don't talk about the water," he said, speaking in the voice of the ancient matriarch. He often would stop mid-sentence and suddenly start acting, taking on the persona of characters in his plays. This could be disconcerting to the uninitiated, but by this point, Kreidler was used to it. He understood that in between everything else Wilson was doing, he was already writing the next play.

He should have been fine-tuning *Hedley*, which was about to open on May 24. Boston audiences were familiar with Wilson's work, and the Huntington always had an enthusiastic opening-night crowd. But it didn't go over so well. Like *Jitney* (and *Ma Rainey*, *Fences*, *Two Trains*, and *Seven Guitars*), the play ends abruptly with a death, this time after a gun is fired. Ruby accidentally shoots her son in the throat, while Tonya screams out for someone to call 911. The last scene was Wilson's attempt to turn King into a tragic hero straight out of Greek drama. The Fates intervene, and the hero dies, the victim of his tragic flaw. But the scene played as if it were an afterthought. And Wilson didn't have the hometown advantage in Boston. Boston audiences and critics were not as forgiving of Wilson's use of the theater to develop an inchoate play. Writing in the *Boston Globe*, Ed Siegel concluded, "Wilson may yet craft a fine drama from these characters' struggle for honor and comfort, but if so his work has just begun. It is less of a treat this time around, then, to be a test audience."

In the past, Wilson had used the regional theaters as a tryout ground, but he'd had Richards quietly nudging him to focus on things like through line, character development, motivation, and action. Wilson had also developed five of his earlier plays at the O'Neill. As he often said, he "listened" to his characters talk, and the result was often a series of soaring, poetic monologues that stand on their own, but do not necessarily add up to a coherent whole. He had realized this with *Two Trains*, which he didn't workshop at the O'Neill. *Hedley* begged to have gone through the developmental process at the O'Neill, because the changes that happened there were now taking place in regional theaters with paying audience members in the seats. Wilson had not been back to the O'Neill since *Seven Guitars*. Richards had retired as artistic director of the O'Neill the previous summer at the age of eighty. After the split with Wilson and his retirement from the O'Neill, he held the occasional visiting professorship and advised other directors. He won the prestigious Dorothy and Lillian Gish Prize, which included a purse of $200,000, in 2002, and spoke at theater conferences, but he stepped back from directing in his last years.

So Wilson did not have a seasoned director to advise him. He spent the next few months trying to hone and shape *Hedley*. That summer, he mourned the death of Edward T. Owens, the owner of Eddie's Restaurant in the Hill District, who died of a heart attack at age fifty-nine on July 23. Wilson had a love-hate relationship with Owens. He worked there for one day, because Owens fired him when he took an extra-long break and sat in a booth writing. "You're not here to write," the restauranteur told the young poet. But Wilson continued to stop in for a bottomless cup of coffee, and he set *Two Trains* in a diner modeled after Eddie's Restaurant. And he also mentioned it in *Piano Lesson*, noting that "coffee costs a nickel, and you can get two eggs, sausage and grits for 15 cents. He even give you a biscuit with it." Wilson had his issues with certain members of the Hill District community who resented his success, but he lamented changes in the neighborhood and what he saw as the loss of traditions and values. Owens's death was just another chip away at the old order—a loss, in some ways, that lay at the heart of *Hedley*.

The play opened in September at the Mark Taper Forum in Los Angeles and received a frustrated and tepid response similar to the one it garnered in Boston. Calling it Wilson's "grimmest" work, *Los Angeles Times* critic Michael Phillips wrote that "its density (three hours, 15 minutes) tends to flatten rather than deepen the characters." But he also saw the potential and urged Wilson to "get tough with it." But maybe what the playwright needed was someone to get tough with him.

Wilson wasn't particularly fond of Los Angeles. He often told a story about trying to cash a $750 check from the Mark Taper Forum at a bank in Los Angeles. The teller interrogated him because he had a Washington State identification card. She summoned the manager, and they went through a book containing photographs of all the official state IDs. After a long wait, Wilson finally got his money, but the teller refused to give him an envelope. As he told the story, he admitted that the incident was not worth dying over, but it was significant nonetheless. "It's not a little thing," he wrote. "She looked at a man and she said, 'This man does not deserve the same respect as other men deserve.' And that's the sin that caused slavery." Wilson never forgot a slight.

He was, however, prepared for another celebration when the production moved from Los Angeles to Chicago in December 2000. A year had passed since *Hedley* opened the O'Reilly in Pittsburgh, and now the play was set to inaugurate the new Goodman Theatre on North Dearborn Street in the city's revitalized North Loop theater district. The $46 million complex had been in the works for twelve years. It replaced the Goodman's aging performance space located in the back of the Art Institute of Chicago, where it had opened in 1925. Wilson, along with Chicago Mayor Richard M. Daley, was one of six speakers at the ribbon-cutting ceremony on November 9. "This is a glorious and historic day for the arts in Chicago," Wilson said, describing the theater as "a temple, a monument dedicated to cultural arts." He added, "We who work in theater are proud to stand at the end of an art form that goes all the way back to the ancient Greeks."

His comment was eloquent, but it was also deeply personal. With *Hedley*, he aspired to write in the style of ancient Greek tragedy, with Stool Pigeon as the chorus and King as his tragic hero. Even with his meteoric success, he still aimed to prove that he was capable of writing epic tragedy. During the long pre-Broadway run of *Hedley*, he told actor Stephen McKinley Henderson, "I got one for the old man. This is something the old man is going to love." The old man was Lloyd Richards, and despite the fact that Wilson had split with the director, he was still the student, aiming to impress. He wanted Richards to see him write like the ancient Greeks.

The opening was on Monday, December 11, and the Windy City was snowed in under near-blizzard conditions. The storm was accompanied by freak peals of thunder, and only about half of the theater's 856 seats were filled. Mayor Daley had reserved tickets, but he did not attend. Those who did make the trek included benefactors and theater aficionados in a town that fashioned itself as the Broadway of the Midwest. Faye M. Price, who had worked with Wilson at Penumbra in St. Paul in the 1980s (she acted in *Eden*, the theater's first production that inspired Wilson to move to the Midwest), was undeterred by the weather. "It's like the postman," she said. "Nothing is going to stop them from delivering tonight."

Price, a native of Chicago's Hyde Park district who grew up going to the Goodman, was a reminder of Wilson's early days, when his first professional production of *Black Bart* flopped miserably at Penumbra. But Wilson was the star of the Goodman opening. He sat beaming with his family. He was particularly tickled by David Gallo's set. "If you look closely, you'll see that he's built in elements of all of my previous plays into the set," he told a reporter for the *Chicago Tribune*. Indeed, Gallo's set featured a fence, a piano, a horn, and a guitar.

The celebrated actress and singer Leslie Uggams was now playing Ruby. But the production was still plagued with the same issues. Richard Christiansen, the venerable chief critic of the *Chicago Tribune*, praised Wilson's "ambitious attempt to create an epic tragedy from his vision of African-American life," likening his effort to that of Eugene O'Neill. The play had not achieved its lofty goal, he wrote, and "judging from the problems of structure, casting and direction . . . it may never get there."

Casting had been a vexing issue since the Pittsburgh opening. Wilson and McClinton had recast roles in every city. The only actor who remained from the original production was the reliable Charles Brown, as Ruby's suitor, Elmore. Wilson was a playwright searching for a structure; the play started out at three and three-quarter hours, had been cut to three and a quarter hours, but was back at three and a half hours in Chicago. In Chicago, he also inserted a snippet of a speech by President Ronald Reagan talking about trickle-down economics, which was meant to be an ironic statement about misguided federal policies that devastated Black neighborhoods like the Hill District.

With some exceptions, critics seemed to want to take on the role that Richards and the dramaturges played at the O'Neill. Christiansen was compelled to write not one, but two reviews. The second, which ran two weeks after the opening, reiterated the glaring problems, but also went on to extol the effort. "Because Wilson is a poet and a playwright of enormous talent, the play refuses to be diminished. Few modern dramatists have attempted to reach the peak of tragedy that Wilson has set his sights on," he wrote on December 24, his last column of the year. And, he concluded, "Even in failure, there is glory." Wilson put critics on their knees. They wanted to love each new Wilson play.

But Wilson could not afford a glorious failure on Broadway now that he and Sageworks were the lead producers, and time was running out. Wilson thought he had a wild card up his sleeve. Charles S. Dutton—who had blown away the rafters at the O'Neill as Levee in *Ma Rainey*—had committed to step into the title role when the play opened in February 2001 at the Kennedy Center in Washington, D.C., for a brief run before its debut at the Virginia Theatre on Broadway in May. But Dutton—who by now had considerably more star power than he had in his "jail to Yale" days—had a conflict and dropped out at the last minute. As the team raced to find a replacement, preferably a name with box office appeal, it turned out that Dutton's manager also represented Brian Stokes Mitchell, the charismatic baritone who had won the 2000 Tony Award for Best Actor in the revival of Cole Porter's *Kiss Me, Kate*. He had also been nominated in 1998 for his star turn as Coalhouse Walker in the musical adaptation of E. L. Doctorow's *Ragtime*.

Mitchell was well-known in theater circles, but the handsome actor with the finely chiseled cheekbones was not the obvious choice to play a scarred ex-convict. "A lot of people thought it was going to be a big gamble," McClinton admitted. But even though Mitchell didn't get a day off after closing in *Kiss Me, Kate*, he threw himself into the role, shaving his head to get into the gritty character. He put Hedley in the same category as Coalhouse Walker, a proud man who was a victim of racial prejudice at the turn of the twentieth century. "It's very much the same kingly experience in a time and a place where it is not allowed him," he said. "Like Coalhouse, King Hedley is a huge character. He's a Hamlet, a Lear."

The production got another important cast change. Viola Davis, who had been nominated for a Tony Award for playing Vera in *Seven Guitars*, stepped in as Tonya.

Even after five productions (including inaugurating two brand-new theaters), the play was still a diamond in the rough, with the emphasis on rough. Wilson continuously made changes to the script, even after the play closed in Washington and moved into previews in New York. Charles Brown said that the cast received revisions two days before the official Broadway opening on May 1. And that can be maddening for actors. "All of a sudden I'm in a scene and I thought, 'Oh my God, I don't know what my next line is,'" Davis said. "I was searching in my head, and then I went back to what the line was about three months before." The same thing happened to Brown, in the role of Elmore. "I started speaking lines that have been gone for months," he said. "His writing is so rich and so ingrained that when you're into it and you're flowing rhythmically with it and it's in the body, the cellular memory of the original speech comes back."

When the play opened, it clocked in at three hours (the ideal time for a Broadway production). But while he had reduced the time, Wilson hadn't resolved the issues that had been apparent a year and a half ago in Pittsburgh. The mystery at the heart of the play—Hedley's real parentage—was muddled. The plot was murky and hard to follow. The reviews, however, were mixed. Most critics applauded Wilson's effort to turn a dirt yard in the Hill District into ancient Greece and some were forgiving of his failure to meet that goal. "Any drama that consistently aims as high as *Hedley* does, inviting comparison to everything from Aeschylus' *House of Atreus* to the Book of Job, is sometimes going to miss its target and thud to earth," wrote Ben Brantley in the *New York Times*. "The thuds in this New York premiere, it must be admitted, are as audible as the celestial high notes."

This clearly was not going to be another monumental hit like *Fences* or a crowd-pleaser like *Jitney*. It wasn't just that the play was set in the dark, depressing eighties and that its characters were stymied by a dearth of economic opportunity. Wilson hadn't made the story gel in a way that connected with the audience. King was an enigma, even after all the rewrites, and plot points were raised and then left hanging. The reviews singled out Davis as Tonya—who had that showstopping monologue about not wanting to bring a baby into such a bleak, unforgiving world— and Brown, who had been inhabiting the role of Elmore for almost two years.

Mitchell was ill and had to miss a performance the week before the opening, so the reviews came out a day later than usual, after the opening-night party. With no worries about the ritual reading of the reviews, the atmosphere at the Copacabana, the nightclub on Fifty-Seventh Street, was joyous. Wilson always included his family members at these affairs, and Sakina and Azula were there along with an entourage of Wilson's siblings and cousins. And the stars turned out, as they often do: Gregory Hines, James Earl Jones, Bobby Short, Henry Winkler, and Terrence McNally, to name a few. His old friend Claude Purdy was there as well, even though it was clear by now that he would not inherit the torch as Wilson's director of choice. Wilson put on a good face at these events, although he preferred sitting at a corner table smoking, talking to regular folks whose names did not appear in bold in the New York gossip columns. One of those people was Kreidler, who was there with his girlfriend, Pittsburgh actress Erin Annarella. They had had a big fight that night, and Kreidler was a mess. His eighteen-month stint as Wilson's assistant had come to an end. He had grown accustomed to living life on "August Wilson time," and he was set to go back to Pittsburgh to determine his next step. "It's not bad to have had an 18-month stretch when you could never take a day for granted," he said.

Award season in the theater begins in mid-May. For the first time since the debut of *Ma Rainey*, Wilson did not win the New York Drama Critics' Circle Award for Best Play; that went to *Proof*, David Auburn's mathematical puzzle of a play. *Hedley* was nominated for six Tony Awards, including Best Play and Best Direction of a Play. Before the ceremony on June 3, Wilson took a quick trip to Chicago to accept the 2001 Harold Washington Literary Award, named for the city's first African American mayor, who died in 1987. The award was sponsored by the Printers Row Book Fair, which Wilson kicked off with a speech at Dearborn Station. While in Chicago, he took in a production of Athol Fugard's *The Island*, which was produced by a fledgling African American troupe called Congo Square Theatre Company. He was quietly mentoring the company, which was founded by Derrick Sanders, a young director he had met while Sanders was pursuing his MFA at Pitt. The troupe had produced his play *Piano Lesson* earlier in the season. Wilson had, after all, made a huge statement about the scarcity of Black theater companies, and when he saw talent, he offered assistance, sometimes anonymously. He didn't broadcast his support.

Wilson flew back to New York to attend the Tony Awards. At this point, the Hotel Edison on West Forty-Seventh Street seemed like home. He had stayed there for two consecutive months while working on *Hedley*. Wilson was a creature of habit, and he insisted on staying at the fraying hotel, preferably in the same room, and dining in the café. The place was drab, the rooms were shabby, but the matzo ball soup was legendary. He knew the housekeeper by name; after she went home to Jamaica, she brought back a doll for Azula.

The Tony Awards ceremony at Radio City Music Hall was mostly anticlimactic for the *Hedley* creative team. The play was upstaged by the musical *The Producers*, which won twelve awards, breaking the record set by *Hello, Dolly!* with ten in 1964. Mel Brooks, the musical's creator, stopped the show—and created a mini-controversy—when he accepted the award for Best Musical by saying, "I want to thank Hitler for being such a funny guy onstage." And Nathan Lane, who won for Best Actor in a Musical, mortified his costar, Matthew Broderick, by dragging him onstage to share the award with him. "Believe me, without him, I'm nothing," he said, while Broderick, who had lost, tried to put on a good face.

Of course, Wilson basked in his awards when he won them, but he was also rooting for McClinton. The St. Paul native had been working in the theater for twenty-five years, and *Hedley* was his Broadway debut. McClinton was a dedicated foot soldier who worshipped Wilson. "I've worked on Shakespeare, Beckett, and Genet, and they were a walk in the park compared to this play," he said during a public discussion with Wilson. "Sometimes it feels like Muhammad Ali fighting Joe Frazier—he keeps coming at you!" That enthusiasm tickled Wilson. "Marion will go home after rehearsal and read the script every night," he said. "I honestly don't know anyone more passionate than he is about the theater."

McClinton lost to Daniel Sullivan, director of *Proof*, which also won Best Play. The only one to take home the statue from the *Hedley* team was Davis, who won Best Featured Actress in a Play. In one of the more cryptic acceptance speeches of the night, Davis thanked Wilson "for giving me enough humility to know that I'm not the best, I'm just one of the many blessed people in this business." Later, after Davis had won another Tony for a revival of *Fences* and an Academy Award for its movie adaptation, she credited Wilson for convincing her that she was beautiful. "He would always say, 'Viola, you are just so beautiful,'" she said during a *60 Minutes* interview in 2020. "I never felt feminine. I never felt like I could fit into that sort of confines of what it meant, or the stereotypical ways of what being a woman was about until I did *Seven Guitars*."

Hedley was a box office disaster. The play closed on July 1, after two months and just seventy-two performances. Wilson was resigned. "You can only close if you opened," he said shortly after the end of the run. At fifty-six, he had been keeping a schedule that would make a young adult yearn for a long, well-deserved break. He was not a disciplined writer who kept a strict schedule. Wilson wrote when his characters spoke to him. He had been short-circuited by the deadline for the opening of the O'Reilly Theater, and even though it was an honor, he wasn't planning to do that again anytime soon. He was already developing his next play, the one with the central image of Aunt Ester refusing to talk about the water. He had outlined a list of characters and shown it to Kreidler while rehearsing *Hedley* in New York.

He was also itching for something else to do. He had been working on the play cycle for seventeen years, and he desperately wanted to try another genre. Wilson liked to tell a story from his days as a young poet in Pittsburgh that made an enormous impression on him. When he was working at Black Horizons, a "small, slightly built shy man" walked into the rehearsal room at the Weil elementary school. He asked if he could play the piano, and when he sat down, he played brilliantly. But just as soon as he had started, he stopped cold and banged his head on the piano, kicking and screaming, "Limitation of the instrument!" Wilson initially thought the man was incapable of playing a particularly difficult piece, but realized that he had simply done all he could on the piano. "Imagine Pablo Picasso standing in front of a blank canvas with a paintbrush in his hand and suddenly go, 'Limitation of the instrument. There ain't nothing else I can do with this paint and canvas. I done did it all. This is limiting me. I got to find another way to express myself.'"

Wilson wasn't quite at the point where he was banging his head and throwing his fountain pen out the window, but he was restless. He knew he had to finish the cycle, but he was already writing a novel in his mind. The story? "You have a man walking down a dirt road in Mississippi in 1937, and the novel more or less follows him down that road, which leads him many places," he told the *Chicago Tribune* that June. "He's searching for a story, a particular story. He's being guided by some people and misguided by some people." Fiction, he thought, would enable him to open up his work in a way that he couldn't in his plays—the limitation of the instrument. He had already imagined the opening image. "In my first paragraph, I have these birds. The birds fly over and they just darken the whole landscape. This flock of crows—it blocks the sun." He noted that such vivid imagery isn't possible onstage. "You can't do that in the theater. You can't see the blood seeping inside his shoes."

But the novel would have to wait. Wilson had a tradition he followed every time he wrote the last scene of a play. Once he had typed the words "The end," he put another piece of paper in the typewriter or opened another file on his computer and wrote a sentence or two of the next play. He was always working on something.

But it wasn't always easy. He put pressure on himself. Of course, the regional theaters that produced his work would readily give him a slot in any upcoming season, but those artistic directors were willing to wait as long as necessary. Wilson was not. He had said he was writing ten plays, and he was going to do it, even if he paid a personal price. At the end of his preface to the published version of *Hedley*, he wrote, "I often remark that I am a struggling playwright. I'm struggling to get the next play on the page. Eight down and counting. The struggle continues."

CHAPTER SEVENTEEN

An Uphill Battle
in the Basement

Blacks have always, historically, been the custodians for America's hope.

—AUGUST WILSON

Hey, man, it's August."

After the untimely close of *Hedley*, Wilson returned to Seattle, ostensibly to spend more time with the family and to work on those two remaining plays. He had gotten used to having Kreidler around as a sounding board, and he took to calling him several times a week. Wilson was feeling pressured to write his last two plays, and he kept hearing the voice of Aunt Ester. His next play didn't have a title yet, but he was listening to the characters. Set in the 1900s, it was the first play chronologically in the cycle. Kreidler had moved to an apartment in Jersey City with his girlfriend, but he was a bit lost, trying to figure out what to do with his career after what he called "the adventure of a lifetime." He missed the road. He missed his mentor.

Wilson, who was restless himself, would call Kreidler around five or six in the evening, beginning every call with "Hey, man, it's August." The two would stay on the phone until two or three in the morning, talking about theater, the state of the universe, the latest outrage in the news, or cute things Azula said that day. Kreidler was delighted. He hadn't really expected to stay in such close touch, but he lit up when he heard Wilson's voice. Of course, those long conversations gave both men less time to devote to their personal lives at home, but they fed off each other. Wilson talked for hours about his new, yet-to-be-titled play, particularly the character of Caesar Wilkes, a Black constable in the Hill District who stood for law and order. Wilson fashioned him as a middle-class man who had not only assimilated so soon after the end of slavery, but had also become part of the governing ranks. Wilson did not know how to portray such a character who was so different from himself and his friends. "Todd, man, I have to figure this out. He is middle-class. How did he get his money?" he said during one rambling conversation.

One night, a call from Wilson began the usual way—"Hey, man, it's August"—but the playwright quickly handed the phone over to Romero. She invited Kreidler to Seattle for Azula's fourth birthday party. Wilson had trouble asking for things, and yes, he did want Kreidler to attend his daughter's celebration, but he also wanted Kreidler to collaborate on the screenplay for *Fences.* That project was still languishing after nearly a decade and a half, but Scott Rudin was now Wilson's lead producer at Paramount and Eddie Murphy was out of the picture. There had been talk over the years about various Black directors, including the actor Laurence Fishburne, but nothing had happened. This time, McClinton was supposedly the director of choice. By now, Wilson was nonchalant about the whole thing. He had stated his case, and if the movie never got made, then it never got made. He was not one to back down on his principles. (Wilson didn't particularly trust Rudin and complained that the producer would have his assistant call him, but then when he called back immediately, Rudin was "out of the office." This was before Rudin was publicly disgraced in 2021 for a long history of bullying and berating employees and coworkers.) But he had promised Rudin that he would deliver a new screenplay, and he wanted Kreidler's help. Kreidler flew out to Seattle and expected to stay for three or four days. It turned into three weeks.

Rudin had given Wilson notes, but it had been well more than a decade since he had written *Fences,* and he felt that the play was finished.

He didn't want to repeat himself, so he decided to open up the story to encompass the community outside of Troy Maxson's fenced-in yard. He toyed with scenes with Troy and his lover, Alberta, and Troy with the sanitation department boss; his son Cory playing on the football field and working as a stock boy at the A&P; and Rose volunteering at her church.

He and Kreidler settled into a schedule they would continue for the rest of their collaborations together. The day started with a four- or five-hour breakfast at a local eatery, during which they dissected the day's newspaper, item by item. To an outsider, it didn't look like they were doing anything—"We're not very productive," Kreidler said—but the freewheeling conversations were vital to the writing. They frequented restaurants where the atmosphere oozed with Seattle's casual vibe, and Wilson was known in the neighborhood as the guy who left huge tips, not as the famous East Coast playwright. They would eventually wander back to Wilson's Victorian home on East Aloha Street, but the real work didn't begin until about 11:00 p.m., when they retreated to Wilson's basement lair. One night, Kreidler went upstairs for a break and overheard Azula. She was looking for her father. "I think he's asleep," she said.

Wilson's heart wasn't in the *Fences* script, though. He had turned down dozens of other screenwriting offers over the years, including Steven Spielberg's 1997 *Amistad*. Nevertheless, he knew that a film would reach a much wider audience than his plays ever would, which was one reason why he had made the teleplay of *Piano Lesson*. He planned to spend a little time on the screenplay and then jet off to London, where *Jitney* was scheduled to open at the Royal National Theatre in October. His plays had been produced across the pond, but this time, the production featured the American cast that had been together for so long. They got the idiomatic speech and the cultural references correct. They knew these characters. They had grown up surrounded by men like them. McClinton had won the 2000 Obie Award for Direction for the off-Broadway production, and the stellar cast had picked up the Obie Award for Best Ensemble. Wilson was excited about rehearsing in London, and he was also writing his next play in his mind—even if he didn't have a title yet.

But Wilson, like the rest of the world, was short-circuited on September 11, 2001, when two planes crashed into the World Trade Center in New York; another hit the Pentagon; and a fourth crashed in a field in Pennsylvania, thanks to the heroics of the passengers onboard. Wilson canceled his plans to fly to London. That week, he had been conducting a public correspondence with John Lahr, the *New Yorker* critic who had profiled him in the magazine earlier that spring. They were collaborating on a feature called "The Breakfast Table" in *Slate*, the online magazine, trading letters each day. Up until 9/11, the back-and-forth was distinctly Wilsonian, with the two men discussing such seemingly disparate subjects as boxing and gambling; consumerism and playwriting; and the Human Genome Project and Aunt Ester. The mood shifted dramatically after 9/11. "What damnable horror!" Wilson wrote to Lahr. "All words seem inadequate. You say hatred will be given new license. I'm afraid you're right, though God knows it's had more than enough authority already. This tragedy has opened a chasm of vulnerability and our national response, as well as our personal response, will define the character and conscience of our nation for years to come. Yesterday was a different world, and I am mourning for it."

As the days passed, Wilson, like any father, worried for his young daughter. He wrote that when he dropped her off at preschool the morning after the tragedy, he thought of all the children in New York whose parents weren't there to pick them up. The day after the planes hit the Towers, Wilson woke up and "attacked [his] play with a vengeance." He turned to art in the face of catastrophe. "A stabbing need to create something out of this madness. To stand Art up in the face of it. Maybe it's a redemptive act. Maybe it's this belief in the power of art to construct, to inform us of the nobility of our humanity, to bring us closer to our kinship with the gods, and, armed and armored thus, through will and daring, bring about an increase in our humanity."

He also told Lahr that he was against a use of military force to retaliate against a group of "elusive and destructive terrorists" and, instead, urged officials "to rebuild the World Trade Center on the exact spot (Phoenix rising from the ashes) as a testament to the resiliency of the American spirit. This, to my mind, would be the truly heroic thing to do."

Wilson was shaken to the core, like the rest of the country, but he was deeply thoughtful and tried to grasp the roots of this "insane, dastardly, nightmarish, pointless act of terrorism for terrorism's sake." He condemned the atrocity, but he also struggled to understand a nebulous war driven not by territorial disputes, but by "hatred for our arrogant display of power and our seeming callous indifference to the rest of the world's humanity." Wilson feared more innocent deaths as the result of a retaliatory strike.

In October, the Actors Theatre of Louisville, a highly regarded regional theater known for its support of emerging playwrights, mounted a production of *Piano Lesson*, and Wilson explained to a local reporter that his plays are about "the big things: love, honor, duty, and betrayal." But when the reporter asked him what was most important to him about life in America, he didn't pause. "My four-year-old daughter," he said. "We've changed a lot in the past month, as you know. I'm trying to take an assessment of what America is and its possibilities." He also expressed a soupçon of hope. "Blacks have always, historically, been the custodians for America's hope," he added.

For the first time in years, Wilson was finding solace in family. He was tired of moving from city to city as he developed each play, and he made a conscious decision that he would only work on the next play at three theaters, instead of taking it to six or seven before opening on Broadway. He had been deeply, irrevocably saddened, and he was taking stock of life as he came close to completing his cycle.

He wasn't actually writing that play, though. When he went to see *Piano Lesson* in Louisville, he narrated the entire plot of his yet-to-be-named play to director Timothy Douglas—but he also admitted that he hadn't written much of it yet. Wilson had been looking forward to rehearsals of *Jitney* in London, but now he refused to travel overseas, so he could be close to his family, especially Azula. He wasn't in London to celebrate the extraordinary response to *Jitney*, which received glowing reviews: "superb," "dazzling," "finely pitched," and, in the London *Times*, "so funny yet moving that it merits comparison with the work of the great [Sean] O'Casey, or maybe even the greater Chekhov" (whom Wilson admired). The play, which included most of the tightly knit ensemble that had traveled the U.S. and performed off-Broadway, was slated to move from the Royal National Theatre to London's West End, but the producers canceled their plan after 9/11. Anthony Chisholm and the other actors were sorely disappointed, and when they attended a meeting with producers and learned the news, they turned to one another as if to say, "Where is August?" Despite the setback, the production went on to win the 2002 Olivier Award for Best New Play.

Back at home, Wilson was continuing to support the African Grove Institute for the Arts, the nonprofit that was formed after his Dartmouth Black theater summit. He was on hand in May 2002 when a group in Missouri announced that it had formed a chapter of the nonprofit, which aimed to "create an environment to stimulate artistic excellence and the advancement and preservation of African-American arts." Wilson was in Missouri for the opening of the Kansas City Repertory Theatre's production of *Joe Turner*. After each Broadway production, Wilson's plays were produced at numerous regional theaters across the country; when *Fences* closed on Broadway after 525 performances, it was the second most produced play in regional theaters in 1989 (second only to the annual cash cow, Charles Dickens's *A Christmas Carol*). Wilson had broken down barriers at the nation's premier theaters, but success doesn't come without a backlash. Some other Black playwrights privately thought that Wilson, whose work was mainstream and traditional in terms of structure, occupied the one slot allotted each season to an artist of color at regional theaters. His success, some said, blocked access for other playwrights to achieve the same chance, particularly more experimental writers. When she was starting out, playwright Suzan-Lori Parks was often told that her plays were "not like August Wilson's," as if that were something bad. She took such comments as a challenge and went on to great acclaim, winning both the 2002 Tony Award and the Pulitzer Prize for *Topdog/Underdog*.

(The two playwrights admired each other, and Parks wrote a gushing introduction to *Radio Golf* in the elegant 2007 collection of all ten plays.) Wilson never asked to be put on a pedestal, and even if his work was traditional, he supported other playwrights, at the O'Neill and elsewhere. And he had been rankled when an anonymous Black theater professional quoted in Gates's "Chitlin Circuit" article dubbed him the "Black artistic spokesman, the one playwright who could do no wrong" and blamed him for causing funding for Black theater to dry up.

Wilson was not a pioneer in campaigning for the self-sufficiency of Black theaters. In 1966, the Black actor Douglas Turner Ward wrote an op-ed piece in the *New York Times* titled "American Theater: For Whites Only?" The piece pinpointed that "the most immediate, pressing, practical, absolutely minimally essential active first step is the development of a permanent Negro repertory company of at least Off-Broadway size and dimension." Ward was impatient: "Not in the future, but now!" W. McNeil Lowry, vice president of Humanities and Arts at the Ford Foundation, took heed and established a $434,000 grant to form a new Black theater company. Ward became artistic director of the Negro Ensemble Company (NEC) in 1967 and launched an ambitious and artistically successful troupe that performed plays by Black writers with Black casts, achieving Du Bois's call to create a theater "about us, by us, for us, near us." In the 1980s, however, that same foundation and many others started funneling money to mainstream white institutions to encourage cultural diversity, effectively steering funds away from Black theaters like NEC, which began to suffer financially.

Yet amid the carnage, some said, Wilson remained the anointed "Black playwright." Ward, who made that bold statement in his 1966 op-ed, traced Wilson's success to the time when *New York Times* critic Frank Rich gave *Ma Rainey* a "review that all writers—Black, white or green—would hock their children for," he said in a 2002 interview. "With that champion in the primary critical spot, it made August's career. An opinion-maker from the mainstream came in and designated a cultural representative. But the formula that regional theaters have in doing

August is a pernicious thing—'August Wilson' is almost a brand name. His work is approved by the *New York Times* so it's safe to do. At NEC, I wanted to prove the *variety* of Black voices."

That criticism hit a nerve. Wilson thought that he was simply writing his plays, and he privately supported Black theater companies, including the Congo Square Theatre Company in Chicago and, later, the Pittsburgh Playwrights Theatre Company. He had very publicly put himself on the firing block by taking on Brustein to champion the very Black theater artists who were now calling him out. He also sensed—accurately—that some of his oldest friends in Pittsburgh resented his success. Despite all the awards and accolades and honorary degrees, he felt alienated and isolated, a victim of his own success. When he was home in Seattle, he was happiest just hanging out at a sidewalk table at Caffe Ladro, a coffee shop not far from his home. There he chatted up the locals and gave spare change to the various characters who were down on their luck. He knew who he was.

His mood shifted after the failure of *Hedley*, followed by the shock of 9/11, which put the entire nation on red alert. Since Azula was born, he had talked about just wanting to be home in his basement office, writing, sneaking cigarettes, and listening to the blues. And even though his young daughter sometimes called him the "slippery guy," they both had the same stubborn temperament, and he cherished her company. Perhaps that mood is what drew him closer to Kreidler as well. He was a source of comfort and could also act as a shield. After Kreidler had spent time working with him on the *Fences* screenplay, Wilson began to think of him as his surrogate son.

While *Joe Turner* was playing in Kansas City, Kreidler flew out to see the production. His grandfather died suddenly while he was there. Kreidler had told Wilson about his childhood, confiding that his father had been a chilly, unapproachable figure. He had been raised by his mother and his grandparents, and his grandfather had filled in because his father was emotionally absent. Kreidler was distraught. He didn't know what to do. So he called Wilson, an expert on funerals. Wilson walked him through the steps: how to plan the service, the flowers, the wake, the eulogy. Wilson bought his protégé a plane ticket and sent him home to mourn. It was a symbiotic friendship: Kreidler needed guidance and Wilson needed unconditional loyalty and love.

卜卜

Wilson was still rebounding from the dismal response to *Hedley*, the first entirely new play he had launched without his old, familiar support system. No matter what Wilson thought of Richards, the director's magic touch was missing in the final draft of the play. Wilson also missed the hallowed ground of the O'Neill. After Richards retired as artistic director in 1999, he was replaced by James Houghton, founder of New York's Signature Theatre Company, which made its name by producing an entire season dedicated to an individual playwright. Each season was planned years in advance, and Houghton told Wilson that he would mount his plays at Signature in the 2006–2007 season. But at the O'Neill, Houghton shook things up in more ways than one. He moved the playwrights from the Seaside Sanitorium onto the O'Neill campus, bringing them closer to the action, and he did away with the company of actors and directors and cast each play individually. He also inaugurated a writer-in-residence slot. One of the first things he did was fire off a letter to Wilson, arguably the O'Neill's greatest success story. "The minute I got there, I wrote August a note saying, 'August, you're welcome back any time,'" he said. "I think I sent it out snail mail back then. He must have gotten the letter a few days later, and he called me right away. I put a room aside for him, and he came."

The O'Neill feels like home to the initiated, and Wilson was at ease there. He spent much of the summer of 2002 working on *Gem of the Ocean*. He was free to write and did not have the pressure of a staged reading. The great lawn behind the mansion looks out on Long Island Sound; the air is replete with the smell of brine, and the sound of the pounding waves fills the air. It was the perfect setting for Wilson to work on this particular play. The ocean is a mystical force in *Gem*, and the familiar setting was always inspiring. Wilson thrived when he was among his fellow writers, and under the new administration, he slipped right back into the familiar environment.

But shortly after the residency ended, Kreidler got a late-night call from Wilson, which was not unusual. But this time, the playwright was agitated. "Todd, man, I'm in trouble," he began. He was at a benefit in Seattle, and he had just had a conversation with Sharon Ott, then artistic director of the Seattle Repertory Theatre. He casually mentioned the one-man show he and Kreidler often joked about in their rambling conversations, and Ott jumped on it. "She offered me a slot, and I agreed, so I need a show, man." And then he made a request that left Kreidler sleepless for days. "I need a director, and I want you to do it," he said. Kreidler was at once over the moon and scared out of his mind. "I did not sleep that night out of excitement and abject terror," he said. "That is when we knew we had to get serious. We had to do the show."

They would eventually get around to it—on August Wilson time. Wilson, as usual, had several projects going at once. He had agreed to open *Gem* at the Goodman in Chicago the following spring, and despite his time at the O'Neill, he still hadn't finished the play or the *Fences* screenplay. In St. Paul, Penumbra was dedicating an entire season to his plays, and he was scheduled to return to Waterford in October to accept the Monte Cristo Award from the O'Neill Center. The award was named for Eugene O'Neill's childhood home, which was part of the center's campus. Fellow playwright Marsha Norman was scheduled to bestow the honor on Wilson.

But amid this exhausting whirlwind, which had become second nature by now, Wilson was also deep into plans for a star-studded revival of the play that had launched his career. A Broadway revival of *Ma Rainey* was slated to open on February 6, 2003, at the Royale Theatre. The stars? Charles S. Dutton, now fifty-two and thirty pounds heavier, was reprising his role as the hotheaded young trumpet player, Levee, and comedian Whoopi Goldberg was signed to play the title role. Goldberg was appearing on Broadway in her one-woman show in 1982 when the original *Ma Rainey* opened, and over the years, she had expressed interest in playing the title character. She had a seven-month block between projects, as did Dutton. Wilson, along with Mordecai and their production company, Sageworks, set out to raise the $2.5 million to stage the revival. Goldberg, one of only ten people at the time to have won an Emmy, a Grammy, an Oscar, and a Tony (the so-called EGOT), brought her considerable star power to the production—despite the fact that she isn't a singer. When Wilson asked Dwight Andrews to oversee the musical direction, he was thrilled to be back in Wilson's company. "Who is playing Ma?" he asked. Wilson told him it was Whoopi Goldberg. There was a long silence. "I didn't know Whoopi could sing," Andrews said. Another pause. Wilson then said quietly, "We'll have to see." Andrews worked with her, and to his surprise, she followed all of his instructions, but a singer she was not.

The production should have been a box office slam dunk, if not a surefire critical one, but it was doomed from the start. When the show was announced in October, Dutton was still steaming over Wilson's split with Richards, and he didn't help matters when he talked to the press. "I feel that the definitive production of the play has already been done, and directed by the definitive director," he said in a *New York Times* interview. "I'm not looking to do anything different. If it ain't broke, don't fix it." That statement would hardly send ticket buyers rushing to the box office. Why revive the show if the original couldn't be matched? Why have Marion McClinton direct if Richards was the paragon? Goldberg was more upbeat. She had last appeared on Broadway when she replaced Nathan Lane in *A Funny Thing Happened on the Way to the Forum* in 1997. "I figured if I can do that, I can do anything," she said.

The production, with its two marquee names, brought unwanted attention from the show's original 1984 producers, Robert Cole and Frederick M. Zollo. They claimed that their contract gave them sole rights to a revival. The project seemed in jeopardy, but the producers worked it out behind closed doors and came to a "financial arrangement," and Cole and Zollo were listed in the credits.

Still, what seemed like a license to make money soon became a major headache for Wilson. He still had to finish *Gem* before its opening at the Goodman in April, not to mention the one-man show that had put him in a panic the night he called Kreidler. He did manage to get a rough first draft of his new play finished by the end of 2002. "I've known how it ended, so it was simply a matter of writing it," he told the *Guardian*. "Now

I look at the script and there is something on all those pages that used to be blank. It's like you've just given birth. It's painful but it's a joyous process."

The *Ma Rainey* revival, however, was all pain and no joy. Three cast members left the show during rehearsal, and there was more than the usual backstage grumbling about the producers. Goldberg and Dutton went public with the disputes, carping in an astonishing tell-all article in the January 23–30 issue of *Time Out New York*, which was teased on the cover with the headline "Whoopi Goldberg and Charles Dutton on *Ma Rainey* Backstage Brouhaha." They complained about accommodations and billing, among other things, griping publicly about the types of issues that are usually worked out behind the curtain. And Dutton continued to insist that Richards had directed the definitive production, suggesting that McClinton was second-rate. "I've had to get the original out of my system," he said in another *New York Times* interview. "Because, I make no bones about it, for a long time my dream was to come back to Broad-way with as many of the original folks—director, actors, tech—as are left. I had to let it go. I had to say the definitive production happened. It was August's discovery, my discovery, Lloyd's [Richards] re-emergence. It had all those great circumstances." Previews played to a half-empty house. Dutton added some Shakespearean drama to the already acrimonious situation by announcing his swan song in his *Playbill* biography. "I have done the theater some service, and they know it," he wrote. "No more of that!" He was paraphrasing two lines from Othello's final monologue. ("I have done the state some service, and they know't; / No more of that," the Moorish general says.)

The week before the opening, Charles Gordon, who was playing the trombonist, Cutler, burst a blood vessel in his leg; three performances were canceled while his understudy rehearsed. At the same time, McClinton was hospitalized with "frighteningly low" potassium levels, due to existing kidney and high blood pressure issues. Dutton stood in as director to work with Gordon's understudy.

Wilson was a man of limited patience during normal situations, and the pressure was building when it came to opening night on February 6. Given all the turmoil, it was no surprise that the reviews were lackluster, at best. In the *Times*, Ben Brantley said the "hollow new revival . . . rarely gets past the level of an orchestra still tentatively tuning up." With its star wattage and glorious past, *Ma Rainey* had been anticipated as "one of the most exciting revivals in years," Brantley wrote, but qualified instead "as the most poignant heartbreaker of the season." It was wrenching for Wilson, who as executive producer had dedicated the show to three of its original stars, Theresa Merritt, Joe Seneca, and Robert Judd, all deceased.

The opening-night party was a dour affair. Actor Anthony Chisholm was a guest, and at one point during the evening, he was standing in the lobby of the Roosevelt Hotel. Wilson was at the reception counter, and apparently the staff person had said something that angered him. "August went and flew off the handle," Chisholm said. "He exploded like a bomb. He was getting ready to punch someone out." Chisholm and several others in attendance intervened, but Chisholm had seen Wilson launch into a rage on a few other occasions. "It was always with some outsider," he said. Actor James Craven, who is Black, witnessed Wilson explode many times over the years, often when he was out drinking with actors. "If he suspected he was being racially profiled or slighted in any way, he went from zero to sixty," Craven said. "My thing was, 'Okay, Negro, you got some money. You got some fame. You think you can do that, but the rest of us will get shot if you keep that up.' "

The targets of his rage were often inconsequential working stiffs—the coat-check clerk, the receptionist, the waitress—who happened to say the wrong thing at the wrong time. This would not be the first or the last time he flew off the handle in a stressful situation. Sakina had learned to anticipate such outbursts. "I could see it physically coming," she said. "I was always trying to calm him down and defuse situations. I could see him boiling, and then something happened, but the trigger wasn't the cause. It was something brewing inside, like the last straw." He did not thrive in large, crowded ballrooms, where he was the center of attention and had to socialize, nor in any environment that triggered sensory overload. In

Pittsburgh, his childhood peers knew not to cross him, and in the theater, his closest friends often found themselves intervening to save Wilson
from himself.

It was probably for the best that the production, which was set to run
through June 29, closed early on April 6. Goldberg made a diplomatic
exit by citing a conflict in her schedule. Wilson was frayed at a time when
he needed to be focusing on his new play. He summed up the forgettable
experience by calling it "the worst 73 days of my life."

Wilson was more than happy to leave New York and head to Pittsburgh
for his annual birthday party for his mother on March 12. He also wanted
to comfort his brother Richard, the baby of Daisy Wilson's seven children who was nine years younger. Richard had not had an easy time in
life. Growing up in Pittsburgh, he had somehow ended up on the wrong
end of trouble, getting arrested more than twenty times, mostly for petty
crimes. A soft-spoken man with sad eyes, he had settled down and become a devoted father, but his son had been struck and killed by a train
two months earlier. He was crushed by his son's death, and Wilson wanted
to support him. He had convinced his brother to accompany him on a trip
to Syracuse University, where he had agreed to be the featured speaker at
the University Lectures Series on March 18. Richard would do the driving, and Wilson would do the talking.

But on March 17, Wilson got shattering news. Poet and playwright
Rob Penny dropped dead of a heart attack at his home in the Hill District.
Wilson was heartbroken. He had missed Nick Flournoy's funeral when he
was in South Africa with Sakina, and now Penny was gone, too. They had
grown up together on the streets of the Hill in the 1960s; with Flournoy
and Chawley Williams, they formed what they called the Centre Avenue
Poets. His passing shook Wilson deeply. He was pushing sixty, and he was
on the verge of completing the ambitious series of plays he had set out to
write so many years ago. Sakina had grown and flown, and he had a young
daughter and wife at home. He didn't know what was next in his life, but

he knew it had all started in Pittsburgh with his poet friends. His grief ran deep, and it was overwhelming.

But Wilson kept his promises, and he and his brother took off for the Syracuse speech. Wilson charmed the students and professors. He recited an unpublished poem called "Ode to the Greyhound," not his finest work. "Every writer does bad writing," he assured the students. He told many of the stock stories he had cultivated over the years and had filed away for the time he got around to writing the autobiographical one-man show. After the lecture, he took a seat in the audience and stayed as long as the students had questions. This was typical Wilson, sticking around to talk to students, not professors and patrons.

He was back in Pittsburgh in time for Penny's 11 a.m. funeral mass at St. Benedict the Moor on March 22. The place was ingrained in his memories. He had mourned his mother there twenty years ago, almost to the day. He always had something to say at funerals, even for those of people he barely knew, street folks he helped out with spare change. It was one of his principles: always speak highly of the dead and honor their legacy. He was under a lot of personal stress. Rehearsals were about to begin for the Chicago debut of *Gem* and he still hadn't written the one-man show, which was set for mid-May. But he had finally embraced the advice of Richards, his former mentor: be where you are. He focused on the funeral and thought deeply about what he wanted to say when he got the chance.

Wilson was with his brother when he got the disturbing news that Penny's family wanted him to know that everyone was welcome to speak at the funeral except him. Wilson was crushed. This message confirmed what he had suspected all along. His former friends resented his meteoric success and thought that he was just lucky: it could have been any of them. Wilson, after all, was the odd duck who walked around in tweed coats while everyone else was wearing dashikis back in their youth. He had always looked up to Penny and applauded him when he was hired as a professor at Pitt's newly formed Africana Studies department in 1969. There was no similar job for Wilson, the high school dropout with the IQ of 143, yet he did not resent his friend's success at the time. But this snub deepened his feeling of alienation. He never tried to flaunt his fame, but his friends resented his celebrity. This was the price of success. He mourned more than the loss of Penny the day of the funeral as he fell to his knees and wept next to the coffin.

He had come back to Pittsburgh to support his brother, but now Richard ended up supporting him. He later talked to Kreidler about the funeral and indicated that he knew his friends not only envied him but also resented him. But he never told Kreidler that he had been banned from speaking at the funeral. It was too sharp a cut, and he kept his wounds to himself. He never spoke ill of the dead, and he wasn't going to do it now.

Wilson was in a less somber mood when he got to Chicago to rehearse *Gem*. McClinton had recovered after his health crisis during the *Ma Rainey* debacle and was back as director, firmly ensconced as Richards's replacement. The second act was barely a half hour long, Kreidler said, and the pivotal final scene was just a sketch. But Wilson was in a merry mood when he sat down to talk to Chris Jones, then arts reporter for the *Chicago Tribune*. Wilson arrived at the interview wearing a T-shirt that said "I used to be white." He was asked to explain. "I thought I'd give it to Clarence Thomas," he said to Jones. He waited and added, "Or maybe Eminem."

He was trying out material for his upcoming one-man show. He expressed reservations about the engagement at the Seattle Rep. "I'm a writer, not a performer and if I could get out of it, I would," he said dryly. "But I'm an honorable man."

The Goodman production was really a glorified workshop of an unfinished script, and this time the critics weren't buying it. Ben Brantley of the *New York Times*, who didn't "review" the production but wrote about it in a piece labeled "Critic's Notebook," noted *Gem* was but a "waning echo" of the inimitable *Joe Turner*. "Theme overwhelms credible character," he wrote. "The sermon ultimately drowns out the story."

Clearly, Wilson had some rewriting to do, but he had the one-man show on his mind. First, he took a quick trip to New York on May 13 to receive a Lifetime Achievement Award at the New Dramatists' fifty-fourth annual benefit luncheon. New Dramatists, the playwrights center on West Forty-Fourth Street, had been his artistic and physical home in New York for many years when he was an up-and-coming playwright, and Wilson was honored to be back in his old haunt. Dutton was a speaker at the gala, and the staff of New Dramatists was nervous that sparks might fly, given the festering rift over Richards and the recent *Ma Rainey* disaster. The two men were still seething, but somehow they let the animosity dissipate. Dutton improvised his speech and recited line after line from Wilson's plays, as if they were the best of friends. After his speech, the two men embraced, much to the relief of the event's organizers. Nevertheless, Wilson fidgeted nervously during the formal affair. He was clearly not comfortable sitting at the dais during the main event, but he stayed late at the after-party, comfortably chatting with old friends after the benefactors and board members had left and the actors and playwrights remained.

But when he got back to Seattle, he could no longer procrastinate. His show opened on May 22. When he was working on *Gem* in Chicago, he repeatedly asked Kreidler how they were going to pull it off. Kreidler, who was still going by the title of assistant, assured Wilson, "I got a plan, man. I got a plan." He did not, however, have a plan. Kreidler relished every moment he spent with Wilson, but his personal life was a mess. He had recently broken up with his girlfriend. He had quit smoking for six months but started again after the breakup. Wilson had quit and started up again, too, but he was starting to think of Kreidler as the son he never had, and he was furious. "He was so disappointed in me," Kreidler said. "He said, 'You look so fucking stupid, you idiot.' He dressed me down."

Wilson could be toughest with the people he cared about the most. Early in their friendship, Kreidler asked Wilson to read a play he had written, but then time passed, and he didn't hear a word. Finally, when he asked, Wilson just shook his head and said, "Yeah, I read it." Not another word. The silence was damning, but Kreidler took it as encouragement to write something better. Wilson did the same thing with the actor Laurence Fishburne, who had starred in *Two Trains*. Fishburne sent him a play, and Wilson slammed it with silence.

But in Seattle, Kreidler was the one who had to be tough with the playwright. He had been collecting Wilson's stories for several years, but they were just notes jotted down on stray pieces of paper. He flew to Seattle and arrived on Wilson's doorstep early one morning. Kreidler is hypoglycemic, and by his own account, he gets "angry and nasty" if he hasn't eaten. He expected that the two would follow their usual routine, which was to start the day with a five-hour breakfast at some low-key café. But Wilson insisted that they retreat to the basement office right away. Kreidler was not happy. "I just want to get some breakfast," he said. Stomach grumbling, he reluctantly followed Wilson down the stairs. When they had worked together in the past, Kreidler pulled up a chair and sat in what he called his "Bob Cratchit" position, ever the eager assistant. But when he got down the stairs and around the corner, he saw that Wilson had bought him a huge desk and set it up with yellow legal tablets, pens, and a printer. Kreidler was beside himself. "I don't think you could put an Academy Award in my hand and it would have felt any better," he said. Wilson shrugged off Kreidler's effusive thanks and simply said, "You need a place to work, man. Now let's go get something to eat."

Wilson was letting Kreidler know that he accepted him as a peer. "August called those moments 'snapshots of privilege,' moments you collect that define and mark your life," Kreidler said. "I could never express the power of what this gift meant to me."

Since Kreidler had exaggerated about having a plan, they started by carving a structure out of Wilson's repertoire of stories about growing up on the Hill. They had joked about the show for many years. They had watched *The Original Kings of Comedy*, the 2000 stand-up comedy film featuring Steve Harvey, D. L. Hughley, Cedric the Entertainer, and Bernie Mac. They had dissected the routines the way they might analyze a fight: where the jokes land, where there is a need for a pause followed by a sharp jab. They had laughed about potential titles, including *I'm Not Spalding Gray*; *Move Over, Chris Rock*; and *Sambo Takes Over the World.* They had imagined opening the show with the business of throwing forty-one ping-pong balls at the audience, as a reminder of the murder of Amadou Diallo. They realized that was not an appropriate bit, but the idea underlies the ethos of the ninety-minute play. Kreidler wanted to re-create the sense of a great storyteller and capture Wilson's self-deprecating humor as well as his passion for justice. He wanted the audience to feel as if they were present at one of their five-hour breakfasts, where the conversation turned on a dime, but somehow all made sense, with one riff segueing seamlessly into the next. "He was a blues man with a jazz mind," Kreidler said.

The deadline was quickly approaching. Seattle Rep had given the pair a rehearsal space and a stage manager, and by day, they would rehearse the various stories at the theater. After a long dinner, they would retreat to the basement at the house on East Aloha Street, listen to the tape of that day's rehearsal, and try to build a structure out of the series of vignettes. They snuck cigarettes down in the musky writer's lair, and they worked well beyond midnight. "To say the very least, it was an uphill battle in the basement," Kreidler said of the heady time. "It was like the inmates took over the asylum. We'd listen to the rehearsal tapes like game day footage."

Those sessions could go on all night. Meanwhile, Romero was operating around Azula's schedule, which involved a regular bedtime and three square meals a day. One morning, she woke up and Wilson hadn't come to bed the night before. She tiptoed downstairs to what she called the "bachelor pad" and found the two men asleep at their desks. It didn't faze them. After a time, they got up and went out for their five-hour breakfast.

There was always music playing in the background. One night, they were listening to Paul Robeson singing "The House I Live In." The song about religious and racial tolerance was originally performed in the 1942 musical *Let Freedom Sing* and was later sung by Frank Sinatra in a 1945 short film of the same name. Robeson released his version in 1948, making the song more poignant as he asked the question "What is America to me?" in his deep bass-baritone. Wilson and Kreidler started free-associating about the song and what America means to African Americans, and they came up with the idea of starting with a speech about America's legacy of slavery. They wrote the first of a series of monologues that night, and the one-act play begins with Wilson (or an actor playing Wilson) addressing the audience directly. "My ancestors have been in America since the early 17th century. And for the first 244 years, we never had a problem finding a job." After the opening, they tweaked the idea Wilson originally had for the T-shirt. He takes off his coat, revealing the back of a shirt that says "I am an accident. This did not turn out right." He turns around, revealing the front of the shirt, which reads "I am supposed to be white." The image brings down the house every time. (Wilson later had a shirt made for Kreidler that said "I am supposed to be Black.")

At the end of a little more than a week, they had created a loose framework of short scenes, each telling a particular tale from Wilson's youth. The scenes were introduced with slides bearing such titles as "My Ancestors," "Hill District," "Jail," "Something Is Not Always Better Than Nothing," and "Limitation of the Instrument." At one point in the development, Whoopi Goldberg suggested adding a slide that read "Oral Sex," followed by the line "Let's skip that one." That bit stayed in the show.

As the two men fought that uphill battle, they eventually came up with a tight play that illuminated all of the issues that were important to Wilson—loyalty, friendship, honor, commitment, dignity, justice. He mentions many of his friends from his days on the Hill, including his friend Cy Morocco, who couldn't play a note on the saxophone, his ex-junkie mentor, Chawley Williams, and the gentle activist and community organizer Nick Flournoy. He reveals his sometimes wild escapades with women, some of which are highly exaggerated for dramatic effect. (His girlfriend Snookie's husband, for instance, never pulled out a gun and threatened to shoot him, as he claims in the show.)

When it came time to rehearse on the stage, the two had miraculously put together something stage-worthy. They dropped all the titles they had joked about and came up with a new one: *How I Learned What I Learned.* Wilson approved, but he also told Kreidler, "No, man, if it is going to be a one-man show, it should have a long title." They added a wordy subtitle: *And How What I Learned Has Led Me to the Places I've Wanted to Go. That*

I Have Sometimes Gone Unwillingly Is the Crucible in Which Many a Work of Art Has Been Fired. The published version reflects that thought in the description of the setting, which is simply "The crucible in which many a work of art has been fired."

They had a script, which they cobbled together like a jazz session, with a playlist of Wilson's favorite sagas. The playwright proved to be deft at segueing from one scene to the next. Kreidler convinced him that the freshly minted script echoed the way he spoke. "Being with August, you would suddenly make a sharp left," Kreidler said. "You didn't know how you got there, but goddamn it was fun." Wilson was satisfied with the script, but he had stage fright, and now Kreidler had to assure him that he could actually perform it. Kreidler was devoted to his mentor, sometimes so much that he could not distinguish boundaries between his work life and his personal life. "I had a sense of how he felt under siege as a public figure, the stress of that, how much that cost him," he said. "It was a big deal to do the one-man show, considering how introverted he was."

But then there was the matter of the poster. When Wilson agreed to do the show as a gift to Seattle Rep, its artistic director, Sharon Ott, had promised him that the theater would print a poster advertising the play. Wilson suggested that they use a caricature that a Pittsburgh artist had drawn of him, but the theater reported that they had had trouble obtaining the rights to the image and told Wilson they would commission another artist to design the poster. As opening night neared, Wilson had not seen the poster, and he was ultimately told that it wasn't in the budget. That didn't sit well with him, nor with Kreidler.

They both felt that the theater management had disrespected them throughout the process. At twenty-eight now, Kreidler barely looked old enough to get into a bar, and as director, he had trouble arranging time for tech and getting the bare-bones assistance he needed to mount the show. He had directed a few productions for the Pittsburgh Public Theater's Young Company, but this was his professional directorial debut. "Any other theater in the country would kill to do this, and they didn't support us at all," Kreidler said. "It was just unconscionable." The series of slights hit a raw nerve for Wilson, and the poster put him over the edge.

During one rehearsal, Wilson refused to go onstage. It took Kreidler five hours of negotiating and cajoling simply to get him into the theater. In the end, he promised Wilson that they could work the issue of the poster into the show.

Wilson, who was nervous about his stage debut, was a huge hit on opening night of the weeklong run. He pulled the gee-shucks Kreidler onstage during the standing ovation. Kreidler's friend Tim Colbert said he looked "embarrassed and abashed," resembling "a sheep dog in a black sport coat." Over the next few days, Wilson soothed a sore throat from all that talking, and Sakina gave him a simple solution. "Quit telling stories, Dad."

But he had one more story to add before the end of the run. On the last night of performances, he juxtaposed the saga of the poster with a tale about a Pakistani cabdriver who refused to pick him up in New York one night. The two bits ended with him saying, "I am not a shit." Kreidler said, "You could have taken the air out of the room. It reverberated through-out the board [of directors]." In fact, members of the theater's board of trustees peppered Ott and Seattle Rep managing director Ben Moore with questions about the failure to produce a poster. Two months after the pro-duction, they wrote a letter of apology to Wilson and also requested that he delete the episode that criticized the theater in future incarnations of the play.

Of course, in this case, the poster wasn't just a poster. It was emblem-atic of all the other insults the pair had weathered during their time at Seattle Rep. Wilson could be like his first famous character, Levee in *Ma Rainey*. The trumpeter goes ballistic when another musician acciden-tally steps on his shiny new shoes. But his rage came from a deeper place, from a life of constantly being told he was second best. Wilson eventually calmed down, and the story about the poster does not appear in the pub-lished version of the play. But he never forgot the slight. A few years later, before a production of *Ma Rainey* at Seattle Rep, he walked around the lobby, pointing to posters of his plays, noting that there was nothing on the wall to commemorate his performance in *How I Learned*.

During the buildup to the production, Kreidler stayed at temporary housing that Seattle Rep uses for visiting actors. But after the final performance, he and Wilson set out for the Woodmark Hotel and Still Spa in Kirkland, Washington, an upscale waterfront resort about ten miles east of Seattle. They weren't there for a well-earned vacation: Scott Rudin put them up in adjacent suites so they could work on the *Fences* screenplay. "It was a wonderful, insane time, and I slept about two or three hours a night in the best bed I've ever slept in," Kreidler said.

Romero drove them to the hotel. "Nobody wanted to be around us doing that," Kreidler said. Wilson wanted to open up the play and show the Hill District community as it existed in 1957, the vibrant, nurturing place where he grew up. He had talked about the neighborhood in the one-man show, explaining that it was a place that could sustain "three wallpaper and paint stores," which indicates an environment where people maintain clean, comfortable homes. By this time, the Hill District was viewed as an unsafe neighborhood, but Wilson remembered a community populated by a diverse mix of ethnicities, a place where all the adults watched over the children. All the women were "aunts" entitled to praise or scold the neighborhood kids. He envisioned a film with scenes at Bella's Market, the store in front of his home at 1727 Bedford Avenue, with Bella leaning her hand on the scale as she weighed the meat. He didn't want to repeat himself. He wanted to use the film medium to show off the community in ways he couldn't do onstage. He took an epic approach to the medium and began the screenplay with Troy as a teenager fooling around with a girl down by a creek in Alabama, creating a visual image of a story Troy tells in the play. He continued the scene with Troy being whipped by his father and then running away to Pittsburgh, where he lived with other migrants in a shack under the Brady Street Bridge and stole bread to stay alive.

Kreidler was exhilarated by his new role as coauthor, and he and Wilson developed a system of working together at the resort. They wrote during the day in their separate suites, sliding papers under each other's door when they completed a scene. Wilson was burned out, and he delegated long scenes to Kreidler, who thought the new responsibility was awesome. They stayed for ten days and completed a draft that Wilson sent to Rudin, but with diminished expectations. "If you do it, you do it; if you don't, you don't," he said of the producer. He complained again that Rudin never returned his calls. His resignation was prophetic, as his screenplay never got made. When Denzel Washington finally directed and starred in the 2016 film, he reverted to the script of the play, word for word. But the experience was thrilling for Kreidler—and a relief for Wilson. During their whirlwind writing adventure, he looked at his protégé and said, "Todd, at your age, you run to the work. At my age, I am running from it."

CHAPTER EIGHTEEN

Keeping the Tradition Alive

> Black America is a tremendous triumph.
> —AUGUST WILSON

Wilson still had two plays to finish, depicting the first and last decades of the twentieth century. He had written a very rough draft of *Gem of the Ocean* when it debuted at the Goodman in April 2003, and the production, which was directed by McClinton, was lackluster. Wilson's new way of writing during rehearsal was taxing, and the play needed polishing before it opened in July at the Mark Taper Forum in Los Angeles. Set in 1904, *Gem* sets the stage for the rest of the cycle. Wilson also brings Aunt Ester, the offstage character from *Two Trains* and *Hedley*, onstage for the first and only time.

The play unfolds in Aunt Ester's Hill District house at 1839 Wylie Avenue. In *Two Trains*, her home was a mysterious place. Pilgrims showed up at her red door, and if they were lucky, she allowed them to come in, only to send them away with an inexplicable order to throw $20 in the river. She was an enigma who had the power to put people's lives back on track and heal their wounds. But in *Gem*, Aunt Ester lives in a completely ordinary home; biscuits bake in the oven and pig feet simmer on the stove. At this point, she is said to be 285 years old, and she is a no-nonsense, plain-speaking, exacting old lady who demands respect and offers unsolicited advice. She shares the house with Black Mary, her protégé and heir apparent, and Eli, her loyal guardian and gatekeeper.

The play opens when Citizen Barlow, fresh up from Alabama, knocks on her door looking for redemption. He had lied about stealing a bucket of nails and inadvertently caused an innocent man's death. The accused man jumped in the river and drowned, rather than be arrested and tried for a crime he did not commit. He chose to "die in truth rather than to live a lie."

Aunt Ester has a suitor, a former escaped slave named Solly Two Kings. He took his name after he escaped from slavery: Two Kings stands for the biblical monarchs David and Solomon. He was a conductor on the Underground Railroad and carries a chain link from the bonds that once tied him, as well as a walking stick with sixty-two notches, each representing an enslaved person he shuttled to freedom in Canada. He plans to return to the South to rescue his sister, who is struggling in the land of Jim Crow.

The neighborhood constable is Caesar Wilks. He is Black Mary's older stepbrother, and the two have a fractured relationship. She is the eager student of Aunt Ester who aims to learn the history of her ancestors, while Caesar seems to have forgotten the past. Wilson had spent hours imagining this character, his first to break apart from the Black community and assimilate. Caesar is so obsessed with authority and alienated from his ancestry that he audaciously declares that some Black people would be better off in slavery. "It's Abraham Lincoln's fault. He ain't had no idea what he was doing. He didn't know like I know." He then blames Black people for their own struggles. "You try and give them an opportunity by giving them a job and they take it and throw it away." Wilson told Kreidler that it was a difficult character to write, but vital to his cycle.

Wilson also reintroduces Rutherford Selig, the white "People Finder" from *Joe Turner*. He appears in the first scene, delivering tinware and a load of rocks so Eli can build a wall around the house at 1839 Wylie. "I want a wall," Eli says. "See if I can keep Caesar on the other side. The way he going he gonna have everybody in jail."

In the second act, Aunt Ester gives Citizen a "soul-washing" by taking him to the mythical City of Bones. She presents him with a paper boat made from a slave bill of sale and then leads him on a mystical, metaphorical journey under the ocean, where the bones of drowned Africans create a beautiful landscape evoking memories of the Middle Passage. The scene was depicted with flashing lights at the Goodman, and despite the imagery of the words, it was abrupt and incomplete. Wilson hadn't yet found a way to meld the mystical spiritualism of the City of Bones scene with the down-home realism of the rest of the play.

Wilson had created similar otherworldly scenes in *Piano Lesson* and *Joe Turner*, most notably and triumphantly in the unforgettable scene in which Herald Loomis sees the bones walking on water. Wilson said it was his favorite moment as a playwright. After he wrote it, he said, "I thought, as an artist, right there, I'd be satisfied." But he hadn't reached that pinnacle with *Gem*, at least in the Goodman production.

So it was back to the rewrite table when he got to Los Angeles. There was one significant casting change: Phylicia Rashad of *The Cosby Show* fame stepped into the pivotal role of Aunt Ester. She replaced Greta Oglesby, an actress Wilson had seen in a production of *Piano Lesson* at Penumbra. (Wilson said of Oglesby, "I liked Aunt Ester when she didn't go all gospel.") Mordecai was the consulting producer, and the team was looking for star power when the production moved to New York. Anthony Chisholm, who had performed in *Two Trains* and *Jitney* and who was one of Wilson's favorite actors, repeated his role as Solly Two Kings. But Wilson didn't manage to make the play sing in this second outing. As in Chicago, the actors received glowing praise, but the play itself got reviews that were the equivalent of a shrug. Wilson was getting used to the critics and their tendency to end their reviews with an obvious play on words. "The skeleton of the play needs bracing before this *Gem* will be able to shine its brightest," wrote Don Shirley in the *Los Angeles Times*. A few months later, Wilson laughed about it. "When you have a title like that you're asking for trouble. I get 'Polished Gem' or 'Gem Needs Polishing,'" he said.

After the Los Angeles production, the next few months were quiet— at least by Wilson standards. In December, he traveled to Pittsburgh to accept the Heinz Award. He was one of five winners of the tenth-annual award. Funded by the Heinz Family Foundation, the awards were established by Teresa Heinz, widow of the late senator John Heinz (she married Senator John Kerry in 1995), and the prize of $250,000 was one of the largest individual prizes for artists worldwide. Wilson accepted gracefully, but he also said that he treated all awards as equal, regardless of the size of the prize or the patina of the prestige. He had won enough of them by this point. "You hang it up on a wall," he said after he had already won two Pulitzer Prizes. "None of that shit helps you write. If you have an awareness of that, you'd be scared to write." He attended the ceremony at Carnegie Music Hall on December 4, and this time he gave a warm and fuzzy speech instead of the fiery broadside he had delivered in that hall a few years earlier. (The day the award was announced, however, the topic of police brutality against Black men was in the news yet again; the page-one story in the *Pittsburgh Post-Gazette* was printed directly above a news article about a Black man in Cincinnati dying after being repeatedly clubbed by police officers.)

Wilson had invited many of his family members to the ceremony, but Romero and Azula remained in Seattle. He thanked many individually, singling out his youngest brother, Richard, as "my first critic." He also recognized Sakina, calling her his "first inspiration." He talked about his youth and his education at the Carnegie Library, but he also acknowledged his new role as an elder statesman. "I am older, wiser, back in the saddle, riding an old warhorse, searching for the fuel for all the howls and whispers and songs that I might uncover while storming the barricade," he said, thanking the foundation for an award that "empowers my search for the limitations of my art." There were those words again: "limitations of my art." He was feeling boxed in by the task he had created for himself so many years ago, and he was eager to finish so he could free up his imagination for other projects.

Wilson did not have a production scheduled until September. He spent much more time at home in Seattle, writing and hanging out at Caffe Ladro, his favorite coffee shop in his neighborhood. He liked the place because he was known as the guy who shared his cigarettes and talked for hours, not the "famous playwright." He struck up a friendship with a young filmmaker named Jamie Hook, who, in 1995, was the cofounder of the Northwest Film Forum, a film and arts center in the neighborhood. Around the time that Wilson was working on *How I Learned*, Hook was wrapping up *The Naked Proof*, an independent feature about a philosophy student attempting to complete his dissertation. He needed someone to play the narrator, a pompous German philosophy professor. On a lark, he asked Wilson, who surprisingly agreed to play the role. "He said that John Singleton once asked him to be in a movie, and there were two roles: one was a middle-aged cop and one was a theater writer. He said, 'I don't want to be the theater writer. I want to be the cop,'" Hook said. Wilson told him that he was the only director who ever asked him to play a role that wasn't a character like August Wilson.

The group spent half a day filming Wilson, who shows up in the opening scene apologizing for being late. He refused to take payment for playing the role; Hook gave him a pack of Marlboro Lights and took him out to lunch. The film won the Honorable Mention for the New American Cinema Award at the 2003 Seattle International Film Festival, but Hook ran out of money and the film was never distributed, although a trailer exists. It was Wilson's only appearance in a film; he turned all other offers down. "I always knew him as a real gracious, real low-key guy," Hood said.

Wilson owns his scene in the trailer for the film, and he was honing his skills as an actor. In March 2004, he and Kreidler attended the US Comedy Arts Festival in Aspen, where he won the Freedom of Speech Award and also performed his one-man show.

But the time off did not prepare him for the chaos that unfolded after he arrived at Boston's Huntington Theatre Company at the end of the summer for the next production of *Gem*. This was his last chance to rewrite before the play was slated to open in November at the Walter Kerr Theatre on Broadway. Sometime between Los Angeles and Boston, Wilson and McClinton had decided they needed another star, this time in the role of Solly Two Kings. Anthony Chisholm had received rave notices, and he was a "Wilson Warrior." In June, two months before the start of rehearsals, Chisholm got a call from McClinton, who invited him to return to the production, but in the much smaller role of Eli. When he protested, McClinton explained that they needed a bigger name for

Broadway. Chisholm expected to hear that someone with the wattage of Morgan Freeman or Samuel L. Jackson was stepping into his role, but McClinton said they had given the role to Delroy Lindo, who had created an unforgettable presence as the haunting Herald Loomis in *Joe Turner*. Chisholm, a seasoned veteran, was not pleased. "He ain't no household word," he said. He kept McClinton and Wilson waiting for ten days. Eventually he said yes. "Any role on Broadway in an August Wilson play is a gift from God," he said, resigning himself to learning the smaller role. The creative team also recast the role of the constable Caesar with Ruben Santiago-Hudson, who had won the Tony Award for his performance as Canewell in *Seven Guitars*.

Rehearsals started on August 10, but the atmosphere was far from harmonious. Lindo, who is commanding onstage and demanding in rehearsal, got into several arguments with McClinton. They disagreed about how to approach the role. Chisholm, a lanky man with a deep baritone and the ability to get laughs with a nod of his head, had played Solly Two Kings as a gregarious soul who immediately endears himself to the other characters—and to the audience. The character is a direct link to slavery. When he encountered Union soldiers during the Civil War, he realized that they weren't fighting for him. "I told them you get what's in it for you and I'll get what's in it for me. You get yours and I'll get mine. And we'll settle the difference later. We're still settling it." The last line said it all.

The way Chisholm remembered it, Lindo took a dark, somber approach, similar to the brooding way he had played Herald Loomis. "He was playing it all sneaky and stealthy, under the radar," said Chisholm, who claimed that he had made his peace with his lesser role. McClinton had to stop the rehearsal several times to have a long debate with Lindo, and once, he emptied the rehearsal hall and asked the other actors to wait in the greenroom while they worked it out. According to Chisholm, Lindo asked Wilson to change some of the lines, which, given Wilson's temperament and attachment to his work, did not go over well. "I said, 'Man, you don't ask the playwright to change the character to suit you. You gotta get with the character.'" Chisholm also said Lindo suggested calling Lloyd Richards, which was an insult to McClinton and echoed what Dutton had done during the *Ma Rainey* revival. Lindo, however, was not alone in thinking that Wilson's plays were weaker without Richards directing. *Hedley*, after all, had fizzled, both commercially and artistically.

Chisholm was a smoker at the time, and during every break, he stood outside the brick building on Huntington Avenue puffing on a cigarette. Wilson was back to chain-smoking, so they often convened on the sidewalk. After one run-in with Lindo, Wilson was agitated as he smoked. "I am worried, man. I am worried," he told Chisholm. "The play ain't coming together, man." The play was already booked for Broadway. Chisholm did what he could to calm his friend down. "God has a way of bringing things together," he said.

But the theater gods were not on their side. Things weren't exactly humming along by August 31, ten days before the first preview. McClinton was suddenly taken ill again and rushed to the hospital. He was ultimately diagnosed with kidney disease, and the doctors said he would be hospitalized for at least two weeks. It was clear that he would not be able to return to the production. Who could replace him this late in the process? Producer Benjamin Mordecai told Huntington managing director Michael Maso that Wilson's first choice for a replacement was the much-decorated director George C. Wolfe, who at the time was the artistic director of the New York Shakespeare Festival/Public Theater and who had won Tony Awards for his direction of *Angels in America: Millennium Approaches* and *Bring in 'da Noise, Bring in 'da Funk*. Maso knew the chances of that happening were as likely as snow in July. He suggested Kenny Leon, who had previously directed three shows at the Huntington and helmed the recent Broadway revival of *A Raisin in the Sun*, starring Phylicia Rashad and Sean Combs (aka P. Diddy). Rashad won a Tony Award for her performance as matriarch Lena Younger. Leon had played the role of Citizen Barlow in the Goodman production of *Gem* a year earlier, so he knew the play.

Mordecai convinced Wilson to go with Leon, and by a stroke of luck, the Huntington had a hole in its schedule and was able to postpone the opening for two weeks. The production was in total disarray, but Leon agreed to step in. The former director of Atlanta's Alliance Theatre, Leon had recently founded True Colors Theatre Company, and he was in

Washington, D.C., directing Langston Hughes's *Tambourines for Glory*, a show for his new theater that was set to open September 18. That production had also hit roadblocks; two actors left and Leon had to recast their roles. But the chance to direct a new Wilson play was irresistible and potentially a great career booster. Leon arranged his schedule so that he flew back and forth between the two cities, directing two plays simultaneously.

Wilson went to the hospital himself to break the news to McClinton, who was ferociously loyal to his friend of twenty-five years. "August told me to take care of myself, my health. He cried. I cried. We cried some more," McClinton said. "But I understood it and knew the importance, not only of this production, but of his entire play cycle. That's what he had to do."

Maso, who as managing director handled scheduling and contracts and also put out fires, was up front with Leon. "You have one problem," he told him. "Delroy has taken over the room." Leon was anything but a pushover. Tall and bald and strikingly handsome, he had landed on *People*'s "50 Most Beautiful People" list that year. He came in and took over, working double time. He faced the same interruptions during rehearsal as McClinton had. Lindo had become obsessed with research he needed to do for his character's limp, and the rest of the cast was getting increasingly frustrated. Leon had a private meeting with Lindo, but the tension was sucking the air out of the rehearsal space. Eventually, Leon met with Wilson and Maso and reached a decision. Lindo had to be fired.

Rehearsal was set to begin at noon, but the stage manager told the actors to come back an hour and a half later while Wilson and Leon met with Lindo. Chisholm got back to the theater a few minutes early and saw Lindo leaving the building. The actor told him, "They cut me loose, man. They cut me loose." Lindo took the news in stride. "He was a mensch about it," Maso said. Immediately after Lindo left the building, Wilson and Leon asked to speak to Chisholm privately. Of course, they asked the actor to step back into the role he had created in Chicago. Solly Two Kings was a larger, more charismatic role than Eli, a dutiful servant who blended into the furniture. Chisholm had felt let down, and he wasn't going to make this easy. "I said, 'Oh, man. I poured my whole inner self into Eli.' I went into a conversation with myself while the rest of them were holding their breath." Chisholm enjoyed this moment immensely. It seemed like it was an eternity, but it was really only a minute or two. "I said, 'All right, I will do it,' and they let out this huge sigh of relief."

Later, when the cast was ready to go into the technical rehearsal, all of the Huntington staff, the designers, and the crew sat in the audience. Chisholm was in place, ready to start, when Wilson bounded onto the stage, carrying Solly Two Kings's walking stick. "He stuck it in my chest and started crying like a baby. I am telling the God's truth. He said, 'Forgive me, man. Forgive me for taking your role.' I had to peel him off me. I said, 'Come on, man. Any role you write is a piece of fruit on the tree.'"

All was forgiven, but the cast had a new director and two weeks' grace period to get ready to open. Chisholm had to brush up on his lines, and he had a reputation for taking his time with memorization. And the role of Eli was now open, so Leon called the actor Eugene Lee, whom he had worked with in other shows. Wilson had seen Lee perform in regional theater productions of both *Fences* and *Piano Lesson*, and he approved the choice. "I was on the third hole on a golf course in California, and my cell phone rang," Lee said. Leon implored him to get to Boston to fill in at the last minute, and Lee told him that he not only wanted to join the cast for the Huntington, he wanted to continue on to Broadway. They hung up, and he continued his game. "By the time I got to the eighteenth hole, they were sending a script to my house and setting up travel," Lee said. He learned his lines on the flight to Boston and arrived the next evening, four days before the first preview.

The Huntington rose to the occasion to meet the new demands caused by the backstage drama, but the pressure was still intense. The theater also diplomatically told the press that Lindo quit the show for "creative differences." Wilson was chain-smoking Marlboro Lights, sometimes going through as many as five packs a day. He increasingly leaned on Kreidler, and while at the Huntington, he decided to promote him from assistant to dramaturge. "He said, 'You're called my assistant, and nobody has any idea what the fuck it is that you do,'" he told Kreidler. "What do you think if we call you dramaturge?" The change gave Kreidler a raise in pay, but it also gave him status. His new title was credited in the program and in published editions of the play. Kreidler had an office next to Wilson's in the Huntington's complex, and Wilson told him to put his name on the door. "We'll call ourselves the rascals," he said. Leon would pass by their offices and hear the two of them yelling back and forth, spewing out a stream of obscenities. "It was never personal, and it was fun," Kreidler said. "I could get just as worked up as he was."

The relationship between the two men had deepened, and not just because of the new title. Kreidler was a kindred spirit for Wilson, who tended to perseverate over issues large and small. Kreidler helped him blow off steam. Romero had played that role when they first became a couple, but now they had a young daughter. She had designed the costumes for *Gem*, and she was immersed in her own work. It could be emotionally draining to hear Wilson tear apart an issue for days and days. "They would be talking about the play, but then they'd go off," she said. "'Justice! Let's put an end to world tyranny!' I feel what they feel, but just not as deeply. I'm like, 'Okay, but now it's time to put Azula to bed.'"

Wilson didn't handle stress well, and this play was precious to him for many reasons, not simply because it was one step closer to the end of the cycle. It represented a critical historical moment; the characters straddled the world of slavery and freedom. At one point in the play, Solly Two Kings defines freedom: "All it mean is you got a long row to hoe and ain't got no plow. Ain't got no seed. Ain't got no mule." That line captures the essence of the play and of the time period. "The question he asks is whether it's freedom if you can't do nothing with it," Wilson said. "You're still restricted." He knew that his grandmother, Zonia Wilson, was living on a hilltop in Spear, North Carolina, in 1904. He knew that she was a haunted soul during her last years in Pittsburgh, holed up in Charley and Julia Burley's house. He only imagined what her life was like down south; he told interviewers that his mother was the child of sharecroppers, while the real history was more complicated. This play was his gift to his ancestors and to everyone who carried on their tradition. Aunt Ester, he said, "resembles any Black woman in her early seventies—someone you wouldn't look twice at if she stepped outside." And of course, she wasn't really 285 years old. "She represents any old person in the community that keeps its traditions alive. She's not mystical or magical. She can't help you find your way to redemption. You have to find it," he said. He demystifies her in *Gem* and makes it clear that she is carrying on a tradition that she wants to pass on from generation to generation. In Act 1, Scene 5, she tells Black Mary:

> I got a long memory. People say you crazy to remember. But I ain't afraid to remember. I try to remember out loud. I keep my memories alive. I feed them. I got to feed them otherwise they'd eat me up. I got memories go way back. I'm carrying them for a lot of folk. All the old-timey folks. I'm carrying their memories and I'm carrying my own. If you don't want it I got to find somebody else. I'm getting old.

Aunt Ester is passing the tradition down. In the metaphorical journey to the City of Bones, the bones are stronger than in *Joe Turner.* They aren't tragic specters, but rather the embodiment of the persistence, courage, and strength of the descendants of those who died during the Middle Passage. "What we're doing in the play is we're marking it," Wilson said. "There are hundreds of millions of bones of slaves in chains, entangled in ships. The city is part of all of our history, our experience." And it is glorious. "People look at Black American history, and they say, 'Oh, you poor people, what you were subjected to, that's such a horrendous thing. I'm sure you want to forget that.' And I say, no, no, I don't want to forget that, because it's a triumph. Black America is a tremendous triumph."

In fact, when Citizen Barlow begins his symbolic journey to the City of Bones, he hears the whispers of people who made that journey never to return. He repeats their cries. "Remember me," he says. "Remember me." Like Herald Loomis, he sees himself in their incarnation. "They all look like me. They got my face," he says.

Wilson worked out the loose ends in the plot, despite the backstage turmoil. Solly Two Kings ends up as a fugitive after he burns down the mill in protest, and Selig covers for him. The traveling peddler uses his white privilege to help Solly escape, but when they get to West Virginia, Solly wants to go back and free some people who were arrested during the riot at the mill. He turns around and heads back to Pittsburgh. Citizen, who has now become part of Aunt Ester's inner circle, explains why: "Say he didn't feel right being free and the rest of the people in bondage." Solly remains true to the pact he made with himself when he escaped slavery but returned South to rescue others on the Underground Railroad: he can't be free until everyone is free. But he doesn't make it this time. Caesar chases him down and shoots him dead. The final scene points toward the future, with Citizen picking up Solly's cane and saying, "So live." Earlier in the play, Solly recited a passage from William Cullen Bryant's poem "Thanatopsis" that begins with those words. Citizen has taken on Solly's role as a freedom fighter, just as Black Mary will carry on for Aunt Ester.

The cast and the Huntington staff understood the significance of the play and rallied around Wilson. Leon did his part to unite the troupe, ending each rehearsal with the cast and crew holding hands in a sort of prayer circle, with someone reciting a significant line of poetry, a psalm, or a line from one of Wilson's plays. "The work on this play and the work on the cycle is bigger than all of us," Leon said.

Wilson went through many a carton of Marlboro Lights to get him to September 29, the opening night. And despite all the backstage drama, the audience rose to its feet at the end, giving the play a long, enthusiastic standing ovation. It received the kind of rave reviews that Wilson had missed with *Hedley* and the previous two productions of *Gem. Boston Globe* critic Ed Siegel applauded the play's fitting and eloquent status as the anchor of the entire cycle. Wilson, he wrote, "is able to fully join the sadness and pride, hopes and horrors, ambitions and deprivations into a work that not only stands proudly on its own, but also introduces the thematic concerns of the later plays."

It seemed as if the play was on an upward trajectory, despite all the mayhem that led up to the opening. It broke box office records at the Huntington and was set to close in Boston on October 31 and head straight to New York, with previews at the Walter Kerr Theatre beginning November 4 and opening night set for November 11. But before the show even closed in Boston, Mordecai, who was the lead producer, announced that a major investor had pulled out of the $2 million production. He was scrambling to fill the gap of more than $1 million. But Wilson was not a surefire financial bet. Mordecai said that three of his plays had turned a profit in New York: *Fences*, *Piano Lesson*, and *Jitney*, with *Fences* repaying original backers ten times over. The Broadway runs ranged from seventy-two performances for *Hedley* to 525 for *Fences*. Mordecai was also producing *Brooklyn the Musical* at the same time, and that show was struggling to find an audience. With the *Gem* production in limbo, the sets had not been loaded into the theater, and the posters and signs remained stacked in storage. The day before previews were to begin, the producers canceled performances, buying two weeks to obtain more financing.

Wilson had to make a quick jaunt on November 7 to Chicago, where he was receiving the 2004 *Chicago Tribune* Literary Prize as part of the city's Humanities Festival. In lieu of a speech, he performed an excerpt from *How I Learned* and then immediately got on a flight to San Francisco. There, he met with an unlikely angel: Carole Shorenstein Hays, the real estate heiress and producer he had sparred with during the run-up to *Fences*. All was forgiven, though, when she put up the money necessary to open *Gem*. "I am deeply passionate about this beautiful play by one of America's preeminent playwrights," Hays said in a statement. "Our last project together, *Fences*, remains one of the high points of my producing career." Mordecai bowed out, and Hays and Jujamcyn Theaters became the lead producers. Various vendors and creative personnel made financial concessions in order for the show to move forward. "Everyone is making concessions: August will, we will at the theater, everyone will," Rocco Landesman, president of Jujamcyn, said of the deal.

The mad dash for funds was a major embarrassment for many in the theater industry. Wilson, after all, was a preeminent playwright, and the show had a bona fide star in Rashad, who had just won a Tony Award. *Gem* was one of the only new plays set to open on Broadway that year, and the fact that the production struggled to get off the ground was another sign that serious drama was floundering on Broadway. Landesman and others had gone into full throttle to locate funds before Hays agreed to put up nearly $1 million. "The people who produce plays do it because there's something in the play that speaks to them, but the risk-reward is getting worse and worse," Landesman said. "It is just not a hospitable world out there for new work."

Gem finally opened on December 6, and the reviews were glowing. While noting that the characters were not as fully fleshed out as in Wilson's previous plays, Ben Brantley of the *New York Times* described the play as "a touchstone for everything else he has written," an appropriate beginning to the ambitious cycle. "It is a swelling overture of things to come, a battle hymn for an inchoate republic of African-Americans just beginning to discover the price of freedom." Linda Winer of *Newsday* described it as "gloriously humane and hallucinatory," and Clive Barnes in the *New York Post* hailed it as "surely one of the best-acted plays in New York." There were some quibbles, but Wilson was celebrated once again.

The atmosphere at the opening-night party was joyous; given all they had been through, the cast and the design team deserved to raise a toast—or to take off their shoes and dance. But Wilson was like a human pressure cooker, and the long, harrowing buildup to the opening curtain had taken its toll. He hated being the center of attention, and his anxiety rose with the responsibility of making sure his siblings and relatives were taken care of and his friends had a place to stay. The cameras! The reporters! The benefactors! The bright lights! The speeches! He smiled dutifully and provided witty quotes, but at the end of the night, he was spent. Jacqui Shoholm, his friend from St. Paul, watched him as he went to retrieve his coat. The clerk said something she couldn't hear, and Wilson lashed out at the fellow, no longer able to contain all the anxiety that had been building for months.

A week later, though, he was in an entirely different frame of mind. Kreidler was marrying his longtime, on-again, off-again girlfriend, Erin Annarella, and he had asked Wilson to perform the service. Kreidler had thought he had built enough time into his schedule to devote himself to the wedding arrangements, but the postponement of the *Gem* opening occupied him in the weeks before the ceremony. He ended up being absent for much of the planning, the same way Wilson was unavailable before his own wedding to Romero back in 1994. That could not have sat well with either woman.

While working on the plays, it was Kreidler's job to talk Wilson off the ledge when pressure mounted, but on December 12, it was Wilson's job to make sure his young mentee was calm and composed as he took his vows. Wilson took this role seriously. Ritual was important to him, and Kreidler was more than just a dramaturge and a sidekick. Wilson had schooled the aspiring playwright on the business, urging him not to make the same mistakes he had made and not to let anyone take advantage of him. He was critical of his writing when he needed to be, but he also supported him unconditionally.

Kreidler is not religious, but he is spiritual, and he told Wilson that he wanted a wedding that his grandmother would recognize as deeply ritualistic. "I want someone to marry us who represents the best moral and artistic standards," he told Wilson. "You are not a god, but you represent the best possible version of all the things I want to do." Wilson choked up at the request and then threw his heart into standing up for his friend. Kreidler shares Wilson's anxiety about giant social events, and in this case, Wilson eased his friend's nerves. He also adopted his deep, scholarly Dylan Thomas voice when he read the ceremony, putting on a show to make Kreidler's grandmother proud.

But Wilson had little time to celebrate. He had agreed to open *Radio Golf*, the final play in his cycle, at the Yale Repertory Theatre in April. Of course, it wasn't finished; he had written it in his head, but he had barely anything on the page. The Yale debut was another stressor; he wanted to launch the last play at the place where the whole thing began, but without Richards. It was symbolic, but rife with mixed emotions.

But then came another round of disappointing news. *Gem* had been well-received critically, but it was slow going at the box office. The actors were reaching momentum, and word of mouth was beginning to generate interest. But another production that was a critical success at the Manhattan Theatre Club needed a larger home on Broadway. That play was

Doubt, a drama about suspicions of pedophilia in the Catholic Church written by John Patrick Shanley, Wilson's buddy from the O'Neill. The producers pulled the plug on *Gem* to make way for *Doubt*. The cast was not only crushed; they were angry and bitter. The play was an important and eloquent addition to the cycle. *Gem* closed after only seventy-two performances. "We were so proud of that production, and it didn't feel right," Leon said. He tried to console the actors. "It's a business," he told them. The show had ultimately been rescued, only to close prematurely despite rave reviews. And in the end, the irony wasn't lost on anyone. The lead producer of *Doubt* was Carole Shorenstein Hays.

CHAPTER NINETEEN

Wherever You Are, I'm Here

I have strived to live it all seamless—art and life together,
inseparable and indistinguishable.

—AUGUST WILSON

One unseasonably warm day in Seattle, with the sun shining in late January 2005, Wilson was settled in at Caffe Ladro, perched under an awning at his regular outdoor table. He liked to tell visitors that the café was just a mile down the street from where martial artists Bruce and Brandon Lee are buried in Lake View Cemetery. When he first moved to the Capitol Hill neighborhood, he had looked for a place where he felt comfortable, a no-frills location like the Café Edison in New York or Ann's Cafeteria in Boston. Caffe Ladro was low-key, and he was a fixture there when he was in town. The baristas knew him so well they gave him free coffee, and he always left a generous tip. One employee, who happened to be good with fixing things, went over to Wilson's house one day to fix the jukebox in the living room. The jukebox was from the set of *Two Trains*, and it needed a tune-up.

Wilson was home this winter for an uncharacteristic stretch of time. *Gem* was about to close on Broadway, and he, like the members of the cast, was emotionally exhausted from the experience. The last play in the cycle, *Radio Golf*, was set to open at the Yale Repertory Theatre in April, and he had barely written a single scene. "I'm working on it" was all he would say when asked about his progress. The opening coincided with his sixtieth birthday, another milestone. But to the baristas and customers at the café, he was just the guy with the whispery voice who told great stories of bygone eras. He was rarely alone in this alfresco setting. Al Frank, the former Peace Corps volunteer who used to own a bookstore in the neighborhood, sometimes stopped by for a cup of coffee and left four hours later. Mark, a raggedy crack addict who camped out under an awning across the street, often sidled over to bum a few cigarettes.

But Wilson was preoccupied. "Man, where is Gunars?" he asked rhetorically. His friend Gunars Berzins, a self-described "crazy Latvian," had died a few days earlier at age seventy-four. "He was nutty as a fruitcake and he was the first person to say he was crazy," Wilson said. "He might come down the street singing an aria. 'My cat is God! Goering! You Bushwhacker!'" Berzins told everyone who would listen that he had been forced to participate in the Hitler Youth in Nazi Germany and that he was sexually abused during World War II, leaving him emotionally wounded. The man didn't have any boundaries. He talked about visiting prostitutes, providing way too much lecherous information. Most of the regulars at Caffe Ladro cringed and looked busy on their phones when he ambled down the street singing, but Wilson accepted him into his inner circle and nicknamed him General Berzinsky. He closely followed his quirky friend's misadventures, while others simply tried to ignore him. He sympathized when Berzins lost his apartment over a "battle about the damn cat." Berzins was obsessed with watches and wore six of them on his arm; Wilson had just bought him a book about timepieces, but Berzins died before Wilson was able to give it to him. He talked about Berzins at home; when he was in New York for the opening of *Gem*, Azula had asked if he had written to his friend.

If Berzins had been Black and walked the streets of the Hill District, he could have been a character in a Wilson play, one of the wounded yet wise fixtures whose ravings are laced with searing truth. He could have been Hambone in *Two Trains* or Gabriel in *Fences*. Wilson saw the comparison as a compliment to Hambone, Gabriel, and Gunars alike. "Take Hambone," he said. "He's crazy and all, but he refused to compromise. That's admirable. Look at Gabriel. He thinks he's the Angel Gabriel, but he's self-sufficient. He works hard. And Gunars: he understood more things about life than all of those guys put together." Wilson saw the dignity in people who were invisible to others. One day, he was walking in the Capitol Hill neighborhood with Sakina, and he gave a few dollars to a homeless man, who happened to be Black. He didn't just shell out the cash and hurry away. He stopped, looked him straight in the eye, and said, "Walk with your head up. You walk with a line of kings."

Wilson extended the same compassion to Berzins, and he mourned his friend's death in a way one would expect a person to grieve for a family member. Al Frank couldn't abide the old street wanderer, and the baristas at Caffe Ladro thought he was a nuisance. But he stirred something in Wilson's soul at this particular point in his life. "I saw a lot of myself in Gunars," he said. The similarity wasn't readily apparent, but to start, they shared the same birthday, April 27. Berzins would have been seventy-five the day Wilson turned sixty. "He was a passionate man. He was full of life. Whatever his circumstances were, he was living his life. He was singing his songs. Oh, man, a little part of my world has slipped away."

Of course, that world involved writing his final play, and Berzins had been known to tease Wilson about his chosen profession. He would walk down the street, sometimes wearing a Big Bird shirt and a blue wig, waving his arms and exclaiming, "August Wilson! You! You are the best playwright in the neighborhood!" Wilson planned to go to Berzins's memorial service that afternoon.

This wasn't unusual for him. "He has a heart for the man on the corner," Romero said. "He understands their wisdom through their hardships." She was the first to say that she did not share his patience nor his compassion. She wasn't going anywhere near the memorial service. She was practical and had a child to care for and things to accomplish that afternoon. But Berzins's death had gotten Wilson thinking, hard, about his legacy and about what this thing called life really meant. "You stick around long enough, and you look up and it's twenty years later." He had suddenly realized that his work was being taught in schools and that an entire generation of young theater artists had grown up with his plays. "That's what gets me, man. I meet these guys, and they're like twenty-nine years old. Ever since they were aware of theater, I was part of their fabric. I just discovered that, and it surprised me."

He was in a somber, contemplative mood when he took a taxi to the Providence Vincent House, a subsidized residence for needy elderly, for Berzins's memorial. Wilson treated the death of his friend with the seriousness others might reserve for a prophet or a prince. Several employees from Caffe Ladro were in attendance, and other residents of the senior housing center gathered in an antiseptic common room for the service. A few came for the coffee, carrots, and crackers laid out on a bare table. An uncomfortable silence fell over the room when it came time to praise the departed. Wilson, wearing a tweed coat and his signature cap, shifted in his chair and wiped his face with his handkerchief. "Mongolian horses," he said quietly. He then recounted one of his friend's more hallucinogenic tales, a story that began with the decreasing population of Mongolian horses and ended with an apocalyptic vision of drought, famine, and the destruction of the planet. Several people nodded. They'd heard the story before. After the service, Wilson checked in with the Providence Vincent House staff to make sure that Berzins didn't have any debts. His friend was solvent.

Wilson had other things he was supposed to be doing, but he never missed a funeral. He was also spending quite a bit of time reading biography, including one about his beloved Jorge Luis Borges and a new tome about abstract expressionist Willem de Kooning. "I always hated biography, but I'm just old enough now that it's like, let me find out what a life can be."

Life, at this particular moment, was about hanging out at the café and being home, even if Yale Rep was anxiously awaiting the new script. It was hard to cast, produce, and publicize a play with nothing but a brief plot summary. But he was weary. Wilson had dedicated *Gem* to his daughters, ending with the words "May the circle be unbroken." He was aware that he missed a lot of his first daughter's early years. He had a second chance, and he didn't want to miss Azula's childhood, which was slipping away fast. He wanted to be a better parent the second time around, but he wasn't necessarily doing the greatest job. "I don't get the love from him that all of me would like," Romero told the *New Yorker*. "I don't have a partner through the little things in life." She went on. "In his mind, he's a great father, a great man, a great husband. One time, I was saying to Azula, when she was going to sleep, 'I'm going to teach you how to choose a husband for yourself.' And then August said, 'Just like your daddy.' And I was thinking to myself, 'No!'" Sakina had learned that lesson early on: art comes first, family second.

However, there was definitely more "family" structure in the Seattle household. Romero made sure of it. They held regular "family meetings" to talk about everything from racist graffiti Azula had seen at the local park to where to store the shoes. Wilson told stories about his young daughter the same way he regaled listeners with anecdotes about his days on the streets of the Hill. Azula was a stickler for rules—and for changing them. When the family decided where to go out to eat, they agreed that the majority rules on the choice of restaurant. But when Azula was outvoted, she decided that everyone should take a turn. Wilson once told her she cried too much, and she got right back at him. "You are not in my body, and you don't know how I feel," she said. "I think I should be allowed to cry." He agreed. Her argument made sense.

He admired her tenacity—in part because it reminded him of his mother, who was pragmatic and down-to-earth. He once told his mother that he had a toothache, looking for sympathy. Her response was not "Oh, you poor baby," but "Damn fool, go to the dentist." Azula seemed to have inherited Daisy's practicality and was equally uncompromising when it came to matters of principle. A few days before Berzins's funeral, Wilson had taken away his daughter's scooter because she crashed it while riding in the house. She insisted it wasn't her fault because she didn't do it on purpose. The two remained in a standoff for days. She refused to apologize and ask for her toy back, and he refused to give it to her until she did. She thought she was right and wouldn't budge, which also reminded him of his mother—and himself. Romero saw the same characteristics in both

of them. "It's not easy having two stubborn people in the house," she said.
"They butt heads so much."

He clearly delighted in this miniature version of himself, and he did
not talk down to her. When she was born, he started a library for her
and wanted to inspire her to love reading, the way Daisy inspired him.
The collection included the usual children's books, but the shelves also
included titles like *Hitler's Willing Executioners* and an autographed copy
of *The Good War*, a gift from its author, Studs Terkel. When his friend
the novelist Oscar Hijuelos gave him a copy of one of his novels, he asked
him to sign it for Azula. "Sign your novel for me, but make it out to Azula.
It's for her library," he told Hijuelos. (The two often met at the novelist's
Manhattan apartment to watch boxing matches, sometimes joined by an
eclectic group that included musician Lou Reed and an HVAC technician
from New York University.)

One night, he was working on the play in the basement in Seattle
when Azula, seven at the time, walked into his lair and asked him what he
was writing. He read her some lines and she asked what it was called. He
hadn't named the play yet, so she suggested that he call it *The Secrets of the
Radio Sisters*. He mulled that over and answered that there were no "radio
sisters" in the play, but he could compromise and call it *Radio Golf*. Azula
was tickled, and so was Kreidler. He gave Wilson a package of golf balls as
a gift, even though Wilson didn't play the game.

While he certainly liked to regale listeners with cute Azula stories,
there is no question that he was an artist first, a father second. He was also
stressed and less carefree than he had been when he first showed up as the
neophyte at the O'Neill. His work weighed heavily on him. He refused to
take a vacation or travel, unless it involved work. He turned down invita-
tions to parties and leisurely events, unless his family forced him to attend.
He was burdened by the monumental significance of writing that last play,
completing the cycle, keeping his word to himself and to the world. He
grew closer and closer to his protégé, Kreidler, because the younger man
understood the compulsion to put work first. "Our personal relationships
were secondary," Kreidler said. "We didn't kill anyone, but we had lost
friendships, had broken engagements, strained family relationships. But

August demonstrated his love in his own way. He didn't abandon his family, but his time and attention were absorbed by work."

It didn't always seem as if he was working, though. Acquaintances in Seattle often saw Wilson having one of his open, rolling conversations at the café or sitting down at Coastal Kitchen in the middle of the afternoon to eat the restaurant's popular all-day breakfast. "When does he do his writing?" they asked Romero. There was no clear answer. He might take a long bath or read the newspaper for hours. When he read a news story that angered him, it could dominate his attention for hours, or even days. That January, he was obsessed with the aftermath of the earthquake and tsunami that had rocked Indonesia in December, killing more than 220,000 people and leaving thousands of children without parents. There was a movement to adopt those orphans, which frustrated Wilson. "I don't understand that! There were plenty of orphans here before that. People are starving, man," he said. Al Frank was an easy sounding board for these random bursts of indignation, but Kreidler kept him going for even longer when he was around. The subject of their outrage didn't even have to be recent: Wilson once toured the Reynolds Mansion on Sapelo Island in Georgia, and he angrily left the tour when he was told he was not allowed to smoke in the house. "The man made his money on cigarettes," he said years later. "You can't smoke in R. J. Reynolds's house? I put up my little protest and left the building."

Their wives did not share this compulsion to tear apart a single issue. And it was exhausting. "Sometimes I want a snack in the middle of the night and I just tiptoe into the kitchen," Romero said. "If he hears me, he comes running up. He's a talker and can engage you for hours. I care, but not as much as he does."

He could go on for hours about the state of American theater, which he didn't think had improved since he first started out. Or he could engage in a debate about African American assimilation. He had long been convinced that the Great Migration had been a mistake, despite the fact his mother and grandmother had moved out of poverty in Spear, North Carolina, to a more stable and comfortable life in Pittsburgh. He advocated for Blacks to move back to the South, where they would be able to elect African American senators and representatives, thus gaining greater power in Congress. But he, himself, was not budging from Seattle. "People say, 'Why ain't you down there?'" he readily admitted. "I'm a follower. I'm not gonna be the first person moving there."

Wilson was passionate about his beliefs, but to some extent, they were a diversion from the work. He could appear relaxed holding court at his alfresco table, but the stress of the final deadline was eating at him. Romero noticed that all the joy seemed to have been sucked out of the process of writing, and he took any opportunity to avoid the task. And he was suddenly fascinated with painting. He had watched *The Mystery of Picasso*, a 1956 French documentary in which the great Spanish painter turned blank canvases into art for the camera. Wilson was intrigued by the process. He had always drawn, scribbling faces and doodles on his omnipresent notepad. He had recently gotten more serious about it. Sometimes he played around with a computer program that allows the user to paint on top of existing photographs. Romero, a Yale School of Drama–trained visual artist and designer, was impressed with his innate ability. "He does wonderful drawings," she said. "His color sense is marvelous. I think he's really good."

But the painting was yet another diversion. He had never pushed a deadline this close before, and Romero could see the toll the stress was taking on his health. She couldn't convince him to go to the doctor; the tasks most people take for granted were careful negotiations with Wilson. He confided that he would feel relieved when the last play was done, but he still had to sit down and do it. He would retreat into his basement lair late in the evening, and sometimes he emerged with a line or two of dialogue, but sometimes he sat and drew pictures. "I worked real hard and thought I had all this material. I printed it up, and I was so discouraged. It was four pages. Somehow, I thought it should have been forty pages! Or seventeen pages! That took two months to write," he said.

Romero likened his process to a warrior preparing for battle, yet in Wilson's case, he was waging the war with himself. Every play took something out of him. He had boxed himself into a corner with the two productions so close together. He was losing weight, and he was more somber than usual. He didn't look healthy, but some of those around him sensed that his ailments were due to the pressure. "I'm concerned for him, as someone who wants him to last," Romero said. "There's a piece of him that goes with every play. For him, life is art, and he gives everything for it."

Wilson wanted nothing more than to finish the cycle and move on to something new. He had an idea for a comedy that had nothing to do with the cycle, and he couldn't help but laugh when he talked about it. He was tentatively calling it *The Coffin Maker Play*, and he had already drafted a sketch of the plot in his mind. It was about a war between the coffin makers and the undertakers, with appearances by Death, Queen Victoria, the Platters, Fidel Castro, and a magic radio.

And there was also that novel that he had discussed with Charles Johnson. His outline was cryptic. "He said it was about a man who comes into town and goes up to a person and says, 'I am here for the story.' The reply is 'The story is not yet. The story is later,'" Johnson said. Wilson was nervous about switching genres; he had spent the last two and a half decades producing his cycle of interrelated plays, and he struggled with the idea of facing a new medium. He could be tough on self-proclaimed writers who simply talked and talked about their art, but never actually did it. He once agreed to read a "novel" written by a cabdriver he met in Seattle. From the way the guy talked about it, Wilson had been expecting something along the lines of *War and Peace*, but when the man delivered his manuscript, it was a page and a half of scribbling. Wilson yelled at the cabdriver and told him to leave him alone until he actually did the work.

Johnson was more gentle with his friend, but only to a point. Wilson told him repeatedly that he needed guidance to write a novel because he felt as if he were "crossing an ocean without a compass" when he contemplated the task. This topic came up frequently during the pair's monthly dinners, and finally an exasperated Johnson said, "Get a compass!"

He was coming to the end of an era, and the prospect was both terrifying and exhilarating. In more ways than one, he was adrift, not unlike that piano player from Pittsburgh who banged his head on the keyboard, agonizing at what he called "the limitation of the instrument." After all these years, perhaps Wilson had discovered the boundaries of his chosen art form, which was why he was exploring other genres instead of sitting down and grinding out the last play. His passion for painting was more than just an excuse. He had read an article citing a statistic that visual artists live longer than writers, and that simple statement stuck like superglue in his capacious mind. Romare Bearden was a collagist, and he was able to communicate through color and form, and Wilson had always been intrigued by the medium. He wasn't just playing around: he was looking for another instrument to fuel his insatiable passion for self-expression. "See, visual artists live long, and writers die young," he said. "I'm moving over to painting. You can't get me yet! Go buy me some paint!"

Wilson took the time in late February to travel to Kansas City, Missouri, to see the Kansas City Rep's production of *Two Trains*. The theater was now run by Peter Altman, his old friend from Boston's Huntington Theatre, and the production was directed by Lou Bellamy, the founder and artistic director of Penumbra in St. Paul. Several of the Penumbra actors were in the production. James A. Williams (known familiarly as "Jay Dub") was playing the restaurant owner Memphis, and James Craven was cast as Hambone, the man whose singular desire in life is to get the ham he is owed for a job well done. Most actors played Hambone as certifiably insane, unstrung, out of control, and worthy of pity. But Craven took a different approach. He did not want to play the role as a "mumbling, head-down, idiot savant," but rather as a strong man with a singular purpose: to receive the restitution he deserved. "I said that if he is a metaphor for our hopes and dreams, he shouldn't be dragging around," Craven said. "I went onstage, eyes bright, chest up, announcing to the world that I was going to get my ham."

Bellamy and the actors knew that Wilson had a history of exploding when directors imposed interpretations he did not like, so they made sure that Wilson saw the play late in the run, before he could demand changes. He liked what he saw and told Bellamy that it was "amazing." But he didn't like that Craven had put his personal stamp on the role behind his back.

He asked Williams to join the cast of *Radio Golf* at Yale. He didn't say a word to Craven about his performance.

But he did intimate that something was wrong when the group from St. Paul met for dinner at Genghis Khan, a Mongolian barbecue restaurant in Kansas City. He looked thin and drawn, and his tweed coat hung loose on his narrow shoulders. The men stood around on the corner "telling lies," to use their expression, and Wilson lit a cigarette before they went in to eat. He indicated that he wasn't feeling his best, and Craven intuited that something was seriously wrong. But that was the end of it. That conversation began and ended abruptly on the street corner, and the subject was changed.

Shortly after his trip to Kansas City, Wilson met Kreidler in New Haven, where rehearsals were set to begin for *Radio Golf.* The script had not progressed much further than the scanty draft he had compiled back in Seattle. Wilson could talk the actors through the plot, even if it wasn't clear on the page. Set in 1997, *Radio Golf* is about an ambitious African American real estate developer named Harmond Wilks, who aims to use a federal grant for minority-run businesses to build an upscale mixed-use development in the Hill District. The retail section will be anchored by upmarket establishments like Starbucks and Whole Foods, which are known for shutting down the kind of mom-and-pop stores and restaurants that Wilson frequented in his youth. Harmond is also running for mayor of Pittsburgh, and if he wins, he will become the first Black mayor in the city's history. His friend and business partner, Roosevelt Hicks, was recently promoted to vice president of Mellon Bank, and he joins forces with an offstage entrepreneur, who uses him as the front man to buy a radio station. The entrepreneur, who is white, needs a Black partner to qualify for funding offered to minority businesses. Here as in his other plays, white people with financial clout and power are present, yet unseen. Roosevelt is passionate about golf—the quintessential white man's game—and he recalls feeling "free, truly free" the first time he picked up a club.

Wilson conceived the play at the same time he was finishing *Gem*, and he decided to link characters in the two plays that bookend his cycle.

He had put off the 1990s play for last, because he knew he was going to create upper-middle-class Black characters who had achieved financial success but had forgotten their past. This kind of linkage was confusing and convoluted when he tried it with *Seven Guitars* and *King Hedley*, but he wanted to give it another try, especially since *Gem* was still fresh in his mind. Harmond is the grandson of Caesar Wilks, the Black constable from *Gem* who has assimilated into white culture and government. In order to build his development, Harmond must tear down Aunt Ester's home at 1839 Wylie Avenue. She died twelve years earlier in *King Hedley*, and Roosevelt dismisses her sacred home as a "raggedy-ass, rodent-infested, unfit-for-human-habitation eyesore."

An old, weathered resident of the Hill District named Elder Joseph Barlow insists that he owns the house and sets out to paint it, despite the fact that the demolition is already scheduled. Old Joe, as he is called, is the son of Citizen Barlow and Black Mary from *Gem*. Black Mary was Aunt Ester's protégé and successor, the link to the history that is about to be destroyed by the gentrification of the neighborhood. She was also Caesar Wilks's younger sister, so Harmond and Old Joe are first cousins once removed, but they are unaware of their kinship.

The development project can't start until the city declares the area to be officially blighted, and when the ruling occurs, the two business partners do a dance of joy, chanting, "Blight! Blight! The gang's all here!" It's a far cry from the jubilant juba the characters danced in *Joe Turner*, which connects the characters to Africa; the entrepreneurs sing Tin Pan Alley tunes like Irving Berlin's "Blue Skies," which is nothing like the blues from Wilson's earlier plays. Wilson was clear about his intention: his well-heeled characters were so busy assimilating and climbing the ladder that they forgot not only their history, but also their lost song. The blood's memory had stopped flowing.

Wilson also brings back the character of Sterling Johnson from *Two Trains*. In 1969, he was an optimistic activist fresh out of jail, "the new Black man" who represented change. In *Radio Golf*, he is an independent contractor and handyman who can see through the political machinations that are driven by money and greed, not community spirit or respect for the past. He makes an impression on Harmond, who does have a conscience and wants to do the right thing—while making a fortune at the same time. His wife, Mame, runs his public relations campaign for mayor, and he ignores her advice when she asks him to delete a reference to police violence in an op-ed that is set to run in the *Pittsburgh Post-Gazette*. "An innocent man gets shot by the police and the officer gets away with it and he gets a promotion?" he says, telling his wife, "Yeah, I'm angry! Aren't you?"

But by the time the play got into rehearsal, most of the plot existed solely in Wilson's mind. And the debut at Yale Rep was loaded with significance for Wilson. It was not just the last play in the cycle. Wilson hadn't premiered a play at Yale since *Two Trains* in 1990. He also didn't have a director he knew and trusted. McClinton was still ailing back in St. Paul, and Leon was directing *Margaret Garner*, an opera composed by Richard Danielpour with a libretto by Nobel laureate Toni Morrison, which was set to premiere in May at the Detroit Opera House. When Wilson heard about Leon's scheduling conflict, he said, "Damn, you gotta do Toni Morrison." He had once distributed copies of Morrison's Nobel Prize acceptance speech to friends at the O'Neill, and this particular opera was loosely based on the story of the escaped slave Margaret Garner, whom Morrison had used as the inspiration for her 1987 masterpiece, *Beloved*.

The job ultimately went to Timothy Douglas, a director who had graduated from the Yale School of Drama. He was the associate director of the Actors Theatre of Louisville, where he had met Wilson while he was directing *Piano Lesson*. Douglas viewed the assignment as "a rite of passage, both personally and professionally," but he didn't have much to go on during the early stages of production. He didn't even have a script at his first design budget meeting.

On the first day of rehearsals, Wilson let Douglas explain the plot, and he muddled through, doing the best he could. Wilson didn't add much, but he told Douglas, "You're doing great." He dusted off the poem he had written in 1985, when Yale produced *Fences*, and he read it to the cast. (It's the same poem he also resurrected at the ceremony in St. Paul years earlier. It came in handy.) The poem, called "Home," ends with an expression of gratitude and humility: Wilson refers to his work as a "bloodless execution of the alphabet."

For Douglas, the rehearsal process was not exactly a bloodless execution, but it was frustrating. Wilson was rewriting during rehearsals, and he handed Douglas a new scene every day. "They veered off far enough. I didn't know where it was going," Douglas said. He didn't even know how the story would end, so he told the actors to "treat each scene as a one-act play." That is especially difficult, because actors can't build a character without a sense of motivation and destiny. Wilson wasn't certain himself precisely what he wanted the characters to be. When costume designer Susan Hilferty delivered sketches, he said, "Oh, this is what they look like!"

Wilson clearly wasn't comfortable writing middle-class characters because, in his heart, he was still a penniless poet who related more to the Gunars Berzinses of the world than he did to the golfers in his play. "For me, *Radio Golf* is basically about the Black middle class, and what I see as their failure to return the sophistication and expertise and resources they have gained to the communities and the people they belong to," he said. "They've forgotten who they are."

Wilson had said goodbye to poverty a long time ago. He lived a comfortable life and easily could have retreated quietly into a life of leisure. He had the elegant home and the means of a successful man, but he wasn't comfortable with what those accoutrements symbolized. He was poised and professional while doing televised interviews, looking and sounding like a diplomat or a professor, but he was more at home among the residents of places like the Providence Vincent House in Seattle. He code-switched easily from the King's English to the dialect he heard growing up on the Hill. He didn't know how to write poetic dialogue for his characters in *Radio Golf*, partly because he rejected their values. They had lost touch with their ancestors, and as such, it was hard to put words into their mouths.

While the play was still in its inchoate state, he had been infuriated by the caustic comments of America's most famous upper-middle-class Black father, Bill Cosby, who had played the cuddly Dr. Cliff Huxtable on his eponymous television sitcom. At the NAACP *Brown v. Board of Education* fiftieth-anniversary commemoration in 2004, Cosby gave a speech castigating Black youth and their parents without once mentioning the circumstances in which they lived. Among other things, he took Black parents to task for spending hundreds of dollars for sneakers while refusing to spend $250 for Hooked on Phonics. Cosby criticized Black youth for using controversial language, "stealing Coca Cola," and "getting shot in the back of the head over a piece of pound cake." Their parents, he said, were even worse for failing to give their children normal names like Bill. "The lower-economic people," Cosby said, "are not holding up their end in this deal." He wondered why even more Black people were not incarcerated. "God is tired of you," he said in what became known as "The Pound Cake Speech."

Wilson put similar ideas into the mouth of his character Roosevelt Hicks, and he also took on Cosby publicly. In an interview with *Time* magazine that coincided with the opening of *Radio Golf*, he dismissed the comedian, who would later experience a host of legal problems. "A billionaire attacking poor people for being poor," Wilson said. "Bill Cosby is a clown. What do you expect? I thought it was unfair of him."

Cosby's rant, which was widely reported and debated, was clearly on Wilson's mind as he wrote and rewrote. But Wilson wasn't working round the clock on the play, even as it inched closer to the opening, with previews starting on April 22 and the formal opening set for April 29, two days after his sixtieth birthday. He and Kreidler took a quick two-day trip to Millersville University in Lancaster, Pennsylvania, to speak and perform as part of the small school's 150th anniversary. He granted interviews, sat in on an African American literature class, and performed excerpts from his one-man show. He spent time connecting with students and announced that he planned to retire in March 2006. "I'm going home," he said. "I have a seven-year-old. I am going home to raise my kid and organize my CDs." While the quote is endearing, Kreidler maintains that Wilson had no intention of retiring. He couldn't. His work was his life.

But what really needed to be organized at that point was his play. The cast was used to the way Wilson worked, and he and Kreidler often huddled together during rehearsal, conspiring about ways to clarify the script. Wilson had been uneasy about returning to Yale Rep, as he hadn't been there since he and Richards parted ways. But James Bundy, Yale Rep's artistic director, welcomed him back enthusiastically. And on the verge of his sixtieth birthday, Wilson was nostalgic. That is why he read his poem "Home" to the cast and crew. "I had this baseball analogy," he said of the poem. "I've gone to first base, second base, third base, and now I've made it back here."

But the play itself wasn't ready for the Major Leagues. Wilson was worried on opening night, but the concern was partly for Mordecai, his friend and producing partner. Mordecai had been diagnosed with cancer, and he wasn't doing well. Wilson was fiercely loyal to the producer, even after the fiasco with the funding for *Gem*. Mordecai was the only person who attended every single opening of Wilson's plays—Wilson noted that even his second and third wives occasionally had to miss an opening night, but Mordecai was always there. He went to visit his friend at four o'clock on the afternoon of the opening, and Mordecai promised him that he would be there to celebrate the last play. It turned out that he was too sick to attend. Wilson had supported Mordecai during an earlier illness, when he was hospitalized with meningitis. "He showed up at the hospital," Sherry Mordecai, the producer's wife, said. "He said, 'I knew I had to be here.'"

But the opening went on without Mordecai, and it was far from triumphant. The play simply wasn't done, and not only was the dialogue stilted, the plot was convoluted. That was not particularly unusual for the first production of a Wilson play, but in the past, the plays were overwritten and had to be cut by at least an hour, often more. This play was two hours and twenty-five minutes long, and it was more like a series of sketches than a play.

By this point in his career, critics were so wowed by Wilson's grand, noble ambition that he was immune to nasty reviews written in acid ink, the kind that shook a playwright's confidence. While the notices were mostly negative, all the critics applauded Wilson's unprecedented effort to complete the ten-play cycle. (Only Eugene O'Neill attempted such a lofty project, mapping out an eleven-play series called *A Tale of Self-Possessors*

Dispossessed; only two of those plays survive, *A Touch of the Poet* and *More Stately Mansions*. O'Neill destroyed fragments of unfinished plays in the series before his death in 1953.) The critics also gushed about how appropriate it was that Wilson had come "home" to Yale, while gently noting that the play itself was far from complete.

The problems were obvious. In writing about the middle class, Wilson abandoned the poetic language that had become his signature. Roosevelt, Harmond, and his wife, Mame, spoke as if they were ordering sushi or shopping at Pottery Barn. The play, at its heart, probes the perils of assimilating versus the nobility of maintaining—and cherishing—the link to the past. This was not a new idea for Wilson: that's what Aunt Ester is all about, and he had expressed it in interview after interview, most notably when he pushed back against Bill Moyers in 1988. Nevertheless, the characters were underdeveloped, and the plot—with a mayoral election, a major urban development, and the radio station—was convoluted. Wilson was telegraphing the ideas he had expressed while castigating Bill Cosby, rather than making the characters embody them. The most potent image in the play took place offstage, with Elder Joseph Barlow tenaciously continuing to paint Aunt Ester's house as the bulldozers approach.

Wilson knew he had to rewrite, and the clock was ticking. But he suffered another blow on May 8. Benjamin Mordecai died at age sixty, just nine days after *Radio Golf*'s official opening at Yale, where he was still associate dean and chair of the Yale School of Drama's department of theater management. Wilson and Mordecai had made a pact with each other. Once *Radio Golf* premiered, the two men and their families were going to take a cruise down the Nile to celebrate their sixtieth birthdays and the completion of the cycle. Wilson had invited Kreidler and his wife; the trip was his wedding gift to the couple.

Wilson was bereft. He would dedicate the published version of *Radio Golf* to him: "To Benjamin Mordecai, who was there from the beginning—good company, a friend, a brother." Wilson was not feeling that great himself. When he embraced Sherry Mordecai, the producer's widow, after his friend's death, she noticed that he looked drawn and tired. He held her close and told her, "I will be next." He contemplated death in his plays, and he had lost so many of his friends in recent years. It's no accident that he was thinking about mortality when he dedicated the published version of *Hedley* to his lifelong friends, the Pittsburgh poets. "For Rob Penny and Nicholas Flournoy—fallen oaks of the Centre Avenue tradition. And for Chawley P. Williams—don't you leave me here by myself."

Wilson now had a single purpose: finish the play. On May 10, the ill-fated *Gem* received five Tony nominations, including Best Play. Phylicia Rashad got the nod for Best Leading Actress, and Romero was nominated for her costume designs. Wilson was feeling less than sanguine about Broadway, which was increasingly dominated by musicals. The commercial theater, he thought, was about one thing: the bottom line. "It's not a conspiracy or anything," he said shortly after *Gem* closed. "They gotta make some money. That's the bottom line. To think otherwise is to delude yourself. That's what's happened in the commercial theater. With some exceptions, it's about that." In his view, drama didn't stand a chance in the fiercely commercial environment where musicals reigned. And despite his own success, he did not think that the institution had become more open to non-white playwrights in the last two decades. "The situation, I believe, in American theater has gotten worse," he told the television interviewer Charlie Rose. "I'm not sure we should call it American theater because I don't think it is representative of America. What we basically have is a European American theater." When reminded that such Black directors as George C. Wolfe and Kenny Leon ran prominent nonprofit theaters, Wilson fired back, "Just putting a Black person in charge doesn't make that a Black theater." Rose suggested that Wilson was angry, a term that made him cringe because it evoked a stereotype. "Anger implies you're out of control," he replied. "I would call it a passionate concern."

That year, the goofy musical *Spamalot*, a laugh-a-minute adaptation of the 1975 cult film *Monty Python and the Holy Grail*, topped the Tony list with a total of fourteen nominations. Denzel Washington, who played Brutus in a production of *Julius Caesar*, was passed over for Best Leading Actor in a Play. James Earl Jones was nominated for playing a crotchety professor in a revival of *On Golden Pond*, which was loaded with irony for Wilson. He had battled with Jones during *Fences*, and he had called his Black theater summit at Dartmouth "On Golden Pond." And, in his fiery speech at the TCG conference, he had denounced such nontraditional casting as Jones playing a role immortalized by Henry Fonda in the screen adaptation. Wilson kept his feelings to himself, though, and he skipped the June 5 ceremony at Radio City Music Hall and stayed in Seattle. Romero and Sakina attended. Wilson had instructed Sakina to accept the award for Best Play, but he didn't expect to win. He told her to say, "My dad is just as shocked as all of you." But Wilson was right. He didn't win, and *Gem* was shut out that year. The award for Best Play went to *Doubt*, and its star, Cherry Jones, walked away with Best Leading Actress.

Wilson had taken to sitting on the porch at his home on East Aloha Street, and he was in constant contact with Kreidler, plotting out the *Radio Golf* rewrites before the upcoming opening in Los Angeles. Unable to ignore his ailing health, he underwent an array of medical tests, including a biopsy, at the University of Washington Medical Center. Kreidler got the call on June 13. He and his new wife were in the process of moving to Chicago, and Sakina was visiting with them at the time. Wilson had inoperable liver cancer, and the doctor had given him five months to live. "It wasn't a surprise," Kreidler said. "We were expecting bad news."

Sakina had been terrified of this day for most of her life. She was proud of him when he quit smoking for a few years, but even as a child, she could see that his lifestyle was far from healthy. She was interested in homeopathic medicine, and she worried about the rich foods he ate and all those cigarettes and cigars. "I was always afraid with my dad and his health," she said. When he was living in St. Paul with then wife Judy Oliver, his daughter tensed up every time the phone rang. "I always feared that Judy would call me to tell me he had a heart attack."

This diagnosis was just as dire, but Wilson did not wallow. He had one thing left to do, and that was to finish his play. He also never turned down the chance to praise the dead, so when *American Theatre* magazine asked him to contribute to an "In Memoriam" tribute for his friend Mordecai, he wrote a quick paean. "Now, haunted by the specter of my own death, I find solace in Ben's life, a life he lived with dignity and purpose magnified by his indomitable spirit," Wilson wrote. "There is a grace beyond matter. It is our way of knowing, and accepting, the splendor of death with its voluminous atlas. We find it when we must." His tribute would not appear until the September issue.

He did not, however, make a public announcement about his illness. Kreidler flew out to Seattle immediately. Even though he was newly married, he planned to stay as long as necessary and moved into temporary quarters on the third floor of Wilson's spacious home. Wilson gave the news to Kenny Leon, who had been picked to direct the next production of *Radio Golf.* Director Timothy Douglas had been devastated when he was told he would not continue with the production, but he had been a placeholder all along. Leon was told the diagnosis on a need-to-know basis, one of only a few people who were let in on the news. Wilson sent a handwritten letter to his friend Charles Johnson, informing him that he was using the time he had left to finish his play. He referred to Eugene O'Neill, who had never finished his cycle. He would not end up the same way. He shared the dream he once had of retiring quietly from the theater with a big stack of books, playing with his daughter, writing that novel, staying away from reporters, and living in peace.

As late spring turned to summer, Wilson surrounded himself with only a few close confidants. Sakina moved into the house to help care for her father's medical and personal needs. Wilson and Kreidler got to work on the play. For Kreidler, the role of dramaturge was a blessing. If he focused on the play, he wouldn't have to confront the inevitable. Wilson had to inform the Mark Taper Forum about the situation, so he confided in Gordon Davidson, the longtime artistic director who was about to retire and had chosen to end his tenure with Wilson's last play. Davidson then told Jack Viertel, the creative director of the Broadway producing giant Jujamcyn Theaters. Viertel immediately spurred an effort to rename one of the group's theaters for Wilson, with the support of Rocco Landesman, co-owner of the theatrical producing and theater ownership group. They chose the Virginia Theatre on Fifty-Second Street, which had been named for the wife of former Jujamcyn owner James H. Binger. Viertel worked out the details with Binger family members, who were understanding and supported the name change.

In early summer, Viertel flew to Seattle to talk to Wilson about the new theater. He brought a rendering of the marquee, which displays Wilson's distinctive signature. The playwright was touched. He still had some energy, but he wasn't sure how long it would last, so he wrote an acceptance speech for the ribbon cutting of the theater, just in case he couldn't be there to celebrate. He gave the speech to Sakina and told her to read it if he wasn't able to do it himself. Even as he was getting weaker and weaker, he still wanted to pay respect and give proper thanks. "I have a robust imagination and I have imagined for myself many things," he wrote, sitting on the front porch that had become his summer office. "I have imagined a wife and two beautiful daughters, and I have imagined a sustained career for myself in the theater. But not in my wildest imagination could I have ever imagined this. This is the capstone of my entire career and the capstone end to my spirit, to my being and the end to the measure and meaning of my life."

Viertel was just one of an invitation-only stream of visitors who made their way to the Seattle porch. Wilson's siblings, including Richard and older sister Donna, came out. They drove from Pennsylvania, because Richard was afraid of flying. Marion McClinton made the journey from St. Paul. Wilson reconnected on the phone with a friend, a former boxer named Mike Morgan, with whom he had worked at Little Brothers of the Poor when he was still an aspiring playwright. Wilson's first two wives, Brenda Burton and Judy Oliver, called and each had long, private conversations with him. Sakina made sure to clear the porch during those calls. Wilson hadn't talked to Burton in years, but he made his peace with her. He had remained friends with Oliver after their divorce, and he was able to thank her for being there at the beginning.

Wilson also called Richards on a day he was feeling up to it. Richards was reticent about the details. "I thought we might have had another conversation, but it did not happen and it will not happen," he told an interviewer. "Whatever we had, that was it. We completed our relationship at this place, and in this time."

But while many of his closest friends wanted to spend time with him, he remained clear: the play was his first priority. Sakina and Romero acted as gatekeepers and turned away phone calls and visits. The atmosphere in the house, however, was tense. Under all the stress, bottled-up emotion came to the surface. Wilson's older daughter and his third wife often disagreed about matters both trivial and large, and there was constant conflict, according to Kreidler. The tension made Kreidler uncomfortable, but Wilson never wavered from the simple fact that the work was now the center of the universe for him. He let others vie for his sympathy and attention, but his focus was on completing the cycle.

The diagnosis had come late, and the cancer was debilitating. Wilson was quickly losing weight, and the failure of his liver led to edema. His belly was swollen, while his face was shrunken. He was clearly in a lot of pain, but he refused standard chemotherapy. He wanted to be able to focus on the play. He had seen his mother suffer when she died, and he wanted to avoid that kind of pain—both for himself and for those around him. He also wanted to be clearheaded about the play. His doctors had recommended an experimental treatment called chemoembolization, in which cancer-fighting drugs are injected directly into a tumor, followed by a liver transplant, but it turned out that the cancer was too far advanced for the procedure. Those closest to him wanted him to pursue chemotherapy, but both Sakina and Kreidler said that he would have had to quit smoking, and he refused. He couldn't enjoy a good meal or sex or a walk to the café, and smoking was the one bodily pleasure he had left.

And then there was the work. He didn't forget that the play had received some of the worst notices of his career, and when rehearsals began in Los Angeles, he used all of his energy to write a better play. While top administrators at the Mark Taper knew about his illness, the actors remained in the dark. Kreidler communicated script changes through fax, telephone, and email, and he flew back and forth to Los Angeles to check in. "On the one hand, it was strangely calm and focused and collected," Davidson said of the process. "On the other hand, we had this specter hanging over us, because he didn't want anyone to know."

Three of the actors from Yale continued with the cast, and while they weren't told that anything was wrong, they knew how Wilson worked. They were used to having him in the rehearsal room and getting his freshly typed rewrites the next day. "We had our suspicions because he hadn't been around," James A. Williams said. Sakina flew down to meet with the cast, and actor Anthony Chisholm noticed a faraway look in her eyes. It didn't seem right to him. He noticed the same thing when Romero came to visit a few days later. "Something was happening," said Chisholm. "I could feel it." But Wilson didn't want to distract attention from the production, and he insisted that the actors remain unaware of his condition so they could focus on their roles.

Leon shuttled between Los Angeles and Seattle, similar to the way he flew between Washington, D.C., and Boston during the crisis with *Gem*. They met on the porch and talked about the play. Sometimes they talked about life, particularly about the respect African American theater artists needed to demand. During one visit, Leon brought a CD of new music for the show. The stereo in the house wasn't working, so Leon suggested they sit in his rental car, which was parked in the driveway. At this point, Wilson was a sliver of himself, and he required a walker to move from place to place. He was in serious pain, but Leon could see the determination in his eyes as he made his way to the car. As the music played, Leon asked Wilson what he thought, and he could read the look on his withered face. "He wasn't feeling it," he recalled. "He said, 'No, that ain't quite it.'" The music was always critical in an August Wilson play, and even as he faced certain death, the playwright was exacting to the very end.

While the main focus was on the play, Wilson also wanted to protect those closest to him before he passed. Once, when Kreidler was in Los Angeles working on the production, he asked to speak with Kreidler's wife. She sat with him on the porch and he told her that Kreidler needed to learn to ask for things and to demand the things he deserved as a theater artist. He felt that Kreidler was too much of a pushover, and he asked Annarella to make sure that he learned to stand up for himself once his mentor was gone.

His desire to protect Kreidler went further. The two would sit on the porch together for hours, sometimes wearing their matching Borsalino fedoras, just like the old times. He wanted to go back to Pittsburgh one last time with his young protégé, but they both knew that wasn't going to happen. One night, they sat outside and Wilson brought up the one-man show, *How I Learned*. He and Kreidler had collaborated closely, fighting that uphill battle in the basement. Wilson told him that he was leaving him the play and he wanted him to direct another production with another actor. Kreidler was shocked. That very pronouncement confirmed the fact that his friend was really dying. "I said, 'Fuck it, there is no show without you.'" Wilson channeled his mother, Daisy, and replied, "Man, you gotta eat." The next day, Wilson called actor Ruben Santiago-Hudson, who had won the Tony Award for his performance in *Seven Guitars*. He told Santiago-Hudson that he was leaving the play to Kreidler, and he wanted him to star in a new production, with Kreidler directing. That cemented the deal. Kreidler finally directed that production—but it took him ten years to be emotionally ready to take it on. (The August Wilson Estate, however, maintains the copyright to the play.)

Wilson put off managing his affairs because he was rewriting. *Radio Golf* began previews in Los Angeles on July 31, with the official opening on August 11. While the play still had flaws, all the rewriting and the change in directors had paid off, to some degree. And Wilson did have some fun with the script; he includes many dates in the dialogue, which represent the birthdays of his siblings and friends. Although the play doesn't have the soaring monologues that had become his signature, it does provide some redemption and hope in the final scene. Harmond exposes corruption at city hall involving the illegal auction of seized property, which destroys his chances to be elected mayor. He cannot stop the demolition of 1839 Wylie Avenue, but he sides with the community members who are painting Aunt Ester's house as a final tribute before the house and all it represents is destroyed.

The play received a mostly positive review in the *Los Angeles Times*. The production, critic Daryl H. Miller wrote, "maintains a beautiful balance as the action hovers between the ancient, almost magical pull of Africa and the greedy, clamoring demands of the still-not-united United States." But it was not the play Wilson would have written if he had been healthy. The dialogue is stilted, and the language is far from poetic. It reads as if it were written by committee.

Wilson was unable to attend the opening, even though Davidson, who was ending his thirty-eight-year career at the Taper, had offered to fly him to Los Angeles on a private plane. It was getting harder and harder to keep his illness a secret, especially given his absence at the opening of his new play. Wilson was always at openings, surrounded by family and friends. On August 25, Wilson realized that he could no longer hide his condition from the press, and he called Christopher Rawson, the drama critic of the *Pittsburgh Post-Gazette* who had been his longtime champion and a friend. He told Rawson that he only had a few months to live. "It's not like poker, you can't throw your hand in," he said. "I've lived a blessed life. I'm ready." He had called to arrange what he called "an exit interview," but the paper learned that the news was about to break elsewhere, so it ran a page-one story the following day. Wilson had not called to announce his illness publicly, and some who were close to him felt betrayed when the news broke.

The story went national. Within two days, it had run in every major newspaper across the country. A few days later, on September 2, Jujamcyn Theaters officially announced the renaming of the Virginia Theatre as the August Wilson Theatre. The new marquee, with the writer's signature in bright neon, was set to be unveiled at a ceremony on October 17. Wilson would be the first African American with a Broadway theater bearing his name. It wasn't clear if Wilson would last long enough to see it happen, but the significance was not lost on some copy editors, who picked up the story under the headline "The Great White Way No More."

While all of this was unfolding, Wilson was still confined to his make-shift office on the porch. He could no longer dissect the day's headlines over an all-day cup of coffee and a smoke, but he was aware of world events. While he had been on the phone with Rawson, Hurricane Katrina was decimating New Orleans and the surrounding area, leaving 80 percent of the city under water for weeks. The storm caused more than 1,700 deaths and billions of dollars of damage, and the inadequate response from federal, state, and local governments was widely criticized.

Images of stranded storm victims, most of them African American, were broadcast worldwide, creating an outcry of rage. Dead bodies floated in storm-flooded streets, and evacuees were stranded at the sweltering Superdome, while patients in nursing homes were abandoned. The levees were breached, which surely would have reminded Wilson of his hotheaded character in *Ma Rainey*. This was precisely the kind of news story that infuriated Wilson. Sakina had friends in New Orleans, and she checked in on them to ensure they had survived the devastation, but she tried to shelter her father from the news. She knew how indignant he could get, and she wanted him to save his energy. "Daddy, don't watch that," she said, but he still managed to catch the news and talk about the injustice of it all, just with less energy than he had in the past.

Now that the play had opened, Wilson set his attention on planning his last act: his funeral. He called Dwight Andrews, who had been the musical director for his early plays. He had been the associate pastor at Christ Church at Yale when Wilson first met him, and the playwright often discussed theology with him. Before the split between Wilson and Richards, Andrews was used to late-night calls from Wilson. One began "Hey, man, there's this piano," when Wilson was formulating the idea for *Piano Lesson*. When he heard Wilson's voice, Andrews immediately thought that he was calling to ask him to work as musical director on a new play, but after a moment, he heard how frail and breathless his friend sounded. Wilson said, "Hey, man, I am sick and I need you to do my service, put me down properly." His voice was hollow and weak. Andrews, of course, said yes and offered to go out for a visit in Seattle. Wilson never called back.

He also called McClinton and asked him to deliver the eulogy. Those two friends were the only people Wilson asked to participate in the service, and Sakina kept in contact with them to make sure they were ready when the time came. He didn't sign his will until September 26, when he was close to the end.

Wilson knew he wasn't going to get to sail down the Nile or even go back to Pittsburgh before he died. But he did want to take one quick trip. He and his immediate family, along with Kreidler and his wife and his assistant Dena Leviton, took a ferry to the San Juan Islands off the coast of

Seattle. He was no longer able to walk, so he got around on a red scooter that he called his sports car. They spent the night, and when they returned to the house on East Aloha Street, his health deteriorated even further. One night, Sakina rushed him to the hospital. She told him to preserve his breath, but he kept repeating, "It is beautiful. It is beautiful." He passed away on October 2.

His death was memorialized the next day on page one of newspapers across the country. The actors whose careers he launched or nurtured—Angela Bassett, Laurence Fishburne, Courtney B. Vance, Viola Davis, Samuel L. Jackson, Delroy Lindo, Ruben Santiago-Hudson, to name a few—sang his praises. Other playwrights marveled at his accomplishments. Tony Kushner, the author of the wildly ambitious and brilliant two-part saga *Angels in America*, told the *New York Times*, "Heroic is not a word one uses often without embarrassment to describe a writer or playwright, but the diligence and ferocity of effort behind the creation of his body of work is really an epic story." Newspapers from the *Palm Beach Post* to the *Pittsburgh Post-Gazette* ran editorials along with their obituaries. Every major regional theater in the country put out a statement. August Wilson, the quirky, soft-spoken poet from the Hill District, was gone.

Years earlier, when he spent hours over dinner and coffee with Charles Johnson, Wilson had expressed the world-weary question often posed by artists at some point or another: Does any of it matter? Sometimes Wilson answered that question with more than a hint of despair, especially when he read a story or heard of an incident in which "people still think all Black men are violent and lazy and stupid." But the outpouring of grief that accompanied his death might have changed that. All over the country, major American newspapers that had paid little attention to plays outside the Western canon were now mourning the loss of a true American master. That got Johnson thinking, deep in the middle of his own grief. He wished he could tell his friend that, in the end, he had made a difference, so he wrote about it in an essay called "Night Hawks" that he published many years later. He said he finally realized that, yes, all the work did matter. "The love of beauty had been our lifelong refuge as Black men, a raft that carried us both safely for sixty years across a turbulent sea of violence, suffering, and grief to a far shore we'd never dreamed possible in our youth, one free of fear, and when his journey was over laid him gently, peacefully to eternal rest."

His legacy was abundantly clear when his body was flown back home to Pittsburgh. Hundreds of friends and fans came out for the viewing at the funeral home on October 7. His best man, James Yoshimura, didn't go to the service; he was too crushed, and the act of seeing his friend buried would have cemented the fact that he was really gone. On Saturday, October 8, about four hundred invited guests gathered for a two-hour service at the Soldiers and Sailors Memorial Hall in Oakland, not far from Central Catholic, where Wilson had been tormented as a teenager. The guests, who included theater luminaries, producers, relatives, and friends, packed the stately auditorium for the service, which was led by Andrews, now a professor of music theory at Emory College of Arts and Sciences and pastor of the First Congregational Church in Atlanta. "I was sad until I remembered how much I learned from him," Andrews told the crowd. "I was sad until I remembered how his plays teach us for eternity."

Wilson had left instructions, and McClinton, who had his own health struggles, delivered a stirring eulogy, noting that sending his friend off was "the hardest thing I've ever had to do in my life." He reminded the mourners that "August Wilson changed the lives of young men and women, of old men and women, of men and women in between, Black, white, red and yellow. If they came from Mars, he changed them." He added, Wilson "loved his people and he would not let them not love themselves."

Romero had invited four actors to read excerpts from the plays: Charles S. Dutton performed a monologue from *Fences*; Phylicia Rashad quoted the venerable Aunt Ester from *Gem*; Anthony Chisholm read from *Joe Turner*; and Ruben Santiago-Hudson performed from *Two Trains*. Dutton, who had feuded with Wilson, but ultimately reconciled with him, told the attendees that his plays "encompassed the entire African-American experience." His legacy, he noted, "is as important as Martin Luther King's legacy, as important as Malcolm X's legacy, and as important as Nat Turner."

When the ceremony wrapped up, the sound of a lone trumpet echoed from the back of the hall. At Wilson's request, Wynton Marsalis played "Danny Boy," the Irish dirge that was one of the playwright's favorite tunes. People rummaged for their handkerchiefs; tissues were passed down the aisles. But then, after Marsalis blew out the last mournful notes—"Oh, Danny boy, I love you so"—he switched up the tempo and launched into "When the Saints Go Marching In." Suddenly the mood shifted, and the people began to dance in the aisles. They put their hands together and stomped their feet, marching as they followed the casket down the center aisle and out the doors. Wilson had done it again. He had people on their feet, laughing and crying and whooping and hollering.

After the ceremony, the traditional parade of cars followed the hearse, but the procession did not head directly to the cemetery. The cars headed east down Centre Avenue to the Hill District, where they snaked through the streets that Wilson had walked as a boy, past the sites of Eddie's Restaurant, Crawford Grill, Pan Fried Fish, West Funeral Home, the brick home at 1727 Bedford Avenue, and the lot on Wylie Avenue where Aunt Ester was said to live. All along the route, residents stood outside in the autumn drizzle, holding up professionally printed signs that said things like "August we love you" and "May all your fences have gates." The scene was reminiscent of the crowd that turned up to honor Prophet Samuel in *Two Trains Running*. "Look like they had more people watching than was in the funeral," Risa says in Act 2. "They was lined up on both sides of the street."

The procession ended at Greenwood Cemetery, and Wilson was laid to rest in a plot at the top of a hill. Daisy Wilson is buried down the hill, with her tombstone located in a direct straight line from her son's memorial. Zonia Wilson's grave is nearby. Zonia came north as a young woman, leaving a painful past behind her in North Carolina in search of a better life. Eller Cutler, Wilson's great-grandmother, is buried in the AME Cemetery in Plum Tree, North Carolina, 450 miles due south. The line of ancestry—the blood's memory—that Wilson celebrated in his plays is immortalized by the perfect placement of the graves.

The drizzle let up a bit when the mourners gathered by the graveside to hear Andrews recite a final prayer. Chisholm was the first to pick up the shovel and throw dirt on the grave. A spiritual man, he said that he felt a kinetic energy in the air as he poured the dirt. He recalled the final scene in *Fences*, when Gabriel couldn't get a note out of his trumpet, so instead enacted *"a slow, strange dance, eerie and life-giving."* The mourners took turns covering the grave, and someone left a harmonica at the site, embossed with the name of the bluesman Robert Johnson. Wilson's gravestone takes a cue from the Buddha. It reads, "Wherever you are, you are. I'm here." August Wilson was gone. At last, he had found his way home, long after he had found his song.

Afterword

On March 1, 2020, several hundred theater aficionados gathered at the Pillsbury House and Theatre, a cultural and community service center on Chicago Avenue in Minneapolis. They were there to celebrate the life of director Marion Isaac McClinton, who died on November 28, 2019, after a long struggle with kidney disease that sidelined him during *Gem of the Ocean*. Actors, directors, family, and friends crammed into the standing-room-only ninety-nine-seat theater for a passionate series of tributes, performances, and musical interludes. The event stretched long into the evening, as members of both the Broadway and Twin Cities theater communities praised McClinton—and by extension, his colleague August Wilson. Upstairs, tables were laden with food donated by the community. Children colored pictures in a family-friendly room. McClinton's prized *Jitney* jacket was displayed in a memorabilia room. Tears and laughter flowed as people who hadn't seen one another in years honored a life well lived.

Two and a half months later, two blocks down, George Floyd was murdered.

The story of Floyd's death—he suffocated in front of a convenience store at Chicago Avenue and Thirty-Eighth Street as a Minneapolis police officer knelt on his neck for nine minutes and twenty-nine seconds—sparked national outrage and widespread protests. A witness, seventeen-year-old Darnella Frazier, filmed the murder on her cell phone, and the video went viral, galvanizing a movement for racial justice. In the middle of a global pandemic, people who didn't attend rallies and who might have once been unaware of—or wary of—the Black Lives Matter movement were suddenly spurred to action.

But the murder of Floyd, which was punctuated by his poignant cries for his mother as he struggled to breathe, would not have surprised Wilson. He had known, from the minute he moved out of Daisy's house, that Black men on the street stood a strong chance of a dangerous and violent run-in with the police. He had been outraged at the shooting of Amadou Diallo in 1999. The police were an offstage, yet menacing, force in all of his plays. In *Two Trains Running*, Memphis recalls the tragedy of a young man named Begaboo, who was shot in the head by a policeman. His friends staged a protest. "Raised all kind of hell. Trying to get the cop charged with murder. They raised hell for three weeks. After that it was business as usual. The only thing anybody remember is the funeral," Memphis says.

That play opened on Broadway in 1992, almost thirty years before George Floyd's murder spurred global action. Wilson did not need a viral video to understand the reality of police violence toward young African American males. He wrote from his own experience and from that of his community. He was neither a seer nor a prophet; he was a truth teller, a griot who accurately depicted the ordinary lives of honorable people whose stories were ignored by the mainstream culture. It took a pandemic and a horrific murder for the dominant culture to finally grasp what Wilson had been saying all along in his unparalleled cycle.

He single-handedly wrote the history of African Americans in those ten plays. *Joe Turner* is the indisputable masterpiece, one of the greatest American plays of the twentieth century. *Fences*, *Piano Lesson*, and *Gem of the Ocean* are now classics. The characters in *Jitney* are irresistible. In both *Jitney* and *Two Trains*, Wilson vividly captured the speech rhythms and the spirit of highly opinionated men sitting around talking, invoking their dreams and disappointments, while making the audience want to sit down and join the conversation. He was not as successful with his female characters, but even so, he gave Rose (in *Fences*) and Vera (in *Seven Guitars*) showstopping monologues. Even in his weakest play, *King Hedley II*, Tonya's monologue eloquently portrays the heartache of a mother's worst nightmare. He didn't have the gift of time with *Radio Golf*, but he wrote the best play he could, as he was dying. A few of the plays fell short, but in the theater, he had a damn good batting average. His work opened the door for other Black playwrights and made it impossible for theaters to continue presenting season after season of plays written almost exclusively by white men.

But it wasn't easy, and his success came with a price. He never asked to be "*the* Black artistic spokesperson," and he never set out to examine every aspect of Black culture. He wrote what he knew, which is precisely what he told other writers to do.

It took the mainstream theater community years to embrace the gist of his impassioned speech "The Ground on Which I Stand." Theater professionals zeroed in on the controversy over nontraditional casting and missed the other points he was making about the culture at large. He often said he felt like he had been given a visitor's pass at the theaters that produced his work. The staffs of these theaters treated him with respect, even reverence, but he saw who was in the boardrooms, the administrative offices, the scene shops, and the box offices; the resident theaters were largely run by white men and, in a few instances, white women. In 2005, he told Charlie Rose, "When I go to these theaters . . . I count thirty-three people who work at that theater, you know, carpenters, electricians, whoever, people working in the press office, they're all white. They're simply all white, everywhere you go." He qualified that: "Security guards are all Black. I've never seen a white security guard in any of these theaters." He said that on national television fifteen years before Floyd's death, and precious little changed. In his 1996 speech, he said that out of the sixty-six members of the League of Resident Theatres, only one could be identified as Black; in 2022, of the seventy-nine LORT theaters, there were no Black institutions. (Wilson was not talking about theaters with Black artistic directors; he was talking about theaters like

Penumbra, which are run by Black artists and are committed to producing work by Black playwrights.)

In 1991, around the time Wilson was working on *Two Trains*, I co-authored a series called "The Fine Arts: A World Without Color" for the *Boston Globe*. It underscored the fact that the boards, staffs, and programs at the nation's major arts institutions were, with few exceptions, almost exclusively white. The series, which ran over four days on page one, was applauded by communities of color and lambasted by some arts leaders. "How dare you question our integrity?" some asked. I interviewed Wilson for that series, and he said the same thing he told Charlie Rose. After it ran, some institutions made efforts—a play here, an exhibit there, a cellist hired by a prestigious orchestra—but not much substantially changed.

Now, after George Floyd's murder, *every single one* of those institutions has inaugurated some form of "Equity and Anti-Racism" initiative. Diversity consultants who have been around all along are suddenly in high demand. I suspect Wilson would have felt at least a dash of cynicism about the overnight impetus to change; he had, after all, pointed out the lack of diversity in the arts quite publicly and he was hardly universally supported.

But his personal, if not his institutional, mark on the nation's culture is indelible. Two weeks after he died, the Virginia Theatre on West Fifty-Second Street was christened the August Wilson Theatre. It opened on November 6, 2005, with the long-running *Jersey Boys*, which was as far removed from an August Wilson play as could be. But in August 2021, Antoinette Chinonye Nwandu's play *Pass Over* had a short run at the theater. That play is about two men who are haunted by police violence, and it was inspired by the death of Trayvon Martin. And in December 2021, Jeremy O. Harris's *Slave Play* enjoyed a short revival at the August Wilson Theatre. In 2022, another theater was renamed for an African American: the newly renovated Cort Theatre on West Forty-Eighth Street was christened the James Earl Jones Theatre.

That film of *Fences* was made in 2016, almost thirty years after it was optioned by Paramount and more than a decade after Wilson's death. It took a film icon with the wattage of Denzel Washington as director and star to get the green light. Washington scrapped the screenplays Wilson had written and was faithful to the play; Viola Davis won the Academy Award for Best Supporting Actress. Maybe someday, another director will dig up Wilson's screenplay and make the film he envisioned. In 2020, director George C. Wolfe's film adaptation of *Ma Rainey* debuted on Netflix, with Viola Davis as Ma Rainey and Chadwick Boseman as Levee. Boseman died tragically before the film debuted, adding pathos to its eventual release. Denzel Washington has committed to filming the rest of the cycle, so many more people will get to see the plays years after Wilson's death.

He died too young at sixty, and it is a significant loss that we will never be able to read that novel he had started or see *The Coffin Maker Play* he imagined writing or view his visual art. In 2004, he told the *New York Times* that he had several film ideas—"and they don't necessarily deal with Black characters," he said. We'll never know what he would have created. He had been surrounded by death his entire life, and in his later years, he watched his old friends from Pittsburgh pass, one by one. He expressed that loss in his dedication to *King Hedley II*, when he implored Chawley Williams, "Don't you leave me here alone."

And so many in the August Wilson universe have passed in the years since his death. Lloyd Richards died on June 29, 2006, his eighty-seventh birthday. As Roc Dutton said, there would be no "August Wilson" without Lloyd Richards, but theirs was a symbiotic relationship. Richards nurtured and launched Wilson, but he also reinvigorated his directing career with Wilson's plays. Richards's death was followed by a string of others. Claude Purdy died on August 3, 2009, followed by Chawley Williams on December 2, 2009. Many of the original "Wilson Warriors" have passed: Theresa Merritt, Joe Seneca, Roscoe Browne. The inimitable Anthony Chisholm, who was generous and forthcoming in several interviews for this book, passed on October 16, 2020. This list feels distinctly Wilsonian: with each passing, memories are lost. I was about to get on a plane to interview McClinton in November 2019 when his ex-wife kindly called from the hospital to tell me not to come: McClinton had just died.

But Wilson's legacy remains. Since 2015, there has been an Annual August Wilson Birthday Celebration Block Party on Bedford Avenue, an all-day family event with food, music, dancing, and child-friendly activities. Once left derelict, his childhood home at 1727 Bedford was named to the National Register of Historic Places in 2013, thanks to the efforts of his nephew Paul Ellis. In 2018, Denzel Washington spearheaded a $5 million fundraising drive to restore the house. The project was completed in August 2022, and the building where Wilson grew up is now a multiuse community arts center, with a restoration of the two-room residential space and the addition of artist studios and community gathering spaces. The voluminous August Wilson Archive opened at the University of Pittsburgh in March 2023; this biography was already in production when the archive opened, so I only got to spend a few days perusing documents. It is a treasure trove for future researchers.

Even years after his death, his very name still reveals fissures in the national culture—and in his hometown of Pittsburgh. In 2009, the August Wilson African American Cultural Center opened on Liberty Street in Pittsburgh's downtown Cultural District. The center struggled financially and was eventually taken over by a nonprofit consortium. But in February 2019, the consortium shortened the name to simply the August Wilson Cultural Center. Black activists, including Wilson's indomitable cousin Renee Wilson, protested the removal of "African American" from the name, and a month later, the name was changed back to the original designation. In April 2022, the center opened *August Wilson: The Writer's Landscape*, a permanent interactive exhibit that celebrates his life and work.

And the plays continue to stir up mini-controversies. In 2009, Lincoln Center mounted a revival of *Joe Turner's Come and Gone*, the first Broadway revival since Wilson's death in 2005. Bartlett Sher, a white man, directed. Black directors and some actors were furious, but the August Wilson Estate, run by Constanza Romero, approved the production. Marion McClinton criticized the choice as "straight up institutional racism," while other directors said that, given the precedent, they might never get to direct a Broadway production of a Wilson play again. The cast, however, collaborated closely with Sher, and the production received rave reviews.

It's not clear what Wilson would have made of the remount. By the end of his life, he was beginning to consider hiring white directors for his plays, according to a source close to him. He wanted the best director available. His insistence on a Black director for the movie of *Fences* was ironclad; he knew the film would expose his work to more people than had ever seen it onstage. And a film is forever.

During Wilson's lifetime, all of his Broadway debuts were directed by men. Since then, female directors have added a new resonance to the plays, giving more depth to his female characters. In the 2022 Broadway revival of *Piano Lesson*, directed by LaTanya Richardson Jackson, the character of Berniece (played by Danielle Brooks) was a complex woman with wants and needs that were not acknowledged in the original production. And in the Huntington Theatre Company's 2022 revival of *Joe Turner*, directed by Lili-Anne Brown, the character of Bertha did not just bake biscuits and stand by quietly; as played by Shannon Lamb, she ran that household and put her husband in his place when appropriate.

Wilson most certainly would have had an opinion about a contretemps in December 2020 at an elite private school in Charlotte, North Carolina. The Black mother of a ninth-grader assigned to read *Fences* objected because she thought the subject was too mature for that age group and because Wilson's characters frequently use the N-word when referring to one another. The student was expelled because of his mother's interference. That same issue had arisen when Carole Shorenstein Hays and her white patrons objected to the use of the racial slur in *Fences*. Wilson wasn't having it then, and it would be interesting to hear his thoughts on the contretemps, which made national headlines. The good news is that *Fences* is required reading in many schools.

Wilson, who won a Tony Award and two Pulitzer Prizes during his lifetime, continues to receive plaudits and acclaim. Signature Theatre in New York mounted three of his plays in its 2006–2007 season, which had been planned before Wilson died. His estate initially canceled the series of productions, but ultimately agreed to move ahead with productions of *Seven Guitars*, *Two Trains Running*, and *King Hedley II*. The O'Neill added eight new residential cottages that were officially opened in 2015; one of them is named for Wilson. The Broadway production of *Jitney* in 2017 won the Tony Award for Best Revival of a Play. In 2021, the U.S. Postal Service embossed Wilson's image on a Black Heritage stamp, the forty-fourth in a series that includes Harriet Tubman, Martin Luther King, Malcolm X, and Jackie Robinson. He stands, arms crossed, Borsalino fedora tipped jauntily on his head, gazing confidently at the viewer.

At the end of his life, Wilson was awed that young people had grown up reading his work—and they continue to do so. He was unfailingly kind to aspiring thespians and writers. In 1986, he spent an afternoon mentoring ten high school students in the Huntington Theatre Company's Young Critics Institute, a now defunct program designed to introduce adolescents to all aspects of theater. Wilson listened carefully to them and treated them with respect. When one student asked about Wilson's secret to writing dialogue, he said, "You don't make your characters talk; you listen to them as they talk. It's kind of like saying to them, 'OK, what do you want to say?' and then writing it down."

I was a young critic myself when I met Wilson at the O'Neill in 1987. I had received a grant from the New England Foundation for the Arts to attend the National Critics Institute, which coincided with the National Playwrights Conference. Wilson didn't have a play there that summer, but he made a visit and spent an afternoon with the fellows in the Critics Institute. We got to talking after his presentation, sitting under the beloved old beech tree. I told him that I had seen *Joe Turner* at the Huntington and he asked if I had seen *Fences* on Broadway. Being green and subsisting on a freelancer's pitiful wages, I blurted out, "My mother saw it, but I can't afford a ticket." The minute I said it, I wished I could take it back. The next day, I received a note in the O'Neill office: there were two tickets waiting for me at the 46th Street Theatre for that Sunday's matinee.

Even after his death, Wilson continues to inspire young artists. The National August Wilson Monologue Competition was founded in 2007 by director Kenny Leon and Todd Kreidler. It started in Atlanta, but branched out to thirteen regions nationwide. High school students prepared a monologue from a Wilson play and the winners from each region performed in a national competition at the August Wilson Theatre on Broadway, with such "Wilson Warriors" as Ruben Santiago-Hudson and

Phylicia Rashad serving as judges. It was open to any high school student, regardless of race, and the winners received scholarships. (The August Wilson Estate took over the competition in 2022, adding a design contest and renaming it "The August Wilson Legacy Project." It is based at the Goodman Theatre in Chicago. The original founders, who started the event in the throes of grief and built it to a national phenomenon without ever taking a penny, are no longer involved.)

The competition as conceived by its founders received widespread attention in the 2020 Netflix documentary *Giving Voice*. Directed by James D. Stern and Fernando Villena, the ninety-minute film follows several of the competitors, showing the obstacles they confront and the effect that Wilson's words have on their dreams and aspirations. The young monologuists draw from Wilson's oeuvre, and their voices capture what Wilson learned from Romare Bearden. They turn Black Americans into kings and queens.

Wilson had his demons, but his output was remarkable, and he changed the face of American theater. The high school students in the monologue competition understood that, as evidenced in their moving testimonials at the end of the documentary. A young woman named Callie Holley, who went on to study acting at New York University's Tisch School of the Arts, gazes into the camera and says, "August gave me the chance to put myself out there for the very first time and showed me, 'You're worth seeing. *You're worth seeing.*'" And Gerardo Navarro, who finished in first place and was accepted by Carnegie Mellon University to study acting, goes further. Wilson's work, he says, "speaks for everyone and it speaks for those that are not seen. I have talks amongst my friends where we talk about the lack of representation, and we think that is because we are the change. We *have* to be the change." Wilson, who was never too busy to encourage young artists, would undoubtedly agree. His work inspires that change. The blood's memory flows on in the next generation.

AUTHOR'S NOTE

I first met August Wilson at the Eugene O'Neill Theater Center in 1987, and the descriptions of the O'Neill are from my direct experience as a fellow in the National Critics Institute and numerous visits to the O'Neill over the years. I also interviewed Wilson many times as a critic and arts reporter for the *Boston Globe*. I spent several days interviewing him in Seattle in January 2005 for a *Boston Globe Magazine* profile, "One Man. Ten Plays. 100 Years." The wide-ranging interviews covered his entire life. Many of the quotations in this book are drawn from those interviews, as is the opening scene in Chapter 19.

Many of Wilson's intimate letters and early plays and poetry are paraphrased because the August Wilson Estate declined authorization of this book. I hope readers will get a sense of his eloquence nonetheless.

ACKNOWLEDGMENTS

I once had an editor at the *Boston Globe* who had an endearing ritual. In the rare case when you produced a piece that really sang, he sidled over to your desk and put his hands together and bowed. And then he walked away, without uttering a word. None were needed.

So I find myself in my editor's position, hands poised in namaste to the scores of generous, patient people who helped birth this book. There are too many to name, so if I inadvertently forgot someone, please know I bow to you, too.

First and foremost, I owe a debt to Renee Wilson, advocate extraordinaire, brilliant amateur genealogist, mountain climber, chef, mother, grandmother, cousin, and loyal friend. Together with Pittsburgh resident Gordon Everett and Toe River Valley native Alan Singleton, we climbed Spear Tops Mountain during an autumn rainstorm and paid homage to Eller Cutler and the ancestors. Renee, keep doing what you do.

I grew up at the *Boston Globe*. Here's a shout-out to fellow Globies, past and present—friends, colleagues, editors, saints and scoundrels alike. John Koch, Matthew Gilbert, Michael Saunders, Lylah Alphonse, Stephen Kurkjian, Glenda Buell (RIP), and the rest of you who were there at deadline.

The Boston theater community has been invaluable to me over the decades, and I particularly thank Michael Maso and Temple Gill at the Huntington Theatre. Frank Rich said the right thing at the right time to keep me going on my research.

Thanks to Lane Zachary for guidance on the proposal and to Paul Sennott for his law expertise. Thanks to so many at Simon & Schuster: editor Dawn Davis for believing in this book from the start (*Bon Appétit!*); the incomparable Bob Bender who graciously took on a project in the works and who is a font of knowledge about everything from baseball to the blues; the all-knowing and resourceful Johanna Li; general counsel extraordinaire Felice Javit; and production-editorial team Jonathan Evans and Rob Sternitzky.

I am blessed to have many friends in journalism and the theater who are astute readers: John Koch and Sharon Basco, Ed Siegel, Jeffrey Hatcher, Melinda Lopez, Elijah Wald, I salute you.

My mother was a reference librarian who taught me to love literature and to be precise. I applaud my remarkable mother and her colleagues. In particular: Bill Daw, Megan Ashley Massanelli, Leah Mickens, Diael Thomas, and Joe Wozniak at the University of Pittsburgh; Susan Hallgren and Mary Ludo at the University of Minnesota for research assistance and a much-appreciated grant; Matthew Rowe at Yale University's Beinecke Rare Book Manuscript Library; Jeremiah Manion and Wanda Joseph-Rollins at the *Boston Globe*; Jeremy Megraw at the Billy Rose Theatre Division of the New York Public Library; Leigh Focareta at the Carnegie Library of Pittsburgh; and researcher Henry Shull.

I thank everyone at ArtScape, a vibrant artist's community at the Bradford Mill in West Concord, MA, especially Ann Sussman, Tatiana Murnikova, and John Boynton. Thank you for giving me a room of my own during a global pandemic.

My brothers and sisters in biography: I salute the Boston Chapter of Biographers International, all of you, but especially Ray Shepard. And my sisters in the Concord Women's Writers Group: thanks for listening.

There are so many in the August Wilson universe who gave me their time and memories. Todd Kreidler is a walking encyclopedia of all things Wilson—and an extraordinary colleague whom I am blessed to know.

In Pittsburgh: Nelson Harrison, my spiritual and street-savvy guide, who, in his eighties, drives like a teenager out to impress the ladies; Curtiss Porter, who did a double take when I showed up at a diner with Nelson; Reginald Howze; Sala Udin; and so many more.

In St. Paul: too many to name, but a bow to Terry Bellamy, the original Levee who ought to be in charge of all of it; Jacqui Shoholm, quiet force of inspiration who did more than anyone knows; Lou Bellamy; James

Craven; Mike Henley at Little Brothers of the Poor; and Tess Gallagher, who welcomed me into her Airbnb and introduced me to Juan and Zulie Jaimes, the current owners of Wilson's home on Holly Avenue who graciously gave me a tour.

At the O'Neill: First, an overdue thank-you to the New England Foundation for the Arts, which gave me a grant to attend the National Critics Institute in 1987, when I was a mere babe and aspiring drama critic. I first met August Wilson there. The inimitable wordsmith Jeffrey Hatcher (also a newbie) and I sat under a tree with Wilson for hours, mesmerized by stories about Pittsburgh. The O'Neill launched so many playwrights, and I was there when I was launching my career. In short, thanks to: George White, Jean Passanante, Lori Robishaw, photographer Vinnie Scarano, every single playwright including James Yoshimura, John Patrick Shanley, Herman D. Farrell III, Carl Capotorto, Laura Maria Censabella, Lucy Thurber, Douglas Post, etc. The O'Neill directors focused solely on the playwrights, and Bill Partlan and Amy Saltz were just as generous with me. Scott Richards was incredibly wise and kind and had a front-row seat to the early Wilson years. And a special bow to Lloyd Richards, who always made me feel like I was in the principal's office but for good reason. He taught us all.

Actors. They made these plays happen, and they made this book come alive. James Earl Jones (and his son Flynn Earl and his assistant Coddy Granum), thank you for welcoming me to your home and letting me pass Flynn's test. Anthony Chisholm, I will never be able to walk by the diner on Ninth Avenue without thinking of you. RIP. Stephen McKinley Henderson; Ebony Jo-Ann; Julie Boyd; Anna Deavere Smith; Eugene Lee; and all of the "Wilson Warriors."

And, of course, family and friends. Marc Lipson and Ellen Climo gave me a place to revise the manuscript and welcomed me into their extended family when it was most necessary. You are forever family. Claire Bowin, who is always there. Wes Boyd, who knows why. Skip Gates and all who listened to me, you get the hands in prayer. Carol Hartigan and Anne and Ken Harrison: you were there at the start and continue to be a guiding light. Jennifer Mendenhall and Michael Kramer welcomed me into their home and let me conduct interviews in their living room—and entertain actors and directors on their patio.

Bennet Ih, I offer you gratitude and grace. Godspeed.

Aidan, Marisa, and Devlin: Always.

My hands are pressed together in thanks to all of you, named and unnamed. Namaste.

ORDER OF PRODUCTIONS

BROADWAY OPENING

Ma Rainey's Black Bottom	1984
Fences	1987
Joe Turner's Come and Gone	1988
The Piano Lesson	1990
Two Trains Running	1992
Seven Guitars	1996
King Hedley II	2001
Gem of the Ocean	2004
Radio Golf	2007
Jitney	2017 (off-Broadway, 2000; Pittsburgh, 1982)

CHRONOLOGICAL BY PLOTS

Gem of the Ocean	1900s
Joe Turner's Come and Gone	1910s
Ma Rainey's Black Bottom	1920s
The Piano Lesson	1930s
Seven Guitars	1940s
Fences	1950s
Two Trains Running	1960s
Jitney	1970s
King Hedley II	1980s
Radio Golf	1990s

All interviews conducted by the author.

PROLOGUE

1 *"To arrive at this moment"*: August Wilson, Heinz Award Acceptance Speech, *Pittsburgh Post-Gazette*, December 6, 2003.

1 *Wilson had cut short a trip*: Richard Kittel interview, June 6, 2017.

1 *He sported a black turtleneck*: Charles McCollester photograph in the collection of Mark Clayton Southers, March 22, 2003.

2 *He had also foolishly agreed*: Todd Kreidler interviews, May 29–30, 2017.

2 *"There will come a day"*: August Wilson, conceived with Todd Kreidler, *How I Learned What I Learned* (New York: Samuel French, 2018), 25.

2 *As a boy, Wilson had attended*: Laurence A. Glasco and Christopher Rawson, *August Wilson: Pittsburgh Places in His Life and Plays* (Pittsburgh: Pittsburgh History & Landmarks Foundation, 2011), 8.

2 *The church commissioned a giant statue*: St. Benedict the Moor Parish, https://sbtmparishpgh.com/history.

2 *had infuriated Wilson*: Samuel G. Freedman, "A Voice from the Streets," *New York Times*, March 15, 1987.

2 *He stopped briefly outside the church*: McCollester photograph.

3 *Smith led thousands in protest marches*: Tim Grant, "Leader Who Got Blacks, Women in Unions," *Pittsburgh Post-Gazette*, April 2, 2011.

3 *living in a shady basement apartment*: Glasco and Rawson, *Pittsburgh Places*, 65.

3 *Penny had preceded Wilson*: Central Catholic High School records.

3 *Wilson was accepted two years*: Central Catholic High School 1959–1960 yearbook.

3 *Wilson saw him take a dare*: Kittel interview.

4 *Penny called himself Brother Oba*: Letter from Vernell A. Lillie, Bob Gore, and Rob Penny to August Wilson, July 20, 1987, Kuntu Repertory Theatre Records, Curtis Theatre Collection, Archives & Special Collections, University of Pittsburgh Library System.

4 *Together in 1968*: Ervin Dyer, "Founder of Kuntu Repertory; Poet, Teacher and Activist," *Pittsburgh Post-Gazette*, March 18, 2003.

4   *Penny was able to turn his poetry acumen*: Ibid.

4   *Penny and another Pitt professor*: Curtiss Porter interview, August 17, 2019.

4   *Penny had taken to wearing dashikis*: Dyer, "Founder of Kuntu Repertory."

4   *wore musty tweed sports coats*: Kittel interview.

4   *a coat went for thirty-five cents*: Chip Brown, "The Light in August," *Esquire*, April 1, 1989.

5   *All the mourners were invited*: Sala Udin interview, June 5, 2017.

5   *Sala Udin*: Ibid.

5   *Mark Clayton Southers*: Mark Clayton Southers interview, June 5, 2017.

5   *Wilson was aware*: Constanza Romero interview, January 27, 2005.

5   *Wilson had noticed*: Kreidler interview.

5   *"I have this sort of love-hate"*: Christopher Rawson, "Can Pittsburgh Support Its Playwrights?" *Pittsburgh Post-Gazette*, October 11, 1998.

6   *A crowd had gathered*: Joe Mandak, "Marchers Decry Alleged Police Brutality, War," *Citizens' Voice* (Wilkes-Barre, Pennsylvania), March 23, 2003.

6   *Wilson was just a boy*: Udin interview.

6   *"NO Redevelopment Beyond This Point"*: Glasco and Rawson, *Pittsburgh Places*, 63.

6   *Wilson's younger cousin Renee Wilson*: Renee Wilson interview, July 13, 2019. The author interviewed Renee Wilson numerous times over three years.

6   *One of the dead*: Mandak, "Marchers Decry."

6   *Renee had also called*: Renee Wilson interview.

7   *He followed the funeral procession*: Ibid.

ONE The Blood's Memory

8   *"When your back is pressed to the wall"*: Brown, "Light in August."

8   *In the dark hours of June 9, 1923*: *Asheville Citizen-Times*, June 17, 1923; *Statesville Record and Landmark*, June 18, 1923.

8   *She had raised many children*: The 1900 U.S. Federal Census lists eight children living in her household, but notes that she has eleven children. The 1910 U.S. Federal Census puts the number at thirteen. Grandchildren moved in and out of the house, and census takers wrote down what they were told, which depended on who answered the door.

8   *her husband, Jacob Cutler*: The 1900 U.S. Federal Census states that Cutler was born in 1835 in Mississippi. Eller Cutler is listed as widowed on the 1910 U.S. Federal Census.

8   *it wasn't often . . . walk in the woods*: *Asheville Citizen-Times*, September 2, 1899. A first-person account of people ascending the "rugged mountain." It reads, "The shrubs became so thick and so low that we had to get on our hands and knees and crawl." The author climbed the mountain on October 7, 2019, with Renee Wilson and local resident Alan Singleton, who pointed

out the site of Eller Cutler's homestead. Singleton played on the mountain as a child and his parents' generation talked about the Cutlers. The stone hearth was still intact, but the dwelling was gone.

9   *the only Black family*: 1900 and 1910 U.S. Federal Census.

9   *Justice was mortally wounded . . . chest and abdomen*: North Carolina Death Certificates, North Carolina State Archives, Raleigh, North Carolina.

9   *last will and testament . . . "shooting me without a cause"*: North Carolina, U.S., Wills and Probate Records, 1665–1998, Ancestry.com.

9   *He died at 4:30 a.m.*: North Carolina Death Certificates, North Carolina State Archives, Raleigh, North Carolina.

9   *According to published reports*: Asheville Citizen-Times, June 17, 1923; Statesville Record and Landmark, June 18, 1923.

9   *One tale claims . . . good Christians blush*: Oral history related to the author by Alan Singleton, October 7, 2019.

9   *The law of the land*: Avery County Historical Society and Museum.

10   *In 1864, a man named . . . and a piano*: Will Records and Cross Index, 1782–1964, North Carolina Superior Court (Rutherford County), Rutherford, North Carolina, Ancestry.com.

10   *By 1880, Calvin Twitty . . . illiterate*: 1880 U.S. Federal Census, Ancestry.com.

10   *born around 1868*: Sarah "Eller" Cutler's date of birth varies from document to document. The 1880 U.S. Federal Census lists her birth date as "about 1867"; the 1900 U.S. Federal Census lists "August 1868" as her date of birth. The 1920 U.S. Federal Census lists it as "about 1864," and the 1930 U.S. Federal Census lists it as "around 1860," which is certainly too early. Since the 1900 Federal Census is the most specific, all ages for Eller are calculated using a birth date of 1868.

10   *He identified himself*: 1880 U.S. Federal Census, Ancestry.com.

10   *He claimed that he fought*: General Affidavit, filed by H. L. Williams, Claim of Calvin Twitty Co. F. 40 U.S. C. Troops, September 10, 1892, Record and Pension Office, War Department, National Archives.

10   *officials in Washington*: Letter to Attorney, September 12, 1892, Record and Pension Office, War Department, National Archives.

10   *his son William*: "A Runaway Log Train," Asheville Weekly Citizen, November 12, 1891.

10   *He walked away with $10,000*: Oxford Public Ledger, Oxford, North Carolina, January 22, 1892.

11   *worth a shade more than $306,000*: CPI Inflation Calculator, https://www.in 2013dollars.com/us/inflation/1892?amount=10000.

11   *"The old darkey"*: Oxford Public Ledger, Oxford, North Carolina, January 22, 1892.

11   *He was born around 1835*: 1880 U.S. Federal Census.

11   *a sizeable tract of land he had purchased*: Deed, Watauga County Register of Deeds, Boone, North Carolina.

11   *it takes its name from Estatoe*: Muriel Earley Sheppard, *Cabins in the Laurel* (Chapel Hill: University of North Carolina Press, 1935), 4.

11   *In 1923, there were only*: 1920 U.S. Federal Census, courtesy of North Carolina historian Michael C. Hardy.

11   *Cutler Falls*: Southern Appalachian Highlands Conservancy, December 20, 2013, https://southernappalachian.wordpress.com/tag/protected-waterfall/.

11   *Eller worked*: North Carolina State Board of Health, Bureau of Vital Statistics. Eller is listed as the midwife on the births of her grandchildren, Daisy Zerola Cutler and Detroit Cutler (who later used the name Ray Wilson), and Burleson is listed as the attending physician.

11   *"granny woman"*: Oral history provided by Hardy and the Avery County Historical Society and Museum.

11   *Born in 1896*: https://www.findagrave.com/memorial/28428626/zonia-wilson.

11   *she later told her children . . . consensual relationship*: Renee Wilson interview.

12   *Eller is listed as the midwife*: Birth certificates, North Carolina State Board of Health, Bureau of Vital Statistics.

12   *In April 1923*: Avery County Courthouse, Newland, North Carolina, 1923 docket.

12   *April 1924 . . . six months in jail*: Avery County Superior Court, Criminal Docket, April 1924.

12   *In 1923, violence erupted*: Ben Dixon MacNeill, "More Troops Ordered to Spruce Pine Early Today," *News and Observer*, October 1, 1923.

12   *"run the Blacks out of the county"*: Muriel Earley Sheppard, *Cabins in the Laurel* (Chapel Hill: University of North Carolina Press, 1935), 135.

13   *Spear remains a town . . . Eller's time*: The author visited all of these places in October 2019.

13   *The land is now the property*: Mountain Xpress, "Conservancy Nonprofit SAHC Purchases Spear Tops Mountain Tract in Avery County," December 17, 2011; South Appalachian Highlands Conservancy, https://appalachian.org /yellow-mountain-gateway-357-acres-preserved/.

13   *The trail is posted*: Author visit.

13   *She died on that mountain*: North Carolina State Board of Health, Bureau of Vital Statistics, Standard Certificate of Death, May 9, 1935, Ancestry.com.

13   *he told interviewers*: August Wilson interviews, January 27–29, 2005.

13   *passed on by his mother*: Renee Wilson interview.

13   *daughter of sharecroppers*: August Wilson, "Feed Your Mind, the Rest Will Follow," *Pittsburgh Post-Gazette*, March 28, 1999.

13   *There were no sharecroppers*: Michael C. Hardy interview, October 7, 2019.

14   *She is "the embodiment of African wisdom"*: Maureen Dezell, "Gem of the Theater: A 10-Play Odyssey Continues with 'Gem of the Ocean,'" *Boston Globe*, September 5, 2004.

14   *Wilson said that Aunt Ester "resembles any Black woman"*: Ibid.

14 *Wilson never visited Spear*: August Wilson interview.

15 *He came from Cleveland County*: U.S., World War I Draft Registration Cards, 1917–1918, Ancestry.com. When he enlisted for the draft, he listed a wife and child on his enrollment form.

15 *Everett Mills*: North Carolina, U.S., Birth Indexes, 1800–2000, Ancestry.com; U.S., Social Security Applications and Claims Index, 1936–2007, Ancestry .com.

15 *Lucille*: North Carolina, U.S., Death Certificates, 1909–1976, Ancestry.com. Lucille Wilson's death certificate lists Bynam Wilson and Mary Young as her parents.

15 *a poem many years later*: August Wilson: The Ground on Which I Stand, dir. Sam Pollard, *American Masters*, PBS, 2015.

15 *The character Bynum*: Wilson's grandfather's name is most frequently spelled Bynam, yet the character name is spelled Bynum.

15 *Zonia later told*: Renee Wilson interview.

15 *Great Migration*: Digital Public Library of America.

16 *Monday morning of June 9, 1928*: "Tennessee State Marriages, 1780–2002," Tennessee State Library and Archives, Nashville, Tennessee, USA, Ancestry .com.

16 *They bought two one-way tickets . . . who knew everyone born in those parts*: Avery County Historical Society and Museum.

16 *Upon arriving in Elizabethton . . . a minister of God*: "Tennessee State Marriages, 1780–2002."

16 *They lived off the land . . . gathered water*: Renee Wilson interview; Hardy interview.

16 *Eller never learned to read*: 1930 U.S. Federal Census, Ancestry.com.

16 *She sent her grandchildren*: Renee Wilson interview.

17 *Years later, Daisy had*: Ibid.

17 *school in Elk Park*: Conrad Ostwalt and Phoebe Pollitt, "The Salem School and Orphanage: White Missionaries, Black School," *Appalachian Journal* 20, no. 3 (1993): 271.

17 *Daisy later regretted*: Wilson, "Feed Your Mind."

17 *The family legend*: Renee Wilson interview; August Wilson interview.

17 *But the 1930 U.S. Census . . . homemaker*: "1930 U.S. Federal Census."

17 *Zonia's sister Lillian and her husband, Arthur*: Ibid.

17 *on May 9, 1935*: Certificate of Death, North Carolina State Board of Health, Bureau of Vital Statistics, Ancestry.com.

17 *Her granddaughters Daisy and Faye*: Hardy interview.

17 *Uncle Arthur*: Renee Wilson interview.

TWO The Crossroads of the World

18 *"I happen to think that the content"*: August Wilson, *Seven Guitars* (New York: Plume, 1997), "A Note from the Playwright."

18 *In 1930, there were only*: 1930 U.S. Federal Census, courtesy of Hardy.

18 *Pittsburgh's population was bursting*: "Historical Census Statistics on Population Totals by Race, 1790 to 1990, and by Hispanic Origin, 1970 to 1990, for Large Cities and Other Urban Places in the United States," U.S. Census Bureau, https://www.census.gov/library/working-papers/2005/demo/POP-twps 0076.html.

18 *Since 1910, the city's Black population*: Ibid.

18 *"wide-hipped and full of grace"*: Wilson, "Mother's Prayer."

19 *she had been called*: Renee Wilson interview.

19 *a boardinghouse on Clark Street*: "1940 U.S. Federal Census," Ancestry.com. Daisy is listed as Zerola Wilson, using her middle name, as a lodger. Her sister Faye is listed in the same house as Navada Walker, along with her two children.

19 *melting pot of nationalities*: Wilson, *How I Learned What I Learned.*

19 *"an amalgam of the unwanted"*: Ibid.

19 *"the crossroads of the world"*: Ida Alexander Herbert, "A Salute to Fifty Years of Progress," *New Pittsburgh Courier*, November 9, 1974. The term is often attributed to poet Claude McKay, but a digital search of his archives at the Beinecke Rare Books and Manuscript Library at Yale University and the Schomburg Center for Research in Black Culture at the New York Public Library did not find any source attributing the term to McKay, but there are numerous sources attributing it to Dee.

20 *A jazz renaissance began*: Colton Harper, "The Crossroads of the World: A Social and Cultural History of Jazz in Pittsburgh's Hill District, 1920–1970," dissertation, University of Pittsburgh School of Music, 2001, https://sites .google.com/site/pittsburghmusichistory/; Nelson Harrison interview, August 7, 2019.

20 *Bill "Bojangles" Robinson visited*: "Bill Robinson, Actor and Ambassador of Good Will, Spends a Weekend in Smoketown," *Pittsburgh Courier*, January 6, 1940.

20 *one of Eckstine's schoolmates*: "Timeline," Romare Bearden Foundation, https:// beardenfoundation.org/timeline/.

20 *Bynam sat the young man down*: Renee Wilson interview.

20 *In 1942, he registered*: "U.S., World War II Draft Cards Young Men, 1940–1947," Ancestry.com.

21 *He was more specific*: "Pennsylvania, U.S., Veteran Compensation Application Files, WWII, 1950–1966," Ancestry.com.

21 *Ray found work . . . died in 1971*: Renee Wilson interview; Bill Moyers, *A*

World of Ideas: Conversations with Thoughtful Men and Women About American Life Today and the Ideas Shaping Our Future (New York: Doubleday, 1989), 188.

21 *a two-room rear apartment*: Ervin Dyer and Monica Haynes, "Real-Life Drama Surrounds Wilson's Childhood Home," *Pittsburgh Post-Gazette*, January 26, 2003.

21 *Louis and Bella Siger*: Wilson later used the names of his childhood neighbors as offstage people mentioned in his plays.

21 *Dr. Albert Goldblum*: Orin Goldblum interview, July 16, 2021.

21 *brothers Frank and Johnny Butera*: Lillian Thomas, "Keeper of Time," *Pittsburgh Post-Gazette*, May 31, 2001.

21 *She had desperately wanted a boy*: John Lahr, "Been Here and Gone," *New Yorker*, April 8, 2001, 55.

21 *Kittel was not Freda's father*: Renee Wilson interview.

21 *a European pastry chef . . . a Polish immigrant*: Allegheny County Department of Court Records, Wills/Orphans' Court Division, Marriage License Bureau: Application for Marriage License and Marriage Certificate.

22 *Kittel showed up every now and then*: Lahr, "Been Here and Gone."

22 *Life couldn't have been . . . hot-water heater*: Dyer and Haynes, "Real-Life Drama."

22 *"prosperity and growth" . . . "what we will"*: August Wilson, "Living on a Mother's Prayer," *New York Times*, May 4, 1996.

22 *Kittel was not the father*: Kittel interview; Renee Wilson interview.

22 *The growing family*: Kittel interview.

23 *she left the baby*: Kittel interview; Renee Wilson interview.

23 *dedicated his play*: August Wilson, *The Piano Lesson* (New York: Plume, 1990), dedication page.

23 *Life at home was far from . . . on credit*: Lahr, "Been Here and Gone."

23 *He later told a friend*: Kreidler interview.

23 *Bella Siger was a vital part*: Glasco and Rawson, *Pittsburgh Places*, 74.

23 *She had only a sixth-grade education*: August Wilson, "Feed Your Mind."

23 *When he was five*: August Wilson interview.

23 *"editorials, essays"*: Wilson, "Feed Your Mind."

24 *"I thought I was cut out of the world of books"*: August Wilson interview.

24 *his grandfather Bynam disappeared*: Renee Wilson interview.

24 *Burley was a former champion welterweight*: International Boxing Hall of Fame, http://www.ibhof.com/pages/about/inductees/modern/burley.html.

24 *"I grew up without a father"*: Ronald K. Fried, "The Black Boxing Legend Who Inspired 'Fences,'" *Daily Beast*, December 24, 2016, https://www.thedailybeast.com/the-black-boxing-legend-who-inspired-fences.

24 *"Any one of the adults could tell you"*: Dinah Livingston, "Cool August: Mr. Wilson's Red Hot Blues," *Minnesota Monthly*, October 1987; reprinted in

Conversations with August Wilson, eds., Jackson R. Bryer and Mary C. Hartig (Jackson: University Press of Mississippi, 2006), 42.

25 *One day . . . "Where is your mother?"*: Ibid., 45.

25 *"Sunday morning"*: Ibid.

25 *"At six o'clock"*: Ibid., 46.

25 *"I've been threatening"*: Ibid.

26 *"We came to school to learn" . . . knew the answer*: Udin interview.

26 *Daisy was a loyal parishioner*: Renee Wilson interview.

26 *Daisy had a good relationship*: Renee Wilson interview.

26 *"He was a great stutterer" . . . "his words out"*: Reginald Howze interview, June 7, 2017.

26 *his grandmother Zonia died*: https://www.findagrave.com/memorial/28428 626/zonia-wilson; author visit to grave, August 2019.

26 *died alone in 1980 . . . no known survivors*: *The Courier* (Waterloo, Iowa), October 28, 1980.

26 *Her grave is marked*: https://www.findagrave.com/memorial/28428626/zonia -wilson.

27 *His older sister, Freda*: Renee Wilson interview.

27 *"at times possessed"*: August Wilson, *Three Plays* (Pittsburgh: University of Pittsburgh Press, 1991), 216.

27 *Kittel was still rarely around*: Lahr, "Been Here and Gone."

27 *In May 1952*: Allegheny Department of Court Records, Criminal Division.

28 *and promptly sued*: Ibid.

28 *Daisy strongly believed*: Herb Boyd, "Interview with August Wilson," *The Black World Today*, April 26, 2000. Reprinted in *Conversations with August Wilson*, ed. Jackson R. Bryer and Mary C. Hartig (Jackson: University Press of Mississippi, 2006), 42.

28 *"That was something that deeply"*: James Yoshimura interview, December 5, 2017.

28 *grew angry if anyone*: Romero interview.

28 *He was enamored*: Wilson, "Feed Your Mind."

28 *"Well, son, I'll tell you"*: Langston Hughes, "Mother to Son," Poetry Foundation, https://www.poetryfoundation.org/poems/47559/mother-to-son.

28 *One day, the whole family*: Wilson told this story repeatedly. He included it prominently in *How I Learned*.

28 *"God damn it"*: Livingston, "Cool August," 47.

29 *"Daisy, go get"*: Ibid.

29 *"Something is not always better"*: Ibid.

29 *Freddy understood*: Wilson, *How I Learned*, 17.

29 *"She reached into her apron"*: August Wilson interview.

29 *white customers at Woolworth's . . . a paper bag*: Boyd, "Interview with August Wilson," 237.

29 *He was a bit of a loner*: Sala Udin essay, in Glasco and Rawson, *Pittsburgh Places*, xvii.

29 *he and the other children*: Ibid., xvii; Udin interview.

29 *In 1955, the Pittsburgh City Council . . . 32.9 percent were white*: Diana Nelson Jones, "Traces of a Lost Neighborhood," *Pittsburgh Post-Gazette*, June 18, 2018.

30 *"To kids, this was frightening"*: Udin in Glasco and Rawson, *Pittsburgh Places*, xvii.

30 *Many of the neighborhood's*: "Progress Demands These Lower Hill Landmarks," *Pittsburgh Courier*, August 27, 1955.

30 *Most of the Black families*: Ibid.

30 *the Wilson family cut a hole in the ceiling*: Dyer and Haynes, "Real-Life Drama."

30 *In fourth grade*: August Wilson interview.

30 *"The nuns said"*: Ibid.

30 *"He had a reputation" . . . "when he got angry"*: Howze interview, June 7, 2017.

31 *"She would stop the class"*: August Wilson interview.

31 *A trip to buy a new pair*: Lahr, "Been Here and Gone," 55.

31 *it was his one memory*: Ibid.

31 *named him as his son*: Allegheny County Department of Court Records, Wills/Orphans' Court Division.

31 *an intimate, curious letter*: Jean Passanante, letter from August Wilson, January 14, 1986.

31 *He later said that he sleuthed around*: August Wilson interview.

32 *She frequently sent him*: Ibid.

32 *"I was the only one"*: Ibid.

32 *He craved the role*: Wilson, *How I Learned*, 40–43. Wilson told this story repeatedly in interviews and included a long version in his one-man show.

32 *didn't even get a speaking role*: Ibid.

32 *His friend Howze*: Howze interview.

32 *he didn't mention it*: Kreidler interview.

33 *"Brief. Electric"*: Wilson, *How I Learned*, 41.

33 *In 1931, when Daisy*: *Pittsburgh Press*, September 3, 1931.

34 *He made neckties . . . a spotless record*: William Allen, *Pittsburgh Press*, March 22, 1953.

34 *Bedford's sentence was commuted*: "Fine Pardons Numbers Baron," *Pittsburgh Press*, April 21, 1954.

34 *He had a car . . . more comfortable than ever*: Kittel interview.

34 *The family moved to Hazelwood*: Livingston, "Cool August," 42.

34 *enrolled Freddy at St. Stephen's . . . in his class*: Ibid.

35 *Someone threw a brick*: August Wilson interview.

THREE Something Is Not Always Better Than Nothing

36 *"From my early childhood"*: August Wilson, "Feed Your Mind."

36 *One night, hoodlums smashed*: Kittel interview.

36 *new rental home*: Ibid.

36 *In the 1940s*: "Pittsburgh, the 'Smoky City,'" Popular Pittsburgh, February 11, 2015, https://popularpittsburgh.com/darkhistory/.

37 *Freddy had made a few friends*: Livingston, "Cool August," 44. Wilson mentioned two friends from the neighborhood, boys named Ba Bra and Earl.

37 *"Looking back on it"*: Dennis Watlington, "Hurdling Fences," *Vanity Fair*, April 1989; reprinted in Bryer and Hartig, ed., *Conversations with August Wilson*, 83.

37 *"Never before in the entire history"*: James Baldwin, "Sweet Lorraine" (1969), in *Lorraine Hansberry in Her Own Words: To Be Young, Gifted and Black*, adapted by Robert Nemiroff (New York: Vintage Books, 1995), xviii.

37 *At five foot seven and 175 pounds*: Michael Feingold, "August Wilson's Bottomless Blackness," *Village Voice*, November 27, 1984; reprinted in Bryer and Hartig, ed., *Conversations with August Wilson*, 13.

37 *The monsignor at St. Stephen's*: Central Catholic records.

38 *He would study law*: Kittel interview; August Wilson interview; Brown, "Light in August."

38 *IQ of 143*: Brown, "Light in August."

38 *Established in 1927 . . . "men of service"*: "Fast Facts," Central Catholic High School, https://www.centralcatholichs.com/pages/fast-facts.

38 *Almost all the students*: Brandon Haburjak interview and tour, Central Catholic High School, August 7, 2019.

38 *only a handful of African American students*: Central Catholic High School 1959–1960 yearbook.

38 *The students at Central Catholic were tracked*: Haburjak interview.

38 *placed in 3F*: Central Catholic 1959–1960 yearbook.

38 *He walked up the four flights*: Haburjak interview.

39 *he called the class . . . Pledge of Allegiance*: August Wilson interview.

39 *The school was stifling . . . natural light*: Central Catholic tour.

39 *Brother Dominic*: Watlington, "Hurdling Fences."

39 *"It was like I was contaminated"*: August Wilson interview.

39 *a student named Tom Kennedy*: Ibid.

39 *"He ate his lunch"*: Ibid.

39 *At recess, the boys*: Feingold, "August Wilson's Bottomless Blackness," 13.

40 *"The neighborhood I grew up in"*: Ibid.

40 *Rob Penny . . . before Freddy enrolled*: Central Catholic 1956–1957 yearbook.

40 *Samuel Howze . . . "invited to find another school"*: Udin interview.

40 *He arrived almost every morning*: Feingold, "August Wilson's Bottomless Blackness," 13.

40   *One morning, Brother Vincent . . . his own protection*: August Wilson interview.

41   *He tried out for the football team . . . wouldn't budge*: Kittel interview.

41   *Brother Dominic became a mentor*: Watlington, "Hurdling Fences," 83.

41   *he walked into the Hazelwood branch*: August Wilson, "Feed Your Mind."

41   *"That word 'power'"*: Ibid.

41   *after school cutting the lawn*: Ibid.

41   *neighbor named Herbert Douglas . . . 1948 Olympics*: Christopher Harris, "Olympian Herb Douglas Remembers the Legacy He Built in Sports and Business," *Ebony*, March 9, 2017.

42   *"I was proud of the fact"*: August Wilson, "Feed Your Mind."

42   *the Milwaukee Braves were in town*: Robin Adams Sloan, *Indianapolis News*, December 14, 1984.

42   *"One thing I took"*: August Wilson, "Feed Your Mind."

42   *He took out The Complete Poems*: Ibid.

42   *"the teachers, the principal"*: Ibid.

42   *"I began to understand"*: Ibid.

42   *"It opened a world"*: Ibid.

42   *He wrote a poem*: Watlington, "Hurdling Fences."

42   *"You shouldn't just write"*: Ibid.

43   *he started writing nature poems*: Ibid.

43   *"I'm gonna quit" . . . he walked out*: Livingston, "Cool August," 43.

43   *His mother was not pleased*: Kittel interview.

43   *In the school's 1959–60 yearbook*: Central Catholic High School 1959–60 yearbook.

43   *"you're not gonna be a lawyer"*: Livingston, "Cool August," 43.

43   *Clifford B. Connelley Trade School*: "History," Energy Innovation Center History, https://www.eicpittsburgh.org/about/history/.

44   *When Freddy showed up*: Livingston, "Cool August," 43.

44   *"They're doing fifth-grade work!"*: Ibid.

44   *He clashed with the sheet metal teacher*: August Wilson interview.

44   *"I don't want to be an auto mechanic"*: Livingston, "Cool August," 43.

44   *referred to as Mr. Biggs*: Ibid., 43. In some interviews, Wilson referred to this teacher as "Mr. B," but in private, he called him Mr. Biggs.

44   *Freddy sensed Mr. Biggs*: Ibid., 43.

45   *he had taken Napoleon . . . "What do we do next?"*: Ibid., 44.

45   *He called it "Napoleon's Will to Power"*: Moyers, *A World of Ideas*, 185.

45   *he hired his sister*: Ibid.

45   *Mr. Biggs asked him to stay . . . "your research?"*: Ibid.

45   *Freddy pointed out . . . who was incensed*: Ibid.

45   *Freddy tore the paper . . . he gave up*: Ibid.

46   *"I dropped out of school"*: Wilson, "Feed Your Mind."

46   *He was naive enough*: Ibid.

46 *"I felt suddenly liberated"*: Ibid.

46 *books on "cultural anthropology"*: Ibid.

47 *"My mother was through with it"*: August Wilson interview. It is interesting to note that he referred to his mother as "Mrs. Kittel" during this interview and many others. At the time, Daisy was not married to Frederick Kittel and was living with David Bedford. He allowed interviewers and colleagues to believe that the two were married.

47 *"She told him he was no good"*: Lahr, "Been Here and Gone," 57.

47 *when he was seventeen, he enlisted*: Charles Johnson, *Night Hawks: Stories* (New York: Scribner, 2018), 168. In an interview, Johnson confirmed that Wilson spoke about his military service, but never said that he actually took the exam. In *Pittsburgh Places*, Rawson and Glasco write that he did, indeed, take the test, and his score was "off the charts." One version of the story contends that he quit in anger, while another says that after he took the test, the top brass discovered that, at seventeen, he was underage and gave him an early release. That story cannot be true because the minimum age for enlisting is seventeen, with parental consent.

47 *There are no military records*: National Archive, National Personnel Records Center.

47 *"Anyone who goes into the army"*: David Savran, *In Their Own Words: Contemporary American Playwrights* (New York: Theatre Communications Group, 1988), 301.

48 *"I got six [years]"*: August Wilson, *Fences* (New York: Plume, 1986), 94.

48 *he went off to Los Angeles*: Kittel interview.

48 *a poem called "LA 1963"*: August Wilson, *In Concert: Gerry Rhodes, Poet August Wilson, Poet Mark Martin, Guitarist (Bluegrass, Blues, Ragtime), presented by Mill River Productions and Statue of Life, February 21, 1976*, CD recording at Detre Library & Archives, Heinz History Center, Pittsburgh.

FOUR A Period of Reinvention

49 *"His art was anchored"*: Johnson, *Night Hawks*, 168.

49 *One late afternoon in January . . . bathed in a watery glow*: Peggy Martin interview, August 14, 2019.

49 *"I was mesmerized"*: Ibid.

49 *She beckoned . . . obscure words*: Ibid. Wilson was going by the name "August" in 1964, even though later he said he changed his name in April 1965.

50 *They were not romantically . . . discovered in a book*: Ibid.

50 *His mother had moved twice*: Glasco and Rawson, *Pittsburgh Places*, 72.

50 *His wife, Maryanna Jodzis Kittel*: Obituary notice, *Pittsburgh Press*, January 7, 1964.

51 *She and Kittel went*: Butler County Marriage Bureau, Butler County Courthouse.

51 *"My mother was very practical"*: Kittel interview.

51 *A few months after the civil ceremony*: "Vital Statistics, Divorce Suits Filed," *Pittsburgh Press*, August 22, 1964; Allegheny County Department of Court Records, Civil/Family Division.

51 *a small, nagging suspicion . . . years later*: Renee Wilson interview.

51 *On March 5, 1965*: Larry Oakes, "Honored Playwright Offers St. Paul Soliloquy," *Star Tribune*, August 6, 1987.

51 *He worked odd jobs*: August Wilson, conceived with Todd Kreidler, *How I Learned What I Learned* (New York: Samuel French, 2018), 14, 15, 17.

51 *He bought woolen coats*: Nathan Oliver poem, in Glasco and Rawson, *Pittsburgh Places*, 11.

51 *"He was always in businessman appropriate"*: Kittel interview.

52 *"A lot of people thought"*: Ibid.

52 *"How you gonna eat?"*: August Wilson interview.

52 *"She thought I was a failure"*: Ibid.; Brown, "Light in August."

52 *He went home one day*: Kittel interview.

52 *Daisy was not amused*: Ibid.

52 *one of about fifty-five thousand . . . "a third-world country"*: Wilson, *How I Learned*, 11; "Historical Census Statistics on Population Totals by Race for Large Cities." The number is Wilson's estimate; in 1960, there were 100,692 African Americans living in Pittsburgh, not all of them in the Hill District, so his estimate is reasonable.

52 *Lena Horne*: Mark Whitaker, *Smoketown: The Untold Story of the Other Great Black Renaissance* (New York: Simon & Schuster, 2018), 137.

52 *George Benson*: Ibid., 325.

52 *"nine drugstores" . . . Mainway Supermarket*: Wilson, *How I Learned*, 12.

53 *So often was his pen on paper*: Vera Sheppard, "August Wilson: An Interview," *National Forum: The Phi Kappa Phi Journal* (Summer 1990), reprinted in *Conversations with August Wilson*, ed. Jackson R. Bryer and Mary C. Hartig (Jackson: University Press of Mississippi, 2006), 101.

53 *Daisy took him in*: Kittel interview.

53 *one last visit*: Lahr, "Been Here and Gone," 57.

53 *"He suddenly looked up"*: Ibid.

53 *He left each of his five "beloved" . . . Barbara*: Allegheny County Department of Court Records, Wills/Orphans' Court Division.

53 *she contested the will*: Allegheny County Department of Court Records, Wills/Orphans' Court Division.

53 *The family did hold a wake . . . requiem mass*: *Pittsburgh Press* obituary notice, April 2, 1965.

53 *they buried him*: St. Stanislaus Cemetery records.

54 *There is one unmarked grave*: Ibid.

54 *what happened on April 1, 1965*: Lahr, "Been Here and Gone," 57.

54 *the paper was called*: Ibid.

54 *a used Royal Standard manual*: Ibid.

54 *He bought it at McFarren's Typewriter Store*: Ibid. The profile misstates the date as April 1, 1964, but Wilson told the story repeatedly, always using April 1, 1965, the date of Kittel Sr.'s death. See Glasco and Rawson, *Pittsburgh Places*, 65.

54 *typed out various versions*: Ibid.

54 *didn't change it legally*: State of Minnesota, Ramsey County District Court, Second Judicial District.

55 *began speaking with an affected Welsh accent*: Porter interview.

55 *Many of the Pittsburgh poets*: Ibid.

55 *"As I bedded down"*: Wilson, *Three Plays*, viii.

55 *allowed them to shoot up*: Lahr, "Been Here and Gone," 58.

55 *Chawley Williams . . . protected him*: Ibid.

55 *"When I met August"*: Ibid.

56 *He described one incident . . . "none of that shit"*: Ibid.

56 *Cy Morocco . . . spit out a note*: Wilson, *How I Learned*, 28–32.

56 *"He was a joke among the musicians"*: Harrison interview.

56 *"the original homeless man" . . . when he was homeless*: Wilson, *How I Learned*, 33–34.

56 *Barbara Peterson . . . Pittsburgh Public Schools*: Ibid., 14.

57 *"That was my first real lesson in life"*: Ibid.

57 *Her boyfriend was in jail . . . her way around obstacles*: Kreidler interview.

57 *One favorite haunt . . . "'not here to write'"*: L. A. Johnson, "Long-Time Owner of Popular Restaurant in Hill District," *Pittsburgh Post-Gazette*, July 27, 2000.

57 *The seniors called him Youngblood*: Wilson, *How I Learned*, 43.

57 *He had picked up*: Sheppard, "August Wilson: An Interview," 101.

57 *"They talked philosophy"*: Ibid.

58 *He had a string of odd jobs*: Wilson, *How I Learned*, 14, 15, 17.

58 *"I quit"*: Ibid., 15.

58 *stormed off a landscaping job*: Ibid., 16.

58 *He quit a job at Klein's Restaurant*: Ibid., 18.

58 *the older man gave him the name*: Ibid., 13.

58 *"As a twenty-year-old Black man"*: Ibid.

58 *ended up in jail . . . sing a tune*: Ibid., 19–21.

59 *the original, unpublished version*: Huntington Theatre Company rehearsal script, 2016 production, 22.

59 *in the posthumously published version*: Wilson, *How I Learned*, 21.

59 *touched him deeply . . . darkest of nights*: Ibid.

59 *One day in 1965*: Wilson, *Three Plays*, ix.

59 *"Nobody in Town"*: Spencer and Clarence Williams, Bessie Smith recording, 1923.

60 *"The universe stuttered"*: Wilson, *Three Plays*, ix.

60 *not popular in Pittsburgh's vibrant music scene*: Whitaker, *Smoketown*, 324.

60 *"Suffice it to say"*: Wilson, *Three Plays*, ix.

60 *"The blues . . . wellspring of my art"*: August Wilson, foreword to Myron Schwartzman, *Romare Bearden: His Life and Art* (New York: Harry N. Abrams, 1990), 8.

61 *"I began to look"*: Brown, "Light in August."

61 *"best literature that the Blacks have"*: Carol Rosen, "August Wilson: Bard of the Blues," *Theatre Week*, May 27, 1996; reprinted in Bryer and Hartig, *Conversations with August Wilson*, 198.

61 *Columbia blue label*: https://www.discogs.com/release/3292604-Bessie-Smith -If-You-Dont-I-Know-Who-Will-Nobody-In-Town-Can-Bake-A-Sweet-Jelly -Roll-Like-Mine.

61 *her real name*: Willa Mae Montague interview, June 10, 2017.

61 *"I never saw Billy"*: Ibid.

61 *a waitress . . . Reginald Howze*: Wilson, *How I Learned*, 22–27.

62 *One night in 1966*: Wilson, *How I Learned*, 29–32.

62 *a window on the side street*: Harrison interview. The window still exists in the boarded-up building.

62 *"Aw, man, it ain't got no words!"*: Miles Marshall Lewis, "An Interview with August Wilson," *The Believer*, November 1, 2004, https://believermag.com /an-interview-with-august-wilson/.

62 *"enabled" . . . "art to do"*: Ibid.

62 *"It remains" . . . growing music collection*: Wilson, *How I Learned*, 29–32.

62 *he went to see a free screening*: Kittel interview.

62 *his younger brother Richard . . . "You have to clean yourself up"*: Ibid.

63 *he attended the Epiphany school . . . "by the white kids"*: Ibid.

63 *Wilson identified as Black . . . ignore the questions*: Ibid.

63 *Richard frequently stopped by . . . "two voices"*: Ibid.

63 *cycle of petty crimes*: Kittel interview.

63 *"He told me to be my own man"*: Ibid.

64 *the Hill artists got a home . . . any given night*: Thomas O'Neil, "Halfway Gallery—A Need Fulfilled," *Pittsburgh Post-Gazette*, May 14, 1966.

64 *When it opened*: Brown, "Light in August."

64 *Signals Press published . . . "For Malcolm X and Others"*: "May We Speak," ed. Gerald Rhodes (Pittsburgh: Signals Press, 1968), Bob Johnson Papers, 1949– 2003, Curtis Theatre Collection, Archives & Special Collections, University of Pittsburgh Library System.

64 *"Or rather only imagine"*: Ibid.

65 *"a flock of saints" . . . "glutton of this time"*: Ibid.

65 *"I live and turn my wheel"*: Ibid.

65 *in his speech "The Ground on Which I Stand"*: August Wilson, *The Ground*

on Which I Stand (New York: Theatre Communications Group, 2001; speech originally delivered June 26, 1996), 11.

65 *the Afro-American Institute of Pittsburgh . . . powerful rhetoric*: Roger Stuart, "Controversial Leader to Arrive for Program Here," *Pittsburgh Post-Gazette*, February 21, 1968; Curtiss Porter, "Soul 'n Fury: Black Unity Theme," *New Pittsburgh Courier*, March 16, 1968; Curtiss Porter, "Soul 'n Fury: Unity and Culture," *New Pittsburgh Courier*, March 23, 1968.

65 *"When you see a revolution, going on"*: Porter, "Unity and Culture."

65 *The activist/artist gave a thundering ovation . . . militant speech*: Ibid.

66 *He had a copy of* Black Magic: Poetry, 1961–1967: August Wilson interview.

66 *"I wore that book out"*: Ibid.

66 *became aware of Baraka's groundbreaking*: David Savran, *In Their Own Words: Contemporary American Playwrights* (New York: Theatre Communications Group, 1988), 292.

66 *"We talked about doing theater"*: Livingston, "Cool August," 80.

66 *Riots broke out*: "Pittsburgh Hit by Gangs in Hill District," *Pittsburgh Post-Gazette*, April 6, 1968.

66 *looters swarmed the Mainway Supermarket*: Jack Ryan, "Hill Takes on Appearance of Battlefield," *Pittsburgh Post-Gazette*, April 8, 1968, 1.

66 *"It was the first place to burn"*: Wilson, *How I Learned*, 12.

66 *staged a photo*: Frank Hightower, https://www.ffhphotographyarts.com/p4 80376171.

66 *Governor Raymond P. Shafer . . . were arrested*: "Guard, State Troopers Sent in to Quell Hill District Disorder," *Pittsburgh Post-Gazette*, April 8, 1968, 1.

67 *Black Horizons Theatre*: Various sources identify it as either Black Horizon Theatre or Black Horizons Theatre. The August Wilson Archive at the University of Pittsburgh uses Horizons, and it is used most commonly in periodicals.

67 *he didn't see his first professional production*: Glasco and Rawson, *Pittsburgh Places*, 13.

67 *with electric performances*: George Anderson, "Striking Play from South Africa," *Pittsburgh Post-Gazette*, November 11, 1976.

67 *meetings at a place called the Pan Fried Fish . . . jitney station next door*: Udin interview.

67 *Porter contends*: Porter interview.

67 *Wilson was chosen by default*: Livingston, "Cool August," 50.

67 *"Read the play"*: Harrison interview.

67 *"It never occurred to us"*: Christopher Rawson, "Wilson Again Proves Home Is Where the Art Is," *Pittsburgh Post-Gazette*, December 5, 1999.

68 *He took out a book on directing*: Livingston, "Cool August," 50.

68 *"There are beasts in our world"*: Amiri Baraka, *Four Black Revolutionary Plays* (New York: Marion Boyars, 2009), 56.

68 *"outrageously wicked"*: Wilson, *How I Learned*, 9.

68 *Wilson solicited donations*: Livingston, "Cool August," 50.

68 *Wilson later said . . . tape*: August Wilson interview.

69 *Larry Neal . . . "iconology"*: Larry Neal, "The Black Arts Movement," *The Drama Review* 12, no. 4 (1968): 29.

69 *Curtiss Porter remembers*: Porter interview.

69 *"For Once a Virgin"*: August Wilson, *In Concert.*

69 *Porter recalls*: Porter interview.

69 *"He felt left out"*: Kreidler interview.

69 *"You didn't write that"*: August Wilson interview.

70 *"August wasn't really Black"*: Lahr, "Been Here and Gone," 57.

70 *"Muhammad Ali" and "For Malcolm X and Others"*: Sandra S. Shannon, *The Dramatic Vision of August Wilson* (Washington, D.C.: Howard University Press, 1995), 201.

70 *"Muhammad Ali is a lion"*: Ibid., poem by August Wilson.

71 *took over Pitt's computer center . . . their demands*: "Negro Students Hold Pitt Computer Center," *Pittsburgh Post-Gazette*, January 16, 1969.

71 *took a road trip . . . among others*: "August Wilson 1969 Oberlin College," YouTube, https://www.youtube.com/watch?v=uxHxCo7Z16A.

71 *Rob Penny got a job . . . the administration*: Porter interview.

71 *Wilson wanted to use the funds*: Kreidler interview.

71 *"August was pissed"*: Ibid.

71 *"Doing community theater"*: Savran, *In Their Own Words*, 290.

72 *He took his share of the money*: Kreidler interview.

72 *the couple conceived a child*: Ibid.

72 *They married soon after*: Allegheny County Department of Court Records, Wills/Orphans' Court Division, Marriage License Bureau: Application for Marriage License and Marriage Certificate.

72 *A reception was held*: Kittel interview.

72 *Wilson's father-in-law*: Obituary for Elder Joseph Burton, *Pittsburgh Post-Gazette*, April 15, 2000.

72 *His friends from the arts scene*: Porter interview.

72 *David Bedford died*: Obituary notice, *Pittsburgh Post-Gazette*, September 1, 1969.

72 *Wilson considered him*: Kreidler interview.

72 *Daisy's children looked up to him*: Kittel interview.

72 *He doted on his daughter*: Kittel interview.

73 *member of the Nation of Islam*: Ibid.

73 *He wore the requisite . . . "each other"*: Brown, "Light in August."

73 *he saw a bearded, bespectacled Black man*: Jacqui Shoholm interview, September 7, 2018.

73 *Purdy had just returned . . . Wole Soyinka*: New Federal Theater biography, https://newfederaltheatre.com/nft-artist/claude-purdy/.

73 *Purdy and his new girlfriend*: Elva Branson Lee interview, July 17, 2019.

74 *The opening act*: Harrison interview.

74 *she was frustrated*: Kreidler interview.

74 *"He had the tools of the trade"*: Kittel interview.

74 *"It was a source of pain for him"*: Kreidler interview.

74 *she filed for divorce . . . Allegheny County*: Allegheny County Court of Common Pleas, Pittsburgh.

74 *Pittsburgh Housing Authority*: Allegheny County Court of Common Pleas, Civil Division, Pittsburgh.

74 *"She moved out"*: Lahr, "Been Here and Gone," 59.

75 *"A house divided"*: Feingold, "August Wilson's Bottomless Blackness," 15.

75 *Burton kept to herself*: Kittel interview.

75 *"It was pure trauma"*: Kreidler interview.

75 *"Soon she figure she got a heathen"*: August Wilson, *Ma Rainey's Black Bottom* (New York: Plume, 1985), 91.

75 *"dressed as befitting a member of an Evangelist church"*: Wilson, *Three Plays*, 283.

75 *"You done gone over to the devil"*: Ibid., 287.

75 *"You shining"*: Ibid., 289.

FIVE A Road Marked with Signposts

76 *"I called to my courage"*: August Wilson, foreword to Schwartzman, *Romare Bearden*, 13.

76 *His friend Claude Purdy*: Branson Lee interview.

76 *His brothers and sisters*: Kittel interview; Lahr, "Been Here and Gone," 59.

76 *He talked about the loss*: Charles Johnson interview, March 8, 2005.

77 *"I laughed. I cried"*: August Wilson, *Oxherding Tale* (New York: Scribner, 2005), jacket cover.

77 *"I didn't value and respect"*: Nathan L. Grant, *American Drama* 5 (Spring 1996); reprinted in *Conversations with August Wilson*, ed. Jackson R. Bryer and Mary C. Hartig (Jackson: University Press of Mississippi, 2006), 183.

77 *"Morning Statement"*: August Wilson interview; Lahr, "Been Here and Gone," 60.

77 *"The poem didn't pretend"*: Ibid.

77 *"I was wrassling with poems"*: Brown, "Light in August."

78 *He consciously decided*: Savran, *In Their Own Words*, 292.

78 *His friend Nick Flournoy*: Rawson, "Home Is Where the Art Is."

78 *"What the hell is this?"*: Ibid.

78 *"I would describe . . . everyone"*: Kim Powers, "An Interview with August Wilson," *Theater* 16 (Fall–Winter 1984); reprinted in Bryer and Hartig, ed., *Conversations with August Wilson*, 5.

78 *his first play*, Recycle: Wilson originally named the play *Recycling*, but later

changed the name to *Recycle*. Notebooks, August Wilson Archive, University of Pittsburgh.

78 *That summer, he and Penny*: Laurence Glasco, "Chapter IX: 'I Can't Take It!': August Wilson Leaves Pittsburgh," *August Wilson Journal* 1, no. 1 (2019), http://augustwilson.pitt.edu/ojs/augustwilson/article/view/26.

78 *The two poets had a grandiose plan*: Bob Hoover, "Wilson Draws on Youth in Hill," *Pittsburgh Post-Gazette*, June 1, 1987.

78 *Penny later said*: Ibid.

78 *Other sources contend*: Glasco, " 'I Can't Take It!' "

79 *The play . . . having a conversation*: Sandra S. Shannon, *The Dramatic Vision of August Wilson* (Washington, D.C.: Howard University Press, 1995), 205–6.

79 *Maisha Baton . . . "wet with laughing"*: Maisha Baton, "The Testimonial: August Wilson & Me: The Early Years," Acting Now, Johnson Papers; Maisha Baton interview, March 8, 2005.

80 *Baton spoke the first line . . . "two of you"*: Ibid.

80 *"daughterless"*: August Wilson, Poem, *In Concert*.

80 *He visited Sakina . . . gave her the money*: Sakina Ansara Wilson interview, May 31, 2017; Kittel interview.

81 *series of poems*: August Wilson, unpublished script, Johnson Papers.

81 *a teacher named Vernell Lillie*: Edward L. Blank, "Black Drama Keys on Love Expression," *Pittsburgh Post-Gazette*, January 23, 1977.

81 *means "way"*: Jean Bryant, "Taking the Lead," *Pittsburgh Post-Gazette*, March 15, 1994.

81 *"the cultural tradition"*: Kuntu Repertory Theatre program, Johnson Papers.

81 *Kuntu's first season*: Bryant, "Taking the Lead."

82 *formed the Kuntu Writers Workshop*: Christopher Rawson, "A Pair of Premieres," *Pittsburgh Post-Gazette*, October 2, 1998.

82 *"He could, just with a twinkle"*: Vernell Lillie interview, March 8, 2005.

82 *he penned "The Greatest Blues Singer"*: August Wilson, *King Hedley II* (New York: Theatre Communications Group, 2005), preface, vii.

82 *"social context of the artist" . . . "drowning"*: Ibid.

82 *"The Wood of the Cross"*: August Wilson, Notebook 485, August Wilson Archive. There is no copy of *Placebo* in the archives, but Wilson wrote extensive notes about the trilogy in his notebooks.

82 *St. Paul actor Terry Bellamy . . . into the world*: Terry Bellamy interview, August 31, 2018.

83 Coldest Day of the Year . . . *uncertain future*: August Wilson, script, Johnson Papers.

83 *a bill of three one-act plays*: Flyer advertising the program, Johnson papers.

83 The Homecoming *takes place*: August Wilson, script, Johnson papers.

83 *The blind son*: Elijah Wald, *The Blues: A Very Short Introduction* (Oxford, UK: Oxford University Press, 2010), 28–30.

83 *the usual story*: Elijah Wald interview, June 10, 2021.

84 *Morton did . . . collaboration*: Wald interview.

84 *The theater had opened . . . Malvolio*: "About the Public," Pittsburgh Public Theater, https://www.ppt.org/ppt_home/about.

85 *"I thought"*: Savran, *In Their Own Words*, 392.

86 *His friend Claude Purdy*: Wilson, *Romare*, 8.

86 *"What for me had been so difficult"*: Ibid.

86 *"He showed me a doorway"*: Ibid., 9.

86 *she hired him to direct*: Edward L. Blank, "Black Drama Keys on Love Expression," *Pittsburgh Press*, June 13, 1977.

87 *In a 1971 review*: Mel Gussow, "In New England Winter," *New York Times*, January 27, 1977.

87 *Wilson clashed with Lillie*: Glasco, "'I Can't Take It!'"

87 *In his version, Black Bart*: Wilson, *Black Bart and the Sacred Hills*, script, Johnson Papers.

87 *"sheer artistic madness"*: Baton interview.

87 *"It was fun"*: Ibid.

88 *Branson recalled that Purdy*: Branson Lee interview.

88 *Purdy, in particular*: Jacqui Shoholm email, July 23, 2021.

88 *Johnson had originally . . . write the script*: Harrison interview.

88 *Johnson sent the script*: Peter M. Carnahan, letter, June 1, 1977, Johnson Papers.

88 *drew up a production budget*: "Black Bart Weekly Production Costs," "Black Bart Pre-Production Budget," Johnson Papers.

88 *Johnson repeatedly urged Harrison*: Harrison interview.

88 *they scheduled auditions . . . July opening*: Auditions flyer, Johnson Papers.

89 *The center had received*: Macelle Mahala, *Penumbra: The Premier Stage for African American Drama* (Minneapolis: University of Minnesota Press, 2013), 4.

89 *Purdy invited Wilson*: Ibid., 60.

89 *He secretly hoped Penumbra*: Jacqui Shoholm interview, September 7, 2018.

89 *He also had his eyes on the Guthrie*: Branson Lee interview.

SIX Learning to Listen

90 *"I was sitting in a room"*: Douglas J. Keating, "The August Wilson Play That Got Him on His Way," *Philadelphia Inquirer*, June 14, 1998.

90 *Wilson asked if they could go*: Shoholm interview.

91 *Wilson stayed with Purdy*: Ibid.

91 *The grand hotel*: "About the Commodore," Commodore, https://www.thecommodorebar.com/about-us.

91 *He went to see Eden*: Shoholm interview.

91 *its executive director*: Mahala, *Penumbra*, 4.

91 *She was a city planner*: Shoholm interview.

91 *She had seen Purdy's*: Ibid.

91 *performed at the Downtown Dinner Theater*: Ira Letofsky, "Great White Hope Opens at Downtown Dinner Theater," *Star Tribune*, March 10, 1976.

91 *She asked Purdy if he*: Shoholm interview.

92 *"This guy is the real thing"*: Ibid.

92 *She introduced Wilson*: Ibid.

92 *his "true heart"*: Brown, "Light in August."

92 *"I said, 'Here is who I am'"*: Peter Vaughan, "2 Early One-Act Plays by Wilson Will Be Presented at Fundraiser," *Star Tribune*, September 15, 1989.

92 *He had sent the script*: Letter from Lynn Holst, New Play Development Coordinator, New York Shakespeare Festival, October 12, 1978, Johnson Papers.

92 *Johnson received a polite*: Ibid.

92 *On March 5, 1978*: Larry Oakes, "Honored Playwright Offers St. Paul Soliloquy," *Star Tribune*, August 6, 1987.

93 *she blessed the move*: Kittel interview.

93 *population of the state of Minnesota*: "Historical Census Statistics on Population Totals by Race, 1790 to 1990, and by Hispanic Origin, 1970 to 1990, for the United States, Regions, Divisions, and States," U.S. Census Bureau. In 1980, there were 53,344 Blacks residing in Minnesota.

93 *He started showing up*: Abdul Salaam El Razzac interview, September 6, 2018.

93 *"He was the dude"* . . . *quiet presence in the background*: Ibid.

93 *the artists at Penumbra*: Mahala, *Penumbra*, 1–42; Lou Bellamy interview, September 14, 2018.

93 *In addition to* Eden . . . *"some fun too"*: Mahala, *Penumbra*, 18.

94 *pay the actors $150 a week*: Lou Bellamy interview.

94 *he said that some days*: Terry Bellamy interview.

94 *"being a female"*: Mahala, *Penumbra*, 82.

94 *"The Black Arts Movement"*: Ibid.

95 *"a mother or a prostitute"*: Ibid.

95 *"aware how much my"*: Ibid.

95 *"It was a place"*: Carlyle Brown interview, September 6, 2018.

95 *He arranged a trip*: Sakina Ansara Wilson interview.

95 *"It was like, 'Wow'"*: Ibid.

95 *Shoholm connected him*: Oakes, "Honored Playwright."

95 *titles like* Eskimo Insult Duel: August Wilson interview; Shannon, *Dramatic Vision*, 203.

95 *In* Profiles in Science: August Wilson, *Profiles in Science: William Harvey*, unpublished and undated, August Wilson Archive.

96 *a senior curator called Wilson*: August Wilson interview.

96 *"I could write a better"* . . . *"never forget you"*: Ibid.

96 *He was enamored*: August Wilson, notecard attached to script of *Eskimo Insult Duel*, August Wilson Archive.

96 *Purdy arranged for a reading*: Program, Inner City Cultural Center, May 8, 1978, Johnson Papers.

96 *"It was a mess"*: Shoholm interview.

97 *Larry Neal's essay*: Neal, "The Black Arts Movement," 29.

97 *"The one thing which we did not"*: Shannon, *Dramatic Vision*, 211.

97 *he had told his younger brother*: Kittel interview.

97 *two couples formed . . . some point as well*: Shoholm interview.

97 *"She was lively and funny"*: Yoshimura interview.

97 *Shoholm, an experienced city planner . . . for good luck*: Shoholm interview.

98 *he picked up a rejected script*: Kreidler interview.

98 *"Sometimes I can hear him"*: Brown, "Light in August."

98 *His friend Rob Penny*: Watlington, "Hurdling Fences," 85.

98 *Wilson applied*: Eugene O'Neill Theater Center Archives.

98 *"He had all this East Coast energy"*: James Craven interview, November 2, 2018.

98 *Craven, in fact*: Ibid.

98 *Craven came back . . . on Broadway*: Ibid.

99 *"A musical satire"*: Press release, Penumbra Theatre Company Archives, Givens Collection of African American Literature, University of Minnesota Libraries.

99 *Wilson had seen a production*: Joan Herrington, *"I Ain't Sorry for Nothin' I Done": August Wilson's Process of Playwriting* (New York: Limelight Editions, 1998), 30–31; Baraka, *Four Black Revolutionary Plays*, 57–79.

99 *"It's wild and zany"*: Ibid.

100 *The musical opens*: August Wilson, *Black Bart and the Sacred Hills*, script, Johnson Papers.

100 *"there is a large cast"*: Michael Phillips, "Wild Spoof," *St. Paul Pioneer Press*, July 17, 1981.

100 *On opening night*: Lou Bellamy interview.

100 *"cartoon-like parody"*: Phillips, "Wild Spoof."

100 *One night, the motorcycle*: Lou Bellamy interview.

100 *"I will never do a play"*: Ibid.

100 *"It's zany. I think"*: August Wilson interview.

101 *Oliver knew*: Mike Henley interview, September 5, 2018.

101 *Little Brothers of the Poor*: http://littlebrothers.org/.

101 *Wilson fit right in*: Henley interview.

101 *His two brothers . . . stable lifestyle*: Kittel interview.

101 *hanging out of his mouth*: Henley interview.

101 *his record was respectable*: https://www.boxerlist.com/boxer/mike-morgan /15155/.

101 *Wilson was earning*: Henley interview.

101 *filed for bankruptcy*: District of Minnesota, United States Bankruptcy Court, Minnesota.

101 *Wilson appeared at*: Minnesota Second Judicial Court records.

101   *He and Oliver married*: Minnesota Official Marriage System records.

101   *in a ceremony . . . photos*: Shoholm interview; Jacqui Shoholm photo.

102   *"They would have verbal arguments"*: Henley interview.

102   *"He enjoyed the time" . . . "best time of his life"*: Ibid.

102   *"He was older"*: Dunn interview.

102   *"Americanized Homer dialogue"*: Phillips, "Wild Spoof."

103   *He spent many hours . . . shoes shined*: Dunn interview.

103   *One of the members . . . "'photocopiers'"*: Ibid.

103   *"Oppressed by the socioeconomic conditions"*: The Playwrights' Center Records, Performing Arts Archives, University of Minnesota Libraries.

104   *"That was the first person"*: Shannon, *Dramatic Vision*, 124.

104   *"It was like"*: Ibid.

104   *summed up as an examination*: Newsletter, Playwrights' Center Records.

104   *"I was going to write three plays"*: August Wilson interview.

104   *"I wasn't a playwright" . . . not his* father's house: Ibid.

105   *"One day, I was at a place called Nora's"*: Ibid.

106   *It was given a staged reading*: Terry Bellamy interview.

106   *Some of the actors . . . completed filming*: Shoholm interview; Terry Bellamy interview.

106   *On December 1, 1981 . . . Ma Rainey*: Eugene O'Neill Theater Center Archives.

SEVEN   The Launchpad of American Theater

107   *"Your belief in yourself"*: August Wilson, Program for *Ma Rainey's Black Bottom*, Kuntu Repertory Theatre, March 12, 1985, Johnson Papers.

107   *He had boarded the van*: Jean Passanante interview, December 15, 2017.

108   *White learned . . . $1 a year*: Jeffrey Sweet, *The O'Neill: The Transformation of Modern American Theater* (New Haven, CT: Yale University Press, 2014), 13.

108   *he invited a group of playwrights*: Ibid., 16.

109   *"blatant attempt to disregard"*: Judy Oliver, "Black Playwrights," *Star Tribune*, March 12, 1982.

109   *"CONGRATULATIONS YOUR PLAY"*: Passanante interview.

110   *The O'Neill contract*: Agreement, Eugene O'Neill Theater Center, August Wilson Archive.

110   *Wilson called Passanante*: Ibid.

110   *"People showed up . . . felt that way"*: August Wilson interview.

111   *Constance Grappo . . . "subtler"*: Wilson, *Ground* (PBS).

111   *"My sense was that"*: Passanante interview.

111   *"The Great Black Hope"*: Jeffrey Hatcher interview, December 8, 2017.

111   *"The characters were alive"*: Brown, "Light in August."

111   *Richards didn't immediately recognize*: Sweet, *The O'Neill*, 151.

112   *They held contests*: Doug Post interview, December 28, 2017.

112   *"The O'Neill is like a club"*: Steve Robman interview, November 9, 2017.

112   *"You could lay on the floor"*: Lee Blessing interview, November 28, 2017.

113   *"Could you read* Ma *next?"* . . . *the rest of his life*: Kreidler interview.

114   *"How did I feel?"*: August Wilson interview.

114   *Olivetti 93 DL*: August Wilson, letter to Stan Chervin, October 1, 1983, Stan Chervin personal files.

114   *"its warmth and redress"*: Wilson, *Ma Rainey*, xv.

114   *"*Ma Rainey *is very long"*: Passanante interview.

114   *Wilson's friends in St. Paul*: Shoholm interview; Lou Bellamy interview.

114   *"He inhabited every character"*: Passanante interview.

115   *"When you listen to four plays"*: Amy Saltz interview, July 17, 2018.

115   *"The O'Neill was an intimidating"* . . . *in the car's trunk*: Ibid.

115   *"August was a mythmaker"*: Ibid.

116   *"He was the anointed playwright"*: James Nicholson interview, January 26, 2018.

116   *Wilson told his friend Charles Johnson*: Johnson interview.

116   *During the four weeks*: The author was in residence at the National Critics Institute in 1987.

117   *He emerged from the shower*: Laura Maria Censabella interview, November 26, 2017.

117   *He passed notes* . . . *"little napkins"*: Julie Boyd interview, January 9, 2018.

117   *Late one night*: Tom Aberger interview, July 25, 2018.

117   *"He was intense"*: Barnet Kellman interview, December 18, 2017.

117   *"old jug band shit"*: Wilson, *Ma Rainey*, 26.

118   *refers to them as "boys"*: Ibid., 20.

118   *paid $100 plus room and board*: Vinnie Scarano interview, December 18, 2017.

118   *Wilson and Scarano would go down to the beach*: Ibid.

118   *"That is not going to happen to me"*: Ibid.

119   *his director, Bill Partlan*: Bill Partlan interview, October 11, 2017.

119   *he had made few, if any*: Ibid.

119   *Wilson had written* . . . *second act*: Hoover, "Wilson Draws on Youth."

119   *Partlan and Feingold wanted to massage*: Partlan inerview.

119   *"He said that he had to hear it"*: Ibid.

119   *Wilson did not make any changes*: Ibid.

120   *Dutton had been convicted* . . . *the African Americans disappear overnight*: Greg Donaldson, "Real Life Drama," *Newsday*, May 8, 1990.

120   *"to Yale"*: Ibid.

120   *Angela Bassett*: Partlan interview.

120   *"We heard these stories"*: Samuel G. Freeman, "Mother of an Era," *New York Times*, February 2, 2003.

120   *"The writing was beautiful* . . . *the action"*: Partlan interview.

120   *Partlan agreed to stage*: Ibid.

120 *"You are not allowed to pace"* . . . *"leaning back"*: Ibid.

121 *"huge cuts"*: Ibid.

121 *Partlan had one last rehearsal*: Ibid.

121 *Wilson's mother . . . Curtiss Porter*: Porter interview.

121 *The press office was aware*: Frank Rich interview, November 15, 2017.

121 *"God bless you"*: August Wilson interview.

122 *Dutton was on fire*: Sweet, *The O'Neill*, Vinnie Scarano photograph, 1982, 150.

122 *The audience members*: Partlan interview.

122 *Scarano slipped him a joint*: Scarano interview.

122 *He joined the parties*: Sweet, *The O'Neill*, 142.

122 *He played softball*: Wendy MacLeod interview, January 17, 2018.

122 *One day near the end of the conference*: Nicholson interview.

122 *"If you were doing something wrong"*: Boyd interview.

122 *The* Times *had arrived* . . . Playing in Local Bands: Frank Rich, "Where Writers Mold the Future of Theater," *New York Times*, August 1, 1982.

123 *"the talent to go all the way"*: Ibid.

123 *"It is quite unusual"*: Ibid.

123 *"I was electrified"*: Ibid.

123 *"Mr. Wilson . . . who gave the American theater its past"*: Ibid.

123 *"Lloyd never gave me instructions" . . . no conspiracy with Richards*: Rich interview.

124 *"Lloyd knew what he was doing"*: August Wilson interview.

124 *subsequent productions*: The author saw a production of *Ma Rainey* by Boston's Huntington Theatre Company in 2012 and attended a production with Wilson at the Seattle Repertory Theatre in 2005.

124 *A 2003 Broadway revival*: https://www.ibdb.com/broadway-production/ma -raineys-black-bottom-13462.

124 *Wilson got a call*: Partlan interview.

124 *Playwright Jeffrey Hatcher*: Hatcher interview.

124 *"The whole time I was there" . . . " 'bring your lawyer' "*: August Wilson interview.

124 *The producer interested . . . Wilson was furious*: Partlan interview.

125 *"I am the theater"*: https://www.nycommunitytrust.org/newsroom/the-legacy -of-helen-merrill-a-love-of-theater-lives-on/.

125 *"I must be a playwright, too"*: Sweet, *The O'Neill*, 152.

EIGHT Living on Mother's Prayer

126 *"It is only when you encounter"*: August Wilson, "Living on Mother's Prayer."

126 *"Although I haven't yet found out"*: Frank Rich quoted by August Wilson, interview, 2005.

127 *The perky press release*: Press release, Allegheny Repertory Theatre, Johnson Papers.

127 *In a September 27, 1982, letter*: August Wilson, letter to Bob Johnson, September 27, 1982, Johnson Papers.

127 *"the 1982 recipient"*: Bob Johnson, Johnson Papers.

127 *He ended up casting*: *Jitney!* program, Johnson papers.

127 *"I thought, 'What the hell'"*: Udin interview.

127 *"breathtakingly realistic cast"*: Donald Miller, "'Jitney' Characters Try to Cope with Their Bumpy Rides in Life," *Pittsburgh Post-Gazette*, November 5, 1982.

127 *Wilson took Daisy*: August Wilson interview.

128 *The jitney driver told Wilson*: Ibid.

128 *still a rough sketch*: Videotape, Penumbra Theatre production of *Jitney!*, 1984–85 season, Penumbra Theatre Company Archives. The author compared the differences between the original script and the subsequent rewrite, which underwent revisions in a series of productions from 1996 to 2000.

128 *that jitney station had closed*: Glasco and Rawson, *Pittsburgh Places*, 87.

128 *COurt 1-9802*: August Wilson interview.

128 *Chawley Williams . . . "digitarian"*: John Lahr, "John Lahr and August Wilson," *Slate*, September 10, 2001, https://slate.com/human-interest/2001/09/john-lahr-and-august-wilson-2.html.

128 *Youngblood is the name*: August Wilson, *How I Learned*, 43.

129 *"They were saying, 'Daddy is dead'"*: Udin interview.

129 *the "best premiere"*: Jim Davidson, "'Ghost Sonata' Tops Small Theater '82," *Pittsburgh Press*, January 2, 1983.

129 *he and Oliver had moved . . . father and daughter as well*: Shoholm interview. Despite numerous attempts by the author, Judy Oliver chose not to be interviewed for this biography.

129 *She learned . . . he knew it*: Sakina Ansara Wilson interview.

130 *"To my daughter"*: Wilson, *Three Plays*, 194.

130 *The comparable award*: CPI Inflation Calculator.

130 *March 13*: "In the Wings," *Star Tribune*, March 13, 1983.

130 *Wilson and Oliver flew . . . devastated*: Sakina Ansari Wilson interview.

130 *younger brother Richard*: Kittel interview.

130 *He arrived back*: Ibid.

130 *Richard remembers . . . "bury any of you"*: Ibid.

130 *Among the extended family . . . family lore*: Renee Wilson interview.

131 *"When the sins of our fathers"*: August Wilson, *Fences* (New York: Plume, 1986), x.

131 *Wilson threw himself . . . death left in his life*: August Wilson interview.

131 *As a child . . . "mysterious and unfathomable condition"*: Wilson, "Living on Mother's Prayer."

131 *There was a two-day wake*: Daisy Kittel obituary, *Pittsburgh Press*, March 17, 1983.

131 *Her mother Zonia's grave*: Author visit to Greenwood Cemetery, Pittsburgh, August 6, 2019.

132 *"She's like, 'That's nice'"* . . . *" 'you're a writer' "*: August Wilson interview.

132 *She had smiled*: Jacqui Shoholm photograph.

132 *"They sheltered us from a lot of indignities"*: Livingston, "Cool August," 42.

132 *"an alien place"* . . . *"good directions"*: Wilson, "Living on Mother's Prayer."

133 *Daisy left her estate . . . property*: Allegheny County Department of Court Records, Wills/Orphans' Court Division.

133 *He marveled at Daisy's beauty . . . life full of promise*: August Wilson, letter to Jean Passanante, January 14, 1986, files of Jean Passanante.

133 *"most profound grief imaginable"*: Wilson, *How I Learned*, 25.

133 *Founded in 1949*: "Our History," New Dramatists, https://newdramatists.org/our-history.

134 *Wilson was accepted unanimously*: Tom Dunn interview, September 5, 2018.

134 *New Dramatists . . . late-night hours*: Joel Ruark interview, January 8, 2018; tour of building and library.

134 *He joined a group . . . impersonation*: Casey Childs interview, January 9, 2018.

135 *Sherry Kramer . . . good morning to the staff*: Sherry Kramer interview, December 4, 2017.

135 *he managed to get a collection*: Stan Chervin interview, January 18, 2018.

135 *engaging letter . . . left it on a bus*: August Wilson letter to Stan Chervin, October 1, 1983, Stan Chervin personal files.

136 *"I came up with the idea"*: Shannon, *Dramatic Vision*, 211.

136 *cat named Maxwell*: Brown, "Light in August."

136 *He had one goal . . . they were smashed*: Yoshimura interview.

137 *Like Wilson, Yoshimura*: Ibid.

137 *"That does not work"*: Ibid.

137 *"You are the* other*"*: Ibid.

137 *fine scotch*: Ibid.

137 *"The bottle of scotch"*: Ibid.

137 *Wilson did not question*: Ibid.

137 *"I read my play very badly"*: Ibid.

137 *"He was humble"*: Ibid.

138 *He never suggested . . . " 'you gotta fix it' "*: Ibid.

138 *Some critics . . . the griping stopped*: Censabella interview.

138 *"My impression was"*: Yoshimura interview.

138 *"He was an encyclopedia"*: Ibid.

138 *When Yoshimura's wife . . . scuffed-up*: Ibid.

139 *shut down . . . "deeply wounded"*: Ibid.

139 *the play needed cuts*: Partlan interview.

139 *he stayed up all night*: Ibid.

139 *Helen Hayes . . . "enough theater for one night"*: Sweet, *The O'Neill*, 157.

139   *Wilson took out a long monologue*: Partlan interview.

140   *"He begins to howl"* . . . *"That's the way that go"*: Wilson, *Fences*, 101.

140   *"How thick the fog is"*: Eugene O'Neill, *Long Day's Journey into Night* (New Haven: Yale University Press, 1989), 108.

140   *"The fog came in"*: Partlan interview.

140   *Shanley said* . . . *"Nobody can touch that"*: Sweet, *The O'Neill*, 163.

140   *Wilson had written* . . . *Tennessee Williams*: John Breglio, *I Wanna Be a Producer: How to Make a Killing on Broadway . . . or Get Killed* (New York: Applause, 2016), 146.

140   *skipped a production* . . . *"one bit"*: Yoshimura interview.

141   *Wilson made a promise*: Shoholm interview.

141   *Kramer turned to Wilson* . . . *"a theater named after him"*: Kramer interview.

142   *His sister Freda Ellis*: Adrian McCoy, "August Wilson's Sister Served in Many Roles," *Pittsburgh Post-Gazette*, September 1, 2015.

142   *Wilson often asked Richard*: Wilson, "Heinz Award Acceptance Speech."

142   *sibling issues*: Renee Wilson interview.

142   *In an elegiac letter* . . . *villages of Africa*: August Wilson, letter to Lloyd Richards, March 1, 1984, Lloyd Richards Papers, James Weldon Johnson Collection in the Yale Collection of American Literature, Beinecke Rare Book and Manuscript Library.

143   *Perched on Chapel Street*: "Our Story," Calvary Baptist Church, https://cbcn hct.org/index.php/en-us/about.

143   *Robert Cole* . . . *"exploded on every level"*: Cole interview.

144   *Wilson politely referred*: Ibid.

144   *a producer had to arrange the rights*: Ibid.

144   *"August Wilson's funny, poetic, stabbing"*: Malcolm L. Johnson, "Ma Rainey's Burning, Visceral Attack on American Racism," *Hartford Courant*, April 7, 1984.

144   *"Mr. Wilson has lighted"*: Frank Rich, "Theater: Ma Rainey's Black Bottom," *New York Times*, April 11, 1984.

144   *After the review ran* . . . *produce the play*: Cole interview.

145   *It cost $700,000*: Ibid.

145   *Hotel Edison*: "Our Hotel," Hotel Edison, https://www.edisonhotelnyc.com /our-hotel.

145   *There was no room service*: Michael Fine, "Despite Pulitzer, August Wilson Has Challenges," Gannett News Service, *Burlington Free Press*, May 7, 1990.

145   *New York*: "Our Hotel," Hotel Edison, https://www.edisonhotelnyc.com/our-hotel.

145   *most of the cast*: Enid Nemy, "A 'Ma Rainey' Quartet Plays Its Own Special Music," *New York Times*, October 28, 1984.

146   *"this young actor brings"*: Rich, "Theater: Ma Rainey's Black Bottom."

146   *"Where the hell was God"*: Wilson, *Ma Rainey*, 98.

146   *"That speech shuts down the empty religiosity"*: Dwight Andrews interview, July 17, 2018.

146 *infuriated the church ladies*: Ibid.

146 *"He a white man's"*: Wilson, *Ma Rainey*, 98.

146 *deliberately named this character Levee*: Lou Bellamy interview.

146 *Richards called on actress Ebony Jo-Ann*: Ebony Jo-Ann interview, January 2, 2018.

147 *"He said, 'Here is what'"*: Cole interview.

147 *"I talked to Lloyd privately"*: Ibid.

147 *His wife, Barbara Davenport*: "New Plays," Eugene O'Neill Theater Center, https://www.theoneill.org/newwork.

147 *"My brother and I were raised"*: Scott Richards interview, November 10, 2019.

147 *"He took me home and said"*: Ibid.

147 *He peppered his son*: Ibid.

148 *One night, Theresa Merritt was locked*: Shannon, *Dramatic Vision*, 220.

148 *Wilson later remarked*: Ibid.

148 *But Scott Richards insisted*: Richards interview.

148 *"I don't think it was a personal thing"*: Ibid.

148 *"far from a perfect play"* . . . *"seeming ease"*: Nels Nelson, " 'Ma Rainey' at the Zellerbach," *Philadelphia Daily News*, September 24, 1984.

149 *"I was always the first one"*: Rawson, "Home Is Where the Art Is."

149 *"Everyone felt relief"*: Richards interview.

149 *"The play is a searing inside account"*: Frank Rich, "Wilson's 'Ma Rainey' Opens," *New York Times*, October 12, 1984.

149 *"stirring and entertaining"*: Douglas Watt, " 'Ma Rainey's': Mostly, It Swings," New York *Daily News*, October 12, 1984.

149 *"nothing much happens"*: Clive Barnes, *New York Post*, October 12, 1984.

150 *"God can kiss my ass!"*: Wilson, *Ma Rainey*, 98.

150 *"leftover from history"*: Ibid., 57.

151 *"The four men"*: Nemy, "A 'Ma Rainey' Quartet."

151 *He was one of the most* . . . *Wilson's death in 2005*: Ibid.; Breglio, *I Wanna Be a Producer*, 141–53.

152 *"the Black Shakespeare"*: Peter Vaughan, "Terry Bellamy Casts of Early 'Irresponsibility' to Earn Honors," *Star Tribune*, December 8, 1984.

152 *A rave review* . . . *"simmers and boils"*: Peter Vaughan, " 'Jitney' Carries Audiences into Deeply Moving Drama," *Star Tribune*, December 17, 1984.

152 *The production lost*: Breglio, *I Wanna Be a Producer*, 147.

152 *"The street's postmortem"*: Ibid.

152 *"more than 90 percent"*: Ibid., 149.

153 *Awards, he later noted* . . . *"fuel to the fire"*: Christopher Rawson, "Playwright Wilson Wins Heinz Award," *Pittsburgh Post-Gazette*, December 2, 2003.

153 *"There were nights"*: Robert Feldberg, "Dutton Satisfied Hunger for a Role Once Tasted," *The Record*, February 2, 2003.

153 *It was Hank Aaron*: Sloan, *Indianapolis News*, December 14, 1984.

153 *"You know, Mr. Aaron"*: Ibid.

154 *"When I was 14"*: Ibid.

154 *a certain slugger: Hank Aaron*: Wilson, *Fences*, 34.

NINE A Fastball on the Outside Corner

155 *"Some people build fences"*: Wilson, *Fences*, 61.

155 *It was an unseasonably*: Weather Report, *Hartford Courant*, May 3, 1985.

155 *"All of these people . . . given myself"*: Watlington, "Hurdling Fences," 88.

156 *In one stanza . . . "alphabet"*: August Wilson, "Home," poem dated April 27, 1985, Lloyd Richards Papers.

156 *"This is no sophomore slump"*: Malcolm L. Johnson, " 'Fences' Is Riveting at Yale Rep," *Hartford Courant*, May 4, 1985.

156 *a thank-you note . . . tribute to their lives*: August Wilson, letter to Lloyd Richards, May 3, 1985, Lloyd Richards Papers.

156 *he dedicated . . . "who adds to whatever he touches"*: Wilson, *Fences*, v.

156 *He originally conceived*: Livingston, "Cool August," 54.

156 *"The first lines I wrote"*: Ibid.

157 *"How come you ain't never liked me?"*: Wilson, *Fences*, 37.

157 *"Like you?"*: Ibid., 38.

157 *"Don't you try to go through life"*: Ibid.

158 *"half his head blown away"*: Ibid., 26.

158 *"a pot to piss in"*: Ibid., 28.

158 *"A motherless child"*: Ibid., 79.

158 *described the play as "absorbing"*: Frank Rich, "Theater: Wilson's 'Fences,' " *New York Times*, May 7, 1985.

159 *"sound like stock replicas"*: Ibid.

159 *"The reason for the shortfall"*: Ibid.

159 *"As Mr. Wilson's extraordinary voice"*: Ibid.

159 *a talkback with the audience . . . "Portugal"*: Report on the audience talkback, May 8, 1985, Lloyd Richards Papers.

159 *Wilson had not been home for seventy-three days*: August Wilson, letter, June 25, 1985, Lloyd Richards Papers.

159 *proud of the play*: Ibid.

159 *producer Bob Cole thought*: Robert Cole interview, January 8, 2018.

160 *another letter to Richards . . . Richards's direction*: August Wilson, letter, June 27, 1985, Lloyd Richards Papers.

160 *She told him: "I have the f-word"*: Cole interview.

160 *they left saying, "Well, it's a play about a Black family"*: James Earl Jones and Penelope Niven, *James Earl Jones: Voices and Silences* (New York: Charles Scribner's Sons, 1993), 326.

160 *nine-page, handwritten critique . . . "less futile"*: James Earl Jones, letter to Lloyd Richards, August 22, 1985, Lloyd Richards Papers.

160 *"I immediately dismissed that . . . The Great White Hope"*: James Earl Jones interview, March 23 and 24, 2017.

161 *"I said, 'Where are you, August?' . . . he was very generous"*: Yoshimura interview.

161 *He told Benjamin Mordecai*: Sherry Mordecai interview, March 29, 2018.

161 *On October 3, the Goodman announced . . . "Chicago run"*: Richard Christiansen, "'Fences' Gets New Look for Goodman," *Chicago Tribune*, October 3, 1985.

161 *that changed three weeks*: Richard Christiansen, "Program Note," *Chicago Tribune*, October 25, 1985.

162 *Richards never allowed . . . directorial choices*: Hatcher interview.

162 *"expertly constructed"*: Sarah Miles Watts, "GeVa Builds 'Fences' into a Monument," *Democrat and Chronicle*, February 24, 1986.

162 *Judy Oliver and Jacqui Shoholm*: Shoholm interview.

163 *"second viewing . . . another crack at the play"*: Richard Christiansen, "August Wilson: A Powerful Playwright Probes the Meaning of Black Life," *Chicago Tribune*, February 9, 1986.

163 *not able to earn a living*: Ibid.

163 *"particularly formidable"*: Rich, "Wilson's 'Fences.'"

163 *seasonably frigid day*: Weather report, *Chicago Tribune*, February 10, 1986.

163 *compared the play . . . his character*: Richard Christiansen, "*Fences* Carries Memorable Impact," *Chicago Tribune*, February 11, 1986.

163 *"is a man of almost mythic power"*: Ibid.

163 *will "live long in memory"*: Ibid.

163 *"August Wilson, it is clear"*: Ibid.

163 *Wilson was harboring hopes*: Christiansen, "A Powerful Playwright."

163 *musical called* Mr. Jelly Roll *. . . workshop*: Ibid.

164 *Broadway producer Margo Lion . . . someday*: Tonya Pinkins, "*Jelly's Last Jam*—The August Wilson Play That Almost Was and the George C. Wolfe Musical It Became," *Playbill*, December 14, 2021.

164 *Carole Shorenstein Hays . . . saw* Fences: John Breglio.

164 *According to the play's star, Jones*: Jones and Niven, *Voices and Silences*, 326.

164 *According to John Breglio*: Breglio interview; Breglio, *I Wanna Be a Producer*, 147.

165 *"I realized . . . crisis"*: Jones and Niven, *Voices and Silences*, 326–27.

165 *"Troy Maxson was my father . . . deeply"*: Steven Winn, "Second Acts/San Francisco's Carole Shorenstein Hays Has Built a Career on Broadway by Taking Calculated Risks," *SFGate*, October 31, 2004.

165 *"I don't know . . . responsible person"*: Christiansen, "A Powerful Playwright."

165 *"I thought it would look good"*: Winn, "Second Acts."

166 *"We've never looked . . . sums for her to use"*: Ibid.

166   *"Don't you ever make my little girl"*: Sherry Mordecai interview.

166   *Jones saw an ally . . . "'killing each other'"*: Jones and Niven, *Voices and Silences*, 327–28.

167   *"main flaw" . . . secondary role*: Tim Appelo, "Fences Captures Complex Truth," *Seattle Times*, March 20, 1986.

167   *"Such richness!" . . . Euripides*: Joe Adock, "Rep's Richly Realized 'Fences' Stands as a Tribute to Humanity," *Seattle Post-Intelligencer*, March 21, 1986.

167   *Broadway theatrical unions charge*: Paul Dean (Theatrical Business Manager, IATSE Local One) interview, October 17, 2017.

167   *he frequently enjoyed the company*: The author interviewed several women who had affairs with Wilson but chose to remain off the record. This was a well-known fact among scores of theater professionals interviewed for this book. Few, if any, would talk on the record, but dozens talked about it behind his back while he was alive and after he died. A few women interviewed resented him for his adultery and promiscuity, as did some men. Others engaged in affairs themselves and preferred to keep out of other people's business. It was not uncommon at the O'Neill that married theater professionals had affairs while they were in residence; the close quarters of cast and crew, as well as the summer camp atmosphere, the coed bathrooms, and the intimate, yet fleeting nature of the National Playwrights Conference, created a ripe atmosphere. As far as the author could tell, all of the affairs were consensual, but some did involve younger women and there was an uneven power dynamic between Wilson and those lovers.

168   *Altman saw an opportunity*: Peter Altman interview, December 17, 2020.

169   *an unusual arrangement*: Breglio interview.

169   *In a letter dated April 22, 1986*: Letter from John Breglio to Gary DaSilva (Lloyd Richards's attorney), April 22, 1986, Lloyd Richards Papers.

170   *On May 5, Richards fired off*: Letter from Lloyd Richards to Gary DaSilva, May 5, 1986, Lloyd Richards Papers.

170   *"For openers . . . insulting"*: Ibid.

170   *"short fuse and little tolerance"*: Ibid.

170   *"negotiating techniques"*: Ibid.

170   *"a unique and talented . . . few peers"*: Ibid.

170   *"August has a meaningful . . . theatrical realization"*: Ibid.

170   *"practically any director can do it"*: Ibid.

170   *"There is not anyone . . . has done"*: Ibid.

170   *he would be one of ten artists*: Elizabeth Mehren, "Gualala Poet Wins Whiting Award," *Los Angeles Times*, November 7, 1986.

170   *"I respect the writer . . . joyous price to pay"*: Letter from Richards to DaSilva, May 5, 1986.

171   *"We are all conscious . . . a good risk"*: Ibid.

171   *"I stood with . . . producing the play"*: Ibid.

171 *"These circumstances . . . other playwrights"*: Ibid.

171 *No one at the Boston theater*: Maso interview; Altman interview.

171 *a typewritten letter written . . . clear the air*: August Wilson letter to Lloyd Richards, July 6, 1987, Lloyd Richards Papers.

171 *in December 1986, Wilson and Breglio*: Letter and contract sent to Lloyd Richards in care of his attorney, December 16, 1986, Lloyd Richards Papers.

172 *Jones still wasn't satisfied*: Jones and Niven, *Voices and Silences*, 327.

172 *Jones felt he was "being stonewalled"*: Ibid., 328.

172 *"She was white, Jewish, rich, and young"*: Ibid., 329.

172 *Hays and Kamlot . . . appropriate for the characters to use*: Breglio, *I Wanna Be a Producer*, 150–51.

172 *Jones agreed with Wilson*: Jones interview.

173 *Hays and Kamlot met . . . open on Broadway*: Breglio, *I Wanna Be a Producer*, 151.

173 *Hays asked him to reconsider*: Carole Shorenstein Hays letter to Lloyd Richards, February 13, 1987, Lloyd Richards Papers.

173 *emphasizing that she was confident*: Ibid.

173 *he and Hays still didn't like*: Jones interview; Jones and Niven, *Voices and Silences*, 331.

173 *"It's between you and me"*: Wilson, *Fences*, 89.

174 *"How does it feel"*: Ibid.

174 *Hays suggested an alternate ending*: Sweet, *The O'Neill*, 160.

174 *"a young green kid"*: Ibid., 159.

174 *"He said, 'I will not'"*: Ibid., 160.

174 *On Wednesday, February 25, Hays sent . . . attention to him*: Memo from Carole Shorenstein Hays to Lloyd Richards, February 25, 1987, Lloyd Richards Papers.

174 *change Rose's line*: Ibid.

175 *"You a womanless man"*: Wilson, *Fences*, 79.

175 *critical shortcoming*: Carole Shorenstein Hays, "Addendum to Previous Memo," February 27, 1987, Lloyd Richards Papers.

175 *"Troy assumes a batting posture"*: Wilson, *Fences*, 89.

175 *considering canceling*: Handwritten note from Lloyd Richards to August Wilson, February 1987, Lloyd Richards Papers.

175 *Richards asked Kamlot*: Ibid.

175 *The next morning, Hays called . . . "leaving"*: Ibid.

175 *She called back forty-five minutes later*: Ibid.

175 *"These are the forces . . . Fences"*: Ibid.

175 *"excited, entertained"*: Ibid.

176 *they also encouraged it*: The author spent many years as a theater critic at the *Boston Globe* and has direct experience with press agents showing up asking for reviews and then taking quotes out of context.

176   *"The fact that a play lingers"*: Handwritten note from Richards to Wilson.

176   *disillusion . . . two and a half hours*: Ibid.

177   *"I was a little boy"*: Sweet, *The O'Neill*, 160.

177   *the little girl . . . too old for the role*: Ibid., 160–61.

177   *"It was a bitter"*: Ibid., 161.

177   *"Courtney, in forty years"*: Ibid., 160.

177   *"He couldn't understand . . . instigator of it"*: Jones interview.

178   *Wilson lunged*: Ibid.

178   *"Some words . . . didn't in his writing"*: Ibid.

178   *"The white man"*: Wilson, *Fences*, 35.

178   *"If they got a white fellow . . . team"*: Ibid., 34.

178   *"I said . . . pain in the ass"*: Jones interview.

178   *"I was always on guard . . . his father"*: Ibid.

178   *Jones readily admits*: Ibid.

178   *"I didn't like him . . . keeping them separate"*: Ibid.

179   *she fired Richards*: Ibid.

179   *"She had to fire them" . . . "worked it out"*: Ibid.

179   *"I realized later"*: Breglio, *I Wanna Be a Producer*, 152.

180   *Wilson and members of the cast*: Sakina Ansara Wilson interview.

180   *"clunkier dramaturgy"*: Frank Rich, "Family Ties in Wilson's 'Fences,'" *New York Times*, May 27, 1987.

180   *"a major writer"*: Ibid.

180   *it was his least favorite*: Sandra S. Shannon and Dana Williams, eds., *August Wilson and Black Aesthetics* (New York: Palgrave Macmillan, 2004), reprinted in Bryer and Hartig, ed., *Conversations with August Wilson*, 251.

180   *one of the most financially*: Breglio, *I Wanna Be a Producer*, 152.

181   *He noticed Dove*: Rita Dove interview, January 8, 2021.

181   *He wrote her a letter . . . accomplishments*: August Wilson letter to Rita Dove, March 9, 1994, Rita Dove personal collection.

181   *Wilson had a conversation*: Dove interview.

181   *"quasi low-key and elevated . . . being cool"*: Ibid.

181   *"We recognized . . . spot together"*: Ibid.

182   *The first word of the poem*: August Wilson, "Meeting Rita Dove at the Pulitzer Luncheon," Rita Dove personal collection.

182   *Minnesota governor Rudy Perpich . . . gymnasium that evening*: "State Officials Applaud Ex-Cook Whose Play Charmed a Select Circle," *Star Tribune*, May 28, 1987.

183   *"This is a talent"*: Ibid.

183   *"is not my home"*: Ibid.

183   *"Now we can pay our bills"*: Ibid.

183   *a cloudy, drizzly evening*: Weather report, *New York Times*, June 7, 1987.

183   *designed by Pauline Trigère*: Winn, "Second Acts."

183 *When Glenn Close . . . "asleep"*: 1987 Tony's Acceptance Speech for Fences—Best Play, video, https://www.youtube.com/watch?v=ak_qxlD0FeY.

184 *"I think I'm going"*: Ibid.

TEN Shining Like New Money

185 *"You should always respect"*: Romare Bearden.

185 *"Revolutionary Greetings, Mbulu"*: Letter from Vernell A. Lillie, Bob Gore, and Rob Penny to August Wilson, July 20, 1987, Kuntu Repertory Theatre Records.

185 *petitioned Pittsburgh mayor Richard Caliguiri*: Ibid.

186 *"It could be to St. Paul"*: Larry Oakes, "Honored Playwright Offers St. Paul Soliloquy," *Star Tribune*, August 6, 1987.

186 *Mayor George Latimer*: Ibid.

186 *He just replaced a few words . . . "city of St. Paul"*: Ibid.

186 *"I have carried . . . I'm home"*: Ibid.

186 *he and John Breglio*: Breglio, *I Wanna Be a Producer*, 152–53.

186 *"Bubble Hill" . . . professional recording studio*: Braden Kell, "More Bubble Trouble," *New York Post*, January 14, 2007.

187 *He had smashed*: UPI, "Eddie Murphy Extends Contract with Paramount," *The Times* (Streator, Illinois), August 26, 1987.

187 *His manager had called*: Breglio, *I Wanna Be a Producer*, 152.

187 *Wilson and Breglio . . . fireplace*: Ibid., 153.

187 *James Earl Jones . . . Othello*: Jones interview.

187 *Bubble Hill was a slang*: Sarah Paynter, "His Own Zumanda: Inside Eddie Murphy's $20 Million House Fit for a King," *New York Post*, March 25, 2021.

187 *Murphy kept his guests . . . agreed to the terms*: Breglio, *I Wanna Be a Producer*, 153.

187 *Wilson later described . . . "Neither do I"*: August Wilson, "I Don't Want to Hire Nobody Just 'Cause They're Black," *Spin*, October 1990, 70.

187 *paying Wilson $1 million . . . screenplay*: Breglio, *I Wanna Be a Producer*, 153.

188 *"Eddie Murphy thinks"*: "Eddie on the Fence," *Hartford Courant*, September 13, 1987.

188 *"I wanted to hire somebody"*: Wilson, "I Don't Want to Hire Nobody," 70.

188 *"August Wilson" . . . "eras of time"*: Freda Ellis, Speech Delivered in the Pittsburgh Council Chambers, September 21, 1987, Kuntu Repertory Theatre Records.

188 *a whirlwind two-day schedule*: "August Wilson's Itinerary," Kuntu Repertory Theatre Records.

188 *a three-day expense account . . . appointments*: "Expenditures: August Wilson," Kuntu Repertory Theatre Records.

189 *Wilson's friends drove him to the event*: Bob Hoover, "Playwright Has Quick Trip Home," *Pittsburgh Post-Gazette*, September 28, 1987.

189 *laudatory document . . . "creativity"*: Proclamation for August Wilson Day, September 26, 1987, Kuntu Repertory Theatre Records.

189   *"It is very hard to express"*: Walter Ray Watson Jr., "Playwright Celebrated on Homecoming," *New Pittsburgh Courier*, October 10, 1987.

189   *It was held at Pitt's Forbes*: Ibid.

190   *Poet Maisha Baton . . . the Black experience*: Ibid.

190   *"Wilson is of mixed parentage"*: Ibid.

190   *"As Pittsburghers . . . proud of"*: Ibid.

190   *"abrupt starts and intense"*: Ibid.

190   *"Perhaps this is" . . . "thank you"*: Ibid.

190   *"Yo, Bro" . . . "mood of life"*: Ibid.

191   *he joined his family . . . after the service*: Kathleen Healy, "An Unphotographed Chapter in a Playwright's Homecoming," *Pittsburgh Post-Gazette*, October 12, 1987.

191   *Wilson said he got the inspiration*: Herrington, "I Ain't Sorry," 79.

192   *"The moment that I got my desk"*: J. Wynn Rousuck, "'Jitney': Vehicle for a Friendship," *Baltimore Sun*, January 3, 1999.

192   *working on a poem*: Herrington, "I Ain't Sorry," 79.

192   *"In Bearden I found"*: August Wilson, foreword to Schwartzman, *Romare Bearden*, 9.

192   *"It showed a man"*: Livingston, "Cool August," 54.

192   *"the sons and daughters"*: Wilson, *Three Plays*, 203.

192   *He later told Todd Kreidler*: Kreidler interview.

192   *"Foreigners in a strange land"*: Wilson, *Three Plays*, 203.

192   *"I wanted to find out . . . story of Joe Turner"*: Livingston, "Cool August," 54.

193   *Joe Turney, not Turner*: W. C. Handy, ed., introduction and notes by Abbe Niles, *Blues: An Anthology* (New York: Albert & Charles Boni, 1926), 41.

193   *"Dey tell me"*: Ibid.

193   *He originally named the play*: August Wilson script, *Mill Hand's Lunch Bucket*, Lloyd Richards Papers.

193   *"coming up from the country"*: Wilson, *Three Plays*, 209.

193   *"That boy done carried"*: Ibid.

194   *Wilson told the playwright*: Douglas Post interview, December 28, 2017.

194   *"This old People Finding"*: Wilson, *Three Plays*, 241.

194   *"He's not evil at all" . . . "the community"*: Powers, "An Interview with August Wilson," 8.

195   *"old wild-eyed, mean-looking"*: Ibid., 236.

195   *"killed somebody gambling over a quarter"*: Ibid., 222.

195   *"he is unable to harmonize"*: Ibid., 216.

195   *"old mumbo jumbo nonsense"*: Ibid., 205.

195   *"heebie-jeebie stuff"*: Ibid., 206.

195   *dying alone . . . "no immediate survivors"*: Obituary for Bynam Wilson, *The Courier*, October 28, 1980.

195   *"Ain't you ever heard"*: Wilson, *Fences*, 51.

196   *"They walk out their front door"*: Ibid.

196   *"reconnect and reassemble"*: Wilson, *Three Plays*, 203.

196   *African juba*: Handy and Niles, *Blues: An Anthology*, 34.

196   *"bones walking"*: Ibid., 250.

196   *"My legs won't stand"*: Wilson, *Three Plays*, 252.

196   *"He looked at me"*: Andrews interview.

197   He recalled the *"Valley of the Bones"*: Ibid.

197   *"There was a noise"*: Ezekiel 37:7, New International Version.

197   *"He took the material . . . Middle Passage"*: Andrews interview.

197   *"I was intimidated" . . . play justice*: Saltz interview.

197   *"August would walk in circles" . . . choreography*: Ebony Jo-Ann interview, January 2, 2018.

198   *"Herald Loomis, you shining!"*: Wilson, *Three Plays*, 289.

198   *Carl Capotorto . . . "new idea"*: Carl Capotorto interview, December 12, 2017.

198   *"As it turns out"*: Jim Davidson, "A Playwright Who Stirs the Imagination," *Pittsburgh Press*, November 4, 1984.

198   *"The first words" . . . "wrong move"*: Freedman, "A Voice from the Streets."

199   *"There's nothing . . . won't disappear"*: Don Aucoin, "Playwright Adds to His Cycle of Black History in America," *Boston Globe*, May 11, 1986.

199   *"worried about disappointing that audience"*: Ibid.

199   *"at once a teeming canvas"*: Frank Rich, " 'Joe Turner' at Yale Rep," *New York Times*, May 6, 1986.

199   *"a metaphorical force"*: Ibid.

200   *"The Broadway system" . . . "nurture theater"*: Jeff McLaughlin, " 'Joe Turner' to Tour After Huntington Run," *Boston Globe*, September 12, 1986.

200   *many in the house that night*: The author was in the audience and reviewed the play for the *Tab* newspapers, a chain of local newspapers in the Boston area.

200   *"an ax blade"*: Jay Carr, "A Powerful Portrayal of the Black Experience," *Boston Globe*, October 2, 1986.

201   *"Herald Loomis, you shining!"*: Wilson, *Three Plays*, 289.

201   *"one of the most powerful"*: Ibid.

201   *"befitting a member"*: Wilson, *Three Plays*, 283.

201   *"conspiracy of boundless joy"*: Wilson, *How I Learned*, 42.

202   *Wilson had dedicated the play*: Wilson, *Three Plays*, 194.

202   *"A woman like you"*: Ibid., 226.

202   *"A woman can't be"*: Ibid.

202   *"Your mother was a woman"*: Ibid., 244.

203   "The Juba . . . Holy Ghost": Ibid., 249.

203   *"networking that is going on"*: Dan Sullivan, " 'Turner' Paints a Portrait of Pain at the Old Globe," *Los Angeles Times*, February 6, 1988.

203   *"It left this viewer" . . . "escaped this viewer"*: Ibid.

204 *"There was lots of shiny men"*: Wilson, *Three Plays*, 213.

204 *"I don't do it lightly"*: Ibid.

204 "a man driven": Ibid., 216.

204 *"They Black"*: Ibid., 252.

205 *"I woke up one morning"*: Ibid., 285.

205 "Having found his song": Ibid., 288–89.

205 *with a gross of $11 million*: W. Speers, "Newsmakers," *Philadelphia Inquirer*, March 25, 1988.

205 *Jones had warned his replacement*: Jones interview.

206 *During one matinee . . . "bitch was white!"*: Ibid.

206 *Bearden died on March 12*: C. Gerald Fraser, "Romare Bearden, Collagist and Painter, Dies at 75," *New York Times*, March 13, 1988.

206 *"I have often thought"*: Wilson, *Bearden: His Life and Art*, 9.

206 *"There are occasions"*: Frank Rich, "Panoramic History of Blacks in America in Wilson's 'Joe Turner,'" *New York Times*, March 28, 1988.

206 *"The clash between"*: Ibid.

206 *photos of a beaming*: "People/Wilson on Broadway Again," *Pittsburgh Post-Gazette*, March 29, 1988.

206 *Veteran producer Elliot Martin . . . $60,000 a week*: Jeremy Gerard, "Despite Praise, 'Turner' May Be Forced to Close," *New York Times*, April 21, 1988.

207 *after word hit the press*: "'Joe Turner' Not Closing," *New York Times*, April 27, 1988.

207 *One day, Wilson and Oliver buzzed*: Shoholm interview.

208 *About a month later . . . college expenses as well*: Ibid.

208 *This act of kindness . . . Shoholm said*: Ibid.

208 *472 Holly Avenue . . . bathroom floor intact*: The author toured the home in October 2018, courtesy of the current owners. The home contains a log of the history of the home, dating back to the original owners.

209 *look at colleges . . . rent as well*: Sakina Ansara Wilson interview.

210 *Black action society . . . "current situation"*: August Wilson interview.

210 *Morgan awarded him*: Morgan State University, Honorary Degrees Awarded, https://commencement.morgan.edu/honorary-degrees/.

210 *he admitted that he couldn't*: Malcolm L. Johnson, "August Wilson's New Play Explores Lessons of a Legacy," *Hartford Courant*, November 27, 1987.

210 *"I like St. Paul"*: Ibid.

ELEVEN What Do You Do with Your Legacy?

211 "Everybody got stones": August Wilson, *The Piano Lesson* (New York: Plume, 1990), i.

211 *Late one night . . . "Black community"*: Andrews interview.

211 The Piano Lesson (Homage to Mary Lou): Romare Bearden Foundation,

https://beardenfoundation.org/prints/homage-to-mary-lou-piano-lesson -1984/.

211 *"This will be my next play"*: Herrington, *"I Ain't Sorry,"* 21.

212 *"I thought that the woman"*: Mervyn Rothstein, "Round Five for a Theatrical Heavyweight," *New York Times*, April 15, 1990.

212 *"Then the question"*: Ibid.

213 "On the legs . . . realm of art": August Wilson, "The Setting," *Piano Lesson*, i.

213 *"She say it got blood on it"*: Ibid., 10.

213 *Wilson himself didn't know*: Rothstein, "Round Five."

213 *Robman concerned himself*: Steve Robman interview, November 9, 2017.

213 *"It was obvious"*: Ibid.

213 *"Some of the plays"*: Ibid.

214 *"I wish sometimes"*: Hatcher interview.

214 *Feingold became*: Herrington, *"I Ain't Sorry,"* 58.

214 *"You know, you skipped"*: Ibid.

215 *"In the original ending"*: Ibid., 59.

215 *Wilson talked to another playwright*: Ibid.

215 *Years later . . . "journey for me"*: Carla Sosenko, "Samuel L. Jackson on Revisiting the Broadway Play That Landed Him in Rehab," *Newsweek*, September 7, 2022.

216 *"I wanted Boy Willie"*: August Wilson, "How to Write a Play Like August Wilson," *New York Times*, March 10, 1999.

216 *"unruly and unfinished" . . . "what comes before"*: Frank Rich, "Wilson's 'Piano Lesson,'" *New York Times*, December 10, 1987.

216 *"These flaws co-exist"*: Ibid.

217 *was drawn to the twenty-nine-year-old*: Christopher Akerlind interview, January 30, 2018.

217 *"My dad made a point"*: Sakina Ansara Wilson interview.

217 *"We were working"*: Akerlind interview.

217 *"he made it clear"*: Maso interview.

217 *"promise and power" . . . "clarity"*: Kevin Kelly, "'Piano Lesson' Is Rough, but Memorable," *Boston Globe*, January 14, 1988.

218 *"You trying to tell me . . . 'love you?'"*: Wilson, *The Piano Lesson*, 67.

218 *"The theater suddenly" . . . "mythic power Wilson is suggesting"*: Kelly, "Piano Lesson Is Rough."

218 *Kelly was dead-on*: The author saw the same production.

218 *Richards, who was almost seventy*: Richards interview, November 10, 2019.

219 *"It was hard to pin"*: Ibid.

219 *compared Wilson to Eugene O'Neill*: Peter Vaughan, "Raves for Wilson," *Star Tribune*, January 20, 1989.

219 *"soars with lyric beauty"*: Ibid.

219 *The creative team*: Andrews interview.

219   *"She doesn't play anything" . . . "ancestors"*: Ibid.

219   "It is an old urge": Wilson, *The Piano Lesson*, 106.

220   *"If you want to tell her" . . . "celebration"*: Wilson, *The Piano Lesson*, 90–91.

220   *"Everything up to that point"*: Sylvie Drake, "Wrestling with Ghosts in 'The Piano Lesson,'" *Los Angeles Times*, May 6, 1989.

220   *first National Black Theatre Festival . . . Woodie King Jr.*: Mervyn Rothstein, "Festival Sets Goals for Black Theater: New Togetherness," *New York Times*, August 17, 1989.

221   *"This is the kind of thing"*: Ibid.

221   *"this terrible scream of pain"*: Ibid.

221   *represented with* Malcolm X: Tony Brown, "Festival to Showcase Theater by Blacks," *Charlotte Observer*, August 2, 1989.

221   *"where you stand around"*: Lou Bellamy interview.

222   *One day, Wilson . . . "'You can't be doing that'"*: Ibid.

222   *"Claude understood it"*: Shoholm interview.

222   *which caused some sniping*: Hatcher interview.

223   *"Don't you have to adopt"*: Bill Moyers, "August Wilson on Blackness and the Blues," A World of Ideas, https://billmoyers.com/content/august-wilson/, 187.

223   *"We got the American part . . . we are Americans"*: Ibid.

223   *"The cultural environment of my life"*: Ibid., 188.

223   *"does not reflect Black America"*: Ibid., 190.

224   *"Don't you grow weary"*: Ibid., 194.

224   *"How could one grow weary"*: Ibid.

224   *" 'Piano Lesson': Harmony at Last"*: Sylvie Drake, " 'Piano Lesson': Harmony at Last," *Los Angeles Times*, January 19, 1990.

224   *He pointed out*: Ray Loynd, "Wilson Seeking Black Director for His Film Version of 'Fences,'" *Los Angeles Times*, January 9, 1990.

224   *"White people have set"*: Ibid.

224   *"Until the industry"*: Ibid.

225   *"The reality is"*: Ibid.

225   *he announced that he would be leaving*: Mervyn Rothstein, "Lloyd Richards Is Leaving Yale Drama School and Rep," *New York Times*, January 29, 1990.

225   *"I will go on"*: Ibid.

225   *The collaboration between*: Jacques le Sourd, "The Art of Business on Broadway," *Daily Times*, March 3, 1994.

226   *"I said to him" . . . "took that out"*: Christopher Rawson, "Actors Talk August," interview series, April 21, 2021, https://americantheatrecritics.org/chris-rawson-actors-talk-august-interview-series/.

226   *He was in the middle of an interview*: Peter Vaughan, "St. Paul Dramatist's Award Is His Second," *Star Tribune*, April 13, 1990.

226   *"By the look on her face"*: Laurie Goldstein and Megan Rosenfeld, "Pulitzer

Surprises: Getting the Word: August Wilson: Writing Plays from the Blues," *Washington Post*, April 13, 1990.

226 *"It's a surprise"*: Vaughan, "St. Paul Dramatist's Award."

227 *"That's good company"*: Goldstein and Rosenfeld, "Pulitzer Surprises."

227 *honorary high school diploma*: David Malehorn, "How I Found August Wilson's Carnegie 'Diploma,'" *Pittsburgh Post-Gazette*, October 9, 2011.

227 *"This certifies"*: Ibid.

227 *"Tinkle the keys"* . . . *"I don't play"*: Goldstein and Rosenfeld, "Pulitzer Surprises."

228 *"O'Neill-like excess"*: Frank Rich, "A Family Confronts Its History in August Wilson's 'Piano Lesson,'" *New York Times*, April 17, 1990.

228 *"deprofessionalize"* . . . *"American theater"*: "Yale Drama School Dropping Brustein," *New York Times*, June 22, 1978.

228 *"Protocol required"*: "Lesson of 'The Piano Lesson,'" *Reimagining American Theatre* (New York: Hill & Wang, 1991), 99.

228 *comment in a 1988* New York Times *article*: Hilary De Vries, "New Paths for Regional Theaters," *New York Times*, December 3, 1989.

228 *"McTheatre"*: Brustein, "The Lesson of 'The Piano Lesson,'" 99.

229 *"overwritten exercise"*: Ibid.

229 *"a kitchen-sink production"*: Ibid.

229 *"much ado about a piano"*: Ibid., 101.

229 *"sit on the edge"*: Ibid., 100.

229 *"never come on like menacing"*: Ibid.

229 *"Wilson is reaching a dead end"* . . . *"his other work"*: Ibid., 103.

229 *"I will simply ask"*: Ibid., 103–4.

229 *"Has anyone ever told"*: Mervyn Rothstein, "Passionate Beliefs Renew Theater Fight over Art and Profit," *New York Times*, May 15, 1990.

230 *Oliver produced . . . of all of his plays*: Peter Vaughan, "2 Early One-Act Plays by Wilson Will Be Presented at Fundraiser," *Star Tribune*, September 15, 1989.

230 *a terse statement*: Associated Press, "Chronicle," *New York Times*, July 19, 1990.

231 *"It's real hard to maintain"*: Ibid.

231 *an arrangement he worked out*: Shoholm interview.

231 *one night with a man*: Lou Bellamy interview.

231 *The dedication*: August Wilson, *Two Trains Running* (New York: Plume, 1992), dedication page.

TWELVE Pick Up the Ball

232 *How beautiful it is*: Tennessee Williams, *The Glass Menagerie* (New York: Dramatists Play Service, 1948), 7.

232 *"Where's Lonne Elder?"*: John Lahr, "Blood's Memory," *The Guardian*, October 15, 2001.

233 *she broke ties*: Shoholm interview.

233 *"My mother was friends"*: Richards interview.

233 *"We were not shopping around"*: Romero interview.

233 *Al Frank . . . "half big brother and half mentor"*: Al Frank interview, February 14, 2005.

234 *Lion had optioned*: Pinkins, "Jelly's Last Jam," December 14, 2021.

234 *Morton had told Lomax*: Alan Lomax, *Mister Jelly Roll: The Fortunes of Jelly Roll Morton, New Orleans Creole and the Inventor of Jazz* (New York: Duell, Sloan and Pearce, 1950), 120.

234 *a musical with a cast of twelve*: August Wilson, *St. Louis Blues*, private collection.

235 *They had several meetings*: Letter to Dwight Andrews from Theater Emory, March 18, 1989, Stuart A. Rose Manuscript, Archives & Rare Book Library, Emory University; "Project Proposal for St. Louis Blues Workshop," memo from Dwight Andrews, July 3, 1990, Stuart A. Rose Manuscript, Archives & Rare Book Library, Emory University.

235 *"One of the first things"*: Andrews interview.

235 *They discussed whether*: Ibid.

235 *submitted a proposal*: "Project Proposal for St. Louis Blues Workshop."

235 *Purdy was just as gung ho*: Shoholm interview.

236 *He did, however, think*: Kreidler interview.

236 *"We are an African people"*: August Wilson, "I Don't Want to Hire Nobody Just 'Cause They're Black," *Spin*, October 1990, 71.

236 *"The skills of Black lawyers"*: Ibid., 70.

237 *"We shook hands"*: Spike Lee, "TopSpin," *Spin*, October 1990, 8.

237 *"No white in the world"*: Richard Brooks, "Black and White Movies," *The Observer*, May 17, 1992.

237 *"There's too much attention"*: James Greenberg, "Did Hollywood Sit on Fences?" *New York Times*, January 27, 1991.

237 *a brief author's note*: Christopher Rawson, "Wilson's 'Trains' Rides a Healing Theme," *Pittsburgh Post-Gazette*, May 7, 1990.

238 *"fail to accumulate"*: Kevin Kelly, "Heart and Mind Are in Right Place in 'Two Trains,'" *Boston Globe*, April 5, 1990.

238 *"is waiting at the station"*: Ibid.

238 *"Setting it in 1968"*: Kevin Kelly, "August Wilson's True Stories," *Boston Globe*, April 29, 1990.

238 *"By 1969, there was a new Black man"*: Ibid.

238 *meatloaf with two sides*: Wilson, *Two Trains*, 1.

239 *"He gonna give me my ham"*: Ibid., 14. The character of Hambone says the refrain on his first entrance and repeats it throughout the play.

240 *"make you right with yourself"*: Wilson, *Two Trains*, 22.

240 *"If you drop the ball"*: Wilson, *Two Trains*, 109.

241 *"it's an evening"*: Kevin Kelly, " 'Trains': All Steamed Up, No Place to Go," *Boston Globe*, November 1, 1990.

242 *"You start at the beginning"*: Rothstein, "Round Five."

242 *"It's like a heavyweight fighter"*: Ibid.

242 *"My plays are talky"*: Matt Wolf, "Poet of Broadway," *The Guardian*, January 24, 1996.

242 *a local writer approached him*: Johnson interview.

243 *Wilson and Johnson . . . "guacamole"*: Johnson, *Night Hawks*, 163–76.

243 *They frequently exchanged*: Ibid., 164.

243 *"This experience"*: Ibid., 165.

243 *"My dad hated" . . . "attention, either"*: Sakina Ansara Wilson interview.

244 *"Every page"*: Johnson, *Night Hawks*, 169.

244 *"Nothing we've done"*: Ibid., 171.

244 *a quote Wilson cherished*: Ibid., 163, 167.

245 *couldn't keep track*: Richard Christiansen, "Checking In," *Chicago Tribune*, February 10, 1991.

245 *"the consummate actor"*: Kevin Kelly, "Ed Hall's Acting Had Heart and Soul," *Boston Globe*, August 1, 1991.

245 *"It would have an all-male"*: Christiansen, "Checking in."

246 *"The guys looked up" . . . " 'Come on in' "*: Megan Rosenfeld, "The Voices of August Wilson: The Playwright Listens—and Stays True—to the People in His Post," *Washington Post*, November 10, 1991.

246 *The paperwork was filed*: Ramsey County District Courts Records Center.

247 *"vivid and uplifting"*: *Time*, jacket blurb, *Two Trains*.

247 *"unassailable authenticity"*: *Variety*, jacket blurb, *Two Trains*.

247 *"easily Mr. Wilson's most"*: Frank Rich, "*Two Trains Running*; August Wilson Reaches the 60's with Witnesses from a Distance," *New York Times*, April 14, 1992.

247 *"sometimes seems the battered"*: Ibid.

248 *heart-to-heart conversation*: Christopher Rawson, "Actors Talk August," interview series, April 21, 2021, https://americantheatrecritics.org/chris-rawson-actors-talk-august-interview-series/.

248 *"I've told the world"*: Ibid.

249 *On April 29, 1992*: Seth Mydans, "The Police Verdict; Los Angeles Policemen Acquitted in Taped Beating," *New York Times*, April 30, 1992; Katherine Schulten, "The Rodney King Verdict and the L.A. Riots," *New York Times*, April 30, 2015.

249 *"I'd like to thank"*: "1992 Tony Awards, Larry Fishburne: Best Featured Actor in a Play," May 31, 1992, https://www.youtube.com/watch?v=fVBfWkcLDKA.

250 *Born in 1954 . . . find his way as an artist*: Rohan Preston, "Marion McClinton, a Man Made by Theater," *Star Tribune*, August 9, 2014.

250 *"flipped out"*: Lou Bellamy interview.

250   *his favorite staging*: Mahala, *Penumbra*, 69.

250   *through his attorney*: Breglio interview.

250   *a three-story home*: Wilson gave the author a tour of the home, January 26, 2005.

251   *Romero was eager to decorate*: Lahr, "Been Here and Gone," *New Yorker*, April 8, 2001, 65.

251   *He crossed the street*: Johnson, *Night Hawks*, 169.

251   *he quit smoking*: Peter Vaughan, "Five-Year Span Between Plays Was Too Long," *Star Tribune*, January 24, 1995.

251   *Sakina had always wanted . . . cold turkey*: Sakina Ansara Wilson interview.

252   *Set on the shore*: Atlas Obscura, "Seaside Sanatorium, Waterford, Connecticut," https://www.atlasobscura.com/places/seaside-sanitorium.

252   *"It was a building"*: Sweet, *The O'Neill*, 237–38.

253   *Seaside was included*: Atlas Obscura, "Seaside."

253   *Wilson shuffled in . . . "regular guy"*: Herman Daniel Farrell III interview, February 5, 2018.

254   *Wilson bought it*: Post interview.

254   *"I never got a sense"*: Ibid.

254   *"anonymous donor"*: Ibid.

254   *"It was a world"*: Saltz interview.

254   *One foggy night*: Post interview; Farrell interview.

255   *"He put his elbows"*: Farrell interview.

255   *"I come from" . . . "forced on them"*: Lucy Thurber interview, March 12, 2018.

256   *"To Lucy"*: Ibid.

256   *One day . . . role for Wilson*: Post interview.

256   Dunking Sadness: Douglas Post, *Dunking Sadness*, Post's private papers.

257   *preproduction began*: Christopher Rawson, "History Lesson," *Pittsburgh Post-Gazette*, September 23, 1994.

257   *Post and other playwrights*: Post interview.

257   *"There's no question"*: Ibid.

257   *168 locals . . . cameo as a neighbor*: Christopher Rawson, "Sitting In on 'The Piano Lesson,'" *Pittsburgh Post-Gazette*, October 3, 1994.

258   *a scathing letter . . . "financial status"*: Thomasina L. West, "An Open Letter to August Wilson," *Pittsburgh Post-Gazette*, June 3, 1994.

258   *"Why not?"*: Christopher Rawson, "Nothing in Common," *Pittsburgh Post-Gazette*, August 2, 1994.

258   *in real life, Karl Lutz . . . particular business owner*: Sean D. Hamill, "Real Story Behind August Wilson 1968 Violence Play Character," *Pittsburgh Post-Gazette*, April 7, 2018.

258   *"I never consciously"*: August Wilson interview.

258   *an Italian-Swiss television crew*: Ibid.

258   *"They somehow thought"*: Ibid.

258   *he was thrilled to have Richards . . . on the crew as well*: Rawson, "History Lesson."

259   *"On the legs of the piano"*: Wilson, "Setting," *The Piano Lesson.*

259   *Van Ryker's suggestion infuriated*: Lahr, "Been Here and Gone," 63.

259   *"He was screaming"*: Ibid.

259   *"I don't function dictatorially"*: Ibid.

259   *"I remember even then"*: Sakina Ansara Wilson interview.

259   *August 15 to apply for the marriage license*: Certificate of Marriage, Washington State Archives—Digital Archives, Department of Health, Marriage Certificates, 1968–1996.

260   *the wedding . . . wear to the ceremony*: *Minneapolis Star Tribune*, August 21, 1994.

260   *blue suit*: Sakina Ansara Wilson interview.

260   *"This is supposed to be" . . . "It's too nice"*: Yoshimura interview.

260   *"By the way" . . . "knock him in the head"*: Ibid.

261   *They wrapped the film*: Rawson, "Sitting In on the 'Piano Lesson.'"

261   *"You be a writer" . . . "I did it"*: August Wilson interview.

THIRTEEN "You a Big Man"

262   *"An artist must be free"*: Langston Hughes, *Not So Simple: The "Simple" Stories by Langston Hughes* (ed. University of Missouri Press, 1996).

262   *In December 1994*: Richards interview.

262   *"He was incredibly nervous"*: Ibid.

263   *"My guess is"*: Ibid.

263   *"In the old days"*: August Wilson tribute to Lloyd Richards, private collection of Jeffrey Hatcher. The speech is also reprinted in Sweet, *The O'Neill*, 274–75.

264   *unique profit-sharing formula*: Letter from Benjamin Mordecai to Ric Pappas, August 15, 1994, Lloyd Richards Papers.

264   *"incredulous and unacceptable"*: Letter from Gary DaSilva to John Breglio, November 17, 1994, Lloyd Richards Papers.

264   *Wilson and Mordecai quickly agreed*: Memo from Benjamin Mordecai to Ric Pappas, November 28, 1994, Lloyd Richards Papers.

264   *a laid-back director*: Katharine Q. Seelye, "Walter Dallas, 'Heartbeat' of Philadelphia Theater, Dies at 73," *New York Times*, May 22, 2020.

264   *"Now Lloyd is old enough"*: Watlington, "Hurdling Fences," 87.

264   *Wilson's attorney had requested*: Letter from Lloyd Richards to Benjamin Mordecai and August Wilson, January 16, 1995, Lloyd Richards Papers.

265   *a missive . . . "paths for the work"*: Ibid.

265   *"I fully realize" . . . not a genuine partnership*: Ibid.

265   *A partnership called Sageworks*: The partnership was formed in April 1995 between Benjamin Mordecai Productions, Inc., and David Bedford Films, Inc., an entity Wilson formed and named after his stepfather.

265 *"found nothing there to entice him"*: Letter from Albert DaSilva to August Wilson, January 18, 1995, Lloyd Richards Papers.

265 *Constanza Romero said that*: Sweet, *The O'Neill*, 168.

265 *"Lloyd told me"*: Ibid., 169.

266 *"It was a betrayal"*: Richards interview.

266 *"My father didn't hang out"*: Ibid.

266 *"When he gave it to me"*: Saltz interview.

267 *"You're intrigued"*: Herrington, *"I Ain't Sorry,"* 39.

267 *"He still wanted to learn"*: Saltz interview.

268 *"her little fast behind"*: August Wilson, *Seven Guitars* (New York: Plume, 1997), 30.

268 *"lead the Black man out of bondage"*: Ibid., 68.

268 *"big man"*: Ibid., 18. Hedley says this early in the play and repeats the phrase throughout.

268 *"He was shaking"*: Saltz interview.

268 *"Floyd touched me"*: Wilson, *Seven Guitars*, 14.

268 *"He didn't know"*: Saltz interview.

268 *He kept writing . . . found the scene*: Ibid.

269 *"The energy was coming"*: Ibid.

269 *"I think I meant"*: Herrington, *"I Ain't Sorry,"* 116–17.

270 *Sakina was worried*: Sakina Ansara Wilson interview.

270 *"August began to assert"*: Andrews interview.

270 *"He wanted to hear"*: Ibid.

270 *"It's usually an open forum"*: Herrington, *"I Ain't Sorry,"* 118.

271 *bitterly cold evening*: Weather report, *Chicago Tribune*, January 21, 1995.

271 *"Some critic or someone" . . . "fault lines"*: Andrews interview.

271 *He asked Saltz*: Saltz interview.

271 *"I happen to think"*: Wilson, "A Note from the Playwright," *Seven Guitars*.

272 *"not all right in my head"*: Ibid., 67.

272 *"You have to assemble"*: Carol Rosen, "August Wilson: Bard of the Blues," *Theatre Week*, May 27, 1996; reprinted in Bryer and Hartig, *Conversations with August Wilson*, 203.

272 *"Bynum says"*: Ibid.

272 *"far from finished" . . . "muffled"*: Christopher Rawson, "Striking the Right Note," *Pittsburgh Post-Gazette*, February 9, 1995.

273 *"patina of age"*: Christopher Akerlind interview, January 30, 2018.

273 *"It felt non-epic"*: Ibid.

273 *"Put them all in a hat"*: Hevrdejs and Conklin, "The Democratic Way," *Chicago Tribune*, February 26, 1995.

273 *Mordecai wrote to Richards*: Letter from Benjamin Mordecai to Lloyd Richards, April 25, 1995, Lloyd Richards Papers.

273 *"hardly seemed tactful"* . . . *"assistant"*: Letter from Lloyd Richards to Benjamin Mordecai, April 27, 1995, Lloyd Richards Papers.

274 *he wrote the role of Hedley*: Fax, August Wilson to Lloyd Richards, October 4, 1995, Lloyd Richards Papers.

274 *"spectacle character"*: Bonnie Lyons, "An Interview with August Wilson," *Contemporary Literature* (University of Wisconsin Press, Spring 1999, 40), reprinted in Bryer and Hartig, ed., *Conversations with August Wilson*, 208.

274 *production notes . . . nodding off during the performance*: Jane E. Neufeld memo, September 16, 1995, Lloyd Richards Papers.

275 *he sent a two-page fax*: Fax, August Wilson to Lloyd Richards, October 4, 1995.

275 *"I loved Zakes"*: Keith David interview, January 20, 2021.

275 *Wilson said the same thing*: Fax, Wilson to Richards, October 4, 1995.

275 *"August made a decision"*: Maso interview.

275 *"You a big man"*: Wilson, *Seven Guitars*, 79.

275 *"August Wilson is a big man"* . . . *"he wasn't"*: Maso interview.

276 *"There is something"* . . . *"inner life"*: Letter from Lucy Kroll to Lloyd Richards, October 17, 1995, Lloyd Richards Papers.

276 *"contains an overabundance"*: Robert Hurwitt, "Slow, Blue 'Guitars,'" *San Francisco Examiner*, November 16, 1005.

277 *"one stop on the pre-Broadway"*: Ibid.

277 *"draws his portrait"*: Ibid.

277 *"fuzzy enunciation"* . . . *"foreshadow danger"*: Peter Haugen, "Long-Playing 'Seven Guitars' Moves with Soulful Music," *Sacramento Bee*, November 18, 1995.

277 *wrote down two words*: August Wilson, postcard, August Wilson Archive.

277 *character of Hedley "has a lot of truth"*: Jesse Hamlin, "Theater," *San Francisco Examiner*, November 12, 1995.

277 *"You can't really fire people"*: Richards interview.

277 *He exploded*: Boyd interview.

277 *"It was probably"*: Ibid.

278 *he left abruptly*: "Actor Leaves 'Seven Guitars,'" *Sacramento Bee*, November 23, 1995.

278 *claiming that it was second-rate . . . truth, responsibility, and justice*: August Wilson letter to Lloyd Richards, December 30, 1992, Lloyd Richards Papers.

278 *He suggested that he give the actors*: Ibid.

278 *"Every playwright"*: Sweet, *The O'Neill*, 169.

278 *one word . . . "one is never satisfied"*: Jan Breslauer, "August Wilson: Seven Plays Running," *Los Angeles Times*, January 14, 1996.

279 *"How can you dump the guy?"*: Wilson, *Ground* (PBS).

279 *"If it wasn't for Lloyd"*: Ibid.

279 *"It was hard for me"*: Ibid.

280   *"He learned a lot of things"*: Patti Hartigan, "One Man. Ten Plays. 100 Years.," *Boston Globe Magazine*, April 3, 2005.

280   *A speech about insomnia*: Bruce Weber, "Sculpturing a Play into Existence," *New York Times*, March 24, 1996.

280   *"I don't know if I'll do another play"*: Ibid.

280   *"Rogerisms"*: Andrews interview.

280   *During the Los Angeles run*: Jane E. Neufeld memo, February 29, 1996, Lloyd Richards Papers.

281   *"mutual affection" . . . "bristly element"*: Weber, "Sculpturing a Play."

281   *such A-listers as Gregory Hines*: Cast party photographs, private collection of Renee Graham.

281   *"without whom my life"*: August Wilson, *Seven Guitars,* dedication page.

281   *"It was a very cool reception"*: Saltz interview.

281   *"The feeling was like"*: Richards interview.

281   *"a play whose epic proportions"*: Vincent Canby, "Unrepentant, Defiant Blues for 7 Voices," *New York Times*, March 29, 1996.

281   *"It's like a session number"*: Clive Barnes, quoted in "Seven Saluted," *Los Angeles Times*, April 14, 1996.

282   *Photographs from the opening-night*: Photographs, private collection of Renee Graham.

282   *"August was like" . . . decisively*: Andrews interview.

FOURTEEN The Ground on Which I Stand

283   *"The Negro is sort of a seventh son"*: W. E. B. Du Bois, *The Souls of Black Folk.*

283   *"I'm going home"*: Christopher Rawson, "Traveling Home by 'Jitney,'" *Pittsburgh Post-Gazette*, June 10, 1996.

283   *threatened to sue . . . closed doors*: Letter from Albert DaSilva to John Breglio, April 11, 1986; letter from John Breglio to August Wilson, April 12, 1996; letter from Albert DaSilva to John Breglio, April 16, 1996; letter from John Breglio to August Wilson, April 17, 1996; letter from Albert DaSilva to John Breglio, June 5, 1996; letter from John Breglio to August Wilson, June 6, 1996. August Wilson Archive.

283   *"I'm not sure I want to invest my life"*: Ibid.

284   *actor Judd Hirsch*: Wilson, *Ground*, 11.

284   *Peter Zeisler . . . shake things up*: Isaac Butler, "Breaking Ground: How the Speech Came to Be and What Set It in Motion," *American Theatre*, June 20, 2016.

285   *The actors' union defined . . . "not germane"*: Alan Eisenberg, "Nontraditional Casting: When Race and Sex Don't Matter," *New York Times*, October 23, 1988.

285   *He recruited the husband-and-wife team*: Butler, "Breaking Ground."

285 *"We said, 'Are we correct' "*: Rebecca Rickman interview, February 24, 2021.

285 *"I have been waiting"*: Ibid.

285 *"We just had to talk"*: Butler, "Breaking Ground."

286 *"I think he wanted"*: Rickman interview.

286 *"I have no problem"*: Anthony Chisholm interview, October 18, 2017.

286 *"As part of the process"*: Butler, "Breaking Ground."

286 *wearing a tailored gray suit*: Photo of Wilson before the speech, Lewis Center for the Arts, Princeton University, https://arts.princeton.edu/events/august -wilson-symposium-diversity-opportunity-american-theater/.

287 *Matthews Theatre . . . Othello*: Eric Quinones, "Firestone Library Exhibition Marks 75th Anniversary of McCarter Theater," *Princeton University News*, January 31, 2005.

287 *"I wish to make it clear"*: Wilson, *Ground*, 9–10.

287 *"the kiln in which"*: Ibid., 12.

287 *"I have strived"*: Ibid., 13.

288 *"big house"*: Ibid., 19.

288 *"I stand myself"*: Ibid., 20.

288 *"Funding agencies"*: Ibid., 23–24.

289 *"Quite possibly"*: Ibid.

289 *"I say raise the standards"*: Ibid., 24.

289 *"an aberrant idea"*: Ibid., 29.

290 *In 1988 . . . Les Misérables*: Eisenberg, "When Sex and Race Don't Matter."

290 *of the sixty-six members*: Wilson, *Ground*, 17.

290 *Du Bois called for*: W. E. B. Du Bois, "Krigwa Players Little Theatre: The Story of a Little Theatre Movement," *Crisis*, July 1926, 134–36.

290 *"Where is the common ground" . . . "air and expanse?*: 26.

291 *"I think I would leave" . . . "the next week"*: Shannon and Williams, *Black Aesthetics*, 252.

291 *"The ground together"*: Wilson, *Ground*, 45–46.

291 *"He was shocked"*: Rickman interview.

292 *"It blew the conference up"*: Butler, "Breaking Ground."

292 *"proudest moment of my life"*: Don Shirley, " 'Colorblind' Casting Has Wilson Seeing Red," *Los Angeles Times*, September 1, 1996.

292 *"rambling jeremiad"*: Robert Brustein, "Subsidized Separatism," *American Theatre*, October 1996, reprinted in *The American Theatre Reader* (New York: Theatre Communications Group, 2009), 163.

292 *"I fear Wilson is displaying"*: Ibid., 165.

292 *"By choosing to chronicle"*: Ibid., 166.

293 *"rabid identity politics"*: Ibid., 167.

293 *"I don't think Martin Luther King"*: Ibid.

293 *"It is Brustein's failure"*: August Wilson, "A Response to Brustein," *American Theatre*, October 1996, reprinted in *The American Theatre Reader*, 170.

293   *"eloquent, honest, and brave"*: Frank Rizzo, "Playwright Wilson Blasts Cultural Limits in the Theater," *Hartford Courant*, July 14, 1996.

293   *"confer in a city"*: Wilson, *Ground*, 37–38.

294   *He connected with . . . his participation*: Victor Leo Walker II interview, July 22, 2021.

294   *"modest proposal"*: Patti Hartigan, "Brustein, Wilson Tiff Obscures Real Issues," *Boston Globe*, October 4, 1996.

294   *She got a phone call*: Anna Deavere Smith interview, October 18, 2017.

294   *After reading both men's . . . conversation at NYU*: Ibid.

295   *she contacted Sullivan . . . among others*: Anna Deavere Smith, "Ringside," Opening Plenary Speech, Theatre Communications Group Conference, June 23, 1916, private collection of Anna Deavere Smith.

295   *a giddy Henry Louis Gates Jr.*: Conversation with author, January 27, 1997.

296   *"Wilson will take the fight"*: Smith, "Ringside."

296   *"It has been some time"*: "August Wilson/Robert Brustein Debate," transcript, *Fresh Air*, NPR, February 5, 1997, https://www.npr.org/programs/fresh-air/1997/02/05/13008066/fresh-air-for-february-5-1997. The author covered the debate for the *Boston Globe*, so many of the details in the discussion were observed by the author.

296   *made him sweat*: Robert Brustein interview, March 22, 2017.

296   *"workings of the human soul"*: "August Wilson/Robert Brustein Debate."

296   *"If Mr. Wilson" . . . "versus separatism"*: Ibid.

296   *"We are not advocates"*: Ibid.

296   *"TCG staffers descended upon me"*: Smith, "Ringside."

297   *"I think you have"*: Ibid.; "August Wilson/Robert Brustein Debate."

297   *"Are you aware"*: Ibid.

297   *"It was a question"*: Ibid.

297   *"I make this self-definition"*: Ibid.

297   *"I am an actor"*: Ibid.

298   *"However that person"*: Ibid.

298   *"This is an academic exercise" . . . "as usual"*: Elmo Terry-Morgan, "The Making of the African Grove Institute for the Arts," *Black Theatre's Unprecedented Times* (published electronically by Black Theatre Network News), 24. Files of Victor Leo Walker II.

298   *"I learned that behind"*: "August Wilson/Robert Brustein."

298   *The minute he said it*: Brustein interview.

298   *"I consider myself"*: Ibid.

298   *"I thought it was a failure"*: Smith interview.

298   *"This is how we get written"*: Ibid.

299   *"I was so worried"*: Romero interview.

299   *used the occasion*: Sakina Ansara Wilson interview.

299   *some fifteen to twenty . . . would not show up*: Walker interview.

299 *"Both August and I"*: Brustein interview.

299 *"The Chitlin Circuit"* ... *a week in Atlanta*: Henry Louis Gates Jr., "The Chitlin Circuit," *New Yorker*, February 3, 1997, 44–55.

300 *Garrett, known as "the Godfather"*: Chris Jones, "'Chitlin Circuit' Fare Draws Fire—But Also Big Audiences," *Chicago Tribune*, February 19, 1998.

300 *"If O.J. can play"*: Ibid., 46.

300 *"Once the white mainstream"*: Ibid., 45.

300 *A few years later*: Christine Dolen, "Play Rights," *Miami Herald*, March 31, 2002.

301 *"He neither looks"*: Gates, "The Chitlin Circuit," 45.

301 *He later told Dartmouth professor*: Walker interview.

301 *Wilson told Walker* ... *scheduled for March 1998*: Ibid.

301 *"Why Dartmouth?"*: Patti Hartigan, "Advocating Black Theater N.H. Summit Will Plumb Racial, Economic Issues," *Boston Globe*, March 6, 1998.

301 *"He was mesmerized"*: Romero interview.

301 *Romero had originally* ... *"blue" in Spanish*: Ibid.

302 *"In Spanish, that's like blue-a"*: Ibid.

302 *Wilson and his partners*: Walker interview.

302 *the Ford Foundation*: Patti Hartigan, "Harvard to Launch Arts Forum," *Boston Globe*, November 24, 1997; Janny Scott, "Arts Forum on Race, Guns and the Internet," *New York Times*, June 24, 1998.

302 *forged ahead* ... *Lloyd Richards*: Ibid.

303 *"I don't think this is a good"*: Ibid.

303 *"They're styling"* ... *"diversionary bull"*: Hartigan, "Advocating Black Theater."

304 *opening-night ceremony*: Video, Penumbra Theatre Company Archives.

304 *She had agreed* ... *in the background*: Romero interview.

304 *"Is we free yet?"*: Elmo Terry-Morgan, "Call and Response: Making of the African Grove Institute," *Black Theatre's Unprecedented Times* (Black Theatre Network), 1999, 33.

304 *"The first day"* ... *clashing egos*: Walker interview.

304 *Tension was rife* ... *other participants*: Ibid.

305 *the room was filled*: Mel Gussow, "Energizing the Future of Black Theater," *New York Times*, March 9, 1998.

305 *Carlyle Brown's* ... *about Black people*: Carlyle Brown, *The African Company Presents Richard III* (New York: Dramatists Play Service, Inc., 1994).

305 *"Beneath the Necessity of Talk"*: Walker interview.

306 *"I am not following that"*: Ibid.

306 *"Sister, you just brought it"*: Ibid.

306 *The group approached*: Ibid.

306 *panel discussion focused on*: Photo, "The Urban Circuit Play," *Black Theatre's Unprecedented Times*, 54.

306 *the group also announced a partnership*: Victor Leo Walker II, "AGIA and Its Vision for the New Millennium," *Black Theatre's Unprecedented Times*, 92.

306 *Wilson signed on . . . did not last long*: Walker interview; Keryl McCord interview, July 6, 2021.

307 *Wilson felt that the Getty*: Walker interview.

307 *Crossroads Theatre canceled*: Laurie Granieri, "U.S. Losing Black Theatres," *Central New Jersey Home News*, October 7, 2001.

307 *Such theaters as Jomandi*: Ibid.

307 *"The concrete results"*: Shannon and Williams, *August Wilson and Black Aesthetics*, 243.

FIFTEEN A Master Jitney Driver

308 *"We need these stories"*: Marion Isaac McClinton, "Introduction," *Jitney* (New York: Overlook Press, 2001).

308 *"It did not matter"*: Ibid.

309 *when he talked to audience . . . remount it*: Christopher Rawson, "Traveling Home by 'Jitney,'" *Pittsburgh Post-Gazette*, June 10, 1996.

309 *He decided to rewrite . . . expand the story*: Ibid.

309 *Pittsburgh Public announced McClinton*: Christopher Rawson, "On Stage," *Pittsburgh Post-Gazette*, August 30, 1995.

310 *Richards typically recommended*: Hatcher interview.

310 *According to actors from St. Paul*: Craven interview; Terry Bellamy interview; Lou Bellamy interview.

310 *Purdy's widow*: Shoholm interview.

310 *"These people" . . . his approach*: Lou Bellamy interview.

311 *Purdy directed Bellamy to go hot*: Terry Bellamy interview.

311 *"He moves to kiss"*: Wilson, *Ma Rainey*, 82.

311 *"White folks don't understand"*: Ibid.

311 *"They were supposed to do a dance"*: Terry Bellamy interview.

311 *Bellamy is convinced . . . "Playwrights don't want to hear that"*: Ibid.

312 *"If you want to direct"*: Ibid.

312 *The three men thought*: Craven interview.

312 *"Black Bart didn't work"*: Ibid.

312 *Wilson had another blowup*: Ibid.

312 *"August said that Claude"*: Ibid.

313 *"Of all human relations"*: Wilson, "Mother's Prayer."

313 *"I don't have the human guide"*: Randy Gener, "August Wilson's New Main Man," *Village Voice*, April 24, 2001.

313 *"You don't take on"*: Elaine Dutka, "Not an Assignment, an Honor," *Los Angeles Times*, September 10, 2000.

313 *a welcoming dinner . . . "really uncanny"*: Chisholm interview.

314 *"When I wrote the play"*: Christopher Rawson, "'Jitney' Brings Playwright Home," *Pittsburgh Post-Gazette*, June 10, 1996.

314 *He had gotten close . . . families*: Chisholm interview.

314 *his mother, Edith Chisholm*: Neil Genzlinger, "Anthony Chisholm Dies at 77; Acclaimed in August Wilson Roles," *New York Times*, October 20, 2020.

314 *"We got into a conversation . . . other life"*: Ibid.

315 *"The guy was about one hundred"*: Chisholm interview.

315 *"We have to go" . . . finished polishing it*: Ibid.

316 *Wilson did not ask him . . . despondent*: Ibid.

316 *Brustein had challenged Wilson*: "August Wilson/Robert Brustein Debate."

316 *the theater held off announcing*: Patti Hartigan, "Wilson's 'Jitney' to Open at a Black Theater, as Planned," *Boston Globe*, January 30, 1997.

316 *"I'm kind of glad"*: Ibid.

316 *Wilson added a scene*: Herrington, "I Ain't Sorry," 127.

317 *"It was like he was playing"*: Chisholm interview.

317 *"He was practically twerking"*: Ibid.

317 *"I said, 'Can the character'"*: Stephen McKinley Henderson interview, October 18, 2017.

317 *"In general, director Dallas"*: Christopher Rawson, "'Jitney' Takes a Ride to Jersey," *Pittsburgh Post-Gazette*, April 24, 1997.

318 *"Walter would say"*: Chisholm interview.

318 *"It got so ridiculous"*: Ibid.

318 *Southers delivered a difficult*: Southers interview.

318 *Flournoy was the most loyal*: Todd Kreidler interview.

318 *He worked as a community activist*: Brown, "Light in August," *Esquire*, April 1, 1989.

318 *Wilson told Sakina*: Sakina Ansara Wilson interview, May 31, 2017.

318 *"We got Marion back"*: Henderson interview.

318 *"August knew when it had"*: Ibid.

319 *"We're going to scrap"*: Christopher Rawson, "Scenes from August Wilson," *Pittsburgh Post-Gazette*, March 24, 1998.

319 *"You are my son"*: August Wilson, *Jitney* (New York: The Overlook Press, 2003), 60.

320 *In the original play*: Videotape, Penumbra Theatre production of *Jitney!*, Penumbra Theatre Company Archives, Givens Collection of African American Literature, University of Minnesota Libraries.

320 *"A house?" . . . "chance to pick out"*: Wilson, *Jitney*, 74.

320 *the Boston production*: The author saw the Boston production.

320 *Sakina objected*: Chisholm interview.

321 *"Wilson mourns"*: Lloyd Rose, "'Jitney': An Intense Ride," *Washington Post*, January 20, 1999.

321 *"No one stepped forward"*: J. Wynn Rousuck, "For Playwright Wilson, the Ideas Keep Percolating," *Baltimore Sun*, reprinted in *Atlanta Constitution*, April 28, 2000.

321   *"Whenever you're working on a show"*: Robin Pogrebin, "Bouquets of Star-Studded Praise Can't Keep Small Shows from Closing," *New York Times*, December 26, 2000.

322   *"The only reason Jitney"*: Henderson interview.

322   *"The old world's in a hell of a fix"*: Bob Hoover, "'Lynching Rope' Replaced with Police Bullets, Playwright Wilson Says," *Pittsburgh Post-Gazette*, March 21, 2000. The author noted that Wilson struck his hand on the podium twenty times, but the paper ran a clarification on April 2, 2000, explaining that Wilson, in fact, had pounded the podium a symbolic forty-one times.

322   *"a 90-minute angry assault"*: Ibid.

322   *"We've replaced . . . bleeding"*: Ibid.

323   *"marginal human beings"*: Ibid.

323   *"to find the courage"*: Ibid.

323   *"urban symphony"*: Ben Brantley, "Finding Drama in Life, and Vice Versa," *New York Times*, April 26, 2000.

324   *"feels hammered on"*: Ibid.

324   *"the slippery guy"*: Lahr, "Been Here and Gone," 53.

324   *"For Azula Carmen Wilson"*: Wilson, *Jitney*, dedication page.

SIXTEEN The Struggle Continues

325   *"You can only"*: Christopher Rawson, "Playwright August Wilson Still Has Miles to Go," *Pittsburgh Post-Gazette*, July 5, 2001.

325   *Eddie Gilbert invited*: Rawson, "Home Is Where the Art Is."

325   *"crown jewel"*: Marylynn Uricchio, "Crystal Clear in the Cultural District," September 27, 1999.

325   *On October 27, 1999*: Christopher Rawson, "On Stage," *Pittsburgh Post-Gazette*, October 27, 1999.

326   *He talked about the play*: Kreidler interview.

326   *They had just finalized*: Rawson, "Home Is Where the Art Is."

326   *Wilson was fiddling . . . was a demotion*: Kreidler interview.

326   *"Do you know" . . . people to navigate*: Ibid.

327   *About an hour . . . into his memory*: Ibid.

327   *Kreidler had had a chilly . . . studying for class*: Ibid.

328   *"The streets that Balboa"*: Wilson, *King Hedley* II (New York: Theatre Communications Group, 2007), vii.

329   *"You have to make your spirit larger"*: August Wilson, "Feed Your Mind."

329   *"I was at Hillary's"*: Rawson, "Home Is Where the Art Is."

329   *"Daddy, medal on"*: Ibid.

329   *"Pittsburgh, far away"*: Ibid.

329   *never understood the 1980s*: Johnson interview.

330   *era of "hip-hop"*: Johnson, *Night Hawks*, 165–66.

330 *he planned to listen . . . rooted in the blues*: Lewis, "An Interview with August Wilson."

330 *"All the ideas and attitudes"*: Ibid.

330 *He peppered his younger brother*: Kittel interview.

330 *"It's not so much a breakdown"*: Boyd, "Interview with August Wilson."

330 *aimed to write a Greek tragedy*: Rawson, "Miles to Go."

330 *"When I look at the situation"*: Lyons, "Interview with August Wilson," 208.

331 *"I think the Black kids"*: Ibid.

331 *"uncommon woman" . . . "electric"*: August Wilson, *Seven Guitars* (New York: Plume, 1997), 55.

332 *"strives to live by his own moral code"*: Wilson, *King Hedley* II, 5.

332 *"I ain't gonna be"*: Ibid., 79.

332 *"I ain't sorry"*: Ibid., 59.

332 *"longtime, but sporadic flame"*: Ibid., 5.

332 *he asked Kreidler to consult*: Kreidler interview.

333 *"We did it, man"*: Ibid.

333 *launched into tales . . . "back to rehearsal"*: Ibid.

334 *"You fall under the spell"*: Ibid.

334 *"He had that ability"*: Ibid.

334 *"I'm thirty-five years old"*: Wilson, *King Hedley II*, 39.

335 *"go back and pick up the ball"*: Wilson, *Two Trains*, 109.

335 *"duty to life"*: August Wilson, *Gem of the Ocean* (New York: Theatre Communications Group, 2006), 68.

335 *"The path to her house"*: Wilson, *King Hedley II*, 8.

335 *"Lock your doors"*: Ibid., 19.

335 *"Got one job"*: Ibid., 54.

336 *Kreidler started writing*: Kreidler interview.

336 *"Forty-one bullets"*: Ibid.

336 *a novel idea*: Ibid.

336 *"I've spent three months"*: Rawson, "Home Is Where the Art Is."

337 *Wilson and Romero . . . always an issue*: Marylynn Uricchio, "Premiere at the Public," *Pittsburgh Post-Gazette*, December 20, 1999.

337 *"Sure enough, at intermission"*: Ibid.

337 *many of Wilson's friends*: Christopher Rawson, "On Stage," *Pittsburgh Post-Gazette*, December 22, 1999.

337 *"Bear down, buckle up"*: Christopher Rawson, "Wilson's 'Hedley' a Thrilling Ride," *Pittsburgh Post-Gazette*, December 16, 1999.

337 *"craggy, thickly forested"*: Ibid.

337 *same category . . . "the family"*: Ibid.

338 *"No Wilson play"*: Christopher Rawson, "Counting Chickens," *Pittsburgh Post-Gazette*, December 24, 1999.

338 *a guest list that included*: Hearst Newspapers, "Stars Will Be Shining at

Nation's 2000 Party," printed in the *Arizona Republic*, December 12, 1999.

338 *"This is perfect"*: Rawson, "Home Is Where the Art Is."

338 *He arranged to have lunch . . . "the easy part"*: Kreidler interview.

339 *"ready enough" . . . "as long as it takes"*: Altman interview.

339 *Kreidler took . . . "my life"*: Kreidler interview.

340 *"There was a lot" . . . two jazzmen*: Altman interview.

340 *"I want everybody to know"*: Wilson, *King Hedley II*, 61.

340 *"It ain't for you"*: Ibid., 90.

341 *"There's a lot of things"*: Kreidler interview.

341 *"Wilson may yet craft"*: Ed Siegel, "Wilson Loses Touch in 'Hedley,'" *Boston Globe*, May 26, 2000.

342 *prestigious Dorothy and Lillian Gish Prize*: https://gishprize.org/recipients/lloyd-richards/.

342 *"You're not here to write"*: Johnson, "Long-Time Owner."

342 *"coffee costs a nickel"*: August Wilson, *The Piano Lesson* (New York: Plume, 1990), 19.

342 *"grimmest" . . . "get tough with it"*: Michael Phillips, "A Dream Deferred," *Los Angeles Times*, September 15, 2000.

343 *"It's not a little thing"*: Wilson, *How I Learned*, 44.

343 *"This is a glorious and historic day"*: Robert K. Elder, "Goodman Theatre Basks in the Spotlight of Grand Day," *Chicago Tribune*, November 10, 2000.

343 *"I got one for the old man"*: Henderson interview.

343 *Windy City was snowed in . . . but he did not attend*: Lee Carlozo, "Goodman Making Snowy, Showy Debut," *Chicago Tribune*, December 12, 2000.

344 *"It's like the postman"*: Ibid.

344 *"ambitious attempt" . . . "may never get there"*: Richard Chistiansen, "Wilson's Epic Drama Dream Still Eluded Him," *Chicago Tribune*, December 12, 2000.

345 *"Because Wilson is a poet" . . . "there is glory"*: Richard Christiansen, "The Near-Triumph of August Wilson's 'King,'" *Chicago Tribune*, December 24, 2000.

345 *Charles S. Dutton . . . dropped out*: Elaine Dutka, "Quick Takes," *Los Angeles Times*, January 13, 2001.

345 *"A lot of people thought"*: Mervyn Rothstein, "Needed a Rest, but Got a Break," *New York Times*, April 29, 2001.

345 *"It's very much . . . Lear"*: Ibid.

346 *"All of a sudden I'm in a scene"*: David Finkle, "Acting 'King Hedley II': It Just Makes You Soar," *New York Times*, June 3, 2001.

346 *"I started speaking lines"*: Ibid.

346 *"Any drama" . . . "high notes"*: Ben Brantley, "The Agonized Arias of Everyman in Poverty and Pain," *New York Times*, May 2, 2001.

347 *atmosphere at the Cocacabana . . . Claude Purdy*: Christopher Rawson, "Lighting Up Broadway," *Pittsburgh Post-Gazette*, May 1, 2001.

347 *"It's not bad to have"*: Ibid.

348 *He had stayed there . . . doll for Azula*: Rawson, "Miles to Go."

348 *"I want to thank Hitler"*: Robin Pogrebin, "'Producers' Shatters Tony Award Record with 12 Prizes," *New York Times*, June 4, 2001.

348 *"Believe me, without him"*: Ibid.

348 *"I've worked on Shakespeare"*: Don Shewey, "Sharing the Stage with August Wilson," *New York Times*, April 29, 2001.

348 *"Marion will go home"*: Ibid.

349 *"for giving me enough"*: "Viola Davis Wins 2001 Tony Award for Best Featured Actress in a Play," YouTube, https://www.youtube.com/watch?v=Gi4nPZKJ-LA.

349 *"He would always say"*: Jon Wertheim, "Viola Davis' Journey to Triple Crown-Winning Actress," *60 Minutes*, December 6, 2020.

349 *"You can only close"*: Rawson, "Miles to Go."

349 *shown it to Kreidler*: Kreidler interview.

349 *"small, slightly built shy man"*: Wilson, *How I Learned*, 31.

350 *"Limitation of the instrument"*: Ibid., 32.

350 *"Imagine Pablo Picasso"*: Ibid.

350 *"You have a man"*: Patrick T. Reardon, "On the Road to a Novel," *Chicago Tribune*, April 23, 2001.

350 *"In my first paragraph" . . . "blood seeping inside his shoes"*: Ibid.

350 *"I often remark"*: Wilson, *King Hedley II*, xi.

SEVENTEEN An Uphill Battle in the Basement

351 *"Blacks have always, historically"*: Judith Egerton, "'Piano' Man," *Courier-Journal*, October 21, 2001.

351 *"Hey man, it's August"*: Kreidler interview.

352 *"Todd, man, I have"*: Ibid.

352 *including the actor Laurence Fishburne*: Christopher Rawson, "Scenes from August Wilson," *Pittsburgh Post-Gazette*, March 24, 1998.

352 *McClinton was supposedly*: Christopher Rawson, "On Stage," *Pittsburgh Post-Gazette*, January 29, 2003.

352 *Wilson didn't particularly trust*: August Wilson interview.

352 *Rudin was publicly disgraced*: Tatiana Siegel, "'Everyone Just Knows He's an Absolute Monster': Scott Rudin's Ex-Staffers Speak Out on Abusive Behavior," *Hollywood Reporter*, April 7, 2021.

353 *open up the story*: Kreidler interview; Rawson, "Home Is Where the Art Is."

353 *"We're not very productive"*: Kreidler interview.

353 *"I think he's asleep"*: Ibid.

353 *He had turned down dozens*: Breglio interview.

354 *"What damnable horror"*: August Wilson, "The Breakfast Table," *Slate*, September 11, 2001.

354   *Wilson, like any father*: Ibid.

354   *"attacked [his] play"*: Ibid.

354   *"A stabbing need"*: Ibid.

354   *"elusive and destructive"* . . . *"heroic thing to do"*: Ibid.

355   *"insane, dastardly"*: Ibid.

355   *"hatred for our arrogant"*: Ibid.

355   *"the big things"*: Egerton, " 'Piano' Man."

355   *"My four-year-old daughter"*: Ibid.

355   *"Blacks have always"*: Ibid.

355   *he narrated the entire plot*: Timothy Douglas interview, March 8, 2005.

356   *"so funny yet moving"*: "News and Notes," *Star Tribune*, November 25, 2001.

356   *Anthony Chisholm and the other actors*: Chisholm interview.

356   *to "create an environment"*: Robert Trussell, "Stage Notes," *Kansas City Star*, May 12, 2002.

356   *it was the second most produced play*: Barbara Isenberg, *Los Angeles Times*, December 24, 1989.

356   *"not like August Wilson's"*: Maya Phillips, "August Wilson, American Bard," *New York Times*, December 3, 2020.

357   *elegant 2007 collection*: The ten-play collection was published in 2007 by Theatre Communications Group and includes ten slim hardbacks in a cardboard box, with introductions to each play by writers including Phylicia Rashad, Frank Rich, Toni Morrison, Tony Kushner, and Laurence Fishburne.

357   *"Black artistic spokesman"*: Gates Jr., "The Chitlin Circuit," 46.

357   *"the most immediate"* . . . *"but now"*: Douglas Turner Ward, "American Theater: For Whites Only?" *New York Times*, August 14, 1966.

357   *established a $434,000 grant*: Sam Zolotow, "Ford Fund Aids Negro Theater; Grant of $434,000 to Set Up Ensemble Company Here," *New York Times*, May 15, 1967.

357   *began to suffer*: Laurie Granieri, "U.S. Losing Black Theatres," *Central New Jersey Home News*, October 7, 2001.

357   *"review that all writers"* . . . *"variety of Black voices"*: Christine Dolen, "Lack of Venues Draining Black Theater Movement," *Miami Herald*, March 31, 2002.

358   *Wilson walked him through the steps*: Kreidler interview.

359   *"The minute I got there"*: Sweet, *The O'Neill*, 240.

360   *"Todd, man, I'm in trouble"*: Kreidler interview.

360   *"She offered me a slot"* . . . *"I want you to do it"*: Ibid.

360   *"I did not sleep"*: Ibid.

361   *"Who is playing Ma?"* . . . *"We'll have to see"*: Andrews interview.

361   *"I feel that the definitive"*: Jesse McKinley, "On Stage and Off," *New York Times*, October 25, 2002.

361   *"I figured if I can do that"*: Ibid.

361   *They claimed that their contract*: Ralph Blumenthal and Jesse McKinley, " 'Ma

Rainey' Broadway Revival Is Threatened by Contract Dispute," *New York Times*, November 14, 2002.

361 *"I've known how it ended"*: John O'Mahony, "American Centurion," *The Guardian*, December 14, 2002.

362 *"Whoopi Goldberg and Charles Dutton"*: *Time Out New York*, January 23–30, 2003.

362 *"I've had to get the original"*: Samuel G. Freeman, "Mother of an Era," *New York Times*, February 2, 2003.

362 *"I have done the theater"*: *Ma Rainey's Black Bottom, Playbill*.

362 *"I have done the state"*: William Shakespeare, *Othello*, Act 5, Scene 2.

362 *Charles Gordon . . . high blood pressure issues*: Jesse McKinley, "On Stage and Off," *New York Times*, January 31, 2003.

363 *"hollow new revival . . . tuning up"*: Ben Brantley, "Old Blues, New Riffs," *New York Times*, February 7, 2003.

363 *"one of the most exciting" . . . "heartbreaker of the season"*: Ibid.

363 *"August went and flew off"*: Chisholm interview.

363 *"If he suspected"*: Craven interview.

363 *"I could see it physically"*: Sakina Ansara Wilson interview.

364 *"the worst 73 days"*: Chris Jones, " 'Gem' of Theater Tries Comedy," *Chicago Tribune*, April 25, 2003.

365 *"Every writer does bad writing"*: Sean Mills, "Cultural Differences Discussed by Writer," *Daily Orange*, March 18, 2003.

365 *when he got the disturbing news*: Kittel interview; Sala Udin interview, June 5, 2017.

366 *wept next to the coffin*: Southers interview.

366 *He later talked to Kreidler . . . speaking at the funeral*: Kreidler interview.

366 *"I used to be white" . . . "maybe Eminem"*: Jones, " 'Gem' of Theater."

366 *"I'm a writer, not a performer"*: Ibid.

366 *"waning echo" . . . "drowns out the story"*: Ben Brantley, "Future as Prologue in Two New Dramas," *New York Times*, May 20, 2003.

367 *Dutton improvised . . . late at the after-party*: Joel Ruark interview, January 8, 2018.

367 *"I got a plan"*: Kreidler interview.

367 *"He was so disappointed"*: Ibid.

367 *"Yeah, I read it"*: Ibid.

368 *Fishburne sent him a play*: Richard Natale, "Into the Looking Glass," *Los Angeles Times*, October 30, 2000.

368 *"angry and nasty"*: Kreidler interview.

368 *"I just want to get some breakfast"*: Ibid.

368 *"I don't think" . . . "something to eat"*: Ibid.

368 *"August called those moments"*: Ibid.

369 *"He was a blues man"*: Ibid.

369 "To say the very least . . . game day footage": Ibid.

369 One morning, she woke up: Romero interview.

370 "My ancestors": Wilson, How I Learned, 7.

370 "I am an accident": Ibid., 8.

370 Whoopi Goldberg suggested: Kreidler interview.

370 "Oral Sex": Wilson, How I Learned, 40.

370 His girlfriend Snookie's husband: Willa Mae Montague interview, June 10, 2017.

370 "No, man": Kreidler interview.

371 "The crucible": Wilson, How I Learned, 5.

371 "Being with August": Kreidler interview.

371 "I had a sense": Ibid.

371 "Any other theater": Ibid.

372 "embarrassed" . . . "black sport coat": Tim Colbert, "August Wilson Takes the Stage and Leaves 'Em Wowed," Pittsburgh Post-Gazette, June 1, 2003.

372 "Quit telling stories, Dad": Ibid.

372 "I am not a shit": Kreidler interview.

372 they wrote a letter of apology: Letter from Sharon Ott and Ben Moore to August Wilson, August 5, 2003, August Wilson Archive.

373 [[Trailing phrase TK]]:The author attended the performance of Ma Rainey with Wilson in January 2005.

372 "You could have taken": Ibid.

373 "It was a wonderful": Ibid.

373 "Nobody wanted to be around": Ibid.

373 sustain "three wallpaper": Wilson, How I Learned, 12.

373 He envisioned a film . . . stay alive: Kreidler interview. All details of the screenplay were provided by Kreidler.

374 "If you do it": Ibid.

374 "Todd, at your age": Ibid.

EIGHTEEN Keeping the Tradition Alive

375 "Black America": Dezell, "Gem of the Ocean."

376 "die in truth": Wilson, Gem of the Ocean, 45.

376 "It's Abraham Lincoln's fault": Ibid., 34.

376 "You try and give them an opportunity": Ibid.

376 "I want a wall": Ibid., 14.

377 "I thought, as an artist": Rawson, "Miles to Go."

377 "I liked Aunt Ester": Christopher Rawson, "August Wilson Wants to Finish His 10-Play Cycle," Pittsburgh Post-Gazette, December 6, 2003.

377 "The skeleton of the play": Don Shirley, "Wilson's 'Gem of the Ocean' Opens," Los Angeles Times, August 1, 2003.

377 *"When you have a title"*: August Wilson interview.

378 *"You hang it up on a wall"*: Brown, "Light in August."

378 *news article about a Black man*: John Nolan, Associated Press, "350-Pound Man's Death in Police Custody Roils Cincinnati," *Pittsburgh Post-Gazette*, December 2, 2003.

378 *"my first critic"*: Wilson, "Heinz Award Acceptance Speech."

378 *"first inspiration"*: Ibid.

378 *"I am older"* . . . *"limitations of my art"*: Ibid.

378 *a young filmmaker named Jaime Hook*: Jamie Hook interview, September 16, 2022.

379 *who shows up in the opening scene*: Trailer, *The Naked Proof*, https://www.you tube.com/watch?v=CIRPnZ1kJNs.

380 *"He ain't no household word"*: Chisholm interview.

380 *"Any role on Broadway"*: Ibid.

380 *"I told them you get"*: Ibid.

380 *"He was playing it"*: Ibid.

380 *"I said, 'Man'"*: Ibid.

381 *"I am worried, man"*: Ibid.

381 *"God has a way"*: Ibid.

381 *Producer Benjamin Mordecai*: Maso interview.

382 *"August told me"*: Preston, "Marion McClinton, a Man Made by Theater."

382 *"You have one problem"*: Maso interview.

382 *Lindo had become obsessed*: Chisholm interview.

382 *"They cut me loose"*: Ibid.

382 *"He was a mensch"*: Maso interview.

382 *"I said, 'Oh, man'"* . . . *"'I will do it'"*: Chisholm interview.

383 *"He stuck it in my chest"*: Ibid.

383 *"I was on the third hole"*: Eugene Lee interview, May 30, 2017.

383 *"By the time I got"*: Ibid.

383 *"creative differences"*: Catherine Foster, "The Story Behind This Play Is a Gem," *Boston Globe*, September 24, 2004.

383 *"He said, 'You're called'"*: Kreidler interview.

384 *"We'll call ourselves"* . . . *"worked up as he was"*: Ibid.

384 *"They would be talking"*: Romero interview.

384 *"All it mean is"*: Wilson, *Gem*, 28.

384 *"The question he asks"*: Dezell, "Gem of the Theater."

384 *"resembles any Black woman"*: Ibid.

385 *"She represents any old person"*: Ibid.

385 *"I got a long memory"*: Wilson, *Gem*, 43.

385 *"What we're doing"*: Ibid.

385 *"People look at Black American history"*: Ibid.

385 *"Remember me"*: Wilson, *Gem*, 66.

386 *"Say he didn't feel right"*: Ibid., 82

386 *"So live"*: Ibid., 85.

386 *"The work on this play"*: Foster, "This Play Is a Gem."

386 *"is able to fully join"*: Ed Siegel, "Crown Jewel: Phylicia Rashad Shines in August Wilson's Powerful 'Gem of the Ocean,'" *Boston Globe*, October 1, 2004.

387 *announced that a major investor*: Jesse McKinley, "Financial Woes Plague Two Broadway Hopefuls," *New York Times*, October 27, 2004.

387 *Mordecai said that three*: Benjamin Mordecai interview, March 8, 2005.

387 *producers canceled performances*: Jesse McKinley, "Trying to Rescue 'Gem,'" *New York Times*, October 28, 2004.

387 *he met with an unlikely angel*: Michael Phillips, "'65 as Told by a Master Story-teller," *Chicago Tribune*, November 8, 2004.

387 *"I am deeply passionate"*: Michael Kuchwara, "Curtain Up! 'Gem of the Ocean' Now Scheduled to Arrive on Dec. 6," Associated Press, November 16, 2004.

387 *Mordecai bowed out . . . "everyone will"*: Jesse McKinley, "Investor Comes to the Rescue of Wilson Play," *New York Times*, November 13, 2004.

388 *"The people who produce"*: Jesse McKinley, "Plays Without Music Find Broad-way Harsh," *New York Times*, December 7, 2004.

388 *"a touchstone" . . . "price of freedom"*: Ben Brantley, "Sailing into Collective Memory," *New York Times*, December 7, 2004.

388 *"gloriously humane"*: Linda Winer, *Newsday*, quoted in "Reviews of 'Gem of the Ocean,'" *Atlanta Constitution*, December 12, 2004.

388 *"surely one of the best-acted"*: Clive Barnes, *New York Post*, quoted in "Reviews of 'Gem of the Ocean,'" *Atlanta Constitution*, December 12, 2004.

388 *watched him as he went*: Shoholm interview.

389 *"I want someone to marry us"*: Kreidler interview.

390 *"We were so proud"*: Kenny Leon interview, February 28, 2018.

NINETEEN Wherever You Are, I'm Here

391 *"I have strived"*: Wilson, *Ground*, 13.

391 *One unseasonably . . . a few cigarettes*: August Wilson interview. Many of the details and quotes in this chapter are from a series of interviews conducted for the author's article "One Man. Ten Plays. 100 Years.," *Boston Globe Magazine*, April 3, 2005.

391 *One employee*: Robert Schulze interview, March 8, 2005.

392 *"I'm working on it"*: August Wilson interview.

392 *"Man, where is Gunars?"*: August Wilson interview.

392 *"He was nutty as a fruitcake"*: Ibid.

392 *"battle about the damn cat"*: Ibid.

393 *"Take Hambone"*: Ibid.

393   *"Walk with your head up"*: Sakina Ansara Wilson interview.

393   *"I saw a lot of myself"* . . . *"slipped away"*: August Wilson interview.

393   *"August Wilson!"*: Ibid.

393   *"He has a heart"*: Romero interview.

393   *"You stick around long enough"* . . . *"surprised me"*: August Wilson interview.

394   *"Mongolian horses"* . . . *destruction of the planet*: Ibid.

394   *"I always hated biography"*: Ibid.

394   *"May the circle"*: Wilson, *Gem of the Ocean*, dedication page.

395   *"I don't get the love"* . . . *"thinking to myself, 'No!'"*: Lahr, "Been Here and Gone," 65.

395   more *"family" structure* . . . *argument made sense*: August Wilson interview.

395   *"Oh, you poor baby"*: Ibid.

396   *"It's not easy"*: Romero interview.

396   *the shelves also included*: Michael Blowen, "Dreaming with Words," *Boston Globe*, October 25, 1998.

396   *"Sign your novel for me"*: Oscar Hijuelos, "A Last Round with August Wilson," *New York Times*, October 9, 2005; Kreidler interview.

396   The Secrets of the Radio Sisters: Charlie Rose, *Charlie Rose*, PBS, May 18, 2005, https://charlierose.com/videos/9260.

396   *He gave Wilson a package*: Kreidler interview.

396   *"Our personal relationships"*: Ibid.

397   *"When does he do his writing?"*: Romero interview.

397   *"I don't understand that!"*: August Wilson interview.

397   *"The man made his money"*: Ibid.

397   *"Sometimes I want a snack"*: Romero interview.

398   *"People say, 'Why ain't you'"*: August Wilson interview.

398   *Romero noticed*: Romero interview.

398   *fascinated with painting*: August Wilson interview.

398   *"He does wonderful drawings"*: Romero interview.

398   *Romero could see*: Ibid.

398   *"I worked real hard"*: August Wilson interview.

399   *"I'm concerned for him"*: Romero interview.

399   The Coffin Maker Play: August Wilson interview.

399   *Death, Queen Victoria*: August Wilson, *Coffin Maker*, undated script fragments, August Wilson Archive.

399   *"He said it was about"*: Johnson interview.

399   *He once agreed to read*: August Wilson interview.

399   *"crossing an ocean"* . . . *"Get a compass!"*: Reardon, "On the Road to a Novel."

400   *"See, visual artists live long"*: August Wilson interview.

400   *"mumbling, head-down"*: Craven interview.

400   *"I said that if he is a metaphor"*: Ibid.

400   *Bellamy and the actors*: Ibid.

401   *But he did intimate*: Ibid.

401   *"free, truly free"*: August Wilson, *Radio Golf* (New York: Theatre Communications Group, 2007), 13.

402   *"raggedy-ass, rodent-infested"*: Ibid., 48.

402   *"Blight! Blight!"*: Ibid., 50.

403   *"An innocent man"*: Ibid., 29–30.

403   *"Damn, you gotta"*: Leon interview.

403   *"a rite of passage"*: Douglas interview.

403   *"You're doing great"*: Christopher Rawson, "When August Calls," *Pittsburgh Post-Gazette*, September 22, 2005.

403   *He dusted off the poem*: Ibid.

404   *"bloodless execution"*: Wilson, "Home."

404   *"They veered off far enough"*: Rawson, "When August Calls."

404   *"treat each scene"*: Ibid.

404   *"Oh, this is what"*: Ibid.

404   *"For me,* Radio Golf *is basically about"*: Charles Isherwood, "August Wilson's 100-Year Memory," *New York Times*, April 27, 2005.

405   *Cosby gave a speech . . . "tired of you"*: Bill Cosby, transcript of speech to the NAACP, 2004, Blackpast, https://www.blackpast.org/african-american-history /2004-bill-cosby-pound-cake-speech/.

405   *"A billionaire attacking"*: Clarence Page, "A New Century, a New 'Color Line,'" *Chicago Tribune*, May 1, 2005.

405   *"I'm going home"*: Rebecca J. Ritzel, "MU Helps Teach Playwright a 'Lesson,'" *Intelligencer Journal*, April 1, 2005.

405   *Kreidler maintains that Wilson had no intention of retiring*: Kreidler interview.

406   *"I had this baseball analogy"*: Michael Kuchwara, "Chronicling the Black Experience," Associated Press, April 24, 2005.

406   *He went to visit . . . "'had to be here'"*: Sherry Mordecai interview.

406   *This play was two hours and twenty-five minutes*: Michael Phillips, "Playing Through," *Chicago Tribune*, May 1, 2005.

407   *Benjamin Mordecai died*: Charles Isherwood, "Benjamin Mordecai, Stage Producer and Manager, Dies at 60," *New York Times*, May 10, 2005.

407   *made a pact*: Sherry Mordecai interview.

407   *"To Benjamin Mordecai"*: Wilson, *Radio Golf*, dedication page.

407   *"I will be next"*: Sherry Mordecai interview.

408   *"For Rob Penny"*: Wilson, *King Hedley II*, dedication page.

408   *"It's not a conspiracy"*: August Wilson interview.

408   *"The situation" . . . "passionate concern"*: Charlie Rose, *Charlie Rose*, PBS, air date May 18, 2005.

409   *"My dad is just as shocked"*: Sakina Ansara Wilson interview.

409   *"It wasn't a surprise"*: Kreidler interview.

409   *"I was always afraid" . . . "heart attack"*: Sakina Ansara Wilson interview.

409   *"Now, haunted by the specter"*: August Wilson, *American Theatre*, September

2005, quoted in Frank Rizzo, "Mordecai Tribute Draws Hundreds of Theater Notables," *Hartford Courant*, September 22, 2005.

410 *Director Timothy Douglas*: Rawson, "When August Calls."

410 *Wilson sent a handwritten . . . living in peace*: Johnson interview.

410 *Viertel immediately spurred*: Jesse McKinley, "Theater Is to Be Renamed for a Dying Playwright," *New York Times*, September 2, 2005.

411 *Viertel flew to Seattle*: Kreidler interview.

411 *"I have a robust imagination"*: Michael Kuchwara, Associated Press, "A Broadway Theater Renamed for August Wilson," *Seattle Times*, October 17, 2005.

411 *"I thought we might"*: Sweet, *The O'Neill*, 170.

412 *The atmosphere in the house*: Kreidler interview.

412 *His doctors had recommended*: Christopher Rawson, "August Wilson Says He's Dying," *Pittsburgh Post-Gazette*, August 26, 2005.

412 *Those closest to him*: Sakina Ansara Wilson interview; Kreidler interview.

412 *"On the one hand"*: Diane Haithman, "Playwright Wilson Has Liver Cancer," *Los Angeles Times*, August 27, 2005.

413 *"We had our suspicions"*: Karen Wada, "He's Absent, Yet He's There," *Los Angeles Times*, September 16, 2005.

413 *"Something was happening"*: Chisholm interview.

413 *During one visit . . . "'ain't quite it'"*: Leon interview.

413 *he asked to speak*: Kreidler interview.

414 *"I said, 'Fuck it'" . . . Kreidler directing*: Ibid.

414 *"maintains a beautiful balance"*: Daryl H. Miller, "On the 18th Hole," *Los Angeles Times*, August 12, 2005.

415 *"It's not like poker"*: Rawson, "Wilson Says He's Dying."

415 *"exit interview" . . . the following day*: Christopher Rawson, "Let's Celebrate the Life That Is August Wilson," *Pittsburgh Post-Gazette*, September 4, 2005.

415 *some who were close to him*: Kreidler interview.

415 *Hurricane Katrina*: Katherine Schulten, "Hurricane Katrina and New Orleans, Then and Now," *New York Times*, August 3, 2010.

416 *"Daddy, don't watch"*: Sakina Ansara Wilson interview.

416 *"Hey, man, I am sick"*: Andrews interview.

416 *He didn't sign his will*: August Wilson Will, King County Superior Clerk's Office.

416 *took a ferry*: Sakina Ansara Wilson interview.

417 *"It is beautiful"*: Ibid.

417 *"Heroic is not a word"*: Charles Isherwood, "August Wilson, Theater's Poet of Black America, Is Dead at 60," *New York Times*, October 3, 2005.

417 *"people still think"*: Johnson, *Night Hawks*, 171.

417 *"The love of beauty"*: Ibid., 176.

418 *His best man*: Yoshimura interview.

418 *"I was sad"*: Ramesh Santanam, "Hundreds Turn Out to Mourn August Wilson," Associated Press, October 9, 2005.

418   *"the hardest thing"* . . . *"not love themselves"*: Bob Hoover, "August Wilson's Final Act," *Pittsburgh Post-Gazette*, October 9, 2005.

418   *"encompassed the entire"* . . . *"Nat Turner"*: Santanam, "Hundreds Turn Out."

419   *"Look like they had more people"*: Wilson, *Two Trains Running*, 81.

419   *Chisholm was the first*: Chisholm interview.

420   *"a slow, strange dance"*: August Wilson, *Fences* (New York: Plume, 1986), 101.

420   *"Wherever you are"*: Author visit to grave, August 2019.

AFTERWORD

422   *"Raised all kind of hell"*: Wilson, *Two Trains Running*, 85.

423   *"When I go to these theaters"*: Charlie Rose, *Charlie Rose*.

423   *of the seventy-nine LORT theaters*: Author interview with Matt Schultz (LORT management associate), May 18, 2022.

425   *"and they don't necessarily"*: Jason Zinoman, "On Stage and Off," *New York Times*, March 19, 2004.

425   *"Don't you leave me"*: Wilson, *King Hedley II*, dedication page.

425   *an Annual August Wilson Birthday*: https://www.augustwilsonbirthdaycelebration.com.

426   *his childhood home at 1727 Bedford*: Diana Nelson Jones, "August Wilson's Childhood Home Joins National Register," *Pittsburgh Post-Gazette*, May 29, 2013, https://augustwilsonhouse.org/index.html.

426   *Denzel Washington spearheaded*: "Names and Faces," *Detroit Free Press*, September 29, 2018.

426   *Black activists*: Charlie Deitch, "August Wilson Center Responds to Petition," *Pittsburgh Current*, March 1, 2019.

426   *Black directors . . . collaborated closely*: Patrick Healy, "Race an Issue in Wilson Play, and Its Production," *New York Times*, April 22, 2009.

427   *The Black mother*: Marie Fazio, "A Black Student's Mother Complained About 'Fences.' He Was Expelled," *New York Times*, December 15, 2020.

427   *His estate initially canceled . . . King Hedley II*: Jesse McKinley, "Arts, Briefly; Wilson Plays Cancelled," *New York Times*, November 4, 2005, https://www.signaturetheatre.org/About/Playwrights---Residencies/August-Wilson.aspx.

428   *"You don't make your characters talk"*: Patti Hartigan, "Young Critics in the Spotlight in Huntington Student Program," *Boston Globe*, October 10, 1986.

428   *National August Wilson Monologue Competition*: https://truecolorstheatre.org/august-wilson-monologue-competition/.

429   *The August Wilson Estate . . . no longer involved*: Chloe Rabinowitz, "'August Wilson Legacy Project' National Partnership Announced," *Broadway World*, February 25, 2022.

429   *A young woman named . . . "be the change"*: *Giving Voice*, directed by James D. Stern and Fernando Villena.

BIBLIOGRAPHY

ARCHIVES AND SPECIAL COLLECTIONS

Bob Johnson Papers, 1949–2003, Curtis Theatre Collection, Archives & Special Collections, University of Pittsburgh Library System.

Kuntu Repertory Theatre Collection, Curtis Theatre Collection, Archives & Special Collections, University of Pittsburgh Library System.

Lloyd Richards Papers, James Weldon Johnson Collection in the Yale Collection of American Literature, Beinecke Rare Book and Manuscript Library.

New Dramatists Library.

Penumbra Theatre Company Archives, Givens Collection of African American Literature, University of Minnesota Libraries.

The Playwrights' Center Records, Performing Arts Archives, University of Minnesota Libraries.

PUBLISHED PLAYS

Wilson, August. *Ma Rainey's Black Bottom.* New York: Plume, 1985.

Wilson, August. *Fences.* New York: Plume, 1986.

Wilson, August. *Joe Turner's Come and Gone.* New York: Plume, 1988.

Wilson, August. *The Piano Lesson.* New York: Plume, 1990.

Wilson, August. *Three Plays.* Pittsburgh: University of Pittsburgh Press, 1991.

Wilson, August. *Two Trains Running.* New York: Plume, 1992.

Wilson, August. *Seven Guitars.* New York: Plume, 1997.

Wilson, August. *Jitney.* Woodstock & New York: The Overlook Press, 2003.

Wilson, August. *King Hedley II.* New York: Theatre Communications Group, 2005.

Wilson, August. *Gem of the Ocean.* New York: Theatre Communications Group, 2006.

Wilson, August. *Radio Golf.* New York: Theatre Communications Group, 2007.

Wilson, August. *August Wilson Century Cycle.* New York, Theatre Communications Group, 2007.

Wilson, August, conceived with Todd Kreidler. *How I Learned What I Learned.* New York: Samuel French, 2018.

UNPUBLISHED PLAYS

Wilson, August. *Black Bart and the Sacred Hills.* 1977. Bob Johnson Papers.

Wilson, August. *The Coldest Day of the Year.* 1977. Bob Johnson Papers.

Wilson, August. *Eskimo Insult Duel.* August Wilson Archive.

Wilson, August. *Fullerton Street.* August Wilson Archive.

Wilson, August. *The Homecoming.* 1976. Bob Johnson Papers.

Wilson, August. *How Coyote Got His Special Power and Used It to Help the People, Eskimo Insult Duel.* August Wilson Archive.

Wilson, August. *The Janitor.* August Wilson Archive.

Wilson, August. *Malcolm X.* Undated script. Penumbra Theatre Company Archives.

Wilson, August. *Margaret Mead.* August Wilson Archive.

Wilson, August. *Mill Hand's Lunch Bucket.* 1982. New Dramatists Library.

Wilson, August. *Profiles in Science: William Harvey.* August Wilson Archive.

Wilson, August. *Recycle.* August Wilson Archive.

Wilson, August. *St. Louis Blues.* 1986. Private collection.

Wilson, August. *Science Clubhouse.* August Wilson Archive.

Wilson, August. *Why I Learned to Read.* August Wilson Archive.

POETRY

Rhodes, Gerald, ed. *Signals.* Bob Johnson Papers.

Wilson, August. "In Concert: Gerry Rhodes, Poet August Wilson, Poet Mark Martin, Guitarist (Bluegrass, Blues, Ragtime), presented by Mill River Productions and Statue of Life, February 21, 1976." CD recording at Detre Library & Archives, Heinz History Center, Pittsburgh.

BOOKS AND PLAYS

American Theatre Magazine Staff, eds. *The American Theatre Reader.* New York: Theatre Communications Group, 2009.

Baraka, Amiri. *Four Black Revolutionary Plays.* New York: Marion Boyars, 2009.

———. *Raise, Race, Rays, Raze: Essays Since 1965.* New York: Random House, 1969.

Breglio, John. *I Wanna Be a Producer: How to Make a Killing on Broadway . . . or Get Killed.* New York: Applause, 2016.

Brown, Carlyle. *The African Company Presents Richard III.* New York: Dramatists Play Service, Inc., 1994.

Brustein, Robert. *Reimagining American Theatre.* New York: Hill & Wang, 1991.

Bryer, Jackson R., and Mary C. Hartig, eds. *Conversations with August Wilson.* Jackson: University Press of Mississippi, 2006.

Du Bois, W. E. B. *The Souls of Black Folk.* Amazon Classics, 2017.

Fugard, Athol, John Kani and Winston Ntshona. *Siswe Bansi Is Dead.* New York: Viking, 1976.

Gates, Henry Louis, Jr. *The Signifying Monkey.* Oxford: Oxford University Press, 1988.

Glasco, Laurence A., and Christopher Rawson. *August Wilson: Pittsburgh Places in His Life and Plays.* Pittsburgh: Pittsburgh History & Landmarks Foundation, 2011.

Gottlieb, Peter. *Making Their Own Way: Southern Blacks' Migration to Pittsburgh, 1916–1930.* Champaign: University of Illinois Press, 1987.

Handy, W. C., ed., introduction and notes by Abbe Niles. *Blues: An Anthology.* New York: Albert & Charles Boni, 1926.

Hansberry, Lorraine. *A Raisin in the Sun.* New York: Penguin, 1988.

Herrington, Joan. *"I Ain't Sorry for Nothin' I Done": August Wilson's Process of Play-writing.* New York: Limelight Editions, 1998.

Hughes, Langston. *Selected Poems of Langston Hughes.* New York: Vintage, 1959.

Johnson, Charles. *Oxherding Tale.* New York: Scribner, 2005.

———. *Night Hawks: Stories.* New York: Scribner, 2018.

Jones, James Earl, and Penelope Niven. *James Earl Jones: Voices and Silences.* New York: Charles Scribner's Sons, 1993.

Lahr, John. *Tennessee Williams: Mad Pilgrimage of the Flesh.* New York: W. W. Norton and Company, 2014.

Mahala, Macelle. *Penumbra: The Premier Stage for African American Drama.* Minneapolis: University of Minnesota Press, 2013.

Moyers, Bill. *A World of Ideas: Conversations with Thoughtful Men and Women About American Life Today and the Ideas Shaping Our Future.* New York: Doubleday, 1989.

Nadal, Alan. *May All Your Fences Have Gates.* Iowa City: University of Iowa Press, 1994.

Nemiroff, Robert, adaptor. *Lorraine Hansberry in Her Own Words: To Be Young, Gifted and Black.* New York: Vintage Books, 1995.

Post, Douglas, *Dunking Sadness.* Unpublished, 1994.

Reed, Ishmael. *Mumbo Jumbo.* New York: Integrated Media, 2013.

Savran, David. *In Their Own Words: Contemporary American Playwrights.* New York: Theatre Communications Group, 1988.

Schwartzman, Myron. *Romare Bearden: His Life and Art.* New York: Henry N. Abrams, Inc., 1990.

Shannon, Sandra G. *The Dramatic Vision of August Wilson.* Washington, D.C.: Howard University Press, 1995.

Shannon, Sandra G., and Dana Williams, eds. *August Wilson and Black Aesthetics.* New York: Palgrave Macmillan, 2004.

Sheppard, Muriel Earley. *Cabins in the Laurel.* Chapel Hill, N.C.: University of North Carolina Press, 1935.

Sweet, Jeffrey. *The O'Neill: The Transformation of Modern American Theater.* New Haven: Yale University Press, 2014.

Wald, Elijah. *The Blues: A Very Short Introduction.* Oxford: Oxford University Press, 2010.

Washington, M. Bunch. *The Art of Romare Bearden: The Prevalence of Ritual.* New York: Harry N. Abrams, 1973.

Whitaker, Mark. *Smoketown: The Untold Story of the Other Great Black Renaissance.* New York: Simon & Schuster, 2018.

Wilson, August. *The Ground on Which I Stand.* New York: Theatre Communications Group, 2001.

Wolfe, Peter. *August Wilson.* New York: Twayne Publishers, 1999.